Rajasthan

**Monique Choy
Sarina Singh**

LONELY PLANET PUBLICATIONS
Melbourne • Oakland • London • Paris

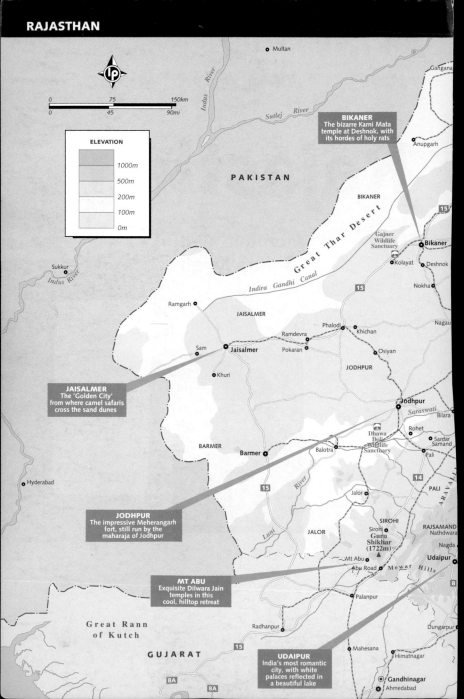

RAJASTHAN

PAKISTAN

ELEVATION

1000m
500m
200m
100m
0m

Great Thar Desert

BIKANER
The bizarre Karni Mata
temple at Deshnok, with
its hordes of holy rats

JAISALMER
The 'Golden City'
from where camel safaris
cross the sand dunes

JODHPUR
The impressive Meherangarh
fort, still run by the
maharaja of Jodhpur

MT ABU
Exquisite Dilwara Jain
temples in this
cool, hilltop retreat

UDAIPUR
India's most romantic
city, with white
palaces reflected in
a beautiful lake

Multan

Gangana

Anupgarh

Sukkur

Indus River

Indus River

Sutlej River

Indira Gandhi Canal

BIKANER

Gajner
Wildlife
Sanctuary

Bikaner

Kolayat

Deshnok

Nokha

Nagau

Ramgarh

JAISALMER

Ramdevra

Phalodi

Khichan

Sam

Jaisalmer

Pokaran

Osiyan

Khuri

JODHPUR

Jodhpur

Saraswati

Bilara

Rohet

BARMER

Barmer

Balotra

Dhawa
Doli
Wildlife
Sanctuary

Sardar
Samand

Pali

Hyderabad

River

Jalor

PALI

ARAVALLI

JALOR

SIROHI

Sirohi

Guru
Shikhar
(1722m)

RAJSAMAND
Nathdwara

Nagda

Udaipur

Mt Abu

Abu Road

Mewar Hills

Palanpur

Great Rann
of Kutch

Radhanpur

Dungarpur

GUJARAT

Mahesana

Himatnagar

Gandhinagar

Ahmedabad

Abohar
Bathinda
Thanesar
Haridwar

UTTAR
PRADESH

Sirsa
10
Karnal
Rampur

Suratgarh
Panipat
1

HARYANA
Sonipat
Meerut

GANGANAGAR
Hisar

CHURU
Rajgarh

**SHEKHAWATI
REGION**
The extraordinary painted
havelis (mansions) of
the merchant class

DELHI
24

Sardarshah

Churu
JHUNJHUNU
Rewari

JAIPUR
The 'Pink City', with
its fascinating
palace and busy
artisan quarters

Ratangarh
11
Fatehpur
Jhunjhunu

Didwana
Sikar
Nawalgarh
Nim Ka
Thana
Kot Putli
Bansur
Alwar
Deeg
Mathura
2

SIKAR
Shahpura
JAIPUR
Sariska
Tiger
Reserve
ALWAR
Bharatpur
Agra

Sambhar
Salt Lake
Amber
11A
11
Keoladeo
Ghana
National Park
BHARATPUR

NAGAUR
Merta
Jaipur
Sanganer
Basi
Dausa
SAWAI
MADHOPUR
Dholpur

**KEOLADEO GHANA
NATIONAL PARK**
World Heritage–listed
sanctuary, home to over
400 bird species

Pushkar
Ajmer
Kishangarh
Dudu
Phagi
Chatsu
DHOLPUR

RANGE
Beawar
AJMER
Kekri
Deoli
12
TONK
Tonk
Ranthambhore
National Park
Sawai
Madhopur
3

BHILWARA
BUNDI
**PUSHKAR CAMEL
FESTIVAL**
The world-famous
shindig held near
Pushkar's sacred lake

Deogarh
Bundi
BARAN
25
Jhansi

Bhilwara
Mandalgarh
Bijolia
Kota
Baran
Shivpuri

Rajsamand
CHITTORGARH
Chittorgarh
Rana
Pratap
Sagar
KOTA
Darrah
Wildlife
Sanctuary
Guna
26

Chappan Hills
Nimach
Chambal River
Jhalawar
JHALAWAR
Aklera

UDAIPUR
Jaisamand
Lake &
Wildlife
Sanctuary
Gandhi
Sagar
Rajgarh

MADHYA
PRADESH

DUNGARPUR
BANSWARA
CHITTORGARH
The majestic fort, a
symbol of Rajput
chivalry and honour

Galiakot
Banswara
12
Bhopal

Ratlam
Ujjain
3
12

Rajasthan
3rd edition – October 2002
First published – January 1997

Published by
Lonely Planet Publications Pty Ltd ABN 36 005 607 983
90 Maribyrnong St, Footscray, Victoria 3011, Australia

Lonely Planet offices
Australia Locked Bag 1, Footscray, Victoria 3011
USA 150 Linden St, Oakland, CA 94607
UK 10a Spring Place, London NW5 3BH
France 1 rue du Dahomey, 75011 Paris

Photographs
Many or all images in this guide are available for licensing from
Lonely Planet Images.
W www.lonelyplanetimages.com

Front cover photograph
Hundreds of pilgrims flock to the ghats during the annual Hindu
pilgrimage to holy Pushkar Lake (Dallas Stribley)

ISBN 1 74059 363 4

Printed by Craft Print International Ltd, Singapore

**Although the authors
and Lonely Planet try
to make the informa-
tion as accurate as
possible, we accept
no responsibility for
any loss, injury or
inconvenience sus-
tained by anyone
using this book.**

Contents – Text

Contents – Maps

The Authors

Monique Choy

On Monique's travels she has sipped tea with a Templar knight on the Camino de Santiago in Spain, cast a line for barramundi with Yolngu people in Arnhemland and tussled with an angry ghost on a former island of the banished in the Maldives.

She now lives in the town of Cockatoo, near Melbourne, Australia, where she attempts to keep her organic garden alive between trips overseas. She has contributed to Lonely Planet's *Aboriginal Australia & the Torres Strait Islands*, *Australia*, *Out to Eat – Melbourne* and *Tibet*.

Sarina Singh

After finishing a business degree in Melbourne, Sarina bought a one-way ticket to Delhi. In India she completed a corporate traineeship with the Sheraton but later ditched hotels for newspapers, working as a freelance journalist and foreign correspondent. After four years in the subcontinent she returned to Australia, pursued postgraduate journalism qualifications and co-wrote and directed a television documentary.

Sarina has worked on Lonely Planet's *Aboriginal Australia & the Torres Strait Islands*, *North India*, *Mauritius, Reunion & Seychelles*, *Africa on a shoestring*, *Sacred India*, three editions of *India*, the first two editions of *Rajasthan* and the *Out to Eat* restaurant guides to Melbourne and Sydney. She has also contributed to various international publications, including the *Sunday Times* and *National Geographic Traveler*.

FROM MONIQUE

Very special thanks to Mark Goudkamp for bumping down the road with me, Sarina Singh for support and advice, Sam Milward at Anokhi, Jack Reece at Help in Suffering, John and Faith Singh and Aparna Bordia at Intach, Ramesh Jangid at Apani Dhani, Laxmi Kant Jangid at the Hotel Shiv Shekhawati, Bablu in Udaipur and the friendly folk at the RTDC. Thanks also to the many readers who wrote in with great tips and advice, and especially the hard-working team at Lonely Planet: Hilary Ericksen, Adriana Mammarella, John Hinman, Jenny Mullaly, Nina Rousseau, and Jody Whiteoak.

This Book

The first edition of *Rajasthan* was researched and written by Michelle Coxall and Sarina Singh, and the second edition by Sarina Singh. The third edition was updated by Monique Choy, with assistance from Patrick Horton on the Delhi and Agra chapters.

FROM THE PUBLISHER

This edition of *Rajasthan* was produced in Lonely Planet's Melbourne office. John Hinman and Jenny Mullaly coordinated editing, and were assisted through editing and proofing by Nina Rousseau. Jody Whiteoak coordinated cartography and design, and was helped by Jack Gavran and Amanda Sierp. Victoria Harrison and Jody took the book through layout, with the help of designers Anna Judd and Birgit Jordan. Isabelle Young created the index, Emma Koch compiled the Language chapter and Shahara Ahmed produced the climate charts. Lonely Planet Images coordinated the illustrative material, and Margie Jung and Maria Vallianos designed the book's cover. Adriana Mammarella, Chris Love and Shahara supervised design, and Hilary Ericksen supervised editing. Thanks to Mark Germanchis and Lachlan Ross for their technical support during layout.

ACKNOWLEDGMENTS

Grateful acknowledgment is made for reproduction permission to HarperCollins Publishers Ltd for the excerpt from *City of Djinns* © 1993 William Dalrymple.

Thanks

Many thanks to the following travellers who used the last edition of *Rajasthan* and wrote to us with helpful hints, useful advice and interesting anecdotes:

Maayan Abas, Shabnam Arora Afsah, Neal Alagia, Juan Allos, Basil Anand D'Souza, Suzanne Anthony, Nina Antonissen, Nick & Sally Archer, Victor Ashe, Sally Atkinson, Sam Attenborough, Peter Baker, Renske Bakker, Angela Bara, David Barrett, Fiona Baverstock, Chris Beall, Carrie Beam, Ronan Beirne, Sally Bennett, Joselyn Besson, Marianne Beyer, Pankaj Bharadwaj, Anna Bielski, Gideon Bierer, Magali Billot, Marieke Bink, Matthew Bird, Alice Birnbaum, Sam Blatt, Christopher Blurton, Anne Boise d'Enghien, Annelies Bongers, Margarita Bonilla, David Bornstein, Angela Botham, James Botham, Tim Bradbeer, Bruce & Lois Bradberry, Karla Branen, Jo Bray, Guy Breton, John Brewski, Mary Brosnan, Judith Brouwer, Sean Broxham, Jeroen Bruggeman, Jim Bryce, Hugh Buck, George Burn, BMC Buttery, Jenny Buyck, Louise Byrnes, H Carlo, RJ Cartman, Rowan Castle, Michelle Catlin, Catherine Causer, Mary-Liz Chaffee, Hugues Charlot, Eugenie & Stephane Charriere, Andrea Cheung, Chris Chihrin, Shiva Choudhary, Victoria Clark, Matthew Claydon, Johan Collier, Bruce Cone, George Cook, Dean Cresswell, Wendy Crouch, Neal Croxford, Charlotte Dadd, Niva Dagani, Nigel Dahl, Keith Dalglish, Pierre-Alain Darlet, Sarah Davis, Tom Day, Nathalie De Sutter, Alann De Vuyst, Roland Denning, Anna Derivi, Prashant Desai, Karin Diderich, Rolf Diepen, David Dixon, Catherine Dobb, Cheryl Donald, Lisa Dransfield, Wim Driessen, Carolin Dufhues, Keely Dunhill. Ilga Eger, Irmin Eggens, Eva Ekelund, Heribert Engemann, Tyler Entwistle, Elodie Et Aurelie Houssier, Luis Etxeberria, Suzy Evan, Lorna Evans, John Fenner, Rosy Fernandes, Bruno Fiechter, Monique Floothuis, Marten Folmer, Barbara Forster, Christine Futia, Rowdy Gale, Jay Gandhi, Mathew Gedigian, Georg Geibler, Aida Ghion, Freya Gibson, Denise & Darren Godfrey, FB Goemann, Sandhya & Jyoti Goenka, Joziena Goldie, Noemie Goldszal, Jesse Goode, Julian Graham, Anthony Gray, Katherine Grech, Catherine Griffiths, Mike Grimmer, Mike & Christabel Grimmer, Martine Groves, Gabrielle Guillemin, Heinz Gunther Fischer, Stuart Gurner, Nir Haimovich, Petra Hammerl, Anthony Harrison, Anthony & Ski Harrison, MSK Harrison, Sara Harrop, Stacie Hartung, James Hastings, Paul Haywood, Wayne Herd, Eva Herkenrath, Itai Hermelin, Mark Hodgetts, Rhonda Hoff, Jelka Hopster, Trudy Howson, Blanche Hunt, Ed Hunter, Otto Insam, Rhoda Isaacs, Kate Israel, Shirley Jackson, Jon Jacobs, Ronnie Jaeger, Parela Jagger, Justin Jagosh, Ramesh C Jangid, Corinne Jaworenko, Karen Jedema, Graham Jeffs, Darina Jevosova, Denn John, Martha Johnson, Glyn Jones, Steve Jones, Bo Jonsson, Anna Kajerman, Haemish Kane, Cheyne Keith, Sarah Keller, Andrea Kellmann, Jenni Kesti, AJ King, Victoria Knighton, Brian Kong, Ruth Konig, Thor Kuhlmann, Karen Kwok, Valentina

Lacmanovic, Melanie Ladwig, Yoann Lancien, DC Langmead, Nora I
Langton, Aja Larsson, Sarah Lathrop, Winnie Lau, Cassandra Leather-
man, Lucie Leblanc, Olaf Lechtenfeld, Jennifer Letham, Toby Leyland,
David & Mary Lloyd, Graham Lupp, Paul Maas, Iona Mackenzie, Mike
Madick, Shirley Mancino, Susmita Mandal, Mirelle Marivoet, Lois
Mason, Philippa Matherson, Silke Matussek, Nina Mayorek, Janine
McDonald, Cynthia McMillan, Kaysha McMonagle, Christine Melzer,
Brent Menke, Connie Menzies, Marc Miller, Daniele Minns, Michal
Miron, Dorothear Mittcalf, Suzanne Molineaux, Angus Moncur,
George Moorcroft, Seana Moorhead, Guy Moorhouse, Clare Myers,
Jamie Nairn, Dhroeh & Sangeetha Nankoe, Jakhan Nguyen, Mattew
O'Neill, Julie Odell, Bryne Oerstavik, Laura Orlando, Bill O'Toole,
Magdalena Pabijan, John Page, Navinder Pandher, Benoit Paradis,
Deepa Parry-Gupta, Arnold Parzer, Giorgio Perversi, Odile Pfauvadel,
Leland Phillips, Emma Pleasance, Max Popp, Rod Priest, Jorg
Puhlmann. S Raghunath, Georg Raiser, Simon Ralfe, Sudad Rasool, TS
Rathore, Llor Razon, Rien Reuser, Hannah Richardson, Larry Rinaldi,
Georges Ripka, Aaron & Laura Ritchey, Rami Rivlin, Marika Roath,
Suzanne Roberts, Chris Robson, Eugeni Sainy, Neil Salt, John Sanders,
Nicola Scatassi, Alois & Jacky Schallberger, Monika Scheiber, Markus
Schilling, Anne Schnurr, Dirk Schoeps, A Schomeecker, Joerg Schulze,
Katja Schwieger, Charlotte Senay, Ravi Shah, Gilad Shalom, Dr Sharik,
Nidhi Sharma, Vina Shukla, Els Heerink Siemerink, AJ Singh, Thsunder
Singh, Galit Sivan, Mythili Sivaraman, Paola Smeriglio, Melanie Smith,
Paul Sobkin, Jonas Soderlund, Estibalitz Solana, Markus Sommer,
Alfred Staffels, Leticia Subira, John & Lynn Sullivan, Adam Sutcliffe,
Jude Talbot, Amit Taneja, John Taylor, Lisa Taylor, Alexandra Terhorst,
Christina Themar, Julie Thomas, Nick Thompson, Marg Thornell, Tonny
Tornblom, Simone Torreggiani, Stephanie Torrington, Aloma Treister,
Meagan Twomey, Kelly Udall, Reni & Nadine van Brandenburg,
Caroline & Herman van den Wall Bake, Siemen van der Kamp, Celine
& Justine van Lamsweerde, Ingrid van Loon, Anton van Veen, Ellen
van Vossen, Serinde van Wijk, Bart Vandelplassche, Ray VarnBuhler,
Isabel Vietta, Claske Vingerling, Tim Vivian, Hanna Vogt, Joachim von
Usslar, Joost Wagenaar, Scott Waight, Russell Wakefield, Felicity
Waley-Cohen, Val Walker Jones, Birgit Walter, Gundula Walther,
Simon Ward, Jane Wayne, Julie Webb, Helen Webster, Lynn Weddle,
Joshy Wedgwood, Carol Welsby, Kate White, Dr Aaron Wiegand,
Peter Wiles, Mark Wilkinson, Melinda Williams, Safaa Wood, Susan
Wood, Elaine Wycherley, Noriko Yamazaki, Marcus Yorke, Andreina
Zagari, Jane Zaring, Ems Zuidgeest

Foreword

ABOUT LONELY PLANET GUIDEBOOKS

The story begins with a classic travel adventure: Tony and Maureen Wheeler's 1972 journey across Europe and Asia to Australia. There was no useful information about the overland trail then, so Tony and Maureen published the first Lonely Planet guidebook to meet a growing need.

From a kitchen table, Lonely Planet has grown to become the largest independent travel publisher in the world, with offices in Melbourne (Australia), Oakland (USA), London (UK) and Paris (France).

Today Lonely Planet guidebooks cover the globe. There is an ever-growing list of books and information in a variety of media. Some things haven't changed. The main aim is still to make it possible for adventurous travellers to get out there – to explore and better understand the world.

At Lonely Planet we believe travellers can make a positive contribution to the countries they visit – if they respect their host communities and spend their money wisely. Since 1986 a percentage of the income from each book has been donated to aid projects and human rights campaigns, and, more recently, to wildlife conservation.

Although inclusion in a guidebook usually implies a recommendation we cannot list every good place. Exclusion does not necessarily imply criticism. In fact there are a number of reasons why we might exclude a place – sometimes it is simply inappropriate to encourage an influx of travellers.

UPDATES & READER FEEDBACK

Things change – prices go up, schedules change, good places go bad and bad places go bankrupt. Nothing stays the same. So, if you find things better or worse, recently opened or long-since closed, please tell us and help make the next edition even more accurate and useful.

Lonely Planet thoroughly updates each guidebook as often as possible – usually every two years, although for some destinations the gap can be longer. Between editions, up-to-date information is available in our free, quarterly *Planet Talk* newsletter and monthly email bulletin *Comet*. The *Upgrades* section of our website (W www.lonelyplanet.com) is also regularly updated by Lonely Planet authors, and the site's *Scoop* section covers news and current affairs relevant to travellers. Lastly, the *Thorn Tree* bulletin board and *Postcards* section carry unverified, but fascinating, reports from travellers.

Tell us about it! We genuinely value your feedback. A well-travelled team at Lonely Planet reads and acknowledges every email and letter we receive and ensures that every morsel of information finds its way to the relevant authors, editors and cartographers.

Everyone who writes to us will find their name listed in the next edition of the appropriate guidebook, and will receive the latest issue of *Comet* or *Planet Talk*. The very best contributions will be rewarded with a free guidebook.

We may edit, reproduce and incorporate your comments in Lonely Planet products such as guidebooks, websites and digital products, so let us know if you don't want your comments reproduced or your name acknowledged.

How to contact Lonely Planet:
Online: e talk2us@lonelyplanet.com.au, W www.lonelyplanet.com
Australia: Locked Bag 1, Footscray, Victoria 3011
UK: 10a Spring Place, London NW5 3BH
USA: 150 Linden St, Oakland, CA 94607

Introduction

Rajasthan, the Land of Kings, truly embodies all the fairy-tale notions that its name evokes. This is the home of the Rajputs, the ruling warrior clans who controlled this part of India for over 1000 years. The three Rajput clans claim descent from the sun, the moon and the flames of a sacrificial fire, and their highly evolved code of chivalry and honour is akin to that of medieval European knights. Fiercely independent and renowned for their valour and pride, they preferred to die an honourable death than to suffer the ignominy of capture. When defeat was inevitable, this translated into occasions of grim mass suicide known as *jauhar*, in which hundreds of women hurled themselves onto funeral pyres, while their men rode out to face certain death at the hands of the enemy.

The Rajputs entrenched themselves in this harsh desert land in enormous forts

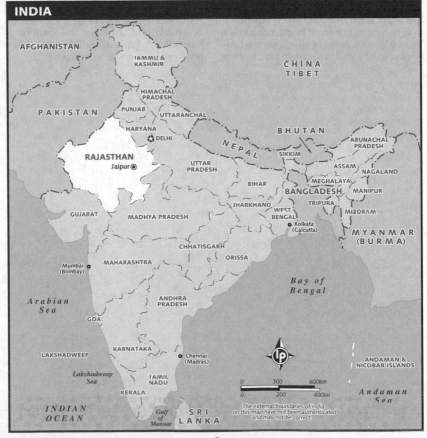

INDIA

AFGHANISTAN

CHINA
TIBET

JAMMU &
KASHMIR

PAKISTAN

HIMACHAL
PRADESH

PUNJAB

UTTARANCHAL

HARYANA

DELHI

BHUTAN

NEPAL

ARUNACHAL
PRADESH

RAJASTHAN

Jaipur

UTTAR
PRADESH

SIKKIM

ASSAM

NAGALAND

BIHAR

MEGHALAYA

MANIPUR

BANGLADESH

JHARKHAND

TRIPURA

GUJARAT

MADHYA PRADESH

WEST
BENGAL

MIZORAM

Kolkata
(Calcutta)

MYANMAR
(BURMA)

CHHATISGARH

ORISSA

Mumbai
(Bombay)

MAHARASHTRA

Bay of
Bengal

Arabian
Sea

ANDHRA
PRADESH

GOA

LAKSHADWEEP

KARNATAKA

Chennai
(Madras)

ANDAMAN &
NICOBAR ISLANDS

Lakshadweep
Sea

TAMIL
NADU

KERALA

0   300   600km
0   200   400mi

The external boundaries of India
on this map have not been authenticated
and may not be correct.

Andaman
Sea

INDIAN
OCEAN

Gulf
of
Mannar

SRI
LANKA

such as those at Chittorgarh, Jodhpur and Jaisalmer. Many of their sumptuous palaces are now open to visitors, offering a glimpse into the decadence of the princes' lives in their last glory days of the 19th and early 20th centuries.

Modern Rajasthan is fiercely proud of its feudal heritage, but it has left the state one of the poorest in India, cursed also by its harsh environment, where drought regularly threatens the livelihoods of ordinary people. The majority of Rajasthanis still live a hard life in dry, dusty villages, but they fill their daily lives with colour. Canary yellows, emerald greens, vivid purples, electric blues and splashes of brilliant reds and oranges – the effect is dazzling, and you'll experience it everywhere: in a sea of bright turbans on a crowded bus; a group of village women huddled around a stall in a busy bazaar; or even in the middle of the desert, as a lone iridescent-pink turbaned villager leads his sleepy-eyed camel home across the parched plains.

The state's many festivals also offer the perfect escape from the daily grind. Trade fairs, holy days and seasonal changes are opportunities to put on the glad rags, decorate the camel, and join thousands in celebration. At these times the glorious history of the Rajputs is remembered in stories and songs, part of a rich folk tradition of performing arts, acrobatics, puppetry, music and dance.

Whether you've come here to spot a tiger in a national park, chill out in a former palace or cross the desert on a camel, you'll be enchanted by the people and culture of Rajasthan. In contrast to the sometimes inhospitable land, there is a fine tradition of hospitality here, and you'll be treated as a privileged guest wherever you travel.

Facts about Rajasthan

HISTORY

Early History

Historians believe that Rajasthan may have been one of the earliest settled areas of India. The Harappan culture, which flourished in the Indus Valley in modern-day Pakistan from 2500 to 1700 BC, is generally considered the first major civilisation of India. However, evidence of a pre-Harappan culture has been discovered at Kalibangan, near Ganaganagar in northern Rajasthan. At this site, terracotta pottery and jewellery dating from 3000 BC have been discovered. Kalibangan was later absorbed into the bronze-age Harappan civilisation, which had trade links with Mesopotamia and a taste for fine art. The decline of the culture in the 2nd millennium BC is thought to be a result of flooding in the Indus Valley, or perhaps climatic change that led to a failure of agriculture.

Bhil and Mina tribes next settled the area, developing small kingdoms that battled each other, the first in a long and proud history of warfare in Rajasthan.

Rajasthan remained for the most part independent from the great empires consolidating their hold on the subcontinent in its early history. Buddhism failed to make substantial inroads here; the Mauryan empire (321–184 BC), whose most renowned emperor, Ashoka, converted to Buddhism in 262 BC, had minimal impact in Rajasthan. However, there are Buddhist caves and *stupas* (Buddhist shrines) at Jhalawar, in southern Rajasthan, and Ashoka left behind several rock-cut edicts at Bairat.

Ancient Hindu scriptural epics make reference to sites in present-day Rajasthan. The holy pilgrimage site of Pushkar is mentioned in both the Mahabharata and Ramayana.

Emergence of the Rajputs

The fall of the Gupta empire, which held dominance in northern India for nearly 300 years until the early 5th century, was followed by a period of instability as various local chieftains sought to gain supremacy. Powers rose and fell in northern India. Stability was only restored with the emergence of the Gurjara Pratiharas, the earliest of the Rajput (from 'Rajputra', or Sons of Princes) dynasties that were later to hold the balance of power throughout Rajasthan.

The emergence of the Rajput warrior clans in the 6th and 7th centuries played the greatest role in the history of Rajasthan. From these clans came the name Rajputana, as the princely states were known during the Muslim invasion of India. The Rajputs fled aggressors in their homelands in Punjab, Gujarat and Uttar Pradesh to settle in Rajasthan, subjugating the indigenous tribes, the Bhils and Minas. There is evidence to suggest that some of the Rajput clans can trace their emergence to the arrival of foreign invaders such as the White Huns, who may have been assimilated here, and other invaders and settlers from Central Asia.

Whatever their actual origins, the Rajputs have evolved a complex mythological genealogy. This ancestry can be divided into two main branches: the Suryavansa, or Race of the Sun, which claims direct descent from Rama; and the Induvansa, or Race of the Moon, which claims descent from Krishna. Later a third branch was added, the Agni-kula, or 'Fire Born'. These people claim they were manifested from the flames of a sacrificial fire on Mt Abu. From these three principal races emerged the 36 Rajput clans.

As they were predominantly of lower castes, the Rajputs should not have aspired to warrior status – an occupation reserved for those in the upper echelons of the caste hierarchy. Their (albeit contrived) celestial origins, however, enabled them to claim descent from the Kshatriya, or martial caste, which in the caste hierarchy falls just below that of the Brahmins.

The Rajput clans gave rise to dynasties such as the Chauhans, Sisodias, Kachhwahas and Rathores. Chauhans of the Agnikula Race emerged in the 12th century and were renowned for their valour. Their territories included the Sapadalaksha kingdom, which encompassed a vast area including present-day Jaipur, Ranthambhore (part of Mewar), the western portion of Bundi district, Ajmer, Kishangarh, and even, at one time, Delhi. Branches of the Chauhans also ruled the territories known as Ananta (in present-day Shekhawati) and Saptasatabhumi.

The Sisodias of the Suryavansa race, originally from Gujarat, migrated to Rajasthan in the mid-7th century and reigned over Mewar, which encompassed Udaipur and Chittorgarh.

The Kachhwahas, originally from Gwalior in Madhya Pradesh, travelled west in the 12th century. They built the massive fort at Amber, and later shifted the capital to Jaipur. Like the Sisodias, they belonged to the Suryavansa race.

Also belonging to the Suryavansa race, the Rathores (earlier known as Rastrakutas) travelled from Kannauj, in Uttar Pradesh. Initially they settled in Pali, south of present-day Jodhpur, but later moved to Mandore in 1381 and ruled over Marwar (Jodhpur). Later they started building the stunning Meherangarh (fort) at Jodhpur.

The Bhattis, who belong to the Induvansa race, were driven from their homeland in the Punjab by the Turks, and installed themselves at Jaisalmer in 1156. They remained more or less entrenched in their desert kingdom until they were integrated into the state of Rajasthan following Independence.

The Warrior Legacy

The first external threat to the dominance of the Rajputs was that posed by the Arabs who took over Sind in 713. The Gurjara Pratiharas' response was largely defensive. The Arabs were repulsed by the Gujara Pratiharas, who were led by their king, Nagabhata I, founder of the Pratihara empire. The Arabs also tested their strength against the Rastrakutas. Unfortunately, when not pitting their wits against the Arabs, the Pratiharas and Rastrakutas were busy fighting each other.

By the third decade of the 8th century, a new threat was emerging – the Turks, who had occupied Ghazni in Afghanistan.

Around AD 1001, Mahmud of Ghazni's army descended upon India, destroying infidel temples and removing everything of value that could be carried. The Rajputs were not immune from these incursions; a confederation of Rajput rulers assembled a vast army and marched northwards to meet the advancing Turks. Unfortunately it was a case of too little, too late, and they were decisively and crushingly vanquished. The Pratiharas, then centred at Kannauj, fled the city before the Turks arrived, and in their absence the temples of Kannauj were sacked and desecrated, as were so many others in northern India.

Towards the end of the 12th century, Mohammed of Ghori invaded India to take up where Mahmud of Ghazni had left off. He met with a collection of princely states that failed to mount a united front. Although initially repulsed, Ghori later triumphed, and Delhi and Ajmer were lost to the Muslims. Ajmer has remained a Muslim stronghold, apart from a brief period when it was retaken by the Rathores. Today it is an important Muslim place of pilgrimage.

The Rajputs vs the Sultans of Delhi

Mohammed of Ghori was killed in 1206, and his successor, Qutb-ud-din, became the first of the sultans of Delhi. Within 20 years, the Muslims had brought the whole of the Ganges basin under their control.

In 1297, Ala-ud-din Khilji pushed the Muslim borders south into Gujarat. He mounted a protracted siege of the massive fort at Ranthambhore, ruled at the time by the Rajput chief Hammir Deva. Hammir was reported as dead (although it's unknown if he did actually die in the siege) and upon hearing of their chief's demise, the women of the fort collectively threw themselves on a pyre, thus performing the first instance of *jauhar* (mass suicide) in the history of the Rajputs. In 1303 Ala-ud-din went on to sack the fort at Chittorgarh, held by the Sisodia clan. According to tradition, he had heard of the great beauty of Padmini, the consort of the Sisodian chief, and resolved to carry her off with him (see

Sons of the Sun

Legend has it that the Rajput royal houses are descendants of the heavens, hailing from the moon and the flames of a sacrificial fire. The maharana of Udaipur (Mewar), king of all Rajput kings, is from the illustrious Sisodia clan, which traces its origin to the sun.

Most royal families of India have their own coat of arms, symbolic of their family's history. The focus of the Udaipur royal family's coat of arms is a blazing sun, since their ancestors were born of the sun. There are two figures flanked on either side of the sun: one is a Rajput warrior holding a shield (which signifies the upholding of Mewar) and the other is a Bhil tribal archer.

The Bhil tribes were renowned for their skilled archery and the maharanas of Udaipur relied on them to protect the kingdom. In the past, at the coronation of a maharana, a Bhil chieftain would cut his thumb and place a blood *tika* (a mark devout Hindus put on their forehead) on the maharana before leading him to the *gaddi* (throne of a prince).

SARAH JOLLY

The Mewar Coat of Arms:
'The Almighty protects those who stand steadfast in upholding righteousness'

the boxed text 'Death before Dishonour' in the Southern Rajasthan chapter). Like Ranthambhore before it, Chittorgarh fell to the Muslim leader.

The Rajputs vs the Mughals

The Delhi sultanate weakened at the start of the 16th century, and the Rajputs took advantage of this to restore and expand their territories. The kingdom of Mewar, ruled by the Sisodias under the leadership of Rana Sangram Singh, gained pre-eminence among the Rajput states. Under this leader, Mewar pushed its boundaries far beyond its original territory, posing a formidable threat to the new Mughal empire which was emerging under the leadership of Babur (r. 1527–30).

Babur, a descendent of both Timur and Genghis Khan, marched into Punjab from his capital at Kabul in Afghanistan in 1525 and defeated the sultan of Delhi at Panipat. He then focused his attention on the Rajput princely states, many of which, anticipating his designs, had banded together to form a united front under Rana Sangram Singh.

Unfortunately, the Rajputs were defeated by Babur. The Rajputs sustained great losses, with many Rajput chiefs falling in

the fray, including Rana Sangram Singh, who reputedly had 80 wounds on his body which he had suffered during this and previous campaigns.

The defeat shook the foundations of the princely states. Mewar's confidence was shattered by the death of its illustrious leader, and its territories contracted following subsequent attacks by the sultan of Gujarat.

Now Marwar, under its ruler Maldeo, emerged as the strongest of the Rajput states, and it recorded a victory against the claimant to the Mughal throne, Sher Shah. However, none of the Rajputs were able to withstand the formidable threat posed by the most renowned of the Mughal emperors, Akbar (r. 1556–1605).

Recognising that the Rajputs could not be conquered by mere force alone, Akbar contracted a marriage alliance with a princess of the important Kachhwaha clan which held Amber (and later founded Jaipur). The Kachhwahas, unlike their Rajput brethren, aligned themselves with the powerful Mughals, and even sent troops to aid them in times of battle.

Akbar also used conventional methods to assert his dominance over the Rajputs, wresting Ajmer from the Rathores of Marwar. All the important Rajput states eventually acknowledged Mughal sovereignty and became vassal states, except Mewar, which fiercely clung to its independence, refusing to pay homage to the infidels.

An uneasy truce was maintained between the Rajputs and the Mughal emperors, until the reign of Aurangzeb (r. 1658–1707), the last great Mughal emperor, when relations were characterised by mutual hostility.

Aurangzeb devoted all his resources to extending the Mughal empire's boundaries. Punitive taxes, which he levied on his subjects in order to pay for his military exploits, combined with his religious zealotry eventually secured his downfall.

The Rajputs were united in their opposition to Aurangzeb; the Rathores and Sisodias raised arms against him. It didn't take long for revolts by his enemies to break out on all sides and, with his death in 1707, the Mughal empire's fortunes rapidly declined.

The Rajputs vs the Marathas

Following the death of Aurangzeb and the dissolution of the Mughal empire came the Marathas. They first rose to prominence with Shivaji who, between 1646 and 1680, performed feats of arms and heroism across central India. The Maratha empire continued under the Peshwas, hereditary government ministers who became the true rulers. They gradually tightened their stranglehold on the weakening Mughal empire, first by supplying troops and then by actually taking control of Mughal land.

The Marathas conducted numerous raids on the Rajputs, and the latter, too busy fighting among themselves, laid themselves open to attack, resulting in numerous defeats in battle, the loss of territories and the inevitable decline of the Rajput states.

Expansion of British Powers

Since establishing its first trading post in India in 1612, the East India Company, a London trading company that had a monopoly on trade in India, had been gradually consolidating its power. The British victory in the Battle of Plassey (1757), close to Calcutta, confirmed their dominance in the east, and after the collapse of the Mughal empire they moved to fill the power vacuum with a series of battles and alliances with local rulers. By the early 19th century, India was effectively under British control. From 1784 onwards, the British government in London began to take a more direct role in supervising affairs in India, although the territory was still notionally administered by the East India Company until 1858.

Meanwhile, the Marathas continued to mount raids on the Rajputs. Initially the British adopted a policy of neutrality towards the feuding parties. However, they eventually stepped into the fray, negotiating treaties with the leaders of the main Rajput states. British protection was offered in return for Rajput support.

Weakened by habitual fighting between themselves and their skirmishes with the Marathas, one by one the princely states forfeited their independence in exchange for this protection. British residents were gradually installed in the princely states. The British ultimately eliminated the Maratha threat, but by this stage the Rajputs were effectively reduced to puppet leaders and lackeys of the British.

While the Rajput leaders enjoyed the status and prestige of their positions, discontent was manifesting itself in the rest of India. Anger was growing throughout the country due to the influx of cheap goods such as textiles from Britain, which destroyed many livelihoods, as well as the dispossession of many rulers and the taxes imposed on landowners. This anger found expression in the 1857 Uprising when soldiers and peasants took over Delhi for four months and besieged the British Residency in Lucknow for five months before they were finally suppressed. There were also uprisings in Rajasthan among the poor and middle classes, but the Rajput royals supported the British and were rewarded for their loyalty by retaining their titles after the British government assumed control of the country from the East India Company in 1858.

The 1857 Uprising was a precursor to widespread opposition to British rule that occurred throughout India. It was Mohandas Gandhi, later known as Mahatma Gandhi, who galvanised the peasants and villagers into the nonviolent resistance that was to spearhead the nationalist movement.

Road to Independence

By the time WWII had ended, Indian independence was inevitable. The war dealt a deathblow to the myth of European superiority, and Britain no longer had the power nor the desire to maintain a vast empire. Within India, however, a major problem had developed: the large Muslim minority had realised that an independent India would also be a Hindu-dominated India.

Thus the country was divided along religious lines, with the Muslim League, which was led by Muhammad Ali Jinnah, speaking for the Muslims, and the Congress Party, led by Jawaharlal Nehru, representing the Hindu population.

Gandhi was absolutely opposed to severing the Muslim-dominated regions from the prospective new nation. However, Jinnah was intransigent: 'I will have India divided, or India destroyed' was his uncompromising demand. The new viceroy, Louis Mountbatten, made a last-ditch attempt to convince the rival factions that a united India was a more sensible proposition, but the decision was reluctantly made to divide the country. Independence was finally instituted on 15 August 1947, with the concomitant partitioning of the nascent country. The result was a Hindu-dominated India and a Muslim-dominated West and East Pakistan.

Emergence of the State of Rajasthan

It took time for the boundaries of the proposed new state of Rajasthan to be defined. In 1948, it comprised the southern and southeastern states of Rajputana. With the merger of Mewar, Udaipur became the capital of the United State of Rajasthan. The maharana of Udaipur was invested with the title of *rajpramukh* (head of state). Manikya Lal Varma was appointed prime minister of the new state, which was inaugurated on 18 April 1948.

Almost from the outset the prime minister came into opposition with the *rajpramukh* over the constitution of the state government ministry. Varma wanted to form a ministry of all Congress members. The *rajpramukh* was keen to install his own candidates from among the *jagirdars*, or feudal lords. *Jagirdars* traditionally acted as intermediaries between the tillers of the soil (peasants) and the state, taking rent or produce from the tenants and paying tribute to the princely ruler. They were symbols of the old feudal order, under which millions of inhabitants of Rajputana had been held in serfdom. Varma was keen to abolish the age-old system of *jagirdari* and, with Nehru's support, installed his own Congress ministry and do away with this feudal relic.

Still retaining their independence from India were Jaipur and the desert kingdoms of Bikaner, Jodhpur and Jaisalmer. From a security point of view, it was vital to the new Indian Union to ensure that the desert kingdoms, which were contiguous with Pakistan, were integrated into the new nation. The Rajput rulers were offered handsome privy purses, or ongoing government stipends, to sweeten the deal. The princes finally agreed to sign the Instrument of Accession, and the kingdoms of Bikaner, Jodhpur, Jaisalmer and Jaipur were merged in 1949. The maharaja of Jaipur, Man Singh II, was invested with the title of *rajpramukh*. Jaipur became the capital of the new state of Rajasthan. Heera Lal Shastri was installed as the first premier of Rajasthan.

Later in 1949, the United State of Matsya, comprising the former kingdoms of Bharatpur, Alwar, Karauli and Dholpur, was incorporated into Rajasthan. As a result, Rajasthan became the second-largest state in India, exceeded in geographical area only by the central Indian state of Madhya Pradesh. It attained its current dimensions in November 1956, with the additions of Ajmer-Merwara, Abu Rd and a part of Dilwara, originally part of the princely kingdom of Sirohi that had been divided between Gujarat and Rajasthan.

Indira Gandhi (daughter of India's first prime minister, Jawaharlal Nehru) came to

India–Pakistan Standoff

In 1998 the BJP, led by Prime Minister Atal Behari Vajpayee, assumed national power and promptly blasted its way into world headlines by defiantly detonating five nuclear devices in the Rajasthan desert near Pokaran. This shattered any hopes of a peaceful resolution to the Kashmir crisis that had plagued international relations with Pakistan throughout the 1990s. Pakistan furiously responded to India by testing its own nuclear devices, igniting global concern about a nuclear arms race in south Asia.

The tension between the two rivals escalated again when the Indian national parliament was hit by a suicide bomber in December 2001, killing 12 people. India blamed Pakistan-based Kashmiri militants for the attack, and began a heavy build-up of troops along the border with Pakistan, including in Rajasthan. At the time of writing the situation in Rajasthan was stable, with the focus of hostilities firmly in Kashmir. However, only a handful of travellers were venturing out to the western desert-towns of Jaisalmer, Bikaner and Barmer, despite assurances from tourist authorities that there was no danger to visitors.

power in 1966 and abolished the privy purses and privileges granted to the Rajasthan princes in 1971.

Rajasthan Today

During the 1990s India was swept up in a wave of Hindu nationalism, and Rajasthan was no exception. In 1990 state government was won by a coalition of the Janata Dal and the staunchly Hindu revivalist Bharatiya Janata Party (BJP). They retained state power until the most recent elections in 1998 when they lost control to the Congress, however in the same year the BJP assumed power nationally.

Many of the former rulers of Rajasthan continue to use the title of maharaja (or a similar title) for social purposes. The only power it holds today is as a status symbol. Since the abolition of the privy purses, the princes have had to support themselves financially. Some princes hastily sold heirlooms and properties for a pittance, in a desperate attempt to pay bills.

While a handful squandered their family fortunes, others refused to surrender their heritage, and turned to politics (see the boxed text 'The Rani of Rambagh' in the Jaipur chapter), business or other vocations. Many converted their palaces into hotels, now prime tourist destinations, such as the Lake Palace Hotel in Udaipur, the Rambagh Palace in Jaipur and the Umaid Bhawan Palace in Jodhpur. The revenue from such

hotels has enabled the maharajas to maintain their properties, sustain time-honoured family traditions and continue to lead a comfortable lifestyle. However, not all the princes' palaces were on the tourist circuit and they could not rely on tourism as a source of income. Many palaces and forts are today falling into decay.

GEOGRAPHY & GEOLOGY

The state of Rajasthan covers some 342,239 sq km in the northwestern region of India.

Hills of Rajasthan

The state is dissected by the Aravalli Range, which extends diagonally across Rajasthan from the northeast to the southwest, inhibiting the movement of the Thar Desert eastwards. In places, the Aravalli is over 750m high, although the average elevation of the state is between 100m and 350m above sea level. The highest point of the range is known as Guru Shikhar (1721m). The Aravalli may be the oldest existing mountain range in the world. There is a second hilly spur, the Vindhyas, in the southernmost regions of Rajasthan.

Rivers

The Aravalli Range effectively divides Rajasthan's two principal river systems. The Chambal, which is the only perennial river in the state, rises in Madhya Pradesh from the northern slopes of the Vindhyas, entering

Rajasthan at Chaurasigarh. It forms part of the eastern border between Rajasthan and Madhya Pradesh. Supplemented by its tributaries, the Kali Sindh, Alnia, Kunu, Parbati, Eru, Mej, Chakan and Banas, it flows northwestwards, draining into the Yamuna River, which in turn courses across northern India, entering the sea at the Bay of Bengal.

The southern region of Rajasthan is drained by the Mahi and Sabarmati Rivers, while the Luni, which rises about 7km north of Ajmer in the Aravalli at the confluence of the Saraswati and Sagarmati Rivers, is the only river in western Rajasthan. It flows for 482km before draining into the Arabian Sea at the Rann of Kutch in Gujarat. The Luni is seasonal, and comparatively shallow, although at places it is over 2km wide. Its main tributaries are the Lilri, Raipur, Sukri, Bandi, Mitri, Jawai Khari, Sagi and Johari, which all rise in the Aravalli.

Marusthali – Region of Death

The arid desert region in the west of the state is known as Marusthali, or the Region of Death. This sandy wasteland extends between the Aravalli Range to the east and the Sulaiman Kirthar Range to the west. This is the Thar Desert, the eastern extension of the great Saharo-Tharian desert expanse. It encompasses 68% of the state's geographical area and represents 61% of the area covered by desert in India.

In Rajasthan, the arid zone includes the districts of Jaisalmer and Bikaner, the northwestern regions of Barmer and Jodhpur districts, the western section of Nagaur and Churu districts, and the southern portion of Ganganagar district. The desert, the greatest part of which lies in Rajasthan, also extends into the neighbouring states of Gujarat, Punjab and Haryana, and across the international border into Pakistan.

The sandy plains are periodically relieved by low, rugged and barren slopes. The sand dunes of Marusthali, which comprise about 60% of the desert region, are formed partly by the erosion of these low eminences and partly from sand carried from the Rann of Kutch in Gujarat by southwesterly winds.

It is hard to imagine that this now desolate region was once covered by massive forests, and was host to various large animals. In 1996, two amateur palaeontologists discovered animal fossils, which date from some 300 million years ago, in the Thar Desert. They include those of dinosaurs and their ancestors. In the Akal Wood Fossil Park, 16km from Jaisalmer, fossils from nearly 185 million years ago have been recovered. Plant fossils from 45 million years ago indicate that the desertification of Rajasthan is relatively recent and ongoing.

Semiarid Transitional Plain

It is difficult to identify exactly where the desert region merges into the semiarid region, which encompasses about 25% of the geographical area of the state. The semiarid zone is characterised by a larger distribution of rock protrusions and numerous short water-courses. It lies between the Aravalli Range and the Thar Desert, extending westwards from the Aravalli, and encompassing the Ghaggar River Plain, parts of Shekhwati, and the Luni River Basin.

Eastern Plains

The Eastern Plains, a large undulating region characterised by various low eminences, to the east of the Aravalli Range, comprises two distinct areas: the Plain of Mewar, which contains the Banas River Basin, to the north of Udaipur; and, the Chappan Plains, to Udaipur's south. The Plain of Mewar encompasses sections of Bhilwara and Bundi, all of Tonk district and most of Ajmer, Jaipur, Sawai Madhopur and Dholpur districts. It is drained by the Banas River and its tributaries, which flow southeastwards before joining the Chambal River on the Madhya Pradesh–Rajasthan border. The Chappan Plains comprise the two southernmost districts of Banswara and Dungarpur, and are drained by the Mahi River and its tributaries, which eventually flow into the Arabian Sea.

Hadoti Plateau

This zone falls to the east and southeast of the Eastern Plains, and is characterised by hill folds and ridges, most notably around Chittorgarh, Bundi and Ranthambhore. It is the major catchment area for the Chambal River, which is flanked, particularly in the environs of Dholpur, by rugged, precipitous gorges. The region between the Banas and Chambal Rivers is scarp land, composed of sandstone, while the area encompassing Jhalawar, Kota, parts of Chittorgarh, Bhilwara and Bundi forms a tableland traversed by the tributaries of the Chambal. The valleys formed by these rivers are rich in black soil.

CLIMATE

The climate of Rajasthan can be neatly divided into four seasons: pre-monsoon, monsoon, post-monsoon and winter. Monsoon *(kharif)* and winter *(rabi)* are the two main growing seasons.

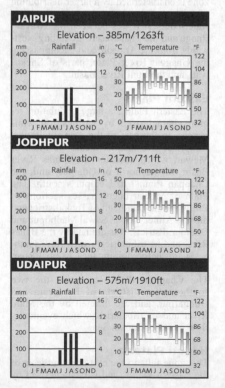

Pre-monsoon, which extends from April to June, is the hottest season, with temperatures ranging from 32° to 45°C. There is little relief from the scorching onslaught of the heat, particularly in the arid zone to the west and northwest of the Aravalli Range, where temperatures often climb above 45°C, particularly in May and June. Mt Abu registers the lowest temperatures at this time. In the desert regions, the temperature plummets as night falls. Prevailing winds are from the west and sometimes carry *andhis* (dust storms). The only compensation is that the winds are usually accompanied by a slight reduction in temperatures, and sometimes by light showers.

The monsoon is a welcome arrival in late June in the eastern and southeastern regions of the state, finally falling in mid-July in the desert zones. It is preceded by dust and thunderstorms. Unless the rains are insubstantial, the monsoon is accompanied by a decrease in temperatures, with average maximum temperatures of between 29.5° to 32.2°C in the south and southeast of Rajasthan, and an average of above 37.7°C in the northern and northwestern regions. Over 90% of Rajasthan's precipitation occurs during the monsoon period, and humidity is greatest at this time, particularly in August, although the humidity is less evident in the desert zone.

The third season is the post-monsoon season. The monsoon has generally passed over the entire state by mid-September. It is followed by a second hot season, with relatively uniform temperatures registered across the state. In October, the average maximum temperature is 33° to 38°C, and the minimum is between 18° and 20°C.

The fourth season – of most interest to visitors – is the winter or cold season, from December to March. There is a marked variation in maximum and minimum temperatures, and there are regional variations across the state. January is the coolest month of the year. There is slight precipitation in the north and northeastern regions of the state, and light winds, predominantly from the north and northeast. At this time, relative humidity ranges from 50% to 60% in the morning, and 25% to 35% in the afternoon.

There is a wide variation in the distribution of rainfall across the state, with a reduction in the volume of rain as you proceed further west. In the southeast, over 1500mm can be expected, with most rain (about 90% of the annual rainfall) falling during the monsoon period (mid-June to mid-September), and an average of 55 days of rain. At the western extremity of Rajasthan, less than 100mm may be registered in any one year, and rainfall is received on an average of only 15 days in the year.

Drought

Periodic droughts, along with their threat of famine, are common in Rajasthan. They are caused by the unreliability of the monsoon; in any five years, two may be considered drought years. In the desert regions, it is not uncommon for one in every three years to be stricken by drought.

In 1999, 2000 and 2001 the state was struck by three consecutive years of severe drought, leading to shortages in drinking water, decreased agricultural output, and food shortages. The drought affected 40 million Rajasthanis in 2001 and 74% of villagers lost more than half their crops due to water shortages. In July 2001 the rains finally came and half a million people who had been forced to migrate from the worst affected areas were able to return home.

Droughts highlight the urgent need for water-conservation strategies and many villages are making impressive gains by reviving traditional water-harvesting techniques. However, the state still faces a water crisis. You can help by using water wisely – see Responsible Tourism in the Facts for the Visitor chapter for more information.

ECOLOGY & ENVIRONMENT
Desertification

One of the greatest threats faced by the inhabitants of Rajasthan is desertification. While this is in part a natural phenomenon that has occurred over the ages as geological factors have given rise to warmer and drier climates, the process has also been exacerbated by the burgeoning human and animal population trying to use the ever-diminishing resources. The Thar Desert is the most densely populated desert in the world, with an average of 61 people per sq km. Further pressure is placed on this fragile region by the density of livestock.

An acute shortage of water, salinity, erosion, periodic droughts, overgrazing, over-cultivation and overconsumption of scanty vegetation for fuel and timber all either contribute to or are a consequence of the continuing desertification of Rajasthan. As inhabitants scour the landscape for wood fuel, some species of vegetation are severely threatened. The roots of the phog plant *(Calligonum polygonoides)*, which is one of the few species found on sand dunes, are used for fuel, and the removal of this plant is severely affecting the stability of the sand dunes. Once common in Jodhpur district, phog has now completely gone. Rohira has all but disappeared from the arid zone. The wood of this plant, known locally as Marwar teak, is highly prized for furniture construction, and was traditionally used in the carved architraves and window frames of havelis (mansions).

There is a Marwari proverb that illustrates the destructive effects of overgrazing:

Oont chhode Akaro, Bakri chhode Kangro

The camel consumes everything other than ak (a thorny shrub) but the goat devours even that, leaving only the pebbles

The success of crops is threatened by drought; scorching heat; sandy, nutrient deficient soils; intermittent dust storms that smother and destroy crops; and few underground water resources. Although Rajasthan is 10.4% of the total Indian area, it has only about 1% of India's available water resources.

In western Rajasthan, even in good years, cultivation barely meets subsistence requirements. Rainfall is low and the main river system that runs through this region, the Luni, is not perennial. Ground water is often unfit for animal and human consumption, and irrigation is practically nonexistent.

It is not just the arid zones that are threatened due to overutilisation of resources. The dense forests that covered the Aravalli Range prior to Independence are thinning rapidly. Before Independence, villagers were forbidden from encroaching on these forests, which were the preserves of the maharajas and barons who hunted large animals there. However, following Independence, huge stands of trees were felled to meet increasing timber, fuel and fodder requirements, and this trend is continuing.

The alarming disappearance of the forests of the Aravalli has provoked government intervention, and some areas are now closed periodically to enable the forest to regenerate. However, the closed regions are poorly policed by lowly paid guards who are often bribed by pastoralists desperate for fodder. Local inhabitants are also entitled to take dry wood from the forests. However, there is simply not enough wood for everyone, so villagers ringbark healthy trees, returning later to remove the dead timber.

Pollution

Pollution and deforestation are damaging many parts of Rajasthan, especially the southern region. Marble mining has been particularly harmful. Industrial waste has caused air, water and noise pollution. To address the issue of water pollution, the government has introduced policies that restrict building and development around lakes and rivers.

It's too late, unfortunately, for the village of Bichri, 15km from Udaipur. Most of the village's canals are contaminated with sulphurous sludge released indiscriminately by chemical plants in the district. Over 350 hectares of prime wetland has been made a desolate wasteland, and the water in dozens of wells in the vicinity of the factories is unfit for human consumption. The companies continued to manufacture highly toxic chemicals without official permission. In spite of a Supreme Court order to store effluents safely, chemical waste was released into streams or mixed with soil and deposited in various places in a crude attempt to hide it, with the result that these toxic effluents have seeped into the ground water.

Plastic Waste

Almost everywhere in Rajasthan plastic bags and bottles clog drains, litter city streets and deserts and even stunt the growth of grass in parks. Of growing concern are the number of cows, elephants and other creatures that consume plastic waste, resulting in a slow and painful death. The antiplastic lobby estimates that about 72% of the plastics used in India are discarded within a week and only 15% are recycled. It's up to individuals (including travellers) to restrict their use of plastic, and responsibly recycle bottles and bags. For more information see Responsible Tourism in the Facts for the Visitor chapter.

Conservation

According to scientists, the most efficient way to combat desertification is afforestation. Not only will it provide food, fodder, fuel and timber, but trees stabilise the earth and act as windbreaks, lessening the damage caused by sandstorms. The sparse vegetation in the arid zone is both in a very degraded condition and extremely slow growing, a further cause for alarm.

The first official recognition of the advancement of the Thar Desert and its alarming ramifications for the inhabitants of the arid zone occurred in 1951. As a direct result, the Desert Afforestation Research Station was established in Jodhpur in 1952, which in 1959 became the Central Arid Zone Research Institute, to conduct research into the problems of desertification. This is the most important institute of its type in south Asia.

The institute's endeavours include stabilising shifting sand dunes; establishing silvipastoral and fuelwood plantations; planting windbreaks to reduce wind speed and subsequent erosion; rehabilitating degraded forests; and starting afforestation of barren hill slopes.

Some of the work carried out at the institute has been criticised by conservationists. They claim that, rather than protecting and preserving the desert ecosystem, massive attempts to irrigate and afforest the arid zone alter its fragile composition.

Indira Gandhi Canal Project

The Indira Gandhi Canal, also known as the Rajasthan Canal, was initiated in 1957 and is still not completed. It includes an amazing 9709km of canals, with the main canal stretching 649km. Critics suggest that the massive project, which is connected with the Bhakra Dam in Punjab, was concerned more with economics than with ecological concerns and conservation.

The canal has opened up large tracts of the arid western region for cash crops, managed by wealthy landowners rather than the rural poor. Environmentalists say the soil in the command areas has been destroyed through over-irrigation, and maintain that the canal has also been a key factor in the introduction of chemical fertilisers and pesticides to the regions opened up to agriculture. Indigenous plants have suffered, further adding to the degeneration of the arid zone. Also, sections of the canal are built on traditional grazing grounds, to which graziers are now denied access. It's been suggested that traditional local food crops, which require less irrigation, and *gochars* (traditional grazing grounds) could have been established instead.

The Indira Ghandi Canal has also been blamed for breeding malaria-carrying mosquitoes and for the extinction of the desert lizard, which couldn't cope with the increased moisture in its habitat.

An afforestation project along the Indira Gandhi (Rajasthan) Canal has come under attack. The indigenous phog plant, which has already completely disappeared from some regions in the arid zone, is being uprooted and replaced with fast-growing species such as *Eucalyptus hybrid* and *Acacia tortilis*. Phog, with its deep and wide-spreading root system, is an important stabiliser of sand dunes. Further, people who have been allocated land in the areas irrigated by the canal have uprooted this shrub to raise crops. This has caused heavy silting of a portion of the canal in Jaisalmer district, and shifting sand dunes

have become prevalent, rendering much of this area a wasteland.

Animal husbandry is the traditional livelihood of the majority of the inhabitants of the 11 desert districts of Rajasthan, forming the major staple of the economy. Intensive planting of non-native species in the name of afforestation reduces traditional grazing grounds. In addition to upsetting the finely balanced desert ecosystem, such species are of little nutritional or practical use to villagers. Environmentalists argue that development should work not counter to, but in harmony with, the desert ecosystem. It should promote the generation and conservation of desert species that are finely attuned and adapted to the fragile environment and provide food, fodder and fuel.

FLORA

Vegetation in the desert zone is sparse. Only a limited range of grasses and very slow-growing thorny trees and shrubs have adapted to the hostile conditions. The most common tree species are the ubiquitous khejri *(Prosopis cineraria)* and various strains of acacia. Rajasthan also has some dry teak forest, dry mixed deciduous forest, bamboo brakes and subtropical hill forests. Forest stocks are dwindling, however, as inhabitants scour the landscape for fuel and fodder. Forests, most of which are in very poor condition, only cover just over 9% of the state, mostly to the east of the Aravalli Range.

The hardy khejri, held sacred by the Bishnoi tribes of Jodhpur district (see the boxed text 'Village Activists' in the Western Rajasthan chapter), is extremely drought resistant due to its deep root system. The thorny twigs are used for barriers to keep sheep and goats away from crops. The leaves are dried and used for fodder. The bean-shaped fruit can be eaten ripe or unripe. The latter, when cooked, is known as *sangri*. The wood is used to make furniture and the branches are burnt for fuel. The twigs are used in the sacred fire burnt at marriage ceremonies.

Another tree that is distributed across the arid zone is rohira *(Tecoma undulata)*. Its pods have medicinal value in the relief of abscesses and the wood is used in furniture construction. The Central Arid Zone Research Institute has had some success with the introducion of faster-growing exotic species to the desert zone, including various acacia species.

Grasses of the arid zone include sewan *(Lasiurus sindicus)*, which is found over large areas, dhaman *(Cenchrus ciliaris)*, boor *(C. jwarancusa)* and bharut *(C. catharticus)*. The last of these is abundant in times of drought, when it serves as a staple for the poor.

There are various species of shrubs in the arid zone, including phog. Its root system stabilises sand dunes; the wood (when green) is used in construction; branches serve as camel fodder; and the pods, known as *lasson*, are eaten as vegetables. Other shrub species include the leafless khair *(Capparis decidua)*, ak *(Calotropis procera)* and thor *(Euphorbia caduca)*. Khair not only has strong and durable wood that is resistant to white ants, but produces a fruit that can be eaten fresh or preserved. Ak prospers in sandy soil, and both ak and thor produce a juice that is taken as a cough elixir. The leaves of thor, known as papri, are eaten as a vegetable.

FAUNA

Despite the inhospitable terrain, Rajasthan hosts a wide variety of mammals and birds.

Mammals of the arid zone have adapted to the hostile environment. Some supplement their fluid intake with insects, which are composed of between 65% and 80% water, and water-bearing plants. Others retain water for longer periods. Means of adapting to the extremes in temperature include burrowing in the sand or venturing out only at night, when the temperature plummets.

Antelopes & Gazelles

Despite the paucity of blackbuck antelope numbers in most parts of Rajasthan, there are still substantial populations in Jodhpur district, where these animals are afforded special protection by the Bishnoi tribes (see the boxed text 'Village Activists' in the Western Rajasthan chapter). Mature male blackbucks feature fine-spiralling horns, up to 60cm long.

It is also partly due to the efforts of the Bishnoi that populations of chinkaras, or Indian gazelles, are still found in the arid zone. Chinkaras are slighter than blackbucks, standing some 100cm tall, and live in smaller herds, sometimes with no more than three members. They are very well-adapted to the desert, thriving on wild grasses and various types of shrubs.

Another member of the *Bovidae* family found in Rajasthan is the nilgai, or bluebull, a large, stocky animal whose front legs are longer than its rear legs, giving it

Conservation Organisations

Several organisations work to regenerate the ecosystem and promote environmentally sustainable development. The following organisations can be contacted for information on their projects:

Tarun Bharat Sangh (Young India Organisation) This organisation is involved in water-harvesting projects, constructing small dams to collect rain-fed water. Traditional technology and local labour and materials are used; dams are shared by communities via small irrigation channels. Write to Rajendra Singh, Tarun Bharat Sangh, PO Bhikampura Kisori, District Alwar 301022.

Ubeshwar Vikas Mandal This organisation is concerned with the afforestation of hilly areas. Email e chand67@bppl.net.in.

Central Arid Zone Research Institute This institute focuses on the problems of desertification. It has a small pictorial museum with a photographic exhibition illustrating the institutes' work. Write to Central Arid Zone Research Institute (CAZRI), Jodhpur 342003.

an ungainly, sloping stance. Nilgais are found in most parts of India, and in Rajasthan are found on open plains (although not in the extreme west of the state) and in the foothills of the Aravalli Range.

Cat Family

Tigers were once found along the length of the Aravalli Range. However, due to hunting by Rajasthan's princely rulers and animal poachers trading in illegal skins, and the reduction of their habitat, they are now found only at Ranthambhore and Sariska National Parks. These parks are both administered by Project Tiger, a government programme initiated in 1973–74 to establish a number of protected sanctuaries across India.

The leopard, or panther, is rarely seen, but inhabits rocky declivities in the Aravalli, and parts of Jaipur and Jodhpur districts.

A much smaller specimen of the cat family is the jungle cat, which is about 60cm

Tigers are still an endangered species

long, excluding the tail. It is notable for its long limbs and short tail, and is able to kill animals larger than itself. It is generally nocturnal, but may be seen at the Keoladeo Ghana National Park near Bharatpur.

Smaller than the jungle cat is the Indian desert cat, about the size of a domestic moggie, but covered in spots, other than on the tail, flanks and cheeks, which are striped. The desert cat was once well distributed in the Thar Desert, but is now rarely seen.

Dog Family

Jackals are renowned for their unearthly howling, which enables them to locate each other and form packs. Once quite common in Rajasthan, they were found close to villages, where they preyed on livestock. Jackal numbers have been drastically reduced due to habitat reduction and their being hunted for their skins. They are nocturnal, and feed on rodents, lizards, small mammals and carrion.

The wolf once roamed in large numbers in the desert zone, but was hunted almost to the point of extinction by farmers. Over recent decades, wolves have begun to reappear due to concerted conservation endeavours. Wolves protect themselves from the scorching heat by digging burrows in sand dunes. In the desert zone, they live in pairs rather than packs. Their prey is domestic animals, rodents, small mammals and birds.

The desert fox is a subspecies of the red fox, and was once prolific in the Thar Desert, but its numbers are now drastically reduced. A close cousin of the desert fox is the Indian fox, which used to be found in the arid zone, although not in the extreme west. It is now found in Rajasthan only in national parks.

Rodents

The largest rodent in Rajasthan, or in all of India for that matter, is the crested porcupine. In the arid zone, the crested porcupine is found near hills and fixed sand dunes. It is seldom seen, as it only ventures out at night, and is herbivorous.

There are several varieties of gerbils in the arid zone, including the nocturnal ratod, the blight of farmers as it wreaks havoc on crops. The ratod is the largest gerbil in the Thar Desert, and is widely distributed, although it is not found on sand dunes. It is about the same size as a house rat.

Desert gerbils are smaller but they descend in vast numbers on crops, causing untold damage. Their burrowing contributes to desertification: in the arid zone between 12,000 and 15,000 burrows per hectare have been identified. Each burrow opening shifts 1kg of soil, which is carried by the high-velocity winds, contributing to soil erosion and dust storms. A distinctive characteristic of the desert gerbil is that when it senses danger, it thumps the earth with its hind feet; the entire colony then flees to its burrows.

There are various species of rats and mice in the desert region. The mole rat owes its name to its mole-like appearance, accentuated by its diminutive ears. It has a short tail and a reddish-brown coat. This destructive little fellow gnaws the bark around the main stems of trees from its underground burrow, eventually killing the tree.

Monkeys

Two types of monkey are found in Rajasthan, the rhesus monkey and the more gangly langur. The rhesus is found predominantly in the vicinity of the Aravalli Range. It has a distinctive red face and red rump, and lives in large groups headed by a dominant male. Rhesus monkeys are often found in or near human habitations, upon which they have become dependent for food.

The sacred langur, which represents Hanuman, the divine monkey god, in Hindu mythology

The langur is covered by brownish-grey fur and has a black face with prominent eyebrows. It is herbivorous and, like the rhesus monkey, can often be found near human settlements.

Bats

Bats that are found in Rajasthan include a subspecies of the pigmy pipistrelle, the *Pipistrellus mimus glaucillus*, a diminutive bat that lives between the walls of houses or beneath tree bark.

The disconcerting-looking Indian false vampire is a carnivore, living on small rodents, other rats, lizards and small birds. It has enormous ears in proportion to its head, and powerful wings. It is found in eastern Rajasthan.

Insectivores

The nocturnal Indian shrew, found throughout Rajasthan, predominantly in the Aravalli Range and the semiarid Shekhawati region, is also known as a musk rat, but does not belong to the rodent family, and can be distinguished from a rat by its prominent, flexible nose.

Other insectivores include two species of hedgehog: the Indian hedgehog and the desert hedgehog. Both are nocturnal creatures. The desert hedgehog is larger, and is prolific in the desert region. It protects itself from predators by rolling into a ball, with its sharp quills a deterrent to attack.

Other Mammals

The wild boar belongs to the pig family. Once prolific in Rajasthan, its numbers are now confined to the southeastern Aravalli Range, around Mt Abu, and in the vicinity of the Indira Gandhi Canal. It has tiny eyes, small tusks, a stocky frame and a short, fine tail. The hunting of wild boar was a favourite occupation of the maharajas.

The sloth bear inhabits forested regions, and can be found on the western slopes of the Aravalli Range. It is some 150cm long and stands 75cm at the shoulder. It is covered in long black hair, other than on the muzzle. It feeds on vegetation and insects, although it has been known to eat carrion.

Indian hedgehogs are commonly found in the Jodhpur and Shekhawati districts

The striped hyena resembles a dog but has feline-like features, such as its teeth. It is found in Rajasthan on rocky terrain, and is a nocturnal creature, feeding on carrion and occasionally killing ailing sheep or goats.

The desert hare is found in desert grasslands, and poses a nuisance to farmers, as it feeds on crops. It also ringbarks saplings by tearing the bark near the base of the stem, a bane to conservationists who are engaged in reafforestation.

Two types of mongoose can be found in Rajasthan: the small Indian mongoose and the Indian grey, or common, mongoose. The small Indian mongoose is found in the arid zone and lives on insects, small rodents, lizards, birds and even snakes. The Indian grey mongoose is larger than its cousin, and enjoys poultry. It also climbs trees to divest nests of eggs.

A subspecies of the small Indian civet inhabits the Thar Desert. It is a long, lean animal with an elongated head and short limbs, and is nocturnal. It feeds on poultry, insects, lizards, rodents and eggs.

Birdlife

There is an abundance of birdlife in Rajasthan and no less than 450 species have been identified in the state. The Keoladeo Ghana National Park, near Bharatpur in eastern Rajasthan, is an internationally renowned bird sanctuary.

Forests The forests of the Aravalli Range provide a habitat for orioles, hornbills, kingfishers, swallows, parakeets, warblers, mynahs, robins, flycatchers, quails, doves, peacocks, barbets, bee-eaters, woodpeckers and drongos, among others.

Lorikeets, which are found nowhere else in the state, can be seen in the Sitamata-Pratapgarh area. The forests of Darrah are home to the Alexandrine parakeet. Birds of prey include numerous species of owls (great horned, dusky, brown fishing and collared scops, and spotted owlets), and eagles (spotted and tawny), white-eyed buzzards, black-winged kites and shikras.

Wetlands The wetlands in eastern Rajasthan include the Keoladeo Ghana National Park. Other wetlands include those that are encompassed by Sariska and Ranthambhore national parks, Jaisamand Lake in Udaipur district and Sadar Samand Lake in Jodhpur district. The species mentioned here are found at Keoladeo Ghana National Park.

Migratory species include spoonbills, herons, cormorants, storks, openbills, ibis and egrets.

The peacock is the national bird and is frequently represented in Rajasthani art

Wintering waterfowl include the common, marbled, falcated and Baikal teal; the pintail, gadwall, shoveler, coot, wigeon, bar-headed and greylag goose; and the common and brahminy pochard. Waders include snipe, sandpipers and plovers. Several terrestrial species include the endangered Siberian crane, which only winters at Keoladeo; the monogamous sarus, which inhabits the park year-round; and the beautiful demoiselle crane. Species resident throughout the year include moorhens, egrets, herons, storks and cormorants.

Birds of prey include many types of eagles (greater spotted, steppe, imperial, Spanish imperial, fishing), vultures (white-backed and scavenger) and owls (spotted, dusky horned and mottled wood). Other birds of prey include the pallid and marsh harrier, sparrowhawk, kestrel and goshawk.

Grasslands Some of the better grassland zones for bird-watching are the Tal Chhapar Sanctuary in Churu district (northern Rajasthan); Sorsan, near Kota (southern Rajasthan); Sonkalia, near Ajmer (eastern Rajasthan); and in the environs of the Indira Gandhi Canal (western Rajasthan).

Common birds of the grasslands include various species of lark, including the short-toed, crested, sky and crowned finch-lark. Quails, including grey, rain, common and bush, can also be seen, as can several types of shrike (grey, rufous-backed and bay-backed), mynahs, drongos and partridges. Migratory birds include the lesser florican, seen during the monsoon, and the houbara bustard, which winters at the grasslands. Birds of prey include falcons, eagles, hawks, kites, kestrels and harriers.

Desert The Thar Desert also has a prolific variety of birdlife. At the small village of Khichan, about 135km from Jodhpur, vast flocks of demoiselle cranes descend on fields in the morning and evening from the end of August to the end of March. Other winter visitors to the desert include houbara bustards and common cranes.

Water is scarce, so water holes attract large flocks of imperial, spotted, pintail and Indian sandgrouse in the early mornings. Other desert dwellers include drongos, common and bush quail, blue-tailed and little green bee-eaters and grey partridges.

Birds of prey include eagles (steppe and tawny), buzzards (honey and long-legged), goshawks, peregrine falcons and kestrels. The most notable of the desert and dry grassland dwellers is the impressive great Indian bustard, which stands some 40cm high and can weigh up to 14kg.

Endangered Species

While some of Rajasthan's wildlife is perishing as a consequence of encroachment on its habitat, other species are falling at the hands of poachers.

Tigers It is estimated that during the 1990s more than 20 tigers were slaughtered at Ranthambhore National Park. After the skin is removed, the bones inevitably find their way to China, where they form the basis of 'tiger wine', believed to have healing properties. The penis is coveted for its alleged aphrodisiac powers.

National parks and sanctuaries are proving to be lucrative hunting grounds for poachers. Frequently, only main roads in parks are patrolled by guards (who are often poorly paid), so poachers can trespass without fear of detection. In July 1992, Badia, one of Ranthambhore's more committed trackers, was brutally murdered – allegedly by poachers, who have still not been convicted. In 2000 then US president Bill Clinton brought world attention to the issue when he visited Ranthambhore and urged Indian businessman to help preserve the tiger population.

Strict measures have been implemented to stop the international trade in tiger skins and bones, including severe penalties for offenders. Nevertheless, the smaller animals on which tigers prey are still hunted by local villagers, and the survival of this beautiful, endangered animal still hangs in the balance.

Other Fauna Although they are not necessarily in immediate danger of extinction,

Stalked, Slaughtered & Stuffed

The Rajput is fond of his dog and his gun. The former aids him in pulling down the boar or hare,and with the stalking horse he will toil for hours after the deer.

Colonel James Tod, *Annals & Antiquities of Rajasthan*

The Rajputs, particularly the princes, were once passionate hunters and were greatly admired for their shooting prowess. *Shikhar* (hunting) was considered an important part of an Indian prince's upbringing, right up until the first half of the 20th century. A handful of princesses were even encouraged to excel at this elite sport. Children as young as 10 years old, lugging heavy rifles, would participate in hunts, eager to return to the palace with a creature of some sort.

Indeed, in India hunting was the 'sport of kings' and many princes toured the world in search of new and unusual beasts to add to their prized collections. Stuffed tigers, lion-skin rugs (complete with head), zebra-fur lamps and mounted animal trophies filled many of Rajasthan's palaces. Many palaces still contain a depressing collection of animal 'ornaments'.

Some maharajas argued that hunting was necessary to maintain a crucial balance of wildlife. Others claimed it was their duty to protect their subjects from the many dangerous animals that lurked around villages. But hunting was primarily pursued as a pleasure sport.

Hunting was not the sport of Indian princes alone. The British were voracious hunters and organised elaborate shooting expeditions. During their heyday in India, the British Raj, English lords and other dignitaries often joined the maharajas on bloody killing sprees through the jungles, and these jaunts served to cement the good relations between them. Trudging through the forest atop elephants, they were mainly in search of the big jungle cats – lions, tigers, panthers and leopards. But almost anything that came in their path was fair game, from wild boar to spotted deer.

Today hunting is illegal in India. Now it is the lucrative international poaching trade that threatens some of India's wildlife with extinction. Sadly, there have been recent reports of hunting animals for sport in Rajasthan – if you do come across any such cases, report them immediately to the local authorities.

large mammals, such as the spotted deer, blackbuck, sambar, chowsingha, bluebull, wild boar and chinkara are hunted for their meat, skins or antlers. Smaller mammals such as mongooses, squirrels, jungle cats, hares and jackals are killed for their fur. The skins of reptiles supply the lucrative handbag, shoe and belt market.

Fish are indiscriminately killed by dynamiting rivers or by poison. Monkeys are trapped and exported to foreign private collectors. Birds and small mammals are captured in nets. Large carnivores such as tigers and leopards are poisoned with baits, or killed or wounded in spring traps. Wild boars are killed by baits that explode inside them.

In recent years only one pair of the endangered Siberian cranes has been wintering at Keoladeo Ghana National Park. The birds migrate from their summer range in Siberia and their numbers have declined alarming – 30 years ago there were an estimated 200 birds wintering in Rajasthan. It is thought that the birds are killed for meat and sport as they fly over Afghanistan and Pakistan.

The habitat of the animals of the Thar Desert is being steadily destroyed by overgrazing and overutilisation of the desert resources. Some mammals that once thrived in the arid zone have now completely vanished from this region, such as the wolf, cheetah, caracal and wild ass. Several other species are on the endangered list, including the desert fox, jackal, panther, blackbuck (Indian antelope) and chinkara (Indian gazelle).

The great Indian bustard's numbers have dwindled alarmingly due to hunting and because its eggs are trampled by livestock. Its numbers have also declined in the Desert

National Park. The World Conservation Union (IUCN) estimates that the number of great Indian bustard in the park has decreased from between 200 and 400 in 1985 to between 50 and 100 in 2001. Even so, this remains one of the largest populations of the bustards in India.

NATIONAL PARKS & WILDLIFE SANCTUARIES

Rajasthan has several world-renowned wild-life sanctuaries and national parks, as well as numerous other reserves. Some of these, such as Ranthambhore and Sariska, were originally the hunting reserves of the maharajas. Others, such as the Desert National Park in western Rajasthan, have been established to protect and preserve the unique plants and animals found in the arid zone.

Bird lovers shouldn't miss Khichan, a small village that lies only a few kilometres from the large town of Phalodi, between Jodhpur and Jaisalmer. It has not yet been listed as a wildlife sanctuary, but from late

Major National Parks & Wildlife Sanctuaries

National Park/ Wildlife Sanctuary	location	features	best time to visit
Darrah WS	southern Rajasthan	leopards, chinkaras, spotted deer, wild boar, wolves, sloth bears	Feb–May
Desert NP	western Rajasthan	Indian bustard, blackbucks, nilgais, wolves, desert foxes, crested porcupines	Sept–Mar
Dhawa Doli WS	western Rajasthan	blackbucks, partridges, desert foxes	Oct–Feb
Gajner WS	western Rajasthan	desert cats, desert foxes, chinkaras	Oct–Mar
Jaisamand WS	southern Rajasthan	crocodiles, leopards, chinkaras, beautiful *chhatris* (cenotaphs)	Nov–June
Keoladeo Ghana NP	eastern Rajasthan	400 bird species, including migratory birds such as Siberia cranes & waterbirds (wetlands)	Oct–Mar, July–Aug
Kumbhalgarh WS	southern Rajasthan	wolves in packs of up to 40, chowsinghas, four-horned antelopes, leopards, horse riding	Oct–June
Mt Abu WS	southern Rajasthan	deciduous & subtropical forest, wild boars, sambars, leopards	Mar–June
National Chambal WS	southern Rajasthan	gharials, wolves, chinkaras, blackbucks, wild boars, caracals	Oct–Mar
Ranthambhore NP	eastern Rajasthan	tigers, chitals, leopards, nilgais, chinkaras, birdlife, ancient fort	Oct–Apr
Sariska Tiger Reserve	eastern Rajasthan	tigers, leopards, chitals, chinkaras, a fort & temples	Nov–June
Sitamata WS	southern Rajasthan	ancient teak trees, deer, sambars, leopards, flying squirrels, wild boars	Mar–July
Tal Chhapar WS	northern Rajasthan	blackbucks, chinkaras, desert foxed, harriers, eagles, sparrowhawks	Sept–Mar

August/early September to the end of March, it's possible to witness the spectacular sight of hundreds of demoiselle cranes descending on the fields around the village, where they feed on grain distributed by villagers.

Further details about the national parks and sanctuaries listed here are provided in their respective chapters.

GOVERNMENT & POLITICS
National
India is a constitutional democracy. There are 29 states and six union territories (which are administered by the president in Delhi, through an appointed administrator). The constitution (which came into force on 26 January 1950) details the powers of the central and state governments as well as those powers that are shared. If the situation in a particular state is deemed to be unmanageable, the central government has the right to assume power there. This controversial right, known as President's Rule, has been enforced in recent years, either because the law-and-order situation has gotten out of hand – notably in Punjab from 1985 to 1992, in Kashmir in 1990 and in Assam in 1991 – or because there is a political stalemate, such as occurred in Goa, Tamil Nadu, Pondicherry, Haryana and Meghalaya in the early 1990s.

Parliament is bicameral; the lower house is known as the Lok Sabha (House of the People) and the upper house is known as the Rajya Sabha (Council of States).

The Lok Sabha has 545 members, and elections (using a first-past-the-post system) are held every five years, unless the government calls an election earlier. All Indians over the age of 18 have the right to vote. Of the 545 seats, 125 are reserved for the Scheduled Castes (the official term for Dalits or Untouchables) and Tribes.

The upper house consists of 245 members; members are elected for six-year terms and a third of the house is elected every two years. The president appoints 12 members and the rest are elected by state assemblies using a regional quota system. The president, whose duties are largely ceremonial, is elected by both houses and the state legislatures (presidential elections are held once every five years). The president must act on the advice of a council of ministers, chosen by the prime minister. The president may dissolve the lower house but not the upper one.

State
Rajasthan is divided into six separate administrative zones: Mewat (Alwar region), Marwar (Jodhpur region), Mewar (Udaipur region), Dhundhar (Jaipur region), Hadoti (Kota region) and Shekhawati (Sikar region).

After the formation of the state of Rajasthan, executive and legislative powers were wielded by the *rajpramukh*, Man Singh II of Jaipur, who was assisted in the execution of his duties by the state ministry, members of which he appointed. It was not until February 1952 that the first general election to the state assembly was held. Until then, Rajasthanis had been under monarchical rule and had little experience of democratic processes. The title of *rajpramukh* was replaced by that of governor in 1956, a position that held little political weight.

After the abolition of the privy purse in 1971 by then prime minister Indira Gandhi, a number of maharajas entered the political arena.

Since Rajasthan has had an elected government, it has been ruled by Congress, the Janata People's Party, and by a coalition of the BJP and the Janata Dal. At various times it has also been subjected to President's Rule. In the 1993 state election, the BJP–Janata Dal coalition led by Bhairon Singh Shekhawat retained power. However, in the last state elections in 1998, 75% of the seats were won by the Congress Party, and Ashok Gehlot became the new chief minister.

ECONOMY
Prior to Independence, princely rulers derived revenue from rent, customs duty, transit duty imposed on traders and merchants passing through their respective kingdoms, and excise duty on liquor and narcotic drugs. Some maharajas derived revenue from state owned railways, or from forestry and mining. After the annual tribute payable to the British government was deducted,

remaining revenue was spent on maintaining the state's army, on law enforcement, and on sustaining the princes' often extravagant lifestyles. Little of the funds derived from tax and nontax sources was spent on public amenities or civic services such as health and education.

In the immediate post-Independence period, Rajasthan was one of India's poorest states, a situation exacerbated not only by its feudal legacy, but by the ravages wreaked on the region by periodic droughts and famines.

Currently, the per capita income is still below the national average.

Agriculture

Today agriculture is one of the most important sectors in Rajasthan's economy, accounting for 33% of the state's gross domestic product (GDP), and employing 70% of the workforce. The major crops are cereals such as wheat, *bajra* (millet occasionally used in bread making but more frequently pounded with spice to make pappadams), *juar* (also a variety of millet), gram and barley. Rajasthan is the largest producer of *bajra* in India, and the second-highest producer of sesame. The state also produces 35% of India's mustard and rapeseed. There are two main growing seasons – *kharif* (monsoon) and *rabi* (winter). In the dry western region only *kharif* crops are grown.

The availability of water has a significant effect on agriculture and the regular droughts have a massive impact on agricultural output. Agriculture uses 83% of Rajasthan's water resources.

Despite massive expenditure on irrigation, agricultural output has fluctuated rather dramatically over the years. Actual grain production has increased since 1951, but some years have much greater crop yields than others.

Substantial funds have been directed towards afforestation, to inhibit the advancement of desertification and soil erosion, and address the state's fuelwood deficits.

In recent years the government has also directed increased funds to assisting farmers with water-conservation technology.

The number of livestock has risen dramatically to some 48 million head – more than double the figure of 1951. This represents an alarming trend, as overgrazing is substantially contributing to environmental degradation and desertification. Rajasthan produces 40% of India's raw wool, employing around three million people.

Industry

Production of textiles is the most important contributor to the industrial sector, and Rajasthan is one of India's major textile producers. There are around 30 textile mills in the state, employing about 50,000 people. Rajasthan's textile exports increased from Rs 5534 million in 1995–96 to Rs 8046 million in 1998–99.

Rajasthan produces about 13% of India's cement, 94% of the country's gypsum and 84% of its asbestos. Precious metals and gems are another contributor – all of India's garnets and emeralds are mined in Rajasthan and the state produces 76% of its silver ore. The production of sugar and salt also contributes to the state economy, as does the mining of marble and sandstone, a trade in which the states of Rajputana have been engaged for centuries. Rajasthan's main industrial centres are Jaipur, Kota, Udaipur and Bhilwara, and the state's medium- and large-scale industries employ around 170,000 people.

Handicrafts

The handicrafts sector is the focus of a great deal of government and nongovernmental organisation (NGO) support in Rajasthan, as it employs some of the poorest and lowest-caste people in the state. The Rajasthan Small Industries Corporation aims to encourage and promote the local handicraft sector. It operates the Rajasthali showrooms, which can be found in Rajasthan and beyond selling local handicrafts. It has also trained thousands of people in handicraft production, such as carpet weaving.

There are about 66,000 families in Rajasthan weaving on handlooms, many of whom belong to scheduled castes. The Rajasthan Handloom Development Corporation runs programmes in human-resource development for weavers.

The state is also the biggest producer of woollen *khadi* (homespun fabric) in India, and is the third-largest producer of *khadi* overall. An estimated 425,000 people are employed in *khadi* production and village-based industries.

The state government has exempted most craft items from sales tax. It is difficult to estimate the revenue earned from this sector as it doesn't go into the state coffers. In 1999, there were over 200,000 small-scale industries (which were employing more than 767,000 people) in Rajasthan, such as carpet making, cotton and wool spinning, block printing, gem cutting and polishing, ivory carving, pottery and brassware production, leather-goods production, marble carving and enamelling.

Tourism

Tourism has emerged as one of Rajasthan's prime revenue earners. About six million foreign and domestic tourists visit Rajasthan annually, spending almost Rs 10 billion in the state each year. Around 40% of international tourists visiting India have Rajasthan on their itinerary, amounting to around 700,000 people. However, the global downturn in tourism after the September 11 attacks in the US caused a serious slump in foreign arrivals. The situation was worse in Rajasthan as tensions between India and Pakistan mounted in the months following the attacks on the Indian parliament in December 2001, and troops were massed on Rajasthan's border with Pakistan. Tourism authorities turned their attention to the domestic market in an attempt to bolster tourist numbers in the state.

In 2000, the government of Rajasthan made tourism a compulsory high-school subject to increase awareness of the state's heritage and its vast economic potential.

POPULATION & PEOPLE

According to the 2001 national census, the population of Rajasthan is 56.5 million, an alarming increase of some 42 million since the first census was conducted in 1951,

shortly after Independence. Rajasthan has the eighth-largest population of any Indian state, and its population growth rate (28.33%) is still higher than the national average (21.34%).

There are various hypotheses for this phenomenal growth. Despite the state still being periodically ravaged by drought, the population is rarely decimated by famine, as improved transport infrastructure and communications enable the stricken inhabitants to receive aid in the form of grain and fodder. Further, Rajasthan is still a relatively poor state, and there is a correlation between poverty and the size of families. The perpetual desire for 'an heir and a spare' encourages parents to keep trying for two male offspring. The child sex ratio is rather dismal – the number of girls per 1000 boys under six years old dropped from 916 in 1991 to 909 in 2001 (see also the boxed text 'Female Infanticide' later in this chapter).

While the average number of people per square kilometre is about 165, densities vary drastically according to region (the lowest being in the desert region). Rajasthan's population is overwhelmingly rural, with 43.3 million people living in the countryside, as opposed to 13.2 million in urban areas.

Hindus represent around 89% of the state's population. Scheduled Castes (formerly known as Untouchables) and Scheduled Tribes form around 17% and 12% of the state's population respectively.

Less than 10% of Rajasthan's population is Muslim, most of whom are Sunnis. There is a small affluent community of Shi'ia Muslims in southeastern Rajasthan known as the Bohras.

The Gujjars, who profess Hinduism, dwell in eastern Rajasthan, including Jaipur, Udaipur, Alwar, Kota and Bharatpur. They are divided into two groups, the Laur and the Khari.

The nomadic Rabari, or Raika, are also Hindu. They are divided into two groups, the Marus, who breed camels, and the Chalkias, who breed sheep and goats.

The affluent Oswals hail from Osiyan, near Jodhpur, and are successful in trade and commerce. They are predominantly Jain,

Adivasis of Rajasthan

Tribal, or Adivasi, groups were the original inhabitants of the area now called Rajasthan. The main Adivasi tribes are the Bhils and the Minas, who were forced into the Aravalli Range by the Aryan invasion. Smaller tribes include the Sahariyas, Damariyas, Garasias and the Gaduliya Lohars.

Bhils

The Bhils are an important tribal group and traditionally they inhabited the southeastern corner of the state – the area around Udaipur, Chittorgarh and Dungarpur – although the largest concentrations of Bhils are found in neighbouring Madhya Pradesh.

Legend has it that the Bhils were fine archers, hence their name, which can be traced to the Tamil word *vil*, meaning 'bow'. Bhil bowmen are mentioned in both the Mahabharata and the Ramayana. They were highly regarded as warriors, and the Rajput rulers relied on them to thwart the invading Marathas and Mughals. In fact, some scholars suggest that the Rajputs owe their warrior propensities to the Bhils, whom they emulated.

Although originally food gatherers, these days the Bhils have taken up small-scale agriculture, or have abandoned the land altogether and taken up city residence and employment. The literacy rate of the Bhils, particularly the women, used to be one of the lowest in the country, which made them prime targets for exploitation and bonded labour. This trend is now being reversed and the fortunes of the Bhils are improving. Several Bhils, including one Bhil woman, have even entered state parliament, becoming members of the legislative assembly.

Those Bhils who can afford it engage in polygamy. Marriages of love, as opposed to arranged marriages which are the norm in India, are condoned.

The Baneshwar Fair is a Bhil festival held near Dungarpur in January/February each year, and large numbers of Bhils gather for several days of singing, dancing and worship. Holi is another important time for the Bhils.

Witchcraft, magic and superstition are deeply rooted aspects of Bhil culture.

Minas

The Minas are the second-largest tribal group in the state after the Bhils, and are the most widely spread. They live in the regions of Shekhawati and eastern Rajasthan. Scholars still disagree as to whether the Minas are an indigenous tribe, or whether they migrated to the region from Central Asia. The name Mina is derived from *meen* (fish), and the Minas claim descent from the fish incarnation of Vishnu. Originally they were a ruling tribe, but their slow downfall began with the rise of the Rajputs and was completed when the British government declared them a 'criminal tribe'

although a few profess Vaishnavism. Oswal women are compelled to observe strict *purdah* or seclusion.

EDUCATION

In 1951, the literacy rate in Rajasthan stood at just 8.02%, but Rajasthan has made a remarkable improvement in literacy rates in recent years. In the 2001 census it recorded the highest percentage increase in literacy of any Indian state, rising from 38.55% in 1991 to 61.03% in 2001, as compared to a rise of only 13.17% throughout the country. Even female literacy, which lagged at

20.44% in 1991 more than doubled to 44.24% in 2001. However, Rajasthan is still slightly behind the national average of 65.38% literacy (54.46% for females).

The District Primary Education Programme has focused in recent years on achieving universal primary education in Rajasthan and today almost every village in the state now has a primary school. Special 'Rajiv Gandhi Swaranjayanti Schools' have also been opened to ensure that no child has to walk for more than 1km to get to school.

At the formation of the state of Rajasthan, the state had only one university,

Adivasis of Rajasthan

in 1924, mainly to stop them trying to regain their territory from the Rajputs. In their skirmishes with the Rajputs, the Minas resorted to various unorthodox means such as demanding 'protection money' from villagers to curtail their *dacoit* (bandit) activities.

Following Independence, their ignominious status as a criminal tribe was lifted, and they took to agriculture. However, their culture was by this time more or less destroyed, and they have now been given protection as a Scheduled Tribe.

As with the Bhils, the literacy rate among the Minas has been very low, but is improving.

Marriage is generally within the tribe. This is arranged by the parents, and most marriages take place when the children are quite young.

Gaduliya Lohars

The Gaduliya Lohars were originally a martial Rajput tribe, but these days they are nomadic blacksmiths. Their traditional territory was Mewar (Udaipur) and they fought with the maharana against the Mughals. With typical Rajput chivalry, they made a vow to the maharana that they would only enter his fort at Chittorgarh after he had overcome the Mughals. As he died without achieving this, the clan was forced to become nomadic. When Nehru was in power he led a group of Gaduliya Lohars into the fort at Chittorgarh, with the hope that they would then resettle in their former lands, but they preferred to remain nomadic.

Garasias

The Garasias are a small Rajput tribe found in the Abu Road area of southern Rajasthan. It is thought that they intermingled with the Bhils, as bows and arrows are widely used by the Garasias.

The marriage ceremony is curious in that the couple elope, and a sum of money is paid to the father of the bride. If the marriage fails, the bride returns home, with a small sum of money to give to the father. Widows are not entitled to a share of their husband's property, and so they generally remarry.

Sahariyas

The Sahariyas are thought to be of Bhil origin, and live in the areas of Kota, Dungarpur and Sawai Madhopur in the southeast of the state. They are one of the least-educated tribes in the country and, as unskilled labourers, have been cruelly exploited.

As all members of the clan are considered to be related, marriages are arranged outside the tribe. The food and worship traditions of the Sahariyas are closely related to Hindu customs.

and that was in Jaipur. There are now nine universities in the state.

ARTS

The celebration of beauty in Rajasthan is abundantly evident in its traditional arts and crafts, as well as in everyday domestic items and tools of the Rajputs' trade, such as swords and knives.

Traditionally, the maharajas commissioned fine artistic works to adorn their palaces and to convey a degree of opulence befitting their esteemed status; the flourishing of the arts in Rajasthan is due, in a good degree, to the patronage of Rajasthan's princely rulers.

Today the artisans mainly produce goods for the large number of foreign visitors to Rajasthan, most of whom are less discerning than your average king. Nevertheless, institutions such as the National Awards for Master Craftsmen encourage artisans to strive for artistic excellence and perpetuate Rajasthan's important artistic tradition. For details on handicrafts of Rajasthan, see the special section 'The Colourful Crafts of Rajasthan'.

Music and dance are integral to all celebrations and festivals, and Rajasthan has a rich tradition of regional folk dances. In some dance performances, whole communities participate; others are performed only by men or by women. There is also the tradition of itinerant performers who interpreted popular or religious myths and legends through song, dance and drama, and who, in the past, received patronage at royal courts and performed for the pleasure of kings and their entourages.

Dance

Many tribal groups in southern Rajasthan have maintained old forms of folk dance. The *ghoomer* is a type of ceremonial dance performed only by women on special occasions, such as festivals or weddings.

On the occasion of sacred festivals such as Navratri, women perform the *ghoomer*

Kathak Comeback

Kathak is the best-known classical dance of northern India. Originally, Kathaks were storytellers who danced to depict their stories in the temples of northern India. The advent of Muslim rule brought Kathak out of the temples and into the courts. The diversity among the Hindu courts of Rajasthan and the Muslim courts of Delhi, Agra and Lucknow saw Kathak develop into a much more stylised art, with an emphasis on solo performers and their virtuosity. It also enabled Kathak to become a fusion of Hindu and Muslim influences.

Two schools of Kathak emerged: the Jaipur Gharana and the Lucknow Gharana. The Jaipur Gharana focused on rhythmic movement, while the Lucknow Gharana focused on moods and emotions. Rhythm, timing and footwork are fundamental characteristics of Kathak. The dance is accompanied by the tabla and the *sarangi* (a stringed instrument), as well as the 200 bells on the dancers' feet.

Kathak suffered a period of notoriety when it moved from the courts into houses where *nautch* (dancing) girls tantalised audiences with renditions of the Krishna and Radha love story. It was restored as a serious art form in the early 20th century.

for the deities. This dance varies in different communities and regions. In Udaipur, the dancers join a circle and carry sticks that they rhythmically strike together.

The Bhil tribal people of southern Rajasthan perform a special dance during the festival of Holi in February/March known as the *gir*, which is performed only by men, who hold sticks that they beat together. The *gir-ghoomer* is performed by both men and women, dressed in traditional costume. At the start of the dance, participants form two circles. The women, in a small inner circle, are encompassed by the men in the larger circle, who determine the rhythm of the dance by beating sticks and striking drums. As the dance proceeds, the participants change places, with the men forming the inner circle.

The *dandiya* is performed by both men and women as part of the exuberant Holi celebrations, and is particularly notable in Jodhpur district. Participants form a circle and beat together small sticks accompanied by musicians. Also performed during Holi, in eastern Rajasthan, is the *gindar*, which is danced throughout the night. In an unusual show of tolerance, caste Hindus perform this dance with Dalits.

The *neja* is danced by the Minas of Kherwara and Dungarpur just after Holi. In this dance, a coconut is placed on a large pole, and while the men endeavour to dislodge it, the women rhythmically beat sticks and strike the men with whips!

A form of the classical *kathak* dance, which is more commonly associated with Lucknow in Uttar Pradesh, is performed in Jaipur. Traditionally it was performed by males only, but today it is danced by both boys and girls, the latter dressed as males. Kathak interprets through dance the stories of Krishna and his consort, Radha, and entails dramatic facial expressions, especially through the movement of the eyes and eyebrows, and dexterous movement of the neck and wrists (see the boxed text 'Kathak Comeback').

The *terahtal*, which is derived from the Hindi word for '13', is performed with the aid of 13 cymbals fastened to the bodies of the female dancers, who are accompanied by male singers and drummers. It is performed in honour of the local deity, Ramdev, and can be seen at the Ramdevra Festival which is held in August or September at the small village of Ramdevra, near Pokaran in western Rajasthan.

In the region of Marwar (Jodhpur), the *loor*, or *luvar*, is performed only by women, who stand opposite each other in two lines. At a given beat of the drum they advance rapidly towards each other singing, and then retreat to their original position.

Performed mostly by the Bhil women of Udaipur, the *gauri* dance depicts legends associated with Shiva and Parvati. Participants form a semicircle and perform a series of steps in time with drum beats.

A nomadic tribal people who are traditionally associated with snake charming, the Kalbelias often complement their performances with dances such as the *shankaria*, which portrays a romantic tale. The Siddha Jats of Bikaner are renowned for their spectacular fire dance, performed on hot coals that reputedly leave no burns.

A traditional dance of Shekhawati is the *kacchi ghori*. The dancers, all men, ride mock wooden horses and brandish swords in mock battles. They are accompanied by a singer and musicians.

The *ramlila* and the *rasalila* are performed in honour of Rama and Krishna respectively, and are danced to the accompaniment of harmoniums and drums.

Puppetry

The traditional puppeteers, known as *kathputlis* or *putli-wallahs*, originally hailed from Nagaur district. They emerged in the 19th century, travelling from village to village to secure their livelihood. The skilled puppeteers relay stories through narration, music and dance. The *kathputlis* are among the most impoverished of Rajasthan's traditional entertainers, and are often compelled to work as farm labourers.

Many of the *kathputlis* make their own puppets from wood or clay. Romantic themes are common in the stories they re-enact, such as the story of Dhola Maru (see the boxed text 'The Legend of Dhola Maru' in the Northern Rajasthan chapter).

The puppeteer is usually male, but he is generally assisted in his performance by his wife, who plays the *dholak* (a small drum) and sings. Today there is less demand for the *kathputlis* – although the regions of Lunicha, Kuchaman and Khakholi, on the eastern fringes of the Thar Desert, still have a lively tradition of *kathputli* performers – so they have to go further afield in search of paying audiences, making long journeys throughout northern India in the winter months. Up to a dozen families may set out on these journeys, pitching tents at night and carrying all their possessions on their backs.

Acrobats

Like Rajasthan's puppeteers, its acrobats, who belong to the Nat community, are very poor, and often have to resort to begging. The itinerant Nats travel around the countryside performing acrobatic feats such as tightrope walking and balancing on long bamboo poles for the entertainment of villagers. There is still a substantial community of Nats in Chittorgarh district.

Music

Although Hindi pop songs are as popular in Rajasthan as anywhere else in India, folk music is a vital part of traditional culture. Through songs the legendary battles of the Rajputs are told. The music engenders both a spirit of identity and provides entertainment as relief from the daily grind of wrenching a living from the inhospitable land.

Rajasthani folk songs are commonly ballads that relate heroic deeds or love stories, and religious or devotional songs known as *bhajans* and *banis*. They are often accompanied by percussion instruments such as *ektaras* or *dholaks*. Various communities specialise in professional singing, such as the Dhadhis, the Dholis, the Mangamars, and the Nats, among others. Hindu prostitutes (Patars) and Muslim prostitutes (Kancharis) are renowned for their singing, as are the Muslim Mirasis, who specialise in folk songs called *mands* that almost approximate classical singing.

Percussion Instruments The most common instrument found in the villages of Rajasthan is the *dhol*, or drum. Goat skin is stretched over both ends of the *dhol*, one end being beaten with the hand, and the other with a stick. There is also a smaller version of the *dhol*, the *dholak*, which is one of the most common instruments of northern India. Another type of drum is the *ektara*, which is played during devotional ceremonies by priests. The *ektara* is a gourd over which skin is stretched. This membrane is beaten with a finger or with a stick of bamboo.

Matas are played in pairs by two musicians. A *mata* is an earthenware pot with a skin stretched over the opening. It is a popular instrument of the Bhopas, a caste of professional storytellers. The *chara* is an earthenware pot with an open mouth into which the musician sometimes blows, creating a deep, resonant, booming sound. The sides of the pot are struck with the right hand on which a ring is worn. Sometimes the musician accompanies the performance with dance steps. The *chara* is traditionally played by the Meghwal caste, who are found along the India–Pakistan border.

The *naupat* is played during marriage ceremonies, and consists of two drums, a *nagada*, which is the male form of the drum, and the *jheel*, which is the female form. The *chang* is a large drum played generally by one, but sometimes two, musicians. It is frequently played during the festival of Holi. The drummer beats the centre of the drum

Patrons & Performers

Musicians and minstrels play an integral role in Rajasthani society, not only in providing entertainment, but in maintaining a tradition that is deeply rooted in community life. There are various castes and communities of professional musicians such as the Muslim Manganiyars, Langas and Dholis. They belong to subcastes of the lowest caste.

Musicians receive patronage not only from ruling families, but from ordinary people, both high and low caste, who pay for the performers' services with livestock, cash or a portion of the patron's crop. They play an important role in cultural life and are essential for the ceremonies that accompany birth, marriage and death. The musician's responsibility at a death ceremony includes holding a vigil at the cremation ground for 12 days and reciting lamentations dedicated to the deceased.

As patronage is hereditary, the virtuosity (or lack of it) of the performer does not influence the relationship. A *jajman* (patron) cannot 'fire' a musician, who is attached not just to a single family, but to the entire family line. A breakdown in this relationship is detrimental to the cohesiveness of society, so mechanisms have evolved to ensure the continuation of the bond. A patron can endure social stigma if his family's performer withdraws services. A musician can express displeasure with a patron by refusing to recite *subhraj*, poems dedicated to his family. If this fails to bring the patron around, the musician can take the more drastic step of removing the strings from his instrument and symbolically burying them. The worst insult towards a patron by a musician is to make an effigy of him, which is tied to the tail of a donkey, paraded through the village and repeatedly beaten with a shoe. The patron is then denied the services of all musicians belonging to that caste. As musicians are essential at important social functions, the patron is effectively socially ostracised and may, for example, be compelled to marry his children to members of a lower caste.

In addition to receiving patronage from ordinary people, musicians were also patronised, prior to Independence, by the *jagirdars*, or feudal lords. Most of the musicians who performed for the *jagirdars* belonged to the Damani caste, a subgroup of the Dholis. Unfortunately, when the *jagirdari* system was abolished after Independence, the Damanis lost their patrons. Many were compelled to work in fields unrelated to music, spelling the death knell for various forms of traditional music that had formed part of their repertoire.

with his left hand and the rim of the instrument with a stick held in his right hand. The *duff* is also played during Holi. This is a large tambourine with a rim of iron or wood, and a membrane of goat's skin.

The *nagada* (not to be confused with the male form of the *naupat*) consists of two drums of different sizes that are played together. One drum is iron and the other copper. Buffalo skin is stretched over the larger drum, and camel skin over the smaller. They were traditionally beaten during battles. The *khanzari*, traditionally played by Kalbelias, is a small drum encircled with brass or iron bells. The Kalbelias are a nomadic tribal group who are associated with snake charming. The tabla is a pair of drums and is played by classical musicians throughout India.

Stringed Instruments The two-stringed *rawanahattha*, a bowed instrument, is played by Bhopas in honour of their deity, Pabuji. One of the two strings is made of horse hair, the other formed from several thin threads twisted together to form one string. The bowl is made from a coconut shell, and the main body of the instrument from bamboo.

The *kamayacha* is a stringed instrument played by the professional Muslim caste singers known as Manganiyars, who perform in small groups of three of four. The *kamayacha* is played by drawing a bow across strings of animal gut. The bowl of the instrument is made of wood, with a membrane stretched across it.

A well-known stringed instrument is the *sarangi*, of which there are various types. The *Sindhi sarangi* is used to accompany Sarangiya Langas, Muslim singers who perform for Muslim patrons. A smaller version, the *Gujratan sarangi*, is also played by these singers. Yet another type of *sarangi* is the *jogiya sarangi*, traditionally played by snake charmers who hail from Barmer and Jodhpur districts.

The stringed *srimandal* is very rarely seen today, and only a few musicians in Jaisalmer district still excel at this instrument. It is a rectangular board over which 17 or 18 strings are stretched.

One string, known as the *mandrasa*, is plucked throughout the performance to provide the drone, while the other strings are dexterously plucked to give the melody. Other stringed instruments include the *revaj*, *dusaka*, *apang* and *dilruba*, the last of which is played with a bow.

The five-stringed *tandoora* is played by plucking the strings and beating the rhythm on the bowl of the instrument. It is often used to accompany the dance known as the *terahtal*, which is performed in honour of Ramdev.

The *tambura* is commonly used alongside a main melody instrument such as the violin. This four-stringed instrument provides a secondary melody giving the musicians a constant reference point to follow.

The sitar, which is a classical instrument as opposed to a folk instrument, dates from the 12th century and was introduced to India by the Muslims.

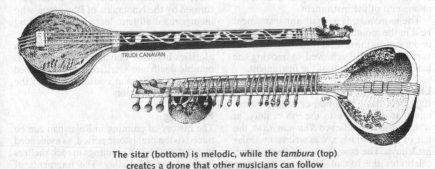

The sitar (bottom) is melodic, while the *tambura* (top) creates a drone that other musicians can follow

Wind Instruments

Rajasthani wind instruments include the *kariya*, a brass instrument once played in the courts of the maharajas, and also on the battlefield. The *mashak* is a wind instrument played by the Bhopas of Bhaironji. The *surnai* is played by the Jogis of the Bhil areas, the Dholis and the Langas of Jaisalmer. The mouthpiece contains a *jhajoor*, or tar-leaf reed.

The *narh* is a four-holed flute made from a type of desert grass known as kangore, and was traditionally played by shepherds to amuse themselves on their lonely vigils. Kangore was once obtained from Pakistan, but hostilities with India have reduced opportunities to obtain it, so there are few *narh* players left in Rajasthan.

Another type of wind instrument is the *satara*, consisting of two flutes which are played simultaneously. One of the flutes contains holes which, as with conventional flutes, enable different pitches to be achieved. Holes are absent in the second flute, which gives a steady drone. The *satara* is a popular instrument with the Bhils and Meghwals, and is played by shepherds.

One of the most well-known instruments of the desert is the *poongi*, also known as a *murli*. This is the traditional snake charmers' flute; the bulge in its centre is formed by a gourd. are enabled by Reeds of different lengths produce different pitches. It is played in the desert regions by folk musicians such as Langas and Manganiyars.

The *bankiya*, found in the Mewar (Udaipur) region, is a form of trumpet, with sound produced by blowing in small holes at one end of the instrument.

The *morchang* is a small iron instrument held in the mouth by the teeth. Breathing in or out causes the central reed to vibrate, and various tones are achieved by moving the hand along the length of the instrument.

Literature

Rajasthan has a tradition of written literature that dates back to the 9th century, at which time it is believed *Khuman Raso*, the tale of a Mewari hero, was written by Dalapat Vijaya. The epic *Prithviraj Raso*, which celebrates the life of Maharaja Prithviraj Chauhan, was written by Chand Bardai in the medieval period. While Rajasthan has produced several talented writers in the post-Independence period, few of their works have been translated into English.

Marwari is the dialect most commonly used by Rajasthani writers. A form of literary Rajasthani, known as Dingal, evolved in the 15th century for the communication of poetry and ballads telling of the exploits of heroes and warriors.

Popular literature is embodied in folk tales related orally by bards down through the centuries. Tales include love stories such as those of Dhola Maru and the tragic tale of the beautiful princess Mumal (see the boxed text 'Mumal & Mahendra' later), tales of heroic exploits, religious legends, and fables and stories recounting the dastardly deeds of notorious *dacoits* (bandits).

In addition there are folk songs and ballads, the latter frequently concerned with the virtue and heroism of deified folk heroes such as Pabuji, who died while fulfilling a promise that took him away from his marriage. *Pabuji-ka-phad* is a style of folk poetry performed by the nomadic Bhopas, devotees of Pabuji, who complement the narrative with painted scrolls showing the various events in his life.

Khyals are a form of folk literature. Tales, legends and historical events are communicated through *khyals*, which may include plays, songs, sayings and storytelling. When sung, they are often accompanied by a tambourine-drum known as a *duff*. The most renowned *khyals* were those performed by the Nautankis of Bharatpur, who incorporated athletic leaps and the beating of drums into their recitations.

The folk literature of Rajasthan, which glorifies heroism, chivalry, virtue and honourable death and sacrifice, has engendered the image in popular consciousness of the brave Rajput warrior.

Painting

The history of painting in Rajasthan can be traced to the prehistoric period, as evidenced by the discovery of paintings in rock shelters in the Chambal Valley. The fragments of

Mumal & Mahendra

Upon first laying eyes on her, Mahendra of Umarkot lost his heart to the beautiful princess Mumal. Every night he raced to her chamber, borne by a swift camel named Chekal. As Mahendra had to travel at night to visit Mumal in the distant village of Lodhruva, near Jaisalmer, he had little energy left to perform his husbandly duties to the satisfaction of his eight wives. Suspecting his nocturnal visits to the princess of renowned beauty, the aggrieved wives beat Mahendra's trusty camel Chekal within an inch of his life, rendering him completely lame. Mumal had to use a camel not of the calibre of Chekal, which subsequently lost its way.

In the meantime, Mumal's sister Sumal, of rather more homely appearance, decided to pay a visit to her sister. Sumal was in the habit of wearing men's clothes, and fell asleep next to Mumal who was exhausted from her midnight vigil awaiting Mahendra. When he finally reached Mumal's apartment, he was confronted by the sight of her lying next to what appeared to be another man. Mahendra fled from the chamber, vowing never to lay eyes on her again, and bitterly cursing the inconstancy of women. Mumal waited every night for her absent lover, finally pining away with grief. When Mahendra heard of her death, and of the misunderstanding that had kept him from visiting her, he went mad.

paintings found on pottery shards recovered from Kalibangan, among other places, indicate the antiquity of its pictorial art tradition.

From the 11th century, pictorial art was recorded on palm leaf, and in subsequent centuries, on paper. These were predominantly religious paintings that illustrated ancient Jain manuscripts. The influence of these early paintings is shown in the paintings of the 15th century. The remnants of paintings dating from this period are evident at the Kumbhalgarh and Chittorgarh forts. Common themes include religious mythology, especially that concerning Krishna and Radha, romance and interpretations of poems written about a *ragamala* (musical mode or melody).

Miniature Painting The most characteristic paintings of Rajasthan are miniatures, small paintings crammed with detail and executed in vegetable and mineral colours, generally on hand-made paper, but also on ivory, marble, wood, cloth and leather. Various schools of miniature painting emerged in the 17th century. Although employing common themes, there were distinct differences in paintings produced in different regions. The most important regional schools of painting were those of Mewar (Udaipur), Marwar (encompassing Bikaner, Jaisalmer

and Jodhpur), Amber (Jaipur; known as the Dhundhar school), Kishangarh and Hadoti (divided into the Bundi and Kota schools).

The Bundi school produced some magnificent work, which other schools tried to emulate, employing rich colours and idealised subject matter, often against a lush jungle background. In the late 18th century, Bundi artists created unusual paintings with half the surface left white, and just a few figures painted against this in pale colours. The Kota school, which emerged in the 19th century, is renowned for its depictions of *shikhars*, or royal hunts.

The artists of Kishangarh also produced distinctive paintings. The Kishangarh school emerged in the second half of the 17th century under the patronage of Raja Man Singh. The school flourished under a later ruler, Sawant Singh, who ascended to the *gaddi* (throne) in 1706. The portrayal of Krishna's consort, Radha, was a common theme, and it is believed that a local beauty, Bani Thani, who had won the heart of Sawant Singh, was the model for these paintings. The greatest works of the Kishangarh school were produced by the master artist Nihal Chand. The Kishangarh school is also known for its romantic miniatures.

Artists of Amber, and the later capital of Jaipur, received patronage from successive

Kachhwaha rulers, so the area was a most prolific centre. Much of the work from Jaipur was influenced by Mughal styles.

In Mewar, the patronage of the royal family and the pursuit of all artistic endeavours afforded a fertile environment for miniature painting to flourish. Mewar is famous for its paintings depicting court life. These were produced for the various maharanas from the early 18th century. The paintings are large and detailed, portraying festivals, ceremonies, elephant fights and hunts. Human faces had distinctive features such as almond-shaped eyes and prominent noses.

The paintings of Jodhpur, belonging to the Marwar school, featured distinctive vivid colours and heroic, bewhiskered men accompanied by dainty maidens. The paintings of Bikaner were greatly influenced by the Mughals, as many master Mughal painters, known as Ustas, were encouraged to attend the Bikaner court.

The Rajasthani painters used colours derived from minerals, ochres and vegetables. The vibrant colours, still evident today in miniatures and frescoes in some of the royal palaces, were derived from crushed semi-precious stones, while the gold and silver colouring is in fact finely pounded pure gold and silver leaf.

Portrait & Courtly Painting Rajput exposure to the Mughal courts in the first half of the 17th century gave rise to a new mode of painting – the royal portrait. Bikaner, with its close association with the Mughals, was one of the first schools to adopt the new style. Throughout the subsequent evolution of Rajasthani painting, while the Rajputs borrowed from the Mughals and adapted their themes, their paintings remained much more idealised, abstract and stylised than those of their Mughal counterparts.

The 18th century saw less emphasis on religious themes and the illustration of manuscripts, and more on secular themes. Paintings commonly depicted maharajas engaged in various activities, including hunting, visiting the *zenana* (women's quarters), attending the *durbar* (royal court) and fulfilling religious obligations, such as presiding at

the Holi celebrations. Mewar became the main centre for the production of these courtly themes.

A distinct difference between the paintings of the Rajputs and those of the Mughals in the 18th century was in the use of colour. While the Mughals used muted colours that gave a sense of shadow and depth, the Rajputs used bold primary colours, which rendered their paintings two-dimensional and abstract. It is not unusual to see Rajasthani miniatures of this period in which the subjects appear to 'float', captured in limbo between the foreground and background, the earth and the sky.

The 19th century heralded a decline in the execution of portraits in Rajasthan, perhaps reflecting a decline in the relative power of the maharajas as the British began to erode their dominance and, as a consequence, to divest them of their heroic status.

Cloth Painting The town of Nathdwara, 48km from Udaipur, is an important centre for the production of *pichwai* paintings, which are religious paintings on home-spun cloth hung behind images of Krishna (who in Nathdwara is worshipped as Sri Nathji). The paintings were introduced by members of a Vaishnavite sect known as the Vallabh Sampradhya.

The large cloths are painted to evoke a particular mood, generally associated with the legends of Krishna, such as the *rasalila*. In the *rasalila*, Krishna, in order to please the *gopis* (milkmaids), manifested himself numerous times and was thus able to dance individually beside every maiden (the circular nature of this dance also makes the *rasalila* a popular theme on the interior of domes in temples and *chhatris*). Traditionally *pichwai* paintings were done in colours derived from natural minerals and vegetables, with red and yellow predominating; today, however, they are mass produced for tourists and are of little artistic value.

Another form of cloth painting is the *phad*, a painted scroll used by the nomadic Bhopas to illustrate the legends of the deified hero Pabuji. The Bhopa, assisted by his wife, the Bhopi, travels from village to village, dancing, singing and pointing to sections of the scroll to assist the narrative. The paintings are executed by a subsect of the Chhipa caste, the Joshis, who hail from the regions of Bhilwara and Chittorgarh.

Domestic Painting The region of Shekhawati, in northern Rajasthan, is reputed for its extraordinary painted havelis (see the special section 'Architecture').

The folk-art form of *mandana* is also evident in Rajasthan, in which houses are decorated with floral and geometric designs in red chalk, or with vegetation motifs that indicate the various seasons.

Sculpture & Stonework

Rajasthan is known for the fine quality of marble and sandstone extracted from the numerous quarries in the state. This has given rise to a tradition of stonemasons and sculptors. Some of the more famous quarries include those at Makrana, from which the marble used in the Taj Mahal was mined. Also built using marble from these mines were the impressive Dilwara Jain temples at Mt Abu.

The quarries of Dungarpur yield a soft chironatic stone that is used for carving images of the deities. When this stone is oiled, it becomes a rich, lustrous black. Due to their divine subject matter, sculptors producing these images are required to work according to guidelines laid down in the *Shilpa-Shashtra*, an ancient Hindu treatise on sculpture and architecture. In most cases, producing an image of a deity can entail the work of two or more sculptors. An apprentice would be responsible for carving the crude image and liberating it from the stone block, but the fine work that imparts expression and dignity to the image is done by a master sculptor.

The finest sculptors of the day were commissioned to work on the beautiful temples of Rajasthan, and some of the best work can be seen in the temples of the Jains. The Dilwara temples at Mt Abu feature exquisite carvings. No less inspiring are the Jain temples within the fort walls at Jaisalmer; the superb Jain and Hindu temples at Osiyan in western Rajasthan, which date from the 8th to the 12th centuries; and the beautiful 15th-century Jain temples at Ranakpur, in southern Rajasthan.

At the palaces of centres such as Ajmer, Udaipur, Jaipur, Jodhpur and Bikaner, very fine examples of *jali* (stone tracery) worked on screens and panels can be seen. *Jali* screens offered protection from the elements while allowing ventilation through the intricate geometric patterns. They were frequently used in the windows of the *zenanas*, enabling the women in *purdah* to view the events of the courts without being seen themselves. *Jali* screens were sculpted from both sandstone and marble.

SOCIETY & CONDUCT
Traditional Culture

Birth The birth of a male child is greeted with great rejoicing and celebration. The birth is broadcast by an elderly female member of the husband's family who beats a

Female Infanticide

Such is the desire to have male children that the mortality rate of female infants is greater than that of males. The dowry system, which requires the parents of the bride to ply the bridegroom's family with gifts, ensures the continued undesirability of girls, and the lower status of women in Rajasthani society.

The practice of killing newborn female infants was not unknown in Rajasthan prior to Independence, particularly among Rajput families where the dowry traditionally involved paying vast sums of money. Some analysts suggest that female infanticide may still take place. Postnatal care of female infants is less vigilant than that of males. More affluent members of society had, until it was outlawed recently, recourse to tests such as amniocentesis and chorionic villus sampling (CVS) that revealed the sex of a foetus, enabling female ones to be aborted. It is not unlikely that, for the right fee, doctors in large cities could still be persuaded to provide this service.

copper thali (plate) to inform the neighbours of the good news. However, the birth of a female child is considered a cause of commiseration, and there is no joyous celebration. A folk saying sums up the typical attitude towards female children: *Beti bhali no ek* (It is not worth having even one daughter).

In order to ward off evil spirits known as *dakins* or *chureils* who prey on young infants, a ceremony is performed shortly after birth. The death of a newborn child is attributed to the malevolent machinations of these spirits.

Around 20 days following birth, at an hour deemed auspicious by the priest, a ceremony known as *panghat poojan* is performed at the local village well in worship of the water god. After this ceremony, the new mother is permitted, to recommence her domestic duties.

The birth of a female child is not considered a calamity in all communities. There are several communities, mostly belonging to the Scheduled Castes and Tribes, which demand a bride price, or *reet*, on the marriage of their daughters. Young men who are unable to pay *reet* are either condemned to bachelorhood, or are compelled to exchange their sisters or female cousins in a multiple marriage transaction.

Adoption A common solution in Rajasthan to the problem of a lack of a male heir, and one resorted to in the past by numerous maharajas, is adoption. The adoption ceremony is performed before a group of representatives from the community. Vermilion is smeared on the forehead of the adoptee, and a turban placed on his head.

Marriage Almost without exception, marriages are arranged by parents, the engagement being announced after a suitable match is found and the horoscopes of the prospective partners compared by a priest and found to be compatible. The father of the girl traditionally sends her future father-in-law a coconut. Once the coconut has been received, the marriage is inevitable. Cross-caste marriages, once socially taboo, are now performed occasionally, and are generally the result of a love match.

Although outlawed by government, child marriages are not uncommon in rural areas. Unicef estimates that 82% of girls in Rajasthan are married before they turn 18, and 48% are married by the age of 15. The Sahariya tribal people arrange marriages while the child is still in the womb. Often a group of children are married simultaneously, to reduce costs, although the newlyweds return to the family home until they reach maturity. On attaining puberty, girls are given gifts by their parents and then dispatched with due ceremony to their in-laws' homes. Several days in the year are considered auspicious for marriage, and on such days, thousands of child marriages are performed throughout Rajasthan. The authorities generally turn a blind eye to these proceedings, after receiving *baksheesh* (a bribe). Some people who have actively opposed this custom have been violently assaulted.

Spring, especially around the festival of Holi, is a popular time for weddings, although the actual date of marriage is determined by a Brahmin priest. Around Holi in Jaipur, Jodhpur and the other towns and cities of Rajasthan, it's not uncommon to see marriage processions along the busy streets. The groom, resplendent in traditional Rajput warrior costume, is borne aloft a white horse – surrounded by his friends and family and the marriage party (known as the *baraat*) – and led by a brightly decorated float, on which a singer and musicians blast out the latest Hindi movie love songs through megaphones. Hired helpers carry heavy and ornate fluorescent lights on their shoulders to in order to illuminate the procession.

Traditionally, the bridegroom proceeded to the home of the bride, where he pierced with a sword a shield-shaped device known as a *toran* over the doorway, and thus symbolically 'won' his bride and entered her family home to claim her. This was not necessarily an easy process, as the bride was allowed to fend off her suitor with a sword. If the husband-to-be survived the attack, he could claim her! Today brides strike their future husbands with bunches of sweets rather than sword strokes.

Following the marriage, according to Rajasthani tradition, the groom is plied with seemingly nonsensical riddles by his new female in-laws. The main object is to unsettle and embarrass him, and often the riddles have a ribald sexual content.

Polygamy Prior to the dissolution of the princely states, it was not unusual for a maharaja to have at least several wives, who were known as *ranis*. Polygamy flourished during the medieval period when more wives ensured more male progeny, and hence more warriors to fight in the not-infrequent battles of the Rajputs.

The ability to support a large harem became a symbol of power and affluence, and even in the 20th century, one maharaja boasted more than 300 women, which constituted a vast drain on the state's financial reserves! Gayatri Devi, the jet-setting wife of the last maharaja of Jaipur, Man Singh II, who socialised with, among others, Queen Elizabeth II of England and Prince Philip, was Man Singh's third wife.

Polygamy is still practised by those members of the Bhil and Mina tribes who can afford to maintain more than one wife.

Dowry System Unfortunately, the dowry system, although illegal, is entrenched in Rajasthan, and the parents of female children can be plunged into terrible debt trying to maintain their honour by sending their daughter to her in-laws' home with appropriate gifts of cash, jewellery, electrical goods such as TVs and radios, and even motor scooters and washing machines.

If the family of the bridegroom believes that the dowry is inadequate, further demands can be made on the bride's family. 'Bride burning', or 'dowry death', is not unknown and, as in other parts of India, the deaths of new brides in 'stove fires' are not uncommon. Some of these are attributed to the greed of in-laws, who kill their daughter-in-law to enable their son to remarry and hence claim another dowry. A poet from Rajasthan has written, 'How is the stove so wise that it distinguishes between a daughter-in-law and mother-in-law?'.

Divorce & Remarriage Traditionally, among the Jats, Gujjars and Scheduled Castes and Tribes, a woman is permitted to remarry following the death of her husband. However, the new husband is required to pay compensation both to the relatives of the former husband and to the bride's parents. Remarriage of widows was once forbidden by the Hindu upper castes, but is gradually becoming more prevalent and accepted. Divorce, also once forbidden, is now also more prevalent among these castes. If a woman wishes for a divorce to marry another man, compensation is payable to the former husband and his family.

Purdah Prior to Independence and the dissolution of the princely states, *purdah*, or isolation of married women, was prevalent among the upper echelons of society, particularly among the Rajputs. Maintaining a woman in *purdah* reflected favourably on her husband, as it was a symbol of his wealth and position.

The women of the royal harems were ensconced in *zenanas*, rarely venturing beyond the palace precincts, and were viewed by no man other than their husband (and the palace eunuchs). If they did leave their cloistered quarters, the women were transported in covered vehicles under heavy escort.

Lower-caste women were veiled from the eyes of men by their head scarves. Only the nomads and tribal women were free from the constraints imposed by *purdah*.

Today *purdah* is considered a relic of the feudal past and, other than in the Muslim communities and among the Oswal Jains, is generally not observed.

Death Twelve days after cremation, if the deceased was the male head of the family, a symbolic turban-tying ceremony is performed, in which his successor is recognised by his family and the community.

In rural areas, a death feast known variously as *mosar*, *barwa*, *kariyawar* or *terwa* is often held 12 or 13 days after death. The mourning relatives are reminded of their obligations to perform a death feast by community leaders who call on the family three

Glorifying the Burning Widow

On 4 September 1987, India was plunged into controversy when a 19-year-old recently widowed woman, Roop Kanwar, burned to death on her husband's funeral pyre at the village of Deorala in the district of Sikar. According to the dead girl's family and the entire village of Deorala, Roop Kanwar voluntarily ascended the funeral pyre and calmly recited prayers while she was consumed by flames. Sceptics have alleged that the young woman, who had only been married seven months, was drugged and forcibly thrown on the fire.

What is equally as shocking as the fact that a young woman should needlessly perish by fire, whether voluntarily or not, is that in the late 20th century the act of *sati* was glorified and the victim deified, not just by superstitious rural folk, but by hundreds of thousands of people around the country. Within one week of Roop Kanwar's death, Deorala had become a major pilgrimage site, attracting *half a million* pilgrims, most of whom left substantial donations for a temple to be built in her honour. Among the pilgrims who visited the site of the calamity were several members of both the state and central governments.

On 27 September, Prime Minister Rajiv Gandhi issued a statement declaring the circumstances of the death of Roop Kanwar 'utterly reprehensible and barbaric'. In December 1987, a law was passed by the central government banning *sati*, with family members of persons committing *sati* to be divested of their right to inherit her property. Persons charged with 'glorifying' *sati* would be prohibited from contesting elections. In addition, *sati melas*, or fairs, were banned.

Despite these measures, the incontestable power of the *sati* still holds sway over the population, both educated and uneducated. In 1996, the 32 people accused of Roop Kanwar's murder were acquitted. Women still reverently pay homage at shrines erected in honour of *satis*, believing that they have the power to make barren women fertile, or cure terminal illnesses. And as recently as November 1999, a 55-year-old Dalit village woman in Satpurva (Uttar Pradesh) performed *sati* after her husband died from tuberculosis.

The reverence in which *sati* is evidently still held is exemplified in the extraordinarily lavish temple of Rani Sati in Jhunjhunu, in Shekhawati, which commemorates the self-immolation of a woman on her husband's funeral pyre in 1595. This temple is said to receive the second highest amount of donations of any temple in India.

days following the death, regardless of the family's financial ability to discharge this obligation. Frequently these unwelcome visitors are conveniently accompanied by the *bohara*, or village moneylender.

Death feasts can be expensive, elaborate affairs, often plunging those who hold them into debt. It has been known for the *bohara* to call on the bereaved family shortly after the death feast and seize their possessions in lieu of payment. However, the custom of *mosar* is entrenched, and to fail in this duty would reflect poorly on both the family and the honour of the deceased person.

In 1922, some 50,000 people were fed at the death feast of Maharaja Madho Singh of Jaipur. Some people celebrate the *mosar* feast in their lifetime, in case their relatives fail to honour them after their death. The state government has enacted laws to limit the guests at a feast, with little success. Once, a clash between police and mourners at a death feast resulted in scores of deaths.

Very affluent families may erect a *chhatri* to commemorate the deceased. This practice was common in Shekhawati, where some of the wealthy merchant families, such as the Poddars, have left a legacy of architecturally impressive and beautiful *chhatris*.

Sati The practice of *sati*, or voluntary self-immolation by a widow on her husband's funeral pyre, is believed to date from the Vedic era. It is named after Shiva's wife Sati, who self-immolated when her father insulted Shiva by refusing to invite him to a feast. In Rajasthan there are numerous instances of *sati*, especially among the ruling Rajputs, when the wives of maharajas threw themselves on their husbands' pyres, both to honour their dead husband, and to avoid the ignominy of widowhood.

Widows, rather than being treated with compassion and solicitude on the deaths of their husbands, were divested of their wealth and rich vestments, cursed and hounded, and considered living symbols of misfortune. There are also examples in Rajput history of not only wives but maids, slaves and other domestic hands perishing on the funeral pyre of a deceased ruler.

There are several examples in Rajput's history of *jauhar* – *sati* performed on a mass scale, when defeat in battle was imminent and the women of the royal court preferred to face death, rather than dishonour, at the hands of the enemy.

In 1846, the princely state of Jaipur was the first state in Rajasthan to outlaw *sati* after prompting by the British government, and it was soon followed by other states. Mewar resisted the ban, and in 1861 Queen Victoria was compelled to issue a proclamation forbidding the practice of *sati*. Intermittent cases of *sati* have taken place over subsequent years.

Traditional Beliefs

Evil spirits, or ghosts, known as *bhuuts* or *dakins*, which possess the minds of their hapless victims, can be dislodged with the assistance of a priest, known as a *jogi* or a *bhopa* (the Bhil name for a priest). *Bhuuts* and *dakins* are also blamed for natural disasters such as droughts, famines and crop failure, and are propitiated accordingly to avert calamity. They are known to frequent crossroads. The Balaji exorcism temple, 80km to the east of Jaipur, is visited by those seeking relief from possession by a *bhuut* or *dakin*.

Barren women are feared by new mothers, as it is believed that a barren woman will conceive if she secures hair or a fragment of clothing from an infant, who will die as a consequence.

The crossing of a cobra or cat in front of a person is considered a bad omen, as is confronting a goldsmith, a cart laden with firewood, or a woman carrying an empty pitcher. A person setting out on a long journey who is confronted by any of these inauspicious signs would do well to delay their journey.

However, meeting a married woman with a pitcher of water is an auspicious sign, auguring well for a good journey. Also considered good luck is the braying of a donkey or the cheeping of a sparrow. Friday is considered a lucky day, and work commenced on this day is guaranteed success. Monday, however, is not considered a good day for commencing new projects, and journeys to the east are never undertaken on a Monday.

It is considered unlucky to have your hair cut on a Tuesday and, consequently, barber stalls generally remain closed on this day throughout the state.

Deceased ancestors are worshipped as *pitars* (in the case of men) and *pitaris* (in the case of women who died before their husbands). On the anniversary of the death of the *pitar* or *pitari*, food must be offered to a Brahmin, a cow, a crow and a dog. These ancestors are also collectively worshipped on a particular fortnight of the year known as Shraddha Paksha.

The Caste System

The caste system, integral to Hinduism, dominates the social organisation of Rajasthan. Although its origins are hazy, it seems to have been developed by the Brahmins, or priest class, to maintain their superiority over the indigenous Dravidians. Eventually the system became formalised into four distinct castes, each with rules of conduct and behaviour. These, in order of hierarchy, are said to have come from Brahma's mouth (Brahmins; priest caste), arms (Kshatriyas; warrior caste), thighs (Vaisyas; caste of tradespeople and artisans) and feet (Sudras; caste of farmers and peasants). These basic castes are then subdivided into numerous lesser divisions. Beneath all the castes are the Dalits and Scheduled Castes (formerly known as Harijans and Untouchables), who have no caste. Hindus cannot change caste – they are born into it and are stuck with it for the rest of their lives.

There are variations on the caste system in Rajasthan, the most important being the Rajput caste. The Rajputs are traditionally warriors claiming lineage to the Kshatriyas. Prior to Independence and the merger of the Rajput states into the Indian Union, the martial Rajputs wielded the most power. The Rajputs comprised various *khamps*, or clans, according to their dynastic families. Due to the integration of the princely kingdoms into the state of Rajasthan, and the abolition of the system of *jagirdari*, the Rajputs were nudged from their positions of power by the Brahmins.

The Brahmins can be subdivided into two groups, Chhanayatis and non-Chhanayatis, between whom intermarriage is traditionally forbidden.

Below the Rajputs in Rajasthan's caste hierarchy, the Vaisyas can be divided into two groups: those who profess Jainism, and those professing Vaishnavism, or worship of the god Vishnu. The Oswals, who hail from Osiyan, fall loosely into this caste classification.

Below the Vaisyas, the Jats today play an active role in the administration and politics of the state. They are generally vegetarian and profess Vaishnavism. There are communities of Jats and Gujjars who are traditionally engaged in farming and animal husbandry. In Rajasthan, the tribal groups, known as Scheduled Tribes, belong to the Dalits, the lowest casteless class for whom all of the most menial and degrading tasks are reserved.

Women in Society

While women in urban areas are making inroads into the professions, rural women in Rajasthan are one of the most economically and socially disadvantaged groups, unable to hold property in their own right, and receiving little, if any, education. Women are becoming a priority in development programmes run by the central and state governments, as well as NGOs and donor countries. Initiated in 1984, the Women's Development Programme mobilises rural women to campaign against issues such as rape, *sati* and child marriage, through *sathins* or workers at the grass-roots level.

The Women & Child Development Department in Jaipur is mostly concerned with administering programmes to increase rural women's awareness of issues that directly impinge on them, including child marriage, *purdah*, dowry, and lack of education for girls. Small meetings known as *jajams* are held at the village level in order to educate the women, who are also provided with access to microcredit.

Legislation has been passed requiring 30% of seats in local elections to *gram panchayats* (one to three villages), *panchayat sammitis* (village clusters) and *zila parishads* (district committees) to be reserved for women across India. The state government of Rajasthan has gone one step further by passing a law that requires 30% of the headpersons of *gram panchayats* and *panchayat sammitis* to be village women.

There are dozens of voluntary organisations in the state working towards the economic and social empowerment of women. The Barefoot College, Urmal Trust and Sewa Mandir all run important programmes.

Village Life

Traditional village huts are known as *jhonpas*. They are generally small, single-storey dwellings, with walls of mud and straw, and a thatched roof. The hearth is usually built in part of the *adgaliya*, or veranda, which fronts the dwelling. There are no windows in *jhonpas*, and the door is generally split bamboo. The floor is packed-earth coated with mud and dung. More affluent village members may build houses of stone. Next to the dwelling is a separate building of the same materials, known as a *chhan* or *dogla*. This is where livestock and grain are kept.

Around the hut, and sometimes around the entire village, is a barrier of thorns, to keep wild animals and livestock from wandering into the domestic area.

[Continued on page 50]

ARCHITECTURE

Visitors to Rajasthan will be amazed by the variety and magnificence of the state's architectural heritage. Famous for its majestic forts, intricately carved temples and ornately decorated *havelis* (mansions), Rajasthan is home to some of the country's best-known buildings. Many of these reflect the state's long and intriguing history; the oldest of these structures being the Buddhist caves and *stupas* (Buddhist shrines) believed to date from the 5th century BC. The most eye-catching of them are the extraordinary forts and palaces of the Rajputs. With its romantic and isolated desert structures, its sacred Jain temples and its colourful crowded cities, Rajasthan is a real paradise for the architecture buff.

Temples

There are temples in southeastern Rajasthan whose architecture was influenced by the Gupta empire, which held sway over northern India from the 4th to the 6th centuries AD. Examples include those at Darrah and Sheetaleshvara Temple at Jhalrapatan.

In the 8th and 9th centuries, a new style of temple architecture emerged with the consolidation of the Gurjara Pratihara dynasty of Mandore. Temples built at this time include those at Chittorgarh and the exquisitely carved temples at Osiyan, in western Rajasthan. Many feature magnificent sculptural work. A common feature of these temples is a single *sikhara* (spire) and a sculpted *mandapa* (outer chamber), before the inner sanctum. In several cases, the main temple is surrounded by a series of small and finely sculpted shrines. Well-preserved examples are the Kalika Mata and Kumbha Shyam temples in the fort at Chittorgarh.

At Kiradu, to the west of Barmer, a group of five temples conform to the architectural style known as Solanki. The most inspiring of these is Someshvara Temple, which has a fine sculpted frieze and a multi-tiered spire.

The 10th century saw the construction of many lovely Jain temples. Among the most impressive and well-known are the Dilwara temples at Mt Abu, which are renowned for their remarkable and exquisite carving. Mahavira Temple near Ghanerao in southern Rajasthan is also of note.

Of the later temples, the 15th-century temples at Ranakpur, 60km from Udaipur, are the finest. The most important of these is Chaumukha Temple. It features a series of *mandapas* adorned with intricate carving, and achieves a breathtaking symmetry. The group of Jain temples in Jaisalmer Fort are also noteworthy. The entrance to the *mandapas* of some of these temples is through beautifully carved *toranas* (gateways).

Inset: Carved roof detail on Jaisalmer Fort's Jain temple (Photograph by David Else)

Forts & Palaces

Secular architecture is no less inspiring than religious architecture, as is evident in the massive and beautiful forts (some doubling as palaces) of Chittorgarh, Jodhpur, Jaisalmer, Bikaner, Bundi, Kota, Amber, Jaipur, Alwar, Deeg, Bharatpur, Ranthambhore, Nagaur and Udaipur. These structures encompass *mahals* (palaces), *zenanas* (women's quarters), *diwan-i-am* (public audience halls), *diwan-i-khas* (private audience halls), *sals* (galleries), *mandirs* (temples) and *baghs* (gardens). The palaces and forts of Rajasthan are the last word in opulence. Sometimes the beauty of the royal edifice was reflected in an artificial pool, or tank, as is evident at Deeg and Alwar. In the later palaces, the Rajputs often borrowed architectural inspiration from the Mughals. The *sheesh mahal*, or mirror palace, which is found in Rajasthan is a Mughal innovation.

Amber Fort was the capital of the Kachhwaha dynasty prior to the foundation of Jaipur. This magnificent fort, dating from the late 16th century, features exquisite tile work, found in many of its chambers. The tradition of fine architecture was maintained when the capital was shifted to Jaipur, evident in the soaring Hawa Mahal, or Palace of the Winds, an impressive edifice which is little more than a facade with hundreds of windows, from which the women of the royal court could watch passing processions. Nearby is the vast City Palace complex, construction of which commenced during the reign of Jai Singh II, founder of Jaipur. The maharaja, known as the Warrior Astronomer, also built the Jantar Mantar, an observatory with a series of huge and amazing devices for observing the celestial bodies and their movements, such as the Brihat Samrat Yantra, the largest sundial in the world.

Havelis

The merchants of Rajasthan built ornately decorated residences, known as *havelis*, and commissioned masons and artists to ensure that they were constructed and decorated in a manner befitting the importance and prosperity of their owners. The Shekhawati district of northern Rajasthan is riddled with havelis, most of which are covered, inside and out, with extraordinarily vibrant murals. The merchants also commissioned the construction of civic buildings such as wells, which benefited the entire community. There are beautiful havelis in Jaisalmer, constructed of sandstone, featuring the fine work of the renowned *silavats* (stonecarvers) of Jaisalmer.

Wells & Tanks

Given the importance of water in a predominantly desert state such as Rajasthan, it is not surprising that wells and reservoirs, often known as tanks or *sagars* (lakes), were frequently beautiful and elaborate edifices. The most impressive *baoris* (wells in which a series of steps

KAREN TRIST

GREG ELMS

MONIQUE CHOY

As well as great craftsmanship, a rich cultural and religious heritage is reflected in Rajasthan's intricately sculpted places of worship: 12th-century Adhai-din-ka-Jhonpra mosque, Ajmer (top left); Jain temple interior, Jaisalmer (top right); 10th-century Hindu temple, Eklingji (bottom)

GREG ELMS

Built on Jagniwas Island, Lake Pichola, the Lake Palace Hotel was once the summer residence of royalty

MARK ANDREW KIRBY

Jaisalmer fort mimics the ideal sand castle

SARINA SINGH

Havelis reflect their former owners' wealth

Beauty incarnate: the Peacock Gateway, Jaipur

The conceit is in the facade of the Hawa Mahal

The Meherangarh fort powerfully imposes itself on the landscape surrounding Jodhpur

MARK ANDREW KIRBY

MARK ANDREW KIRBY

JANE SWEENEY

Water is precious and celebrated in Rajasthan: at Jaisalmer, the town furthest into the desert, the Gadi Sagar (all images) is surrounded by small temples and shrines, and there is a *chhatri*, or cenotaph, in the tank itself (top right)

leads down to the water table) in Rajasthan are probably Raniji-ki-Baori in Bundi and the baori at Abhaneri (near Jaipur); although there are beautiful examples throughout the state. An example is the Mertani *baori* at Jhunjhunu, built in the 18th century, with a series of chambers built into the side walls, supported by pillars (see the boxed text 'The Step-Wells of Rajasthan' in the Southern Rajasthan chapter). In Jaisalmer, in the arid western region of the state, is the Gadi Sagar, which supplied water to the city prior to the construction of the Indira Gandhi Canal. It features pretty, freestanding pavilions in the centre of the lake, and a series of *ghats* (steps) that lead down to the water's edge.

Chhatris

Rajasthan's architectural heritage is also evident in the *chhatris* (cenotaphs), built to commemorate maharajas, and, as is the case in the Shekhawati district, wealthy merchants such as the Poddars and Goenkas. In rare instances, chhatris also commemorate women, such as the Chhatri of Moosi Rani at Alwar. Although built in honour of Maharaja Bakhtawar Singh, his wife is also commemorated here as she earned herself a degree of immortality with the highest sacrifice – committing herself to the flames of her husband's funeral pyre in an act of *sati* (self-immolation).

A *chhatri*, which translates as 'umbrella', generally comprises a central dome, supported by a series of pillars on a raised platform, with a series of small pavilions on the corners and sides. In the Shekhawati district, it is not unusual for the inside of the dome to be completely covered with paintings – a good example is the Chhatri of Thakur Sardul Singh at Parsurampura, which features battle scenes from the Ramayana. There is a series of beautiful chhatris commemorating the Rathore Rajputs at Mandore, the ancient capital of Marwar before Jodhpur was founded. Fine chhatris can also be found in the villages of Dundlod and Ramgarh. Excellent royal chhatris may be seen in Jaipur and flanking Jaisamand Lake, near Udaipur.

Building Conservation

The Indian National Trust for Art & Cultural Heritage (Intach) is a voluntary organisation that works to conserve and restore Rajasthan's built heritage and living culture. Another nonprofit organisation is Les Amis du Shekhawati (Friends of Shekhawati), which works to maintain and restore the beautiful painted havelis of Shekhawati. Visitors can also help by writing to the chief minister of the Rajasthan state government to advise that the work carried out by these organisations is appreciated. If you have a knowledge of architecture, restoration or art, some volunteer work may be available with Intach or Les Amis du Shekhawati – see Volunteer Work in the Facts for the Visitor chapter for further details.

[Continued from page 46]

Water, or its absence, is a big problem in the arid zones, and the burden of carrying water, sometimes more than 3km, belongs to women. A paucity of fuelwood also means villagers have to scour the countryside for a meagre load that is then carried many kilometres back to the hearth. Villagers who own livestock prepare cakes of cow dung in the summer, which is burnt as fuel throughout the year.

Women prepare meals with the aid of a *chakki* (handmill), an *okhli* (mortar) and a *moosal* (pestle). Meals are carried out to the men working in the fields and women also help in the fields during the harvest.

Desert villages are naturally found close to available water sources, and village size is dependent on water availability and land productivity, resulting in small communities that are relatively isolated from each other. To trade their goods and purchase livestock, members of these isolated communities attend regular markets and *melas* (fairs), which are opportunities for intervillage socialising. These colourful fairs can range from small local gatherings to enormous fairs such as the Pushkar Camel Fair.

Dos & Don'ts

India is a country of time-honoured traditions and customs. While you are obviously not expected to get everything right, common sense and courtesy will take you a long way. If in doubt about how you should behave, watch what the locals do (eg, at a temple) or simply ask; people are generally happy to point you in the right direction and appreciate your sensitivity.

Kissing and hugging in public is not on, so contain your passion! Before throwing something away to lighten your backpack, think about donating it to a local charity. Lastly, watch where you're walking at night – any undefined, decent-sized shape is likely to be a sleeping human.

Bathing Public nudity is completely taboo (even if you're getting changed at a swimming pool) so make sure you cover up (even in remote locations). Indian women invariably wear saris when bathing in a river or any place where they are in public view. For female travellers, a sarong is a great alternative for bathing – unless at a hotel swimming pool, where a swimsuit is acceptable.

Eating & Visiting Etiquette It's customary to use your right hand for eating and other social acts such as shaking hands; the left hand is used for less-delicious matters such as wiping your backside and removing grotty shoes. If you are drinking from a shared water container, hold the container a little above your mouth and pour (thus avoiding contact between your lips and the mouth of the container).

If you are invited to dine with a family, it's polite to take off your shoes if they do and wash your hands before taking your meal. The hearth is traditionally the sacred centre of the home, so it's best to approach it only if invited to do so. The same often applies for the kitchen (remove shoes). It's inappropriate to touch food or cooking utensils. At a meal, the etiquette is not to help yourself to food – wait to be served or invited to help yourself. If you are unsure about protocol, simply wait for your host to direct you.

Photography Etiquette Exercise sensitivity when taking photos of people, especially women, who may find it embarrassing and offensive – always ask first. Taking photos inside a shrine, at a funeral, a religious ceremony or of people bathing at ghats (steps or landings on a river) or in rivers may cause offence (see Photography & Video in the Facts for the Visitor chapter).

Religious Etiquette With so many spectacular and ancient religious shrines, most travellers to Rajasthan will visit at least one. These places hold enormous spiritual significance, so please be respectful in your conduct and the way you dress. Do not wear shorts or sleeveless tops (this applies to men and women) and don't smoke. Loud and intrusive behaviour isn't appreciated, and neither are public displays of affection, or kidding around.

Before entering a holy place, remove your shoes (remember to tip the shoe minder a couple of rupees when you retrieve them). Photography is usually prohibited – check before taking photos. Never touch a carving or statue of a deity. In some places, such as mosques and some Hindu temples, you will be required to cover your head. For women, a *dupatta* (scarf) is ideal. Many mosques do not admit non-Muslims, and some don't admit women. Always inquire to see if you are allowed into a particular mosque. Women are required to sit apart from the men. Some Jain temples request the removal of leather items that you may be wearing. They may also stipulate that menstruating women should not enter.

Religious etiquette advises against touching locals on the head, or directing the soles of your feet at a person, religious shrine, or image of a deity, as this may cause offence. It is also offensive to touch someone with your feet.

Taxi & Rickshaw Drivers If you hire a car and driver, keep in mind that many hotels do not permit taxi or rickshaw drivers onto their premises to dine, even if you are paying. This is because the commission racket has created all sorts of problems for many hotels, and while your intentions may be warm hearted, the hotel owners are the ones who may face problems with demanding drivers long after you have departed India.

Although some places don't mind drivers joining guests at hotel restaurants, respect those that refuse entry – if in doubt, ask. If you want to shout your driver a meal, there are plenty of good, independent restaurants not attached to hotels that welcome one and all. And, of course, if you are happy with your driver's services, a tip at the end of your trip goes down well. See also Car in the Getting Around chapter for information about hiring a car and driver.

Treatment of Animals

India's ancient reverence for the natural world manifests itself in myths, beliefs and cults that are an intrinsic part of the cultural fabric. But in a country where millions live below the poverty line, survival often comes before sentiment. In addition, big money is involved in the trade of animal parts for Chinese medicine, which has been a major factor in bringing India's national animal, the tiger, to the brink of extinction.

The World Society for the Protection of Animals (WSPA) is working to raise awareness of cases of cruelty and exploitation, with one recent campaign focusing on dancing bears. Endangered sloth bear cubs are captured from the wild, their muzzles are pierced so lead rope can be threaded through the hole, and their teeth are pulled out. The bears' nomadic handlers ply tourist traps in Agra and Jaipur. WSPA strongly urges visitors not to photograph the performances or give money to the handlers, as this is what leads to such cruelty in the first place.

In 2000 captive snakes were the focus of the campaigns of animal-rights activists, who claimed that the treatment of snakes in captivity was extremely cruel. According to the WWF, around 70,000 snakes (including the endangered king cobra) perish annually due to the dreadful living conditions experienced in captivity.

See also Animal Welfare under Responsible Tourism in the Facts for the Visitor chapter.

RELIGION
Hinduism
Hinduism is the dominant religion of Rajasthan, professed by about 89% of the state's population. It is one of the oldest extant religions, with firm roots extending back to beyond 1000 BC.

Essentially, Hindus believe in Brahman. Brahman is eternal, uncreated and infinite; everything that exists emanates from Brahman and will ultimately return to it. The multitude of gods and goddesses are merely manifestations – knowable aspects of this formless phenomenon – and one devotee may freely pick and choose among them.

Although Hindu beliefs and practices vary widely from region to region, there are several unifying factors. These include common beliefs in *samsara* (reincarnation), karma (conduct or action) and *dharma* (appropriate behaviour for one's station in life), as well as the caste system.

Living a righteous life and fulfilling your *dharma* will enhance your chances of being born into a higher caste and better circumstances. Alternatively, if enough bad karma has accumulated, rebirth may take animal form. But it's only as a human that you can gain sufficient self-knowledge to escape the cycle of reincarnation and achieve *moksha* (liberation). Traditionally, women are unable to attain *moksha*. The best they can do is fulfil their *dharma* and hope for a male incarnation next time round.

Gods & Goddesses According to the scriptures there are around 330 million deities in the Hindu pantheon. All of these are regarded as a manifestation of Brahman, and the particular object of veneration and supplication is often a matter of personal choice or tradition at a local or caste level. Brahman is often described as having three main representations, known as the Trimurti: Brahma, Vishnu and Shiva.

Brahma The only active role that Brahma plays is during the creation of the universe. The rest of the time he is in meditation and is therefore regarded as an aloof figure. His vehicle is a swan and he is sometimes shown sitting on a lotus that rises from Vishnu's navel, symbolising the interdependence of the gods. See also the boxed text 'Dreamer of the Universe' in the Eastern Rajasthan chapter.

Vishnu The preserver or sustainer, Vishnu is associated with 'right action' and behaves as a lawful, devout Hindu. He protects and sustains all that is good in the world. He is usually depicted with four arms, each respectively holding a lotus (the petals are symbolic of the unfolding of the universe); a conch shell (as it can be blown like a trumpet it symbolises the cosmic vibration from which all existence emanates); a discus; and a mace (a reward for conquering Indra, the god of battle). His consort is Lakshmi, the goddess of wealth. His vehicle is

HIRA LAL DANGOL

Vishnu

Garuda – a half-bird, half-beast creature – and he dwells in a heaven called Vaikuntha. Vishnu has 22 incarnations, including Rama, Krishna and Buddha. He is alternatively known as Narayan, and Lakshmi is also known as Mohini.

Shiva Although known as the destroyer, creation could not occur without Shiva. Shiva's creative role is phallically symbolised by his representation as the frequently worshipped lingam. With 1008 names, Shiva takes many forms, including Pashupati, champion of the animals, and Nataraja, lord of the *tandava* (cosmic dance), who paces out the creation and destruction of the cosmos.

Shiva is also characterised as the lord of yoga, a Himalaya-dwelling ascetic with matted hair and a naked, ash-smeared body; a third eye in his forehead symbolises wisdom. Sometimes Shiva has snakes draped around his neck and is shown holding a trident (representative of the Trimurti) as a weapon while riding Nandi, his bull. Nandi (literally, 'enjoyment') symbolises power and potency, justice and moral order.

Other Gods The jolly, pot-bellied, elephant-headed Ganesh is held in great affection. He is the god of good fortune and patron of scribes (the broken tusk he holds is the very one he used to write down later sections of the Mahabharata). His animal mount is a rat-like creature. How Ganesh came to have the head of an elephant is a story with many variations. One legend says that Ganesh was born to Parvati in Shiva's absence – Ganesh grew up without knowing his father. One day as Ganesh stood guard while his mother bathed, Shiva returned and asked to be let into Parvati's presence. Ganesh refused him entry. Enraged, Shiva lopped off Ganesh's head, only to later discover that he had slaughtered his own son! He resolved to replace Ganesh's head with the head of the first live creature that he came across. This happened to be an elephant, so that's how Ganesh came to have an elephant's head. In Rajasthan, the most important temple to Ganesh is at the Ranthambhore Fort. Every year thousands of invitations are sent to the elephant god, care of the Fort, to request Ganesh's presence at weddings!

Krishna is an incarnation of Vishnu sent to earth to fight for good and combat evil. Krishna is widely revered throughout Rajasthan. His alliances with the *gopis* (milkmaids) and his love for Radha (a married woman) have inspired countless paintings and songs. Krishna is depicted as being dark blue in colour and usually carries a flute.

Krishna

Hanuman is the hero of the Ramayana and the most popular god in Rajasthan. He is the loyal ally of Rama and embodies the concept of *bhakti* (devotion). Images of Rama and Sita are said to be emblazoned upon his heart. He is king of the monkeys, therefore assuring them refuge at temples across the country, but he is capable of taking on any form he chooses.

Worship of the snake god, Sheshnag, is also widespread across Rajasthan.

Goddesses Within the Shaivite (followers of Shiva) movement, Shakti – the goddess as mother and creator – is worshipped as a force in her own right. Those who follow her are known as *shaktis*.

Shiva's consort is Parvati, the beautiful. In Rajasthan she is worshipped during the Teej festival, which celebrates her marriage to Shiva. Parvati however has a dark side, when she appears as Durga, the terrible. In this role she holds weapons in her 10 hands and rides a tiger. As Kali, the fiercest of the gods, she demands sacrifices and wears a garland of skulls. The Bhil and Mina tribal people are devotees of Kali. In Rajasthan, she is worshipped by women as Gauri, and honoured during the Gangaur Festival, which takes place across Rajasthan just after Holi. Kali usually handles the destructive side of Shiva's personality.

Saraswati, goddess of learning, is the porcelain-skinned consort of Brahma and is widely considered to be the most beautiful goddess.

Sacred Texts Hindu sacred texts fall into two categories: those believed to be the word of god (*shruti*, meaning heard) and those produced by people (*smriti*, meaning remembered).

The Vedas, introduced to the subcontinent by the Aryans, are regarded as shruti knowledge and are considered the authoritative basis for Hinduism. The oldest of the Vedic texts, the Rig-Veda, was compiled more than 3000 years ago.

The *smriti* texts comprise a large collection of literature spaning many centuries and including expositions on the proper performance of domestic ceremonies as well as proper pursuit of government, economics and religious law. Among the better-known works contained within this body of literature are the Kamasutra, the Ramayana, the Mahabharata and the Puranas, which expand on the epics and promote the notion of the Trimurti. Unlike the Vedas, the Puranas are not limited to initiated males of the higher castes and therefore have wider popular appeal. Also highly popular today are the Mahabharata and the Ramayana, which drew an estimated audience of 80 million when they were serialised by Indian state television in the 1980s.

The Mahabharata Thought to have been composed some time around the 1st millennium BC, the Mahabharata has been the prerogative of the ruling and warrior classes, focusing as it did on the exploits of their favourite deity, Krishna. By about 500 BC it had evolved into a far more complex creation, with substantial additions, including the Bhagavad Gita (in which Krishna gives advice to Arjuna before a great battle). It is in fact the world's longest work of literature, being eight times longer than the Greek epics the *Iliad* and the *Odyssey* combined.

The story centres on conflict between the gods – the heroes (Pandavas) and the demons (Kauravas). Overseeing events is Krishna (an incarnation of Vishnu) who has taken on human form. Krishna acts as charioteer for the Pandava hero, Arjuna, who eventually triumphs in a great battle with the Kauravas.

The Ramayana Composed around the 3rd or 2nd century BC, the Ramayana is believed to be largely the work of only one person, the poet Valmiki. Like the Mahabharata, it centres on conflict between the gods and demons.

Basically, the story tells of Rama, an incarnation of Vishnu who assumed human form to overthrow the demon king of Lanka (Sri Lanka), Ravana. Rama won the hand of the princess Sita in a competition and was chosen by his father to inherit his kingdom. But at the last minute Rama's stepmother intervened and demanded that her son take Rama's place. Rama, Sita and Rama's brother, Lakshmana, were duly exiled and went off to the forests where Rama and Lakshmana battled demons and dark forces. Ravana's sister attempted to seduce Rama. She was rejected and in revenge, Ravana captured Sita and spirited her away to his palace in Lanka. Rama, assisted by an army of monkeys led by the loyal monkey god, Hanuman, eventually found the palace, killed Ravana and rescued Sita. All returned victorious to Ayodhya where Rama was crowned king.

Islam

Muslims, followers of the Islamic religion, represent around 7% of the state's population, therefore constituting the second-largest religious group.

Islam was introduced to the north of India by invading armies (in the 16th century the Mughal empire controlled much of northern India). The religion was founded in Arabia by the Prophet Mohammed in the 7th century AD. The Arabic term *islam* means surrender and believers undertake to surrender to the will of Allah (God). The will of Allah is revealed in the Quran (sometimes spelt Koran). God revealed his will to Mohammed, who acted as his messenger.

Islam is monotheistic; God is unique and has no equal or partner. Everything is believed to be created by God and is deemed to have its own place and purpose within the universe. Only God is unlimited and self-sufficient. The purpose of all living things is submission to the divine will. Although God never speaks to humans directly, his word is conveyed through messengers called prophets, who are charged with calling people back to God. Prophets are never themselves divine. Mohammed is the most recent prophet.

In the years after Mohammed's death a succession dispute split the movement and the legacy today is the Sunnis and the Shi'ias. The Sunnis, the majority, emphasise the 'well-trodden' path or the orthodox way. They look to tradition and the customs and views of the greater community. Shi'ias believe that only *imams* (exemplary leaders) are able to reveal the hidden and true meaning of the Quran. The orthodox view is that there have been 12 *imams*, the last of them being Mohammed. However, since then *mujtahids* (divines) have interpreted law and doctrine under the guidance of the imam, who will return at the end of time to spread truth and justice throughout the world.

Most Muslims in Rajasthan today are Sunnis. There is a small community of Shi'ia Muslims, known as Bohras, in south-eastern Rajasthan. The most important pilgrimage site for Muslims in Rajasthan is the Dargah, the tomb of the Sufi saint Khwaja Muin-ud-din Chishti, at Ajmer.

Jainism

The Jain religion is contemporaneous with Buddhism and bears many similarities to both it and Hinduism. It was founded around 500 BC by Mahavira, the 24th and last of the Jain teachers, known as *tirthankars*, or finders of the path. The Jains tend to be commercially successful and have an influence disproportionate to their actual numbers.

In Rajasthan, Jains number only around 1.8% of the population. There are, nevertheless, numerous beautiful Jain temples in this state, as Jainism was for the most part tolerated by the Rajput rulers, some of whom funded the construction of these temples.

The Jain religion originally evolved as a reformist movement against the dominance of priests and the complicated rituals of Brahmanism. It rejected the caste system. Jains believe that the universe is infinite and was not created by a deity. They also believe in reincarnation and eventual spiritual salvation, or moksha, through following the path of the *tirthankars*.

The Jains constructed extraordinary temple complexes, notable for the large number of similar buildings clustered together in one place. While those in Rajasthan are not quite as spectacular as the hill-top 'temple city' at Palitana, in Gujarat, the Jain temple complexes of Mt Abu, Ranakpur and Jaisalmer, and the Jain temples at Osiyan and Bikaner, are known for their beautiful sculpture and architectural symmetry.

Folk Gods & Goddesses

Rajasthan has numerous folk gods and goddesses, many of whom are deified local heroes. As well as these folk deities, every family pays homage to a *kuldevi*, or clan goddess.

The deified folk hero Ramdev has an important temple near Pokaran in western Rajasthan. He is revered for spurning caste distinctions and for his aid to the poor and the sick.

Pabuji often features in the stories of the Bhopas, Rajasthan's professional storytellers. According to tradition, Pabuji entered a transaction with a woman called Devalde, in which, in return for a mare, he vowed to protect her cows from all harm. The time to fulfil this obligation came, inconveniently, during the celebration of Pabuji's own marriage. Recalling his vow, Pabuji immediately went to the aid of the threatened livestock. During the ensuing battle, he, along with all the male members of his family, perished at the hands of a villain by the name of Jind Raj Khinchi.

To preserve the family line, Pabuji's sister-in-law cut open her own belly and produced Pabuji's nephew, Nandio, before committing *sati* on her husband's funeral pyre. An annual festival is held at Kodumand, in Jaisalmer district, the birthplace of Pabuji, at which Bhopas perform *Pabuji-ka-phad*, poetry recitations in praise of Pabuji.

Gogaji was a warrior who lived in the 11th century and could cure snakebite – victims of snakebite are brought to his shrine by devotees, who include both Hindus and Muslims. Also believed to cure snakebite if propitiated accordingly is Tejaji. According to tradition, while pursuing *dacoits* who had rustled his father-in-law's cows, Teja was confronted by a snake that was poised to strike him. He pleaded with the snake to let him pass so that he could recover the cows, and promised to return later. The snake relented, and Teja duly returned, bloody and bruised from his confrontation with the *dacoits*. The snake was reluctant to bite Teja on his wounds, so Teja offered his tongue. So impressed was the snake that it decreed that anyone honouring

Teja by wearing a thread in his name would be cured of snakebite. Other deified heroes include a father and son, Mehaji and Harbhu.

Goddesses, generally incarnations of Devi, or Shakti, the Mother Goddess, include the fierce Chamunda Mata, an incarnation of Durga; Sheetala Mata, the goddess of smallpox, whom parents propitiate in order to spare their children from this affliction; Kela Devi; and Karni Mata, worshipped at Deshnok, near Bikaner.

Women who have committed *sati* on their husbands' funeral pyres are also frequently revered as goddesses, such as Rani Sati, who has an elaborate temple in her honour in Jhunjhunu, in Shekhawati.

Barren women pay homage to the god Bhairon, an incarnation of Shiva, at his shrines, which are usually found under khejri trees. In order to be blessed with a child, the woman is required to leave a garment hanging from the branches of the tree, and often these can be seen fluttering over shrines to Bhairon. The ubiquitous khejri tree of Rajasthan is worshipped during the festival of Dussehra, and the banyan and peepul trees, both considered sacred, are also worshipped on special days.

Other Religions

In Rajasthan, 1.44% of the population professes Sikhism. Most of Rajasthan's Sikhs live in Ganganagar district.

There is a very small population of Christians in Rajasthan, amounting to only around 0.1% of the population. They are found predominantly in Ajmer and Jaipur, where there are several Catholic and Protestant churches.

The Buddhist population is negligible in Rajasthan, representing only 0.01% of the population.

LANGUAGE

Hindi is India's national language and the official language of Rajasthan, although there are many regional languages and dialects. Most of the regional languages of Rajasthan are closely related to Hindi, and many people are fluent in both, as well as speaking a bit of English.

The major dialects of Rajasthan include Dundhari (Jaipur region), Mewati (Alwar and Bharatpur region), Mewari (Udaipur and Chittorgarh), Hadoti (Bundi, Kota and Jhalawar) and Marwari (Jodhpur, Bikaner, Jaisalmer and Barmer). These Indo-Aryan languages are often collectively called 'Rajasthani', as they share a common ancestor in the classical language of Dingal, noteworthy for its many colourful adjectives. These were put to work by the Bhatts (traditional bards) who composed many poems of glory and bravery in Dingal that survive today. Marwari is the most common dialect of Rajasthan. The use of Rajasthani is now in decline, as Hindi takes over as the major language of the state.

For further information on Rajasthan's languages and for useful words and phrases in Hindi, see the Language chapter and the Glossary at the end of this book.

Facts for the Visitor

HIGHLIGHTS

There are plenty of ancient forts and palaces, beautiful temple complexes and fine national parks and sanctuaries in Rajasthan, but one of the highlights of a visit to this state is simply travelling through what is probably the most colourful region of India.

Temples, Tombs & Shrines

There are many important religious sites in Rajasthan, ranging from the sublime to the bizarre. At Mt Abu, the exquisite Dilwara temples are an important Jain pilgrimage centre, featuring incredibly delicate marble carving. Another beautiful Jain temple can be found at Ranakpur, also in southern Rajasthan, which has 1444 exquisite pillars, no two of which are alike. At Deshnok, near Bikaner, the Karni Mata Temple is home to thousands of rats – they're revered as the incarnate souls of local people.

At the tiny desert town of Osiyan, visitors will find a host of beautifully sculpted medieval temples, while in Pushkar there are some 400 temples, including one of the only Brahma temples in the world. Nearby Ajmer is also a holy town. This is the site of the sacred Dargarh, which is the tomb of a Sufi saint, Khwaja Muin-ud-din Chishti.

Fabulous Forts

The tumultuous history of the Rajputs is etched into the land, with scores of fortresses scattered throughout the state. Every second town seems to feature a *garh* (fort) in its name. Some of these forts are falling into gracious ruin, while others have been lovingly restored, often as luxurious hotels, such as Khimsar Fort located in western Rajasthan and Fort Dhariyawad in southern Rajasthan.

Many have a tragic history, such as Chittorgarh, where *jauhar* (ritual mass suicide) was committed three times by the women of the fort; and Kumbalgarh, where the baby prince Udai Singh was hidden by his wet nurse, who sacrificed her own son to save him.

Some forts and their palaces are preserved as museums, providing a window into the lavish world of the maharajas. Examples include Kota Fort, the magnificent Junagarh in Bikaner and the stunning fort at Amber. Others are simply whimsical fantasies, such as the romantic fort at Jaisalmer and the picturesque little Kankwari Fort at Sariska Wildlife Sanctuary.

Palaces & Havelis

One of the most romantic palaces in the world can be found in Udaipur – the stunning Lake Palace, a vision in white seemingly afloat on Lake Pichola. Udaipur's City Palace is also an incredible place to visit; it's the largest palace complex in Rajasthan. Jaipur's City Palace is another must-see, along with the adjacent Hawa Mahal, or Palace of the Winds – a pink organ-pipe structure that provided a discreet vantage point for the ladies of the court to watch the daily life of the street.

The remote Shekhawati region of northern Rajasthan is famous for its havelis (mansions), which feature paintings on both the internal and external walls. The havelis were built by rich merchants who spared no expense constructing elaborate homes as symbols of their elevated financial and social status. Beautifully carved havelis can also been seen in Jaisalmer and Bikaner.

Kicking Back

Craving some time-out from the rigours of travelling? Well, you're in luck. Rajasthan has plenty of places where you can chill out with like-minded souls. The holy town of Pushkar, in eastern Rajasthan, boasts a beautiful location, with tiny whitewashed buildings and temples along the shore of a small, perfectly round lake.

Jaisalmer is another travellers' favourite. Its massive fort rises like an apparition after the long bus or train journey across the dead flat desert. Contained within its walls are dozens of cobblestone-lined alleyways that conceal temples and bazaars. The Sam sand dunes, 42km from Jaisalmer, are where even the most jaded seen-it-all traveller will find it hard to resist playing Lawrence of Arabia.

If you want to escape the crowds there are also some wonderful off-the-beaten-track hideaways in Rajasthan, such as Siliserh, near Alwar, or the traditional towns of the Shekhawati region. For serious rest and relaxation, you can be treated like royalty in one of the many exquisite former palaces, now converted into hotels.

Festivals

Rajasthanis love a party and there are festivals throughout the year and across the state. In November, Pushkar hosts its annual camel fair, and thousands of people throng to the town to trade camels and other livestock. Jaisalmer has its famous Desert Festival in January or February, and there's the Nagaur Fair, a colourful cattle fair, around the same time. There are scores of other religious and secular festivals – see the boxed text at the start of each regional chapter for details.

Arts & Crafts

Jaipur is a real centre of traditional skills. Arts and crafts from around Rajasthan are assembled in the emporiums of the capital city, and it's a great place to shop, or simply to wander through the artisans' quarters of the old city and watch the master craftsmen at work.

In Sanganer, a small village near Jaipur, you can see vast lengths of colourful fabric drying on the riverbanks, or watch yards of it unfurl as it is held at either end by women from the printing and dyeing communities.

The desert town of Barmer is also renowned for its artisans, while other towns specialise in particular crafts, such as wooden toys in Bassi, *usta* (camel-leather products) in Bikaner and *dhurrie* (carpet) weaving at Salawas near Jodhpur.

Wildlife Sanctuaries

Eastern Rajasthan has the state's most important and notable wildlife sanctuaries. Tigers are the attraction at Ranthambhore

and Sariska, but even if you miss out on seeing these elusive big cats, you are virtually guaranteed sightings of other large mammals such as chinkaras, sambars, nilgai and wild boars. At Keoladeo Ghana National Park near Bharatpur, you can view at close hand hundreds of different species in an idyllic wetland setting.

Camel & Horse Safaris

If you want the ultimate desert experience, you're a perfect candidate to undertake a camel safari around Jaisalmer, Bikaner or Pushkar, or in the Shekhawati region. You can also take extended horse safaris in southern Rajasthan.

SUGGESTED ITINERARIES

Although Rajasthan's places of interest are scattered over a vast geographical area, a good rail network means that you can cover large distances very efficiently, and visit many sites in just a few weeks.

Many first-time visitors to India make the mistake of cramming too much into their itinerary, leaving them frazzled at the end of their trip. Take a few days out for serious rest and relaxation; maybe treat yourself to a sojourn at one of the royal abodes off the beaten track that have been converted into atmospheric hotels. These places are a world away from the hustle and bustle and also offer you a taste of rural life.

Rajasthan's most important sites include Jaipur, the historic fort of Chittorgarh, romantic Udaipur, Ranthambhore National Park, the desert city of Jaisalmer, bustling Jodhpur, and Bharatpur – home of the Keoladeo Ghana National Park. In two weeks or more you could take in all of these, as well as Agra with its Taj Mahal in the neighbouring state of Uttar Pradesh (see the Agra chapter). A short camel trek in the environs of Jaisalmer, or a visit to the holy town of Pushkar, or the beautiful palaces of Deeg or Alwar, en route back to Delhi, might also be possible.

In three to four weeks, you could visit all the above-mentioned places and take in the Shekhawati region of northern Rajasthan, with its magnificent painted havelis, as well as the desert city of Bikaner, which has a stunning fort. Bird lovers should stop at Khichan, between Jodhpur and Jaisalmer, to witness the spectacular sight of thousands of demoiselle cranes descending on the fields around this village to feed on grain distributed by villagers.

In four to five weeks you could enjoy an extended camel trek in the environs of Jaisalmer, Bikaner, Pushkar or Shekhawati and a horse safari in southern Rajasthan, and go to Rajasthan's only hill station, Mt Abu, worth visiting especially for its exquisite Jain temples.

PLANNING
When to Go

The best time to visit Rajasthan is in the winter months (December to February), when the days are warm and sunny (average temperatures across the state are around 25°C), and the nights are cool. However, hotel prices are at a premium in winter. The days begin to heat up in March, but are generally still quite pleasant. The post-monsoon season, from mid-September to the end of November, is reasonably pleasant, if a little warm, with average maximum temperatures in October around 35°C and an average minimum of around 20°C.

The winter season corresponds with some of Rajasthan's most colourful festivals, such as the Desert Festival in Jaisalmer and the Nagaur Cattle Fair. In late February/early March, there's Holi, India's most exuberant festival. Rajasthan's own Gangaur festival is celebrated in March/April, as is Udaipur's Mewar Festival. Jaipur's Elephant Festival is held in March. The famous Pushkar Camel Fair takes place in November.

Winter is also a good time to visit Rajasthan's best-known wildlife sanctuaries: Keoladeo Ghana National Park; Ranthambhore National Park; and Sariska Tiger Reserve & National Park.

Maps

Lonely Planet's *India & Bangladesh Travel Atlas* is a handy reference to the entire Indian subcontinent. Its coverage of Rajasthan is excellent, with symbols clearly showing sites of ancient forts, national parks and sanctuaries and other sites of interest. The Discover India Series has a very good map of Rajasthan at a scale of 1:1,200,000, clearly showing rail routes, major highways and roads. There's also the *Rajasthan Road Atlas*, published by Anada Sahitya Prakashan and Gyan Vigyan Prakashan, which has 1:600,000 maps of each district in the state. It's available in good bookshops in the major cities. Nelles Maps publishes a map of *Western India*, which has pretty good coverage of Rajasthan, but it can be hard to get hold of.

Many of the tourist offices in Rajasthan sell a reasonable map (Rs 2) of the town in which they are located.

What to Bring

The usual travellers' rule applies – bring as little as possible. It's much better to have to buy something you've left behind than find you have too much and need to get rid of it.

If you are only travelling to a single destination, a suitcase is a good option. It's lockable, keeps your clothes flat and is less likely to get damaged by careless luggage handlers at the airport. Heavy luggage presents few problems if all you've got to do is get it into the taxi and to a hotel.

For others, a backpack is still the best carrying container. It's worth paying the money for a strong, good-quality pack with a lock, as it's much more likely to withstand the rigours of travel in Rajasthan.

If you're not a fan of backpacks, an alternative is a large, soft, zip bag with a wide, securely fastened shoulder strap.

Light, cool cotton clothes are the best bet for day wear, with a light sweater or pullover for nights, which can get surprisingly chilly, especially in the winter months. In some centres, such as Jaipur, Pushkar and Udaipur, Western-style clothes can be purchased off the peg at ridiculously low prices, or you can have clothes made to measure in the small tailor shops found in all but the tiniest villages.

It's important to bring clothing that is culturally appropriate (see Dos & Don'ts under Society & Conduct in the Facts about

Rajasthan chapter). A reasonable list would include:

- Underwear and swimming gear
- One pair of cotton trousers
- One pair of shorts (men only)
- One long cotton skirt (women)
- A few T-shirts or lightweight shirts
- Sweater or lightweight jacket for cool winter nights
- One pair of sneakers or shoes plus socks
- Sandals
- Flip-flops (thongs) – handy when showering in shared bathrooms
- A set of 'dress up' clothes for that splurge on a meal or night at the disco

Bedding A sleeping bag, although a bit of a bother to carry, can really come in handy. You can use it to spread over unsavoury-looking hotel bedding (especially at some budget places), as a cushion on hard train seats, and as a seat for long waits on railway platforms. If you are planning to do an overnight camel safari during winter, a sleeping bag is essential.

A less cumbersome option is to bring just a sleeping-bag sheet. Mosquito nets in hotels are rare, so your own sheet will help to keep mosquitoes at bay, as well as keeping you separated from the grimy sheets. An inflatable pillow is also worth considering, especially if you are camping or planning to stay in rock-bottom hotels, which usually have rock-hard pillows to match.

Toiletries Soap, toothpaste, shampoo and other toiletries are readily available in Rajasthan, although hair conditioner often comes in the 'shampoo and conditioner in one' format, so if you don't use this stuff, bring along your own. Astringent is useful for wiping away the grime at the end of the day and is available at most pharmacies. A nail brush and moisture-impregnated disposable tissues are also useful.

Tampons are not easily found (even in the larger cities), so it's certainly worth bringing your own stock. No need to bring sanitary pads – you'll find them in pharmacies at even the smallest towns. It's wise to bring your own condoms, as the quality of local brands is variable. Shower caps can be hard to find (unless you're staying at a five-star hotel), so bring your own. High-factor sunscreen is more widely available, but it's *expensive*! A universal sink plug is useful, as few of the cheaper hotels have plugs. Women should consider bringing a lingerie bag to prevent delicate (and expensive) underwear from being battered or completed ruined by *dhobi-wallahs* (washerpeople) and even hotel laundries.

Men can safely leave their shaving gear at home, as there are plenty of barber shops where you'll get the works for a nominal price. With India's HIV/AIDS problem, however, only choose those barber shops that look clean, and ensure that a fresh blade is used (you may like to bring your own).

Miscellaneous Items See Health later in this chapter for a medical kit check list. Some items to stow away in your pack could include:

- A padlock, especially for budget travellers – most lower-priced hotels have doors locked by a flimsy latch and padlock. You'll find having your own sturdy lock on the door does wonders for your peace of mind. Some travellers bring a heavy-duty chain to secure their pack to the luggage racks of trains and buses.
- A knife (preferably Swiss Army) – it has a whole range of uses, such as for peeling fruit. Make sure you don't pack it in your hand luggage or it will be confiscated by airport security.
- A sarong – can be used as a bed sheet, an item of clothing (recommended for bathing in public places), an emergency towel and a pillow.
- Insect repellent, a box of mosquito coils or an electric mosquito zapper – although you can buy them in Rajasthan (electric stuff is useless during power cuts, however). A mosquito net can be very useful – bring tape with you if it doesn't come with a portable frame.
- A torch (flashlight) and/or candles – power cuts (euphemistically known as 'load shedding') are not uncommon and there's little street lighting at night.
- A voltage stabiliser – for those travellers who may be bringing sensitive electronic equipment.
- A spare set of glasses (although several travellers say good-quality glasses are cheaply available in India) and your spectacle prescription. If you wear contact lenses, bring enough solution to last your trip.

- Earplugs (to shut out the din in some hotels as well as outside traffic noise and barking dogs) and a sleeping mask.
- A sun hat and sunglasses – if you dislike sweaty hats, buy an umbrella in Rajasthan (it provides shade plus air circulation).
- A water bottle – it should always be by your side. It's highly recommended that you use water-purification tablets or filters to avoid adding to Rajasthan's alarming plastic waste problem (see Water Purification under Health later in this chapter).
- High-factor sunscreen and lip balm – though becoming more widely available in Rajasthan, they're expensive!
- String – useful as a makeshift clothes line (double-strand nylon is good to secure your clothes if you have no pegs). You can buy small, inexpensive sachets of washing powder almost everywhere in Rajasthan.
- Women should consider bringing a sports bra if intending to do a camel safari, as the trotting momentum can cause discomfort, even for just a few hours.
- Binoculars – if you plan to do bird-watching and wildlife-spotting.
- A high-pitched whistle – some women carry these as a possible deterrent to any would-be assailants.

RESPONSIBLE TOURISM

Responsible tourism doesn't simply mean behaving in an appropriate manner when you are in another country, although of course common sense and courtesy go a long way when you are travelling (see Dos & Don'ts under Society & Conduct in the Facts about Rajasthan chapter). Being a responsible tourist also means taking the time to understand as much about a region as possible before travelling there, and being aware of your impact on the local community. You can do this by contacting relevant organisations in your own country – for example, Oxfam in the UK and Community Aid Abroad in Australia are good sources of information on fair trade, child labour and economically sustainable tourism. Magazines such as the *New Internationalist* are other useful sources of information. See the special section 'The Colourful Crafts of Rajasthan' for suggestions on ways you can shop smart and support the local community during your stay.

A number of monuments in Rajasthan are suffering irreparable damage from tourism and government indifference. Arguably one of the most threatened is Jaisalmer Fort, which has been listed in the New York–based World Monuments Watch list of 100 endangered sites worldwide. Over the years, as tourism numbers have risen, so too have the number of shops, hotels and restaurants within the fort walls – this has had a detrimental impact. Other monuments in dire need of protection include Amber Fort, Jal Mahal and Hawa Mahal in Jaipur and the painted havelis of Shekhawati. You can help to reverse the damage by volunteering in conservation and restoration efforts – see Volunteer Work later in this chapter for further details.

Meanwhile, in Agra, continuing efforts are being made to reduce the impact of tourism on the Taj Mahal. In addition to the introduction of electric buses and autorickshaws and the creation of a traffic-exclusion zone, the recent hike in the admission fee to the Taj was partly devised to raise revenue for conservation purposes and also to limit visitor numbers to more manageable levels.

Tourism growth has also had negative environmental repercussions. In Udaipur, the large number of hotels around Lake Pichola has contributed to widespread pollution within and around the lake. Travellers can help by encouraging hotel management to dispose of rubbish in an environmentally friendly manner. You can put similar pressure on the camel-safari operators who dump rubbish in the desert during their tours.

Responsible tourism also extends to the people you interact with during your travels. For example, if you happen to be invited to stay with an Indian family, despite all good intentions, the cost of housing and feeding you can be a considerable financial drain to those families on small incomes. That's not to suggest you shouldn't stay – just exercise judgment and help out by contributing to daily living expenses. Also, if you agree to post someone a copy of a photograph, it's considerate to follow through on this (or else don't make promises in the first place). Many Indians urge tourists not to hand out sweets, pens or money to children since it is positive reinforcement to beg. A donation to a charitable organisation, health centre or school is a more constructive way to help in the long term – ask at your hotel if there is a needy organisation in the area.

Consider carefully the following practical advice on responsible tourism.

Say No to Plastic

Many once-pristine regions of Rajasthan are now vanishing under a sea of abandoned plastic mineral-water bottles (see also Ecology & Environment in the Facts about Rajasthan chapter). Unfortunately travellers are largely responsible for plastic waste and can make a significant difference by only purchasing products that use environmentally friendly packaging.

Discarded plastic bags are a very serious problem, especially in the cities. These bags are eaten by cows and other creatures, which results in a slow and painful death. According to the animal shelter Help in Suffering in Jaipur, this is one of the leading killers of cows in Rajasthan's cities.

Please avoid buying anything in plastic bags and bottles and if you must buy plastic, reuse it. Other ways of reducing Rajasthan's plastic peril include buying tea in terracotta cups at train stations (or in your own cup) rather than plastic; bringing your own canteen and purifying water rather than buying it in plastic bottles (see Water Purification under Health later in this chapter); and buying soft drinks in (recyclable) glass bottles and not plastic bottles.

The refusal of many travellers to buy plastic products has already sent a powerful message to tourism officials, but few are making much effort beyond politically correct statements to actually implement environment-protection measures.

Use Water Wisely

Traditionally, Rajasthanis invented ingenious methods of conserving water, saving and reusing every drop. In Jaisalmer, the same water was used to bathe, wash clothes, wash the floor, and finally to water the garden. However, today Rajasthan is facing a

water crisis. In the last few years the state has suffered severe droughts (see Climate in the Facts about Rajasthan chapter) and groundwater levels are dropping by up to three metres per year. Across the state many people face a lack of drinking water, while in Jaisalmer increased water usage is causing the fort to crumble. There are a number of reasons for this, but the increasing number of tourist facilities, particularly bathrooms, designed in line with Western standards is definitely one of them.

You can make a difference by cutting down on the amount of waste water you produce. Washing with a bucket uses, on average, one-third of the water that you use taking a shower. Similarly, using Indian rather than Western toilets cuts down on the water that gets flushed down the drain.

Child Prostitution

It goes without saying: do not support this exploitive industry. The Indian Penal Code and India's Immoral Traffic Act imposes penalties for kidnapping and prostitution, and tourists can be prosecuted for child sex offences upon their return home

If you know, witness or suspect that anyone is engaged in these activities you should report it to police in the country you're in and again to the police when you get home.

Animal Welfare

If you're concerned about the welfare of animals, don't take an interest in snake charming, bear dancing, photographic monkeys and other sideshow acts that exploit animals. You can also help by using transport such as tongas (horse-drawn carriages), which enable the animals to earn a living without the back-breaking labour of carting heavy loads. They're also much kinder to the environment than fossil-fuel powered contraptions. For information on elephant welfare, see the boxed text 'The Elephants of Amber' in the Jaipur chapter.

TOURIST OFFICES
Local Tourist Offices

There are Rajasthan Tourism Development Corporation (RTDC) tourist offices (often called Tourist Reception Centres) in most of the places of interest in Rajasthan, including Jaipur, Ajmer, Alwar, Amber, Bharatpur, Bikaner, Bundi, Chittorgarh, Jaisalmer, Jhunjhunu, Jodhpur, Kota, Mt Abu, Pushkar, Sawai Madhopur and Udaipur. (For contact details see the relevant sections in the regional chapters.) They range from the extraordinarily helpful to the fairly useless. However, you can usually pick up glossy brochures and maps at even the most inefficient of them.

There are also several Rajasthan tourist offices in other Indian cities, including:

Delhi (☎ 011-3381884, fax 3382823) Tourist Reception Centre, Bikaner House, Pandara Rd, New Delhi
Mumbai (Bombay; ☎ 022-2074162, fax 2075603) 230 Dr D Naoroji Rd

There is a Government of India tourist office in Jaipur (see Information in the Jaipur chapter). The Government of India tourist offices, found in the two major international gateways to India that are used by travellers to Rajasthan are:

Delhi (☎ 011-3320005) 88 Janpath, New Delhi
Mumbai (☎ 022-2033144, fax 2014496) 123 Maharshi Karve Rd, Churchgate

Tourist Offices Abroad
The Government of India Department of Tourism maintains a string of tourist offices in other countries where it has brochures and leaflets. These often have high-quality information about Rajasthan, so they are worth getting. However, some of these foreign offices are not always as useful as those within Rajasthan. There are also smaller 'promotion offices' in Japan at Osaka and in the USA at Dallas, Miami, San Francisco and Washington DC.

Australia
(☎ 02-9264 4855, fax 9264 4860, ⓔ goito@ tpgi.com.au) Level 2, Piccadilly, 210 Pitt St, Sydney, NSW 2000
Canada
(☎ 416-962 3787, fax 962 6279) 60 Bloor St W, Suite 1003, Toronto, Ontario M4W 3B8

France
(☎ 01 45 23 30 45, fax 01 45 23 33 45, ⓔ info.fr@india-tourism.com) 11–13 Bis Boulevard Hausmann, 75008 Paris
Germany
(☎ 069-24 29 49-0, fax 24 29 49-77, ⓔ info@india-tourism.de) Baseler Strasse 46, 60329, Frankfurt-am-Main
Italy
(☎ 02-805 3506, fax 7202 1681, ⓔ info.it@india-tourism.com) Via Albricci 9, 20122 Milan
Japan
(☎ 33-571 5062, fax 571 5235) Pearl Bldg, 7-9-18 Ginza, Chuo-Ko, Tokyo 104
The Netherlands
(☎ 020-620 8991, fax 638 3059, ⓔ info.nl@india-tourism.com) Rokin 9–15, 1012 KK Amsterdam
Sweden
(☎ 08-21 50 81, fax 21 01 86, ⓔ info.se@india-tourism.com) Sveavagen 9, 1Tr 11, 11157, Stockholm
UK
(☎ 0171-437 3677, 24-hour brochure line ☎ 01233-211999, fax 0171-494 1048) 7 Cork St, London W1X 2LN
USA
New York: (☎ 212-586 4901, fax 582 3274) 30 Rockerfeller Plaza, Suite 15, New York NY 10112
Los Angeles: (☎ 213-477 3824, fax 380 8855, ⓦ www.tourindia.com) 3550 Wilshire Blvd, Suite 204, Los Angeles, CA 90010

VISAS & DOCUMENTS
Passport
You must have a passport with you for the full period of your trip. Ensure that it will be valid for the entire period you intend to remain overseas. If your passport is lost or stolen, immediately contact your country's representative (see Embassies & Consulates later in this chapter).

Visas
Six-month, multiple-entry visas are now issued to most nationals regardless of whether they intend staying that long or re-entering the country. Note that the visa is valid from the date of issue. This means that if you enter India five months after the visa was issued, it will be valid only for one month, not the full six months.

Visas currently cost A$75 (an extra A$10 service fee applies at consulates) for Australians, US$60 for US citizens and UK£30 for Britons.

A special People of Indian Origin (PIO) card is available to people of Indian descent (excluding those in Pakistan and Bangladesh) who hold a non-Indian passport and live abroad (maximum fourth generation). This card costs US$1000 and it offers multiple-entry for 20 years. People who are of Indian origin can also apply for a five-year multiple-entry visa, which is about a quarter of the cost of the PIO card. Both are valid from the date of issue.

Visa Extensions Fifteen-day visa extensions are available from foreigners registration offices in the main Indian cities (only under very exceptional circumstances, *not* as a matter of routine). You can only get another six months by leaving the country.

In Rajasthan, the **Foreigners Registration Office** (☎ 0141-619391; open 10am-1.30pm & 2pm-5pm Mon-Fri) is located in Jaipur, at the end of the road directly opposite the main entrance to the City Palace Museum.

In Delhi, go to the **Foreigners Regional Registration Office** (FRRO; ☎ 011-6711348; Level 2, East Block 8, Sector 1, RK Puram; open 9.30am-1.30pm & 2pm-4pm Mon-Fri) behind the Hyatt Regency hotel.

If you can't get to a major city, you can try to apply through the police superintendent at district headquarter towns.

Restricted-Area Permits

Due to the hostilities between India and Pakistan, foreigners are prohibited from going within 50km of the India–Pakistan border. Special permission is required from the **District Magistrate** (☎ 02992-52201) in Jaisalmer to travel to most of Rajasthan west of National Highway No 15, due to its proximity to the border with Pakistan, and is only issued in exceptional circumstances. The only places exempted are Amar Sagar, Bada Bagh, Lodhruva, Kuldhara, Akal, Sam, Ramkund, Khuri and Mool Sagar.

Permission is required from the **District Magistrate** (☎ 02992-20003) in Barmer to travel to the Kiradu temple complex, about 35km from Barmer near the border with Pakistan.

Onward Tickets

Many Indian embassies and consulates will not issue a visa to enter India unless you hold an onward ticket, which is taken as sufficient evidence that you intend to leave the country.

Travel Insurance

A travel-insurance policy to cover theft, loss and medical problems is highly recommended. Some policies will offer lower and higher medical-expense options; the higher ones are chiefly for countries such as the USA, which have high medical costs. There is a wide variety of policies available, so check the small print.

Some policies will specifically exclude 'dangerous activities', which can include motorcycling or even trekking. A locally acquired motorcycle licence is not valid under some policies.

You may prefer a policy that pays doctors or hospitals directly rather than you having to pay on the spot and claim later. If you have to claim later make sure you keep all documentation. Some policies ask you to call back (reverse charges) to a centre in your home country where an immediate assessment of your problem is made.

Check that the policy covers ambulances or an emergency flight home.

Driving Licence & Permits

If you are planning to drive in India, get an International Driving Licence from your national motoring organisation. In some cities, such as Delhi, it's possible to hire or purchase motorcycles, and you'll often need to produce a driving licence of some sort (see Motorcycle in the Getting Around chapter). An International Driving Licence can also come in handy for other identification purposes, such as plain old bicycle hire.

Other Documents

A vaccination certificate, while not necessary in India, may well be required for onward travel. Student cards are virtually useless these days – many student concessions have either been eliminated or replaced by 'youth fares' or similar age concessions. Similarly, a Youth Hostel (Hostelling International; HI) card is not generally required for Rajasthan's many hostels, but you do pay slightly less at official youth hostels if you have one.

Copies

All important documents (passport data page and visa page, credit cards, travel insurance policy, air/bus/train tickets, driving licence etc) should be photocopied before you leave home. Leave one copy with someone at home and keep another with you, separate from the originals.

EMBASSIES & CONSULATES
Indian Embassies & High Commissions

India's embassies, consulates and high commissions abroad include the following:

Australia
High Commission: (☎ 02-6273 3999, fax 6273 1308, ℮ hicanb@ozemail.com.au) 3–5 Moonah Place, Yarralumla, ACT 2600
Consulate General: (☎ 02-9223 9500, fax 9223 9246, ℮ indianc@bigpond.com) Level 27, 25 Bligh St, Sydney, NSW 2000

Bangladesh
High Commission: (☎ 02-865373, fax 863662, ℮ ahcindia@spotnet.com) 120 Road 2, Dhanmondi, Dhaka

Bhutan
Embassy: (☎ 02-22162, fax 23195) India House Estate, Thimphu, Bhutan

Canada
High Commission: (☎ 613-744 3751, fax 744 0913, ℮ hicomindia@sprint.ca) 10 Springfield Rd, Ottawa K1M 1C9

France
Embassy: (☎ 01 40 50 70 70, fax 01 40 50 09 96, ℮ culture@ambe-inde.fr) 15 rue Alfred Dehodenoq, 75016 Paris

Germany
Embassy: (☎ 30-800178, fax 482 7034) Majakowskiring 55, 13156 Berlin

Israel
Embassy: (☎ 03-510 1431, fax 510 1434, ℮ indembtel@netvision.net.il) 4 Kaufman St, Sharbat House, Tel Aviv 68012

Your Own Embassy

It's important to realise what your own embassy – that is, the embassy of the country of which you are a citizen – can and cannot do to help you should you get into trouble. Generally speaking, it won't be much help in emergencies if the trouble you're in is remotely your own fault. Remember that you are bound by the laws of the country you are in. Your embassy will not be sympathetic if you end up in jail after committing a crime locally, even if such actions are legal in your own country.

In genuine emergencies you might get some assistance, but only if other channels have been exhausted. For example, if you need to get home urgently, a free ticket home is exceedingly unlikely to materialise – the embassy would expect you to have travel insurance. If all your money and documents are stolen, it might assist with getting a new passport, but a loan for onward travel is out of the question.

Some embassies used to keep letters for travellers or have a small reading room with home newspapers, but these days the mail-holding service has usually been stopped and even newspapers tend to be out of date.

Italy
Embassy: (☎ 06-488 4642, fax 481 9539, ℮ ind.emb@flashnet.it) Via XX Settembre 5, 00187 Rome

Japan
Embassy: (☎ 03-3262 2391, fax 3234 4866, ℮ indembjp@gol.com) 2-2-11 Kudan Minami, Chiyoda-ku, Tokyo 102

Myanmar
Embassy: (Burma; ☎ 01-82550, fax 89562) 545–547 Merchant St, Yangon

Nepal
Embassy: (☎ 071-410900, fax 413132, ℮ indemb@mos.com.np) Lain Chaur, GPO Box 292, Kathmandu

The Netherlands
Embassy: (☎ 070-346 9771, fax 361 7072) Buitenrustweg 2, 2517 KD, The Hague

New Zealand
High Commission: (☎ 04-473 6390, fax 499 0665, ℮ hicomind@globe.co.nz) 180 Molesworth St, Wellington

South Africa
High Commission: (☎ 012-342 5392, fax 341 1571, e attache@power.co.za) Suite 208, Infotech Bldg, 1090 Arcadia St, GPO No 40216, Arcadia 0007, Pretoria

Sri Lanka
High Commission: (☎ 01-421 605, fax 446 403, e hicomind@sri.lanka.net) 36–38 Galle Rd, Colombo 3

Thailand
Embassy: (☎ 02-258 0300, fax 258 4627, e indiaemb@mozart.inet.co.th) 46 Soi 23 (Prasarnmitr), Sukhumvit Rd, Bangkok 10110

UK
High Commission: (☎ 020-836 8484, fax 836 4331, e mailsection@hicomind.demon.co.uk) India House, Aldwych, London WC2B 4NA

USA
Embassy: (☎ 202-939 7000, fax 939 7027, e indembwash@indiagov.org) 2107 Massachusetts Ave NW, Washington, DC 20008

Embassies & Consulates in India

Most foreign diplomatic missions are in the nation's capital, Delhi, but there are also quite a few consulates in the other major cities of Mumbai, Kolkata (Calcutta) and Chennai (Madras). The following are embassies in Delhi (area code of which is 011):

Australia (☎ 6888223, fax 6885199)
1/50-G Shantipath, Chanakyapuri
Bangladesh (☎ 6834668, fax 6839237)
56 Ring Rd, Lajpat Nagar III
Bhutan (☎ 6889807, fax 6876710)
Chandragupta Marg, Chanakyapuri
Canada (☎ 6876500, fax 6876579)
7/8 Shantipath, Chanakyapuri
China (☎ 6871585, fax 6885486)
50-D Shantipath, Chanakyapuri
France (☎ 6118790, fax 6872305)
2/50-E Shantipath, Chanakyapuri
Germany (☎ 6871831, fax 6873117)
6/50-G Shantipath, Chanakyapuri
Iran (☎ 3329600, fax 3325493)
5 Barakhamba Rd
Ireland (☎ 4626733, fax 4697053)
230 Jor Bagh Rd
Israel (☎ 3013238, fax 3014298)
3 Aurangzeb Rd
Italy (☎ 6114355, fax 6873889)
50-E Chandragupta Marg, Chanakyapuri
Japan (☎ 6876581, fax 6885587)
4–5/50-G Shantipath, Chanakyapuri
Myanmar (Burma; ☎ 6889007, fax 6877942)
3/50-F Nyaya Marg, Chanakyapuri

Nepal (☎ 3328191, fax 3326857)
Barakhamba Rd
The Netherlands (☎ 6884951, fax 6884956)
6/50-F Shantipath, Chanakyapuri
New Zealand (☎ 6883170, fax 6873165)
50-N Nyaya Marg, Chanakyapuri
Pakistan (☎ 6110601, fax 6872339)
2/50-G Shantipath, Chanakyapuri
UK (☎ 6872161, fax 6872882)
Shantipath, Chanakyapuri
USA (☎ 4198000, fax 4190017)
Shantipath, Chanakyapuri

CUSTOMS

The usual duty-free regulations apply for India; that is, one bottle of spirits and 200 cigarettes.

You're allowed to bring in all sorts of Western technological wonders, but expensive items such as video cameras and laptop computers are likely to be entered on a 'Tourist Baggage Re-Export' form to ensure you take them out with you when you go.

Note that entering from Nepal does not entitle you to import anything free of duty.

There are certain restrictions on what you can take out of India – see Shopping later in this chapter.

MONEY
Currency

The Indian currency is the rupee (Rs), which is divided into 100 paise (singular – paisa). There are coins of 5, 10, 20, 25 and 50 paise and Rs 1, 2 and 5, and notes of Rs 1, 2, 5, 10, 20, 50, 100, 500 and 1000. The Rs 1 and Rs 2 notes have now been almost supplanted by coins, but you'll still come across the notes in country areas. The Rs 1000 is quite rare.

Although notes have often been punctured by staples, torn notes are not acceptable anywhere, so check them carefully and refuse to accept damaged ones.

Large-denomination notes are often difficult to use because of a maddening lack of change, so it pays to keep a regular supply of smaller notes.

Officially you are not allowed to bring Indian currency into the country or take it out of the country. You can bring in unlimited amounts of foreign currency or travellers cheques, but you are supposed to declare anything over US$10,000 on arrival.

Exchange Rates

To find out the latest exchange rates, visit [W] www.oanda.com or ask at a bank. At the time of writing, the exchange rates were:

country	unit		rupee
Australia	A$1	=	Rs 26.15
Canada	C$1	=	Rs 30.98
euro zone	€1	=	Rs 43.28
Israel	ILS1	=	Rs 10.21
Japan	¥100	=	Rs 37.35
Nepal	Nep Rs 100	=	Rs 65.90
New Zealand	NZ$1	=	Rs 21.66
UK	UK£1	=	Rs 70.61
USA	US$1	=	Rs 49.00

Exchanging Money

Outside Rajasthan's main cities, the State Bank of Bikaner & Jaipur or the State Bank of India are usually the places to change money. In the more remote regions (such as parts of Shekhawati), few banks offer exchange facilities, so use the banks in the main tourist centres before heading out into the desert – although you'll have no trouble changing money at Bikaner or Jaisalmer.

The wait at most banks can be painstakingly long and the staff brusque.

Cash In Delhi and other gateway cities you can change most foreign currencies – Australian dollars, Deutschmarks, yen or whatever – but in Rajasthan it's best to stick with US dollars or pounds sterling. It pays to have some US dollars or pounds sterling in cash for times when you can't change travellers cheques or use a credit card.

Travellers Cheques American Express and Thomas Cook are the most widely traded travellers cheques in Rajasthan. Pounds sterling and US dollars are the safest bet; Yen, Deutschmarks and Australian dollars can be changed in main cities, but not in out-of-the-way places. It's probably best to avoid euros until the currency is better established. Not all places take all brands – so it pays to carry more than one type.

Charges for changing travellers cheques vary from place to place and bank to bank.

A few simple measures should be taken to facilitate the replacement of stolen travellers cheques. See Dangers & Annoyances later in this chapter.

ATMs Mumbai, Delhi, Jaipur, Jodhpur, Udaipur plus a few (but slowly growing) number of larger towns have ATMs (many 24 hours) that accept Cirrus, Maestro, MasterCard and Visa (but not always all cards). However, you should definitely not rely on them as your sole source of cash, especially if you're planning to travel beyond the big cities. Note that many ATMs in Rajasthan don't accept foreign cards. Check with your local bank before departing and confirm that your card can actually access international banking networks.

Credit Cards In most major tourist centres, such as Jaipur and Udaipur, credit cards are accepted but don't expect to be able to use a card in budget hotels and restaurants. You can't rely entirely on credit cards – you'll need some ready cash too.

MasterCard and Visa are the most widely accepted cards, and it might pay to bring both with you. Cash advances on major credit cards can be made at various banks (although not usually in smaller towns). For details about whether you can access home accounts in India, inquire at your home bank before leaving.

International Transfers It's best not to run out of money in Rajasthan, but if you do, you can have money transferred quickly via Thomas Cook's Moneygram service (charges are relatively high as it's only considered an emergency service), or the more competitively priced **Western Union** *(via Sita World Travels;* ☎ *011-3311122; 12 F-Block, Connaught Circus, Delhi; or DHL agencies).* You need to bring along your passport when picking-up money.

Black Market The rupee is a convertible currency, which means the exchange rate is set by the market not the government. For this reason there's not much of a black market, although you can get a couple of rupees more for your dollars or pounds cash. There's little risk involved (provided you check on the spot that you have received the agreed amount), although it's still officially illegal.

Re-Exchange Before leaving India you will probably want to change any leftover rupees back into foreign currency. To do so, you must produce encashment certificates (see Encashment Certificates later) that cover the rupee amount and are less than three months old. You'll also have to show your passport and airline ticket.

You can convert rupees back to major currencies at some city banks and money-changers and at the international airports, although if you want US dollars in cash, some places will only allow you to exchange up to US$500 worth of rupees, and only within 48 hours of leaving the country.

Security

The safest place for your money and your passport is next to your skin, either in a moneybelt around your waist or in a pouch under your shirt or T-shirt. Never, ever carry these things in your luggage. You are also asking for trouble if you walk around with your valuables in a shoulder bag. Bum bags are not recommended as they advertise that you have a stash of goodies; this could make you a target for a mugging. Never leave your valuable documents and travellers cheques in your hotel room. If the hotel is a reputable one, you should be able to use the hotel safe. It is wise to peel off at least US$50 and keep it stashed away separately from your main horde, just in case. Finally, try to separate your big notes from your small ones so you don't publicly display large wads of cash when paying for minor services such as shoe polishing and tipping.

Costs

Costs tend to vary depending on whether or not it's the tourist season. They also shoot up during festivals or other special events when it's not unusual for hotel rates to double.

In addition, be prepared to pay more at the larger cities (such as Jaipur, Delhi and Agra), as well as at popular tourist destinations such as Jaisalmer and Udaipur.

Costs also vary depending on whether you are travelling solo or in a group. It's more economical travelling with one or more people, as you can save money by sharing hotel rooms, taxis or rickshaws and car hire.

Whatever budget you decide to travel on, you can be assured that you'll be getting a whole lot more for your money than in most other countries – Rajasthan is great value.

If you stay in luxurious converted forts and palaces, fly between the main cities of Rajasthan, and spend up big in the emporiums in Jaipur, you can spend a lot of money. It's really easy to blow US$200 a night in a swanky palace hotel without even setting foot outside the door.

At the other extreme, if you stay in dormitories or the cheapest hotels, travel in public buses, and learn to exist on daal and rice, it is possible to see Rajasthan on about US$8 a day.

Most travellers will probably be looking for something between these extremes. If so, for US$20 to US$35 a day on average, you'll stay in reasonable hotels, eat in regular restaurants but occasionally splash out on a fancy meal, and take autorickshaws rather than buses.

Admission Fees Most tourist sites have an admission fee and most levy a fee for the use of cameras and videos. Many sites charge a lower admission fee for Indian residents than they do for foreigners. In case you're wondering, if you're of Indian descent (but not an Indian resident), the foreigners' rate officially applies, although you may escape detection or even be knowingly offered the lower local rate.

In late 2000 the Archaeological Survey of India announced new admission fees for non-Indian tourists at 72 of India's national monuments. The admission price for all World–Heritage monuments was cranked up; for example, admission to the Taj Mahal now costs Rs 750 for foreigners.

Tipping, Baksheesh & Bargaining

In tourist restaurants and hotels, where service is often tacked-on, tipping is optional. In smaller places, where there are no service fees, a tip is greatly appreciated (even if it's just a few rupees). Hotel and train porters expect about Rs 10 to carry bags; Rs 5 for bike-watching; Rs 15 for train conductors or station porters performing miracles for you; and Rs 10 to 15 for extra services from hotel staff. It's not mandatory to tip taxi or autorickshaw drivers.

Baksheesh can be defined as a 'tip' and if you're going to be using a service repeatedly, an initial tip will ensure that standards are kept up. Baksheesh also refers to giving alms to beggars. Giving money to beggars is a matter of personal choice – but please don't hand out sweets, pens or money to children as it encourages begging as a career. Instead you may like to donate to a school or charitable organisation (see also Volunteer Work later in this chapter).

While there are fixed-price stores in major cities, in bazaars and at markets specifically geared to tourists you are generally expected to bargain. The trick with bargaining is that you should have some idea of what you should be paying for any given article. You can find out by checking prices at fixed-priced stores (although these are often on the high side), asking other travellers what they have paid and shopping around before settling on a particular vendor. If all else fails, a general rule of thumb is to take the plunge and halve the original asking price. The shopkeeper will know that you are not going to be taken for a ride and you now begin negotiations. You'll often find that the price drops if you proceed to head out of the shop saying you'll 'think about it'. Always keep in mind that haggling is a form of social interaction, not a vicious contest. It's worth remembering exactly how much a rupee is worth in your home currency, so you don't lose perspective and raise your blood pressure.

Taxes & Service Charges

At most rock-bottom hotels you won't have to pay any hotel taxes. A tax or two (or even more) is usually whacked onto accommodation at mid-range and top-end hotels in Rajasthan, as well as on food and beverages at the more upmarket restaurants. Rooms over Rs 750 are taxed at 10%, but at the time of writing there was talk of raising the threshold to Rs 1000 to alleviate the strain on the tourism industry after the very slow season of 2001–02. Taxes rise to 20% for expensive rooms in top-end hotels. In addition there is a 9.2% tax on food and beverages. Some hotels levy a separate 'service charge' on top of this, usually around 10%.

It is always worthwhile asking before you check in whether you will be taxed, and by how much, to prevent an unpleasant shock when you get the bill. Rates quoted in this book are generally the basic rate only – taxes and service charges are extra.

If you've got a visa enabling you to stay in India for more than 180 days, you must technically get a tax clearance certificate to leave the country. This certificate supposedly proves that your time in India was financed with your own money, not by working in India or by selling things (contact one of India's foreigners registration offices in the major cities). You'll need to show your passport, visa-extension form, any other appropriate paperwork and a handful of bank-encashment certificates.

Encashment Certificates

By law, all money must be changed at official banks or moneychangers, and you are supposed to be given an encashment certificate (money-exchange receipt) for each transaction – ask for it if you don't receive one. It is definitely worth getting them, especially if you want to re-exchange excess rupees for hard currency when you depart India (see Re-Exchange earlier).

The other reason for saving encashment certificates is that if you stay in India longer than 180 days, you have to get a tax clearance certificate. Some shipping agents may also request these certificates.

POST & COMMUNICATIONS

Indian postal and poste restante services are generally very good. Expected letters almost

Indian Parcel Postage Rates

destination	weight	air (Rs)	surface (Rs)
Australia	first 250g	375	360
	each additional 250g	65	30
Asia	first 250g	375	360
	each additional 250g	45	30
Europe	first 250g	450	65
	each additional 250g	410	30
Middle East	first 250g	375	370
	each additional 250g	45	40
North America	first 250g	375	90
	each additional 250g	360	40

always arrive and letters you send do almost invariably reach their destination, though they may take up to three weeks. Even though the Indian postal system is fairly reliable, don't count on a letter or package getting to you if there's anything of market value inside it. American Express (AmEx) in major city locations offers an alternative to the poste restante system. Some cities also offer courier services (such as DHL Worldwide Express) that can arrange speedy and safe air freight around the world (at a higher cost).

Sending Mail

It costs Rs 8 to airmail a postcard and Rs 8.50 to send an aerogramme anywhere in the world from India. A standard airmail letter (up to 20g) costs Rs 9 to Australia and Asia and Rs 11 to North America and Europe. The larger post offices have a speed-post service.

Posting parcels is a somewhat convoluted process:

- Take the parcel to a tailor, or a parcel-stitching wallah (occasionally found just outside post offices) and ask for your parcel to be stitched up in cheap linen. Negotiate the price first and expect to pay upwards of Rs 50 per package, depending on the size.
- At the post office, ask for the necessary customs declaration forms. Fill them in and glue one to the parcel. The other will be stitched onto it. To avoid duty at the delivery end it's best to specify that the contents are a 'gift'.

- Be careful how much you declare the contents to be worth. If you specify over Rs 1000, your parcel will not be accepted without a bank clearance certificate, which is a hassle to get.
- Have the parcel weighed and franked at the parcel counter.

Books or printed matter can go by bookpost, which is considerably cheaper than parcel post, but the package must be wrapped a certain way: make sure that it can either be opened for inspection along the way, or that it is wrapped in brown paper or cardboard and tied with string, with the two ends exposed so that the contents are visible. To protect the books, wrap them in clear plastic first. No customs declaration form is necessary. Bookpost rates are about Rs 230 for 500g, Rs 455 for 1kg and Rs 1010 for 2kg.

Be cautious with places that offer to mail items to your home address after you have bought them. Government emporiums are usually OK but in most other places it pays to do the posting yourself.

Receiving Mail

Ask senders to address letters to you with your surname in capital letters and underlined, followed by poste restante, GPO (main post office), and the city or town in question. Many 'lost' letters are simply misfiled under given (first) names, so always check under both your names. Ask senders to provide a return address, just in case you don't collect your mail. Letters sent via poste restante are generally held for one month before being returned to the sender. You'll need to show your passport to collect mail.

Telephone

Even in the smallest towns, you'll find private PCO/STD/ISD call booths with direct local, interstate and international dialling. These are invariably cheaper than direct dialling from hotel rooms. Usually found in shops or other businesses, they are easy to spot because of the large yellow PCO/STD/ISD signs advertising the service. Many are open 24 hours. A nifty digital meter lets you keep an eye on what the call costs and gives you a print-out at the end.

India's Yellow Pages can be found at [W] www.indiayellowpages.com. For those who may be trying to locate a long-lost friend, you could try your luck at the 1 Billion Indians site ([W] www.1billionindians .com), affectionately dubbed as 'India's People Finder'.

Domestic Calls Telephone numbers in Rajasthan have an annoying tendency to change – don't be surprised if a hotel number in this book is no longer the same. If that's the case, call ☎ 197 for local telephone-number inquiries. The collect-call operator can be reached on ☎ 186.

If you're calling an STD number in Rajasthan within 200km, you can replace the initial 0 with 95 and you'll only be charged local rates.

International Calls Direct international calls from call booths (not hotels) cost an average of Rs 100 per minute, depending on the country you are calling. There are often cheaper rates at certain times of the day. Some places also offer cheaper rates on Indian national holidays. To make an international call, you will need to dial 00 (international access code from India) + country code (of the country you are calling) + area code + local number.

In some centres PCO/STD/ISD booths may offer a 'call-back' service – you ring your folks or friends, give them the phone number of the booth and wait for them to call you back. The booth operator will charge about Rs 5 per minute for this service, in addition to the cost of the preliminary call, although some places have a free call-back service. Advise your caller how long you intend to wait at the booth in the event that they have trouble getting back to you. The number your caller dials will be (caller's country international access code) + 91 (international country code for India) + area code + local (booth) number.

The central telegraph offices in major towns are usually reasonably efficient and some remain open 24 hours. Prices are comparable with PCO/STD/ISD booths.

Also available is the Home Country Direct service, which gives you access to the international operator in your home country. For the price of a local call, you can then make reverse-charge (collect) or phonecard calls, although you may have trouble convincing the owner of the telephone you are using that they are not going to get charged for the call. The countries and numbers to dial are:

country	number
Australia	☎ 0006117
Canada	☎ 000617
Germany	☎ 0004917
Italy	☎ 0003917
Japan	☎ 0008117
The Netherlands	☎ 0003117
New Zealand	☎ 0006417
Spain	☎ 0003417
UK	☎ 0004417
USA	☎ 00017

Fax

Fax rates at the telegraph office at the Jaipur main post office are Rs 60 per page for neighbouring countries; Rs 95 per page to other Asian destinations, Africa, Europe, Australia and New Zealand; and Rs 110 to the USA and Canada. This fax office is open 24 hours. Rates within India are Rs 30 per A4 page.

Many of the PCO/STD/ISD booths also have a fax machine for public use. The going rate for international faxes ranges from Rs 125 to 155 per A4 page. Receiving faxes can range from Rs 10 to 30 per page.

Email & Internet Access

Internet outlets in Rajasthan are spreading faster than rumours. Be warned that some bureaus have poor connections and can be excruciatingly slow. Connections and speed are usually superior in the morning and early afternoon (peak demand seems to fall between 5pm and 9pm making this a slow period). Places to surf the Internet are widespread throughout the larger cities, but every medium-sized town has email facilities, too, even if it's just one computer in a cramped little back office.

It usually costs around Rs 20 to 60 per hour, but prices are constantly falling as the infrastructure improves.

DIGITAL RESOURCES

The World Wide Web is a rich resource for travellers. You can research your trip, hunt down bargain air fares, book hotels, check on weather conditions or chat with locals and other travellers about the best places to visit (or avoid!).

There's no better place to start your Web explorations than the Lonely Planet website (W www.lonelyplanet.com). Here you'll find succinct summaries on travelling to most places on earth, postcards from other travellers and the Thorn Tree bulletin board, where you can ask questions before you go or dispense advice when you get back. You can also find travel news and updates to many of our most popular guidebooks, and the sub-WWWay section links you to the most useful travel resources elsewhere on the Web.

There are many websites relating to India and Rajasthan, but they often come and go with some frequency. You'll find that more than a few are nothing more than glossy (often inaccurate) PR puff. On the plus side, many local newspapers and current-affairs magazines have useful sites, including:

The Hindu W www.thehindu.com
The Hindustan Times W www
.hindustantimes.com

Indian Express W www.indian-express.com
India Today W www.india-today.com
Times of India W www.timesofindia.com

Some good portals and search engines worth trying include:

123 India W www.123india.com
Khoj W www.khoj.com
Rediff On The Net W www.rediff.com

There are also some good sites on Rajasthan:

Rajasthan Diary W www.rajasthandiary.com; presented as an interactive travelogue of the state
Rajasthan Tourism Development Corporation W www.rajasthantourismindia.com; the state tourism authority's website
RajDarpan W www.rajgovt.org; the state government website

And for those of you seeking the perfect Indian name for your unborn child, you may want to check out W www.indiaexpress.com/specials/babynames/ – good luck!

BOOKS

India is one of the world's largest publishers of books in English. You'll find a treasure trove of interesting, affordable books about India by Indian publishers, which are generally not available in the West. Recently published Western books also reach Indian bookshops remarkably fast and with very low mark-ups. If a bestseller in Europe or America has major appeal for India the publisher will often rush out a paperback in India to forestall possible pirates.

Most books are published in different editions by different publishers in different countries. As a result, a book might be a hardcover rarity in one country while it's readily available in paperback in another. Fortunately, bookshops and libraries search by title or author, so your local bookshop or library is best placed to advise you on the availability of the following recommendations. Please note that the following list is by no means exhaustive – there is a bounty of other excellent books, far too many to be included here.

Lonely Planet

Lonely Planet publishes a wide range of detailed guides to India's regions and cities. The award-winning *India* is one of Lonely Planet's most popular titles; this is the most comprehensive guide to the country you'll find. Other useful titles include *Delhi, Mumbai (Bombay), North India, Indian Himalaya* and *Trekking in the Indian Himalaya*. We also comprehensively cover the whole region with guides to *Pakistan, Nepal, Bangladesh, Sri Lanka, Bhutan* and the *Maldives*, as well as the route guide *Istanbul to Kathmandu*. Lonely Planet is also the publisher a handy *Hindi/Urdu* phrasebook, *Healthy Travel Asia & India* and *Read This First: Asia & India*.

World Food India takes you on a mouthwatering tour through Indian cuisine, not only exploring its cultural significance but also its many regional specialities.

Travel Photography: A Guide to Taking Better Pictures is written by internationally renowned travel photographer Richard I'Anson. It's full colour throughout and designed to take on the road.

In Rajasthan by Royina Grewal, is an insider's view of this enthralling state. Another recommended title in Lonely Planet's travel-literature series, Journeys, is William Dalrymple's *The Age of Kali*. Lonely Planet also has some lavishly illustrated offerings, including *Chasing Rickshaws*, a tribute to cycle-powered vehicles and their drivers by Tony Wheeler and photographer Richard I'Anson. There's also *Sacred India*, another full-colour book with stunning images of India's diverse religious culture.

Specialist Guidebooks

The growing interest in the magnificent painted havelis of Shekhawati has spawned a number of books on the region. The definitive title is Ilay Cooper's *The Painted Towns of Shekhawati*. It's not only a practical guide to the region, with maps and notes for easy location and identification of paintings, but has very good essays on the history of the region, painting techniques, layout of the havelis, and more. It may be hard to find, so snap up a copy if you see one.

Another book on this subject is *Rajasthan: The Painted Walls of Shekhavati* by Francis Wacziarg & Aman Nath.

Travel

Robyn Davidson's *Desert Places* is an account of the author's journey by camel with the Rabari (Rajasthani nomads) on their annual migration through the Thar Desert. It gives a compelling insight into both the plight of the nomads and the solo woman traveller in Rajasthan.

Rupa & Co has recently released three slim volumes of Rudyard Kipling's tales about the state, called *Rajasthan Stories*; they're available in bookshops in Jaipur. *Rajasthan, Agra, Delhi* by Philip Ward is a travelogue-cum-travel guide about the 'golden triangle' of Indian tourism.

History & Politics

Annals & Antiquities of Rajasthan by Captain James Tod is probably the text most cited by historians writing about Rajasthan. This classic text was originally published in 1829–32. It comes in a two-volume set, published by Rupa & Co.

Rajasthan: Polity, Economy & Society by BL Panagariya & NC Pahariya is a well-written text that concentrates on the formation and composition of the state of Rajasthan in the post-Independence period, the government of the state to the present day, as well as the state's economy, development and cultural heritage.

By My Sword and Shield by E Jaiwant Paul is about the traditional weapons of Indian warriors, especially the Rajputs.

Culture

Cultural History of Rajasthan by Kalyan Kumar Ganguli is a scholarly text that provides a comprehensive historical and cultural analysis of Rajputana.

Folklore of Rajasthan by DR Ahuja is a handy paperback book about the cultural heritage of Rajasthan and its people, with chapters on folk music and dance, customs and traditions and myths and mythology.

For an assessment of the position of women in Indian society, and that of rural women particularly, *May You Be the Mother of One Hundred Sons* by Elizabeth Bumiller offers excellent insights into the subject.

For those interested in the continuing and often shocking and sad story of India's tribal people, there is the scholarly *Tribes of India – The Struggle for Survival* by Christoph von Führer-Haimendorf.

The Idea of Rajasthan, edited by Karine Schomer et al, is a two-volume set of contemporary essays by various scholars on the historical and cultural influences that have contributed towards Rajasthani identity.

Princely Rule

A Princess Remembers by Gayatri Devi & Santha Rama Rau is the memoirs of the maharani of Jaipur, Gayatri Devi, wife of the last maharaja, Man Singh II. It's easy reading and provides a fascinating insight into the bygone days of Rajasthani royalty. (See the boxed text 'The Rani of Rambagh' in the Jaipur chapter for more information about Gayatri Devi.)

A Desert Kingdom: The Rajputs of Bikaner by Naveen Patnaik is a fine hardback volume with magnificent old photos from the collection of Maharaja Ganga Singh of Bikaner, who ascended the throne in 1885. It includes an interesting commentary and historical analysis of his rule.

Maharana by Brian Masters traces the history of the rulers of Udaipur, the world's oldest ruling dynasty, which spans some 76 generations.

Maharaja: The Spectacular Heritage of Princely India, with text by Andrew Robinson and superb photos by Sumio Uchiyama, portrays the past and present heritage of princely India and covers a range of royal families, predominantly from Rajasthan.

The House of Marwar by Dhananajaya Singh outlines the history of the royal house of Jodhpur from the first ruler in the early 13th century up to the present maharaja. The book contains a small collection of photos.

Pictorial Books

Jaipur: The Last Destination, with text by Aman Nath and beautiful photographs by Samar Singh Jodha, is a magnificent prize-winning hardback volume that has extensive historical notes and essays on Jaipur's maharajas and the textiles, arts and crafts of the 'Pink City'.

Rajasthan: An Enduring Romance is an attractive hardback by Sunil Mehra.

Rajasthan, with text by Gerard Busquet and photos by Pierre Toutain, is predominantly pictorial and reflects the vibrant places, people and colour of Rajasthan.

Rajasthan: India's Enchanted Land is a finely presented paperback volume with photographs by Raghubir Singh and foreword by film director Satyajit Ray. Other attractive souvenir books include *Udaipur – The Fabled City of Romance* by Archana Shankar and *Rajasthan* by Kishore Singh. If you have around Rs 3000 to spend, there's the impressive volume *Rajasthan* by Dharmendar Kanwar.

Arts, Crafts & Architecture

Arts & Crafts of Rajasthan, edited by Aman Nath & Francis Wacziarg, is a beautiful hardback volume, with photographs accompanied by informative and interesting essays.

Arts & Artists of Rajasthan by RK Vashistha is a hardback volume covering the period from the 7th to the 19th centuries, concentrating on the art centres of Mewar (Udaipur), with numerous photographic plates, extensive notes and short biographies of artists.

The City Palace Museum Udaipur, with text by Andrew Topsfield and photos by Pankaj Shah, provides an interesting visual and historical background to the Mewar paintings at this museum.

Ateliers of the Rajput Courts contains beautiful colour plates of Rajasthani miniatures, which are part of the Lalit Kala Akademi series (portfolio No 39). Raj K Tandan wrote the accompanying text. The prints are loose-leaf and so they could easily be framed.

The Royal Palaces of India, with text by George Michell and photographs by Antonio Martinelli, is a comprehensive, detailed guide to the forts and palaces of India. The text is complemented with excellent photographs and some archaeological maps.

The Forts of India by Virginia Fass is a large hardback volume with photographs and substantial historical notes.

Flora & Fauna

A classic text on arid-zone flora is E Blatter & F Hallberg's *The Flora of the Indian Desert*, first published between 1918 and 1921. This is a detailed technical reference book, but the notes on traditional uses of the plants of the Thar Desert are interesting.

The Tiger's Destiny, with text by Valmik Thapar and photographs by Fateh Singh Rathore, deals with the besieged tigers of Ranthambhore National Park.

Specifically dealing with the prolific birdlife of Keoladeo Ghana National Park is *Bharatpur: Bird Paradise*, with text by Martin Ewans and photographs by Thakur Dalip Singh et al.

Mammals of the Thar Desert by Ishwar Prakash is a small hardback volume with detailed descriptions and field notes accompanied by line drawings. Another good paperback is *A Guide to the Wildlife Parks of Rajasthan* by Dr Suraj Ziddi with photographs by Subhash Bhargava.

Environment

The Radiant Raindrops of Rajasthan by Anupam Mishra is an excellent look at the ingenious ways that Rajasthanis have managed their meagre water supply over the generations. You can find it at the People Tree bookshop in Delhi.

Novels

Virgin Princess: An Historical Novel of Mewar (Udaipur, India) – The World's Oldest Dynasty by Jane Richardson is an interesting if badly written romantic tale.

Raj by Gita Mehta is the more convincingly told story of a young Rajput princess contracted in marriage to an arrogant prince. *Inside the Haveli* by Rama Mehta is about a girl from Mumbai who marries into a conservative family in Rajasthan.

FILMS

Latcho Drom (Safe Journey), directed by Tony Gatlif, is a very dramatic movie that traces the lives of gypsy dancers and musicians from India to the Middle East, Eastern Europe and Spain. It opens with stunning Rajasthan desert vistas and evocative scenes of traditional music and dance performed by Rajasthani nomads.

NEWSPAPERS & MAGAZINES

English-language dailies include the *Times of India*, the *Hindustan Times*, the *Indian Express* and the *Statesman*; the *Indian Express* is the best of the bunch. The *Economic Times* is for those interested in business and economic analysis.

Popular news magazines include *Frontline*, *India Today*, *Sunday*, *Rashtriya Sahara*, *Outlook*, the *Week* and the *Illustrated Weekly*. They're widely available at bookshops and newspaper stands.

Major city bookshops and top-end hotels usually stock a healthy collection of international fare (although they can be dated and are pricey by local standards). These include the *Economist*, *Time*, *Newsweek*, the *International Herald-Tribune* and *Der Spiegel*.

Popular women's magazines include *Femina*, *Savvy* and *Gladrags*, as well as Indian versions of *Elle* and *Cosmopolitan*. To get the lowdown on who's who and who's doing what to whom in Bollywood, grab a copy of *Stardust*, *Cineblitz* or *Filmfare*.

There are also other English-language magazines, specialising in everything from sports to information technology.

TV & RADIO

Television viewing was once dominated by the rather dreary national broadcaster, Doordarshan. However, since the arrival of satellite and cable TV (in the early 1990s) India has fast become one of the world's most avid channel-surfing nations. Cable is available at all top-end hotels, most mid-range ones and a handful of budget places. Check local newspapers for programme details.

Running 24 hours, cable TV offers some 50-plus channels, with plenty of Hindi-language ones, including the immensely popular Zee TV. Bollywood buffs are well catered for with multiple movie channels churning out blockbuster after blockbuster.

Meanwhile, those in need of spiritual sustenance can switch to the Maharishi Mahesh Yogi's channel, which offers a devout diet of holy images, *bhajans* (devotional songs) and overall positive vibes. There are also some regional channels that broadcast in local languages.

English-language channels include the BBC (has anyone told them about the Bombay, Madras and Calcutta name changes?!), CNN, Discovery and National Geographic Channels. There are also the Star TV offerings, which include Star Movies (for Hollywood blockbusters), Star Plus (for American sitcoms, soapies and more), Star Sports and Star News; the latter two broadcast in Hindi and English. Also in English, Nickelodeon rolls out various sitcoms, while AXN and HBO screen movies (including some great golden oldies). MTV and Channel V are the premier music channels to watch, featuring everything from *bhangra* (Punjabi disco) to American rap.

Radio programmes on All India Radio (AIR; W www.air.kode.net) include various interviews, music, sports and news features.

VIDEO SYSTEMS
Video in India uses the VHS format, although it is possible to convert to and from PAL and NTSC in the larger cities.

PHOTOGRAPHY & VIDEO
Film & Equipment
Colour print film-processing facilities are readily available in major cities and larger towns. Film is relatively cheap and the quality is usually (but not always) good. Same-day processing is often available. Colour slide film is less widely available than print film. You'll generally only find it in the major cities and tourist traps. Colour slides can be processed (usually in two to three days; specify if you want them mounted or not) in major cities including Delhi and Jaipur, but most travellers prefer to get them developed back home. On average, to develop 24 colour prints costs around Rs 130. To develop slide film, expect to pay Rs 200 for 36 shots mounted in plastic.

Always check the use-by date on local film or slide stock. Make sure you get a sealed packet and ensure you're not handed a roll that's been sitting in a glass cabinet in the sunshine for the last few months: heat can play havoc with film, even if the use-by date hasn't been exceeded. A tip: be wary of street hawkers in India. Some travellers report that old, useless film is loaded into new-looking canisters. The hapless tourist only discovers the trick when the film is developed back home. The best advice is to avoid street vendors and only buy film from reputable stores – and preferably film that's been refrigerated.

Video users can get cartridges (including digital minidiscs, VHS and Super 8) in major cities such as Delhi and Jaipur. Lithium batteries are also available in the larger centres.

Technical Tips
Lonely Planet's *Travel Photography: A Guide to Taking Better Pictures*, written by internationally renowned travel photographer Richard I'Anson, will provide you with comprehensive advice on taking photos while travelling.

The following are some handy hints for better photos:

- The quality of your photos depends on the quality of light you shoot under. Light is best when the sun is low in the sky – around sunrise and sunset.
- Don't buy cheap equipment, but don't load yourself down with expensive equipment you don't know how to use properly either.
- A good SLR camera is advisable, but be aware that the quality of your lenses is the most important thing. Zoom lenses are heavier than fixed-focal-length lenses and the quality isn't as good. An alternative to the zoom is a tele-converter that fits over your lens and doubles the focal length.
- Always carry a skylight or UV filter. A polarising filter can create dramatic effects and cut glare, but don't fit it over a UV filter.
- Take a tripod and faster film (at least 400ASA) rather than a flash. Flash creates harsh shadows. A cable release is useful for shooting with a tripod.
- Settle on a brand of film and know how it works before you head off.

- Keep your film in a cool dark place if possible, before and after exposure. However, in practice, film seems to last, even in Rajasthan's summer heat. Silica gel sachets distributed around your gear will help absorb moisture.
- Bring a camera cleaning kit as the dust, sand and general grime in India can be prolific.
- Expose for the main component of a scene and fill the frame with what you are taking.
- Previsualise – it's one of the most important elements in photographic vision. You must 'see' your picture clearly before you take it.

Restrictions

Be careful what you photograph. India is touchy about places of military importance – this can include train stations, bridges, airports, military installations and sensitive border regions. Temples may prohibit photography in the *mandapa* (forechamber of a temple) and inner sanctum. If in doubt, ask. Some temples, and numerous sites such as museums and forts, levy a camera and video fee that you must pay upfront.

Photographing People

Some people are more than happy to be photographed, but care should be taken in pointing cameras, especially at women. Again, if in doubt, ask. A zoom is a less intrusive means of taking portraits – even when you've obtained permission to take a portrait, shoving a lens in your subject's face can be disconcerting. A reasonable distance between you and your subject will help reduce your subject's discomfort, and will result in more natural shots.

Airport Security

Some travellers invest in a lead-lined bag, as repeated exposure to X-ray (even so-called 'filmproof' X-ray) can damage film. Never put your film in baggage that will be placed in the cargo holds of aeroplanes, as it may be subjected to large doses of X-ray that will ruin it. Some professional photographers never take film through any X-ray machine, but prefer to pack it in see-through plastic containers and carry them by hand through customs. Just be aware that some customs officers may wish to open every single canister before you're allowed through.

TIME

India is 5½ hours ahead of GMT/UTC, 4½ hours behind Australian EST and 10½ hours ahead of American EST. It is officially known as IST (Indian Standard Time), although many affectionately dub it as 'Indian Stretchable Time'.

ELECTRICITY

The electric current is 230-240V AC, 50 Hz. Electricity is widely available, but power cuts are not uncommon – keep a torch (flashlight) or candle handy. Breakdowns and blackouts ('load shedding') lasting from several minutes to several hours are common, especially in the hotter months when demand outstrips supply. If you are bringing any sensitive electrical equipment (eg, a laptop computer), you'll require a voltage stabiliser to safeguard it from the power fluctuations.

Sockets are the three-round-pin variety, similar (but not identical) to European sockets. European round-pin plugs will go into the sockets, but as the pins on Indian plugs are somewhat thicker, the fit is loose and connection is not always guaranteed.

You can purchase small immersion elements, perfect for boiling water for tea or coffee, for around Rs 55. For about Rs 75 you can buy electric mosquito zappers. These take chemical tablets that melt and emit deadly vapours (deadly for the mozzie, that is). They're widely available in various brands, with delightful names such as Good Knight.

WEIGHTS & MEASURES

Although India is officially metricated, imperial weights and measures are still used in some areas of commerce. You will often hear people referring to *lakhs* (one *lakh* = 100,000) and *crore* (one *crore* = 10 million) of people, camels, money or whatever. A metric conversion chart is included on the inside back cover of this book.

LAUNDRY

Getting your sweaty, crumpled clothes washed and ironed in India is an absolute breeze. Your clothes will usually be washed by a *dhobi-wallah* at the *dhobi* ghats (see the boxed text 'India's Washing Wizards'). If you don't think they will stand up to being beaten clean, then hand wash them yourself. Washing powder can be bought very cheaply in small sachets almost anywhere in Rajasthan, and hotels are usually happy to lend you a bucket.

At budget and mid-range hotels clothes can usually be washed by a *dhobi-wallah* (inquire at reception). You simply hand over your dirty clothes in the morning and you'll usually get them back washed and pressed that same evening for a minimal cost (around Rs 10 per item; often a little more in touristy places). Most, if not all, upmarket hotels have an in-house laundry with upmarket charges to match. Many crank up the price for same-day service.

Women should consider bringing a lingerie bag to protect delicate bras and undies if they intend handing them over to either a *dhobi-wallah* or a hotel laundry. A tip: make sure you explain *how* the bag is actually used or else your precious lingerie will promptly be taken out and thrashed just like regular clothes.

TOILETS

All top-end and most mid-range hotels have sit-down flush toilets with toilet paper supplied. Some mid-range and most budget hotels usually have a choice of squat and sit-down toilets (see also the boxed text 'Get to Know Your Bathroom' later in this chapter). In the real rock-bottom category and in places well off the tourist circuit, squat toilets are the norm (and are actually a more hygienic option than the sit-down variety) and toilet paper is rarely provided.

Most upmarket restaurants have sit-down flush toilets, while most budget eateries will make you work those calf muscles.

When it comes to effluent etiquette, it's customary to use your left hand and water,

India's Washing Wizards

Thanks to India's *dhobi-wallahs* (washerpeople) you hardly need more than one change of clothes. You simply give them your dirty clothes in the morning and hey presto, they come back freshly washed and crisply ironed later that very day. And all for a ridiculously low price. But what happened to your clothes between their departure and return?

Well, they certainly did not get anywhere near a washing machine. First of all they're taken to the *dhobi ghat* – a series of steps near a lake or river where the *dhobi-wallahs* ply their trade. Upon arrival at the ghat the clothes are separated – all the white T-shirts are washed together, all the burgundy socks, all the blue jeans. Your clothes are soaked in soapy water for a few hours, following which the dirt is literally belted out of them. No newfangled washing machine can wash as clean as a determined *dhobi*, although admittedly after a few visits to the Indian laundry your clothes do look distinctly thinner and faded. Buttons also tend to get shattered, so bring some spares. Zips, lace, bras and flimsy undies sometimes fare likewise. Once clean, the clothes are dried in the glorious Indian sun, then they're pressed with primitive-looking irons – even your underwear will come back with knife-edge creases.

Even though hundreds, even thousands, of items are washed at the same place each day, the deft *dhobi-wallah's* secret system of marking means your clothes won't get mistakenly bundled into another *dhobi's* load. Apparently criminals have even been tracked down by these tell-tale '*dhobi* marks'.

KEIRAN MANGAN

not toilet paper. A strategically placed tap, usually with a little plastic jug nearby, is available in most bathrooms. If you can't get used to the Indian method, bring your own paper (widely available in cities and towns). However, stuffing paper, sanitary napkins and tampons down the toilet is going to further clog an already overloaded sewerage system. Often a bin is provided for used toilet paper and other items – please use it.

HEALTH

Travel health depends on your predeparture preparations, your daily health care while travelling and how you handle any medical problem that does develop. While the potential dangers can seem quite frightening, in reality few travellers experience anything more than an upset stomach.

In even the smallest Rajasthani town you will find at least one well-stocked pharmacy (selling everything from malaria medication to nail-polish remover). Many are open until late. Many pharmaceuticals sold in India are manufactured under licence from multinational companies, so you'll probably be familiar with many brand names. Always check expiry dates.

There are plenty of English-speaking doctors and pharmacists in urban centres, but fewer in rural areas. Most hotels have a doctor on call – if you're staying at a budget hotel and they can't help you, try contacting an upmarket hotel to find out which doctor they use. If you're seriously ill, contact your country's embassy (see Embassies & Consulates earlier in this chapter), which usually has a list of recommended doctors and dentists.

Treatment at public hospitals is generally reliable, though private clinics do offer the advantage of shorter queues. However, there have been reports that some private clinics have bumped up the level of treatment to higher than is necessary in order to procure larger medical insurance claims (see Dangers & Annoyances later in this chapter).

Finally, many towns have both Ayurvedic and Western clinics; if it's not obvious which philosophy the clinic follows, ask at the outset.

Everyday Health

Normal body temperature (98.6°F); more than 2°C (4 cates a high fever. The norm rate is 60 to 100 beats per min 80 to 100, babies 100 to 140). As rule the pulse increases about 20 b minute for each 1°C (2°F) rise in fever.

Respiration (breathing) rate is also an in cator of illness. Count the number of breath per minute: Between 12 and 20 is normal for adults and older children (up to 30 for younger children, 40 for babies). People with a high fever or serious respiratory illness breathe more quickly than normal. More than 40 shallow breaths a minute may indicate pneumonia.

Predeparture Planning

Immunisations Plan ahead for getting your vaccinations: some of them require more than one injection, while some vaccinations should not be given together. Note that some vaccinations should not be given during pregnancy or to people with allergies – discuss with your doctor.

It is recommended you seek medical advice at least six weeks before travel. Be aware that there is often a greater risk of disease with children and during pregnancy.

Discuss your requirements with your doctor, but vaccinations you should consider for this trip include the following (for more details about the diseases themselves, see the individual disease entries later in this section). Carry proof of your vaccinations, especially yellow fever, as this is sometimes needed to enter some countries.

Diphtheria & Tetanus Vaccinations for these two diseases are usually combined and are recommended for everyone. After an initial course of three injections (usually given in childhood), boosters are necessary every 10 years.

Hepatitis A The hepatitis A vaccine (eg, Avaxim, Havrix 1440 or VAQTA) provides long-term immunity (possibly more than 10 years) after an initial injection and a booster at six to 12 months. Alternatively, an injection of gamma

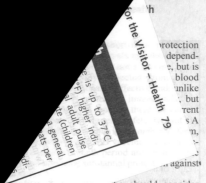

who should consider
... hepatitis B include those on
... , as well as those visiting countries
(including India) where there are high levels of
hepatitis B infection, where blood transfusions
may not be adequately screened or where
sexual contact or needle sharing is a possibility.
Vaccination involves three injections, with a
booster at 12 months. More rapid courses are
available if necessary.

Japanese B Encephalitis Consider vaccination
against this disease if spending a month or
longer in a high-risk area of Rajasthan, making
repeated trips to a risk area or visiting during
an epidemic. It involves three injections over
30 days.

Meningococcal Meningitis Vaccination is recommended for travellers to Rajasthan. A single
injection gives good protection against the
major epidemic forms of the disease for three
years. Protection may be less effective in
children under two years.

Polio Everyone should keep up to date with this
vaccination. It's normally given in childhood. A
booster every 10 years maintains immunity.

Rabies Vaccination should be considered by
those who will spend a month or longer in India
where rabies is common, especially if they
are cycling, handling animals or travelling to
remote areas, and for children (who may not
report a bite). Pretravel rabies vaccination
involves having three injections over 21 to 28
days. If someone who has been vaccinated is
bitten or scratched by an animal, they will
require two booster injections of vaccine; those
not vaccinated require more.

Tuberculosis The risk of tuberculosis (TB) to
travellers is usually very low, unless you will be
living with or closely associated with local
people. Vaccination against TB (BCG) is recommended for children and young adults living in
a high-risk area for three months or more.

Typhoid Vaccination against typhoid may be
required if you are travelling for more than a
couple of weeks in India. It is now available

either as an injection or as capsules to be taken
orally. A combined hepatitis A/typhoid vaccine
was launched recently but its availability is still
limited – check with your doctor to find out its
status in your country.

Medical Kit Check List

Following is a list of items to consider for your
medical kit – consult your pharmacist for
brands available in your country:

☐ **Aspirin or paracetamol (acetaminophen
in the USA)** – for pain or fever

☐ **Antihistamine** – for allergies, eg, hay
fever; to ease the itch from insect bites or
stings; and to prevent motion sickness

☐ **Cold and flu tablets, throat lozenges
and nasal decongestant**

☐ **Multivitamins** – consider for long trips,
when dietary vitamin intake may be
inadequate

☐ **Antibiotics** – consider including these if
you're travelling well off the beaten
track; see your doctor, as they must be
prescribed, and carry the prescription
with you

☐ **Loperamide or diphenoxylate** – 'blockers'
for diarrhoea

☐ **Prochlorperazine or metaclopramide** –
for nausea and vomiting

☐ **Rehydration mixture** – to prevent dehydration, which may occur, for example,
during bouts of diarrhoea; particularly
important when travelling with children

☐ **Insect repellent, sunscreen, lip balm and
eye drops**

☐ **Calamine lotion, sting relief spray or
aloe vera** – to ease irritation from sunburn and insect bites or stings

☐ **Antifungal cream or powder** – for fungal
skin infections and thrush

☐ **Antiseptic (such as povidone-iodine)** –
for cuts and grazes

☐ **Bandages, Band-Aids (plasters) and
other wound dressings**

☐ **Water purification tablets or iodine**

☐ **Scissors, tweezers and a thermometer** –
note that mercury thermometers are
prohibited by airlines

☐ **Sterile kit** – in case you need injections in
a country with medical hygiene prob-
lems; discuss with your doctor

Yellow Fever A yellow-fever vaccine is required if coming from an infected area such as Central Africa and parts of South America. You may have to go to a special yellow-fever vaccination centre.

Malaria Medication Antimalarial drugs do not prevent you from being infected but kill the malaria parasites during a stage in their development and significantly reduce the risk of becoming very ill or dying. Expert advice on medication should be sought, as there are many factors to consider, including the area to be visited, the risk of exposure to malaria-carrying mosquitoes, the side effects of medication, your medical history and whether you are a child or an adult or pregnant. Travellers to isolated areas in high-risk countries may like to carry a treatment dose of medication for use if symptoms occur.

Health Insurance Make sure that you have adequate health insurance. See Travel Insurance under Visas & Documents earlier in this chapter for details.

Travel Health Guides Lonely Planet's *Healthy Travel Asia & India* is handy and pocket size and packed with plenty of useful information including pretrip planning, emergency first aid, immunisation and disease information and what to do if you get sick on the road. *Travel with Children*

from Lonely Planet also includes advice on travel health for younger children.

There are also a number of excellent travel health sites on the Internet. From the Lonely Planet home page there are links at W www .lonelyplanet.com/weblinks/wlheal.htm to the World Health Organization and the US Centers for Disease Control & Prevention.

Other Preparations Make sure you're healthy before you start travelling. If you are going on a long trip make sure your teeth are OK. If you wear glasses take a spare pair and your prescription.

If you require a particular medication take an adequate supply, as it may not be available locally. Take part of the packaging showing the generic name rather than the brand, which will make getting replacements easier. It's a good idea to have a legible prescription or letter from your doctor to show that you legally use the medication to avoid any problems.

Basic Rules

Food Although you should be careful about what you eat and drink, don't become paranoid – sampling the local cuisine is a highlight of travel and Rajasthan has some phenomenal culinary offerings. It's sensible to modify your diet gradually, so resist that urge to feast on deep-fried pakoras the moment you arrive.

Nutrition

If your diet is poor or limited in variety, if you're travelling hard and fast and therefore missing meals or if you simply lose your appetite, you can soon start to lose weight and place your health at risk.

Make sure your diet is well balanced. Cooked eggs, tofu, beans, lentils (daal in India) and nuts are all safe ways to get protein. Fruit you can peel (bananas, oranges or mandarins, for example) is usually safe and a good source of vitamins. Melons can harbour bacteria in their flesh and are best avoided. Try to eat plenty of grains (including rice) and bread. Remember that although food is generally safer if it is cooked well, overcooked food loses much of its nutritional value. If your diet isn't well balanced or if your food intake is insufficient, it's a good idea to take vitamin and iron pills.

In hot climates make sure you drink enough – don't rely on feeling thirsty to indicate when you should drink. Not needing to urinate or voiding small amounts of very dark yellow urine is a danger sign. Always carry a water bottle with you on long trips. Excessive sweating can lead to loss of salt and therefore muscle cramping. Salt tablets are not a good idea as a preventative, but in places where salt is not used much, adding salt to food can help.

Vegetables and fruit should be washed with purified water or peeled where possible. Beware of ice cream that is sold in the street or anywhere it might have been melted and refrozen; if there's any doubt (eg, a power cut in the last day or two), steer well clear. Undercooked meat, particularly in the form of mince, should be avoided.

If a place looks clean and well run and the vendor also looks clean and healthy, then the food is probably safe. In general, places that are packed with travellers or locals will be fine, while empty restaurants are questionable. The food in busy restaurants is cooked and eaten quite quickly with little standing around and is probably not reheated. Although street stalls may look unappetising, the big plus is that you can usually see your food being freshly cooked in front of your eyes.

Water The number one rule is *be careful of the water* and especially ice. If you don't know for certain that the water is safe, assume the worst. Reputable brands of bottled water or soft drinks are generally fine, although in some places bottles may be refilled with tap water. Only use water from containers with a serrated seal – not tops or corks. Take care with fruit juice, particularly if water may have been added. Milk should be treated with suspicion as it is often unpasteurised, though boiled milk is fine if it is kept hygienically. Tea or coffee should also be OK, since the water should have been boiled.

Water Purification The simplest way of purifying water is to boil it thoroughly. Consider purchasing a water filter for a long trip. There are two main kinds of filter. Total filters take out all parasites, bacteria and viruses and make water safe to drink. They are often expensive, but they can be more cost effective than buying bottled water. Simple filters (which can even be a nylon mesh bag) take out dirt and larger foreign bodies from the water so that chemical solutions work much more effectively; if water is dirty, chemical solutions may not work at all. It's very important when buying a filter to read the specifications, so that you know exactly what it removes from the water and what it doesn't. Simple filtering will not remove all dangerous organisms, so if you cannot boil water it should be treated chemically. Chlorine tablets will kill many pathogens, but not some parasites such as giardia and amoebic cysts. Iodine is more effective in purifying water and is available in tablet form. Follow the directions carefully and remember that too much iodine can be harmful.

Be aware that relying on some method of water purification helps the environment, as it stops you adding to Rajasthan's rubbish mountain of used plastic bottles – see Responsible Tourism earlier in this chapter. It also means that bottled water does not have to be trucked out to remote areas for you to purchase. Note that some hotels provide filtered water.

Medical Problems & Treatment

Self-diagnosis and treatment can be risky, so you should always seek medical help. An embassy, consulate or five-star hotel can usually recommend a local doctor or clinic. Although we do give drug dosages in this section, they are for emergency use only. Correct diagnosis is vital. In this section we have used the generic names for medications – check with a pharmacist for brands available locally.

Note that antibiotics should ideally be administered only under medical supervision. Take only the recommended dose at the prescribed intervals and use the whole course, even if the illness seems to be cured earlier. Stop immediately if there are any serious reactions and don't use the antibiotic at all if you are unsure that you have the correct one. Some people are allergic to commonly prescribed antibiotics such as penicillin; carry this information (eg, on a bracelet) when travelling.

Environmental Hazards

Air Pollution Something you'll become very aware of in Rajasthan if you spend a lot of time in urban or industrial environments is pollution.

Air pollution can be a health hazard in India, particularly if you suffer from a lung disease such as asthma. It can also aggravate coughs, colds and sinus problems, as well as cause eye irritation. Consider avoiding badly polluted areas, especially if you have asthma. Alternatively, it might be worth investing in a surgical mask.

Heat Exhaustion Dehydration and salt deficiency can cause heat exhaustion. Take time to acclimatise to high temperatures, drink sufficient liquids and do not do anything too physically demanding.

Salt deficiency is characterised by fatigue, lethargy, headaches, giddiness and muscle cramps; salt tablets may help, but adding extra salt to your food is better.

Anhidrotic heat exhaustion is a rare form of heat exhaustion that is caused by an inability to sweat. It tends to affect people who have been in a hot climate for some time, rather than newcomers. It can progress to heatstroke. Treatment involves removal to a cooler climate.

Heatstroke This serious, occasionally fatal, condition can occur if the body's heat-regulating mechanism breaks down and the body temperature rises to dangerous levels. Long, continuous periods of exposure to high temperatures and insufficient fluids can leave you vulnerable to heatstroke.

The symptoms are feeling unwell, not sweating very much (or at all) and a high body temperature (39° to 41°C or 102° to 106°F). Where sweating has ceased, the skin becomes flushed and red. Severe, throbbing headaches and lack of coordination will also occur, and the sufferer may be confused or aggressive. Eventually the victim will become delirious or convulse. Hospitalisation is essential, but in the interim get victims out of the sun, remove their clothing, cover them with a wet sheet or towel and then fan continually. Give fluids if they are conscious.

Jet Lag When a person travels by air across more than three time zones (each time zone usually represents a one-hour time difference), jet lag is experienced. It occurs because many of the functions of the human body (such as temperature, pulse rate and emptying of the bladder and bowels) are regulated by internal 24-hour cycles. When we travel long distances rapidly, our bodies take time to adjust to the 'new time' of our destination, and we may experience fatigue, disorientation, insomnia, anxiety, impaired concentration and loss of appetite. These effects will usually be gone within three days of arrival, but to minimise the impact of jet lag:

- Rest for a couple of days prior to departure.
- Try to select flight schedules that minimise sleep deprivation; arriving late in the day means you can go to sleep soon after you arrive. For very long flights, try to organise a stopover.
- Avoid excessive eating (which bloats the stomach) and alcohol (which causes dehydration) during the flight. Instead, drink plenty of noncarbonated, nonalcoholic drinks such as fruit juice or water.
- Avoid smoking.
- Make yourself comfortable by wearing loose-fitting clothes and perhaps bringing an eye mask and ear plugs to help you sleep.
- Try to sleep at the appropriate time for the time zone you are travelling to.

Motion Sickness Eating lightly before and during a trip will reduce the chances of motion sickness. If you are prone to motion sickness try to find a place that minimises movement – near the wing on aircraft, near the centre on buses. Fresh air usually helps; reading and cigarette smoke don't. Commercial motion-sickness preparations, which can cause drowsiness, have to be taken before the trip commences. Ginger (available in capsule form) and peppermint (including mint-flavoured sweets) are natural preventatives.

Prickly Heat This is an itchy rash caused by excessive perspiration trapped under the skin. It usually strikes people who have just arrived in a hot climate. Keeping cool, bathing often, drying the skin and using a mild talcum or prickly heat powder or resorting to air-conditioning may help.

Sunburn In the desert you can get sunburnt surprisingly quickly, even through cloud. Use a sunscreen, a hat, and a barrier cream for your nose and lips. Calamine lotion, aloe vera or a commercial after-sun preparation are good for mild sunburn. Protect your eyes with good-quality sunglasses, particularly if you will be near water or sand.

Infectious Diseases

Diarrhoea Simple things such as a change of water, food or climate can all cause a mild bout of diarrhoea, but a few rushed toilet trips with no other symptoms is not indicative of a major problem.

Dehydration is the main danger with any diarrhoea, particularly in children or the elderly as dehydration can occur quite quickly. Under all circumstances *fluid replacement* (at least equal to the volume being lost) is the most important thing to remember. Weak black tea with a little sugar, soda water, or soft drinks allowed to go flat and diluted 50% with clean water are all good. With severe diarrhoea a rehydrating solution is preferable to replace minerals and salts lost. Commercially available oral rehydration salts (ORS) are very useful; add them to boiled or bottled water. In an emergency you can make up a solution of six teaspoons of sugar and a half teaspoon of salt to a litre of boiled or bottled water. You need to drink at least the same volume of fluid that you are losing in bowel movements and vomiting. Your urine is the best guide to the adequacy of replacement – if you have small amounts of concentrated urine, you need to drink more. Keep drinking small amounts often. Stick to a bland diet as you recover.

Gut-paralysing drugs such as loperamide or diphenoxylate can be used to bring relief from symptoms, although they do not actually cure the problem. Only use these drugs if you do not have access to toilets, eg, if you *must* travel. Note that these drugs are not recommended for children under 12 years.

In certain situations antibiotics may be required: diarrhoea with blood or mucus (dysentery), any diarrhoea with fever, profuse watery diarrhoea, persistent diarrhoea not improving after 48 hours and severe diarrhoea. These suggest a more serious cause of diarrhoea and in these situations gut-paralysing drugs should be avoided.

In these situations, a stool test may be necessary to diagnose what bug is causing your diarrhoea, so you should seek medical help urgently. Where this is not possible the recommended drugs for bacterial diarrhoea (the most likely cause of severe diarrhoea in travellers) are norfloxacin 400mg twice daily for three days or ciprofloxacin 500mg twice daily for five days. These are not recommended for children or pregnant women. The drug of choice for children would be co-trimoxazole with dosage dependent on weight. A five-day course is given. Ampicillin or amoxycillin may be given in pregnancy, but medical care is necessary.

Two other causes of persistent diarrhoea in travellers are giardiasis and amoebic dysentery.

Giardiasis is caused by a common parasite, *Giardia lamblia*. Symptoms include stomach cramps, nausea, a bloated stomach, watery foul-smelling diarrhoea and frequent gas. Giardiasis can appear several weeks after you have been exposed to the parasite. The symptoms may disappear for a few days and then return; this can go on for several weeks.

Amoebic dysentery, caused by the protozoan *Entamoeba histolytica*, is characterised by a gradual onset of low-grade diarrhoea, often with blood and mucus. Cramping abdominal pain and vomiting are less likely than in other types of diarrhoea, and fever may not be present. It will persist until treated and can recur and cause other health problems.

You should seek medical advice if you think you have giardiasis or amoebic dysentery, but where this is not possible, tinidazole or metronidazole are the recommended drugs. Treatment is a 2g single dose of tinidazole or 250mg of metronidazole three times daily for five to 10 days.

Fungal Infections These occur more commonly in hot weather and are usually found on the scalp, between the toes (athlete's foot) or fingers, in the groin and on the body (ringworm). You get ringworm (which is a fungal infection, not a worm) from infected animals or other people. Moisture encourages these infections.

To prevent fungal infections wear loose, comfortable clothes, avoid artificial fibres, wash frequently and dry yourself carefully. If you do get an infection, wash the infected area at least daily with a disinfectant or medicated soap and water, and rinse and dry well. Apply an antifungal cream or powder such as tolnaftate. Try to expose the infected area to air or sunlight as much as possible and wash all towels and underwear in hot water, change them often and let them dry in the sun.

Hepatitis The general term for inflammation of the liver is hepatitis. It is quite a common disease worldwide. Several different viruses cause hepatitis, and they differ in the way that they are transmitted. The symptoms are similar in all forms of the illness, and include fever, chills, headache, fatigue, feelings of weakness and aches and pains, followed by loss of appetite, nausea, vomiting, abdominal pain, dark urine, light-coloured faeces, jaundiced (yellow) skin and yellowing of the whites of the eyes. People who have had hepatitis should avoid alcohol for some time after the illness, as the liver needs time to recover.

Hepatitis A is transmitted by contaminated food and drinking water. You should seek medical advice, but there is not much you can do apart from resting, drinking lots of fluids, eating lightly and avoiding fatty foods. Hepatitis E is transmitted in the same way as hepatitis A; it can be particularly serious in pregnant women.

There are almost 300 million chronic carriers of hepatitis B in the world. It is spread through contact with infected blood, blood products or body fluids, for example through sexual contact, unsterilised needles and blood transfusions, or contact with blood via small breaks in the skin. Other risk situations include having a shave, tattoo or body piercing with contaminated equipment. The symptoms of hepatitis B

may be more severe than type A and the disease can lead to long-term problems such as chronic liver damage, liver cancer or a long-term carrier state. Hepatitis C and D are spread in the same way as hepatitis B and can also lead to long-term complications.

There are vaccines against hepatitis A and B, but there are currently no vaccines against the other types of hepatitis. Following the basic rules about food and water (hepatitis A and E) and avoiding risk situations (hepatitis B, C and D) are important preventative measures.

HIV & AIDS Infection with the human immunodeficiency virus (HIV) may lead to acquired immune deficiency syndrome (AIDS), which is a fatal disease. Any exposure to blood, blood products or body fluids may put the individual at risk. The disease is often transmitted through sexual contact or dirty needles – vaccinations, acupuncture, tattooing and body piercing can be potentially as dangerous as intravenous drug use. HIV/AIDS can also be spread through infected blood transfusions. Although India does have the resources to screen blood donations, extreme care should still be

HIV/AIDS in India

In 2000 India recorded the highest number of HIV infections on the planet, with 3.7 million reported cases of HIV – a figure believed to be artificially low as most HIV infections and deaths due to AIDS go unreported. Mumbai has the highest rate of infection in India. In this city an estimated 72% of sex workers (who service an average of 50 clients each per day) are believed to be HIV-positive. Apart from sex workers, truck drivers (nationwide) also fall into the high-risk category.

In a country of more than one billion people, some health officials warn that unless there are dedicated educational programmes and increased condom use throughout India, the number of HIV-positive cases could swell to a staggering 31 million by 2010.

taken, as not all laboratories have adequate controls implemented to ensure that this is done thoroughly. If you do require an injection, ask to see the syringe being unwrapped in front of you, or else take a needle and syringe pack with you. Fear of HIV infection should never preclude treatment for serious medical conditions.

Intestinal Worms These parasites are most common in rural, tropical areas. The different worms have different ways of infecting people. Some (eg, tapeworms) may be ingested on food such as undercooked meat, and some (eg, hookworms) enter through your skin. Infestations may not show up for some time, and although they are generally not serious, if left untreated some can cause severe health problems later. Consider having a stool test when you return home to check for these and determine the appropriate treatment.

Meningococcal Meningitis This serious disease can be fatal. There are recurring epidemics in northern India and Nepal. A fever, severe headache, sensitivity to light and neck stiffness, which prevents forward bending of the head, are the first symptoms. There may also be purple patches on the skin. Death can occur within a few hours, so urgent medical treatment is required. The disease is spread by close contact with people who carry it in their throats and noses and spread it through coughs and sneezes; they may not be aware that they are carriers. Treatment is large doses of penicillin given intravenously, or chloramphenicol injections.

Sexually Transmitted Infections (STIs) HIV/ AIDS and hepatitis B can both be transmitted through sexual contact – see the relevant sections earlier for more details. Other STIs include gonorrhoea, herpes and syphilis; sores, blisters or rashes around the genitals and discharges or pain when urinating are common symptoms. In some STIs, such as wart virus or chlamydia, symptoms may be less marked or not observed at all, especially in women. Chlamydia infection can cause infertility in men and women

before any symptoms have been noticed. Syphilis symptoms eventually disappear completely but the disease continues and can cause severe problems in later years. While abstinence is the only 100% effective prevention, using condoms is also effective. Gonorrhoea and syphilis are treated with antibiotics. The different diseases each require specific antibiotics.

Travellers to Rajasthan should consider bringing along condoms from their home country, which may be more reliable than local brands.

Typhoid This fever is a dangerous gut infection caused by contaminated water and food. Medical help must be sought.

In its early stages sufferers may feel they have a bad cold or flu on the way, as early symptoms are a headache, body aches and a fever that rises a little each day until it is around 40°C (104°F) or more. The victim's pulse is often slow relative to the degree of fever present – unlike a normal fever where the pulse increases. Other symptoms include vomiting, abdominal pain, diarrhoea or constipation.

In the second week the high fever and slow pulse continue and a few pink spots may appear on the body; trembling, delirium, weakness, weight loss and dehydration may occur. Complications such as pneumonia, perforated bowel or meningitis may occur.

Insect-Borne Diseases

Filariasis, leishmaniasis, Lyme disease and typhus are all insect-borne diseases, but they do not pose a great risk to travellers. For more information on them see Less Common Diseases later.

Malaria This serious and potentially fatal disease is spread by mosquito bites. If you are travelling in endemic areas it is extremely important to avoid mosquito bites and to take tablets to prevent this disease. Symptoms range from fever, chills and sweating, headache, diarrhoea and abdominal pains to a vague feeling of ill-health. Seek medical help immediately if malaria is suspected. Without treatment malaria can rapidly become more serious and can be fatal.

There is a variety of medications such as mefloquine, Fansidar and Malarone. You should seek medical advice, before you travel, on the right medication and dosage for you. If medical care is not available, malaria tablets can be used for treatment. You need to use a malaria tablet that is different from the one you were taking when you contracted malaria. Travellers are advised to prevent mosquito bites at all times. The main messages are:

- Wear light-coloured clothing.
- Wear long trousers and long-sleeved shirts.
- Use mosquito repellents containing the compound DEET on exposed areas (prolonged overuse of DEET may be harmful, especially to children, but its use is considered preferable to being bitten by disease-transmitting mosquitoes).
- Avoid perfumes or aftershave.
- Use a mosquito net impregnated with mosquito repellent (permethrin) – it may be worth taking your own.
- Impregnate your clothes with permethrin, which effectively deters mosquitoes and other insects.

Dengue Fever This viral disease is transmitted by mosquitoes and is fast becoming one of the top public-health problems in the tropical world. Unlike the malaria mosquito, the *Aedes aegypti* mosquito, which transmits the dengue virus, is most active during the day, and is found mainly in urban areas, in and around human dwellings.

Signs and symptoms of dengue fever include a sudden onset of high fever, headache, joint and muscle pains (hence its old name, 'breakbone fever') and nausea and vomiting. A rash of small red spots sometimes appears three to four days after the onset of fever. In the early phase of illness, dengue may be mistaken for other infectious diseases, including malaria and influenza. Minor bleeding such as nose bleeds may occur in the course of the illness, but this does not necessarily mean that you have progressed to the potentially fatal dengue haemorrhagic fever (DHF). This is a severe illness, characterised by heavy

bleeding, which is thought to be a result of second infection due to a different strain (there are four major strains) and usually affects residents of the country rather than travellers. Recovery even from simple dengue fever may be prolonged, with tiredness lasting for several weeks.

You should seek medical attention as soon as possible if you think you may be infected. A blood test can exclude malaria and indicate the possibility of dengue fever. There is no specific treatment for dengue. Aspirin should be avoided, as it increases the risk of haemorrhaging. There is no vaccine against dengue fever. The best prevention is to avoid mosquito bites at all times by covering up, using insect repellents containing the compound DEET and mosquito nets – see Malaria earlier for more advice on avoiding mosquito bites.

Japanese B Encephalitis This viral infection of the brain is transmitted by mosquitoes. Most cases occur in rural areas as the virus exists in pigs and wading birds. Symptoms include fever, headache and alteration in consciousness. Hospitalisation is needed for correct diagnosis and treatment. There is a high mortality rate among those who have symptoms; of those who survive many are intellectually disabled.

Cuts, Bites & Stings
See Less Common Diseases later for details of rabies, which is passed through animal bites.

Cuts & Scratches Wash well and treat any cut with an antiseptic such as povidone-iodine. Where possible avoid bandages and Band-Aids, which can keep wounds wet.

Bedbugs & Lice Bedbugs live in various places, but particularly in dirty mattresses and bedding, evidenced by spots of blood on bedclothes or on the wall. Bedbugs leave itchy bites in neat rows. Calamine lotion or a sting relief spray may help.

All lice cause itching and discomfort. They make themselves at home in your hair (head lice), your clothing (body lice) or in your pubic hair (crabs). You catch lice through direct contact with infected people or by sharing combs, clothing and the like. Powder or shampoo treatment will kill the lice and infected clothing should then be washed in very hot, soapy water and left in the sun to dry.

Bites & Stings Bee and wasp stings are usually painful rather than dangerous. However, in people who are allergic to them severe breathing difficulties may occur and require urgent medical care. Calamine lotion or a sting-relief spray will give relief and ice packs will reduce the pain and swelling. There are some spiders with dangerous bites but antivenins are usually available. Scorpion stings are notoriously painful and can actually be fatal. Scorpions often shelter in shoes or clothing.

Ticks You should always check all over your body if you have been walking through a potentially tick-infested area as ticks can cause skin infections and other more serious diseases. If a tick is found attached, press down around the tick's head with tweezers, grab the head and gently pull upwards. Avoid pulling the rear of the body as this may squeeze the tick's gut contents through the attached mouth parts into the skin, increasing the risk of infection and disease. Smearing chemicals on the tick will not make it let go and is not recommended.

Snakes To minimise your chances of being bitten always wear boots, socks and long trousers when walking through undergrowth where snakes may be present. Don't put your hands into holes and crevices, and be careful when collecting firewood.

Snake bites do not cause instantaneous death and antivenins are usually available. Immediately wrap the bitten limb tightly, as you would for a sprained ankle, and then attach a splint to immobilise it. Keep the victim still and seek medical help, if possible with the dead snake for identification. Don't attempt to catch the snake if there is a possibility of being bitten again. Tourniquets and sucking out the poison are now comprehensively discredited.

Women's Health

Gynaecological Problems Antibiotic use, synthetic underwear, sweating and contraceptive pills can lead to fungal vaginal infections, especially when travelling in hot climates. Thrush or vaginal candidiasis is characterised by a rash, itch and discharge. Nystatin, miconazole or clotrimazole pessaries are the usual treatment; some people use a more traditional remedy involving vinegar or lemon-juice douches, or yogurt. Maintaining good personal hygiene and wearing loose-fitting clothes and cotton underwear may help prevent these infections.

Sexually transmitted infections are a major cause of vaginal problems. Symptoms include a smelly discharge, painful intercourse and sometimes a burning sensation when urinating. Medical attention should be sought and male sexual partners must also be treated. For more details see Sexually Transmitted Infections earlier. Besides abstinence, the best thing is to practise safer sex using condoms.

Pregnancy It is not advisable to travel to some places while pregnant as some vaccinations normally used to prevent serious diseases are not advisable during pregnancy (eg, yellow fever). In addition, some diseases are much more serious for the mother (and may increase the risk of a stillborn child) in pregnancy (eg, malaria).

Most miscarriages occur during the first three months of pregnancy. Miscarriage is not uncommon and can occasionally lead to severe bleeding. The last three months should also be spent within reasonable distance of good medical care. A baby born as early as 24 weeks stands a chance of survival, but only in a good modern hospital. Pregnant women should avoid all unnecessary medication, although vaccinations and malarial prophylactics should still be taken where needed. Additional care should be taken to prevent illness and particular attention should be paid to diet and nutrition. Alcohol and nicotine, for example, should be avoided.

Less Common Diseases

The following diseases pose a small risk to travellers, and so are only mentioned in passing. Seek medical advice if you think you may have any of these diseases.

Cholera This is the worst of the watery diarrhoeas and medical help should be sought. Outbreaks of cholera are generally widely reported, so you can avoid such problem areas. *Fluid replacement is the most vital treatment* – the risk of dehydration is severe as you may lose up to 20L a day. If there is a delay in getting to hospital, then begin taking tetracycline. The adult dose is 250mg four times daily. It is not recommended for children under nine years nor for pregnant women. Tetracycline may help shorten the illness, but adequate fluids are required to save lives.

Filariasis This is a mosquito-transmitted parasitic infection found in India and other parts of Asia. Possible symptoms include fever, pain and swelling of the lymph glands; inflammation of lymph drainage areas; swelling of a limb or the scrotum; skin rashes; and blindness. Treatment is available to eliminate the parasites from the body, but some of the damage already caused may not be reversible. Medical advice should be obtained promptly if the infection is suspected.

Leishmaniasis This is a group of parasitic diseases transmitted by sandflies, which are found in India and other parts of the world. Cutaneous leishmaniasis affects the skin tissue causing ulceration and disfigurement, and visceral leishmaniasis affects the internal organs. Seek medical advice, as laboratory testing is required for diagnosis and correct treatment. Avoiding sandfly bites is the best precaution. Bites are usually painless, itchy and yet another reason to cover up and apply repellent.

Lyme Disease This tick-transmitted infection may also be acquired in India. The illness usually begins with a spreading rash at the site of the tick bite and is accompanied by fever, headache, extreme fatigue, aching joints and muscles and mild neck stiffness. If left untreated, these symptoms usually resolve over several weeks but over subsequent weeks or months disorders of the nervous system, heart and joints may develop. Treatment works best early in the illness. Medical help should be sought.

Rabies This fatal viral infection is found in many countries, including India. Many animals can be infected (such as dogs, cats, bats and monkeys) and it is their saliva that is infectious. Any bite, scratch or even lick from an animal should be cleaned immediately and thoroughly. Scrub with soap and running water, and then apply alcohol or iodine solution. Medical help should be sought promptly to receive a course of injections to prevent the onset of symptoms and death.

Tetanus This disease is caused by a germ that lives in soil and in the faeces of horses and other animals. It enters the body via breaks in the skin. The first symptom may be discomfort in swallowing, or stiffening of the jaw and neck; this is followed by painful convulsions of the jaw and whole body. The disease can be fatal. It can be prevented by vaccination.

Tuberculosis This bacterial infection is usually transmitted from person to person by coughing; it may also be transmitted through consumption of unpasteurised milk. Milk that has been boiled is safe to drink, and the souring of milk to make yogurt or cheese also kills the bacilli. Travellers are usually not at great risk of tuberculosis (TB) as close household contact with the infected person is usually required before the disease is passed on. You may need to have a TB test before you travel as this can help diagnose the disease later if you become ill.

Typhus This disease is spread by ticks, mites or lice. It begins with fever, chills, headache and muscle pains followed a few days later by a body rash. There is often a large painful sore at the site of the bite and nearby lymph nodes are swollen and painful. Typhus can be treated under medical supervision. Seek local advice on areas where ticks pose a danger and always check your skin carefully for ticks after walking in a danger area such as a tropical forest. An insect repellent can help, and walkers in tick-infested areas should consider having their boots and trousers impregnated with benzyl benzoate and dibutylphthalate.

WOMEN TRAVELLERS
Attitudes Towards Women

Rajasthan is generally perfectly safe for women travellers, even for those travelling alone. Although foreign women (including those of Indian descent) have been hassled, being ogled (incessantly) is the worst you'll probably encounter, and Rajasthan is, unfortunately, no exception.

The tips provided here are intended to reduce the problems, not to alarm you. (See also Women in Society under Society & Conduct in the Facts about Rajasthan chapter.)

Women travelling with a male partner are less likely to be harassed. However, a woman of Indian descent travelling with a non-Indian male should be prepared to cop disapproving stares; having a non-Indian partner is still not condoned in many parts of India.

Being a woman has some advantages. Women can usually queue-jump without consequence and use 'ladies-only carriages' on trains. There are even special ladies' sections in some cinemas, restaurants and other public places.

For information on what to take, see Planning earlier in this chapter.

What to Wear

Staying safe is a matter of common sense and culturally appropriate behaviour. Close attention to standards of dress will go a long way to minimising problems for female travellers. Refrain from wearing sleeveless blouses, shorts, skimpy or tight-fitting clothing and, of course, the bra-less look. Women who publicly flash ample flesh are not only making themselves an easy target for sexual harassment, they're also making it hard for fellow travellers by painting a poor image of foreign women in general.

Wearing Indian dress, when done properly, makes a positive impression.

Wearing a *choli* (small tight blouse worn under a sari) or a sari petticoat (which many foreign women mistake for a skirt) in public is rather like strutting around half dressed – don't do it. On the other hand, the *salwar kameez* (traditional Punjabi tunic-and-trouser combination) is considered to be respectable attire and has become increasingly popular among female travellers. It's practical, comfortable and attractive and comes in a range of prices. A cotton *salwar kameez* is also surprisingly cool in the hot weather and keeps the burning sun off your skin. The *dupatta* (long scarf) that is worn with this outfit is handy if you visit a shrine that requires your head to be covered.

Safety Precautions

Getting constantly stared at is something you'll simply have to get used to. Don't allow it to get the better of you. Just walk confidently and refrain from returning male stares, as this may be considered a come-on; dark glasses can help. A good way to block out stares in restaurants is to take along a book or letters to write home.

Whenever you wish to keep conversations short, get to the point as quickly and politely as possible. Getting involved in inane conversations with men can be considered a turn-on. Questions such as 'Has anyone ever told you that your eyes are like the sunset?' or 'Do you have a boyfriend?' are strong indicators that the conversation may be going off on a steamy tangent. Some women prepare in advance by wearing a pseudo wedding ring, or by announcing early on in the conversation that they are married or engaged (regardless of whether they are or not). This is a highly effective way of keeping interactions 'lust-free'. If you still get the uncomfortable feeling that he's encroaching on your space, chances are that he is. A firm request to keep away is usually enough to take control of the situation – especially if it's loud enough to draw the attention of passers-by. If this request is ignored, the silent treatment (not responding to questions at all) is usually an effective way of getting rid of unwanted male company.

On trains and buses, sit next to a woman or child if you can. If you find yourself next to a man who tries to take liberties, don't hesitate to return any errant limbs, put some item of luggage in between you or, if all else fails, find a new spot. You're also within your rights to tell him to shove off! It's wise to arrive in towns before it gets dark and, of course, avoid walking alone at night especially in isolated areas.

Other harassment that women travellers in India have encountered includes lewd comments, provocative gestures, jeering, getting 'accidentally' bumped into on the street, and being groped. There have been several reported cases of rape among foreign women. Exuberant special events (such as the Holi festival) can pose problems for women (see Dangers & Annoyances later in this chapter).

GAY & LESBIAN TRAVELLERS

Homosexual relations for men are illegal in India. Section 377 of the Indian Penal Code forbids 'carnal intercourse against the order of nature' (that is, anal sex). The penalties for transgression can be up to life imprisonment. There is no law against lesbian relations.

Although the more liberal sections of certain cities (predominantly the larger centres such as Mumbai and Delhi) are becoming more tolerant of homosexuality, generally gay life is still largely suppressed in India. You may see Indian men holding hands with each other or engaged in other public affectionate behaviour, but don't instantly assume they are gay; this is an accepted expression of nonsexual friendship.

Since marriage is still very highly regarded in India, most gay people stay in the closet or risk being disowned by their families and society.

India's most visible nonheterosexual group is the *hijras* – a caste of transvestites and eunuchs who dress in women's clothing. Some are gay, some are hermaphrodites and some were unfortunate enough to be kidnapped and castrated. As it is traditionally unacceptable to live openly as a gay man, *hijras* get around this by becoming, in effect, a sort of third sex. They work mainly as uninvited entertainers at weddings and celebrations of the birth of male children, and as prostitutes.

As with relations between heterosexual Western couples travelling in Rajasthan – both married and unmarried – gay and lesbian travellers should exercise discretion and refrain from displaying overt affection towards each other in public.

The Mumbai publication *Bombay Dost* is a popular gay-and-lesbian magazine available at a number of bookshops and news stands in the larger cities.

For further information about India's gay scene, there are some excellent websites, including Gay Delhi (W www.members .tripod.com/gaydelhi), Humarahi (W www .geocities.com/WestHollywood/Heights/72 58), Bombay Dost (W www.bombay-dost .com) and Humsafar (W www.humsafar.org).

DISABLED TRAVELLERS

Travelling in Rajasthan can entail some fairly rigorous challenges, even for the able-bodied traveller – long bus trips in crowded vehicles between remote villages, the crush of people in larger towns, and the steep staircases in some budget and mid-range hotels can test even the hardiest traveller. If you can't walk, these challenges are increased many times. Very few buildings have wheelchair access; toilets have certainly not been designed to accommodate wheelchairs; footpaths, where they exist (only in larger towns), are generally riddled with holes, littered with debris and packed with pedestrians, severely restricting mobility. However, seeing the mobility-impaired locals whizz through city traffic at breakneck speed in modified bicycles may serve as inspiration! If your mobility is restricted you will definitely need a strong, able-bodied companion to accompany you, and it would be well worth considering hiring a private vehicle and driver.

Organisations that may be able to assist with information on travel practicalities in India for disabled people include:

Concerned Action Now (CAN; 011-613 2815, fax 610 4865, W www.indev.nic.in/can)

B-4, 3067 Vasant Kunj, Aruna Asaf Ali Rd,
New Delhi 110 070, India
The Royal Association for Disability and Rehabilitation (Radar; ☎ 020-7250 3222, fax 250 0212, [W] www.radar.org.uk) 12 City Forum, 250 City Rd, London EC1V 8AF, UK
Wheelchair Travel (☎ 1800-674 468, [W] www.travelability.com) 29 Ranelagh Dr, Mount Eliza, Vic 3930, Australia

SENIOR TRAVELLERS

Unless your mobility or vision is severely impaired or you're seriously incapacitated in any other way, there is absolutely no reason why the senior traveller should not consider Rajasthan as a potential holiday destination.

It's worth keeping in mind that travelling in Rajasthan can be downright exhausting (even for the most effervescent young traveller), so try not to cram too much sightseeing into a day. In fact, it's not a bad idea to set aside several intermittent days devoted purely to doing absolutely nothing – a tremendous way to recharge your batteries.

If you like your creature comforts, opt for top-end or mid-range hotels (although some mid-range places are far from luxurious) and consider incorporating some organised tours into your trip. Many senior travellers hire a car and driver, which allows greater flexibility (and comfort) in moving around than does public transport. (See Car in the Getting Around chapter.)

No matter what you plan to do in Rajasthan, it's wise to discuss your proposed trip with your doctor (see also Health earlier in this chapter).

TRAVEL WITH CHILDREN

Rajasthan is a very child-friendly destination, not so much because of the facilities available for kids, but rather in the way children are accepted being seen and heard. Indeed, children can often enhance your encounters with local people, as they possess little of the self-consciousness and sense of the cultural differences that can inhibit interaction between adults.

Being a family-oriented society, children are heartily welcomed at most hotels and restaurants. A number of hotels have 'family rooms' or will happily provide an extra bed. Some upmarket hotels also offer babysitting services.

When it comes to meals, although few restaurants offer a special children's menu, many will happily whip up simple requests. Staff don't usually get snooty if your little angels treat the dining area a bit like a playroom (please take the initiative to ensure they don't ruin it for other diners, though).

It's worth bringing along some favourite books, toys and hand-held video games to keep the children occupied when you need some quiet time. If you're staying in a hotel with cable TV, there are several English-language children's channels, including the Cartoon Network.

Despite the acceptance of children, travelling with kids in Rajasthan can be hard work and, ideally, the burden needs to be shared between two adults. Although caution should be exercised at all times, be especially careful near roads, as Indian traffic can be erratic, even in smaller towns. Any long-distance road travel undertaken should include adequate stops, as rough road conditions can make travel more tiring than usual, especially for little ones. Train is usually a more comfortable mode of travel, especially for long trips. Remember to bring enough sunscreen and a wide-brimmed hat, as the midday sun can really pack a punch (even during winter). Always carry sufficient drinking water.

Standard baby products such as nappies (diapers) are available in big cities and even in smaller towns; the larger cities often stock some Western brands too, but they can be expensive. It's wise to bring from home any special items such as medication and baby food if your child is fussy, just in case you can't locate them in Rajasthan. Travellers have also recommended that parents bring a washable changing mat, which comes in handy for covering dirty surfaces.

See Health earlier in this chapter for important tips, and get hold of a copy of Lonely Planet's *Travel with Children* by Cathy Lanigan. The Thorn Tree bulletin board on Lonely Planet's website ([W] www .lonelyplanet.com.au) has a subdirectory on travelling with children.

DANGERS & ANNOYANCES

Like anywhere else, common sense and reasonable caution are your best weapons against theft or worse. The tips we offer are intended to alert you to possible risks in India, most of which are based on travellers' reports. During your trip, it's worth taking the time to chat with other travellers, hotel staff and tour operators in order to stay abreast of the latest potential hazards.

Theft

Never leave those most important valuables (passport, tickets, money) in your room; they should be with you at all times. On trains, keep your gear near you; padlocking a bag to a luggage rack can be useful, and some of the newer trains have loops under the seats that you can chain things to. Never walk around with valuables casually slung over your shoulder. Take extra care on crowded public transport.

Thieves are particularly prevalent on train routes where there are lots of tourists. The Delhi to Agra *Shatabdi Express* service is particularly notorious; Delhi to Jaipur, Jaipur to Ajmer and Jodhpur to Jaisalmer are other routes to take care on. No matter which train you are travelling on exercise caution at all times. Train departure time, when the confusion and crowds are at their worst, is the time to be most careful. One ploy is that just as the train is about to leave, you are distracted by someone while their accomplice is stealing your bag from by your feet. Airports are another place to be careful, especially if arriving in the middle of the night when you are unlikely to be at your most alert.

From time to time there are also drugging episodes. Travellers meet somebody on a train or bus or in a town, start talking and are then offered a *chai* (tea) or something similar. Hours later the traveller wakes up with a headache and all their gear gone, the tea having been full of sleeping pills. Be cautious about accepting drinks or food from strangers, particularly if you're on your own.

Beware, also, of your fellow travellers. Unhappily, there are sometimes more than a

few backpackers who make their money go a little bit further by helping themselves to other people's. If you're staying in a dorm with lockers, use them.

Keep in mind that backpacks are very easy to rifle through. Never leave valuables in them, especially during flights. Remember also that some things, such as film, may be of little or no value to a thief, but to lose them would be a real heartbreak to you.

A good travel insurance policy is essential. If you do have something stolen, you're going to have to report it to the police. You'll also need a statement proving you have done so if you want to make an insurance claim. Insurance companies, despite their rosy promises of full protection and speedy settlement of claims, are just as disbelieving as the Indian police and will often attempt every trick in the book to avoid paying out on a baggage claim. Note that some policies specify that you must report an item stolen to the police within a certain amount of time after you observe that it is missing.

Travellers Cheques If you're unlucky enough to have things stolen, some precautions can ease the pain. All travellers cheques are replaceable, although this does you little immediate good if you have to go home and apply to your bank. What you want is instant replacement. Furthermore, what do you do if you lose your cheques and money and have a day or more to travel to the replacement office? The answer is to keep an emergency cash stash in a totally separate place. In that same place you should keep a record of the cheques' serial numbers, proof of purchase slips, encashment vouchers and your passport number.

AmEx and others tend to make considerable noise about 'instant replacement' of their cheques but a lot of people find out, to their cost, that without a number of precautions 'instantly' can take longer than you think. If you don't have the receipt you were given when you bought the cheques, rapid replacement will be difficult. Obviously the receipt should be kept separate from the cheques, and a photocopy in yet another location doesn't hurt either.

To replace lost AmEx travellers cheques you need a photocopy of the police report and one photo, as well as the proof-of-purchase slip and the numbers of the missing cheques. If you don't have the latter they will contact the place where you bought them. If you've had the lot stolen, AmEx is empowered to give you limited funds while all this is going on. For lost or stolen cheques, it has a 24-hour number in Delhi (☎ 011-6145151) that you must ring within 24 hours of the theft.

Holi Festival

The Hindu festival of Holi isn't dubbed the 'Festival of Colours' for nothing. The festival is celebrated in late February/early March with much zeal (see the boxed text 'Festivals of Rajasthan' later in this chapter for forthcoming dates) and the last day is marked by the exuberant and excessive throwing of coloured *gulal* (powder) and water. Merrymakers will douse anything that moves (pedestrians, buses, rickshaws...good God, even the holy cow gets walloped!). Foreign visitors are also considered fair game for a dousing – especially in tourist spots such as Udaipur, Jaipur and Jodhpur. There have been several reports of toxic substances being mixed with the water, leaving targets with painful and disfiguring scars. There is also an unwritten tradition of guzzling alcohol and consuming cannabis-derived *bhang* during Holi. Female travellers have reported being groped by spaced-out blokes. It's advisable for women to avoid venturing onto the streets alone on the last day of Holi, when this festival reaches its climax.

Contaminated Food & Drink

Sometimes microbes aren't the sole or main risk when it comes to eating and drinking. In Rajasthan *bhang* lassis can pack more of a punch than the hapless traveller would probably expect.

There have also been reports that some private clinics have provided more treatment than is necessary for stomach upsets in order to procure larger medical insurance claims – get several opinions where possible. Worse still, a serious food scare broke out in northern India in 1998, principally in Agra and Varanasi, when numerous travellers became sick and two died after eating at local establishments where their food was adulterated.

Water can also be a potential problem. Always ensure the seal is intact when you buy mineral water and also check that the bottom of the bottle has not been tampered with. You should always crush plastic bottles after using them and help eradicate the possibility of them being resold containing contaminated water. Better still, you could bring along water-purification tablets in order to avoid adding to Rajasthan's alarming waste plastic problem (see Responsible Tourism and Health earlier in this chapter).

Racism

It's not unusual for black travellers to encounter outright racism in India. Speak to African students in India and you'll often hear about racist attitudes towards them, ranging from name-calling to being refused admission to certain restaurants, hotels and nightclubs.

Although skin colour is not always related to caste in India, lighter shades of brown are considered more attractive than dark skin – just have a good look at the matrimonial pages in Indian newspapers and you'll see that being 'fair' is often a prerequisite for a potential spouse.

Although not all black travellers encounter racism during their time in Rajasthan, at the very least they should be prepared for even more incessant (often disapproving) stares than lighter-skinned travellers.

Other Important Warnings

Gem scams are a major problem in Rajasthan, especially Jaipur, and many people have been hoodwinked by dealers who convince them to part with large sums of money for gems to resell at home. Invariably the gems are overpriced, and sometimes they turn out to be glass – see the boxed text 'A Warning!' later in this chapter for further details.

Unfortunately Delhi is one of the worst places in India for scamming travellers, and since most people heading to Rajasthan enter through Delhi, they're often unprepared for the elaborate swindles launched upon them. See the boxed text 'Dodgy Delhi' in the Delhi chapter for some tips on avoiding scams in that city.

EMERGENCIES

Throughout many parts of Rajasthan, local emergency numbers are as follows:

Ambulance	☎ 102
Fire	☎ 101
Police	☎ 100

LEGAL MATTERS

If you find yourself in a sticky legal predicament, immediately contact your embassy (see Embassies & Consulates earlier in this chapter). Foreign travellers are subject to Indian laws and in the Indian justice system it can often seem that the burden of proof is on the accused.

You should carry your passport at all times and the less you have to do with local police the better.

Drugs

India has long been known for its smorgasbord of illegal drugs (mostly grass and hashish), but would-be users should be aware of the severe risks. Apart from opening yourself up to being taken advantage of, the penalties for possession, use and trafficking in illegal drugs are enforced and Westerners have been jailed. If convicted on a drugs-related charge, sentences are a minimum of 10 years for trafficking and at least a year for possession. In addition, there's usually a hefty monetary fine.

Court appearances can be slow – in early 2000 there were an estimated 25 million cases waiting to be heard in courts around India!

Smoking

In 2001 the Indian government banned smoking in public places, including on public transport, at bus and train stations and in restaurants. It also prohibited all forms of tobacco advertising. The ban does not cover snuff and chewing tobacco, which together account for the bulk of tobacco consumption in India.

BUSINESS HOURS

Official business hours are generally from 9.30am to 5.30pm Monday to Friday. Unofficially they tend to be more like 10am to 5pm. Government offices in particular seem to have lengthy lunch hours, which are sacrosanct and can last from noon to late into the afternoon.

Most banks are open form 10am to 5pm Monday to Friday, and from 10am to noon on Saturday – there are variations on these hours, so it pays to check. Travellers-cheque transactions usually cease 30 minutes before the official bank closing time and are sometimes available for only a few hours each day. In some tourist centres there may be foreign-exchange offices, which often stay open longer than banks (eg, Thomas Cook is open 9.30am to 6pm Monday to Saturday).

In the large towns, the main post office is generally open from 10am to 5pm Monday to Friday and on Saturday morning. Many public institutions such as museums and galleries close at least one day during the week – government museums are usually closed on Friday. Tourist reception centres are generally closed on Sunday and every second Saturday.

Shop opening hours vary, but most tend to open from around 10am until late afternoon Monday to Saturday. In the more popular tourist areas, such as Udaipur, Jaisalmer and Pushkar, many shops open at around 9am and don't close until around 7pm, and about half close on Sunday.

PUBLIC HOLIDAYS & SPECIAL EVENTS

Rich in religions and traditions, Rajasthan has scores of vibrant holidays and festivals. Many festivals occur during *purnima* (full moon), which is considered to be traditionally auspicious. Websites that have more -information about festivals in India include W www.hindunet.org/festivals and W www .indiatimes.com (see Festivals under Arts earlier in this chapter).

The 'wedding season' generally falls between the cooler months of November and March (although dates still revolve around auspicious dates set by astrologers). If you visit during this period, you're likely to see a few wedding processions on the street every evening – a merry mix of singing and dancing. They're often accompanied by a procession of fluorescent lights powered by a generator on a cycle-cart, and a loud brass band that almost drowns out the noise of the generator.

Most holidays and festivals follow either the Indian lunar calendar (a complex system determined chiefly by astrologers) or the Islamic calendar (which falls about 11 days earlier each year; 12 days earlier in leap years), and therefore changes from year to year according to the Gregorian calendar.

The holidays and festivals listed below are arranged according to the Indian lunar (and Gregorian) calendar, which starts in

Regional Festival Calendar

Descriptions of regional festivals are included at the beginning of each regional chapter and festivals are marked on the regional maps. A quick reference for dates of the major regional fairs and festivals up to the year 2006 follows:

festival & location	2003	2004	2005	2006
Nagaur Fair, Nagaur	8–12 Feb	28–31 Jan	15–18 Feb	4–7 Feb
Desert Festival, Jaisalmer	15–16 Feb	4–6 Feb	21–24 Feb	10–13 Feb
Baneshwar Fair, Baneshwar	13–16 Feb	1–6 Feb	19–24 Feb	8–13 Feb
Brij Festival, Bharatpur	14–16 Mar	2–4 Mar	21–23 Mar	10–12 Mar
Elephant Festival, Jaipur	17 Mar	6 Mar	25 Mar	14 Mar
Gangaur Fair, Jaipur	4–5 Apr	23–24 Mar	11–12 Apr	1–2 Apr
Mewar Festival, Udaipur	4–5 Apr	23–24 Mar	11–12 Apr	1–2 Apr
Summer Festival, Mt Abu	1–3 June	1–3 June	1–3 June	
Teej, Jaipur	1–2 Aug	19–20 Aug	8–9 Aug	28–29 July
Kajli Teej, Bundi	14–15 Aug	31 Aug–1 Sept	20–21 Aug	11–12 Aug
Ramdevra Fair, Ramdevra (near Pokaran)	4–5 Sept	22–23 Sept	12–13 Sept	2–3 Sept
Dussehra Mela, Kota	3–5 Oct	20–22 Oct	10–12 Oct	30 Sept–2 Oct
Marwar Festival, Jodhpur	8–9 Oct	26–27 Oct	16–17 Oct	6–7 Oct
Pushkar Camel Fair, Pushkar	31 Oct–8 Nov	18–26 Nov	8–15 Nov	29 Oct–5 Nov
Chandrabhaga Fair, Jhalawar	7–10 Nov	25–27 Nov	14–16 Nov	4–6 Nov
Kolayat Fair, Kolayat (near Bikaner)	4–14 Nov	22 Nov–2 Dec	12–21 Nov	2–10 Nov

Food is abundant on Rajasthan's streets. Markets display fresh produce in technicolour (left) and stock stacks of jaggery, a form of raw sugar (top right). Street stalls sell everything from *kachoris* (corn or lentil savouries; centre right) to tasty crisps, samosas and pakoras (bottom).

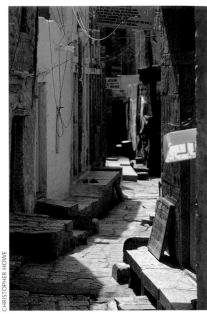

DALLAS STRIBLEY

CHRISTOPHER HOWE

SARA-JANE CLELAND

Stairs to the stars at the Jantar Mantar in Jaipur

It's pedestrians only in Jaisalmer fort's narrow lanes

The rooftops of Udaipur, arguably India's most romantic city, overlook beautiful Lake Pichola

Chaitra (March or April) – contact local tourist offices for the exact dates (especially for Muslim festivals, which have particularly variable dates).

Festivals in Rajasthan generally take one of three forms: purely religious festivals; tourist-oriented festivals; and *melas*, or fairs, such as the Pushkar Camel Fair, which provide opportunities for villagers from the more remote regions to trade livestock and socialise.

The following festivals are celebrated across the entire state of Rajasthan and many are nationwide celebrations. More complete descriptions of regional festivals are included at the beginning of regional chapters.

Chaitra (Mar/Apr)

Gangaur This specifically Rajasthani festival is a celebration of the love between Shiva and his consort Gauri (Parvati), and is a favourite with the women of Rajasthan. Unmarried girls pay homage to Gauri in the hope that they will be blessed with a good husband. Married women pray for the long life and health of their husbands. Images of Gauri are garbed in colourful vestments and carried through the streets in processions. Women perform the *ghoomer* dance, and married women try to be at their husbands' sides during the festival. Jaipur, Bikaner, Jodhpur, Nathdwara and Jaisalmer all host colourful celebrations of Gangaur.

Mahavir Jayanti This Jain festival commemorates the birth of Mahavira, who was the founder of Jainism.

Ramanavami Hindu temples all over India celebrate the birth of Rama. In the week leading up to Ramanavami, the Ramayana is widely read and performed.

Vaisakha (Apr/May)

Muharram This 10-day Muslim festival commemorates the martyrdom of Imam Hussain, Mohammed's grandson.

Baisakhi This Sikh festival commemorates the day that Guru Govind Singh founded the Khalsa, the Sikh brotherhood, which adopted the five *kakkars* (means by which Sikh men recognise each other) as part of their code of behaviour. The Granth Sahib, the Sikh holy book, is read through at *gurdwaras* (Sikh temples). Feasts and dancing follow in the evening.

Sravana (July/Aug)

Teej Also known as the Festival of Swings, which is a reference to the flower-bedecked swings that are erected at this time, Teej celebrates the onset of the monsoon, and is held in honour of the marriage of Shiva and Guari.

Naag Panchami This Hindu festival is dedicated to Ananta, the serpent upon whose coils Vishnu rested between universes. Offerings are made to snake images and snake charmers do a roaring trade at this time. Snakes are supposed to have power over the monsoon rainfall and keep evil from homes.

Raksha Bandhan (Narial Purnima) On the full-moon day of the Hindu month of Sravana, girls fix amulets known as *rakhis* to their brothers' wrists to protect them in the coming year. The brothers give their sisters gifts. A woman can gain the brotherly protection of a man who is not actually her brother by giving him one of these *rakhi*. Political expediency encouraged the maharani of Chittorgarh to honour Emperor Humayun in this manner. Consequently the emperor was compelled to try to save the fort of Chittorgarh from the sultan of Gujarat.

Bhadra (Aug/Sept)

Independence Day This holiday on 15 August celebrates the anniversary of India's independence from Britain in 1947. The prime minister delivers an address from the ramparts of Delhi's Red Fort.

Ganesh Chaturthi This joyful festival celebrates the birth of the popular elephant-headed god, Ganesh, the god of good fortune. It is considered to be the most auspicious day of the year, but to look at the moon on this day is considered unlucky.

Janmashthami The anniversary of Krishna's birth is celebrated with happy abandon – in tune with Krishna's own mischievous moods. Devotees fast all day until midnight.

Shravan Purnima On this day of fasting, high-caste Hindus replace the sacred thread that they always wear looped over their left shoulder.

Asvina (Sept/Oct)

Dussehra The popular festival celebrates Durga's victory over the buffalo-headed demon Mahishasura. In many places it culminates with the burning of huge images of the demon king Ravana and his accomplices, symbolic of the triumph of good over evil. Kota, in southern Rajasthan, celebrates Dussehra with a large *mela*.

Gandhi Jayanti This public holiday, held on 2 October, is a solemn celebration of Mohandas Gandhi's birth anniversary.

Kartika (Oct/Nov)

Diwali (Deepavali) This is the happiest (and noisiest) festival of the Hindu calendar, celebrated on the 15th day of Kartika. At night decorative oil lamps are lit to show Rama the way home from his period of exile. In all, the festival lasts five days. On the first day, houses are thoroughly cleaned and doorsteps are decorated with intricate *rangolis* (chalk designs). Day two is dedicated to Krishna's victory over Narakasura, a legendary tyrant. In the south on this day, a predawn oil bath is followed by the donning of new clothes. Day three is spent worshipping Lakshmi, the goddess of wealth. Traditionally, this is the beginning of the new financial year for companies. Day four commemorates the visit of the friendly demon Bali whom Vishnu put in his place. On the fifth day men visit their sisters to have a *tikka* (mark) put on their forehead. Diwali has also become the 'festival of sweets'. Giving sweets has become as much a part of the tradition as the lighting of oil lamps and firecrackers.

Govardhana Puja A Hindu festival dedicated to the holiest of animals: the cow.

Aghan (Nov/Dec)

Nanak Jayanti The birthday of Guru Nanak, the founder of Sikhism, is celebrated with prayer readings and processions.

Ramadan This 30-day dawn-to-dusk fast is the most auspicious Muslim festival. It was during this month that the Prophet Mohammed had the Quran revealed to him in Mecca. This festival generally occurs between November and December, but can also fall in early January.

Id-ul-Fitr This is a day of feasting to celebrate the end of Ramadan.

Magha (Jan/Feb)

Republic Day This public holiday, on 26 January, celebrates the anniversary of India's establishment as a republic in 1950; celebrations are held in Jaipur.

Phalguna (Feb/Mar)

Holi This is one of the most exuberant Hindu festivals, when people celebrate the end of winter by throwing coloured water and *gulal* (powder) at one another. In tourist places it might be seen as an opportunity to take liberties with foreigners, especially women (see Dangers & Annoyances earlier in this chapter); don't wear good clothes on this day and be ready to duck. On the night before Holi, bonfires are built to symbolise the destruction of the evil demon Holika. Rajasthanis celebrate Holi with particular enthusiasm, and foreign visitors are considered fair game for a dousing with *gulal*. It's great fun, and your best bet is just to give yourself up to the revelry, wear your oldest clothes, and expect to look like a *gulab jamun* (a red, sticky sweet) at the end of the day. Udaipur and Jaisalmer are both excellent venues to celebrate Holi.

Shivaratri This day of Hindu fasting is dedicated to Shiva, who danced the *tandava* (cosmic dance) on this day. Temple processions are followed by the chanting of mantras and anointing of lingams (phallic symbols).

Id-ul-Zuhara This Muslim festival commemorates Abraham's attempt to sacrifice his son.

ACTIVITIES

For more information on the activities listed here, see the relevant sections of the regional chapters.

Camel Safaris

Just about everyone in Rajasthan is offering camel safaris these days. Apart from hotels there are specialist operators, and it's possible to take a safari lasting from one day up to several weeks. A favourite is the Jaisalmer region, in western Rajasthan, and prices vary according to what is provided. Basic safaris start at about Rs 400 per person per day, which includes meals, but you pay more for greater comfort. The Pushkar area is also popular, and a couple of operators in Shekhawati offer camel treks around towns with interesting painted havelis in this semiarid region. Several operators in Bikaner (western Rajasthan) also offer good camel safaris and there are a few operators in Jodhpur.

Horse & Jeep Safaris

Some hotels can arrange horse safaris, such as the Mount Hotel in Mt Abu and Hotel Padmini in Chittorgarh. The Dundlod Fort, in northern Rajasthan, can arrange horse safaris around the Shekhawati region.

For most horse safaris, you are required to bring your own riding hat and boots. The best time to ride is during the cooler months (between mid-October and mid-March).

Many hotels, particularly in western Rajasthan, offer jeep safaris and they are usually available at palace hotels in remote regions, where they are one of the main attractions. One-day jeep village safaris to the Bishnoi villages around Jodhpur are also very popular.

Cycling

Ramesh Jangid, from Apani Dhani in Nawalgarh, northern Rajasthan, can organise cycling tours around the villages of Shekhawati, including informative commentaries on the remarkable paintings of this region. Butterfield & Robinson offers more upmarket organised bicycle tours or you can independently hire a bicycle from one of the numerous rental places found in the larger towns of Rajasthan and tour on your own. (See Bicycle in the Getting Around chapter for more information.)

Wildlife Safaris

The state's major wildlife sanctuaries are in eastern Rajasthan. Wildlife safaris are available by jeep at Sariska Tiger Reserve and at Ranthambhore National Park, although you have to book the latter around two months in advance. Another option at Ranthambhore is a trip in a canter (open-topped truck). At Keoladeo Ghana National Park motorised vehicles are prohibited but you can see the park by cycle-rickshaw or bicycle.

Trekking

Various operators can organise treks in the Aravalli Range. Ramesh Jangid (see Cycling) organises treks that include a guide, all meals, transport and accommodation in village homes, tents and *dharamsalas* (pilgrims' lodgings).

Swimming

Some of the upmarket hotels, including the Hotel Jaipur Ashok in Jaipur, the Shiv Niwas Palace Hotel in Udaipur, the Ajit Bhawan in Jodhpur, the Sawai Madhopur Lodge near the Ranthambhore National Park, and the Gorbandh Palace Hotel in Jaisalmer, allow nonguests to use their swimming pools. Expect to pay anywhere from Rs 100 to 300 for this privilege, which should include a towel.

Boating

There are a number of places where you can take a leisurely ride on a lake or river in Rajasthan. In eastern Rajasthan, you can have a boat ride at the Keoladeo Ghana National Park, Bharatpur, and at the Ana Sagar in Ajmer.

In southern Rajasthan, boats can be rented at Nakki Lake in Mt Abu, at Chambal gardens in Kota, at Fateh Sagar and on Lake Pichola in Udaipur. At Jaisalmer, in western Rajasthan, you can hire boats at Tilon ki Pol.

Golf

It is possible to play golf in Jaipur and Jodhpur (equipment is available for hire).

Polo & Horse Riding

Polo courses are run by Anokhi, an organic farm near Jaipur. The Pratap Country Inn, near Udaipur, has horse-riding lessons for beginners.

COURSES

See the regional chapters for more information on the courses listed here.

Meditation Retreats

The **Dhammathali Vipassana Meditation Centre** runs courses in meditation for both beginners and more advanced students throughout the year at its centre near Galta, about 3km east of Jaipur.

The **Brahma Kumaris Spiritual University** is at Mt Abu, and has introductory courses in raja yoga meditation. Residential courses are also offered, but these need to be organised through one of the 4500 or so overseas branches of the university before your arrival in India.

Yoga

Yoga courses are available at a number of places in Rajasthan, including **Yoga Sadhana Ashram** and **Madhavanand Girls College**, both in Jaipur.

Focus the mind & body at one of
Rajasthan's yoga schools

Ayurveda
In Jaisalmer, the **Ayurveda Hub & Research Institute** runs courses in the ancient Indian arts of herbal medicine and healing.

Astrology
Those fascinated by the mysterious future can take lessons in astrology, held by Dr Vinod Shastri, the General Secretary of the **Rajasthan Astrological Council & Research Institute** in Jaipur. There are lessons for beginners for Rs 3000 per person; advanced courses are available on application.

Music & Dance
It is possible to learn traditional music and dance at the **Maharaja Sawai Mansingh Sangeet Mahavidyalaya** in Jaipur. In Pushkar the **Saraswati Music School** offers lessons in classical tabla (drums) and singing. In Udaipur you can take sitar (an Indian stringed instrument), tabla and flute lessons at **Prem Musical Instruments**.

Painting, Pottery & Printing
In Jhunjhunu, in the heart of the Shekhawati region, you can learn traditional Shekhawati painting from local artists.

In Jaipur, Mr Kripal Singh gives lessons in Indian painting and pottery. Also in Jaipur, Anokhi runs courses in hand-block printing.

VOLUNTEER WORK
Numerous charities and international aid agencies have branches in India and, although they're mostly staffed by locals, there are some opportunities for foreigners. Don't assume it's your right to volunteer your services at any place. You are more use to the charity concerned if you write a few weeks in advance and, if you're needed, stay for long enough to be of help. A week on a hospital ward may go a little way towards salving your own conscience, but you may actually hinder, rather than help, the people who work there long term.

Flexibility in what you are prepared to do is also vital. Some charities are inundated with foreign volunteers wanting to help babies in an orphanage for instance, but few are willing to work with adults with physical or mental disabilities.

Overseas Volunteer Placement Agencies
For long-term posts, the following organisations may be able to help or offer advice and further contacts:

Australian Volunteers International
(☎ 03-9279 1788, fax 9419 4280,
🖳 www.ozvol.org.au) PO Box 350,
Fitzroy, Vic 3065, Australia

Co-ordinating Committee for International Voluntary Service (☎ 01 45 68 49 36,
fax 42 73 05 21, 🖳 www.unesco.org/ccivs)
Unesco House, 1 Rue Miollis, 75732 Paris Cedex 15, France

Global Volunteers (☎ 651-407 6100,
800-487 1074 toll-free, fax 651-482 0915,
🖳 www.globalvolunteers.org) 375 East Little Canada Rd, St Paul, MN 55117-1628, USA

Peace Corps (☎ 703-235 9191,
1800-424 8580 toll free, fax 235 9189,
🖳 www.peacecorps.gov), 1111 20th Street NW, Washington, DC 20526, USA

Voluntary Service Overseas (VSO; ☎ 020-8780 7200, fax 8780 7300, 🖳 www.vso .org.uk) 317 Putney Bridge Rd, London SW15 2PN, UK

Volunteer Work Information Service
(VWIS; ☎/fax 01273-711406,
🅦 www.workingabroad.com)
2nd floor, 59 Landsdowne Place, Hove,
BN3 1FL, East Sussex, UK

Help in Suffering

This animal hospital in Jaipur is supported by Animaux Secours, Arthaz, France. The philosophy of Help in Suffering is to create a 'friendly, rabies-free, healthy street-dog population'. It also treats sick animals, and does a tremendous job to help creatures great and small, from puppies to elephants. If you see an animal in distress in Jaipur, this is the place to call.

Qualified vets and vet nurses interested in volunteering at Help in Suffering should write to **Help in Suffering** *(☎ 0141-760803, fax 761544; Maharani Farm, Durgapura, Jaipur, 302018, Rajasthan)*. You need to stay at least three months, preferably longer. Visitors are welcome at the shelter in Jaipur, and donations are also gratefully accepted. See the Jaipur chapter for details.

Intach & Jaipur Virasat

The Jaipur branch of **Indian National Trust for Art, Culture and Heritage** *(Intach; ☎ 0141-407018, fax 750864; 🅦 www.intach.net; B14/A Bhawani Singh Marg, Jaipur, 302001, Rajasthan)* and Jaipur Virasat, a local heritage organisation linked to it, are working to preserve the vast cultural and physical heritage of Rajasthan's capital, and to increase local awareness of heritage issues.

You can volunteer to work in various capacities, depending on your skills. The focus is on restoration and conservation work, but you can also help if you have skills in promotion, art or administration. You need to stay for a minimum of one month – email with details of your skills a few weeks in advance to see if there's anything available for you. The organisations also run guided heritage walks around Jaipur (see the Jaipur chapter for details).

SOS Worldwide

SOS, which has its headquarters in Vienna, runs over 30 programmes across India and has been working in India since 1965. The society looks after orphaned, destitute and abandoned children, cared for by unmarried women, abandoned wives and widows. In Jaipur, SOS has a garden-surrounded property, and cares for around 120 children and young adults aged from birth to 25 years. Children live in 'families' of up to 10 children with a 'mother' in semidetached homes on the grounds, and are all provided with education.

Volunteers are welcome there to teach English, help the children with their homework and simply join in their games. Monetary donations are also gratefully accepted, as are clothes in good condition, games and sporting equipment. It is also possible to sponsor a child. Prospective sponsors should specify the age and sex of a child they would like to sponsor, and will receive details of the child, progress reports and a photograph. For more information contact **SOS Children's Village** *(☎ 0141-202393, fax 200140; 🅔 soschild@satyam.net.in; opposite Pital Factory, Jhotwara Rd, Jaipur, 302016, Rajasthan)*, or contact the programme coordinator in Delhi *(☎ 011-4355835, fax 435 7298; 🅦 www.soscvindia.org)*.

Les Amis du Shekhawati

Les Amis du Shekhawati (Friends of Shekhawati) aims to safeguard and preserve Shekhawati's rich artistic heritage, including both the remarkable paintings of this region and the havelis themselves. The society's work includes educating local villagers about the social and artistic importance of the paintings of Shekhawati, as well as undertaking restoration work and promoting the region. Ramesh Jangid (see Nawalgarh in the Northern Rajasthan chapter), the president of the association, welcomes volunteers. You can be involved in painting restoration, promotion or teaching English or French to trainee guides. For further information, or if you'd like to become a member of the association, contact Les Amis du Shekhawati through the ecofarm **Apani Dhani** *(☎ 0159-7422239, fax 7424061; 🅦 www.apanidhani.com; Nawalgarh, 333042, Rajasthan)*.

ACCOMMODATION

There is accommodation in Rajasthan to suit all pockets, from dorm beds for US$1 a night to some of India's most luxurious hotels, many of which have been converted from forts and palaces. In the desert village of Khuri, 40km from Jaisalmer, it's possible to stay in a *jhonpa*, a traditional mud hut with a thatched roof; in Pushkar, one place offers accommodation in treehouses; or you can always sleep under the stars on the Sam sand dunes. Be warned that these days the word 'palace' or 'castle' has been tacked onto literally hundreds of hotel names in Rajasthan, but most are not authentic royal abodes.

Some hotels operate on a 24-hour system (ie, your time starts from when you check in). Others have fixed check-out times (from an ungenerous 9am to a more civilised 1pm): it pays to ask before checking in. Some hotels even offer a handy half-day rate – ideal for breaking long journeys.

Credit cards are accepted at most top-end hotels and a rapidly growing number of midrange ones, however, very few budget hotels will take them. Some hotels may request an upfront payment based on your estimated length of stay. If your expenses don't match the prepaid amount you'll receive a refund at the time of check-out.

Although rare, some of the ultracheap, understaffed lodgings refuse to accept foreigners because of the hassle of the foreign registration 'C forms' (these must be submitted to the local police station within 24 hours of a foreigner checking in).

Although most prices quoted here are for single and double rooms, many hotels will put an extra bed in a room to make a triple for about an extra 25%.

Even budget rooms usually have a ceiling fan. 'Air-cooled' is the next step up – this means you get a large (usually noisy) fan built into a frame within a wall. It's a water-filled cooling system, which is less effective during the humid monsoon months. At some places you may have to fill the air cooler with water yourself, though usually you can expect the staff to do it. The most efficient method of keeping cool is air-conditioning,

Get to Know Your Bathroom

Certain terminology is commonly used in the places-to-stay sections throughout this book; rooms with a private, attached bathroom are listed as 'with private bathroom', and rooms where you must share a bathroom down the hall are listed as 'with shared bathroom'. However, several other terms may be used throughout the country. 'Common bath', 'nonattached bath' or 'shared bath' means communal bathroom facilities. 'Attached bath' or 'private bath' indicates that the room has its very own bathroom, which means you can belt out your favourite tune in the shower without being snickered at over the breakfast table.

'Running' or 'constant' water indicates that there is water available around the clock (although this is not always the case in reality). 'Bucket water' means that water is, as the name suggests, available in buckets. Many hotels usually only have running cold water in their guest bathrooms but can provide hot water in buckets (sometimes only between certain hours and sometimes at a small charge).

Hotels that advertise 'room with shower' can sometimes be misleading. Even if a bathroom does indeed have a shower, it's a good idea to actually check that it works before accepting the room. Some hotels surreptitiously disconnect showers to save costs, while the showers at other places render a mere trickle of water.

A geyser is a small hot-water tank, usually found in cheaper hotels. Some geysers need to be switched on an hour or so before use, and they don't work during power cuts.

Keep in mind that some hoteliers refer to squat toilets as 'Indian-style' and sit-down flush toilets as 'Western-style'. In some places you may come across the curious hybrid toilet, which is basically a sit-down flush toilet with footpads on the edge of the bowl! (See also Toilets earlier in this chapter.)

and it is offered in many mid-range places and all top-end hotels. However, you probably won't find air-conditioning necessary during the winter.

Tourist Bungalows

The Rajasthan Tourism Development Corporation (RTDC) has a good network of hotels (commonly referred to as 'tourist bungalows') throughout the state. Once they were great value, but these days, the conditions and services of most are below average. Nevertheless, many offer cheap dormitory accommodation (Rs 50 per person per night). There are also usually three types of rooms available, all with a private bathroom: ordinary rooms (the cheapest option apart from the dormitory) have ceiling fans and sometimes only have cold water (hot water comes by the bucket); deluxe rooms have air coolers; and super-deluxe rooms are usually carpeted and have air-conditioning. Generally there is a nonveg restaurant (with filling thalis) on the premises, and sometimes a bar. Frequently the local tourist office (often called the Tourist Reception Centre) is also located on the same premises – handy for information.

Railway Retiring Rooms

Railway retiring rooms are like regular hotels or dormitories except they are at the train stations. To stay here you are generally supposed to have a train ticket. The rooms are extremely convenient if you have an early train departure, although they can be noisy if it is a busy station. They are often very cheap and in some places also excellent value. Retiring-room details are at the end of the budget hotel section of each town.

Cheap Hotels

There are cheap hotels all over Rajasthan, from filthy, uninhabitable dives (with rock-bottom prices) to quite reasonable places. Ceiling fans, mosquito nets, private toilets and bathrooms are all possibilities, even in rooms that cost Rs 150 or less per night for a double. Many of the cheaper hotels have hot water in a bucket; some may have showers, but most are mere trickles.

Don't expect cheap hotels to be completely flawless – even if budget or mid-range hotels in this book are described as 'clean', they're unlikely to be absolutely spotless. Indeed, even in some respectable mid-range hotels, it's usual for rooms to have minor imperfections and in some places you may even find yourself sharing the room with cockroaches or other creepy-crawlies.

You may hear locals categorise hotels as 'Western' or 'Indian'. The 'Indian' hotels are usually more modestly furnished and thus cheaper. Most also have squat toilets (not only because they are cost-effective, but also because they are generally considered to be more hygienic). 'Western' hotels invariably have a sit-down flush toilet and may be more fancy inside. However, don't instantly assume that the 'Western' hotels are superior; you can often find modern, well-maintained 'Indian' hotels and dishevelled, poorly run 'Western' hotels.

Some cheap hotels allow guests to sleep on the rooftop (which resembles a large flat balcony) for a nominal charge. This should include a pillow, sheet or blanket, and use of a shared bathroom.

Some of the cheaper hotels lock their gates at night, so let the appropriate staff member know if you intend coming back late.

It's also worth making a mental note that some hotel rooms have a master switch on the outside of each room (usually near the door). If you return to your room to find that the lights, TV and geyser don't work, check that your master switch has not been turned off.

Expensive Hotels

Rajasthan has a disproportionate number of expensive hotels, largely due to its tourist appeal. As well, many former maharajas have been compelled to convert their beautiful forts and palaces into swanky hotels to bring in the tourist dollars. In Jaipur and some other major centres, there are also five-star hotels belonging to international groups such as the Holiday Inn and Sheraton. The Oberoi Group has exclusive boutique hotels in a few locations, including Jaipur and Sawai Madhopur.

While the top-end hotels in Rajasthan are certainly comfortable, the service at some leaves a little to be desired, especially considering the high tariffs. The staff can be rather indifferent and you sometimes feel more like a number than a name.

If you're interested in staying at a top-end hotel, it's sometimes cheaper to book them through a travel agent in your home country, who may be able to swing you a good-value package deal.

Palaces, Forts & Castles

Rajasthan is famous for its delightful palace hotels. The most famous are the Lake Palace and Shiv Niwas Palace hotels in Udaipur, the Rambagh Palace in Jaipur and the Umaid Bhawan Palace in Jodhpur. But it does't cost a fortune to stay in a palace – there are plenty of other erstwhile royal abodes that are more moderately priced.

As palaces and forts were not originally designed for tourism purposes, the size and quality of rooms can vary wildly. If it is at all possible, try to look at a few rooms before you check in.

Throughout the state there are many finely appointed historical buildings that have been converted into tourist accommodation. They are known as 'heritage hotels' and include havelis, forts and former royal hunting lodges. Many of the RTDC tourist offices have a brochure that lists heritage hotels, or you can check out the website 🅦 www.heritagehotels.com.

Homestays

Staying with an Indian family can be an enriching education. It's a change from dealing with tourist-oriented people, and a good opportunity to experience everyday Indian life.

Rajasthan's homestay programme, known as the Paying Guest House Scheme, operates in most major towns of Rajasthan. The cost is from around Rs 100 per night upwards, depending on the level of facilities offered, but most cater to the budget end of the market. Meals are usually available with prior notice.

The scheme is administered by the RTDC, and tourist offices have comprehensive lists of the participating families. The Tourist Reception Centre in Jaipur sells a handy booklet (Rs 5) listing all the paying guest houses in Rajasthan.

About Touts

Hordes of accommodation touts operate in Rajasthani towns – Jaipur, Jodhpur, Udaipur, Jaisalmer, Pushkar and Ajmer are probably the worst places for this, and of course you'll strike the commission racket in Delhi and Agra as well. Touts are usually most prevalent at airport terminals and bus and train stations. Very often they are rickshaw-wallahs. Their technique is simple – they take you to Hotel A and pocket a commission for taking you there rather than to Hotel B. The problem with this procedure is that you may well end up not at the place you want to go to but at the place that pays the best commission. Some very good cheap hotels simply refuse to pay the touts and you'll then hear lots of stories about the hotel you want being 'full', 'closed for repairs', 'no good any more' or even 'burnt down'. Nine times out of 10 they will be just that – stories.

Think twice before agreeing to stay in a hotel recommended by touts or rickshaw-wallahs, as some travellers have warned that they stayed in such hotels only to be subsequently badgered to take part in rip-off insurance and import schemes or to accept the sightseeing services of a particular taxi or rickshaw driver.

Touts do have a use, though – if you arrive in a town when some big festival is on, or during peak season, finding a place to stay can be almost impossible. Hop into a rickshaw, tell the driver the hotel price range you want, and off you go. The driver will know which places have rooms available and, unless the search is a long one, you shouldn't have to pay the driver too much. Remember he will be getting a commission from the hotel too.

Seasonal Variations

In the high season (December to March) most hoteliers crank up their prices to two to three times the low-season price. In some locations and at some hotels, there are even higher rates for the brief Christmas/New Year period, or during major festivals such as the Camel Fair in Pushkar or Diwali in Mt Abu. Advance reservations are advisable. It's also worth noting that if things improve in the tourism industry, prices listed in this book could rise steeply.

Conversely, in the low season (May to August) prices at even normally expensive hotels can be surprisingly reasonable.

FOOD

Perhaps the best way of cutting to the heart of this extraordinary culture is by exploring its protean gastronomy. Dining in Indian restaurants abroad cannot prepare you for the experience of eating Indian food in India, as the food is inextricably particular to the place and is not easily exported. It reflects the multilayered culture that fascinates every visitor, and it actually changes shape as you move between each neighbourhood and town. Yes, you stand a good chance of getting a dose of the runs at some stage of your visit, but – with equal measures of good sense and adventure – a few desperate dashes to the toilet will seem like a trifling inconvenience compared with the culinary rewards and cultural insights you will glean.

Considering the paucity of fresh fruit and vegetables in the arid zones, Rajasthan serves up a surprising variety of regional dishes and there is a myriad of specialities unique to the state. These days, many restaurants cater to the Western tastes of travellers and you have to actively hunt down a local place in order to be fed some authentic Rajasthani cuisine.

Local restaurants, known elsewhere in the country as dhabas, are known here as bhojanalyas, from bhojan (food or meal), and alya (place). These simple eateries are great for travellers who are on a tight budget, but make sure you get food that has been freshly cooked, not just reheated.

Thalis

Thalis are the traditional all-you-can-eat meals, which are a combination of curry dishes, relishes, pappadams, yogurt, pooris (deep-fried bread) or chappatis, and rice. Thali is actually the name of the plate on which the meal is served. Most of the RTDC hotels, for example, serve a decent thali for quite a reasonable price.

In southern Rajasthan, many restaurants serve lightly spiced and sweet Gujarati thalis – one of the most famous regional varieties.

Vegetable Dishes

Rajasthan has interesting vegetarian dishes including govind gatta, a lentil paste with dried fruit and nuts, which is rolled into a sausage shape, sliced and deep fried; papad ki sabzi, which is simply a pappadam with vegetables and masala (mixed spices); and alu mangori, which is a ground lentil paste that is dried in the sun and then put in a curry with alu (potatoes) – once rolled by hand, it is now often forced through a machine in the same way as macaroni. A common vegetarian snack is alu samosa, pastry cones stuffed with spicy potato.

Mogri is a type of desert bean and it is creatively made into a curry known as mogri mangori. A sweeter version is methi mangori – methi is the leaf of a green desert vegetable. Kachri is a type of desert fruit that is made into a chutney. Dana methi is made with dana (small pea-shaped vegetables) and methi boiled and mixed with sugar, masala and dried fruit. Cheelra ka saag is a gram (legume) flour paste chappati that is chopped up, fried, and then added to a curry.

Kair sangri is served with a mango pickle. Kair is a small, round desert fruit, which grows on a prickly shrub and is a favourite of camels, and sangri are dried wild desert beans. The seeds and beans are soaked overnight in water, boiled and then fried in oil with various masalas, dried dates, red chillies, turmeric powder, shredded dried mango, salt, coriander and cumin seeds. This dish is easily recognised – it looks like a pile of old dry sticks. Don't be scared – it's surprisingly tender.

Meat

The Brahmins and traders in Rajasthan stick mainly to a vegetarian diet, but the Rajputs enjoy a variety of meats, including game. *Shikhar* (hunting) was a favourite pastime when they had nobody to fight and this introduced a variety of game to the dinner table, including venison, quail, duck and wild boar. In the deserts of Jaisalmer, Jodhpur and Bikaner, meats are cooked without water, using milk, curd, buttermilk and plenty of ghee. Cooked this way, they keep for days without refrigeration. In fact, for special occasions, some dishes are left to steep for a few days to intensify the flavours. *Murgh ko khaato* (chicken cooked in a curd gravy), *achhar murgh* (pickled chicken), *kacher maas* (dry lamb cooked in spices), *lal maas* (red meat) and *soor santh ro sohito* (pork with millet dumplings) are classic Rajasthani-desert dishes.

Safed maas (white meat) is another great regional delicacy. The secret is in the gravy – onion, ginger, garlic paste, salt, pepper, cashew-nut paste and cardamom. Chunks of mutton (with bones) are cooked in this gravy and fresh cream is added just before serving.

Maas ka sule, a favourite meat dish among the Rajputs, can be made from partridge, wild boar, chicken, mutton and fish. Chunks of meat are marinated in a paste of turmeric powder, coriander powder, ginger and garlic paste, salt, red-chilli powder, mustard oil and yogurt. The chunks are cooked on skewers in a *tandoor*, then glazed with melted butter and a tangy masala.

Daal & Cereals

In Rajasthan, daal is traditionally *urad* lentils boiled in water then cooked with *garam* (hot) *masala*, red chillies, cumin seeds, salt, oil and fresh coriander. Cereal dishes include *kabooli Jodhpurl*, made with meat, vegetables such as cauliflower, cabbage and peas, and fried *gram* paste balls. *Khichri* is a mix of cereals, including millet, which is added to meat dishes. *Dalia ki khichri* is wheat porridge mixed with masala, a little *gur* (jaggery, or raw sugar) and ghee. *Ghaat* is a corn porridge served with yogurt.

Besan (chickpea flour) is another staple, and is used to make pakoras (fritters), *sev* (savoury nibbles) and other salted snacks known as *farsan*.

Roti (Bread)

A meal is not a meal in India unless it comes with roti. The irresistible chappati, made with whole-wheat flour and water, is cooked on a concave hotplate known as a *tawa*. In Rajasthan you'll also find *sogra*, a millet chappati; *makki ki* roti, a thick cornmeal chappati; and *dhokla*, maize flour which is steamed and formed into balls and cooked with green coriander, spinach and mint, and eaten with chutney. A *purat* roti is a type of Rajasthani filo pastry. The roti is repeatedly coated with oil and folded so that when it is cooked it is light and fluffy.

Bati (baked balls of wholemeal flour) is the state's most remarkable dish. The balls are broken up by hand, soaked in ghee and mixed with a spicy daal. In the villages it's prepared with cinnamon and nutmeg and boiled in water, with a dash of turmeric powder. The balls are then roasted until they turn brown and deep fried in ghee. *Saadi bati* is a baked ball of wheat flour paste. *Bafle bati* is steamed wheat-flour balls. *Cheelre* is a chappati made with *gram* powder paste. *Masala bati* is wheat balls stuffed with *masala*, peas and peanuts.

The other traditional Indian breads are also widely available. *Pooris* are wholewheat discs of stiff dough that, when deepfried, puff up into soft crispy balloons. Other favourites include flaky *parathas* and puffy naan, which is baked in a tandoor.

Pickles, Chutneys & Relishes

Pickles and chutneys, known as *achars*, include *goonde achar*. *Goonde* is a green fruit that is boiled and mixed with mustard oil and *masalas*. *Kair achar* is a pickle with desert bean as its base. *Lahsun achar* is an onion pickle. *Lal mirch* is a garlic-stuffed red chilli. *Kamrak ka achar* is a pickle with *kamrak*, a type of desert vegetable with a pungent, sour taste. *Bathua raita* is a raita made with *bathua* leaves, which are boiled, rinsed, and mixed into a paste with yogurt.

Desserts

There is no dearth of desserts in this desert state, including *lapsi*, which is jaggery with a wheat-flour porridge; *kheer*, or rice pudding with cardamom and saffron, a North Indian favourite; and *maalpua*, a small chappati made from wheat flour, rolled in sugar and fried.

Badam ki barfi is a type of almond fudge made from sugar, powdered milk, almonds and ghee. *Chakki* is a piece of *barfi* (a milk-based fudge) made from *gram* flour, sugar and milk cake. *Churma* is a sweet of *gram* flour, sugar, cardamom, ghee and dried fruits. *Ghewar* is a paste of *urad* cereal, a Rajasthani favourite. *Firni* is a ball-shaped sweet made from *urad* cereal, deep fried and then dipped in syrup. *Sooji halwa* is semolina pudding. *Meetha chaval* is sweet boiled rice. *Alu ki jalebi* is mashed potato, sugar, saffron and arrowroot. The mixture is made into spirals and fried in hot oil, then soaked in a warm sugar syrup. This sweet is served hot.

Moong daal halwa is a popular dessert of finely ground *moong daal*, fried with ghee, sugar, cinnamon and cardamom powder until the mixture turns a light brown. Raisins, chopped cashew nuts and almonds are added before serving.

Ghewar is a paste of *urad* cereal that is crushed, deep-fried and then dipped in a sugar syrup flavoured with cardamom, cinnamon and cloves. It is served hot and topped with a thick layer of unsweetened cream and garnished with rose petals.

Paan

Meals are polished off with *paan*, a sweet, spicy and fragrant mixture of betel nut (also called areca nut), lime paste, spices and condiments wrapped up in an edible betel leaf (from a different plant) and eaten as a digestive and mouth freshener. The betel nut is mildly narcotic and some aficionados eat them the same way heavy smokers consume cigarettes. If you chew a lot of *paan*, over many years the betel nut will rot your teeth red and black, which accounts for the number of people you'll encounter who look like they had their faces kicked in the night before.

There are two basic types: *mitha* (sweet) and *saadha* (with tobacco). Avoid the foul tobacco version, but a parcel of *mitha paan* is an excellent way to finish a satisfying meal without any harm. Pop the whole parcel in your mouth and chew slowly, letting the juices secrete around your gob. When you've chewed the flavour out, spit the remains out onto the street (there really is no point in trying to be discreet).

DRINKS
Nonalcoholic Drinks

Tea & Coffee Indian *chai* (tea) is much loved in Rajasthan and the sharing of this hot beverage is often a part of social and business gatherings. At train stations it is often served in small clay pots, which you then smash on the ground when empty. Unfortunately, these days *chai-wallahs* are increasingly using plastic cups and disposing of them is far less satisfying – you have to find a bin.

Many travellers like Indian *chai*, but some people find it far too sweet. If you ask for 'tray tea', you will be given the tea, the milk and the sugar separately, allowing you to combine them as you see fit. Unless you specify otherwise, tea is 'mixed tea' or 'milk tea', which means it has been made by putting cold water, milk, sugar and tea into one pot and bringing the whole concoction to the boil, then letting it stew for a long time.

It's almost impossible to get a decent cup of coffee in Rajasthan. Even in an expensive restaurant instant coffee is almost always used; however, some top-end hotels are now thankfully introducing espresso machines!

Other Drinks Coca-Cola and Pepsi are bombarding India with advertising and young, hip locals are lapping up their sickly sweet concoctions. These – and local brands such as Thums Up and Limca – are usually safe to drink as long as you're not diabetic. *Masala soda* is the quintessentially Indian soft drink. Available at all drinks stalls, it is a freshly opened bottle of soda pepped-up with a lime, spices, salt and sugar. Orange juice is widely available, but the most popular street juices are made from sweet lemon, and sugar cane, which is pressed in front of you by a mechanised wheel complete with jingling bells.

Jal jeera is the most therapeutic and refreshing indigenous drink. It's made with lime juice, cumin, mint and rock salt. It is sold in large earthenware pots by street vendors as well as in restaurants. *Faluda* is a rose-flavoured Muslim speciality made with milk, cream, nuts and strands of vermicelli. But of course the most popular of Indian drinks is a refreshing sweet or salt *lassi* (yogurt drink). Jodhpur is famous for its sweet *makhania* lassis, delicious thick lassis flavoured with saffron. *Chach* and *kairi chach* are other Rajasthani specialities – the former is a thin salted lassi and the latter is unripe mango juice with water and salt, widely available in summer and allegedly a good remedy for sunstroke.

For information on water, see the Health earlier in this chapter.

Alcoholic Drinks

In 1999 the government of Rajasthan banned the sale of alcohol from the state's restaurants and 74 beer bars, effectively pushing the trade under the table. Officially, only hotels with a horrendously expensive liquor license can serve alcohol, but in practice many smaller eateries are willing to go and fetch you a bottle of beer from the nearest bottle shop. You'll pay for the privilege though; a bottle of beer costs anything from Rs 60 to 200. Alternatively you can drink at RTDC hotels, which often have a seedy bar, and sometimes even a 'beer shop' on the grounds.

Beer and other Indian interpretations of Western alcoholic drinks are known as IMFL – Indian Made Foreign Liquor. They include incarnations of whisky and brandy under a plethora of different brand names. The taste varies from hospital disinfectant to passable imitation whisky. Always buy the best brand. If you fancy a rum and cola, the Indian rum Old Monk is not bad at all. With the continuing freeing up of the economy, it is likely that well-known foreign brands of beer and spirits will become available.

Local drinks are known as country liquor and include toddy, a mildly alcoholic extract from the coconut palm flower; and *feni*, a distilled liquor produced either from fermented cashew nuts or from coconuts. The two varieties taste quite different.

Beware of Those Bhang Lassis!

Although rarely printed in menus, some restaurants in certain parts of Rajasthan (predominantly the tourist hotbeds such as Pushkar, Jaisalmer and Udaipur) clandestinely whip up 'special' lassis, a yogurt and iced-water beverage laced with *bhang*, a derivative of marijuana. Some places also sell *bhang* cookies, and there's even a government-approved *bhang* shop in Jaisalmer. However, there is certainly no standardised preparation of special lassis and cookies. Some are stronger than others and even the weakest ones do not agree with everyone. Some travellers have been stuck in bed for several miserable days; others have been robbed while they were lying in a state of delirium.

If you still want to try one, you can control your intake by only consuming a half or quarter of the serving given to you (share with friends), and topping up later if you feel like it.

Arak is what the peasants (and bus drivers' best boys) drink to get blotto. It's a clear, distilled rice liquor that creeps up on you without warning. Treat with caution and only ever drink it from a bottle produced in a government-controlled distillery. *Never, ever* drink it otherwise – hundreds of people die or are blinded every year in India as a result of drinking arak produced in illicit stills. You can assume it contains methyl alcohol (wood alcohol).

ENTERTAINMENT

When it comes to pubs and bars, nightclubs and other activities you may take for granted, Rajasthan isn't a hive of activity (indeed this is part of the appeal for many tourists). Major cities such as Mumbai and Delhi are about the nearest you'll come to finding them. But one thing Rajasthan is well endowed with is cinemas. Admission is inexpensive, and if you haven't seen a Bollywood blockbuster before, you should try to see at least one during your trip. Jaipur's Raj Mandir Cinema, decked out in 1920s style, would have to be one of the most atmospheric places to see a Hindi film (see Entertainment in the Jaipur chapter).

At some festivals, such as Pushkar Camel Fair, you might be treated to impromptu performances by livestock traders around a campfire. *Kathputlis* (traditional puppeteers) are another attraction. Puppet shows or traditional Rajasthani music and dance performances are held at many hotels.

SPECTATOR SPORTS
Cricket

India's national sport (obsession almost) is cricket. In the past Jaipur's **Sawai Mansingh Stadium** (☎ 0141-514732) has been the venue for two World Cup cricket matches. Cricket matches can be seen here during the winter, tickets generally go on sale 10 days prior to the match, and matches are advertised in English-language papers. Telephone the stadium for details of forthcoming events.

Tennis

Some international tennis tournaments are held at the **Jai Club**, off MI Rd in Jaipur

(near Panch Batti). Matches are generally well advertised, and tickets can often be obtained from sponsors.

Polo

Polo matches are played at the **Rajasthan Polo Club** (☎ 383580; ✉ *jaipurpolo@hot mail.com*), near the Rambagh Palace hotel in Jaipur. Matches are also sometimes held at the polo ground in Jodhpur. The horse polo season extends over winter with the most important matches usually played in March.

During Jaipur's Elephant Festival in March, matches of elephant polo are played. For further details about them, contact the tourist office in Jaipur.

Polo

Horse polo was very popular among the maharajas, especially during the British Raj, and they often provided polo ponies, facilities and training to talented players. Some of them were among the top players in the world, such as Maharaja Man Singh of Jaipur, whose polo team was champion on the European polo circuit in the 1930s. The maharaja had a stable of 39 ponies, which were shipped over to England in 1933. The team was accompanied by a carpenter (to keep them supplied with polo sticks). They stunned the opposition players and spectators with their equestrian flair, winning every important match in the tournament. Sadly the maharaja's passion was to prove fatal, and he died during a polo match in England in 1970.

Emperor Akbar was believed to have been the first person to introduce rules to the game, but polo, as it is played today, was introduced by a British Cavalry Regiment stationed in India during the 1870s. A set of international rules was implemented after WWI.

The game flourished in India until Independence, when patronage decreased and the game became less popular. Today there is a renewed interest in polo, and Rajasthan produces some of the nation's finest players. The Mewar (Udaipur) polo team has been one of the country's most successful both in India and abroad.

A Warning!

Most people who come to Rajasthan can't resist the fantastic shopping, and there are some real bargains out there, but swindling is elevated to an artform in India and it's easy for even the most experienced traveller to get trounced by a tout. It seems that with every book we make the warnings get longer and more explicit, and yet we still get letters from people with tales of woe and they usually concern scams we specifically mention.

While it is a minority of traders involved in dishonest schemes, nearly all are involved in the commission racket, so shop with care – take your time, be firm and bargain hard. Good luck!

Reselling Scams

If you believe any stories about buying anything in India to sell at a profit elsewhere, you'll simply be proving (once again) that old adage about separating fools from their money. Precious stones and carpets are favourites for this game. Merchants will tell you that you can sell the items back home for several times the purchase price, and will even give you the (often imaginary) addresses of dealers who will buy them. You may also be shown written statements from other travellers documenting the money they have made, even photographs of the merchants shaking hands with their so-called business partners overseas – besuited Westerners standing outside big stores in Europe and America. Don't be taken in, it's all a scam. The stones or carpets you buy will be worth only a fraction of what you pay. Often the gem scams involve showing you real stones and then packing up worthless glass beads to give you in their place. Don't let greed cloud your judgment.

These scams are often elaborate productions and can begin when touts strike up conversations in excellent English while you're waiting for a bus or eating in a restaurant, until you develop a friendly relationship with them. It might be several hours (or even days if they know where you hang out and can organise to see you again) before any mention is made of reselling items.

Tip: beware of anyone who wants to become your best friend in areas that see a lot of tourist traffic, eg, hotel and shopping strips and transport hubs. You certainly don't need to avoid and ignore all the locals, but go to a less-touristy area if you're interested in a genuine conversation.

Commissions

In touristy places such as Jaipur, take extreme care with the commission merchants – these guys hang around waiting to pick you up and cart you off to their favourite dealers where whatever you pay will have a hefty margin built into it to pay their commission. Stories about 'my family's place', 'my brother's shop' and 'special deal at my friend's place' are just stories and nothing more.

Whatever you might be told, if you are taken by a rickshaw driver or tout to a place, be it a hotel, craftshop, market or even restaurant, the price you pay will be inflated. This can be by as much as 50%, so try to visit these places on your own. And don't underestimate the persistence of these guys. We heard of one ill traveller who virtually collapsed into a cycle-rickshaw in Agra and asked to be taken to a doctor – he ended up at a marble workshop, and the rickshaw-wallah insisted that yes, indeed, a doctor did work there!

Tip: if you don't want to be swindled at the market, check out government-emporium prices first.

Credit Card Scams

Another trap occurs when using a credit card. You may be told that the merchant won't forward the credit slip for payment until you've actually received the goods, even if it is in three months time – this is total bullshit. No trader will send you as much as a postcard until they have received the full amount for the goods. What you'll find in fact is that within 48 hours of your signing the credit slip, the merchant has telexed the bank in Delhi and the money will have been credited to their account.

Beware if your credit card is taken out the back to be processed. Sometimes the vendor will imprint a few more forms, forge your signature, and you'll be billed for extra items. Have it done in front of you.

Tip: Avoid using credit cards – cash up at the bank before you head out on a shopping spree.

SHOPPING

Rajasthan really is one of the easiest places to spend money – there are so many busy bazaars, colourful arts and crafts, gorgeous fabrics, miniature paintings, and much more. The cardinal rule when purchasing handicrafts is to bargain and bargain hard.

Be careful when buying items that include delivery to your home country. You may well be given assurances that the price includes home delivery and all customs and handling charges. Inevitably this is not the case, and you may find yourself having to collect the item yourself from your country's main port or airport, and pay customs charges (which could be as much as 20% of the item's value) and handling charges levied by the airline or shipping company (which could be up to 10% of the value). If you can't collect the item promptly, or get someone to do it on your behalf, exorbitant storage charges may also be charged.

Unfortunately, the quality of Rajasthan's handicrafts is not always what it could be, particularly with regards to paintings, which are produced in great numbers for tourist buyers. Sellers often claim that the paintings are antiques, however, this is rarely the case.

Avoid buying products that further endanger threatened species and habitats. Note that it is illegal to export ivory products or any artefact made from wild animals.

For information on buying Rajasthani handicrafts, see the special section 'The Colourful Crafts of Rajasthan'.

Exporting Antiques

Articles over 100 years old are not allowed to be exported from India without an export clearance certificate. If you have doubts about any item and think it could be defined as an antique, you can check with branches of the Archaeological Survey of India. In New Delhi, contact the Director of Antiquities, **Archaeological Survey of India** (☎ 3017220, Janpath).

Getting There & Away

Most travellers visiting Rajasthan fly into Delhi and travel overland into the state from there. A few people also fly into Mumbai (Bombay). As getting to Rajasthan is a two-part journey, the first part of this chapter deals with travel from international destinations to India, while the second part concentrates on travel from Delhi and Mumbai into Rajasthan.

India

AIR
International Airports & Airlines
In February 2002 the first international air service to Jaipur airport opened – Indian Airlines flight 895 from Dubai via Delhi. As the infrastructure improves, no doubt other airlines will open international routes to other destinations, but as yet there are no plans in place.

Most people visiting Rajasthan arrive at either the Delhi or Mumbai international airports. Delhi is the most popular gateway, as it's the closest major international airport to Rajasthan. Mumbai is also an option, as it's India's main international airport.

For comprehensive information about arriving in Delhi, see Getting There & Away in the Delhi chapter.

Mumbai's international airport (officially called Chhatrapati Shivaji, but still better known as Sahar) is about 30km north of the city. The taxi trip downtown from Sahar airport, which takes 1½ to two hours, should cost around Rs 260 (Rs 325 from midnight to 5am) if you use the prepaid taxi booth. Don't take an autorickshaw, as they can't enter the downtown area and you'll end up stranded a few kilometres short of the train stations.

India's national carrier, **Air India** (W *www.airindia.com*), also carries passengers on some domestic sectors of international routes. Indian Airlines, the country's major domestic carrier, offers flights to some 16

Warning
The information in this chapter is particularly vulnerable to change: prices for international travel are volatile, routes are introduced and cancelled, schedules change, special deals come and go, and rules and visa requirements are amended. You should check directly with the airline or a travel agency to make sure you understand how a fare (and ticket you may buy) works and be aware of the security requirements for international travel.

The upshot of this is that you should get opinions, quotes and advice from as many airlines and travel agencies as possible before you part with your hard-earned cash. The details given in this chapter should be regarded as pointers and are not a substitute for your own careful, up-to-date research.

neighbouring countries (for specific destinations see the website at W www.indian-air lines.nic.in).

See Getting There & Away in the Delhi and Jaipur chapters for the contact details of international airline offices in each of those cities. The free magazine *Mumbai: This Fortnight*, available at many guesthouses and the tourist office, has a list of major international airline offices in Mumbai.

Buying Tickets
With a bit of research – ringing around travel agencies, checking Internet sites, perusing the travel ads in newspapers – you can often get yourself a good travel deal. Start early as some of the cheapest tickets need to be bought well in advance and popular flights can sell out.

Full-time students and people under 26 years (under 30 in some countries) have access to better deals than other travellers. You have to show a document proving your date of birth or a valid International Student Identity Card (ISIC) when buying your ticket and boarding the plane.

Generally, there is nothing to be gained by buying a ticket direct from the airline. Discounted tickets are released to selected travel agencies and specialist discount agencies, and these are usually the cheapest deals going.

One exception to this rule is the expanding number of 'no-frills' carriers, which mostly sell only direct to travellers. Unlike the 'full-service' airlines, no-frills carriers often make one-way tickets available at around half the return fare, meaning that it is easy to put together an open-jaw ticket when you fly to one place but leave from another.

The other exception is booking on the Internet. Many airlines, full-service and no-frills, offer some excellent fares to Web surfers. They may sell seats by auction or simply cut prices to reflect the reduced cost of electronic selling.

Many travel agencies around the world have websites, which can make the Internet a quick and easy way to compare prices. There is also an increasing number of online agencies which operate only on the Internet.

Online ticket sales work well if you are doing a simple one-way or return trip on specified dates. However, online superfast fare generators are no substitute for a travel agent who knows all about special deals, has strategies for avoiding layovers and can offer advice on everything from which airline has the best vegetarian food to the best travel insurance to bundle with your ticket.

You may find the cheapest flights are advertised by obscure agencies. Most such firms are honest and solvent, but there are some rogue fly-by-night outfits around. Paying by credit card generally offers protection, as most card issuers provide refunds if you can prove you didn't get what you paid for. Similar protection can be obtained by buying a ticket from a bonded agency, such as one covered by the **Air Travel Organisers' Licensing scheme** (ATOL; ⱳ www.atol.org .uk) in the UK. Agencies that accept only cash should hand over the tickets straight away and not tell you to 'come back tomorrow'. After you've made a booking or paid your deposit, call the airline and confirm that the booking was made. It's generally not advisable to send money (even cheques) through the post unless the agency is very well established – some travellers have reported being ripped off by fly-by-night mail-order ticket agencies.

If you purchase a ticket and later want to make changes to your route or get a refund, you need to contact the original travel agency. Airlines issue refunds only to the purchaser of a ticket – usually the travel agency that bought the ticket on your behalf. Many travellers change their routes halfway through their trips, so think carefully before you buy a ticket that is not easily refunded.

Travellers with Specific Needs

If they're warned early enough, airlines can often make special arrangements for travellers such as wheelchair assistance at airports or vegetarian meals on the flight. Children under two years travel for 10% of the standard fare (or free on some airlines) as long as they don't occupy a seat. They don't get a baggage allowance. 'Skycots', baby food and nappies should be provided by the airline if requested in advance. Children aged between two and 12 can usually occupy a seat for around two-thirds of the full fare, and do get a baggage allowance.

The disability-friendly website ⱳ www .everybody.co.uk has an airline directory that provides information on the facilities offered by various airlines.

Departing India

It's important to reconfirm international tickets at least 72 hours before departure; some travellers have reported having their seat cancelled for not doing so.

Airlines recommend travellers check in three hours prior to international flight departures; allow time for getting stuck in India's often congested traffic, especially during peak hours. Most Indian airports have free luggage trolleys, but you'll probably be accosted by porters eagerly offering to lug your load for a tip (Rs 10 is fine). Once inside the airport, you'll be required to have your check-in baggage screened and sealed by security tape before proceeding to check-in. Also remember that airline security has been increased since 11 September – don't pack anything with a blade (even a pair of nail scissors) in your hand luggage – it will be confiscated by airport security. Don't forget to fill out an embarkation card before heading for the customs gate.

Departure Tax The departure tax of Rs 500 (Rs 150 if you are travelling to Bangladesh, Bhutan, Nepal, Maldives and Sri Lanka) is included in the price of virtually all airline tickets – check with your travel agency.

Tickets in Delhi

Although you can get international tickets in Mumbai, it is in Delhi that the real wheeling and dealing goes on. There are a number of bucket shops (unbonded travel agencies that specialise in discounted airline tickets) around Connaught Place, but inquire with other travellers about their current trustworthiness. And if you use a bucket shop, double-check with the airline itself that the booking has been made.

To give you an idea of costs, the table 'Fares from Delhi' presents some fares (flights from other countries to India are provided under country headings later). The list is not exhaustive – many more international destinations are serviced from Delhi (check with travel agencies). Note that fares here are one way and are given in the currency (rupees or US dollars) in which they are quoted in India. Fares may vary considerably according to peak and low seasons, so it's best to consult a travel agency for the best and latest deals.

Fares from Delhi

destination	one-way fare
Bangkok	Rs 17,000
Colombo	Rs 17,000
Hong Kong	Rs 21,500
Kathmandu	US$142
London	Rs 14,000
Los Angeles	Rs 23,000
New York	Rs 22,000

The USA

Discount travel agencies in the USA are known as consolidators (although you won't see a sign on the door saying 'Consolidator'). San Francisco is the ticket consolidator capital of America, although some good deals can be found in Los Angeles, New York and other big cities.

Council Travel (☎ 800-226 8624 toll free; W www.counciltravel.com), America's largest student-travel organisation, has around 60 offices in the USA. **STA Travel** (☎ 800-781 4040 toll free; W www.statravel.com) has offices in Boston, Chicago, Miami, New York, Philadelphia, San Francisco and other major cities.

The high season for flights from the US to India is June to August and again from December to January. Low season runs from March to around mid-May and from September to November. Prices quoted are for return fares to Delhi.

From the US east coast most flights to India are via Europe. Aeroflot offers the cheapest deals; low-season tickets to Delhi start at US$910. With Air France via Paris, low-season fares start at around US$1020. To Mumbai, Air France and Alitalia offer US$1020 fares.

From the US west coast, Asiana Airlines has the best bargain fares. Expect to pay around US$1030 for a low-season advance-purchase fare. Aeroflot and China Airlines also offer cheap deals, around US$1100 in the low season. From Los Angeles to Mumbai costs US$1070 with Korean Air.

Canada

Canadian discount air ticket sellers are also known as consolidators; their air fares tend to be about 10% higher than those sold in the USA.

Travel CUTS (☎ 1866-246-9762; W www.travelcuts.com) is Canada's national student travel agency and has offices in all major cities.

Vancouver to Delhi fares flying Lufthansa via Frankfurt in the low season are CA$2300. Vancouver to Mumbai in the low season costs from CA$2650. During the high season all flights from Vancouver are routed through the US and cost from CA$3630 flying Northwest via Amsterdam. Low-season Montreal to Delhi flights cost CA$2000 with Air France via Paris; and flights from Toronto to Delhi cost CA$2100 with Lufthansa via Frankfurt.

Australia

Two well-known agencies for cheap fares are **STA Travel** (☎ *1300 733 035;* **W** *www.sta travel.com.au*) and **Flight Centre** (☎ *133 133;* **W** *www.flightcentre.com.au*). STA Travel has offices in all major cities and on many university campuses. Flight Centre has dozens of offices throughout Australia.

Quite a few travel offices specialise in discount air tickets. Some travel agencies, particularly smaller ones, advertise cheap air fares in the travel sections of weekend newspapers.

The low season is from 1 February to 21 November. Advance-purchase return tickets from the east coast of Australia to Delhi with Japan Airlines via Tokyo start at A$1250 in the low season. Malaysian Airlines has a ticket to Delhi via Kuala Lumpur for A$1550, or to Mumbai for A$1350. Fares are around A$200 cheaper from Perth and you can expect to pay around $A2000 for the lowest fares in the high season.

New Zealand

Flight Centre (☎ *0800-354448;* **W** *www .flightcentre.co.nz*) has numerous branches throughout the country. **STA Travel** (☎ *0508-782872;* **W** *www.statravel.co.nz*) has offices in Auckland, Hamilton, Palmerston North, Wellington, Christchurch, and Dunedin.

There are no direct flights between India and New Zealand so most airlines offer stopovers in Asia. Low-season return fares to Delhi or Mumbai from Auckland cost from NZ$1500 with Thai Airways International.

The UK & Ireland

Discount air travel is big business in London. There are many advertisements for travel agencies in the travel pages of the weekend broadsheet newspapers, in *Time Out*, in the *Evening Standard* and in the free magazine *TNT*.

A popular travel agency is **STA Travel** (☎ *08701-600 599;* **W** *www.statravel.co.uk*), which has branches across the country. Britain's second largest travel company aimed at young people, Usit Campus, collapsed in January 2002, but there are plenty of other recommended travel agencies still operating, including:

Bridge the World (☎ 0870-444 7474,
  W www.b-t-w.co.uk) 4 Regent Place,
  London W1R 5F
Flightbookers (☎ 0870-010 7000,
  W www.ebookers.com) 177–178 Tottenham
  Court Rd, London W1
Trailfinders (☎ 020-7628 2345, **W** www.trail
  finders.co.uk) 1 Threadneedle St, London
  EC2R 8JX

From London to Delhi, Aeroflot has low-season return fares starting at £315. British Airways and Virgin Atlantic offer direct flights from £495 in the low season. London to Mumbai costs £444 with Emirates Airlines in the low season. Flights from Belfast to Delhi start from around £570 with British Airways and Virgin Atlantic.

Continental Europe

The Dutch travel industry, like travel industries all over the world, was wrenched by the aviation market meltdown of 2001. Major travel agency casualties included NBBS Reizen and Budget Air, both of which ceased trading that year. Surviving the shakeup was **Holland International** (☎ *070-307 6307*), with offices in most cities. The return trip from Amsterdam to Delhi costs around €830.

Travel agencies in Germany include **STA Travel** (☎ *030-311 0950; Goethesttrasse 73, 10625 Berlin*), with branches in major cities across the country. **Unit Campus** (☎ *01805 788336;* **W** *www.usitcampus.de*) has several offices in Germany (you'll find the details on the website), including one at 2A Zuelpicher Strasse, 50674 Cologne. A return fare from Frankfurt to Delhi costs €975.

In France, **Usit Connect Voyages** (☎ *01 42 44 14 00;* **W** *www.usitconnections.fr; 14, rue de Vaugirard 75006 Paris*) and **OTU Voyages** (☎ *0 820 817 817;* **W** *www.otu.fr;*

39 ave Georges Bernanos, 75005 Paris) are good travel agencies with branches across the country. Both companies specialise in travel arrangements for students and young people. From Paris it costs around €1088 return to Delhi.

Africa
There are plenty of flights between East Africa and Mumbai due to the large Indian population in Kenya. A return fare from Nairobi to Mumbai is US$525 with Kenya Airways. Nairobi to Delhi with Indian Airlines is US$820. An Emirates flight from Johannesburg to Delhi is US$465.

Nepal
Royal Nepal Airlines Corporation (RNAC) and Indian Airlines share routes between India and Kathmandu. RNAC and Indian Airlines have one-way flights from Kathmandu to Delhi for US$142.

Pakistan
At the time of writing, flights between Pakistan and India were suspended due to the tensions between the two countries. If things simmer down the route will probably open again.

Southeast Asia
Bangkok, in Thailand, is the most popular departure point from Southeast Asia into India. One-way flights from Bangkok to Delhi cost around US$300 with Indian Airlines, or US$330 with Air India or Thai Airways International. If you're entering from Malaysia, the one-way economy fare from Kuala Lumpur to Delhi is US$609 with Malaysia Airlines. From Singapore, the one-way economy fare to Delhi is US$415 with Singapore Airways, or US$820 with Indian Airlines, Thai Airways International or SriLankan Airlines.

ORGANISED TOURS
In addition to companies that provide standard tours, there are many foreign eco-, leisure- and adventure-travel companies that can provide unusual and interesting trips. There are too many to include here;

the following are just a few that organise tours to India:

Australasia
Community Aid Abroad Tours
(☎ 08-8232 2727, W www.caa.org.au)
PO Box 34, Rundle Mall, SA 5000
Peregrine Adventures (☎ 03-9662 2700,
W www.peregrine.net.au) 258 Lonsdale St, Melbourne, Vic 3000; plus offices in Sydney, Brisbane, Adelaide and Perth
World Expeditions
Australia: (☎ 02-9279 0188, W www.world expeditions.com.au) 5th floor, 71 York St, Sydney, NSW 2000
New Zealand: (☎ 09-522 9161)
21 Reumera Rd, Newmarket, Auckland

UK
Encounter Overland (☎ 1728-862222,
W www.encounter-overland.com)
2001 Camp Green, Debenham, Stowmarket, Suffolk IP14 6LA
Exodus Expeditions (☎ 020-8675 5550,
W www.exodustravels.co.uk) 9 Weir Rd, London SW12 0LT
Imaginative Traveller (☎ 020-8742 8612,
W www.imaginative-traveller.com) 14 Barley Mow Passage, Chiswick, London W4 4PH

USA
Adventure Center (☎ 800-227 8747,
W www.adventure-center.com) 1311 63rd St, Suite 200, Emeryville, CA 94608
Asian Pacific Adventures (☎ 800-825 1680,
W www.asianpacificadventures.com) 9010 Reseda Blvd Suite 227, Northridge, CA 91324
Nature Exhibitions International
(☎ 800-869 0639, W www.naturexp.com)
7860 Peters Rd, Plantation, FL 33324
Sacred India Tours (☎ 562-263 6000,
W www.sacredindia.com) 5150 Candlewood St, Suite 21C, Lakewood, CA 90712

Rajasthan

AIR
Domestic Airports & Airlines
Within Rajasthan, there are airports in Jaipur, Jodhpur and Udaipur. There's also an airport in Jaisalmer, open from 1 October to 31 March. However, this is closed throughout the year when tensions are high along the Pakistan border, as was the case at the

Air Travel Glossary

Alliances Many of the world's leading airlines are now intimately involved with each other, sharing everything from reservations systems and check-in to aircraft and frequent-flyer schemes. Opponents say that alliances restrict competition. Whatever the arguments, there is no doubt that big alliances are the way of the future.

Courier Fares Businesses often need to send urgent documents or freight securely and quickly. Courier companies hire people to accompany the package through customs and, in return, offer a discount ticket which is sometimes a bargain. However, you may have to surrender all your baggage allowance and take only carry-on luggage.

Fares Airlines traditionally offer 1st-class (coded F), business-class (coded J) and economy-class (coded Y) tickets. These days there are so many promotional and discounted fares available that few passengers pay full fare.

Lost Tickets If you lose your airline ticket, an airline will usually treat it like a travellers cheque and, after inquiries, issue you with another one. Legally, however, an airline is entitled to treat it like cash and if you lose it then it's gone forever. Take very good care of your tickets.

Onward Tickets An entry requirement for many countries is that you have a ticket out of the country. If you're unsure of your next move, the easiest solution is to buy the cheapest onward ticket to a neighbouring country or a ticket from a reliable airline which can later be refunded if you do not use it.

Open-Jaw Tickets These are return tickets where you fly out to one place but return from another. If available, this can save you backtracking to your arrival point.

Overbooking Since every flight has some passengers who fail to show up, airlines often book more passengers than they have seats. Usually excess passengers make up for the no-shows, but occasionally somebody gets 'bumped' onto the next available flight. Guess who it is most likely to be? The passengers who check in late. If you do get 'bumped', you are normally offered some form of compensation.

Reconfirmation Some airlines require you to reconfirm your flight at least 72 hours prior to departure. Check your travel documents to see if this is the case.

Restrictions Discounted tickets often have various restrictions on them – such as needing to be paid for in advance and incurring a penalty to be altered or cancelled. Others are restrictions on the minimum and maximum period you must be away.

Round-the-World Tickets These tickets give you a limited period (usually a year) in which to circumnavigate the globe. You can go anywhere the carrying airlines go, as long as you don't backtrack. The number of stopovers or total number of separate flights is decided before you set off and they usually cost a bit more than a basic return flight.

Ticketless Travel Airlines are gradually waking up to the realisation that paper tickets are unnecessary encumbrances. On simple one-way or return trips, reservations details can be held on computer and the passenger merely shows ID to claim their seat.

Transferred Tickets Airline tickets cannot be transferred from one person to another. Travellers sometimes try to sell the return half of their ticket, but officials can ask you to prove that you are the person named on the ticket. On an international flight, tickets are compared with passports.

time of writing. Domestic services into Rajasthan are operated by the government-run Indian Airlines, and Jet Airways. At the time of writing, Sahara Airlines also had plans to open flights into Jaipur in mid-2002.

From Delhi, there are good air services to Rajasthan's main cities. To Jaipur there are four daily flights to Jaipur (US$65), two flights to Jodhpur (US$115) and three flights to Udaipur (US$115). See Getting There & Away in the Delhi chapter for departure times, information about Delhi's domestic airport and contact details for domestic airline offices in Delhi.

Mumbai's Santa Cruz domestic airport (4km from the international airport) has two terminals a couple of minutes' walk apart. Terminal A handles Indian Airlines flights, while terminal B caters to Jet Airways and Sahara Airlines. You're advised to check in one hour before departure. Note that flights on domestic sectors of Air India routes depart from the international airport.

From Mumbai there are four daily flights to Jaipur (US$165), two to Jodhpur (US$160) and three to Udaipur (US$135).

Reservations

The main airlines have computerised booking services and there are hundreds of computerised travel agencies in Delhi, Mumbai and Rajasthan. Phone numbers for city offices in Delhi and Rajasthan are given in the regional chapters. In Mumbai, you can buy tickets to Rajasthan from any of the many travel agencies or from **Indian Airlines** (☎ 2023031, 24-hour reservations ☎ 141, fax 2830832; Air India Bldg, Nariman Point) or **Jet Airways** (☎ 2837555, fax 2855694; Amarchand Mansion, Madame Cama Rd). All airlines require you to give a telephone number and address when booking. The major airlines don't require reconfirmation unless your ticket was bought outside India, in which case the usual 72-hour rule applies.

Tickets can be paid for with rupees, foreign currency or, in most cases, with credit cards. Change is given in rupees. A lost ticket is very bad news – airlines may issue a replacement ticket at their discretion, but a refund is almost impossible.

Indian Airlines offers a 25% discount for students as well as for those aged between 12 and 30.

Check-In

Check-in is an hour before departure. The baggage allowance is 20kg in economy class, 30kg in business. Some flights have security measures such as having to identify your baggage on the tarmac just before boarding and comprehensive clothing and baggage searches (ask if this is required when checking in). Remember also to get a tag for your hand luggage when you check in, or you may later be sent back to the check-in counter to get one (as the tag must be stamped when you clear security).

It's wise to make your domestic-flight booking at least one day ahead of your flight out of India – some travellers have missed their international connections due to the sudden delay or cancellation of their domestic flight.

BUS

There are bus services from Delhi to all the major towns in Rajasthan, including Jaipur (Rs 216/348 for deluxe/air-con, 5½ hrs), Bikaner (Rs 170 express, 10 hrs), Udaipur (Rs 263 express, 14 hrs,), Jodhpur (Rs 180 deluxe, 13 hrs) and Jaisalmer (Rs 250 private, 20 hrs). Buses to Rajasthan depart from the Interstate Bus Terminal at Kashmiri Gate; see the Delhi chapter for more details on services.

In Mumbai, private buses depart from Dr Anadrao Nair Rd, near Mumbai Central station, although traffic north of Mumbai can make bus travel a tedious option. There are no direct government services from Mumbai to Jaipur; you need to change in Udaipur. There are services to a number of Rajasthani towns, including express buses to Udaipur (Rs 232, 16 hrs) and deluxe buses to Mt Abu (Rs 350, 18 hrs).

Apart from the gateway cities of Delhi and Mumbai, there are also regular bus services between other major Indian cities and Rajasthan, such as Agra, Aurangabad and Ahmedabad. See the Getting Around chapter for general information on bus travel.

TRAIN

The Getting Around chapter has comprehensive information on Indian train travel.

The *Palace on Wheels* is a luxury escorted train journey which departs from Delhi and takes in Agra and the major tourist sights of Rajasthan. It costs from US$285 per person for a seven-night trip, including tours, entry fees, accommodation and all meals. See the boxed text 'Palace on Wheels' in the Getting Around chapter for more information.

From Delhi, there are trains to many destinations in Rajasthan including Bikaner (Rs 203/610 in 2nd/1st class, 12 hrs), Jaipur (Rs 77/405, 5¼ hrs), Jodhpur (Rs 278/727, 11 hrs) and Udaipur (Rs 144/756, 19 hrs). There are also trains to Agra (Rs 54/284, 2½ hrs). See the Delhi chapter for more details.

From Mumbai, the *Jaipur Express* leaves Mumbai Central at 6.50pm daily and takes 17½ hours to reach Jaipur. It costs Rs 301/873 for sleeper/air-con three-tier sleeper. There are also trains to Bharatpur, Jodhpur and Abu Road.

Two train systems operate out of Mumbai. For Rajasthan the one you need is **Western Railways** (*inquiries* ☎ 131), which has services to the north from Mumbai Central train station (still usually called Bombay Central). The easiest place to make bookings for Western Railways is at the crowded reservation centre opposite Churchgate train station, open from 8am to 8pm Monday to Saturday and 8am to 2pm on Sunday. The foreign-tourist-quota counter (open 9.30am to 4.30pm weekdays and until 2pm on Saturday) is upstairs, next to the Government of India tourist office, but tourist-quota tickets are only sold 24 hours before departure and you must pay in foreign currency. There's a reservation centre adjacent to Mumbai Central, but it doesn't sell tourist-quota tickets.

CAR

Few people bring their own vehicles to India. If you do decide to bring a car or motorcycle to India, it must be brought in under a carnet, a customs document guaranteeing its removal at the end of your stay. Failing to do so will be very expensive.

For information about travel by motorcycle and organised motorcycle tours in Rajasthan, see the Getting Around chapter.

Rental

It's possible to hire a self-drive car in Delhi (expect to pay around Rs 1500 per day), although on India's dangerous roads, it's really not recommended. If you must hire a car, you'll find some rental agencies listed in the Delhi chapter. Hiring a car and driver is a much better option. Costs start at around Rs 4 per kilometre – see the Getting Around chapter for further details.

If you're thinking of hiring a car in Mumbai to drive up the coast, think again. The route north, National Hwy 8, is one of the most congested roads in the country.

Getting Around

AIR
Domestic Air Services

There are operational airports in Rajasthan at Jaipur, Jodhpur and Udaipur. The airport at Jaisalmer is also open from 1 October to 31 March, although it's closed throughout the year when tensions between India and Pakistan are high (as was the case at the time of writing).

In addition to flights serving Rajasthan from other Indian cities (see Air in the Getting There & Away chapter), there are several air services between the cities of Rajasthan. At the time of writing, only Indian Airlines and Jet Airways offered internal services. You'll find details about these flights in the regional chapters and information on booking in the Getting There & Away chapter.

BUS

The state government bus service is called **Rajasthan Roadways** (**W** *www.rajasthan roadways.com*), otherwise known as the Rajasthan State Road Transport Corporation (RSRTC). Often there are privately owned, local bus services as well as luxury private coaches between major cities. These can be booked with travel agencies.

Fares and journey times differ by transport provider, eg, by the state-owned bus company and the private operators. The fares with private operators can be influenced by the time of year, the condition of the bus and sometimes by your bargaining skills. Similarly, journey times quoted in this guide are approximate – a multitude of factors can influence how long it takes to get from A to B, from traffic jams and accidents to the fearlessness of the driver. This is India.

Classes

Generally bus travel is crowded, cramped, slow and uncomfortable, although the luxury and deluxe services between major destinations are a good way to travel.

Ordinary buses usually have five seats across – three on one side of the aisle, two on the other – although if there are only five people sitting in them consider yourself lucky! There are often mounds of baggage in the aisles, occasionally chickens under seats, and in some more remote places there'll be people travelling 'upper class' (ie, on the roof) as well. These buses tend to be frustratingly slow, are often in an advanced state of decrepitude and stop frequently – often for seemingly no reason – and for long periods.

Express buses are a big improvement in that they stop far less often. They're still crowded, but at least you feel like you're getting somewhere. The fare is usually a few rupees more than on an ordinary bus – well worth the extra.

Deluxe buses have four padded seats across and these will usually recline. Superdeluxe buses offer even greater comfort and have air-conditioning.

Unlike state-operated bus companies, private operators are keen to maximise profits; their priority is therefore speed rather than maintenance – traveller beware.

If you're unlucky you'll strike a bus with a terrible sound-system and a driver who's a big Hindi pop fan with no qualms about pumping up the volume. Some of the more expensive bus services have videos, which are also usually turned up at full volume for hours on end. You can't do anything about

India's mechanical monsters challenge all the rules

this except bring ear plugs or develop a soft spot for the latest Bollywood hits.

Reservations

If you are travelling with someone, work out a bus-boarding plan so one of you can guard the gear while the other storms the bus in search of a seat. Another accepted method is to pass a newspaper or article of clothing through the window and place it on an empty seat, or ask a passenger to do it for you. Having made your 'reservation' you then board the bus after things have simmered down. This method rarely fails.

You can, however, often make advance reservations (sometimes for a small additional fee) which secure you a ticket with a seat number. This usually only applies to the more upmarket services such as express and deluxe. Private buses should always be booked in advance.

At many bus stations there is a separate women's queue. You may not notice this because the sign (if it exists) will not be in English and there may not be any women queuing. Usually the same ticket window will handle the male and female queues. Despite the glares (or even men's refusals to shift in the queue), female travellers should simply sharpen their elbows and confidently make their way to the front, where they will get almost immediate service.

Baggage

Some companies charge a few rupees to store your luggage in an enclosed compartment at the back of the bus. Alternatively, baggage is sometimes carried for free on the roof and if this is the case, it's worthwhile taking some precautions. Make sure it's tied on securely and that nobody dumps a tin trunk on top of your gear. If someone lugs your bag onto the roof, make sure you pay a few rupees for the service. Theft can be a problem, so keep an eye on your bags during any stops en route (which are an ideal time to stretch your legs anyway).

Toilet Stops

On long-distance bus trips, *chai* (tea) stops can be far too frequent or else agonisingly infrequent. When the bus does stop, make sure you know how long it's staying put before you wander off to buy a *chai* or relieve yourself. Long-distance trips can be a real hassle for women travellers as toilet facilities are generally inadequate, to say the least. Forget about modesty and do what the local women do – wander a few yards off or find a convenient bush.

TRAIN

India has the world's biggest rail network under one management: over 60,000km of track. **Indian Railways** (w *www.indianrail.gov.in*) also has 1.6 million staff, which makes it the world's biggest employer. Moving 11 million passengers daily to any of 7085 stations, it's a ride in India's bloodstream. At first the railways can seem as complicated as India – trains range from intercity expresses to country passenger services on narrow-gauge tracks, with 10 classes from air-conditioned executive chair to ordinary wooden bench, and separate reservation offices or chaotic queues. It's simple enough once you get used to it. While sometimes slower than buses, train journeys can be relaxing, fascinating and even a little romantic. And for overnight journeys they are much preferable to buses.

There are tourist quotas for many express trains, and special offices or counters for foreigners in major cities and destinations (you must bring a money-changing receipt or ATM slip when paying with rupees). We've listed important trains here but there are many, many more. The national guide, *Trains at a Glance* (Rs 25), has 200 pages of train information, and there are timetables covering each regional zone. Look for it at station newsstands.

Classes

Shatabdi Express trains offer a same-day service connecting Delhi, Jaipur, Ajmer and Alwar. These are the fastest (the name means 'arrow') and most expensive trains, with only two classes, air-con executive chair and air-con chair. They are comfortable and the fares include meals, but the glass windows cut the views considerably

Indian Train Fares in Rupees

distance (km)	1st class air-con (1A)	2-tier air-con (2A)	3-tier air-con (3A)	chair car (CC)	sleeper (SL)	2nd class (II)
100	542	322	158	114	84	32
200	778	430	243	171	84	54
300	1052	543	329	231	114	73
400	1296	653	405	277	140	90
500	1541	771	482	323	166	107
1000	2506	1253	783	522	270	174
1500	3154	1577	986	658	340	219
2000	3644	1841	1139	800	393	253

compared with the nonair-con classes on slower trains, which have barred windows and fresh air.

Rajdhani Express trains are long-distance express services between Delhi and major towns, and offer air-conditioned 1st class (1A), two-tier air-con (2A), three-tier air-con (3A) and 2nd class. Two-tier means there are two levels of bunks in each compartment, which are a little wider and longer than the counterparts in three-tier. Two- and three-tier air-con cost respectively a half and a third as much as air-con 1st class, and are perfectly adequate for an overnight trip.

Other express trains and mail trains have two-tier air-con coaches, chair car (if the train runs only during the day), nonair-con sleeper (bring your own bedding), nonair-con 2nd class and, finally, unreserved tickets. Sleeper costs only a quarter as much as two-tier air-con. Some trains also have three-tier air-con and nonair-con 1st class, but the latter is being phased out. To find the train you want, you can search through *Trains at a Glance* (which often takes a lot more than just a glance), or ask English-speaking staff at the inquiry counters of big stations. At the smaller stations mid-level officials, such as the deputy station master, usually speak English.

Second-class travel on passenger trains is very cheap at 60% less than 2nd class express. In the cheaper classes the squat toilet is cleaner than the sit-down flush one. Passenger trains travel on slow local routes, stopping at each country station. These are best on quiet days, when you can feel the breeze through the windows and listen to local itinerant singers at a relaxed pace.

Reservations

To make a reservation you must fill out a form stating which class you need and the train's name and number. For overnight journeys it's best to reserve your place a couple of days in advance, particularly if it's a holiday period. If there is no special counter or office for foreigners at the train station (sometimes classed with other minorities such as 'freedom fighters'), you have to adopt local queuing practices. These range from reasonably orderly lines to mosh pits. There are sometimes separate 'ladies' queues', but usually the same window handles men and women. So women can go to the front of the queue, next to the first male at the window, and get served almost immediately.

If the latter is too much, many travel agencies and hotels are in the business of purchasing train tickets for a small commission. But watch out for small-fry travel agents who promise express-train tickets and deliver tickets for obscure mail or passenger trains. Only leave a small deposit, if any, and check the tickets before paying.

Reserved tickets show your berth and carriage number. Efficient railway staff also stick lists of names and berths on each reserved carriage, as well as the carriage number in chalk. Air-con carriages tend to be towards the front of the train.

If you can't buy a reserved seat you can ask if there is a waiting list, or try your luck by getting on anyway. Unless it's a popular express train or it's a busy holiday it usually works out. You can get on without a ticket but it is more polite to buy an unreserved ticket and try to upgrade it (unreserved tickets go on sale an hour before departure). Find a reserved-class carriage and a spare seat of your choice, and wait there for the conductor (officially the Travelling Ticket Examiner or TTE) to find you. Explain you could only buy an unreserved ticket and ask about vacancies. With luck, the conductor will be happy to oblige. You pay the difference between the ordinary fare and the fare of whichever class you're in, plus a small excess charge of around Rs 25. It's a hassle if you don't have enough change, as conductors usually don't have any either.

Costs

Fares operate on a distance basis. The time-tables indicate the distance in kilometres between the stations and from this it is simple to calculate the cost between any two stations. Reserved tickets attract extra fees of around Rs 50. If your journey is longer than 500km, you can take a day's break en route but you must have your ticket endorsed by the station master or ticket collector at the station you stop at.

Bedding is free in air-con classes, and costs Rs 20 in nonair-con first class. Meals are free on *Rajdhani Express* and *Shatabdi Express* trains, and cheap meals are available on other trains.

Important stations have retiring rooms, which are available if you have a valid ticket or a ticket for the train you've just gotten off. They vary in quality, but at best they're very cheap and can even be ruthlessly clean, with either dormitories or private rooms (see also Accommodation in the Facts for the Visitor chapter).

Refunds Tickets are refundable but fees apply. If you present at least two days in advance, a fee of up to Rs 50 applies. Steeper charges apply if you seek a refund less than four hours prior to departure, but

you can get some sort of refund as late as 12 hours afterwards.

When refunding your ticket you officially have a magic pass to go to the front of the queue, as the next person might require the spot you're surrendering. We've never seen if this actually works in practice.

Special Trains

The luxurious *Palace on Wheels* train makes a regular circuit of Rajasthan. For more details see the boxed text 'Palace on Wheels' later in this chapter.

Left Luggage

Most stations have left-luggage rooms which cost a couple of rupees per day for one bag. It's useful if you want to visit but not stay in a town, or to hunt for accommodation unencumbered.

CAR
Rental

Self-Drive At present there are no agencies in Rajasthan offering self-drive vehicles. In Delhi, self-drive car rental is a possibility – by Western standards the cost is quite low, but given India's hair-raising driving conditions it's much, much better and far more economical to hire a car and driver.

If you're still interested in self-drive, expect to pay around Rs 1500 per day (with a two-day minimum). Insurance is extra and so you usually have to leave a deposit (refundable) of Rs 10,000. See the Delhi chapter for details of rental agencies. You officially need either a valid international driving licence or a regular licence from your home country.

Car & Driver Long-distance car hire with driver is an increasingly popular way to get around Rajasthan. Spread among, say, four people it's not overly expensive and you have the flexibility to go where you want when you want.

Almost any local taxi will quite happily set off on a long-distance trip in Rajasthan. Inquiring at a taxi rank is the cheapest and easiest way to organise this. Alternatively, you can ask a travel agency or your hotel to book one for you, but remember that they'll take their cut for this service.

Official rates for a car and driver with the Rajasthan Tourism Development Corporation are Rs 4.80 per kilometre for a nonair-con car, and Rs 6.5 per kilometre for an air-con car, with the usual 250km minimum hire charge per day and a Rs 100/150 per night overnight charge for nonair-con/air-con. More competitive rates are offered by some travel agencies in Jaipur – see Getting There & Away in the Jaipur chapter. Expect to pay around Rs 3.50 per kilometre if you arrange a car directly with a taxi driver – with a Rs 100 overnight charge and a minimum charge for 250km per day. If you're only going one way, remember that you have to pay for the driver to return to your starting point. Your driver may ask you for an advance of a few hundred rupees at the start of the trip to pay for petrol.

Share-Jeeps Share-jeeps supplement the bus service in many parts of Rajasthan, especially in areas off the main road routes, such as many of the towns in Shekhawati.

Jeeps leave, when they are full, from well-established 'passenger stations' on the outskirts of towns and villages; locals should be able to point you in the right direction. They are usually dirt cheap and jam-packed. The average fare for a one-hour trip is around Rs 10, but you may be sharing the limited space with 15 other people and their belongings! Some travellers may find them too claustrophobic for longer trips.

On the Road
Because of extreme congestion in cities and narrow bumpy roads in the country, driving is a slow, stop-start process – hard on you, the car and fuel economy. Service is so-so; parts and tyres are not always easy to obtain, though there are plenty of puncture-repair

Driving the Best Bargain

If you hire a car and driver for an extended period of time, try to get a driver who speaks at least some English and who is knowledgeable about the region(s) you intend visiting.

More than a few travellers have shelled out much more money than is reasonable, paying for the driver's accommodation and meals (even booze!), completely unaware that these costs have already been factored into the fee. Make sure you understand the accommodation/meal arrangement for the driver before paying and ensure that the driver is also clear on this before you set off. In most cases, the charge that is quoted includes an allowance for the driver's daily living expenses (ie, food and lodging).

When it comes to where the driver stays overnight, this is for him to decide and should never be your headache (many choose to sleep in the back seat of the car thus pocketing their accommodation allowance). Some hotels (especially in remote areas) will provide free (or minimal cost) accommodation for drivers, as there is nowhere else to stay. In the cities and towns, many hotels do not permit drivers to stay or eat in guest areas, even if you insist on paying.

Finally, and very importantly, it is imperative to set the ground rules from day one. Many travellers have complained of having their holiday completely dictated by their driver – one couple were bullied into having meals only when it suited the driver. Another set of travellers could only stay at hotels decided by their driver (see also the boxed text 'About Touts' in the Facts for the Visitor chapter). Your holiday is going to be much more pleasant if you don't have prickly relations with your driver. The way to achieve this is by politely, but firmly, letting him know from the outset that you are the boss. That way, he'll know that you won't put up with any bullying.

At the end of your trip, a tip is the best way of showing your appreciation. So how much should you tip? Well, Rs 50 per day is considered fair, but if you are really chuffed with your driver's service, anything above that is going to get a bigger smile.

places. All in all, driving is not pleasurable (especially for longer trips) except in rural areas where there's little traffic.

MOTORCYCLE

Travelling around Rajasthan by motorcycle has become increasingly popular in recent years, and it certainly has its attractions – motoring along the back roads through small untouristy villages, picnics in the wilds, the freedom to go when and where you like – making it the ideal way to travel.

You'll still get a sore bum; you'll have difficult and frustrating conversations; and you'll get fed up with asking directions, receiving misleading answers and getting lost; but you'll also have adventures not available to the visitor who relies on public transport.

These days, there are a number of excellent motorcycle tours on offer in Rajasthan (see Organised Motorcycle Tours), which take the hassle out of doing it solo.

Equipment

You must have either an International Driving Licence or a regular licence from your home country to motorcycle in India.

It's definitely worth bringing your own helmet. Even though Indian helmets may be cheaper, it can be tough finding one that fits well, and the quality is variable. Leathers, gloves, boots, driving goggles, waterproofs and other protective gear should also be brought from your home country.

Organised tours often have a vehicle which transports luggage, but if you're travelling independently, make sure you have a pack that is easy to carry.

Rental

Some places in Rajasthan hire out motorbikes on a daily, weekly or monthly basis (see the regional chapters for details), but the range of machines available is rather limited. Delhi has a much broader range – see that chapter for details.

Purchase

Purchasing a second-hand machine is a matter of asking around and a perfect place to start is with mechanics, who can usually also offer advice about insurance options. See the Delhi chapter for recommended outlets.

To buy a new bike, you officially have to have a local address and be a resident foreign national. When buying secondhand, all you need to do is give an address.

Ownership Papers An obvious tip perhaps, but do not part with your money until you have the ownership papers, receipt and affidavit signed by a magistrate authorising the owner (as recorded in the ownership papers) to sell the machine – not to mention the keys to the bike and the bike itself!

On the Road

It must be said that, given the general road conditions, motorcycling is a reasonably hazardous endeavour, and one ideally undertaken by experienced riders. Hazards range from goats crossing the road to defunct trucks which have been abandoned in the middle of the road. And of course there are the perpetual potholes and unmarked speed humps to contend with. Rural roads sometimes have various grain crops laid out on roads to be threshed by passing vehicles – it can be a real hazard for bikers.

The risk of bike theft is minimal. The worst you're likely to experience is the way people seem to treat parked motorcycles as public utilities – handy for sitting on, using the mirror to comb their hair, fiddling with the switches – none of which is usually intended to do any damage. You'll just have to turn all the switches off and readjust the mirrors when you get back on.

Avoid covering too much territory in one day. A lot of energy is spent simply concentrating on the road, making long days exhausting and potentially dangerous. On the busy national highways expect to average 50km/h without stops; on smaller roads, where driving conditions are worse, 10km/h is not an unrealistic average. On the whole, on good roads you can easily expect to cover a minimum of 100km a day (up to 300km with minimal stops).

Night driving should be avoided at all costs. If you think driving in daylight is difficult, imagine what it's like at night when there's the added hazard of half the vehicles being inadequately lit (or without headlights on at all), not to mention other hindrances such as animals crossing and broken-down vehicles.

For really long hauls, putting the bike on a train can be a convenient option. You'll generally pay about as much as the 2nd-class passenger fare for the bike. The petrol tank must be empty, and there should be a tag in an obvious place detailing name, destination, passport number and train details. When you pack the bike, it's wise to remove the mirrors and loosen the handlebars to prevent damage.

Repairs & Maintenance

Original spare parts bought from an 'authorised dealer' can be rather expensive compared with the copies available from your spare-parts-wallah. Delhi's Karol Bagh is a good place to go for spare parts for all Indian and imported bikes. If you're going to remote regions, take basic spares with you (valves, piston rings etc) as they may not be readily available.

For all machines (particularly older ones), make sure you regularly check and tighten all nuts and bolts, as Indian roads and engine vibration tend to work things loose quite quickly. Check the engine and gearbox oil

Surviving the Roads

In 1951 the number of motorised vehicles on India's roads totalled 300,000. The figure had climbed to 5.4 million by 1981 and swelled to an estimated 45 million by 2001. Road deaths have risen in line with vehicle numbers and are in fact the highest in the world – an estimated 80,000 people each year! According to the Central Road Research Institute, about 10% of road fatalities are pedestrians and cyclists in the major cities. The pavements are a big problem; they are often in a state of severe disrepair, tiny or nonexistent, therefore tempting pedestrians to jaywalk – with deadly results.

The reasons for the high road toll in India are numerous, and many of them fairly obvious. Firstly, there's road congestion and vehicle overcrowding – when a bus runs off the road there are plenty of people stuffed inside to get injured, and it's unlikely too many of them will be able to escape in a hurry.

Secondly, there is India's unwritten 'might is right' road rule which means that vehicles always have the right of way over pedestrians, and bigger vehicles always have the right of way over smaller ones. It's not surprising that so many pedestrians are killed in hit-and-run accidents. (The propensity to disappear after the incident is not wholly surprising since lynch mobs can assemble remarkably quickly, even when the driver is not at fault.)

A substantial number of accidents involve trucks. Being the biggest, heaviest and mightiest vehicles on the road, you either get out of their way or get mowed down. Also, as with so many Indian vehicles, they're likely to be grossly overloaded and not in the best condition. Trucks invariably carry considerably more than the maximum load recommended by the manufacturer. It's a real eye-opener to see the number of trucks crumpled by the sides of the national highways, and these aren't old accidents, but ones that have obviously happened in the last 24 hours.

If you are driving, you need to be alert at all times. Night driving should be avoided altogether. At night there are unilluminated cars and ox carts, while in the daytime there are zigzagging bicycle riders and hordes of pedestrians. Day and night there are the fearless truck drivers to contend with. The other thing you have to endure at night is the eccentric way in which headlights are used – a combination of full beam and totally off (dipped beams are virtually unheard of). A loud horn definitely helps since the normal driving technique is to put your hand firmly on the horn, close your eyes and plough through regardless. Considering the hazards of night driving, it's best to avoid it.

Even though the Indian roads can be a nail-biting experience, it may help if you take solace in the Indian karma theory – it's not so much the vehicle that collided with you as the events of your previous life that caused the accident.

levels regularly – with the quality of oil it is advisable to change it and clean the oil filter every couple of thousand kilometres.

Given the condition of many Indian roads, chances are you'll make constant visits to a puncture-wallah. These phenomenal fix-it men are found almost everywhere, but it's obviously good to have the tools to at least remove your own wheel. Indeed, given the hassles of constant flat tyres, it's worth lashing out on new tyres if you buy a second-hand bike with worn tyres. A new rear tyre for an Enfield costs around Rs 600 to 700.

Organised Motorcycle Tours

Motorcycle tours are a superb, no-hassles way of seeing India. They usually operate with a minimum number of people and some can even be tailor-made. Contact operators directly for prices and other details:

Ferris Wheels (☎/fax 61-2-4267 5500, ⓦ www.ferriswheels.com.au) PO Box 526, Thirroul, NSW 2515, Australia. This company organises tours through Rajasthan on classic Enfields.

Himalayan Motorcycle Tours (☎/fax 44-1256-771773, ⓦ www.himalayanmotorcycles.com) 16 High St, Overton, Hants RG25 3HA, UK. This company is run by an easy-going American expatriate, Patrick Moffat. Patrick conducts upmarket tours of Rajasthan.

Indian Motorcycle Adventures (☎ 64-9-372 7550, ⓔ gumby@ihug.co.nz) 40 O'Brien Rd, Rocky Bay, Waiheke Island, New Zealand. This company offers 20-day tours of Rajasthan.

BICYCLE

Rajasthan offers an immense array of experiences and challenges for a long-distance cyclist. Nevertheless, long-distance cycling is not for the faint of heart or weak of knee. You'll need physical endurance to cope with the roads, traffic and the climate.

Before you set out, read some books on bicycle touring such as the Sierra Club's *The Bike Touring Manual* by Rob van de Plas (Bicycle Books, 1993). Cycling magazines provide useful information including listings for bicycle tour operators and the addresses of spare-parts suppliers. Their classifieds sections are also good places to look for a riding companion.

Your local cycling club may also be able to help with information and advice. In the UK, the **Cyclists Touring Club** (☎ 0870-8730060, fax 01483-426994; ⓦ www.ctc .org.uk; 69 Meadrow, Godalming, Surrey GU7 3HS, UK), has country touring sheets that are free to members. The **International Bicycle Fund** (☎/fax 1-206-7670848; ⓦ www.ibike .org; 4887 Columbia Dr S, Seattle, WA 98108-1919, USA) has two useful publications: *Selecting and Preparing a Bike for Travel in Remote Areas* and *Bikes Can Fly* (about taking bikes on airplanes).

If you're a serious cyclist or amateur racer and want to contact counterparts while in India, there's the Cycle Federation of India; contact the secretary of Yamun Velodrome in New Delhi. If you're after anything bike-related in Delhi head for Jhandwalan market, near Karol Bagh, which has imported and domestic new and second-hand bikes and spare parts.

Using Your Own Bike

Most travellers prefer to buy a bike in India, but by all means consider bringing your own. Mountain bikes are especially suited to India – their sturdier construction makes them more manoeuvrable and less prone to damage, and allows you to tackle rocky, muddy roads unsuitable for lighter machines. Inquire in your home country about air transport and customs formalities. When transporting your bike, remove pedals, all luggage and accessories, turn the handlebars, cover the chain and let the tyres down a bit.

It may be hard to find parts, especially wheels, for touring bikes with 700C wheels. Parts for bicycles with 26-inch wheels (of variable standards) are available.

Carry a good lock and use it. Consider wrapping your bicycle frame in used inner tubes – this not only hides fancy paint jobs, but protects them from knocks and scrapes.

Rental & Purchase

Even in the smallest towns there is usually at least one outlet that rents bikes. However, you may like to buy a bike in India and your best bet is to shop around to get a feel for brands and prices. There are many brands of

Indian clunkers, including Hero, Atlas, BSA and Raleigh. Raleigh is considered the finest quality, followed by BSA, which has many models including some sporty jobs. Hero mountain-style bicycles are on sale in the larger towns.

Once you've decided on a bike you have a choice of luggage carriers – mostly the rat-trap type varying only in size, price and strength. There's a plethora of saddles available but all are equally bum-breaking. Consider bringing you own saddle, rack and good-quality panniers. Get a machine fitted with a stand and bell.

Reselling is usually a breeze. Count on getting about 60% to 70% of what you originally paid, if it was a new bike. A local cycle-hire shop will probably be interested, or simply ask around to find potential buyers.

On the Road

It's obviously more pleasurable to ride on quieter roads – avoid big cities where the chaotic traffic can be a real hazard for cyclists. National highways can also be a nightmare with speeding trucks and buses. Always make inquiries before venturing off road.

Avoid leaving anything on your bike that can easily be removed when it's unattended. You may like to bring along a padlock and chain. However, don't be paranoid – your bike is probably safer in India than in many Western cities.

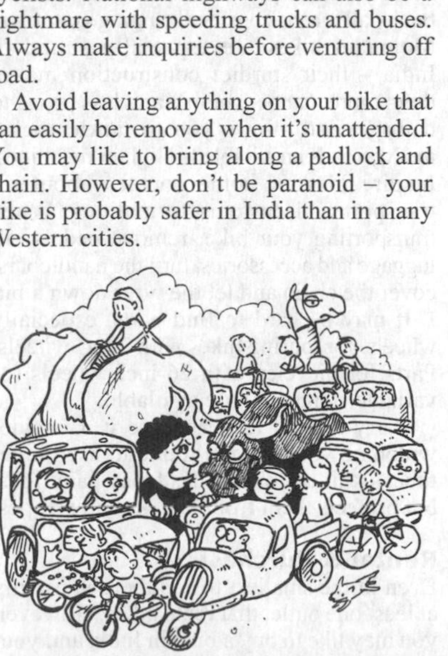

CLINT CURÉ

Cycling in India is not for the faint hearted, but your efforts will be amply rewarded

Distances

If you've never cycled long distances, start with 20km to 40km a day and increase this as you gain stamina and confidence. Be warned that asking directions can send you on a wild-goose chase.

For an eight-hour pedal an experienced cycle tourist will average 70km to 100km a day on undulating plains, or 50km to 70km in mountainous areas on sealed roads; cut this by at least one-third for unsealed roads. The distance you cycle can be dictated by available accommodation; not all villages have a place to stay. If you're cycling in a hot climate, try to get your cycling done by noon as the sun may be too strong in the afternoon. Hotels also fill up in the afternoon and it's usually dark by 6pm, so these are additional reasons to get an early start.

Repairs & Maintenance

For Indian bikes, there are plenty of repair 'shops' (some are no more than a puncture-wallah with his box of tools under a tree), which makes maintenance delightfully straightforward. Puncture-wallahs will patch tubes for a nominal cost. Check the tyres regularly for bits of glass or other sharp objects and dig them out before they make it through to the tube.

If you bring your own bicycle to India, you will need to be prepared for the contingencies of part replacement or repair. Several travellers warn that it is not at all easy locating foreign parts. Ensure you have a working knowledge of your machine. Bring all necessary tools with you as well as a compact bike manual with diagrams – Indian mechanics can work wonders and illustrations help overcome the language barrier. Roads don't often have paved shoulders and are very dusty, so keep your chain lubricated, and bring a spare.

Organised Bicycle Tours

If you want to splash out, **Butterfield & Robinson** *(☎ 416-864 1354; Ⓦ www.butterfield.com; 70 Bond St, Toronto M5B 1X3, Canada)* offers biking expeditions through Rajasthan. The all-inclusive tours last for 12 days, which are divided into walking and

PALL BEINSSEN

HIFA PUNJABI

ANDERS BLOMQVIST

Goats for sale, bedecked elephants parading, pet parrots perched atop young devotees; animals are intrinsic to Rajasthan's fairs and festivals, where celebration meets commerce

These ships of the desert refuel when they can

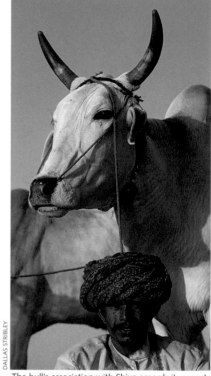

The bull's association with Shiva accords it respect

The serenity of the desert night balances the crush and hoopla of Pushkar Camel Fair

riding days. Expect to pay at least US$5975 per person (US$6800 for singles).

HITCHING

Hitching is never entirely safe in any country, and we don't recommend it. Travellers who decide to hitch should understand that they are taking a small but potentially serious risk. People who do choose to hitch are safer travelling in pairs and let someone know where they are planning to go.

In India hitching is not a realistic option. There are not that many private cars streaking across India so you are likely to be on board trucks. You are then stuck with the old quandaries: 'Will the driver expect to be paid?'; 'Will they be unhappy if I don't offer to pay?'; 'Will they be unhappy with what I offer or will they simply want too much?'.

It is a very bad idea for women to hitch. A woman in the cabin of a truck on a lonely road is taking a huge risk.

LOCAL TRANSPORT

Although there are comprehensive local-bus networks in most major towns, unless you have time to familiarise yourself with the routes, you're better off sticking to taxis, autorickshaws or cycle-rickshaws, or hiring bicycles.

A basic rule applies to any form of transport where the fare is not ticketed, fixed or metered: agree on the fare beforehand. If you fail to do that you can expect enormous arguments and hassles when you get to your destination. And agree on the fare clearly – if there is more than one of you make sure it covers all of you (the price quoted should be per vehicle, not per person). If you have baggage make sure there are no extra charges, or you may be asked for more at the end of the trip. If a driver refuses to use the meter, or insists on an extortionate rate, simply walk away – if he really wants the job the price will drop. If you can't agree on a reasonable fare, find another driver.

Other useful tips when catching taxis/rickshaws include the following:

- Always have enough small change, as drivers rarely do, which can be a real hassle especially

at night when shops/banks (where you can get change) are closed.
- If you are staying, or dining at a top-end venue and you need to catch a rickshaw, try walking a few hundred metres down the road to avoid the drivers who hang outside assuming you're a cash cow.
- Finally, it's a good idea to carry around a business card of the hotel in which you are staying, as your pronunciation of streets, hotel names etc may be incomprehensible to drivers. Some hotel cards even have a nifty little sketch map clearly indicating their location.

Fares are often steeper (as much as double the day fare) at night and some drivers charge a few rupees extra for luggage. Many autorickshaw drivers are right into the commission racket – see the boxed text 'About Touts' in the Visitor chapter.

To/From the Airport

There are usually prepaid taxi and/or autorickshaw booths at all the airports in Rajasthan. These are the easiest ways to get into town.

Taxi

There are taxis in most towns in Rajasthan, and many of them (certainly in the major cities) are metered. Getting a metered fare is another thing. First of all the meter may be 'broken'. Threatening to get another taxi will usually fix it immediately, except during rush hours. It's best to get a prepaid taxi, if they're available.

Secondly, the meter will almost certainly be out of date. Fares are adjusted upwards so much faster and more frequently than meters are recalibrated that drivers almost always have 'fare adjustment cards' indicating what you should pay compared to what the meter indicates. This is, of course, wide open to abuse. You have no idea if you're being shown the right card or if the taxi's meter has actually been recalibrated and you're being shown the card anyway.

The only answer to all this is to try to get an idea of what the fare should be before departure (ask at the information desks at the airport or your hotel). You'll begin to develop a feel for what the meter says, what the cards say and what the two together should indicate.

Autorickshaw
An autorickshaw is a noisy three-wheel device powered by a two-stroke motorcycle engine with a driver up front and seats for two (or sometimes more) passengers behind. They don't have doors and have just a canvas top. They are also known as scooters or autos.

They're generally about half the price of a taxi, are usually metered and follow the same ground rules as taxis.

Because of their size, autorickshaws are often faster than taxis for short trips and their drivers are decidedly nuttier. Hair-raising near-misses are guaranteed and glancing-blow collisions are not infrequent; thrill seekers will love them!

Tempo
Somewhat like a large autorickshaw, these ungainly looking three-wheel devices operate rather like minibuses or share-taxis along fixed routes. Unless you are spending large amounts of time in one city, it is generally impractical to try to find out what the

routes are. You'll find it much easier and more convenient to go by autorickshaw.

Cycle-Rickshaw
This is effectively a three-wheeler bicycle with a seat for two passengers behind the rider. They can be found in many of Rajasthan's towns and are a cheaper (if slower) alternative to autorickshaws. They are also much more environmentally friendly.

Fares must always be agreed upon in advance. Avoid situations where the driver says 'As you like'. He's punting on the fact that you are not well acquainted with correct fares and will overpay. No matter what you pay in situations like this, it will invariably be deemed too little and an unpleasant situation often develops. This is especially the case in popular tourist destinations such as Agra and Jaipur. In these places the riders can be as talkative and opinionated as any New York cabby.

It's quite feasible to hire a rickshaw-wallah by time, not just for a straight trip. Hiring one for a day or even several days can make good financial sense. Make sure that your watches are synchronised before you set out!

Palace on Wheels

The RTDC *Palace on Wheels* is a special train service for tourists which operates weekly tours of Rajasthan, departing from Delhi every Wednesday from September to the end of April. The itinerary takes in Jaipur, Chittorgarh, Udaipur, Sawai Madhopur (for Ranthambhore National Park), Jaisalmer, Jodhpur, Bharatpur (for the Keoladeo Ghana National Park) and Agra. It's a hell of a lot of ground to cover in a week, but most of the travelling is done at night.

Originally this train used carriages that had belonged to various maharajas, but these became so ancient that new carriages were built to look like the originals. They were also fitted with air-conditioning. The result is a very luxurious mobile hotel and it can be a memorable way to travel. The train has two dining cars and a well-stocked bar. Each coach, which is attended by a splendidly costumed captain and attendant, contains four coupés (either double or twin share) with private bathroom with running hot and cold water.

The cost includes tours, entry fees, accommodation on the train plus all meals. Rates per person per day from October to March are US$485/350 for a single/double and US$285 for triple occupancy (the third person sleeps on a fold-away bed). In September and April the tariff is lower: US$395/295/260 for a single/double/triple. It's a very popular service and bookings must be made in advance at **RTDC Tourist Reception Centre** (☎ 011-338 1884, fax 338 2823; Bikaner House, Pandara Rd, New Delhi, 110011) or at **RTDC Tourism, Swagatam Campus** (☎ 0141-203531, fax 201045; w www.palaceonwheels.net) near the train station in Jaipur.

Tonga

In many towns, you'll come across horse-drawn carriages known as tongas. Prices are generally comparable with cycle-rickshaws, and this is a good transport choice if you're concerned about animal welfare. The old-fashioned tongas are becoming increasingly marginalised in favour of autorickshaws and other pollution-belching motorised machines. This forces tonga-wallahs into freight work (such as carrying heavy loads of vegetables), which is a much harder life for the horses.

Bicycle

Bikes are the ideal way of getting around the sights in a city or even for making longer trips. Even in the smallest towns there is usually a shop that rents some sort of bicycle. They charge from around Rs 3 to 5 per hour or Rs 15 to 25 per day. Shops in tourist traps such as Jaisalmer, however, can charge much more.

ORGANISED TOURS
RTDC Tours

In most of the larger cities and places of tourist interest in Rajasthan, including Jaipur, Jodhpur, Udaipur and Jaisalmer, the RTDC operates city tours or tours to places of interest in the environs. These tours are usually very good value, particularly where the tourist sights are spread out over a wide area, as in Jaipur.

The big drawback is that many of these tours try to cram far too much into too short a period of time. They can also be cancelled without notice.

The RTDC also offers a range of package tours. These include a six-day Mewar tour, which leaves Delhi every Saturday and takes in Jaipur, Chittorgarh, Ranakpur, Udaipur, Ajmer and Pushkar (Rs 5500 per person); a three-day Golden Triangle tour, which leaves Delhi every Tuesday and takes in Siliserh, Sariska, Jaipur, Bharatpur, Fatehpur Sikri and Agra (Rs 3100 per person); a

three-day Hawa Mahal tour, which leaves Delhi every Friday and takes in Agra, Fatehpur Sikri, Bharatpur, Deeg, Sariska and Jaipur (Rs 3100 per person); the seven-day desert-circuit tour, which leaves Delhi every Monday and takes in Bikaner, Jaisalmer, Jodhpur, Ajmer and Pushkar (Rs 6200 per person); a four-day wildlife tour, which leaves on request and visits Sariska, Ranthambhore, Deeg and Bharatpur (Rs 4000 per person); and the 15-day Rajasthan tour, which leaves on the first and third Thursday of every month and covers the entire state (Rs 12,000 per person). The tariff includes transport, accommodation (usually at RTDC hotels), sightseeing and guide; entry charges are extra. The tariff for children is lower. There must be a minimum of four people for these tours to operate. For more information, contact the **RTDC Tourist Reception Centre** (☎ *011-338 1884, 338 3837, fax 338 2823; Bikaner House, Pandara Rd, New Delhi, 110011).*

Other Tours

There is a plethora of travel agencies offering various excursions in Rajasthan. One of the few outfits in Rajasthan that promotes sustainable tourism is **Alternative Travels** (☎ *01594-22239, fax 24061; Apani Dhani, Nawalgarh, Shekhawati).* Ramesh Jangid of Alternative Travels can organise camel and cycling trips around the painted towns of Shekhawati, treks in the Aravalli Range and homestays with villagers. For more details, see Organised Tours under Nawalgarh in the Northern Rajasthan (Shekhawati) chapter.

Other agencies include the **Rajasthan Travel Service** (☎ *365408, fax 376935;* w *www.rajasthantravelservice.com; ground floor, Ganpati Plaza, MI Rd, Jaipur),* **Sita World Travels** (☎ *402020, fax 205479;* w *www.sitaindia.com; Station Rd, Jaipur)* and **Indo Vacations** (☎ *364263, fax 412600;* w *www.indien-reise.com; 206 Shri Gopal Tower, Krishna Marg, C-Scheme, Jaipur),* which organises women-only tours.

Jaipur

*Je na dekkhyo Jaipario
to kal main akar kaai kario?*
If one has not seen Jaipur,
what is the point of having been born?

☎ 0141 • postcode 302006 • pop 2.3 million

Although Jaipur is today among the most tumultuous and polluted places in the state, this vibrant capital of Rajasthan rarely disappoints the visitor. It is a city of contrasts, where camels wait at traffic lights next to autorickshaws and Ambassador cars. And film hoardings, depicting many times larger-than-life moustachioed heroes, their faces contorted into desperate grimaces as they battle their adversaries, loom down over luxury car showrooms, while artisans engage in such traditional crafts as block printing, gem cutting and polishing, puppet making, and *dhurrie* (carpet) weaving. Women resplendent in iridescent lime green, hot pink and sunflower-coloured saris thread their way through the crowded bazaars of the old city. Providing stunning backdrops are the ancient forts of Amber, Nahargarh, Jaigarh and Moti Dungri, dramatic testaments to a bygone era which lend a lingering romance to this chaotic city.

Among Jaipur's highlights is the fascinating City Palace, which has a fine museum with priceless exhibits that date from the successive reigns of the Kachhwaha rulers. Nearby is the Jantar Mantar, the observatory built by the founder of Jaipur, Jai Singh II, in the second quarter of the 18th century. It looks more like an outdoor exhibition of modern art than an observatory, but astrologers and astronomers still consult the strange devices here to make their celestial calculations.

The old city is a fascinating place to wander around, with its colourful bazaars and artisans' quarters. As it is laid out on a grid pattern, it's fairly easy to orient yourself here. The *chaupars*, or three main squares in the old city, are great places to be around sunset, when the pink walls give off a rosy hue and you can sit and watch the chaos

Highlights

- The colourful bazaars and emporiums, lively places stacked with handicrafts
- The City Palace complex, a maze of courtyards, gardens and buildings
- Hawa Mahal, the beautiful facade of the Palace of Winds, was built for the women of the court
- Amber Fort, a stunning example of Rajput architecture 11km from Jaipur

unfold around you, as vendors make their way home.

History

The city of Jaipur is named after its founder, the great warrior-astronomer Maharaja Jai Singh II (r. 1688–1744), who came to power at the age of 11 upon the death of his father, Maharaja Bishan Singh. The maharaja had been informed by astrologers upon his son's birth that the boy would achieve great things in his lifetime, and Bishan Singh ensured that he received the very best education in the arts, sciences, philosophy and military affairs.

At 15 years of age, the prodigal prince matched his wits against the Mughal emperor Aurangzeb, who summoned the lad to the Mughal court to explain why he had failed to report to the Deccan to fight the Marathas as he had been ordered. When the emperor grasped the lad's hand the youth retorted that, as the emperor had extended the traditional gesture of protection offered by a bridegroom to his new wife by taking his hand, it was incumbent upon Aurangzeb to protect the young ruler and his kingdom in a similar fashion. Impressed by his wit and pluck, Aurangzeb conferred on Jai Singh the title 'Sawai', meaning 'one and a quarter', a title that was proudly borne by all of Jai Singh's descendants.

Jai Singh could trace his lineage back to the Rajput clan of Kachhwahas, who consolidated their power around the 12th century. They built the impressive Amber Fort, which lies about 11km to the northeast of present-day Jaipur. The dominion of the Kachhwahas spread, eventually encompassing a large area abutting the kingdoms of Mewar (Udaipur region) and Marwar (Jodhpur region).

The Kachhwahas clan recognised the expediency of aligning themselves with the powerful Mughal empire, and subsequently enjoyed the patronage of the Mughal emperors. However, Jai Singh incurred the displeasure of Aurangzeb's successor, Bahadur Shah, who came to power following Aurangzeb's death in 1707.

Bahadur Shah's accession was contested by his younger brother, Azam Shah, and Jai Singh unfortunately supported Azam's bid for power. Bahadur Shah responded by demanding his removal from Amber Fort, and he installed Jai Singh's younger brother Vijay Singh in his place. This naturally rankled Jai Singh, who eventually dislodged his brother. Soliciting the support of other large Rajput states, Jai Singh formed a formidable front against the Mughal ruler, and eventually reconsolidated his rule.

The wealth of the kingdom increased exponentially, and this, plus the need to accommodate the burgeoning population and a paucity of water at the old capital at Amber, prompted the maharaja in 1727 to commence work on a new city which he named after himself – Jaipur.

It was a collaborative effort that used his vision and the impressive expertise of his chief architect, Vidyadhar. Jai Singh's strong grounding in the sciences is reflected in the precise symmetry of the new city, which, unlike the many unplanned and labyrinthine cities in northern India at the time, was laid out according to strict principles of town planning set down in the *Shilpa-Shastra*, an ancient Hindu treatise on architecture. The small villages that lay in the vicinity were incorporated into the new city, which was dissected by wide boulevards flanked by stalls of equal size forming seven rectangles, called *mohallas*, of varying size.

The most central of the seven rectangles comprises the City Palace complex, containing the palace itself, the administrative quarters, the Jantar Mantar (Jai Singh's remarkable observatory) and the *zenana mahals*, or the women's palaces. Here the maharaja's 28 wives and several concubines were installed. He held the dubious honour of maintaining more wives and concubines than any of his predecessors, although most of these alliances were actually motivated more by political expediency than by amorous compulsions.

The precocious Maharaja Jai Singh II came to power as a child

The city was not just an aesthetic triumph; its stout walls protected its inhabitants from would-be invaders, encouraging merchants and tradespeople to flock here, further serving to enhance the city's growth and prosperity. Jai Singh's interest in the arts, sciences and religion fostered their development in Jaipur, and the royal court became a centre of intellectual and artistic endeavour.

Following Jai Singh's death in 1744, power struggles between his many offspring laid the kingdom open to invasion by neighbouring Rajput kingdoms, which encroached on and appropriated large tracts of territory. The kingdom maintained good relations with the British Raj, although the British gradually began to undermine the independence of the state, exercising greater control over its administration.

In 1876 Maharaja Ram Singh had the entire old city painted pink (traditionally the colour of hospitality), to welcome the prince of Wales (later King Edward VII). This tradition has remained, and today all residents of the old city are compelled by law to preserve the pink facade. Maharaja Ram Singh also built Ramgarh Lake to supply water to the ever growing city.

During the 19th and 20th centuries, the spacious and carefully planned city contained within Jai Singh's original city walls could not contain the population, and the city spread beyond its walled perimeters.

In 1922, Man Singh II, Jaipur's last maharaja, took the throne following the death of his adoptive father, Sawai Madho Singh II. During his reign, civic buildings such as schools, hospitals and the vast Secretariat complex were built outside the old city.

Following Independence in 1947, the status of the princely state was set to change forever. In March 1949, Jaipur merged with the Rajput states of Jodhpur, Jaisalmer and

Festivals of Jaipur

Several important festivals are unique to Jaipur. For statewide and nationwide festivals, see Public Holidays & Special Events in the Facts for the Visitor chapter.

January

Jaipur International Festival In celebration of Jaipur's heritage, this festival aims to revive and conserve the vibrant culture and traditions of the region. Performances are held throughout the old city, including classical, traditional and contemporary dance, theatre and music as well as sports events, workshops and exhibitions. Contact the **Indian National Trust for Art and Cultural Heritage** (Intach; ☎ 407018) for more details.

March–April

Gangaur Women across the state celebrate the love between Shiva and his consort Gauri (Parvati) during this popular festival. It commences on the day following Holi, and continues for 18 days. Wooden images of Gauri are bedecked in beautiful costumes and jewels and are worshipped. An elaborately garbed image of the goddess is carried on a palanquin from the Tripolia, at the City Palace, through the streets of the old city.

Elephant Festival During Jaipur's elephant festival, gaily caparisoned elephants lumber through the streets, and matches of elephant polo are held at Chaughan Stadium in the old city. One of the more bizarre spectacles is a tug-of-war between elephants and men.

July–August

Teej This festival heralds the onset of the monsoon, and is celebrated across Rajasthan in honour of the marriage of Shiva and Gauri. It is a favourite with Rajasthani women. At this time, flower-bedecked swings are hung from trees, and songs celebrating love are sung by maidens.

Bikaner, becoming the Greater Rajasthan Union. Jaipur was honoured above the other former states when the title *rajpramukh*, meaning head of state, was conferred on Man Singh II, who was invested with administrative supervision of the new province. The title was later revoked, and Man Singh II was posted as Indian ambassador to Spain. In 1956 Jaipur became the capital of the state of Rajasthan.

The population has expanded from just 300,000 in 1950 to over two million today, and while the city remains prosperous and retains vestiges of its former grandeur, unplanned urban sprawl has disfigured what was possibly one of the most beautiful cities in India. All of the seven original gates into the old city remain, but unfortunately much of the wall itself has been torn down for building material. There is now a preservation order on the remainder.

Orientation

The walled 'Pink City', or old city, is in the northeast of Jaipur; the new parts have spread to the south and west. The city's main tourist attractions are in the old city, which is partially encircled by a crenellated wall pierced at intervals by gates – the major gates are Chandpol (*pol* means 'gate'), Ajmeri Gate and Sanganeri Gate. Broad avenues, over 30m wide, divide the 'Pink City' into neat rectangles, each of which is the domain of a particular group of artisans or commercial activities. The principal shopping precinct in the old city is Johari Bazaar, the jewellers' market.

There are three main interconnecting roads in the new part of town – Mirza Ismail (MI) Rd, Station Rd and Sansar Chandra Marg. Along or just off these roads are most of the budget and mid-range hotels and restaurants, the main train station, the bus station, many of the banks and the modern shopping strip. Panch Batti, midway along MI Rd, is a landmark intersection near the southwest corner of the old city.

Information

Tourist Offices There are tourist offices on platform No 1 of the train station (☎ 315714;

open 24hrs daily), on platform No 2 of the bus station (open 10am-5pm Mon-Fri & every 2nd Sat), at the airport (open for flight arrivals) and in the elephant compound at Amber Fort (open 9am-4.30pm daily).

The main **Tourist Reception Centre** (☎ 410598; MI Rd; open 8am-8pm Mon-Fri & every 2nd Sat), operated by the Department of Tourism, is in the Rajasthan Tourism Development Corporation (RTDC) Tourist Hotel compound. You can buy a range of literature here, including a reasonable map of Jaipur (Rs 2) and even posters (Rs 15). It also sells a handy booklet listing all families who have registered with the Paying Guest House Scheme in Rajasthan (Rs 5). The staff at all the tourist offices are quite helpful, but the office at the train station is probably the most efficient.

Also in the RTDC Tourist Hotel compound are the offices of the **Gujarat Tourism Development Corporation** (☎ 362017; open 10am-6pm Mon-Fri); and an office for **Uttaranchal Tourism** (☎ 378892; open 10am-1.30pm & 2pm-5pm Mon-Sat), which both promote the new state.

The **Government of India tourist office** (☎ 372200; open 9am-6pm Mon-Fri, 9am-1.30pm Sat) is located in the grounds of the Hotel Khasa Kothi, near the train station. It has lots of glossy brochures, but is aimed at travellers planning trips outside Rajasthan.

Bookings for RTDC hotels around Rajasthan, accommodation in the tourist village during the Pushkar Camel Fair, and reservations for the *Palace on Wheels* train (see the boxed text 'Palace on Wheels' in the Getting Around chapter) can be made at the **RTDC Central Reservations Office** (☎ 203531, fax 201045; RTDC Tourism, Swagatam Campus, near train station).

Any applications for visa extensions should be lodged at the **Foreigners Registration Office** (☎ 619391; open 10am-1.30pm & 2pm-5pm Mon-Fri), which is located in the City Palace complex – see Visas & Documents in the Facts for the Visitor chapter for more details.

Money There are plenty of places at which you can change money here in Jaipur.

JAIPUR

JAIPUR

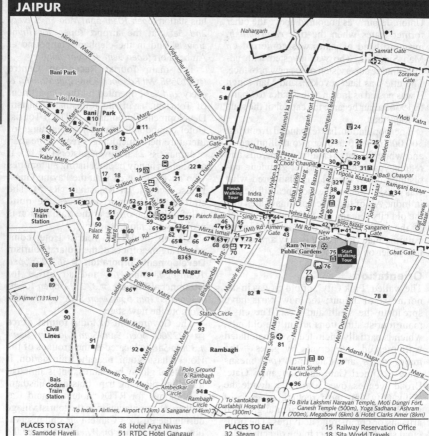

PLACES TO STAY
3 Samode Haveli
4 Hotel Khetri House
5 Hotel Bissau Palace
6 Jag Vilas
7 Hotel Meghniwas
8 Shahpura House
9 Madhuban; Madhavanand
   Girls College
10 Umaid Bhawan Guest
   House; Sajjan Niwas
   Guest House
11 Jaipur Inn
13 Hotel Jaipur Ashok
14 RTDC Hotel Swagatam;
   RTDC Central
   Reservations Office
16 Rajputana Palace
   Sheraton; Bookwise
17 RTDC Hotel Teej
21 Jai Mangal Palace
22 Alsisar Haveli
34 Hotel Kailash
37 LMB Hotel & Restaurant
40 Hotel Sweet Dream

48 Hotel Arya Niwas
51 RTDC Hotel Gangaur
54 Atithi Guest House; Aangan
   Guest House; Chic Chocolate
55 Karni Niwas; Hotel Neelam
56 Mansingh Hotel
60 Hotel Pearl Palace
62 RTDC Tourist Hotel; Tourist
   Reception Centre; Gujarat
   Tourism Development
   Corporation; Uttaranchal
   Tourism
65 Evergreen Hotel; Hotel
   Pink Sun; Ashiyana Guest
   House; Amrapali Travels
78 Nana-ki-Haveli
79 Rajasthan Palace Hotel
82 Hotel Diggi Palace
85 Devi Niwas; Chirmi
   Palace Hotel
88 Jai Mahal Palace Hotel
91 Rajmahal Palace
94 Rambagh Palace; Bank of
   Rajasthan; Polo Bar
95 Narain Niwas Palace Hotel

PLACES TO EAT
32 Steam
42 Ganesh Restaurant
44 Indian Coffee House
45 Lassiwala; Goyal Colour
   Lab; Himalaya
   (Ayurvedic Store)
47 Chanakya Restaurant
64 Handi Restaurant
69 Dasaprakash
71 Surya Mahal; Natraj
   Restaurant; Jal Mahal;
   McDonalds; Pool
   Club & Cafe
72 Dawat; Bake Hut; Pub 2K2
73 Niro's; Book Corner
84 Four Seasons
86 Rendezvous

OTHER
1 Royal Gaitor
2 National Institute of
   Ayurveda
12 Kripal Kumbh

15 Railway Reservation Office
18 Sita World Travels
19 Mewar Cyber Cafe &
   Communication
20 Main Bus Station
23 Chaughan Stadium
24 Govind Devji Temple
25 Foreigners Registration
   Office
26 City Palace & Maharaja
   Sawai Mansingh II
   Museum
27 Bicycle Hire
28 Jantar Mantar
   (Observatory)
29 Rajasthan Astrological
   Council & Research
   Institute; Maharaja Sawai
   Mansingh Sangeet
   Mahavidyalaya
30 Iswari Minar Swarga Sal
   (Heaven Piercing Minaret)
31 Hawa Mahal
33 Jama Masjid
35 Galta

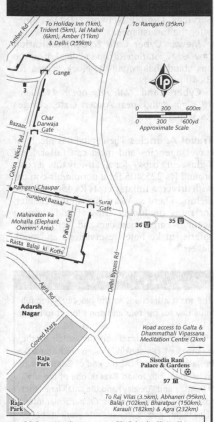

To Holiday Inn (1km),
Trident (5km), Jal Mahal
(6km), Amber (11km)
& Delhi (259km)

To Ramgarh (35km)

Ganga

Char
Darwaja
Gate

Bazaar

0   300   600m
0   300   600yd
Approximate Scale

Ghora Nikas Rd

Ramganj Chaupar

Surajpol Bazaar

Suraj
Gate

Mahavaton ka
Mohalla (Elephant
Owners' Area)

Pahar Ganj

Rasta Balaji ki Kothi

Delhi Bypass Rd

36   35

Agra Rd

Adarsh
Nagar

Covind Marg

Raja
Park

Raja
Park

Road access to Galta &
Dhammathali Vipassana
Meditation Centre (2km)

Sisodia Rani
Palace & Gardens

97

To Raj Vilas (3.5km), Abhaneri (95km),
Balaji (102km), Bharatpur (150km),
Karauli (182km) & Agra (232km)

36 Surya Mandir
38 Music N Sports
39 Shree Sanjay Sharma
   Museum
41 Lufthansa
43 Rajasthali
46 UTI Bank (ATM)
49 Polo Victory Cinema
50 Government of India
   Tourist Office
52 British Airways
53 Jaipur Towers: Thomas
   Cook; Air France; KLM
   Airlines; Kuwait Airways;
   Jetair Ltd; Interglobe Air
   Transport; Delhi
   Express Travels
57 Main Post Office;
   Philatelic Museum
58 Ganpati Plaza: Swaad;
   Pizza Hut; Baskin 31
   Robbins; Rajasthan Travel
   Service; Ganpati Books;
   Sentosa Colour Lab;
   Health Spa; Air India
59 Galundia Clinic; Chic
   Chocolate; Tata
   Finance Amex
61 Jet Airways
66 Juneja Art Gallery
67 DHL Worldwide Express
68 Bank of Rajasthan
70 Raj Mandir Cinema
74 Cyber Land; Books &
   News Mart
75 Modern Art Gallery
76 Zoo
77 Central Museum
   (Albert Hall)
80 Museum of Indology
81 Sawai Mansingh
   Hospital
83 HDFC Bank (ATM)
87 Mojari
89 Soma
90 Kerala Ayurveda Centre
92 Anokhi
93 Birla Planetarium
96 Dolls Museum
97 Vidyadharji-ka-Bagh

Thomas Cook (☎ 360801; ground floor, Jaipur Towers, MI Rd; open 9.30am-6pm Mon-Sat) changes travellers cheques and major currencies and offers advances against major credit cards. A short walk east, **Tata Finance Amex** (☎ 364154; MI Rd; open 9.30am-6pm Mon-Sat year-round & 10am-4pm Sun Nov-Mar) can change travellers cheques and currency. These agencies charge a minimum of Rs 50 for travellers cheques other than their own brands.

A few branches of the **Bank of Rajasthan** (☎ 381416; Rambagh Palace; open 7am-8pm daily; ☎ 362969; MI Rd; open 9am-7pm Mon-Fri, 9am-5pm Sat) change travellers cheques and currency, and they're open convenient hours.

There are a number of 24-hour ATMs in town where you can withdraw money against your credit card. The UTI Bank's centrally located ATM at Panch Batti offers advances on MasterCard, and ATMs at Ashoka Marg and the airport take Visa and MasterCard.

Post The main **post office** (☎ 367037; MI Rd; open 10am-6pm) has a speedy service handling **parcel postage** (open 10am-4pm Mon-Sat) at counter No 11. See Post & Communications in the Facts for the Visitor chapter for postal rates. There's a handy parcel-packing-wallah in the foyer of the post office – to pack, stitch and wax seal a small/large parcel he'll ask for around Rs 40/100, and he can advise you on the most economical way to send your stuff when the parcel counter is busy. There's also a philatelic museum at the post office; see Other Museums later in this chapter.

DHL Worldwide Express (☎ 362826, 1600 111345 toll-free, fax 368852; C-scheme, G-68 Geeta Enclave; open 9am-7.30pm Mon-Sat) is in a small lane off MI Rd and can arrange air freight, starting at Rs 3500 for a 10kg box and Rs 5500 for a 'jumbo' 25kg box to Australia (around Rs 500 more for Europe and the USA). Make sure you ask to pay up-front any customs charges for the destination country unless you want the receiver to find a nasty surprise in the mail.

Telephone There are plenty of public call offices (PCOs) scattered around Jaipur, which are usually cheaper than the hotels for long-distance calls. The international collect-call operator can be reached on ☎ 186.

It is not unusual for telephone numbers to change in Rajasthan. Jaipur has tackled this problem with an excellent automated Jaipur 'changed telephone number' service in English (☎ 1952) and in Hindi (☎ 1951). For local telephone number inquiries call ☎ 197.

Email & Internet Access Jaipur is awash with places advertising Internet access, and the cost of access is constantly dropping as the communications infrastructure improves. The lowest rates (Rs 15 per hour at the time of writing) are available in the south of town, although unless you're in the area it's hardly worth the effort of getting there. The quality of the connections also varies greatly – providers with Integrated Services Digital Network (ISDN) lines offer the fastest speeds.

Mewar Cyber Cafe & Communication (☎ 206172; Station Rd; open 24hrs), near the bus stand, has round-the-clock access for Rs 40 per hour.

Cyber Land (MI Rd; open 11.30am-10.30pm daily), near Ajmeri Gate, charges Rs 30 per hour.

Travel Agencies The capital has plenty of travel agencies and most can tailor local sightseeing trips – for a half-day tour it costs around Rs 225/405 for a normal/air-con car with driver; a full day costs Rs 450/650. See Getting There & Away, later in this chapter, for rates on longer trips. The following agencies can arrange cars and jeep or camel safaris, make hotel reservations and book tickets.

Pink City Walking Tour

The following walking tour will take you through the main attractions in the old city – for full details see the individual listings later. Allow about half a day for the tour and don't forget to bring plenty of water, a hat and your camera.

Entering the old city from **New Gate**, turn right into **Bapu Bazaar**, on the inside of the southern city wall. Brightly coloured bolts of fabric, shoes of camel skin, trinkets and aromatic perfumes make this bazaar a favourite destination for Jaipur's women. At the end of Bapu Bazaar you'll come to **Sanganeri Gate** on your right, but turn left here into **Johari Bazaar**, one of the city's main shopping strips. Johari Bazaar (closed for part of Sunday and Tuesday) and the small lanes that dissect it are where you will find Jaipur's jewellers, goldsmiths and silversmiths. Of particular interest are the artisans doing enamelling, or *meenakari*. This highly glazed and intricate work in shades of ruby, bottle green and royal blue is a speciality of Jaipur. On Johari Bazaar you can also find cotton merchants, with their bolts of white cloth. Interspersed with the uniform shopfronts are the grand pink havelis, or mansions, of Jaipur's wealthy merchants.

You'll pass the **Jama Masjid** to your left, with its tall minarets, and you'll soon come to the old city's major square – **Badi Chaupar**. Across the square to the north is **Siredeori Bazaar**, also known as Hawa Mahal Bazaar. The latter name is derived from the extraordinary **Hawa Mahal** (Palace of the Winds), a short distance to the north on the left-hand side of the street. The building is best admired from the outside, but you can go inside via the rear entrance if you head back to Badi Chaupar and turn right (west) into Tripolia Bazaar and right again down a small lane (see Hawa Mahal later for further details).

Back on **Tripolia Bazaar**, continue west and you'll be confronted by stall after stall crammed with domestic kitchen utensils, textiles, trinkets and ironware. The stalls are closed on Sunday.

A few hundred metres along is **Tripolia Gate**, the triple-arched gate after which the bazaar takes its name. This is the main entrance to the **Jantar Mantar** and **City Palace**, but only the maharaja's

Indo Vacations (☎ 364263, fax 412600,
W www.indien-reise.com) 206 Shri Gopal
Tower, Krishna Marg, C-Scheme
Rajasthan Travel Service (☎ 365408, fax
376935, W www.rajasthantravelservice.com)
Ground floor, Ganpati Plaza, MI Rd
Sita World Travels (☎ 402020, fax 205479,
W www.sitaindia.com) Station Rd

Photography For reliable film processing
try **Goyal Colour Lab** *(MI Rd; open 9.30am-
8.30pm Mon-Sat, 10am-4pm Sun)*, opposite
the Natraj restaurant (there's another branch
in Nehru Bazaar). It sells lithium batteries
and print and slide film and can develop
24-exposure print film in one hour for
Rs 140. It takes about two days to develop
slide films and costs Rs 200 for 36 slides
(which includes mounting).

Another reputable outlet is **Sentosa
Colour Lab** *(☎ 388748; ground floor, Ganpati
Plaza)*, which offers one-hour processing of
24-exposure print film for Rs 129 and can
develop a 36-exposure slide film for Rs 225
(including mounting) in one day.

Bookshops National English-language
dailies and a good selection of maps, magazines, postcards and books on India (with
particular emphasis on Rajasthan) can be
found at **Books Corner** *(MI Rd; open 10am-
11pm daily)*, near Niro's restaurant. There are
some French-language books for sale too.
Here you will also find the monthly publications *Jaipur Vision* (Rs 20) and *Jaipur City
Guide* (Rs 30), which are tourist booklets
that cover similar ground. In the same block
as Books Corner, heading towards the old
city, is the **Books & News Mart** *(MI Rd; open
9.30am-8.30pm Mon-Sat)*, which also has a
fair selection of books on Rajasthan. On the
ground floor of Ganpati Plaza you'll find
Ganpati Books *(open 11am-9pm Mon-Sat)*,

Pink City Walking Tour

family is permitted entrance via its portals. The public entrance to the palace complex is via the less
ostentatious **Atishpol** (Stable Gate), a little further along. To the north of the City Palace is the
Govind Devji Temple, surrounded by gardens. Here Jai Singh installed an image of Govinda Deva
(an incarnation of Krishna) the patron deity of his family. Govinda Deva has a sweet tooth and is
unveiled seven times daily to receive treats brought by devotees.

After visiting the City Palace complex, head back to Tripolia Bazaar and resume your walk west.
To your right you'll see the **Iswari Minar Swarga Sal** (Heaven-Piercing Minaret), an apt name as this
is the highest structure in the old city. The minaret was erected by Iswari Singh, who succeeded Jai
Singh. Lacking the military prowess and courage of his warrior father, Iswari Singh took his own life
rather than confront the advancing Maratha army. His ignominious end was overshadowed by the
sacrifice of his 21 wives and concubines, who performed *jauhar* by immolating themselves upon his
funeral pyre.

Cross the road and you'll see a small archway directly opposite the minaret. If you head west from
here, the next lane on the left is **Maniharon ka Rasta**, where you can see many colourful stalls
selling lac bangles.

Back on Tripolia Bazaar, continue west to **Choti Chaupar**, where villagers from outlying regions
come to sell and trade their produce. Cross this square and you'll find yourself in **Chandpol Bazaar**.
Follow this road until you reach a traffic light, where you turn left into the bustling **Khajane Walon
ka Rasta**. Here you'll find Jaipur's marble carvers at work. Continue down Khajane Walon ka Rasta
until you reach a broad road, just inside the city wall. Cross the road and pass out of the old city
through **Singhpol** – this gate is just two tall pink columns with no arch. Turn right here and then
take the first street on your left. You'll soon emerge at **Panch Batti**. If you turn left here, along MI
Rd, you can revive yourself at one of Jaipur's best restaurants, or cross the intersection to take in a
movie at **Raj Mandir**.

which stocks a reasonable range of English titles. There is an excellent selection of books about India, including an extensive collection of titles on Rajasthan, at **Bookwise** *(Rajputana Palace Sheraton)*. You can buy and exchange second-hand books at some of the budget hotels.

Medical Services One place that comes highly recommended by a number of travellers is the **Galundia Clinic** *(☎ 361040; MI Rd)*, opposite All India Radio. Dr Chandra Sen runs a highly professional service and is well versed in dealing with travellers' ailments. Importantly, he is also on call 24 hours (mobile ☎ 9829-061-040) and will visit you at your hotel. He works with most travel insurance companies and a normal consultation costs Rs 300. This should be your first port of call if you get sick. Dr Sen has a small number of beds, although should you need to be hospitalised, you may end up at the **Sawai Mansingh Hospital** *(☎ 560291; Sawai Ram Singh Marg)* or the **Santokba Durlabhji Hospital** *(☎ 566251; Bhawani Singh Marg)*. Most hotels can also arrange a doctor on site.

Emergency The following numbers apply to most other towns in Rajasthan too.

Ambulance	☎ 102
Fire	☎ 101
Police	☎ 100

Dangers & Annoyances Many travellers have reported problems with commission merchants in Jaipur. The town is particularly notorious for gem scams. See the boxed text 'A Warning!' under Shopping in the Facts for the Visitor chapter. The touts' latest tactic is to accuse you of hating Indians if you refuse to talk to them. They're particularly aggressive around the City Palace, at train and bus stations and at Amber fort. Usually they'll leave you alone if you steadfastly ignore them, but if this doesn't work you can report them to the tourist police stationed at all these places. Often simply threatening to report them is enough to do the trick.

KELLI HAMBLET

The sandstone Palace of the Winds is Rajput artistry at its most indulgent

Hawa Mahal

Built in 1799, the Hawa Mahal *(Palace of the Winds; admission Rs 5, still camera foreigner/ citizen Rs 30/10, video Rs 70/20; open 9am-4.30pm daily)* is one of Jaipur's major landmarks, although it is actually little more than a facade. This five-storey building, which looks out over the main street of the buzzing old city, is a stunning example of Rajput artistry with its pink, delicately honeycombed sandstone windows, of which there are 953. It was originally built to enable the women of the royal household to watch the everyday life and processions of the city. The palace was built by Maharaja Sawaj Pratap Singh and is part of the City Palace complex.

Most people come here to see the beautiful facade, but you can also climb to the top for a view of the city below; peer through the latticed windows to experience the fascinating interplay of gazes set up by the structure. The entrance is from the rear of the building. To get there, go back to Badi Chaupar (the intersection on your left as you face the Hawa Mahal), turn right and then take the first right again through an archway. There's also a small **archaeological museum** *(open 9am-4.30pm Sat-Thur)* located there.

[Continued on page 149]

THE COLOURFUL CRAFTS OF RAJASTHAN

Rajasthan is full of visual spectacle, but perhaps the most lasting impression that visitors take away with them is that of colour. The people have a passion for decoration and historically they have taken full advantage of their position on trade routes to learn new skills of artistry from other lands. In the painted houses of Shekhawati in northern Rajasthan, in turbans, in the long skirts known as *ghagharas* worn by Rajasthani women, in their *odhnis*, or headscarves, right down to the bright embroidered details on their leather *jootis* (shoes), Rajasthanis celebrate life by dyeing and embellishing everything in their daily lives. Nowhere is this more apparent than in the lively markets and bazaars, where the skills of the artisans are on display. In a land characterised by desert wastelands and sandy monotone landscapes, the people of Rajasthan have created beauty amid the starkness, introducing a rainbow of colours which challenge the bleached, arid terrain.

Textiles

Rajasthan is famous for its vibrantly coloured textiles. Cotton cloth is produced by the *Julaha*, or weaver, caste. Textiles and clothes are on sale in markets throughout the state, from the Western-inspired designs of Pushkar and Jaipur to the more traditional favourites, such as the cloth from the village of Kaithoon, in Kota district, known as *masuria*. It is woven from both cotton, and silk and saris made of this cloth fetch top prices around the country.

The basic cloth receives one or several of various treatments to achieve its rich blaze of colour, including dyeing, block printing and numerous forms of embroidery and appliqué.

Tie-Dyed Cloth

Of the dyeing processes, the method producing the most intricate and interesting result is that of *bandhani*, or 'tie and dye'. Parts of the fabric are knotted, so that when the fabric is dyed the knotted sections retain their original colour. Alternatively, after the fabric is knotted, it is bleached, so the unknotted sections are paler than the knotted sections.

The intricate work of tying the cloth is the preserve of women and girls. Different patterns are created by different methods. In the *bandhani* form of tie-dye, a pale background is covered with large splotches. This effect is achieved by knotting the dyed cloth and then bleaching it, with the knotted sections retaining their colour. A worker in this form of tie-dye is known as a *Bandhej*.

Another form of tie-dye, called *loharia* (which translates as 'ripples'), is striped diagonally and is used in saris and turbans. Diagonal patterns of dots are formed by the *jaaldar* and *beldar* processes. *Loharia* pieces are named according to the number of colours employed: *panchrangi*

Inset: The elaborate handiwork of *mehendi* (henna) artists (Photograph by Pramod Mistry)

141

features five colours (from *panch*, meaning 'five'); and *satrangi* features seven different colours. The cloth is worn as turbans and saris.

Ekdali features small circles and squares; *shikari* employs animal and human motifs, which are drawn before the cloth is dyed. In *tikunthi*, circles and squares appear in groups of three; in *chaubasi*, they appear in groups of four; and in *satbandi*, in groups of seven. The dominant colours used in *bandhani* tie-dye are yellow, red, green and pink.

One of the most intricate designs is produced when the cloth is first folded, and then pressed with wooden blocks embedded with nails, which causes raised impressions on the cloth. These raised points are then gathered up and tied, and the cloth dyed. The brilliant results are worn as *odhnis*. *Pomacha* and *sikari-bandhej odhnis* are also highly sought. The former features lotus motifs against a white or pink background. A yellow background indicates that the wearer has recently given birth. *Sikari-bandhej odhnis* are produced in Sikar, in the region of Shekhawati, and feature designs of birds and animals.

Printed Cloth

There are two forms of printing – block printing, and reverse or resist printing. In block printing, wooden blocks known as *buntis* or *chhapas*, on which incisions form the basic design, are dipped in dye and applied directly to the cloth. Anokhi, a clothing and textile oulet in Jaipur, runs courses in traditional block printing from its farm near Jaipur. In the second mode, resist printing, part of the cloth is covered with a dye-resistant substance such as wax, and the cloth is then dyed. The waxed sections retain their original colour, and the wax is washed off. These original-colour sections are then block printed.

The village of Sanganer, near Jaipur, is famous for its block-printed fabric. The Sanganeri prints, generally featuring floral motifs, are exported around the world. Every day, thousands of metres of fabric can be seen drying in long swathes on the banks of the Saraswati River.

The village of Bagru, near Jaipur, is also renowned for its block prints, which feature predominantly zigzag motifs. The city of Barmer, in western Rajasthan, produces resist-printed cloth featuring geometric designs in blue and red on both sides, which is known as *ajrakh*. It is generally worn only by men as shawls and turbans. Jaisalmer specialises in resist printing, which is only executed at night and in the winter months when it is cold enough.

In Nathdwara, in southern Rajasthan, finely printed cloth depicting religious themes, particularly centred around the life of Sri Nathji, the presiding deity, was used, along with *pichwai* paintings (religious paintings on homespun cloth), to adorn temples. Today, the tradition continues with pilgrims purchasing these cloths as religious mementos.

Dyes

Before the introduction of synthetic dyes, all colours were derived from natural sources such as vegetables, minerals and even insects. Yellow was derived from turmeric and buttermilk; green from banana leaves;

PRAMOD MISTRY

orange from saffron and jasmine; black from iron rust; blue from the indigo plant; red from sugar cane and sunflowers; and purple from the kirmiz insect. Colours were either *pacca* (fast) or *kacha* (fleeting). Fast colours were generally more muted than fleeting colours, consisting of browns, blues and greens, while the vibrant yellows, oranges and pinks were generally *kacha* colours.

Embroidery & Appliqué

The third method of adorning cloth is embroidery and appliqué, and this usually takes place after the cloth has been printed or tie-dyed. During the period of the Mughals, embroidery workshops known as *kaarkhanas* were established to train artisans so that the royal families would have an abundant supply of richly embroidered cloth. Finely stitched tapestries were also executed for the royal courts, inspired by miniature paintings.

Barmer, south of Jaisalmer, is famous for its embroidery. In Bikaner, designs using double stitching result in the pattern appearing on both sides of the cloth. In Shekhawati, the Jats embroider motifs of animals and birds on their *odhnis* and *ghagharas*. Chain stitch is employed against a bold background in Alwar district. Tiny mirrors are stitched into garments in Jaisalmer. Beautifully embroidered cloths are also produced

Top: Embroidery is an art practised throughout India

for domestic livestock, and ornately bedecked camels are a wonderfully common sight at the Pushkar Camel Fair.

Wall hangings made from segments of intricately embroidered fabric, some with mirrorwork, are popular buys. Pieces can range from small cushion-sized squares to bedspread-sized pieces. Prices range from a couple of hundred rupees up to several thousand.

Carpets & Weaving

Before the emergence of the Muslims in India, the tradition of carpet making was unknown in the country. Floor coverings consisted of small mats, called *jajams*, on which only one person could sit. Carpet weaving took off in the 16th century under the patronage of the great Mughal emperor Akbar, who commissioned the establishment of various carpet-weaving factories, including one at Jaipur.

In Jaipur pile carpets were produced under the tutorship of Persian weavers. Some of these carpets were enormous. Vast looms had to be constructed in order to produce carpets for the royal durbar halls. There is an exquisite collection of carpets both at the museum in the City Palace, and at the Central Museum, both in Jaipur.

In the 19th century, Maharaja Sawai Ram Singh II of Jaipur established a carpet factory at the Jaipur jail, and soon other jails introduced carpet-making units. Some of the most beautiful *dhurries*, or flat cotton carpets, were produced by prisoners in jails – Bikaner jail is still well known for the excellence of its *dhurries*.

Following the demise of the princely states, both the quality and quantity of carpets declined without the patronage of the royal families. However, recent government training initiatives have seen the revival of this craft, and fine quality carpets are being produced in Bikaner, Jodhpur, Jaipur, Kota and other centres. In the village of Salawas, near Jodhpur, a cooperative of weavers sells high-quality *dhurries*. Medium-fine quality knotted carpets have 150 to 160 knots per square inch, and cost around Rs 3000 for a 1.3m x 2m carpet.

Jewellery

In even the poorest villages of Rajasthan, women, and often men, can be seen bedecked in elaborate silver folk jewellery – bracelets, rings, earrings, nose rings, toe rings, ankle bracelets, and pendants worn on the forehead and breast. The quality of the jewellery indicates the relative economic status of the wearer (or, for a woman, more accurately, of her husband) – one woman may wear ornaments weighing up to 5kg!

Very rarely are these objects of pure silver. Usually the silver is mixed with copper to make it more malleable, although it is still of a very high grade – generally above 90%. Villagers and tribal groups of different regions can be identified by their ornaments, which also indicate the caste to which they belong.

Traditional silver folk jewellery, which is quite chunky, is sold by weight in the bazaars of towns and cities, and there is often a silversmiths'

SARINA SINGH

RICHARD I'ANSON

COREY WISE

DALLAS STRIBLEY

Textiles have always played an important role in Indian culture and trade. Rajasthan's rich textile tradition includes fine embroideries (top left), brocadework (right & bottom), appliqué (bottom) and vibrant sari fabrics (centre left).

SARINA SINGH

FRANCES LINZEE GORDON

RICHARD I'ANSON

SARINA SINGH

Wood was traditionally used for decorative carvings in and on havelis (centre left); today it is largely used in producing the beautifully detailed puppets you'll see for sale (top left & bottom). Pottery is the oldest of crafts, and despite the introduction of plastics is still very much in use today (right).

GREG ELMS

DALLAS STRIBLEY

CHRISTOPHER WOOD

PAUL BEINSSEN

Tie-dyeing and block printing are frequently used to embellish fabrics (top & centre right). Crushing tiny bugs by foot (bottom right) is the traditional method of creating vermilion dye in India, perhaps the only country where bright red cloth could be camouflage in a sea of chillies (bottom left).

DALLAS STRIBLEY

COREY WISE

CHRIS BEALL

ANTONY V GIBLIN

The wearing of jewellery is a sign of status in India; the quality of the materials is a measure of relative wealth. From the richest to the poorest, women in Rajasthan ornament their bodies with metals, gems and beads.

quarter in the main market. Jaipur's silver jewellers ply their trade in Johari Bazaar. In Ajmer, you can buy other silver items such as cigarette boxes and pill boxes. Pushkar is lined with shops selling silver jewellery, much of it designed with Western tastes in mind.

Meenakari

The princely rulers invested much of their wealth in ornaments of silver and gold, usually encrusted with precious and semiprecious gems. It was the founder of Amber, Maharaja Man Singh I, who introduced the beautiful *meenakari*, or enamelwork, to Rajasthan at the end of the 17th century. Man Singh enticed five master *meenakari* workers from Lahore to his royal court, and established a tradition of fine enamelwork that continues in Jaipur to this day.

The oldest extant example of *meenakari* work is the Jaipur staff. It is 132cm long and comprises 33 segments of gold, each of which features exquisite enamelwork depicting floral and animal designs. The handle of the staff is solid jade. The maharaja bore this staff with him to Delhi when he was summoned to the royal court by Emperor Akbar.

Both silver and gold can be used as a base for *meenakari*. However, only a limited number of colours, including gold, blue, green and yellow, can be adhered to silver, whereas all available colours can be applied to gold, making it the preferred medium of enamellers.

Jaipur enamellers use the *champlevé* method, in which engravings are made on the object to be enamelled; these are then flooded with the enamel colour. Each colour has to be individually fired, so those colours which are most resistant to heat are applied first, because they will be refired with the addition of each new colour. As a rule, white is the first colour applied, and red the last.

The final piece of art is the product of a succession of master artisans: the *sonar*, or goldsmith; the *chattera*, who engraves the piece; and the *minakar*, or enameller.

Kundan jewellery features precious gems on one side and *meenakari* work on the reverse, requiring the expertise of a *kundansaz*, who applies the gems.

Jaipur's *meenakari* has particularly vibrant colour. The rich ruby red the *minakars* produce is highly prized. Jaipur is also an important gem cutting and polishing region.

Woodwork

Given the paucity of wood in most parts of Rajasthan, it is not surprising that stone sculpture is more prevalent than woodcarving. Nevertheless, there is a tradition of woodcarving which dates back many centuries. Unfortunately, few of the medieval pieces have survived, having succumbed to Rajasthan's arid climate or to white ants.

Shekhawati was an important centre for woodcarving. Here the woodcarvers' talent can be seen in finely wrought doors, and door and window frames. Artisans in Shekhawati also produced *pidas* – low, folding chairs featuring decorative carving. Bikaner was also an

important centre for woodcarving, known for its ornately carved doors and lintels, and particularly for latticed *jalis* (screen windows).

The heads of puppets were usually carved from wood, and then painted with the requisite (ferocious, heroic or lovelorn) expression. Wooden boxes featuring several layers of lacquer were popular in the 19th century, a craft which was probably introduced from Sind (now in Punjab).

Lacquered ware is produced in Jaipur, Jodhpur, Sawai Madhopur and Udaipur. Jaipur and Jodhpur are known for their *lac* (resin) bangles and bracelets – Jaipur's Maniharon ka Rasta is the centre of the bangle trade. The wooden item to receive the lacquer treatment is first rubbed with liquid clay, and then, when dry, the design is stencilled with the aid of charcoal. Liquid clay, applied with very fine brushes of squirrel hair, is then used to trace the design, which becomes raised with each successive layer. The surface is then coated with paint, and gold leaf applied.

The village of Bassi, near Chittorgarh, is known for the production of wooden puppets and toys, particularly for images of Ishar and Gauri (Parvati), which feature in the Gangaur Festival, and the bright *kavads*, or minitheatres, used by storytellers to relay the tales of the gods.

Bottom: Water pots are carried with amazing balance and grace

Carved wooden horses, honouring the trusty steed of the deified hero, Ramdevji, are offered at his temple during the annual Ramdevji Festival. The woodcarvers of Barmer use *sheesham* and *rohira* wood. *Rohira*, known locally as 'Marwar teak' and possessing excellent qualities for carving, has now unfortunately almost vanished from the desert.

Pottery

According to tradition, the first potter was created by Shiva, who required a vessel for ceremonial purposes on the occasion of his wedding to Sati. This potter was named Rudrapal, and it is from him that the potters' caste, known as the *Kumbhars*, are descended. Many potters today still take the name Rudrapal, in honour of their legendary forebear.

Of all the arts of Rajasthan, pottery has the longest lineage, with fragments of pottery recovered from Kalibangan dating probably from the Harappan era (around 2500 BC). Prior to the beginning of the first millennium, potters in the environs of present-day Bikaner were decorating red pottery with black designs.

PETER DAVIS

Today, different regions of Rajasthan produce different types of pottery, the most famous of which is the blue pottery of Jaipur. Blue-glazed pottery originated in China and later passed to Persia, from where it was introduced to India by the Muslims. The blue-glazed work was first evident on tiles which adorned the palaces and cenotaphs of the Mughal rulers. Later the technique was applied to pottery.

In most centres the production of this highly glazed pottery declined during the era of the Mughal emperor Aurangzeb. However, the tradition was revived in Jaipur in the mid-19th century.

A wide range of items is available, including bowls, plates, tiles, vases, incense burners, mugs, door knobs and ashtrays. The pieces are decorated with images representing legends, ornamental devices and floral motifs, and depictions of animals. They are then painted with a coat of cobalt or copper oxide. After receiving a final coat of glaze, they are baked in a kiln for up to three days.

Most villages in Rajasthan have their own resident potter, who not only produces domestic vessels, but is required to produce clay images of the deities for ceremonial purposes. The most striking of these sacred images are produced in the village of Molela, north of Udaipur in southern Rajasthan. Here potters work with terracotta formed from clay and donkeys' dung, continuing a tradition that dates back to the Harappan era.

Leatherwork

Leatherworking has a long history in Rajasthan. As working with leather is considered an 'unclean' profession, it is performed by the lowest caste in the Hindu caste hierarchy, the Sudras. Tanning is carried out by the Chamar caste. Cobblers throughout Rajasthan belong to a caste known as *Mochis*. Leather shoes known as *jootis* or *mojdis* are produced in Jodhpur and Jaipur, among other centres. *Jootis* often feature ornate embroidery known as *kashida* – in Jodhpur, the embroidery is applied direct to the leather, while in Jaipur it is worked on the velvet with which the shoes are covered. Embroidery is always done by women. Other ornamentation includes fancy stitching on the uppers, and appliqué. Strangely, there is no 'right' or 'left' foot: both shoes are identical but, due to the softness of the leather, eventually they conform to the shape of the wearer's foot.

Alwar is known for its beautiful leather book bindings, a craft which flourished under Maharaja Banni Singh in the early 19th century. One of the finest covers, for the famous copy of *Gulistan (A Rose Garden)* by Shekh Muslihud-din-Sadi, can be seen in the Alwar museum at the City Palace complex. Bikaner is known for its *usta* (camel leather) products, especially *kopis*, or camel-hide water bottles. The trade is centred around Usta St.

Smart Shopping

Handicraft production is a large sector of the Rajasthani economy, and many people depend on it for their livelihoods. Unfortunately, some artisans are exploited by unscrupulous middlemen who underpay the producers and then sell their work to tourists at inflated prices. However, you can be sure you're putting your money to excellent use by shopping at cooperatives. These have been set up to protect and promote the income of day labourers and handicraft producers at the grass-roots level. For the customer, the quality and price of products on sale is superior to other shops and the prices are fixed so you don't have to haggle.

There are a few outlets in Rajasthan that are particularly concerned with promoting small producers – see the regional chapters for full details. In Jaipur, check out Mojari, a fabulous shoe shop producing a wide range of shoes for export. It's a UN-supported project to help poor leatherworkers reach wider markets. Anokhi is another outlet in Jaipur well worth visiting. This clothing and textile manufacturer produces high-quality items and provides good conditions for its workers. At Ranthambhore National Park, in eastern Rajasthan, the Dastkar Craft Centre promotes handicrafts produced by low-caste women in local villages.

Another well-known outlet is the Urmul Trust's Abhivyakti shop in Bikaner. The trust provides health care and education to remote villages and sells high-quality crafts produced by local artisans through its shop. Tilonia, near Kishangarh in eastern Rajasthan, is the home of the Bare-foot College, another grass-roots nongovernmental organisation (NGO) which promotes self-reliance, such as the use of solar technology, in poor communities. The showroom offers excellent handicrafts at reasonable prices, with the profits going back to the artisans themselves.

[Continued from page 140]

Jantar Mantar

Next to the City Palace entrance is the Jantar Mantar *(Observatory; admission Rs 10, Mon free, still camera foreigner/citizen Rs 50/20, video Rs 100/50; open 9am-4.30pm daily)*, begun in 1728 by Jai Singh whose passion for astronomy was even more notable than his prowess as a warrior. Before commencing Jantar Mantar, he sent scholars abroad to study foreign observatories. This observatory is the largest and best preserved of the five he built, with 13 different instruments for calculating the movement of celestial bodies. It was restored in 1901. The others are in Delhi (the oldest, dating from 1724), Varanasi and Ujjain. The fifth observatory, at Mathura, has disappeared.

Jantar Mantar (or 'instrument of calculation') is a curious if somewhat compelling collection of sculptures. In fact, each construction has a specific purpose, for example, measuring the positions of the stars, altitude and azimuth, and calculating eclipses.

The most striking instrument is the **Brihat Samrat Yantra** sundial, an imposing yellow edifice to the far right of the observatory complex which has a 27m high gnomon arm set at an angle of 27°. The shadow this casts moves up to 4m in an hour, and aids in the calculation of local and meridian pass time and various attributes of the heavenly bodies, including declination (the angular distance of a heavenly body from the celestial equator) and altitude. It is still used by astrologers and is the focus of a gathering during the full-moon days of June and July, when it is used to help predict the monsoon rains, and subsequent success or failure of crops.

If you tour the *yantras* (instruments) in a clockwise direction, immediately to the left as you enter the compound is the **Laghu Samrat Yantra**, a small sundial made of red sandstone and white marble. This does not measure as precisely as the Brihat Samrat Yantra, but does calculate the declination of celestial bodies, and the shadow cast by its gnomon enables local time to be determined. Nearby is the **Dhruva Darshak Yantra**, used to find the location of the Pole Star.

The large circular object nearby, known as the **Narivalaya Yantra**, is actually two small sundials. The two faces of the instrument represent the northern and southern hemispheres, and enable calculation of the time within a minute's accuracy.

The two large disks that are suspended from the wooden beams nearby comprise the **Yantra Raj**, a multipurpose instrument which, among other things, can help determine the positions of constellations and calculate the Hindu calendar. A similar looking instrument, the **Unnatansha Yantra**, lies in the northeastern corner of the observatory complex. This metal ring is divided into four segments by horizontal and vertical lines. A hole where these lines intersect, in the centre of the instrument, aids in the calculation of the altitude of celestial bodies.

Nearby is the **Dakhinovrith Bhitti Yantra**, which serves a similar function to the Unnatansha Yantra in helping to determine the placement of heavenly bodies.

West of the Brihat Samrat Yantra, near the southern wall of the observatory, you come to a cluster of 12 yellow instruments known as the **Rashi Yantras**. Each *rashi*, or individual instrument, represents one of the 12 zodiac signs. The gradient of each *rashi* differs in accordance with the particular sign represented and its position in relation to the ecliptic.

The **Jai Prakash Yantra**, resembling two huge slotted bowls, was the last instrument installed at the observatory and was invented by Jai Singh, after whom it was named. The instrument is used in celestial observations, but can also verify the calculations determined by other instruments at the observatory.

The two other sunken concave structures in the western section of the observatory compound comprise the **Kapali Yantra**. The eastern Kapali Yantra is inscribed with lines to which astronomers refer in their deliberations; it is used more for graphical analysis than calculation, as opposed to the western Kapali Yantra, which is used to determine the position of a celestial body. Between the two bowls stands the **Chakra Yantra**, a pair of metal wheels that can be fitted with a brass tube in order to calculate the declination of celestial bodies.

Two other impressive instruments are the **Ram Yantras**, which look like miniature coliseums made of 12 upright slabs and 12 horizontal slabs. They are used in the calculation of the altitude and azimuth of celestial bodies. Between them is another circular instrument used for calculating azimuth, particularly of the sun, the **Digansha Yantra**. It can also be used to determine the time of sunrise and sunset.

City Palace Complex

In the heart of the old city, the City Palace *(foreigner adult/child 5-12 years Rs 150/80, citizen Rs 35/20; palace & museum open 9.30am-5.30pm daily)* occupies a large area divided into a series of courtyards, gardens and buildings. The outer wall was built by Jai Singh, but other additions are more recent, some dating to the start of the 20th century. Today the palace is a blend of Rajasthani and Mughal architecture. The son of the last maharaja and his family still live in part of the palace.

Before the palace proper lies the **Mubarak Mahal** (Welcome Palace), built in the late 19th century by Maharaja Sawai Madho Singh II as a reception centre for visiting dignitaries. It now forms part of the **Maharaja Sawai Mansingh II Museum** and contains a collection of royal costumes and superb shawls including Sanganeri block prints, royal shawls, Kashmiri *pashmina* (goats' wool) shawls, folk embroideries and Benares silk saris (no smoking allowed). One remarkable exhibit is a set of the voluminous clothes of Sawai Madho Singh I (r. 1750–68), who was over 2m tall, 1.2m wide and weighed 250kg!

The **Maharani's Palace**, once the queen's apartments, houses a collection of weaponry. Note the extraordinary frescoes on the ceiling of this room: those beautifully preserved colours were actually derived from semi-precious jewel dust. The priceless collection of weapons dates back to the 15th century, and includes gruesome Rajput scissor-action daggers – when the dagger entered the body, the handles were released to spread the

blades. The dagger was then withdrawn, virtually disembowelling the hapless victim.

Other exhibits include swords with pistols attached to their blades; beautiful crystal, ivory and silver-handled daggers; armour of chain mail, one complete set of which can weigh up to 35kg; and a sword encrusted with rubies and emeralds presented by Queen Victoria to Maharaja Sawai Ram Singh, the ruler of Jaipur from 1835 to 1880. There is also an assortment of guns, including some that also serve as walking sticks; a gun the size of a small cannon for use on camel back; and double-barrelled pistols, which held bullets that were made of lead, dipped in poison and packed with gunpowder.

Between the armoury and the art gallery is the **Diwan-i-Khas** (Hall of Private Audience). In its marble-paved gallery stand two silver vessels which Maharaja Madho Singh II took to London filled with holy Ganges water. As a devout Hindu, the maharaja was reluctant to risk ritual pollution by imbibing English water. These enormous vessels each have a capacity of over 9000L, stand 160cm tall and are the largest sterling-silver objects in the world. There are a number of crystal chandeliers hanging from the ceiling; they are covered with plastic to protect them from dust and pigeon droppings and are only uncovered on certain festive occasions.

The art gallery is housed in the former **Diwan-i-Am** (Hall of Public Audience), beyond and to the right of the Diwan-i-Khas. It retains a beautifully preserved painted ceiling, on which the original semi-precious stone colours have barely faded and from which is suspended an enormous crystal chandelier. Exhibits include a copy of the entire Bhagavad Gita handwritten in tiny script, and miniature copies of other holy Hindu scriptures small enough to be easily hidden in the event that Aurangzeb tried to destroy the sacred texts. There are also beautiful handwritten books in Persian and Sanskrit; early manuscripts on palm leaf; miniature paintings of the Rajasthani, Mughal and Persian schools depicting religious themes, most notably scenes from the Ramayana; various ornate *howdahs* (elephant saddles); and exquisitely detailed paper cuttings incised with a thumbnail.

The **Chandra Mahal** is still occupied by the royal family, but you can visit the ground floor, which only has a few exhibits. Note the exquisite **Peacock Gate** in the courtyard outside.

The ticket to the complex includes entry to Jaigarh (see Around Jaipur), but is only valid for two days from purchase. Photography opportunities are limited because cameras and videos are prohibited inside the palace museums. If you're still interested, a video costs Rs 150 for everyone, but a Rs 50 camera fee is only levied on citizens! There are guides for hire inside the palace complex for around Rs 150 per hour.

New City

By the mid-19th century it became obvious that Jai Singh's well-planned city could not accommodate the growing population. During the reign of Maharaja Ram Singh (1835–80) the city spread beyond its walls and civic facilities such as a postal system and piped water were introduced. The maharaja commissioned the landscaping of the **Ram Niwas Public Gardens**, on Jawaharlal Nehru Marg, and the construction in the gardens of the impressive **Albert Hall**, which now houses the Central Museum (see Other Museums later in this chapter).

These civic improvements were continued by Jaipur's last maharaja, Man Singh II, who is credited with the university, the Secretariat, residential colonies, schools, hospitals and colleges. Unplanned urban growth is spoiling this once beautiful city, with private interests and political expediency outweighing aesthetic considerations. Buildings are being constructed with little regard for Jaipur's rich architectural heritage.

There is a small **zoo** (admission Rs 7; open 8.30am-5.30pm Wed-Mon in summer, 9am-5pm Wed-Mon in winter) in the Ram Niwas Public Gardens with a collection of unhappy looking animals. Nearby, an old theatre houses Jaipur's **Modern Art Gallery** (admission free; open 10am-5pm Mon-Sat) on the first floor of the Ravindra Manch building, which has a small collection for viewing.

To the south, looming above J Nehru Marg to the left, is the small and romantic fort of **Moti Dungri**. It has also served as a prison, but today remains in the possession of the erstwhile royal family, and entry is prohibited.

Birla Lakshmi Narayan Temple (admission free; open 6am-noon & 3pm-8.30pm daily) is a large, modern marble edifice at the foot of Moti Dungri fort. The wealthy industrialist Birla, born in Palani, Rajasthan, bought the land on which the temple now stands from the maharaja for a token Rs 1. Stained-glass windows depict scenes from Hindu scriptures. Ganesh, the protector of households, is above the lintel, and the fine quality of the marble is evident when you enter the temple and look back at the entrance way – Ganesh can be made out *through* the marble, which is almost transparent. The images of Lakshmi and Narayan were carved from one piece of marble. Many of the deities of the Hindu pantheon are depicted inside the temple, and on the outside walls great historical personages and figures from other religions are shown, including Socrates, Zarathustra, Christ, Buddha and Confucius. There is a small **museum** (admission free; open 8am-noon & 4pm-8pm daily) next to the temple. The collection includes household objects and clothing of the Birla family. It costs Rs 2 to park a vehicle at the temple.

Just down the street is **Ganesh Temple** (open 5am-9pm Thur-Tues, 5am-11pm Wed). If you don't like crowds avoid the temple on Wednesday (the auspicious day), when there are throngs of devotees. Photography is not allowed. You can buy *ladoos* (ball-shaped sweetmeats) to offer Ganesh at the sweet stalls outside the temple.

The **Birla Planetarium** (admission Rs 17; open 11am-8pm daily, closed last Wednesday of month) is at the BM Birla Science & Technology Centre, near Statue Circle. Show entitled 'The Violent Universe' run for 35 minutes. Most are in Hindi (at 11am, 1pm, 3pm, 5pm and 7pm). An English commentary is only given in a 6pm session. Next door, there's a **science museum** (admission Rs 8). Parking costs Rs 5 for a car or autorickshaw.

Other Museums

The somewhat dusty collection of the **Central Museum** (foreigner/citizen Rs 30/5, Mon free; open 10am-4.30pm Sat-Thur) is housed in the architecturally impressive Albert Hall in the Ram Niwas Public Gardens, south of the old city. Photography is prohibited. Exhibits include a natural-history collection, models of yogis adopting various positions, tribal ware, dioramas depicting various Rajasthani dances, and sections about the decorative arts, costumes, drawings, musical instruments and tribal costumes.

Inside the old city, the **Shree Sanjay Sharma Museum** (☎ 323436; 1670 Maniharon ka Rasta; foreigner/citizen Rs 80/35; open 10am-5pm Mon-Sat) houses an extraordinary private collection, including many rare manuscripts and some wonderful and historic Indian art from around the country. There's a set of 18th-century paintings of yoga postures showing which poses to strike if you're drowning, going deaf or suffering from gas. There's also a display of exquisite old shoes, including a few pairs with pointy nodes in the soles (for acupressure) and one embedded with nails (for atonement). The museum is signposted off Chaura Rasta; photography is not permitted.

The rather ramshackle **Museum of Indology** (☎ 607455; 24 Gangwal Park; admission Rs 40; open 8am-6pm daily) is another mind-boggling private collection of rare folk-art objects and other bits and pieces of interest – there's everything from a map of India painted on a rice grain, to manuscripts (including a Quran copied by hand by Aurangzeb), old stamps, tribal ornaments, fossils, tantric art, currency notes, clocks, old nut-cutters, a 200-year-old mirrorwork swing from Bikaner and much more. The museum is a private home (although the living quarters have been swallowed up by the collection), and is signposted off J Nehru Marg, near JK Lon Hospital. There are plans to move the collection to a new building on Amber Rd, 6km from Jaipur, in 2003. It costs Rs 20 per shot to take photos and entry includes a guided tour.

Close to the Museum of Indology, in the Deaf, Dumb & Blind compound on J Nehru Marg, is the little **Dolls Museum** (admission by donation; open 10am-5pm Mon-Sat). The collection includes dolls wearing traditional costumes from around India and the world, including two leprechauns from Ireland!

Around the back of the main post office, there's a **philatelic museum** (admission free; open 10am-1.30pm & 2pm-4pm Mon-Sat) that houses a collection of old stamps (some of which are for sale).

Nahargarh

Nahargarh (Tiger Fort), overlooks the city of Jaipur from a sheer ridge to the north and is floodlit at night. The fort was built in 1734 by Jai Singh and extended in 1868. A 9km road runs up through the hills from Jaipur, and the fort can be reached along a zigzagging 2km path which starts from the northwest of the old city. The glorious views fully justify the effort. Inside the fort you can visit the **Madhavendra Bhawan** (admission Rs 5; open 10am-6pm daily), housing the nine apartments of Maharaja Ram Singh's nine wives. The rooms are linked by a maze of corridors and retain some delicate frescoes, as well as toilets and kitchen hearths.

It costs Rs 30/70 for foreigners to use a still camera/video, Rs 10/20 for citizens. The **Durg Cafeteria** (open 10am-10pm; veg thalis Rs 57) is above the entrance to the Bhawan, while Padao Restaurant, 300m west, sells drinks from the ramparts around sunset (see Entertainment, later).

Royal Gaitor

The collection of cenotaphs at the Royal Gaitor (admission free; open 9am-4pm daily) is accessible via the Zorawar or Samrat gates in the northern wall. It's a beautiful, peaceful place just outside Jaipur's old city walls, containing the cenotaphs of the maharajas of Jaipur from Jai Singh II, the founder of Jaipur, to that of the last maharaja, Man Singh II. The more ancient cenotaphs, including that of Jai Singh, are in a walled compound to the rear. A caretaker may be required to open the gate for you here.

There's a charge of Rs 10/20 for using a still or video camera.

Sisodia Rani Palace & Vidyadharji-ka-Bagh

Six kilometres from the city on Agra Rd (leave by the Ghat Gate), this palace with its surrounding terraced gardens *(admission Rs 5; open 8am-6pm daily)* was built for Maharaja Jai Singh's second wife, the Sisodia princess. The palace is closed, but the outer walls are decorated with murals depicting hunting scenes and the Krishna legend. Video cameras are not permitted.

Vidyadharji-ka-Bagh *(Agra Rd; admission Rs 5; open 8am-6pm daily)*, a garden built in honour of Jai Singh's chief architect and town planner, Vidyadhar, is about 200m before Sisodia Rani Palace. Video cameras are not allowed.

Regular local buses leave from Ghat Gate for the Sisodia Rani Palace (Rs 5). Ask the bus driver to drop you at the Vidyadharji-ka-Bagh, and then continue on to the palace. An autorickshaw will cost around Rs 150 return from the city centre to visit both.

Galta & Surya Mandir

Galta, known locally as Monkey Temple, is perched between the cliff faces of a rocky valley, and is a fairly desolate and barren, if somewhat evocative, place. At sunset hundreds of monkeys converge on the temple and you can buy peanuts at the gate to feed to them.

The temple houses a number of sacred tanks, into which some daring souls jump from the adjacent cliffs. The water is claimed to be 'several elephants deep'. The walls are decorated with frescoes, although very heavy rains in 1991 destroyed many of the original paintings.

There are some original frescoes in reasonable condition in the chamber at the end of the bottom pool, including those depicting athletic feats, the maharaja playing polo, and the exploits of Krishna and the *gopis* (milkmaids).

On the ridge above Galta is the Surya Mandir (Temple of the Sun God), which rises 100m above Jaipur and can be seen from the eastern side of the city. A 2.5km walking trail climbs up to the temple from Surajpol (see Jaipur map), or you can walk up from the Galta side. There are fine views over the surrounding plains.

Astrology

It costs Rs 300 for a 20-minute consultation with Dr Vinod Shastri *(☎ 613338, ☎ 603339; ℮ vshastri@sancharnet.in; open 9am-8pm daily)*, the general secretary of the Rajasthan Astrological Council & Research Institute. You need your exact time and place (city or town) of birth to get a computerised horoscope. A semidetailed five-year prediction costs Rs 300 (Rs 900 for full details), while a 30-year prediction is a hefty Rs 3000! Dr Shastri can be found in his shop near the City Palace, Chandani Chowk, Tripolia Gate. It's highly advisable to make an advance appointment.

Dr Shastri also conducts astrology lessons for beginners. The charge is Rs 3000 per person for 10 one-hour lectures, given over a period of five days (a minimum of five people are needed). More advanced lessons are also available.

These days, many hotels are cashing in on foreigners' interest in fortune-telling.

Ayurvedic Clinics

The **Kerala Ayurveda Centre** *(☎ 382757, fax 383363; ℮ kahc@datainfosys.net; 26 Srirampura Colony, opposite CM House, Civil Lines; open 8am-noon & 4pm-8pm daily)* offers Ayurvedic massage and therapy at its pricey but professional clinic. Treatments include *sirodhara*, where 3L of medicated oil is streamed steadily over your forehead for half an hour to reduce stress, tone the brain and help with sleep disorders. Massages (by male or female masseurs) cost from Rs 500 for 50 minutes.

If you're seeking treatment for a specific ailment, you can visit the **National Institute of Ayurveda** *(Madho Vilas)*, near Samrat Gate. This government hospital provides free Ayurvedic therapies, including oil massages, steam baths and purification programmes. However, you must first consult a doctor who will determine the appropriate treatment for your condition. Simple accommodation (Rs 100) is available for those who need long-term treatment.

JAIPUR

The Rani of Rambagh

The life story of Gayatri Devi, the celebrated maharani of Jaipur, is an allegory of 20th-century Rajasthan, capturing the state's ambivalence towards its transition from princely rule to part of post-Independence, democratic India.

In her heyday, Gayatri Devi was an icon of royal glamour, adored by gossip columnists and dubbed by *Vogue* magazine as one of the most beautiful women in the world. She was born in 1919, a princess from the small state of Cooch Behar (now in West Bengal). At the age of 19 she fell in love with Man Singh II, the last maharaja of Jaipur. Although Man Singh already had two wives, they were married in 1939 and settled down to the life of luxury enjoyed by Indian royalty of the time. There were polo matches, hunting jaunts, decadent dinner parties and summers in England.

Man Singh converted his former hunting lodge, 3km southwest of the old city, into the magnificent Rambagh Palace for Gayatri Devi. Today the palace is surrounded by Jaipur's sprawling suburbs, but it was once a secluded retreat well beyond the limits of the city centre. Here the couple entertained some of the world's richest and most famous people, including Eleanor Roosevelt and Jackie Kennedy.

By this time, however, the Man Singhs were adjusting to their new role in post-Independence India. Rajasthan's ancestral rulers had been stripped of their powers, but many were still held in high regard by a large proportion of their former subjects. Banking on this support, Gayatri Devi, like many other royals, decided to enter politics. She stood against the Congress Party in the national elections in 1962 and swept the board. Her stunning victory is now listed in the *Guinness Book of World Records* as the largest margin ever recorded (a staggering 175,000 votes) in a democracy. In the 1967 and 1971 elections she retained her seat.

However, Indira Gandhi's Congress was quick to act against the royals who were successfully challenging its hold on power. The privileges that the maharajas were promised following Independence (notably the privy purses or stipends paid to the royals from public funds) were abolished and investigations into their financial affairs were mounted. In the early 1970s Gayatri Devi was convicted of tax offences and served five months in Delhi's notorious Tihar Jail. On her release she penned her autobiography, *A Princess Remembers*. Now in her eighties, Gayatri Devi retains residential quarters at the Rambagh Palace, which, in 1958, was the first former palace in Rajasthan to be converted into a hotel (see Places to Stay).

Beauty Parlours

Jaipur has lots of beauty parlours for women and some for men. At **Health Spa** (☎ 388691; *Ganpati Plaza*) facial massages start at Rs 250 and you can get *mehendi* (henna) applied for Rs 150 per hand (front and back).

Golf

Rambagh Golf Club (☎ 384482; *Bhawani Singh Rd; open 6am-6pm daily*), near the Rambagh Palace, charges Rs 600/100 per foreigner/citizen per day, plus Rs 50/100 for a caddie and Rs 100 for equipment. You have to buy the balls.

Courses

There are a surprising number of courses on offer to travellers in Jaipur. Along with those listed below, Dr Vinod Shastri runs classes in Indian astrology; see Astrology earlier.

Meditation Vipassana is one of India's oldest forms of meditation; it is 'a logical process of mental purification through self-observation that strives to achieve real peace of mind and lead you to a happy, useful life'.

The **Dhammathali Vipassana Meditation Centre** (☎ 680220; e *dhammjpr@datain fosys.net*) runs courses (for a donation) in meditation for both beginners and more advanced students throughout the year. Courses are for a minimum of 10 days, throughout which you must observe 'noble silence' – no communication with others. This serene meditation centre is tucked away in the hilly countryside near Galta, about 3km east of the city centre. Accommodation is provided in single rooms (some with private bathroom) and vegetarian meals are available. Courses are offered in Hindi, English, German, French, Spanish, Japanese, Hebrew, Italian, Korean, Portuguese, Mandarin and Burmese. Bookings are essential.

Yoga There are several places in Jaipur that conduct yoga classes, including the **Yoga Sadhana Ashram** (☎ 514821; Bapu Nagar; open Wed-Mon), off University Marg (near Rajasthan University). Classes incorporate breathing exercises, yoga *asanas* (poses) and exercise. Most of the classes are in Hindi, but some English is spoken in the 7.30am to 9.30am class. A minimum of one week is recommended and membership costs Rs 600 per month (plus Rs 30 registration).

Alternatively you could try the casual classes held at **Madhavanand Girls College** (☎ 200317; C-19 Behari Marg, Bani Park), next door to the Madhuban guesthouse. There are free daily classes from 6.30am to 7.30am.

Music & Dance Lessons in music and dance are available at **Maharaja Sawai Mansingh Sangeet Mahavidyalaya** (☎ 611397; open 8am-10am & 4pm-8pm Mon-Sat), behind Tripolia Gate. The sign is in Hindi – ask locals to point you in the right direction. Tuition is given in traditional Indian instruments such as tabla, sitar and flute. It costs Rs 250 per month in a small group for regular students. There is also tuition in *kathak*, the classical Indian dance. Classical Indian vocal tuition can also be undertaken. For details contact the school principal, Mr Shekhawat.

Painting & Pottery Mr Kripal Singh (☎ 201127; B-18A Shiv Marg, Bani Park) is a highly respected artist offering lessons in Indian painting, including miniatures and frescoes. The lessons are free, but you must supply your own materials (Mr Singh can advise you on this). You'll need to reserve eight hours a day for at least a week. He also gives free lessons in pottery (although it's not possible during the monsoon) and

has an excellent range of pottery for sale. Advance bookings are essential.

Block Printing The textile outlet **Anokhi** (☎ 750862; e courses@anokhi.com) offers an introductory course on block printing, using blocks that you design yourself. The five-day courses (minimum two people, maximum four people) are run from its organic farm just outside Jaipur and cost US$130 per day, including accommodation on the farm, vegetarian meals, equipment and pick-up and drop-off from Jaipur. Bookings are essential.

Polo Anokhi (see above) also offers introductory polo classes for experienced riders. The courses (minimum two people, maximum four) run for five days and cost US$150 per day, including accommodation, meals, instruction, equipment and horse hire. Bookings are essential one month in advance; email e sales@travelindia.com with 'Anokhi Polo' in the subject line.

Organised Tours

The sights in and around Jaipur are very spread out and many people opt for an organised tour to see them all in one go. It's possible to book approved government day tours of the city and environs with English-speaking guides. The tours visit the Hawa Mahal, Amber Fort (see Around Jaipur later), Jantar Mantar, City Palace, Birla Lakshmi Narayan Temple and the Central Museum.

The half-day tours (Rs 90) are a little rushed but otherwise OK. Times are 8am to 1pm, 11.30am to 4.30pm and 1.30pm to 6.30pm. The full-day tours (Rs 135) are from 9am to 6pm, with a lunch stop at Nahagarh. There's also a tour from 10am to 5pm in an air-con bus (Rs 160). Admission fees to monuments are extra. Tours depart daily from the tourist office at the main train station throughout the year according to demand, picking up passengers en route at RTDC hotels. Ring ☎ 375466 for more details, or book through the tourist office (see Information earlier).

Approved guides for local sightseeing can be hired through the tourist officer at the Tourist Reception Centre. A half-day tour (four hours) Rs 250. A full-day tour (eight hours) is Rs 350. An extra fee of Rs 100 to 150 for both tours is levied for guides speaking French, German, Italian, Japanese or Spanish.

The community group Jaipur Virasat, in association with the **Indian National Trust for Art, Culture and Heritage** (Intach; ☎ 407018; e intach@sify.com), organises City Heritage Walks, run by volunteers, to increase awareness of the city's fascinating history. The two-hour guided walks take you through the walled city and focus on typical Jaipur architecture, local artisans and the homes of famous people. The walks are free (donations appreciated) and leave on Saturday from Albert Hall (the Central Museum) at 8.30am in winter and 8am in summer. Bookings are essential.

The **Rajasthan Travel Service** (☎ 365408; MI Rd) is on the first floor of the Ganpati Plaza. It offers a full-day bus tour of Jaipur city and Amber for Rs 175 per person, or you can see one of these on a half-day tour for Rs 75. It also has a 'Jaipur by Night' tour of Birla Mandir and Chokhi Dhani tourist village for Rs 600 per couple, including dinner at the village.

If you want a taste of rural Rajasthan, the **Hotel Bissau Palace** (☎ 304391; e bissau@ sancharnet.in) organises tours to its erstwhile hunting pavilion, The Retreat (which Prince Charles and Princess Diana once visited). It is located about 27km from Jaipur. From here you are whisked away by camel or camel cart to nearby villages. It costs Rs 1500 per couple or Rs 600 per person for four people. This includes transport, the village tour and lunch. Advance bookings are essential and you can arrange to be picked up from your hotel.

Places to Stay

Getting to the hotel of your choice in Jaipur can be a headache. Autorickshaw drivers besiege almost every traveller who arrives by train (less so if you come by bus). If you don't want to go to a hotel of their choice, they will either refuse to take you at all or they'll demand at least double the normal

fare. If you do go to the hotel of their choice, you'll pay through the nose for accommodation because the manager will be paying them a commission of at least 30% (and the charge won't go down for subsequent nights). The way to get around this 'Mafia' is to go straight to the prepaid autorickshaw stands, which have been set up at both the bus and train stations, where rates are set by the government. Alternatively, check to see if your hotel will pick you up.

Most hotels give discounts of 25% to 40% in the low season, so it's well worth bargaining. The Tourist Reception Centre (see Information, earlier) has a list of places participating in the Paying Guest House Scheme in Jaipur. The cost ranges from around Rs 125 to 1000 per night.

Places to Stay – Budget

Jaipur Inn (☎ 201121, fax 200140; e jaipurinn@sancharnet.in; B-17 Shiv Marg, Bani Park; camp sites per person Rs 50, dorm beds Rs 80, singles/doubles with shared bathroom Rs 150/250, air-cooled rooms Rs 400/500, air-con rooms Rs 600/700) is a long-time favourite. Rooms are fresh and comfortable, and free room and board is exchanged for creative contributions, including artwork, architectural help, cooking or interior design. If you have your own tent you can camp, or you can stay in the rather cramped dorm, featuring a unique tiled roof with mini-skylights designed by a Dutch visitor. There's free pick-up from the train or bus station and you can use the washing machine for Rs 100. The restaurant (see Places to Eat) sports fine views.

Hotel Pearl Palace (☎ 373700, fax 214415; e pearlpalaceindia@yahoo.com; Hari Kishan Semani Marg; singles/doubles with private bathroom from Rs 250/350), off Sanjay Marg, has an enthusiastic following. Some of the rooms have balconies and the food is excellent and cheap (veg thalis go for only Rs 40). You can eat in the dining room with its amazing mural or on the rooftop where there are views over the small Hathroi Fort next door. The owners have ambitious plans to erect a decorated pergola shaped like a giant peacock on the roof.

Hotel Diggi Palace (☎ 373091, fax 370359; diggihtl@datainfosys.net; singles/doubles with shared bathroom from Rs 125/150, with private bathroom from Rs 250/300, air-con rooms from Rs 700/750), just off Sawai Ram Singh Marg, is another popular travellers' hang-out in the former residence of the *thakur* (similar to a lord or baron) of Diggi. Bare but acceptable doubles with shared bathroom come with free hot water by the bucket, or there's doubles with private bathroom and geyser. There's a good restaurant, Internet access and a beautiful lawn area where you can chill out. Autorickshaw tours can also be arranged (Rs 100/150 for two people for a half/full day).

Atithi Guest House (☎ 378679, fax 379496; e atithijaipur@hotmail.com; 1 Park House Scheme Rd; singles Rs 350-750, doubles Rs 400-800), between MI and Station Rds, offers clean rooms with private bathroom. Despite its central location, the rooms are quiet and home-cooked veg meals are available on the pleasant terrace. This is one place rickshaw drivers hate because the owner won't pay commission (always a good sign). Hot water is available in the morning and evening.

Aangan Guest House (☎ 373449, fax 407458; e aangan25@hotmail.com; singles/doubles with private bathroom from 150/250), next door to Atithi Guest House, is cheaper but a little dank and dingy.

Karni Niwas (☎ 365433, fax 375034; e karniniwas@hotmail.com; C-5 Motilal Atal Marg; singles Rs 300-750, doubles Rs 350-800) is in the lane behind the huge Hotel Neelam. It's a homey place run by a nice family, offering clean rooms with private bathroom, some with balcony. Meals are available and free pick-up from the train or bus station is offered.

Evergreen Guest House (☎ 363446, fax 204234; e evergreen34@hotmail.com; singles/doubles with private bathroom from Rs 125/150, with air-con up to Rs 450/500), just off MI Rd in the area known as Chameliwala Market, is something of an institution. It's a huge place with 100 rooms around a pleasant garden area – a good spot to meet other backpackers – but the cleanliness and service are erratic. Amenities include a small swimming pool, Internet access and a reasonably priced restaurant (wood-oven pizzas are around Rs 85).

Ashiyana Guest House (☎ 375414; singles/doubles with shared bathroom Rs 70/150, with private bathroom from Rs 120/175), near the Evergreen, is a much smaller, family-run affair offering grubby rooms. Hot water is Rs 10 per bucket.

Hotel Pink Sun (☎ 376753; singles/doubles with shared bathroom Rs 75/125, with private bathroom Rs 130/175), next door to Ashiyana, is not as good. Hot water here is Rs 5 a bucket.

Devi Niwas (☎ 363727; singh_kd@hot mail.com; Dhuleshwar Bagh, Sadar Patel Marg, C-Scheme; singles/doubles with private bathroom Rs 150/250) is an unpretentious little place run by a family. It has just a handful of good-value rooms with private bathroom and home-cooked meals (thalis Rs 40).

Sajjan Niwas Guest House (☎ 311544, fax 206029; e sajjan_niwas@hotmail.com; Behari Marg, Bani Park; singles/doubles with shared bathroom Rs 150/200, with private bathroom from Rs 200/300) is another great-value pick with spacious, airy rooms. The shared bathrooms have bucket hot water. Meals are available.

Hotel Kailash (☎ 565372; Johari Bazaar; singles with private bathroom Rs 175-375, doubles with private bathroom Rs 195-425), opposite the Jama Masjid, is one of the few places to stay within the old city. It's nothing fancy (the rooms are cramped), but it's friendly. Hot water is only available from 7am to 9am.

Hotel Sweet Dream (☎ 314409, fax 311495; Nehru Bazaar; singles/doubles with private bathroom Rs 270/350, with air-cooling Rs 400/500, with air-con Rs 700/800) is another option in the old city, just inside the walls. Some rooms are better than others so look at a few first. There's a pleasant rooftop veg restaurant here.

Hotel Arya Niwas (☎ 372456, fax 361871; e aryahotel@sancharnet.in; singles/doubles with private bathroom Rs 350/450, with air-con Rs 550/750), just off Sansar Chandra Marg, is another hang-out that's popular with travellers. It has a self-service veg restaurant and clean rooms, although some are a little claustrophobic. There are many reasons for staying at this well-run place, although the touts who are drawn to its perimeter are not among them.

Jai Mangal Palace (☎ 378901, fax 361236; Station Rd; singles/doubles Rs 350/400, with air-cooling Rs 450/500, with air-con Rs 700/740) is found right opposite the bus station. There's a swimming pool here (summer only), as well as a restaurant and a bar. The rooms are OK, but nothing flash.

Hotel Khetri House (☎ 448238; doubles Rs 400-1200), outside Chandpol, not far from the Hotel Bissau Palace, was built for the maharaja of Khetri and is now in a state of dusty decay. Some people will love this extraordinary place and some will find it downright spooky. Rooms are enormous and slightly smelly, with tatty old Art Deco furniture and claw-foot baths. The other-worldly atmosphere is enhanced by a creaky caretaker. All rooms have air-coolers and running hot water, and meals are available.

RTDC Tourist Hotel (☎ 360238; MI Rd; singles/doubles with private bathroom from Rs 200/300), near the main post office, has a certain faded appeal, although it's looking quite shabby these days. Many of the bathrooms have an Indian-style toilet. Meals are available.

RTDC Hotel Swagatam (☎ 200595, fax 201045; MI Rd; dorm beds Rs 50, singles/doubles with private bathroom Rs 350/450, deluxe singles/doubles Rs 550/650) is the closest budget hotel to the train station. It has a rather institutional feel to it, with drab standard rooms or deluxe air-cooled rooms with TV.

Retiring rooms (gents-only dorm Rs 60, singles/doubles with private bathroom Rs 150/300; doubles with air-con Rs 500) at the train station are reasonable.

Places to Stay – Mid-Range

Madhuban (☎ 200033, fax 202344; e madhuban@usa.net; D-237 Behari Marg, Bani Park; singles Rs 550-1500, doubles Rs 650-1800) is heartily recommended if you crave a homey atmosphere with no hassles at all.

The more expensive rooms have fine antique furnishings and even some of the cheaper rooms are elegantly decorated. Ring ahead to arrange a free pick-up from the bus or train station. There's an indoor restaurant, or you can eat out in the pleasant garden where there's a puppet show most evenings. For your dessert try the thin and crispy fried Rajasthani *maalpuas* – delectable!

Umaid Bhawan Guest House (☎ 206426, fax 207445; e email@umaidbhawan.com; Behari Marg, via Bank Rd, Bani Park; singles/doubles from Rs 450/550, suites Rs 1250/1500), behind the Collectorate, is a family-run place that has a lovely personalised feel and enthusiastic service. Many of the atmospheric rooms open out onto balconies; also, free pick-ups are available from the train or bus station.

Hotel Meghniwas (☎ 202034, fax 201420; C-9 Sawai Jai Singh Hwy, Bani Park; singles/doubles from Rs 1000/1200) is yet another marvellous choice. All of the rooms are air-conditioned and Nos 206 and 211 are more like mini-apartments – perfect for long-term guests (Rs 1750 a double). There's also a good restaurant and a pool to splash in.

Jag Vilas (☎ 204638; e info@jagvilas.com; C-9 Sawai Jai Singh Hwy, Bani Park; singles/doubles 1200/1400), next door to Meghniwas, is a modern place with just eight spotless rooms overlooking the pool or garden. Rooms have modem jacks; breakfast is available for Rs 100, while lunch or dinner costs Rs 200.

Hotel Bissau Palace (☎ 304391, fax 304628; e bissau@sancharnet.in; singles/doubles Rs 900/990, with air-con Rs 1500/1800, suites Rs 2700) is a popular choice, perfect if you want to stay in an old palace but can't afford the Rambagh and its ilk. There's a swimming pool, tennis court, a lovely wood-panelled library and two restaurants (one on the rooftop with splendid views; guests only). The cheapest rooms are quite small, while better air-con rooms and suites are also available. Village tours can be arranged (see Organised Tours earlier).

Shahpura House (☎ 202293, fax 201494; e shahpurahouse@usa.net; D-257 Devi Marg, Bani Park; singles/doubles from Rs 600/700, suites 1800/2200) is another good choice, with well-kept rooms decorated in traditional style. All the rooms are different (some have private balconies) and there's a restaurant.

Nana-ki-Haveli (☎ 615502, fax 605481; e nanakihavelijaipur@yahoo.com; Fateh Tiba; singles/doubles Rs 1100/1200, with air-con Rs 1400/1500), just off Moti Dungri Marg, is a friendly place with a homey touch. Meals are available; the set lunch is Rs 250, dinner is Rs 275.

Chirmi Palace Hotel (☎ 365063, fax 364462; e chirmi@vsnl.com; Dhuleshwar Bagh, Sadar Patel Marg; singles/doubles from Rs 650/745) has decent rooms; some have more character than others so try to have a look at a few first. There's a cute restaurant and local sightseeing trips can be arranged.

LMB Hotel (☎ 565844, fax 562176; Johari Bazaar; e info@lmbsweets.com; singles/doubles Rs 1125/1425) is in the old city above the well-known restaurant of the same name. The rooms are not spectacular, but all have air-con.

Narain Niwas Palace Hotel (☎ 561291, fax 561045; e kanota@sancharnet.in; Narain Singh Rd; singles/doubles from Rs 1500/2000, suites Rs 2500), in Kanota Bagh, just south of the city, is a comfortable choice. There's a pool, lovely garden, a restaurant (the set lunch or dinner is Rs 300) and a bar. The owners also operate the **Royal Castle Kanota**, 15km southeast of Jaipur.

Rajasthan Palace Hotel (☎ 661542, fax 602114; 3 Peelwa Garden, Moti Dungri Marg; doubles Rs 250-1500) has a quiet lawn area, a pool and a restaurant. The cheaper rooms are good value.

Alsisar Haveli (☎ 407167, fax 364652; e alsisar@satyam.net.in; Sansar Chandra Marg; singles/doubles Rs 1700/2000, suite Rs 2400) is a gracious 19th-century mansion set in well-manicured gardens, but it's more pricey than other mid-range options and the service is sloppy. There's a restaurant and a relaxing garden area.

Nahargarh, above the old city, is quite a romantic choice, although there is just one basic double room on offer for a hefty Rs 500. It's located in the fort's parapets,

behind the cafeteria, and the views out over Jaipur from the bed are unparalleled. Reservations should be made with the Tourist Reception Centre (☎ 202586).

RTDC Hotel Gangaur (☎ 371641, fax 371647; singles/doubles from Rs 600/700, with air-con 900/1000) is just off MI Rd. There are three restaurants here, including one specialising in Chinese fare.

RTDC Hotel Teej (☎/fax 205482; Collectorate Rd; dorm beds Rs 50, singles/doubles Rs 550/650, with air-con 800/900), opposite the Moti Mahal Cinema, is a bit more homey than most RTDC joints. There's a gloomy bar and a restaurant.

Places to Stay – Top End

Jaipur has plenty of top-notch hotels, but considering the price, the service at many is not up to scratch. Sometimes you get the distinct feeling that you're just a number, not a name.

Raj Vilas (☎ 680101, fax 680202; w www .oberoihotels.com/Rajvilas/jaipurm.htm; Goner Rd; singles/doubles US$350/370, tents US$450, villas US$900-1500), just 8km from the city centre, scores top marks when it comes to attentive, yet unobtrusive service. This would have to be the slickest hotel in Jaipur, if not Rajasthan. Run by the Oberoi Group, it has 71 rooms spread over 32 acres (golf buggies are available to trundle you around) yet it still manages to retain a personal touch. The rooms and colonial-style tents are immaculate and tastefully appointed with all imaginable mod-cons. There's a pricey restaurant with a British chef; nonguests have to pay a minimum of Rs 500/750 for lunch/dinner. Check the website for special offers.

Rambagh Palace (☎ 381919, fax 381098; w www.tajhotels.com/palace/rambagh_jai pur/new.htm; Bhawani Singh Marg; singles/doubles US$240/260, suites US$325-1000), a Taj Group hotel, was previously the palace of Maharaja Man Singh II of Jaipur. The maharani still lives in separate quarters in the hotel grounds. Nonguests can dine in the restaurant or take tea on the veranda. There's also a good bar. The set breakfast is US$6, lunch is US$10 and dinner is US$15.

Samode Haveli (☎ 632370, fax 631397; W www.samode.com/home/haveli; singles/ doubles Rs 1950/3100, suites Rs 3950), in the northeast corner of the old city, is one of the most interesting places to stay. This 200-year-old building was once the town house of the rawal (nobleman) of Samode, who was also the prime minister of Jaipur. Several of the suites are truly astonishing, featuring intricate mirrorwork, ornate paintings, tiny alcoves and recesses and soaring arches. Rooms are ordinary.

Trident (☎ 670101, fax 670303; e reserva tions@tridentjp.com; singles/doubles US$135/ 145, suites US$250), north of the city, is another place run by the Oberoi Group. It is not as upmarket as the Raj Vilas, but is still exceptionally well kept and managed. There's a bar, a pool, a restaurant and a palmist. It is opposite the Jal Mahal (Water Palace); see Around Jaipur later in this chapter.

Jai Mahal Palace Hotel (☎ 223636, fax 220707; W www.tajhotels.com/palace/jaima hal_jaipur/new.htm; cnr Jacob Rd & Ajmer Marg; singles/doubles US$135/155) is another Taj hotel, south of the train station. It has fine gardens, gracious hospitality and good facilities, including a multicuisine restaurant, bar, coffee shop and pool. You can get your future told by the astrologer in the evening (Rs 350).

Rajmahal Palace (☎ 383260, fax 381887; e rajmahalpalace@sancharnet.in; Sadar Patel Marg; singles/doubles US$38/65, suites US$80), in the south of the city, is a more modest edifice than either the Rambagh or Jai Mahal. There are 21 appealing rooms and suites, a restaurant, badminton courts, swimming pool and jogging track. This was formerly the British Residency, and was also temporarily the home of Maharaja Man Singh II and the maharani after their residence, the Rambagh Palace, was converted into a luxury hotel.

Mansingh Hotel (☎ 378771, fax 377582; e mansingh.jaipur@mailcity.com; singles/ doubles Rs 1995/3000, suites Rs 8500), off Sansar Chandra Marg in the centre of town, has good rooms and large two-bedroom suites. There are two restaurants featuring veg and nonveg cuisine, a bar, swimming pool, spa and health club.

Holiday Inn (☎ 672000, fax 672335; e hi jaiin@sancharnet.in; Amber Rd; singles/doubles Rs 2000/3400, suites from Rs 2100/4200) is in rather bleak surroundings about 3.5km north of the city centre. Standard rooms are comfortably appointed and rates include a buffet breakfast. There's a swimming pool, 24-hour coffee shop, bar and Indian and Rajasthani restaurants.

Rajputana Palace Sheraton (☎ 401140, fax 401122; e rajputana.sheraton@welcom group.com; Palace Rd; singles/doubles from US$130/140, Presidential suite US$700) is a swanky hotel between Station and Palace Rds, near the train station. The entrance is on Palace Rd. Amenities include several restaurants, a swimming pool, health club, 24-hour coffee shop and a disco.

Hotel Clarks Amer (☎ 550701, fax 550013; e clamer@pinkline.net; singles/doubles from US$70/85) is a bit inconveniently located about 10km south of the town centre on the way to the airport. There's a swimming pool, 24-hour coffee shop and restaurant.

Hotel Jaipur Ashok (☎ 204491, fax 204498; Jai Singh Circle, Bani Park; singles/ doubles Rs 1600/2500, suites Rs 3500) is about 1km north of the train station. It's modern, somewhat luxurious and completely devoid of character. There's a pool (open to nonguests for Rs 175), a coffee shop, restaurant and bar.

Places to Eat

Jaipur has a very good range of restaurants, many of which offer a mishmash of Indian, continental and Chinese cuisine. There's a cluster of eateries to be enjoyed on MI Rd, just east of Panch Batti, or, if you feel like lashing out, there are plenty of fine restaurants at the top-end hotels.

Niro's (☎ 374493; MI Rd; open 9.30am-11am, noon-4pm & 6pm-11pm daily; mains around Rs 160), was established in 1949 and is a long-standing favourite with Indians and Westerners alike. It still fills up fast (book ahead on weekends), although many will tell you that it's trading on past glory. The expensive menu includes both veg and nonveg Indian, Chinese and continental food. Hot sellers include the chicken tikka masala (Rs 165) and the chicken pepper steak sizzler (Rs 165). An American ice-cream soda will set you back a cool Rs 75.

Surya Mahal (☎ 369850; MI Rd; open 8am-11pm) is a great choice, although it could lose the Western easy-listening music on the stereo. It's less upmarket than other restaurants on this strip, and the prices reflect this, but the food is just as good. There is a range of South Indian dishes, and specials such as the delicious *makki ki roti sarson ka saag* (mustard vegetables with chickpea flour) and a free glass of *chach* (buttermilk) for Rs 75.

Jal Mahal (MI Rd; open 10am-11pm daily), next door to Surya Mahal, is a little take-away ice-cream parlour. A cone of mango tango is Rs 18, a virgin pink waffle sundae is Rs 25 and an Italian thick shake is Rs 13.

Natraj Restaurant (☎ 375804; MI Rd; open 9am-11pm), a little further east towards the old city, is a very good vegetarian place, with an extensive menu featuring northern Indian, continental and Chinese cuisine. The vegetable bomb curry (Rs 80) is a blast, and there are plenty tempting Indian sweets to take away.

Dawat (☎ 378651; open noon-3.30pm & 6.30pm-11pm daily) is down the lane next to Niro's and specialises in Chinese food. Singapore noodles are Rs 65 and sweet-and-sour chicken is Rs 110. There are also some Indian dishes. The food here is OK but nothing to write home about.

Lassiwala (MI Rd; open 8am-4pm daily), opposite Niro's, with its name in brass, is a simple little place that whips up a mighty good lassi. A thick, creamy glassful is Rs 10/20 for a small/jumbo.

Chanakya Restaurant (☎ 372275; MI Rd; open noon-4pm & 6pm-11pm daily; dishes Rs 40-175), further west down MI Rd, on the opposite side to Niro's, is a pure veg restaurant that gets rave reports from travellers. The food is indeed very good and the attentive staff helpfully explain the various menu items. The filling Rajasthani thali is Rs 160.

Dasaprakash (☎ 371313; MI Rd; open 11am-11pm daily; dishes under Rs 80), which

specialises in reasonably priced South Indian cuisine, also offers fresh juices such as pomegranate (Rs 60). Check out the employee of the month on the plaque near the door.

Handi Restaurant (☎ 364839; MI Rd; open 12.30pm-3pm & 6pm-11pm daily; dishes around Rs 80), opposite the main post office, is tucked away at the back of the Maya Mansions building. The furnishings are nothing flash, but it offers scrumptious barbecue dishes and specialises in tandoori and Mughlai cuisine at reasonable prices. In the evenings it sets up a cheap kebab stall at the entrance to the restaurant.

Copper Chimney (☎ 372275; open noon-4pm & 6pm-11pm daily; Indian mains veg Rs 60-105, nonveg Rs 90-170), next door to Handi, has satiating Indian, continental and Chinese cuisine. Try the *lal maas* – it's a Rajasthani speciality of mutton in a thick spicy gravy (Rs 115). Copper Chimney also offers free delivery to your hotel.

Rendezvous (☎ 410377; C-84 Prithviraj Rd, C-Scheme; open 11am-11pm Tues-Sun) is a Western-style café with a real espresso machine. The English owners can whip up delicious cakes and light meals to go with your latte (Rs 30) or macchiato (Rs 25). There are also books, games and magazines to while away an afternoon.

Swaad (☎ 388700; Ganpati Plaza, MI Rd; open 11am-11pm; mains around Rs 150, desserts Rs 50-100), at the swanky Ganpati Plaza, is recommended for a minor splurge. It serves interesting Indian, continental and Chinese cuisine in pleasant surroundings. Travellers' favourites include the *subz malaai kofta-palak* (cottage cheese and herbs with a spinach gravy, Rs 65) and the sizzlers (Rs 115-175).

LMB (☎ 566844; Johari Bazaar; open 8am-11.30pm daily; mains Rs 50-105) is a *sattvik* (pure vegetarian), an air-con restaurant near the centre of the old city, has been going strong since 1954. The '50s decor is looking slightly jaded; food and service get mixed reports from travellers. The LMB sweet shop, next door, sells 'softy cones' for Rs 10.

Steam (☎ 325698; Chaura Rasta; open 11am-11pm daily; dishes under Rs 60) is close to the City Palace and offers a calming refuge from the chaos outside. It's an uncluttered space with candles on the tables and good, reasonably priced food, including Western, Chinese and South Indian cuisine. Thalis start at Rs 40.

Chic Chocolate (☎ 204138; MI Rd; open 8.30am-9.30pm Mon-Sat), around the corner from Atithi Guest House, is a clean pastry shop that does excellent vegie-studded cheese toast (Rs 20) and delicious fruit trifles (Rs 16). It also bakes its own bread.

Bake Hut (☎ 369840; open 9am-10.30pm daily) is another great pastry shop, that offers sweet treats such as chocolate donuts (Rs 8), slices of Black Forest cake (Rs 19) and little lemon tarts (Rs 13). Birthday cakes are baked to order.

Indian Coffee House (MI Rd; open 8am-9.30pm daily; coffee Rs 6.50), off the street, is good if you are suffering withdrawal symptoms from the lack of a decent cup of coffee. It has a somewhat seedy ambience, like a place where shady deals are consummated. Hold your breath as you pass the urinal near the entrance.

Four Seasons (☎ 375221; D-43A Subhash Marg, C-Scheme; open 11am-11pm daily; burgers Rs 35-50, pizzas Rs 50-80, thalis Rs 80-95) is a multicuisine vegetarian restaurant serving moderately priced food in nice surroundings. A speciality is the *rawa masala dosa* (ground rice and semolina South Indian pancake with fresh coconut, onions, carrots and green chillies) for Rs 55.

Jaipur Inn (☎ 201121; B-17 Shiv Marg, Bani Park; buffet dinner Rs 100) boasts one of the city's only rooftop restaurants, with superlative views over the capital. It has an Indian veg buffet dinner (nonguests should book in advance) and a bonfire in winter.

Ganesh Restaurant (Nehru Bazaar; open 9am-11pm daily), near New Gate, is the best-kept secret in Jaipur. This basic outdoor restaurant is in a fantastic location – it's actually on the old city wall. There's no English menu and not much English is spoken, but if you're looking for a local eatery with cheap, tasty food you'll love it. There's no sign – just head up the staircase to the left of Punjab Tailors.

If you're desperately homesick, you'll find **Pizza Hut** (☎ 388627; lunch special Rs 95) and **Baskin 31 Robbins** (open 11am-11.30pm daily; cones Rs 35) at Ganpati Plaza, and there are two **McDonald's** in Jaipur. One is in Panch Patti is right next to Raj Mandir and the other is 9km south of town at Bardiya Shopping Centre, Gaurav Tower, Malviya Nagar.

Entertainment

Despite being the capital of Rajasthan, Jaipur's entertainment scene is surprisingly limited. Many hotels put on some sort of evening music, dance or puppet show.

Raj Mandir Cinema (☎ 374694; tickets Rs 20-79; just off MI Rd, is *the* place to go if you're planning to take in at least one Bollywood flick. This opulent cinema is a Jaipur tourist attraction in its own right and is usually full, despite its immense size. It's a good idea to book, which you can do one day in advance (between 4pm and 5pm at window No 7). However, if you join the appropriate queue (there are separate ones for ladies and gents) around 45 minutes before the start of the movie you should secure a seat. Shows start at 11.45am, 3pm, 6.15pm and 9.30pm – but double-check as these timings may have changed. There are various ticket categories: pearl (Rs 20), ruby (Rs 40), emerald (Rs 49) and diamond (Rs 79); an additional Rs 1 utility fee is charged on all tickets. Avoid the cheaper tickets, which are very close to the screen. English-language movies are occasionally screened at some cinemas in Jaipur – check the newspapers for details.

Pub 2K2 (☎ 379946; Maharaja Hotel, MI Rd; open 11am-1am daily) is probably your best bet for a drink. It's a two-storey bar, down the lane near Niro's, with groovy orange decor and a good range of drinks, including beer, Bloody Marys and pina coladas (Rs 75 each).

Padao Restaurant (☎ 448044; open 6pm-8pm winter, 6pm-10pm summer) is another great option. This open-air RTDC place is right on the ramparts of Nahagarh (Tiger Fort), which looms over the town to the north. It's very simple, offering only beer

(Rs 70) and a few snacks, but the view over Jaipur is spectacular and you can watch the city light up as the sun goes down.

Polo Bar at the Rambagh Palace (see Places to Stay) is Jaipur's most exclusive watering hole, but you'll pay for the privilege of drinking here. A bottle of beer is Rs 209 and a 'polo special' cocktail is Rs 275.

Bowling alleys seem to be the latest rage with Jaipurians. **Megabowl** (☎ 722608; admission Rs 30, bowling fee Rs 70/100 per game Mon-Fri/Sat & Sun; open 1pm-11pm daily) has the best alley but is somewhat inconveniently located in Malviya Nagar at Gaurav Tower, Bardiya Shopping Centre. This modern complex also has various video games and the rather lifeless **Space Station** disco, which closes at 11pm (no alcohol allowed). There's even a fortune-teller here (Rs 50 for 5 minutes).

Pool Club and Cafe (MI Rd, open 8am-11pm daily) is an underground joint with snooker (Rs 90 per hour) and pool (Rs 50).

Spectator Sports

Maharaja Man Singh indulged his passion for polo by building an enormous **polo ground** (Ambedkar Circle, Bhawan Singh Rd) next to the Rambagh Palace, which is still the site of polo matches today. A ticket to a match also gets you into the lounge, which is adorned with historic photos and memorabilia. See the boxed text 'Polo' in the Facts for the Visitor chapter for more on this favourite sport of Rajasthan's royals. The polo season extends over winter, with the most important matches played during January and March – contact the **Rajasthan Polo Club** (☎ 383580; e jaipurpolo@hotmail .com) for ticket details.

During Jaipur's elephant festival in March (for dates see the boxed text 'Festivals of Jaipur' earlier) you can see elephant polo matches at the Chaughan Stadium in the old city. Contact the Polo Club or RTDC (see Information, earlier) for details.

Shopping

Jaipur is *the* place to shop until you drop! It has a wild and wonderful array of handicrafts ranging from grimacing papier-mache puppets to exquisitely carved furniture.

You'll have to bargain hard though – this city is accustomed to dealing with tourists with lots of money and little time to spend it. Shops around the tourist traps, such as the City Palace and Hawa Mahal, tend to be more expensive. The Pink City Walking Tour (see earlier) will take you through some of the traditional artisans quarters of Jaipur. For useful tips on bargaining, see Tipping, Baksheesh & Bargaining under Money in the Facts for the Visitor chapter. At some shops, such as government emporiums, you cannot haggle because the prices are fixed. Most of the larger shops can pack and send your purchases home for you – although it might be cheaper if you actually do it yourself (see Post under Information, earlier in this chapter).

Many rickshaw-wallahs are right into the commission business and it's almost guaranteed that they'll be getting a hefty cut from any shop they take you to. Many unwary visitors get talked into buying things for resale at inflated prices, especially gems. Beware of these 'buy now to sell at a profit later' scams; see the boxed text 'A Warning!' in the Facts for the Visitor chapter.

Shops in Jaipur are usually all open by 10.30am and close at around 7.30pm. Most are shut on Sunday.

The state government emporium, **Rajasthali** (MI Rd; open 11am-7.30pm Mon-Sat), is opposite Ajmeri Gate. Here there's a good selection of artefacts and crafts from all over the state, including enamelwork, embroidery, pottery, woodwork, jewellery, puppets, block-printed sheets, miniatures, brassware, mirrorwork and more. You can get a rough idea of how much things should cost here, before trying your bargaining skills at the markets.

Well worth visiting is **Anokhi** (☎ 750860; 2 Tilak Marg; open 10am-7pm daily) near the Secretariat. It has a terrific range of high-quality textiles, such as block-printed fabrics, tablecloths, bed covers, cosmetic bags and scarves, as well as a range of well-designed clothing with Indian and Western influences. The pieces are produced just outside Jaipur at an unusually ethical factory, built on the grounds of an organic farm.

Anokhi provides excellent working conditions, including limited working hours, free health care and transport for its 200 workers, as well as a creche and educational funding for their children. There are plans to open a café at the shop. Block printing and polo courses are also offered at the farm – see Courses earlier for details.

Soma (☎ 222778; 5 Jacob Rd, Civil Lines; open 10am-8pm Mon-Sat, 10am-6pm Sun) sells similar high-quality textiles.

Mojari (☎ 377037; Bhawani Villa, Gulab Path, Chomu House, off Sadar Patel Marg; open 10am-6pm Mon-Sat) is another fantastic outlet selling beautiful, funky shoes for around Rs 400 to 600. Named after the traditional decorated shoes of Rajasthan, Mojari is a United Nations–supported project to help 3500 rural leatherworkers' households, traditionally among the poorest members of society. There is a wide range available here including embroidered shoes, appliqued shoes, open-toed shoes, mules, sandals, unusual cuts, creative stitching – even shoes with bells on! They meet export quality standards but are based on traditional leatherworking skills and design. For those with a shoe fetish this is heaven, although you may have trouble finding your size.

Kripal Kumbh (☎ 201127; B-18A Shiv Marg, Bani Park) is a great place to buy Jaipur's famous blue pottery produced by the well-known potter Mr Kripal Singh. Vases go for Rs 60 to 400 and a small incense holder costs Rs 40. You can also learn how to make blue pottery here (see Courses earlier in this chapter).

Juneja Art Gallery (☎ 367448; Lakshmi Complex, MI Rd; open 10am-8pm daily), not far from the main post office, has a fabulous range of contemporary paintings, many by Rajasthani artists. There are regular shows of contemporary artists changing almost weekly. Prices range from Rs 200 to 60,000. At the time of research, Juneja was planning to open another branch near the Holiday Inn.

For Ayurvedic preparations, try **Himalaya** (☎ 364495; MI Rd; open 10am-8pm Mon-Sat), near Panch Batti, which exports internationally and has been selling herbal remedies and beauty products for 70 years. It can help

you with a wide variety of ailments, including diarrhoea, poor memory, acne, hangovers and sexual disorders. There are even have treatments for your pet.

Music N Sports (☎ 312134; 73 Chaura Rasta; open 10.30am-8pm Mon-Sat) sells a range of musical instruments, including sitars, tablas, hand cymbals (Rs 50), bamboo flutes (from Rs 25), dancing bells on ankle cuffs (Rs 150 per pair) and harmoniums (Rs 2000 to 18,000).

The cutting, polishing and selling of precious and semiprecious stones is centred around the Muslim area of Pahar Ganj, in the Surajpol Bazaar area. Silver jewellery is also made here. There are numerous factories and showrooms strung along the length of Amber Rd between Zorawar Gate and the Holiday Inn to catch the tourist traffic. Here you'll find block prints, blue pottery, carpets and antiques, but don't expect to find any bargains.

Getting There & Away

Air It's best to book air tickets through travel agencies, where you will usually get a better price than going directly through the airlines. See Travel Agencies, earlier, for details. In Rajasthan you can fly to Udaipur and Jodhpur daily.

Indian Airlines (☎ 743500) Nehru Place, Tonk Rd
Jet Airways (☎ 360450) Umaid Nagar House, MI Rd, opposite Ganpati Plaza
Sahara Airlines (☎ 377637) Shalimar Complex, MI Rd

International Airlines There's a single international flight from Jaipur airport which began in early 2002 – Indian Airlines flight 895 to Dubai via Delhi at 8.30am daily. Services to other international destinations may open in the future, but at the time of writing there were no concrete plans.

Some of the international airlines that serve India have offices in the conveniently located Jaipur Towers building on MI Rd (in the same building as Thomas Cook).

Air France (☎ 370509) Jaipur Towers, MI Rd
Air India (☎ 368569) Ganpati Plaza, MI Rd

Domestic Flights from Jaipur

Airline schedules can be erratic, so check that the information below is still current. Prices for all airlines may have risen by the time you read this.

flight	service	departures	arrivals	fare (US$)
Indian Airlines				
Jaipur–Ahmedabad	CD7269	6.10pm Mon, Wed, Fri	7.10pm	105
Jaipur–Delhi	CD7472	8.30pm daily	9.10pm	65
Jaipur–Delhi	IC895	8.30am daily	9.10am	65
Jaipur–Jodhpur	CD7471	7am daily	7.40am	90
Jaipur–Kolkata	CD7269	6.10pm Mon, Wed, Fri	9.55pm	220
Jaipur–Kolkata	CD7267	7.50pm Tues, Thur, Sat	9.55pm	220
Jaipur–Mumbai	CD7471	7am daily	10.30am	155
Jaipur–Mumbai	IC612	8.30pm daily	10.05pm	155
Jaipur–Udaipur	CD7471	7am daily	8.50am	90
Jet Airways				
Jaipur–Delhi	9W3301	9.45am daily	10.45am	65
Jaipur–Delhi	9W722	6pm daily	6.40pm	65
Jaipur–Mumbai	9W3401	7.35am daily	11.05am	165
Jaipur–Mumbai	9W372	7.30pm daily	9.05pm	165
Jaipur–Udaipur	9W3401	7.35am daily	8.40am	90

Alitalia (☎ 369120) opposite HMT Showroom, MI Rd

British Airways (☎ 370374) near All India Radio, MI Rd

KLM (☎ 367772) Jaipur Towers, MI Rd

Kuwait Airways (☎ 372896) Jaipur Towers, MI Rd

Lufthansa (☎ 561360) 126–127 Sarogi Mansion, MI Rd

Many other international airlines are represented by the following agencies, which are all located in Jaipur Towers:

Delhi Express Travels (☎ 360188) represents Thai

Interglobe Air Transport (☎ 379235, fax 418886) open 9.30am-1pm & 1.45pm-6pm Mon-Sat; represents United Airlines, South African Airways, SAS, Syrian Arab Airlines, Pakistan International Airlines (PIA), Air New Zealand, Delta and Varig

Jetair Ltd (☎ 368640, fax 374242) open 9.30am-1pm & 1.30pm 6pm Mon-Sat, represents American Airlines, Royal Jordanian Airlines, Austrian Airlines, Gulf Airways, Biman Bangladesh and Kenya Airlines

Bus Rajasthan State Road Transport Corporation (RSRTC) buses all leave from the main bus station on Station Rd, and stop to pick up passengers at Narain Singh Circle (you can also buy tickets here). Some services are deluxe (essentially nonstop). There is a left-luggage office at the main terminal and a prepaid autorickshaw stand.

The deluxe buses all leave from platform No 3, which is tucked away in the right-hand corner of the bus station. These deluxe buses should be booked in advance at the reservation office (open 24 hours daily), also on platform No 3. There's a deluxe air-con service to Delhi for Rs 348.

It's best to get an express or deluxe bus – private buses are generally not as reliable when it comes to schedules, although they are usually cheaper. For any express-bus inquiries ring ☎ 206143; for deluxe buses call ☎ 205790.

A number of the private travel agencies in Jaipur book deluxe 2 x 2 (two seat by two seat) services to the major cities (generally services run overnight). There is a cluster of these offices along Motilal Atal Marg, near the Polo Victory Cinema.

There are no direct RSRTC services to Mumbai, so you will need to change at Udaipur. Numerous private agencies operate direct services to these cities.

Train The computerised railway **reservation office** (☎ 201401; open 8am-2pm & 2.15pm-8pm Mon-Sat, 8am-2pm Sun) is reasonably efficient. It is in the building to your right as you exit the main train station and is for advance reservations only. Fill in a reservation form available at counter No 771, then join the queue for 'Freedom Fighters and Foreign Tourists' at counter No 769.

For same-day travel, buy your ticket at the train station on platform No 1, window No 9. The railway inquiries number is ☎ 131.

There's a prepaid autorickshaw stand at the road entrance to the train station, as well as a tourist information office and a cloak room on platform No 1 – it costs Rs 10 to deposit a bag for 24 hours.

Double-check these train schedules, as they may have changed.

Car There are currently no operators renting self-drive cars in Rajasthan. You'll have to hire one in Delhi if you're mad enough to try this – see Getting There & Away in the Delhi chapter for details.

You can arrange a car directly with the driver at the taxi stand at the train station. Usually the drivers need only a day's notice for a long trip. A reasonable price is Rs 3.50 per kilometre, with a 250km minimum per day and Rs 100 per night overnight charge.

RSRTC Bus Services from Jaipur

destination	duration (hrs)	express (Rs)	deluxe (Rs)	private (Rs)
Abu Road	10	181	190	150
Agra	5½	103	123	90
Ajmer	2½	53	66	60
Alwar	4	62	–	–
Bharatpur	4½	71	88	80
Bikaner	8	123	168	100
Bundi	6	83	–	80
Chittorgarh	8	126	–	120
Delhi	5½	113	216	130
			348*	
Jaisalmer	12	186	246	250
Jodhpur	7½	131	160	100
Kota	5	98	120	90
Mt Abu	12	186	–	180
Pushkar	3½	57	–	100
Sawai Madhopur	4	52	–	–
Udaipur	10	162	201	150
Shekhawati District				
Churu	5	87	–	–
Jhunjhunu	5	75	–	80
Nawalgarh	3½	40	58	60
Sikar	3	60	–	50

* Deluxe air-con service

Major Trains from Jaipur

destination	train No & name	departures	distance (km)	duration (hrs)	fare (Rs)
Abu Road	9106 *Ahmedabad Mail*	4.55am	441	8	99/154/713 *
Ahmedabad	9106 *Ahmedabad Mail*	4.55am	626	12½	132/205/951 *
Agra	2308 *Jodhpur Howrah Express*	11.20pm	310	7	77/120/564 *
Bikaner	2468 *Jaipur–Bikaner Intercity*	3pm	517	10	113/348 +
Bikaner	4737 *Jaipur–Bikaner Express*	9pm	517	10	113/176/831 *
Chennai	2968 *Jaipur–Chennai Express*	7.30pm Tues, Fri, Sun	2007	38½	256/397/1851 *
Delhi	2414 *Jaipur–Delhi Express*	4.25pm	305	5¼	77/120/564 *
Delhi via Alwar	4860 *Jodhpur–Delhi Express*	6am	305	5¼	77/120/347 ◆
Delhi via Alwar	2016 *Shatabdi Express*	5.55pm Mon–Sat	305	4¼	495/985 ★
Jodhpur	2461 *Mandore Express*	2.45am	320	5¼	79/123/573 *
Jodhpur	2307 *Jodhpur Howrah Express*	4am	320	6¼	79/123/573 *
Jodhpur	2465 *Intercity Express*	5.20pm	320	5½	79/237 +
Kota	2956 *Jaipur–Mumbai Express*	2.10pm	286	3½	71/111/535 *
Mumbai	2956 *Jaipur–Mumbai Express*	2.10pm	1205	18	200/310/1440 *
Sawai Madhopur	2956 *Jaipur–Mumbai Express*	2.10pm	177	2	52/84/423 *
Sikar	9734 *Shekhawati Express*	5.45pm	105	3½	33/84/337 *
Udaipur	9615 *Chetak Express*	10.10pm	439	12¼	99/154/713 *
Varanasi	4854 *Marudhar Express*	1.25pm Mon, Thur, Sat	971	14½	174/270/783 ◆
Varanasi	4854 *Marudhar Express*	1.25pm Tues, Wed, Fri, Sun	971	13¼	174/270/783 ◆

Trains depart daily unless otherwise indicated.
* general/2nd-class sleeper/2-tier air-con   ◆ general/2nd-class sleeper/3-tier air-con
+ general/air-con chair   ★ air-con chair/executive chair

See the Car & Driver section in the Getting Around chapter for more information.

For those who prefer booking tickets through a travel agency, **Amrapali Travels** (☎ 375100, fax 377906; open 9.30am-7.30pm Mon-Sat, 10am-3pm Sun), near the Evergreen Hotel, offers nonair-con cars for Rs 4 per kilo-metre (minimum 250km per day and Rs 100 per night overnight charge). **Rajasthan Travel Service** (☎ 365408, fax 376 935) hires out vehicles for Rs 5/6 per kilometre for normal/air-con (minimum 250km per day and Rs 70 overnight charge). Rates with the RTDC are from Rs 4.80 per kilometre (Rs 100 overnight charge) for a nonair-con car, and from 6.50 per kilometre (Rs 150 overnight charge) for an air-con car, with the usual 250km minimum per day.

Getting Around

To/From the Airport Only local buses ply the route between the airport and the city, and the bus stop is 300m from the airport, which is far from convenient if you have a heavy bag. There's a prepaid taxi booth inside the terminal – it's Rs 190 to Panch Batti or Rs 200 to Bani Park. An autorickshaw will cost around Rs 80 to 100 to take you into town. Share with others to cut the cost.

Autorickshaw There are prepaid autorickshaw stands at the bus and train stations. Rates are fixed by the government, which means you don't have to haggle. In other cases you should be prepared to bargain hard. If you want to hire an autorickshaw for a sightseeing tour (including Amber), the official rates are Rs 143/280 for a half/full day. This price is per rickshaw, not per person, and don't let drivers tell you otherwise. Make sure you fix a price before setting off to avoid a scene later. A slower, but cheaper and more environmentally friendly option is to hire a cycle-rickshaw or tonga (horse-drawn cart), available at Badi Chaupar in the old city.

Bicycle You can hire bicycles from most bike shops, including one that's about 300m north of Hawa Mahal. It charges Rs 5/50 per hour/day. Some hotels can also arrange bicycle hire or direct you to the nearest rental place.

Around Jaipur

Jaipur is an excellent base from which to visit some of the ancient sites and interesting towns and villages in the precincts. A comprehensive network of local buses makes getting to these regions relatively simple, or it's possible to join an organised tour run by the RTDC that includes a commentary on the various sites visited. See Organised Tours earlier in this chapter for more details.

AMBER
Situated about 11km out of Jaipur on the Delhi to Jaipur road, Amber (pronounced 'Amer') was once the ancient capital of Jaipur state.

The Kachhwahas originally hailed from Gwalior, in present-day Madhya Pradesh, where they reigned for over 800 years. The marital alliance between a Kachhwaha prince, Taj Karan, and a Rajput princess resulted in the granting of the region of Dausa to the prince by the princess's father.

Taj Karan's descendants coveted the hilltop on which Amber Fort was later built,

recognising its virtue as a potential military stronghold. The site was eventually prised from its original inhabitants, the Susawat Minas, and the Minas were actually granted guardianship of the Kachhwahas' treasury in perpetuity.

The Kachhwahas, despite being devout Hindus belonging to the Kshatriya (warrior) caste, recognised the expediency of aligning themselves with the powerful Mughal empire. They paid homage at the Mughal court, cemented the relationship with marital alliances and defended the Mughals in their various skirmishes. For this they were handsomely rewarded. With war booty they financed construction of the fortress-palace at Amber, which was begun in 1592 by Maharaja Man Singh, the Rajput commander of Akbar's army. It was later extended and completed by the Jai Singhs before the move to Jaipur on the plains below.

An impressive sight on the road between Jaipur and Amber is the **Jal Mahal** (Water Palace), situated in the middle of Man Sagar and reached by a causeway. The palace, which was built by Madho Singh in the 18th century, is currently closed. Further south on Amber Rd are the cenotaphs of the maharanis of Jaipur.

Amber fort itself is a superb example of Rajput architecture, stunningly situated on a steep hill right beside the Delhi to Jaipur road. The picturesque **Maota Lake** at the foot of the hillside reflects the fort's terraces and ramparts, but it dries up in the winter months. Around July and August, when the lake is full, boats can be hired for around Rs 40 per person for 15 minutes.

There are three routes up to the fort – as you approach from Jaipur the first entry is for walkers, the second goes via the elephant compound for elephant rides and the third is for motorised vehicles. You can climb up to the fort in about 10 minutes, and cold drinks are available at the top if the climb is a hot one. A jeep costs Rs 120 return and carries up to six people. Riding up on elephants is popular, though daylight robbery at Rs 400 return per elephant. Each elephant can carry up to four people. A quick ride around the palace courtyard costs

JAIPUR

about Rs 20. There's a small **tourist office** (open 9am-4.30pm daily) in the elephant compound.

Amber Fort

The fort (foreigner/citizen Rs 50/10, still camera foreigner/citizen Rs 75/50, video Rs 150/100; open 9am-5pm daily) is divided into four main sections, each with their own courtyard. Entry is through **Suraj Pol** which leads to the **Jaleb Chowk**, or main courtyard. The ticket office is directly across the courtyard from Suraj Pol. From here, an imposing stairway leads up to the main palace, but first it's worth taking the steps just to the right, which lead down to the small **Kali Temple** (open 6am-noon & 4pm-8pm daily). Every day from the 16th century until 1980 (when the government banned the practice) a goat was sacrificed here. It's a beautiful temple, entered by gorgeous silver doors featuring repoussé (raised relief) work. Before the image of Kali lie two silver lions. According to tradition, Maharaja Man Singh prayed to the goddess for victory in a battle with the ruler of Bengal. The goddess came to the maharaja in a dream advising that if he won the battle he should retrieve her image which was lying at the bottom of the sea. After vanquishing his foes, the maharaja recovered the statue and installed it in the temple as Shila Devi (shila means 'slab' and the image is carved from one piece of stone). Above the lintel of the temple is the usual image of Ganesh, this one carved from a single piece of coral.

Heading back to the main stairway will take you up to the second courtyard and the **Diwan-i-Am** (Hall of Public Audience), with a double row of columns each topped by a capital in the shape of an elephant, and latticed galleries above. Here the maharaja held audience and received the petitions of his subjects.

The maharaja's apartments are located around the third courtyard – you enter through the fabulous **Ganesh Pol**, decorated with mosaics and sculptures. The **Jai Mandir**

The Elephants of Amber

If an elephant has its own way, it will live in a hot, wet place, preferably close to a nice deep pool for bathing. Unfortunately, Rajasthan is a long way from the tropics and the elephants that trundle tourists up and down the steep cobbled road to Amber Fort suffer greatly from the hot, dry days and freezing nights of their adopted desert state.

There are around 100 elephants working in rotation at Amber. Every day they have to walk to the fort from their compound, the Mahavaton-ka-Mohalla in Jaipur's old city – a distance of 11km each way. During the hot season temperatures at Amber can reach 45°C and the elephants suffer from sunburn and cracked feet from walking on the hot bitumen roads. Elephants need to drink around 250L of water a day, most of which they drink while bathing. The Amber elephants used to do this at the lake below the palace – until the water level dropped. They also suffer from foot rot, abscesses and blindness caused by vitamin deficiencies.

Many of the mahouts (elephant trainers) are deeply concerned about the health and welfare of their elephants, but unfortunately some resort to metal goads, which sometimes draw blood, to keep their elephants in line. Often this is linked to the poor conditions of the mahouts themselves – low wages mean that there's a high turnover of new recruits and the important relationship between elephant and mahout never has a chance to develop.

If you're concerned about the elephants working the tourist trade at Amber, you can write a letter of support to **Help in Suffering** (☎ 760803, fax 765144; e hisjpr@datainfosys.net; Maharani Farm, Durgapura, Jaipur 302018). This organisation is lobbying the government to speed up its plans to build an elephant compound with bathing facilities close to Amber Fort, and to address the need for enforceable regulations to protect the animals, as well as better training and pay for the mahouts. See also Help in Suffering later for information on this organisation.

(Hall of Victory), to the left, is noted for its inlaid panels and glittering mirror ceiling. Regrettably, much of this was allowed to deteriorate during the 1970s and 1980s, but restoration is now proceeding.

Opposite the Jai Mandir is the **Sukh Niwas** (Hall of Pleasure), with an ivory-inlaid sandalwood door and a channel running right through the room. It once carried water and acted as an ingenious early air-cooling system. Not a single drop of water was wasted, with the overflow passing through conduits to the palace gardens. From the Jai Mandir you can enjoy the fine views from the palace ramparts over **Maota Lake** below. The **zenana**, or women's apartments, are around the fourth courtyard. The rooms have been cleverly designed so that the maharaja could embark on his nocturnal visits to their respective chambers without the knowledge of the other wives and concubines, as the chambers are all independent of each other but open onto a common corridor.

Returning to the Jaleb Chowk you can visit a small **art gallery** *(admission free, open 10am-4.30pm Sat-Thur)*, on your right as you descend the main staircase. It features paintings inspired by *Satsai*, the greatest work of

This stonework inlay is typical of the intricate work seen at Amber Fort

Jai Singh's court poet Bihari (1595–1663). This monumental poem, which consisted of 700 couplets, captures some of the preoccupations of Jai Singh's court as demonstrated in this extract:

Tired with climbing the mountains
Of her breasts,
My gaze proceeded slowly to see
The beauty of her face.
Having met the pit
Of her chin on the way;
It fell into it,
Never to come out again.

At Amber Fort there's also an **RTDC restaurant** *(veg/nonveg thalis Rs 60/90)*, with a pleasant garden, off the Jaleb Chowk, and a Rajasthali government emporium.

Getting There & Away

There are regular buses from Jaipur from both the train and bus stations and near the Hawa Mahal in the old city (Rs 5, 25 minutes). An autorickshaw will charge Rs 100 to 150 for the return trip. RTDC city tours include Amber Fort.

A good option is to hire a taxi from the stand near Jaipur train station – a round trip covering Amber Fort, Jaigarh and Nahagarh will cost around Rs 400 including waiting time (maximum five people). If you time it right, you can arrive at Nahagarh in time for a sunset beer overlooking the city at Padao Restaurant.

JAIGARH

This imposing fort *(foreigner/citizen Rs 20/15, still camera/video Rs 20/100; open 9am-4.30pm daily)*, built in 1726 by Jai Singh, was only opened to the public in mid-1983 and offers a great view over the plains from the Diwa Burj watchtower.

The fort served as the treasury of the Kachhwahas, and some people are convinced that at least part of the royal treasure is still secreted somewhere among its labyrinthine corridors. It's a remarkable feat of military architecture in a fine state of preservation, with water reservoirs, residential areas, a puppet theatre and the world's largest wheeled cannon, Jaya Vana.

AROUND JAIPUR

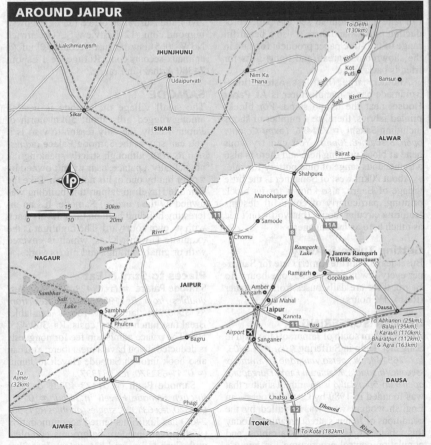

Admission is free if you have a ticket to Jaipur's City Palace that is less than two days old. Vehicles can drive up to the fort, or it's a steep half-hour walk from Amber. The admission charge for cars is Rs 50 and parking outside is Rs 5. English/Hindi guides are available for Rs 100/75 per hour (up to four people).

SANGANER & BAGRU

The small village of Sanganer is 16km south of Jaipur. In addition to its **ruined palace**, Sanganer has a group of **Jain temples** with fine carvings (to which entry is restricted)

and two ruined **tripolias**, or triple gateways. However, the town is most noted for its handmade paper and block-printing outlets (most shops can be found on or just off the main drag, Stadium Rd). A highlight of a visit here is to walk down to the riverbank to see the brightly coloured fabrics drying in the sun. The block printers of Sanganer are famous for small floral prints, and the prints produced here were traditionally used by the royal court.

Salim's Paper (☎ 730222; Gramodyog Rd; open 9am-5pm daily) is the largest hand-made paper factory in India and claims to be one of the biggest in the world. Here you can take a free tour to see the paper production process and there's also a beautiful range of tree-free paper products for sale in the showroom – great (and light) gifts for friends back home.

Another large (but less ostentatious) handmade paper manufacturer is **AL Paper House**, near the tempo stand. For block-printed fabrics, there are a number of shops including **Sakshi** (☎ *731476; Laxmi Colony; open 8.30am-8.30pm*). You can try your hand at block printing here and there is also a tremendous range of blue pottery for sale.

About 20km west of Sanganer is the little village of Bagru, also known for its block printing, particularly of colourful designs featuring circular motifs (but you won't see as much here as in Sanganer).

Getting There & Away

Buses leave from the Ajmeri Gate for Sanganer every few minutes (Rs 5, one hour). To Bagru, there are daily buses from Sanganer (Rs 15, 1½ hours).

HELP IN SUFFERING

Around 10km south of Jaipur, off the road to Sanganer, Help in Suffering (*HIS; ☎ 760803, fax 765144; W perso.wanadoo.fr/animaux -secours/his-india; Maharani Farm, Durgapura; open 9am-5pm daily*) is an animal shelter that was founded in 1980 by Crystal Rogers, an English woman who was appalled by the conditions of Jaipur's street creatures. Today this vibrant organisation runs a rabies- and population-control programme for Jaipur's dogs, operates mobile clinics to rural areas, treats the elephants working at Amber and rescues animals in trouble. It's possible to visit the shelter, where delightfully happy dogs wander the grounds and birds and animals of all descriptions convalesce in the excellent facilities here.

If you find an animal that is in need of some help, you can call HIS. Qualified vets can also volunteer here – see Volunteer Work in the Facts for the Visitor chapter for further details. Donations to Help in Suffering will be put to good use – contact the UK office (e declan@dharney.freeserve.co.uk,

49 Baring Rd, Beaconsfield, Bucks HP9 2NF), the Australian office (e bglasgow@ bigpond.com, 12 Eastview St, Greenwich NSW 2065) or Animaux-Secours (e info@ animaux-secours.com, Refuge de l'Espoir, 74380 Arthaz) in France.

SAMODE

The small village of Samode is nestled among rugged hills about 50km north of Jaipur. Really, the only reason to visit is if you can stay at the **Samode Palace** (*admission Rs 100*), although strictly speaking it's not actually a palace, as it wasn't owned by a ruler but by one of his noblemen. Like the Samode Haveli in Jaipur, this building was owned by the *rawal* of Samode. It's an interesting building built on three levels, each with its own courtyard. The highlight is the exquisite Diwan-i-Khas, which is covered with original paintings and mirrorwork.

Places to Stay & Eat

Samode Palace (*☎/fax 01423-40013; singles/ doubles from Rs 1950/2500, suites from Rs 3500*) has attractive rooms available. Breakfast/lunch/dinner costs Rs 300/425/ 500. The palace admission fee for nonguests is deducted if you have a meal there. You can also book through Samode Haveli in Jaipur (*☎ 0141-632370, fax 631397*).

Samode Bagh (*☎ 01423-40235 or book through Samode Haveli in Jaipur ☎ 0141-632370, fax 631397; singles/doubles Rs 1950/ 2400*) has luxurious tented accommodation (with private modern bathrooms complete with flush toilets and hot water). It is 3km away – a very relaxing place, with lovely gardens and a swimming pool (open also to guests of the Samode Palace).

Getting There & Away

There are a few direct buses to Samode from Jaipur (Rs 30, 1½ hrs), or you can hire a taxi for around Rs 800 return.

RAMGARH

This green oasis, about 35km northeast of Jaipur, has a **pretty lake**, the **Jamwa Ramgarh Wildlife Sanctuary**, with panthers, hyenas, antelopes and wild boars, and a picturesque polo ground. There's also the **Jamwa Maa Di Mandir**, an ancient Durga temple.

Ramgarh Lodge (☎ 01426-552217, 52079; e ramgarh.jaipur@tajhotels.com; singles/doubles with breakfast & dinner US$45/90), the one-time royal hunting lodge overlooking Ramgarh Lake, is the best place to stay. Inside the lodge, there are a number of stuffed beasts, including a bear holding a tray and a tacky elephant's trunk pot-plant holder! Billiards, squash and tennis are available, as well as boating when the lake's water level is high enough. Night-time jeep safaris to the wildlife sanctuary cost Rs 1000 per jeep for one hour (maximum six people).

RTDC Jheel Tourist Village (☎ 01426-52170; singles/doubles with private bathroom Rs 300/400), further away from the lake, is cheaper than Ramgarh Lodge and offers cottage-style accommodation. An extra bed is Rs 100. There's a small dining area with veg thalis for Rs 55. Boating on Ramgarh Lake can be arranged when the water is high enough (Rs 125 per person per hour).

Buses travel daily between Jaipur and Ramgarh (Rs 10, 1 hr).

ABHANERI

About 95km from Jaipur on the Agra road, this village has one of Rajasthan's most awesome *baoris* (step-wells) and is well worth a detour if you're travelling this way. Flanking the mammoth *baori* is a small crumbling palace, now inhabited by pigeons and bats. Admission is free but the caretaker may like a little baksheesh (Rs 10 perhaps) to show you around. In recent years the water level has dropped low enough to reveal 13 levels of steps down to the stagnant water of the *baori*, but there are believed to be even more levels beneath that. You are allowed to take photos of the *baori*, but not of the statues.

Getting There & Away

From Jaipur, catch a bus to Sikandra on the main road to Agra (Rs 30), from where you can take a jam-packed shared jeep (Rs 6) for the 10km trip to Abhaneri, or hire your own jeep (Rs 200 return, including a 30-minute stop).

BALAJI

The extraordinary Hindu exorcism temple of Balaji is about 3km off the Jaipur to Agra road, about 1½ hours by bus from Bharatpur. The exorcisms can be violent and many of those treated will discuss their experiences. To view the exorcisms, go upstairs, where you may see people shaking, and others chained up – they have been exorcised and the chains represent the chaining of the evil spirit. Most exorcisms take place on Tuesday and Saturday. Take off your shoes before entering the temple; you may also like to cover your head with a scarf as a mark of respect. No photography is permitted. The often disturbing scenes at this temple may upset some.

From Jaipur daily express buses go to Balaji (Rs 30, 2 hrs).

KARAULI

Located 182km southeast of Jaipur, Karauli was founded in 1348 and has some important Krishna temples.

The **old city palace** (foreigner/citizen Rs 100/50; open sunrise-sunset daily) was constructed over different periods of time and the oldest portion is about 600 years old. The Durbar Hall has some particularly fine paintings. This palace, which was occupied by the Karauli royal family until around the 1950s, is in need of restoration. Today it is occupied by naughty monkeys and a gaggle of geese. In the old days, geese were used to sound the alert if an intruder entered the palace grounds (they certainly can make one hell of a racket!). There's a **Krishna temple** (open 5am-11.30am & 4pm-8pm daily) in the palace compound.

Bhanwar Vilas Palace (☎ 07464-20024, or in Jaipur 0141-290763, fax 292633; singles/doubles Rs 1600/1700, garden cottages Rs 1200), owned by Maharaja Krishna Chandra Pal, is more like a large country manor than a palace. Rooms are comfortable and meals are available. Excursions to nearby points of interest, including the old city palace, can be organised.

There are buses running between Jaipur and Karauli (Rs 55, 5 hrs), or you can hire a taxi for around Rs 1200.

Eastern Rajasthan

The sites and cities of eastern Rajasthan are all easily accessible from Jaipur, and this region hosts a vast array of attractions. For those who wish to steep themselves in history, there are beautiful palace complexes at Alwar and Deeg, and fine forts at Bharatpur and Ranthambhore. Wildlife and bird enthusiasts are well catered for, with tiger-spotting possibilities at both Ranthambhore National Park and the Sariska Tiger Reserve; both are administered by Project Tiger. Keoladeo Ghana National Park is India's premier bird sanctuary, with an astonishing population of resident and migratory birds in a picturesque wetland setting.

The holy Hindu pilgrimage town of Pushkar, set around a small lake, is one of the most popular travellers' centres in India. You can stay in one of the dozens of tiny whitewashed guesthouses, dine in any one of numerous vegetarian restaurants, have a priest perform a *puja* (offering or prayer) on your behalf, or shop in the fascinating market where you'll find colourful clothes designed to Western tastes. Pushkar is most famous for the camel fair that it hosts annually in October/November.

Ajmer, close to Pushkar, is an important pilgrimage centre for Muslims, who pay homage at the Dargah, a tomb to the Sufi saint, Khwaja Muin-ud-din Chishti. Ajmer is also the site of the prestigious institution of Mayo College, where many of Rajasthan's young princes were educated.

History

Alwar, in northeastern Rajasthan, is possibly the oldest kingdom in kingdom-studded Rajasthan. In 1500 BC it formed part of the Matsya territories of Viratnagar (present-day Bairat), which also encompassed Bharatpur, Dholpur and Karauli.

History blends into mythology, as it was here in the ancient kingdom of Matsya that the Kauravas went cattle rustling, precipitating the war between them and their kinsfolk, the Pandavas. This great battle

Highlights

- Keoladeo Ghana National Park, a World Heritage–listed bird sanctuary
- The Pushkar Camel Festival, Rajasthan's biggest party held in a beautiful temple town with a sacred lake
- Ranthambhore National Park and Sariska Tiger Reserve, where tigers wander the scrub in rare Rajasthani wilderness
- The Dargah in Ajmer, tomb of an important Muslim Sufi, where pilgrims gather from around the country

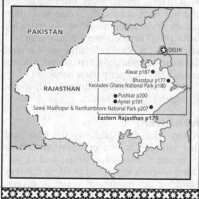

forms the basis of the Mahabharata. The city of Alwar is believed to have been founded by a member of the Kachhwaha family from Amber, but control was wrested from the Kachhwahas by the Nikumbhas. They in turn lost the city to the Bada Gurjara Rajputs of Machari. It then passed to the Khanzadas, under Bahadura Nahara of Mewat, who converted from Hinduism to Islam to win the favour of Emperor Tughlaq of Delhi. At this time, Alwar and Tijara were part of the kingdom of Mewat.

In 1427 descendants of Bahadura Nahara of Mewat bravely defended the Alwar fort against the Muslims. Although the Mewati leader professed the Muslim faith, he chose

174

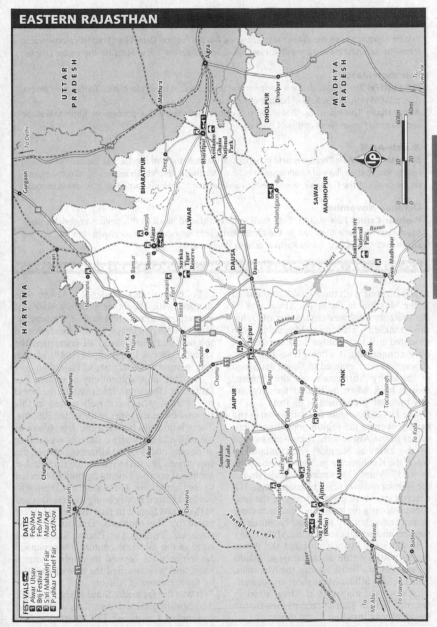

EASTERN RAJASTHAN

FESTIVALS	DATES
1 Alwar Utsav	Feb/Mar
2 Brij Festival	Feb/Mar
3 Sri Mahaviriji Fair	Mar/Apr
4 Pushkar Camel Fair	Oct/Nov

Festivals of Eastern Rajasthan

Eastern Rajasthan hosts the state's most renowned fair, the Pushkar Camel Fair. For festivals celebrated statewide and nationwide, see Public Holidays & Special Events in the Facts for the Visitor chapter.

February–March
Brij Festival The *rasalila* dance is performed at this festival; it takes place in Bharatpur over several days prior to Holi, and is held in honour of Krishna.
Alwar Utsav This tourist carnival showcases cultural activities with a procession, traditional music and dance, a flower show and craft displays.

March–April
Shri Mahavirji Fair This fair is held in honour of Mahavir, the 24th and last of the Jain *tirthankars*, or teachers, at the village of Chandangaon in Sawai Madhopur district. Thousands of Jains congregate on the banks of the Gambhir River, to which an image of Mahavir is carried on a golden palanquin.

October–November
Pushkar Camel Fair Visitors, both from India and abroad, flock to this famous regional festival. Many travellers time their visit to the atmospheric little town to correspond with the fair. See the boxed text 'Camel Fair' under Pushkar later in this chapter.

to ally himself with the Rajputs as opposed to the Muslims in Delhi. As Alwar was on the strategic southwestern frontier of Delhi, this rankled with the Mughals, who mounted military forays into the region, only conquering it after great difficulty. Alwar was later granted to Sawai Jai Singh of Jaipur by Aurangzeb, but the emperor took it back when he visited the city and saw the strategic virtues of its forts.

The Jats of Bharatpur threw their hat in and briefly overran the region, installing themselves in the Alwar fort. They were evicted by the Lalawat Narukas (descendants of Naru, the Kachhwaha prince of Amber) between 1775 and 1782 under the leadership of the Naruka *thakur* (noble) Pratap Singh. His descendants were great patrons of the arts, commissioning the transcription of numerous sacred and scholarly texts and encouraging painters and artisans to visit the Alwar court.

In 1803 the British invested the Alwar *thakur* with the title of maharaja as thanks for support in a battle against the Marathas. This friendly alliance was short-lived, however, since the maharaja of Alwar strongly resented British interference when a British Resident was installed in the city.

Following Independence, Alwar was merged with the other princely states of Bharatpur, Karauli and Dholpur, forming the United State of Matsya, a name that reflected the fact that these states all comprised the ancient Matsya kingdom. In 1949, Matsya was merged with the state of Rajasthan.

Another large ancient city of eastern Rajasthan is Bharatpur, traditionally the home of the Jats, who were well settled in this region before the emergence of the Rajputs. The relationship between the Jats, tillers of the soil, and the warrior Rajputs was at best an uneasy one. Marital alliances between the two groups helped to reduce the friction, but territorial encroachments by both parties led to confrontations. These simmered throughout the centuries, only being overcome when both groups turned to face the mutual threat posed by the Mughals. One of the Jats' strongest leaders was Badan Singh, who ruled in the mid-18th century. He expanded Jat territory far beyond its original boundaries, and was awarded the title of Brij-Raj by the maharaja of Amber.

It was the Jat leader Suraj Mahl who built the beautiful palace and gardens at Deeg and commenced work on the Bharatpur fort, which was completed in the late 18th century after nearly 60 years of work. This was time well spent, as the British unsuccessfully besieged the fort for nearly half a year, finally conceding defeat after substantial losses. The rulers of Bharatpur were the first to enter into an agreement with the East India Company.

The massive fort at Ranthambhore predates that at Bharatpur by many centuries, having been founded in the 10th century by the Chauhan Rajputs. Ranthambhore was held in reverence by the Jains and several temples here were of great spiritual importance. Over the centuries Ranthambhore was subjected to numerous assaults by the Muslims, and in the 14th century the first *jauhar* (ritual mass suicide) was declared in Rajasthan when the women thought their ruler, Hammir Deva, had died on the battlefield.

The Mughal emperor Akbar negotiated a treaty with Surjana Hada, a Bundi ruler who purchased the fort of Ranthambhore from Jhunjhar Khan, and the fort passed to

Jagannatha, under whose leadership the Jain religion flourished. The fort was taken by the Mughals under Aurangzeb, with whom it remained until the 18th century, when it was granted to the maharaja of Jaipur.

Ajmer was also founded by the Chauhans, three centuries earlier than Ranthambhore. In the late 12th century it passed to Mohammed of Ghori, and remained a possession of the sultanate of Delhi until the second decade of the 14th century. Fought over by various neighbouring states over subsequent centuries, it later passed to the Mughals, was briefly taken by the Rajput Rathores, was restored to the Mughals under Akbar, later passed to the Scindias, and came under direct British rule in 1818.

BHARATPUR
☎ 05644 • postcode 321001 • pop 204,456
Bharatpur is famous for its World Heritage–listed bird sanctuary, the Keoladeo Ghana National Park. Many travellers rate this

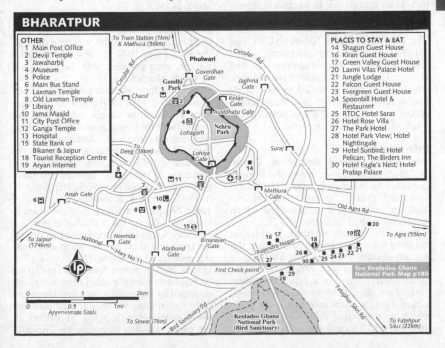

BHARATPUR

OTHER
1 Main Post Office
2 Deviji Temple
3 Jawaharbij
4 Museum
5 Police
6 Main Bus Stand
7 Laxman Temple
8 Old Laxman Temple
9 Library
10 Jama Masjid
11 City Post Office
12 Ganga Temple
13 Hospital
15 State Bank of
   Bikaner & Jaipur
18 Tourist Reception Centre
19 Aryan Internet

PLACES TO STAY & EAT
14 Shagun Guest House
16 Kiran Guest House
17 Green Valley Guest House
20 Laxmi Vilas Palace Hotel
21 Jungle Lodge
22 Falcon Guest House
23 Evergreen Guest House
24 Spoonbill Hotel &
   Restaurant
25 RTDC Hotel Saras
26 Hotel Rose Villa
27 The Park Hotel
28 Hotel Park View; Hotel
   Nightingale
29 Hotel Sunbird; Hotel
   Pelican; The Birders Inn
30 Hotel Eagle's Nest; Hotel
   Pratap Palace

To Train Station (1km) & Mathura (36km)
Circular Rd
Phulwari
Goverdhan Gate
Gandhi Park
Jaghina Gate
Chand
Ketan Gate
Austdhatu Gate
Lohagarh
Nehru Park
To Deeg (38km)
Lohiya Gate
Suraj
Anah Gate
Mathura Gate
Old Agra Rd
To Agra (55km)
To Jaipur (174km)
National
Neemda Gate
Atalbund Gate
Binarayan Gate
Rajendra Nagar
Hwy No 11
First Check point
See Keoladeo Ghana National Park Map p180
Fatehpur Sikri Rd
To Sewar (7km)
Bird Sanctuary Rd
Keoladeo Ghana National Park (Bird Sanctuary)
To Fatehpur Sikri (22km)

0   1   2km
0   0.5   1mi
Approximate Scale

beautiful park as a highlight of their visit to India. Over 400 different birds have been identified in the park and they're everywhere – it's one of the few places in the world where you can hope to spot hundreds of different species within a few days. Even people whose eyes usually glaze over at the mention of bird-watching get excited about this place, and if you're an ornithologist you'll be in ecstasy.

Bharatpur was a Jat stronghold in the 17th and 18th centuries. The Jats maintained a high degree of autonomy, both because of their prowess in battle and their chiefs' marriage alliances with Rajput nobility. They successfully opposed the Mughals on more than one occasion and their fort at Bharatpur, constructed in the 18th century, withstood an attack by the British in 1805 and a long siege in 1825. The siege led to the first treaty of friendship between the states of northwest India and the East India Company.

Bring along mosquito repellent as the little bloodsuckers can be tenacious here.

Orientation

The Keoladeo Ghana National Park lies 5km to the south of the city centre, and is easily accessed by cycle-rickshaw. The fort is on an island in the centre of the old city, which was once surrounded by an 11km-long wall (now demolished). Most people choose to stay in the cluster of hotels to the south, close to the park entrance.

Information

The helpful **Tourist Reception Centre** (☎ 22542; open 10am-5pm Mon-Fri & every 2nd Sat of the month), opposite RTDC Hotel Saras and about 700m from the park entrance, provides tourist literature and sells a reasonable map of Bharatpur (Rs 2).

There are currency exchange facilities at the **State Bank of Bikaner & Jaipur**, near the Binarayan Gate. The main **post office** (open 10am-1pm & 2pm-5pm Mon-Sat) is near Gandhi Park. There is a small **bookshop** (open 6am-6pm daily) at the checkpoint, 1.5km from the main gate inside the park, which has a selection of titles on Indian animal and bird life, and also sells postcards.

There are a few places offering **Internet** services for Rs 60 to 80 per hour. Aryan Internet, in a private home, charges Rs 80 per hour.

Keoladeo Ghana National Park

This beautiful sanctuary ironically came into being as a duck-shooting preserve for Maharaja Suraj Mahl of Bharatpur in the 1850s. He converted a low-lying swamp formed by the confluence of the Gambhir and Banganga Rivers into a reservoir, the Ajun Bund. Flooding during subsequent monsoons soon inundated the surrounding region, creating a shallow wetland ecosystem, the perfect habitat for an astonishing variety of birds.

Keoladeo continued to supply maharajas' tables until as late as 1964. An inscription on a pillar near the small temple in the park bears testimony to this penchant for hunting. On one day alone, almost 5000 ducks were shot by Lord Linlithgow, the viceroy of India, in 1938.

A fence was built around the forests of the wetlands in the latter part of the 19th century to stop feral cattle roaming through the area. From 1944 to 1964, afforestation policies were pursued, with the plantation of stands of acacias.

The post-Independence period was one of great turmoil. Poor local communities were keen to divert the canals, which feed the swamplands for irrigation, and to convert the wetlands into crop lands. Although this tension still exists, the conservationists won the day, and in 1956 the region was declared a sanctuary. In 1982 it was denoted a national park and was listed as a World Heritage site in 1985. The park encompasses an area of some 29 sq km, of which over one-third is submerged during the annual monsoon.

Today Keoladeo is recognised as one of the most important bird breeding and feeding grounds in the world. However, a 1999 United Nations report found that the strain on Keoladeo's fragile ecosystem was being damaged by increased tourism and pressure from surrounding villages. It predicted that some species would soon be extinct in the park, including of course the critically

Siberian Cranes

Park authorities at Keoladeo were concerned when the endangered Siberian crane (*Grus leuco-geranus*) failed to appear during two successive winter seasons in 1994 and 1995. In 1996, on the first day of winter, ornithologists around the world heaved a collective sigh of relief when four of these magnificent birds flew into the park, nearly two months after their usual arrival. In 1998, only one pair came to the park and this pair has returned each season to 2002.

The total population of these graceful white birds wintering in Iran and India is only 15; an estimated 100 of these birds have perished over the last 12 years during their 5000km-long journey from the Orb River basin in Siberia over inhospitable terrain. There are two other populations of Siberian cranes that hail from the Orb River. The most substantial population, numbering almost 3000, winters at the Yangtze River in China, although their habitat is threatened by the Three Gorges dam project and agricultural development. A small population of about a dozen flies to winter grounds along the south coast of Iran's Caspian Sea. The tiny remaining population makes its annual winter journey to India, and it is this group that is hosted at Keoladeo. About 30 years ago more than 200 'Sibes', as they are known, wintered at Keoladeo, and this sharp drop in numbers raises grave fears about their survival as a species. They have been termed 'critically endangered' by the International Union of Conservation of Nature.

Tragically, it is not the natural rigours of the long migration that are blamed for the critical depletion of Sibe numbers, but the Afghanistan war, with Sibes being slaughtered for meat by Afghans. They are also believed to fall prey to hunters in Pakistan, who shoot them for sport. Conservationists can now only wait and hope that these brave journeyers will return to their winter grounds, hopefully in replenished numbers, in future seasons.

endangered Siberian crane. Please keep the birds happy by disposing of rubbish properly, and keeping noise to a minimum.

Keoladeo Fauna During the monsoon period (July to August), and for a month or so following the monsoon, the park is home to vast colonies of birds that come here to breed and feed on the wetland's rich aquatic species. Some of the species that nest at this time include storks, moorhens, herons, egrets and cormorants. Keep your eyes peeled for storks spreading their wings to shield their chicks from the hot sun. Around October the bird population increases with the arrival of wintering migratory birds which usually stay until around the end of February. Among these birds is the highly endangered Siberian crane (see the boxed text 'Siberian Cranes'). This is the best time of the year to visit the sanctuary.

The migratory birds have mostly left by the end of March. At the beginning of April, when the waters begin to recede, there is still a substantial population of birds of prey

(vultures), some kingfishers, and smaller birds such as robins, wagtails and mynahs. Many of these birds feed at the few pools, teeming with fish, that remain in the park during the dry summer months. During the height of summer, when the waters have all but disappeared, the sanctuary is carpeted in dry grasslands that afford habitat to a variety of fauna such as the deer (spotted, sambar, bluebull), jackals, jungle cats, blackbucks, hares and mongoose.

Visiting the Park The park (*foreigner/citizen Rs 200/25, still camera/video Rs free/200; open 6am-6pm daily*) has only one sealed road through it, but has a series of raised embankments that thread their way between the shallow wetlands. Walking or cycling along them affords unique opportunities to observe the rich birdlife at close quarters.

The admission fee for the park entitles you to only one entry. Motorised vehicles are prohibited beyond the second checkpoint, 1.7km inside the park, and it costs Rs 50 to take a car this far. After this gate you can

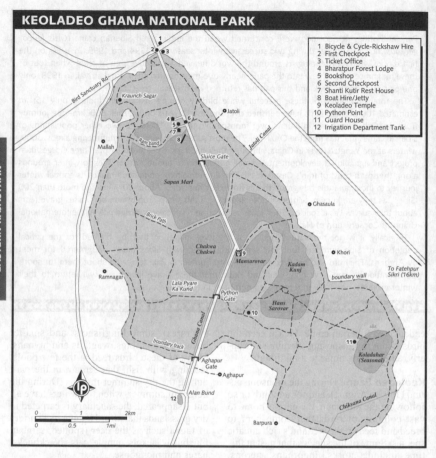

KEOLADEO GHANA NATIONAL PARK

1 Bicycle & Cycle-Rickshaw Hire
2 First Checkpost
3 Ticket Office
4 Bharatpur Forest Lodge
5 Bookshop
6 Second Checkpost
7 Shanti Kutir Rest House
8 Boat Hire/Jetty
9 Keoladeo Temple
10 Python Point
11 Guard House
12 Irrigation Department Tank

choose to get around by foot, bicycle, cycle-rickshaw (see that section later in this chapter), tonga or boat.

When the water level is high enough (usually October to January), boats can be hired near the second gate for Rs 25 per person (minimum three people). They are a very good way of getting close to the wildlife. A horse-drawn tonga costs Rs 100 per hour (maximum six people).

If you hire a guide, most have a pair of binoculars that you can use. Otherwise it's worth hiring binoculars (many hotels rent them out); try to get some with a strap so

you can conveniently hang them around your neck. Most hotels can also arrange a packed lunch.

There's a canteen near the second gate. You can also get a bite to eat at the Bharatpur Forest Lodge (see Places to Stay later), in the park.

A small **display** (admission free) at the ticket office has a map of the park and a photographic display. The southeastern corner of the park is supposedly home to a tiger, and therefore is off-limits, although the tiger's presence is more a matter of legend than hard evidence.

Guides & Cycle-Rickshaws Many people hire a guide for their first trip into the park, then go back with hired bicycles (see Bicycle following) so as to ramble around unaccompanied at their leisure. It's worth hiring one of the government-approved rickshaw-wallahs, as they have been trained in bird identification. Not only are you encouraging local employment, they really do know their birds.

Only cycle-rickshaws authorised by the government (recognisable by the yellow plate bolted onto the front) are allowed in – beware of anyone who tells you otherwise! Although you don't pay admission fees for the drivers, you'll be up for Rs 50 per hour if you take one. A cycle-rickshaw can take a maximum of two people (if you hire a separate guide, he follows on foot or bicycle). More specialised guides can be organised at the park entrance. Official government prices are Rs 70 for one to five people per hour, and Rs 120 for more than five.

In slow years, when there are few travellers about and people's livelihoods are threatened, competition among rival groups of guides at Bharatpur has become deadly. In February 2002 one man was killed and several others seriously injured in a dispute over underquoting tourists for guide services – a matter of Rs 200.

Bicycle After your initial visit to the park with a rickshaw-wallah or trained guide, a fantastic way to see the park on subsequent visits is to hire a bicycle. These can be hired at the park entrance for Rs 20 per day – you must leave your passport or a Rs 1000 deposit. Having a bike allows you to easily avoid the bottlenecks, which inevitably occur at the nesting sites of the larger birds. It's just about the only way you'll be able to watch the numerous kingfishers at close quarters – noise or human activity frightens them away. Some of the hotels rent bicycles (see Places to Stay later). If you plan to visit the national park at dawn (one of the best times to see the birds), you'll have to hire a bicycle the day before.

The southern reaches of the park are virtually devoid of *humanus touristicus*, and

so are much better than the northern part for serious bird-watching.

Old City

Although most people come to Bharatpur for the bird sanctuary, there are a few attractions in the old city worth visiting while you're here.

Lohagarh Built in the early 18th century, Lohagarh (Iron Fort) took its name from its supposedly impregnable defences. Maharaja Suraj Mahl, the fort's constructor and the founder of Bharatpur, built two towers within the ramparts, the Jawahar Burj and Fateh Burj, to commemorate his victories over the Mughals and the British.

The fort occupies an entire small artificial island in the centre of the town, and the three palaces within its precincts are in an advanced state of decay. In fact, the entire fort has a forlorn, derelict feel, and is in need of restoration. The main entrance is the **Austdhatu Gate**. *Austdhatu* means 'eight metals', a reference to the spikes on the gate which are reputedly made of eight different metals.

Museum The government museum *(admission Rs 3, free Mon, still camera/video Rs 10/20; open 10am-4.30pm Sat-Thur)* is housed in the former durbar hall, the maharaja's meeting hall, in the fort. Unfortunately, some areas of the museum are poorly lit and many of the exhibits are not well captioned. The most interesting thing to see here is the *hamam* (bathhouse), which retains some fine carvings and frescoes. There's also a display of sculpture that spans the ages, some pieces dating from the 2nd century AD, as well as a gallery featuring portraits and old photographs of the maharajas of Bharatpur (shoes have to be removed here). Only the exterior of the buildings may be photographed.

Jawaharbij This viewing point is a short walk to the northeast of the museum along a steep path that starts opposite the large water tank. It was from here that the maharajas surveyed their city. It's a nice place capturing the cool breezes in a series of pavilions, the ceilings of which feature badly deteriorating frescoes – scenes of elephants and chariots can be made out. As you would expect, the views down over the city are superlative.

Ganga Temple

Not far from the Lohiya Gate is this exquisitely carved temple dedicated to the goddess Ganga. Construction of the temple commenced in 1845 during the reign of Maharaja Balwant Singh, but it was not completed until 1937, during the reign of Maharaja Brijendra Sawai. The two-storey temple, made of sandstone, features a black-and-white chequered floor and ornately carved arches. The edges of the terrace on which the temple stands, overlooking the busy streets below, are not stable. Do not approach them too closely.

On the laneway leading up to the temple, vendors sell mattress stuffing that's made of Punjabi wool.

Places to Stay & Eat

For details about guesthouses registered with the Paying Guest House Scheme, contact the Tourist Reception Centre (see Information earlier). The prices range from Rs 100 to 300 per night.

Many hotels have bicycles and binoculars for hire and can organise a packed lunch. Most slash tariffs in the low season. The commission system has reared its ugly head in Bharatpur – don't be pressured into accommodation by touts at the train station or bus stand.

Park Precincts The following places are all within easy walking distance (within 1km) of the main entrance to the national park, from where you can hire bicycles or cycle-rickshaws to see the park. The lodgings here are the most popular with travellers and can fill up fast.

RTDC Hotel Saras (*☎ 23700; cnr Fatehpur Sikri & Bird Sanctuary Rds; dorm beds Rs 50, singles/doubles Rs 350/450, with air-cooling Rs 550/650, with air-con Rs 600/700)* has a dusty dorm and slightly shabby rooms with private bathroom and geyser. There's also a restaurant with a wide selection of veg meals and a few token nonveg dishes; chicken *biryani* is Rs 60.

Rajendra Nagar, which runs parallel to Bird Sanctuary Rd, just to the north, has some good budget options away from the noise of the main road.

Kiran Guest House (*☎ 23845; 364 Rajendra Nagar; doubles with shared bathroom Rs 80, with private bathroom Rs 100-200)* is great value. It's a homey place offering free pick-up from the bus or train station. There's a rooftop restaurant with dishes for around Rs 40. Rental bicycles/binoculars are Rs 25/50.

Green Valley Guest House (*☎ 29576; e greenvalley56@hotmail.com; 376 Rajendra Nagar; singles/doubles with private bathroom from Rs 50/100, with geyser Rs 125/150)* is a comfortable, if slightly run-down, place with a nice family atmosphere. The cheaper rooms have hot water supplied by the bucket. Rental bikes/binoculars are from Rs 15/30 and meals are available – the family makes its own milk, butter and curd.

There's a string of budget hotels run by members of the same family, starting just behind the RTDC Hotel Saras.

Jungle Lodge (*☎ 25622; singles/doubles from Rs 200/250)* is the best of these. The small but clean and comfortable rooms with private bathroom and hot water open onto a shady veranda. There's a small lending library, a beautiful garden area and discounts of up to 30% in the low season. Rental bikes/binoculars are Rs 30/70 per day and meals are available.

Falcon Guest House (*☎ 23815, fax 25306; singles/doubles from Rs 150/200, with air-con Rs 500/600)*, near Jungle Lodge, is a peaceful and homey place, run by the friendly Mrs Rajni Singh. Her husband, Tej, is an ornithologist and is happy to answer any bird-related questions when he comes home from work. It has good-sized rooms with private bathroom and bigger rooms with a softer mattress and private balcony. There's a restaurant in the little green garden where you can get home-cooked food such as egg curry (Rs 40) and veg thalis (Rs 70). Bikes are available for hire.

Evergreen Guest House (☎ 25917; singles/doubles Rs 150/250) also on this strip, has six rooms with private bathrooms. Meals are available and there are bikes/binoculars for hire for Rs 30/70.

Spoonbill Hotel & Restaurant (☎ 23571; dorm beds Rs 50, doubles with shared bathroom Rs 100, singles/doubles with private bathroom Rs 150/200) is the first hotel in the string and it has reasonable rooms. The restaurant features both veg and nonveg cuisine including Rajasthani dishes such as *churma*, the royal dish of Rajasthan – sugar, cheese and dried fruit fried in butter. There's a campfire in winter, bike hire is Rs 30 per day (including some mountain bikes), binoculars are from Rs 50 per day, and there's a bird-spotter's guide available for loan for Rs 20 per day.

Most of the other hotels are lined up along Bird Sanctuary Rd, and there are two options in the park itself.

Hotel Rose Villa (☎ 23411; doubles from Rs 200), opposite the Tourist Reception Centre, has just a handful of comfortable rooms. The veg restaurant serves a special herbal tea for coughs and colds (per glass/pot Rs 10/35).

Hotel Eagle's Nest (☎ 25144, fax 22310; Bird Sanctuary Rd; singles/doubles with fan Rs 650/800, with air-con Rs 800/1000), closer to the park, is a clean, comfortable place, and a discount is offered between May and September. There's a large nonveg restaurant, which serves Indian and Chinese food at reasonable prices.

Hotel Sunbird (☎ 25701, fax 28344; singles Rs 250-550, doubles Rs 350-650) is a popular choice. Rooms have a private bathroom and bikes are available for hire (Rs 50 per day). The **Tandoor Restaurant** here whips up a good selection of dishes, such as Kashmiri *biryani* (Rs 80).

Hotel Pelican (☎/fax 24221; singles/doubles with shared bathroom Rs 50/80, with private bathroom Rs 80/125, with air-cooling Rs 100/200) is nearby on the same road. There are tiny but airy rooms with shared bathroom, or better rooms with private bathroom. The restaurant has continental, Indian and Chinese cuisine. Rental bikes cost Rs 20, binoculars Rs 30.

The Birders Inn (☎ 915644, fax 25265; e thebrdinn@yahoo.com; singles/doubles Rs 750/950) offers accommodation and has an atmospheric **restaurant** with Indian, continental and Chinese food.

Hotel Nightingale (☎ 27022, fax 24351; doubles with private bathroom Rs 150-200) has basic rooms in a eucalyptus grove. Bring mosquito repellent as the mossies can be a real hassle. The restaurant serves cheap eats; *palak paneer* is Rs 35.

Hotel Park View (☎ 20802, fax 27800; e bharatpur007@yahoo.com; doubles with shared bathroom Rs 60, with private bathroom Rs 80-150), next door to Hotel Nightingale, is quite good value, with rooms ranging from a clean dungeon to decent doubles with private bathroom. The **restaurant** is pleasant; the Rajasthani *aloo zeera* (potatoes lightly seasoned with cumin) costs Rs 25 and a chicken curry is Rs 45.

Hotel Pratap Palace (☎ 24245, fax 25093; e hotelpratappalace@yahoo.co.in; Bird Sanctuary Rd; singles/doubles with shared bathroom Rs 100/150, with private bathroom Rs 200/300, deluxe Rs 600/700, with air-con Rs 900/1050) is also close to the park entrance. The cheaper rooms aren't bad value, but the more expensive ones are a bit overpriced. A 30% discount is offered between May and August. Breakfast costs Rs 85, and lunch and dinner are Rs 180.

The Park Hotel (☎ 33192, fax 28344; e thepark@yahoo.com; doubles Rs 1500) is a reasonable mid-range option, offering clean and modern motel-style rooms. The hotel offers a 50% discount in the low season (February to October). There's a large garden, a **restaurant** and a **bar**.

Bharatpur Forest Lodge (☎ 22760, fax 22 864; singles/doubles Rs 1900/2700) is inside the park, about 1km beyond the entrance gate and 8km from the Bharatpur train station. This Indian Tourism Development Corporation (ITDC) hotel is looking a little faded. Rooms are certainly comfortably appointed but not really luxurious and the service is lax. However, this is a handy place to stay if you want to get an early start. The **restaurant** is open to nonguests and is handy if you feel peckish while in the park. Lunch or dinner costs Rs 275. There are light bites such as sandwiches (around Rs 35) as well as more substantial meals. A hot chocolate is Rs 40 and a bottle of cold beer is Rs 120.

Shanti Kutir Rest House (☎ 22777; *doubles Rs 600*) is also inside the park, 150m west of the second gate. It rents out rooms if they are not being occupied by government officials. Simple doubles have private bathroom and rates include all meals.

Bharatpur Tucked away down a laneway that's just inside Mathura Gate, **Shagun Guest House** (☎ 32455, fax 24021; *single/ double huts Rs 40/60, rooms with shared bathroom Rs 46/75, with private bathroom Rs 69/89*) is nothing flash but it's a great, chilled-out place to stay, especially if you're strapped for cash. There are cheap grass huts in the garden or rooms in the main house. Bike hire is Rs 28 per day, and electric fans are available. You can get basic meals here (for breakfast Rs 28, for lunch or dinner Rs 30), and the friendly owner, Rajeev, has a wealth of knowledge of the park and Bharatpur.

Laxmi Vilas Palace Hotel (☎ 31199, fax 25259; e *reservation@laxmivilas.com; singles/ doubles Rs 1850/2100, suites Rs 3300*) is at Kakaji-ki-Kothi on the old Agra road, about equidistant between the national park and the town centre. The hotel was originally built for the younger son of Maharaja Jaswant Singh. The comfortable rooms are set around a courtyard where you can enjoy an aperitif or two in the evening. The **restaurant** is open to nonguests; a buffet lunch or dinner is Rs 275.

Getting There & Away

Bus There are local buses to Deeg (Rs 13, one hour), to Jaipur (Rs 71, 4½ hours), and to Agra (Rs 28, one hour), every 30 minutes. There are also two daily services to Fatehpur Sikri (one hour, Rs 11). These buses all leave from the main bus stand on Circular Rd.

Train Bharatpur is on the Delhi to Mumbai broad-gauge line. A good service between Delhi and Bharatpur is the 9024 *Firozpur Janta Express*. It leaves New Delhi station at 2pm, arriving in Bharatpur at 6.20pm (Rs 51/80 2nd-class seat/sleeper, 175km). It leaves Bharatpur at 7.58am, arriving back at the capital at 1.10pm. There are several good services to Sawai Madhopur (Rs 52/234 in 2nd class seat/3-tier air-con, 182km), which go on to Kota (Rs 71/320, 290km) and Mumbai (Rs 200/900, 1210km). To Agra, there's a passenger train in the morning and afternoon (Rs 12, 1½ hours).

Getting Around

Bharatpur has autorickshaws, tongas and cycle-rickshaws. An excellent way to zip around is by hiring a bicycle, which can be done at many of the hotels or at the park entrance – see Visiting the Park earlier for further details.

DEEG
☎ 05641 • postcode 321203 • pop 40,826

The small town of Deeg, about 36km north of Bharatpur, is well off the tourist trail. It boasts massive fortifications, a stunningly beautiful palace and a busy market. Deeg is an easy day trip from Bharatpur, or from Agra or Mathura, both in the adjacent state of Uttar Pradesh.

Built by Suraj Mahl in the mid-18th century, Deeg was once the second capital of Bharatpur state. The Bharatpur maharajas ruled from both Bharatpur and Deeg. At Deeg, the maharaja's forces successfully withstood a combined Mughal and Maratha army of some 80,000 men. Eight years later, the maharaja even had the temerity to attack the Red Fort in Delhi! The booty he carried off included an entire marble building, which can still be seen in the palace grounds.

Suraj Mahl's Palace

Suraj Mahl's Palace, the **Gopal Bhavan** (*foreigner/citizen Rs 100/5; open 8am-5pm daily*) built by Maharaja Suraj Mahl between 1756 and 1763, is one of India's most beautiful and delicately proportioned buildings. Built in both Rajput and Mughal architectural styles, it is in an excellent state of repair and, as it was used by the maharajas until the early 1970s, most of the rooms still contain their original furnishings. These include chaises longues, plenty of antiques, a stuffed tiger, elephant-feet stands, and fine china from China and France.

The mostly two-storey palace is three and four storeys high in places. The eastern facade is fronted by imposing arches to take full advantage of the early morning light. On either side of the palace are two exquisite pavilions. In the northern pavilion is a throne of black marble, while that in the southern pavilion is of white marble. In an upstairs room at the rear of the palace is an Indian-style marble dining table – a long, horseshoe-shaped affair raised just 20cm off the ground. Guests sat around the edge while the centre was used to serve them. In the maharaja's bedroom is an enormous, 3.6m by 2.4m, bed. Taking photographs is not permitted inside the palace.

The palace is flanked by two tanks, to the east the **Gopal Sagar**, and to the west the **Rup Sagar**. The magnificently maintained gardens and flower beds are fed by water from these reservoirs. Among the various buildings in the gardens is the **Keshav Bhavan**, or Summer Pavilion, a single-storey edifice with five arches along each side. An arcade runs around the interior of the pavilion over a type of canal with hundreds of fountains, many of which are still functional, and turned on occasionally, for example at local festivals. Deeg's massive walls (up to 28m high) and 12 bastions, some with their cannons still in place, are also worth exploring.

On the northern side of the palace grounds is the **Nand Bhawan**, an oblong hall enclosed by a grand arcade.

Laxmi Mandir

This very old temple is presided over by a *mataji*, or female priest. There are alcoves on three sides enshrining images of Durga, Hanuman and Gada, and a small shrine to Shiva to one side. The temple is on Batchu Marg, 20 minutes' walk from the palace.

Places to Stay & Eat

Few travellers stop overnight at Deeg and there's only one place worth staying.

RTDC Midway Deeg (*☎ 21000; camp site per person Rs 50; singles/doubles Rs 300/400, air-con doubles Rs 600*), aka the Swaraj Resort, is five minutes' walk from the bus stand and the palace, and has just a handful of rooms. If you have your own tent you can pitch it on the lawn (the rate includes the use of bathroom facilities). Meals are available; a veg thali is Rs 55, a cheese sandwich is Rs 27 and a cup of tea is Rs 5.

Getting There & Away

The roads to Deeg are rough and the buses crowded – often the only space left for passengers picked up en route is on the roof. There are numerous buses between Deeg and Alwar (Rs 27/31 for local/express, 2½ hours). Buses for Bharatpur leave every 30 minutes (Rs 13/15, one hour). There's also an express bus to Mathura (Rs 17, 1¼ hours) and to one to Agra (Rs 45).

ALWAR

☎ 0144 • postcode 301001 • pop 260,245
Alwar was once an important Rajput state, which gained pre-eminence in the 18th century under Pratap Singh, who pushed back the rulers of Jaipur to the south and the Jats of Bharatpur to the east, and who successfully resisted the Marathas. It was one of the first Rajput states to ally itself with the fledgling British empire, although British interference in it's internal affairs meant this partnership wasn't always amicable. Beautiful palace buildings, hunting lodges at Sariska, and the extraordinary collection of *objets d'art* in the government museum bear testament to the wealth of this erstwhile state.

Orientation

The city palace and museum are in the northwest of the city, a steep 1km north of the bus stand. There is a collection of budget hotels a short distance to the east of the bus stand. The main post office is about midway between the bus stand and the train station, the latter on the eastern edge of the town.

Information

Near the train station, the helpful **Tourist Reception Centre** (*☎ 1364, 347348; open*

10am-1.30pm & 2pm-5pm Mon-Fri & every 2nd Sat) is not far from the Hotel Aravali. It can organise guides for local sightseeing and they stock some good maps of Alwar (Rs 2).

The **State Bank of Bikaner & Jaipur** (open 10am-2pm Mon-Fri, 10am-noon Sat), near the bus stand, changes travellers cheques and major currencies.

You can access the Internet at a few places in town, including the **Cyber Cafe** (☎ 702952; Nehru Marg; open 9am-9pm daily) at New Malhotra Transport Co, which charges Rs 35 per hour. Check out Alwar's website at ⓦ www.alwaronline.com.

Bala Quila
This huge fort, with its 5km of ramparts, is perched on the ridge top, 300m above the city. Predating the time of Pratap Singh, it's one of the very few forts in Rajasthan constructed before the rise of the Mughals. Unfortunately, because the fort now houses a radio transmitter station, you can only see inside with special permission from the superintendent of police (☎ 337453), although the Tourist Reception Centre is trying to clear the red tape.

Palace Complex
Below the fort is the large, imposing city-palace complex, its massive gates and its tank lined by a beautifully symmetrical chain of ghats with four pavilions on each side and two at each end. Today, most of the complex is occupied by government offices, but there is a museum (see later), housed in the former city palace. To gain access to the tank and the Cenotaph of Maharaja Bakhtawar Singh, take the steps on the far left when facing the palace. Just outside the palace you can see clerks busily clacking away on typewriters for their lawyer bosses (who have outdoor 'offices' here). The lawyers can be distinguished by their white shirts and black jackets.

Cenotaph of Maharaja Bakhtawar Singh
This double-storey edifice resting on a platform of sandstone was built in 1815 by Maharaja Vinay Singh in memory of his father. The cenotaph is also known as the

Chhatri of Moosi Rani, after one of the wives of Bakhtawar Singh who performed *sati* (self-immolation) on his funeral pyre. Every day several women can be seen paying homage to the maharani at the cenotaph by pouring holy water over raised sculpted footprints of the deceased royal couple. There is fine carving on the interior of the cenotaph (shoes should be removed), but unfortunately the paintings on the ceiling are almost indiscernible.

Museum
This government museum (admission Rs 3, free Mon; open 10am-4.30pm Sat-Thur) is a little difficult to find – it's on the top floor of the palace, up a ramp from the main courtyard. However there are usually plenty of people around who can point you in the right direction. Exhibits include royal vestments in beautiful brocades; stuffed animals, including an enormous bear; Kashmiri lacquer work; and stone sculptures, such as an 11th century sculpture of Vishnu.

A separate exhibition hall has a well-preserved collection of paintings. Photography is not permitted.

Places to Stay
Finding a budget place to stay is not a problem in Alwar. Contact the Tourist Reception Centre (see Information earlier) for details about the three houses involved in the Paying Guest House Scheme (Rs 400 to 1200).

Ashoka (☎ 346780, fax 336767; singles/doubles with private bathroom Rs 150/200, with air-con Rs 300/400, bucket hot water Rs 3) is one of a cluster of cheap hotels that face each other around a central courtyard, about 500m east of the bus stand, set back from Manu Marg. **Ankur** (☎ 333025), **Atlantic** (☎ 343181), **New Alankar** (☎ 330440), **Akash Deep** (☎ 700444) and Ashoka are owned by five brothers. Without wishing to upset any of the brothers, the Ashoka seems to be the best, however, there's really not much difference between them and their prices are comparable.

Imperial Hotel (☎ 701730; 1 Manu Marg; singles/doubles from Rs 180/250, doubles with air-con Rs 675) is at the start of the

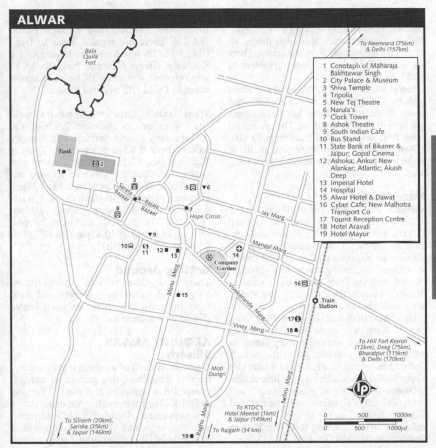

ALWAR

1 Cenotaph of Maharaja Bakhtawar Singh
2 City Palace & Museum
3 Shiva Temple
4 Tripolia
5 New Tej Theatre
6 Narula's
7 Clock Tower
8 Ashok Theatre
9 South Indian Cafe
10 Bus Stand
11 State Bank of Bikaner & Jaipur; Gopal Cinema
12 Ashoka; Ankur; New Alankar; Atlantic; Akash Deep
13 Imperial Hotel
14 Alwar Hotel & Dawat
15 Alwar Hotel & Dawat
16 Cyber Cafe; New Malhotra Transport Co
17 Tourist Reception Centre
18 Hotel Aravali
19 Hotel Mayur

To Neemrana (75km) & Delhi (157km)
Bala Quila Fort
Tank
Sarafa Bazaar
Balaja Bazaar
Hope Circus
Jay Marg
Mangal Marg
Company Garden
Manu Marg
Vivekananda Marg
Train Station
Viney Marg
Nehru Marg
Moti Dungri
Raghu Marg
To Hill Fort Kesroli (12km), Deeg (75km), Bharatpur (115km) & Delhi (170km)
To RTDC's Hotel Meenal (1km) & Jaipur (149km)
To Siliserh (20km), Sariska (35km) & Jaipur (146km)
To Rajgarh (34 km)

EASTERN RAJASTHAN

laneway which leads to the five As. Somewhat musty rooms come with private bathroom and air-cooler. This place could be a little noisy, as it fronts a busy street. There's a decent restaurant here (see Places to Eat).

Hotel Aravali (☎ 332316, fax 332011; e kakkar@datainfosys.net; Nehru Marg; dorm beds Rs 100, singles/doubles with private bathroom from Rs 250/300, suites Rs 2500), is a good choice, although some rooms can be a bit noisy, so ask for a quiet one. Located near the train station, it is run by the Kakkar family (the owner's son, Achal, and his wife, Anika, are helpful and can be

contacted through reception). They arrange tours, for a minimum of two people, of Alwar (Rs 250 per person) or to Sariska and Siliserh (Rs 500 per person). There's a restaurant (see Places to Eat), bar and pool (summer only). If you need a stretch, there are free yoga sessions at 5.30am daily.

Alwar Hotel (☎ 70012, fax 348757; e ukrustagi@rediffmail.com; 26 Manu Marg; singles/doubles with private bathroom Rs 350/500, with air-con Rs 650/750), set in a leafy garden, is another great choice, with clean, quiet rooms. There's a good restaurant (see Places to Eat).

RTDC Hotel Meenal *(☎ 347352; singles/ doubles Rs 400/500, with air-con Rs 600/ 700)* is a respectable mid-range place, although it's a long way from the action. There is a little dining hall; a veg/nonveg thali costs Rs 55/70.

Hotel Mayur *(☎ 701733; singles/doubles from Rs 250/300, with air-con Rs 600/650)* south of the town centre has tatty rooms and is in need of restoration. The restaurant is not bad; half a *kadhai* chicken is Rs 100.

Retiring rooms *(beds Rs 50)* are available at the train station, but you can't get a meal here.

Places to Eat

Narula's *(☎ 333966; open 11am-3pm & 5.30pm-10.30pm daily)*, near the Ganesh Talkies, whips up Indian, Chinese and continental cuisine. This pleasant restaurant, which is underground, offers a good choice of dishes, including tasty veg sizzlers (Rs 50), chicken (half a bird) tikka masalas (Rs 90), French fries (Rs 25) and strawberry milk shakes (Rs 30).

Hotel Aravali *(☎ 332316; Nehru Marg; open 7pm-10.30pm daily; curries Rs 75-100)* serves moderately priced veg and nonveg fare at its restaurant. For a drink, go to the hotel's Guftgu **bar**, where you can guzzle beer (Rs 60 per bottle) while admiring the lilac chairs.

Dawat *(Alwar Hotel, Manu Marg; open Tues-Sun)* serves Indian, continental and Chinese food. The menu includes malai kofta (Rs 50), veg spring rolls (Rs 50) and chicken sandwiches (Rs 40).

Imperial Hotel *(☎ 70012; Manu Marg; dishes under Rs 30)* has vegetarian fare and specialises in South Indian cuisine. A masala dosa is Rs 16 and a daal makhani is Rs 30.

South Indian Cafe *(open 8am-10pm daily)* is opposite the Gopal Cinema, on the road leading to the bus stand. It has cheap and decent dishes such as masala dosas (Rs 20) and veg chowmein (Rs 20).

Getting There & Away

Bus There's a computerised reservation office at the bus stand. Buses for Sariska leave every 30 minutes until 7pm (Rs 11/13 for local/express, one hour). There are also

buses every 30 minutes to Jaipur (Rs 52/62, four hours), which pass through Bairat (Rs 25). There are regular buses to Deeg (Rs 27/31, 2½ hours), and to Bharatpur for Keoladeo Ghana National Park (Rs 38/47 local/express, 4½ hours/3½ hours). Express buses to Delhi (Rs 64) take 4 hours.

Train To Delhi, there's the *Shatabdi Express* (Rs 350 in air-con chair car, 2½ hours) at 7.43pm daily except Sunday. The *Intercity* leaves Alwar at 8.36am, arriving in Delhi at 11.25am (Rs 47/151 in 2nd class/air-con chair). To Jaipur the *Shatabdi Express* departs Alwar daily except Monday at 8.35am, arriving in Jaipur at 10.40am (Rs 375 in air-con chair car) and Ajmer at about 12.45pm (Rs 480). The *Intercity* leaves at 7.45pm, arriving in Jaipur at 10.45pm (Rs 47/151 in 2nd class/air-con chair).

Getting Around

There are cycle-rickshaws, autorickshaws, tempos and some tongas. A cycle-rickshaw from the train station to the town centre should cost around Rs 10.

AROUND ALWAR
Siliserh

If you're in need of a refuge from the mayhem of Rajasthan, this green and tranquil retreat, 20km southwest of Alwar (off the road to Sariska Tiger Reserve), is one of the state's best-kept secrets. Uninhabited hills surround a quiet lake, which you can explore with a paddle boat (Rs 60 per hour for up to four people). There's not much else here except a few cheap restaurants and a restored palace, built by the Alwar maharaja Vinay Singhis, which is situated in a dramatic location overlooking the lake. Inevitably, it is now a hotel.

RTDC Hotel Lake Palace *(☎ 0144-86322; singles Rs 400-800, doubles Rs 500-1900)* is beautiful, if you ignore the rather erratic cleanliness and service. Rooms have private bathrooms and there's a bar and **restaurant**; a veg/nonveg lunch is Rs 150/175.

Getting There & Away A crowded tempo from Alwar will cost about Rs 6 or you can hire a car for around Rs 100.

Kesroli

This pleasant town has a 14th-century fort overlooking agricultural land that has been turned into a hotel. You can see brightly clad villagers working in the fields from the ramparts.

Hill Fort Kesroli (☎ 01468-89352, Delhi ☎ 011-435 6145, fax 4351112; doubles Rs 1500-3400), 12km from Alwar in Kesroli village, is run from the Neemrana Fort Palace (see following). The buffet lunch/dinner is Rs 300/350 and the hotel can arrange sightseeing in Alwar.

From Alwar, you can take a taxi or an autorickshaw to the fort.

Neemrana

This small village lies about 75km north of Alwar on the main Delhi to Jaipur highway, a short distance to the south of the border with Haryana. There's not much of interest in the village itself, but 2km away is the restored fortress palace. Dating from 1464, it was from here that the Rajput maharaja Prithviraj Chauhan III reigned. In usual Rajasthani style, it has been converted into a luxury hotel.

Neemrana Fort Palace (☎ 01494-46006, fax 01494-46005, Delhi ☎ 011-435614, fax 4351112; e sales@neemranahotels.com; singles/doubles from Rs 1100/2200) has suitably luxurious rooms (some rooms are better than others and several even have toilets with views of the countryside). Camel rides are available for Rs 350 per hour and there's Rajasthani folk music every evening. To complete the picture, the hotel has its own helipad.

Getting There & Away Buses on the main Delhi to Jaipur route generally stop at Behror, 14km from Neemrana, and a further 2km from the hotel. A taxi from Behror to the hotel will cost about Rs 200.

SARISKA TIGER RESERVE

☎ 0144

Situated 107km from Jaipur and 200km from Delhi, this national park (foreigner/citizen Rs 200/25, still camera/video free/Rs 200; open 7am-4pm daily 15 Oct 31-Mar, 6am-4.30pm daily 1 Apr-14 Oct) is far less commercialised than Ranthambhore, but you have less chance of spotting a tiger here. It's in a wooded valley surrounded by barren hills, once the private hunting ground of Alwar's royal family. It covers 866 sq km (including a core area of 498 sq km) and has leopards, hyenas, bluebulls, sambars, spotted deer, wild boars, 300 species of birds and, of course, tigers. Project Tiger has been in charge of the sanctuary since 1979.

The sanctuary can be visited year-round, although during July and August your chance of spotting wildlife is minimal, as the animals move on to higher ground. The best time to go is between November and June. There are an estimated 25 tigers at Sariska, and this number is believed to be on the increase. Successful education programmes run in the local communities have helped to stop tiger poaching and improve conservation efforts.

You'll see most wildlife at dawn or sunset, though tiger sightings are becoming more common during the day. To spot a tiger you should plan on two or three safaris.

Wildlife Safaris

While it is possible to take private cars into the park, they are limited to sealed roads only, minimising the chances of spotting wildlife. The best way to visit the park is by jeep. For diesel/petrol jeeps you'll be quoted Rs 600/700 for three hours, or Rs 1500/1800 for a full day. They can take up to five people, and it's worth paying the extra for a petrol jeep as the diesel vehicles are noisy and can scare away the animals. There's an admission fee of Rs 125 per jeep, in addition to the park admission fee. Try to avoid visiting on the days when it is free for citizens (Tuesday and Saturday) as the park can get crowded. Guides are available (Rs 100 for three hours; maximum of five people). It's also possible to arrange guided treks.

Bookings can be made at the **Forest Reception Office** (☎ 841333; Jaipur Rd), directly opposite the Hotel Sariska Palace, which is where buses will drop you.

Kankwari Fort

Deep inside the sanctuary, this small fort offers incredible views over the plains of the national park, dotted with red mud-brick villages. Here Aurangzeb imprisoned his brother, Dara Shikoh, Shah Jahan's chosen heir to the Mughal throne, for several years before he was beheaded.

Hanuman Temple

You can visit a small Hanuman temple in the park. Citizens can enter the park for free between 8am and 3pm Tuesday and Saturday if they're visiting this temple.

Places to Stay & Eat

RTDC Tiger Den Sariska (☎/fax 841344; dorm beds Rs 50, singles/doubles with air-cooling Rs 600/700, with air-con Rs 900/1000, suites Rs 1800/1900) has a nice garden area, but the rooms are a bit run-down and the service is variable. Several travellers advise that you should bring mosquito repellent or a net. There's a bar (beer is Rs 60) and **restaurant** that can make up packed lunches (Rs 145). The veg/nonveg thali is Rs 65/85. Jeep hire can be arranged.

Hotel Sariska Palace (☎ 841322, fax 841323; doubles Rs 3999) which is over 100 years old, is at the end of a long sweeping driveway directly opposite the Forest Reception Office. It's not a glitzy palace, rather a modest but comfortable and serene former royal hunting lodge, set on 20 hectares. The room on the top floor has 360° views over the Aravalli Range. It is possible to take short horse and camel rides around the grounds. The drawing room has an assortment of stuffed beasts, and the dining room is replete with antiques. There's a small lending library and Rajasthani dance programmes at night. A bonfire is lit in winter and jeep hire can be organised.

Nonguests can visit the palace for Rs 100 per person, which is then deducted from your meal price. It's Rs 175 for breakfast and Rs 350 for lunch or dinner.

Forest Rest House (doubles Rs 400) has a guesthouse next door to the Forest Reception Office. It has three double rooms, but bookings should be made in advance through

the chief wildlife warden in Jaipur (☎ 0141-380278; Van Bhawan, near Secretariat).

Getting There & Away

Sariska is 35km from Alwar, which is a convenient town from which to approach the sanctuary. Numerous direct buses run to Alwar from Delhi and Jaipur, and there are buses between Sariska and both Alwar (Rs 13, one hour) and Jaipur (Rs 50, three hours). Buses stop out the front of the Forest Reception Office.

BAIRAT

Around 25km west of Sariska, 85km north of Jaipur, is the ancient Buddhist centre of Viratnagar, or Bairat. Archaeological evidence – the discovery of ancient coins, the remains of a Buddhist monastery, and several rock-cut edicts, a legacy of the great 3rd century BC Buddhist-convert, Ashoka – indicate that this was once an important centre of Buddhism.

Jaipur to Alwar buses pass through Bairat (Rs 35).

AJMER

☎ 0145 • postcode 305001 • pop 485,197
Southwest of Jaipur is Ajmer, a burgeoning town on the shore of the Ana Sagar, flanked by barren hills. Situated in a valley, Ajmer is a major religious centre for Muslim pilgrims during the fast of Ramadan, and has some superb examples of early Muslim architecture. It is famous for the tomb of Khwaja Muin-ud-din Chishti, a venerated Sufi saint who founded the Chishtiya order, which still exists as the prime Sufi order in India today.

The British selected Ajmer as the site for Mayo College, a prestigious school opened in 1875 exclusively for Indian nobility. Today it is open to all boys (who can afford the fees). Other monuments that stand as reminders of Ajmer's colonial past are the Edward Memorial Hall, Ajmer Club and Jubilee Clock Tower.

The main streets of Ajmer are crammed with traffic, pedestrians and busy bazaars. One street sells nothing but silver items. But Ajmer doesn't really have the same

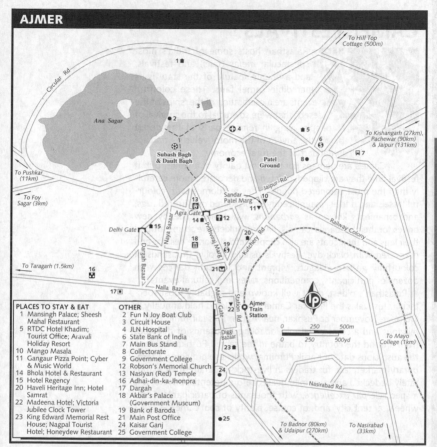

AJMER

Ana Sagar

Subash Bagh & Dault Bagh

Patel Ground

To Hill Top Cottage (500m)

To Kishangarh (27km), Pachewar (90km) & Jaipur (131km)

To Pushkar (11km)

To Foy Sagar (3km)

To Taragarh (1.5km)

To Mayo College (1km)

To Badnor (80km) & Udaipur (270km)

To Nasirabad (33km)

Sandar Patel Marg

Agra Gate

Delhi Gate

Nalla Bazaar

Circular Rd

Naya Bazaar

Dargah Bazaar

Prithviraj Marg

Jaipur Rd

Kutchery Rd

Railway Colony

Madar Gate

Station Rd

Digg Bazaar

Nasirabad Rd

Ajmer Train Station

0   250   500m
0   250   500yd

PLACES TO STAY & EAT
1 Mansingh Palace; Sheesh Mahal Restaurant
5 RTDC Hotel Khadim; Tourist Office; Aravali Holiday Resort
10 Mango Masala
11 Gangaur Pizza Point; Cyber & Music World
14 Bhola Hotel & Restaurant
15 Hotel Regency
20 Haveli Heritage Inn; Hotel Samrat
22 Madeena Hotel; Victoria Jubilee Clock Tower
23 King Edward Memorial Rest House; Nagpal Tourist Hotel; Honeydew Restaurant

OTHER
2 Fun N Joy Boat Club
3 Circuit House
4 JLN Hospital
6 State Bank of India
7 Main Bus Stand
8 Collectorate
9 Government College
12 Robson's Memorial Church
13 Nasiyan (Red) Temple
16 Adhai-din-ka-Jhonpra
17 Dargah
18 Akbar's Palace (Government Museum)
19 Bank of Baroda
21 Main Post Office
24 Kaisar Ganj
25 Government College

EASTERN RAJASTHAN

rustic charm or panache as other Rajasthani towns and is more of a pilgrimage centre than a tourist destination. This is reflected in the dearth of good accommodation.

Although it does have some impressive attractions, Ajmer is really just a stepping stone to nearby Pushkar for most travellers. If you are unable to find accommodation in Pushkar, which is often the case during the camel fair, Ajmer can make a convenient base – if all the hotels in Ajmer are booked out at this time, contact the tourist office (see Information later in this section) to find out about paying-guesthouse options.

History

The town of Ajmer has always had great strategic importance due to its secure position, protected by the Aravalli Range, and its location on the major trade route between Delhi and the ports of Gujarat. It was founded by Ajaipal Chauhan in the 7th century. He constructed a hill fort and named the place Ajaimeru, or 'Invincible Hill'. Ajmer was ruled by the Chauhans until the late 12th century, when Prithviraj Chauhan lost it to Mohammed of Ghori.

[Continued on page 194]

CAMEL FESTIVALS

Rajasthan hosts some of India's most spectacular *melas* (fairs) and festivals, and a unique feature of the state is its incredible camel fairs. These colourful events are a celebration of the 'ships of the desert' that were so crucial to the survival of people living in remote parts of the desert before the advent of the motor vehicle – and are still a vital part of the rural economy.

Camels are perhaps not the most dainty of animals, but at festival time they are clipped, painted and decorated more carefully than the most pampered poodle. They're adorned with colourful tassels and bridles, magnificently embroidered or mirrored rugs, and ornaments known as *gorbandhs,* which are made by new brides for their husbands' camels. Jingling anklets are strung around their legs and their coats are also clipped into elaborate designs and decorated with black dye. Festivals usually involve thousands of colourfully garbed villagers, vibrant and intricate dances with dozens of participants, competitions, races and cultural events.

Rajasthan's oldest, most well known and arguably most spectacular festival is the Pushkar Camel Fair, which is held annually in October–November at Pushkar, near Ajmer. This fair fulfils both a religious and a commercial role, enabling thousands of devotees from around the country to bathe in the sacred Pushkar Lake on the auspicious date of Kartik Purnima, while also providing a temporary marketplace for traders in livestock to parade their elaborately bedecked and groomed beasts before potential buyers. It is a spectacle *par excellence,* with thousands of participants, Ferris wheels, a 'tent city' and, of course, plenty of cool camels.

PAUL BEINSSEN

RICHARD I'ANSON

RICHARD I'ANSON

Camels and people alike wear their finest at the Pushkar Camel Fair (top left & right), where both the beasts and the red-turbanned police keep an eye on proceedings (bottom)

Held in the middle of winter, Bikaner Camel Festival celebrates the renowned strength, beauty and endurance of camels. While a healthy camel can work up to one month without food or water in winter, other festival-goers eat well over the several days of festivities.

The Bikaner Camel Festival, held in January, is the other major event on Rajasthan's camel calendar. Bikaner-bred camels are famous for their great strength and beauty as well as their endurance in harsh desert conditions. The National Research Centre on Camels, where you can visit baby camels and learn everything you ever wanted to know about them (see the boxed text 'Get to Know Your Camel' in the Western Rajasthan chapter), is based here. The festival opens with a camel procession, followed by a camel pageant (something like a beauty competition for camels) and camel dancing. Prizes are awarded to those with the greatest skills in camel milking and camel-hair-cutting.

Jaisalmer's Desert Festival is another festival, organised by tourist authorities, that is held each year in January/February, corresponding with the peak tourist season. Despite its blatant rupee-driven impetus, if you're within camel's spit of Jaisalmer, it's an occasion that shouldn't be missed, with villagers and townspeople donning traditional garb, dozens of elaborately caparisoned camels, traditional dances and music, camel polo matches and more. This is an ideal time to visit the Sam sand dunes near Jaisalmer, when traditional musicians attempt to outdo each other in musical virtuosity, and camel races take place across the dunes. The Mr Desert competition usually attracts a swag of mustachioed hopefuls.

The Nagaur Fair, held in January or February, is ostensibly purely commercial in nature, attracting camel, cattle and horse traders from across Rajasthan, as well as Punjab, Gujarat and Uttar Pradesh. It's no tourist carnival, but an important part of the rural economy. However, this being Rajasthan, it's still a vibrant and joyful event with camel, horse and cattle races, tug-of-war matches, folk musicians and dancers, as well as thousands of villagers letting their hair down.

MARTIN HARRIS

EASTERN RAJASTHAN

[Continued from page 191]

It became part of the sultanate in Delhi. After 1326 Ajmer was continually fought over by surrounding states including the sultans of Delhi and Gujarat and the rulers of Mewar (Udaipur) and Marwar (Jaipur).

Later in its history, Ajmer became a favourite residence of the great Mughals. One of the first contacts between the Mughals and the British occurred in Ajmer when Sir Thomas Roe met with Emperor Jehangir here in 1616.

The city was subsequently taken by the Scindias and, in 1818, was handed over to the British, becoming one of the few places in Rajasthan controlled directly by the British rather than being part of a princely state.

Orientation

The main bus stand is close to the RTDC Hotel Khadim on the east side of town. Most of the hotels are west of the train station. Northeast of the main post office is Naya Bazaar (known for its silver jewellery and tie-dyed fabrics) and Agra Gate. Further north is the large artificial lake Ana Sagar.

Information

The main **tourist office** (☎ 627426; open 8am-6pm Mon-Fri & every 2nd Sat) is in the RTDC Hotel Khadim compound. There's also a small **tourist information counter** (open 10am-5pm Mon-Sat) at the train station.

You can change money at the **State Bank of India** (open 10am-2pm & 2.30pm-4pm Mon-Fri, 10am-1pm Sat), located opposite the Collectorate, but they don't do cash advances on credit cards. The **Bank of Baroda** (Prithviraj Marg; open 10am-3pm Mon-Fri, 10am-12.30pm Sat), opposite the main post office, does issue cash advances on Visa and MasterCard, and changes currency and travellers cheques (but not American Express).

The main **post office** (open 10am-1pm & 1.30pm-6pm Mon-Sat) is less than half a kilometre from the train station.

Cyber & Music World (☎ 628921, Swami Complex; open 10.30am-11pm) offers Internet access in its cramped shop for Rs 20 per hour.

Ana Sagar

Flanked by hills, this artificial lake was created in the 12th century by damming the River Luni. On its bank are the fine parks, the **Dault Bagh** and **Subash Bagh**, with a series of marble pavilions that were erected in 1637 by Emperor Shah Jahan. It's a popular place for an evening stroll. You can hire a boat from the **Fun N Joy Boat Club** (open 9am-7pm daily), on the east side of Dault Bagh. A two-/four-person paddle boat costs Rs 40/60 per half hour. You can also hire a water scooter (Rs 60 for five minutes) here or a motor boat (Rs 15) that will get you to the island in the centre of the lake. This island is where you'll find the Island Restaurant, which sells fast food.

The Dargah

The *dargah* was packed. Tens of thousands of devotees from all over India and beyond were milling around. Ecstatics and madmen were shrieking to themselves, beating their foreheads against the stone railings on the tomb. Blind beggars stumbled around with their alms bowls. Women discreetly suckled young babies under the folds of their saris.

William Dalrymple, *City of Djinns*

Situated at the foot of a hill and in the old part of town, this is one of the most important places in India for Muslim pilgrims. The Dargah (W www.chistyshrineajmer.com; open 5am-9pm winter, 4am-10pm summer) is the tomb of a Sufi saint, Khwaja Muin-ud-din Chishti, who came to Ajmer from Persia in 1192 and died here in 1236. Construction of this shrine was completed by Humayun and the gate was added by the Nizam of Hyderabad. Akbar used to make the pilgrimage to the Dargah from Agra once a year.

You have to cover your head in certain parts of the shrine, so remember to take a scarf or cap although there are plenty for sale at the colourful bazaar leading to the Dargah, along with floral offerings and delicious Muslim toffees.

As you enter the courtyard, removing your shoes at the gateway, a mosque, constructed by Akbar, is on the right. The enormous iron cauldrons are for offerings that are customarily shared by families involved in the shrine's upkeep. In an inner court there is another mosque built by Shah Jahan. Constructed of white marble, it has 11 arches and a Persian inscription running the full length of the building.

The saint's tomb is in the centre of the second court. It has a marble dome and the actual tomb inside is surrounded by a silver platform. The horseshoes nailed to the shrine doors are offerings from successful horse dealers! Beware of 'guides' hassling for donations around the Dargah using the standard fake donation books. Don't be bullied into signing any books or 'visitors registers', which mean that you'll have to make a hefty donation.

This shrine is a hive of activity and you can really get a sense of how deeply significant it is to the Muslim people. The tomb attracts tens of thousands of pilgrims every year on the anniversary of the saint's death, the Urs (when William Dalrymple visited). The anniversary is celebrated in the seventh month of the lunar calendar, Jyaistha (the dates are variable so check with the tourist office). It's an interesting festival but the crowds can be suffocating. As well as the pilgrims, Sufis from all over India converge on Ajmer.

Adhai-din-ka-Jhonpra & Taragarh

Beyond the Dargah, on the outskirts of town, are the ruins of the Adhai-din-ka-Jhonpra mosque. According to legend its construction, in 1153, took just 2½ days (Adhai-din-ka-Jhonpra means 'the 2½-day building'). Others believe it was named after a festival that lasted for 2½ days. It was originally built as a Sanskrit college, but in 1198 Mohammed of Ghori took Ajmer and converted the building into a mosque by adding a seven-arched wall covered with Islamic calligraphy in front of the pillared hall.

Although the mosque is in need of repair, its fine architecture and intricate carving are well worth seeing. The pillars are all different and the arched 'screen', with its damaged minarets, is noteworthy.

Three kilometres and a steep 1½-hour climb beyond the mosque, the Taragarh, or Star Fort, commands an excellent view over the city (accessible by car). It was built by Ajaipal Chauhan, the town's founder. The fort was the site of much military activity during Mughal times and was later used as a sanatorium by the British.

Nasiyan (Red) Temple

The Nasiyan (Red) Temple (*Prithviraj Marg; admission Rs 3; open 8.30am-5.30pm daily*) is a Jain temple built in 1865. It's also known as the Golden Temple, due to its amazing and unique display. Inside the temple gallery is a huge golden diorama, rising through two storeys, which depicts the Jain concept of the ancient world. There's an intricate miniature city, flying animal boats and gilded elephants with many tusks. The hall is decorated with gold, silver and precious stones. It's unlike any other temple in Rajasthan and is worth a visit.

Akbar's Palace

Not far from the main post office, this imposing building was constructed by Akbar in 1570 and today houses the **Government Museum** (*admission Rs 3, free Monday, foreigner/citizen camera Rs 10/5, foreigner/citizen video Rs 20/10; open 10am-4.30pm Sat-Thur*). Exhibits in the limited collection include old weapons, miniature paintings, ancient rock inscriptions and stone sculptures that date back to the 8th century AD.

Places to Stay

Commission rackets are ingrained in Ajmer: you'll be accosted by cycle- and autorickshaw drivers the minute you step off the bus or train. On top of this, the hotels here, especially those in the mid-range category, offer poor service and soulless atmosphere. It's a far better idea to stay in nearby Pushkar. You can visit Ajmer on a day trip from Pushkar, or on the way through.

A good and often cheaper alternative to hotels is the homes participating in Ajmer's Paying Guest House Scheme, which gives you the interesting opportunity to live with an Indian family. Rates range from around

Rs 50 to 800 per night depending on the facilities provided. The tourist office (see Information earlier) has details about these paying guesthouses.

Haveli Heritage Inn (☎ 621607; Kutchery Rd; doubles Rs 350-800) is arguably the best choice in Ajmer. Set in a 100-year-old haveli (mansion), it's a welcoming oasis in the heart of the city. The rooms are large and well-maintained (all with private bathroom and air-cooler) with lovely high ceilings. There's a pleasant courtyard and a real family atmosphere, complete with home-cooked meals.

Hill Top Cottage (☎ 623984; e hilltop cottage@rediffmail.com; 164 Shastri Nagar; singles/doubles/triples/quads Rs 300/400/ 500/800), behind a shopping centre, is just as good, although further out of town. However, they offer free pick-ups from the bus or train stations. Far removed from the crowds and dust, it's not a cottage as the name suggests, but a family-run house on an elevated site with clean rooms. The rooftop sports panoramic views. Breakfast is Rs 25 and a veg lunch or dinner is Rs 50.

RTDC Hotel Khadim (☎ 627490, fax 431 330; dorm beds Rs 50, singles/doubles with private bathroom from Rs 350/450, with air-con Rs 800/900) is not far from the bus stand. There's a range of fairly decent rooms and a restaurant. A veg thali is Rs 55.

Aravali Holiday Resort (☎ 627089; Savitri College Rd; singles/doubles from Rs 100/150), next door, is more homey with just eight simple rooms with a private bathroom (bucket hot water). No meals are available.

Hotel Regency (☎ 620296, fax 621750; e regencyajmer@hotmail.com; singles/doubles with private bathroom Rs 400/450, with air-con Rs 700/740), close to the Dargah, is a dreary grey place, but a reasonable choice in a town starved of hotel talent. There's a good veg restaurant.

King Edward Memorial Rest House (☎ 429936; Station Rd; basic singles from Rs 65, singles/doubles Rs 100/150, deluxe Rs 125/200), known locally as 'KEM', is to the left as you exit the train station. Don't let the grand name fool you. This place is run-down and has lax service. Very few travellers

seem to stay here. The cheapest '2nd class' singles have bucket hot water.

Nagpal Tourist Hotel (☎ 627427; singles/ doubles from Rs 150/300), nearby KEM, is a far more salubrious option. The cheapest singles with private bathroom are small but OK or there are air-con rooms available. Go next door to the Honeydew Restaurant for a feed.

Bhola Hotel (☎ 432844; singles/doubles Rs 150/200), opposite the church near Agra Gate, has no-frills rooms with private bathroom. Self-service bucket hot water is available (no charge). There's a good vegetarian restaurant here (see Places to Eat).

Hotel Samrat (☎ 621257, fax 430229; Kutchery Rd; singles/doubles Rs 200/400, doubles with air-con Rs 725) is just a few minutes' walk from the train station. The rooms are small and a bit musty, but it's very convenient for early-morning bus departures – many of the private bus companies have their offices nearby. Rooms come with private bathroom (some with Indian-style toilet). Some rooms can cop a lot of traffic noise so ask for a quiet room at the back. Only room-service meals are available.

Mansingh Palace (☎ 425702, fax 425858; e mansingh.ajmer@mailcity.com; Circular Rd; singles/doubles from Rs 1995/3000, family rooms Rs 4500), overlooking Ana Sagar, is the only top-end hotel in Ajmer – and it capitalises on this by charging high rates. Rooms are modern and stylish, but not crash hot value. There's also a bar and restaurant (see Places to Eat).

Places to Eat

Ajmer has a lot of independent restaurants and there's a flourishing trade in ice creams and cakes.

Mango Masala (☎ 420724; Sandar Patel Marg; open 9am-11pm daily) is a trendy multicuisine restaurant that goes for an American-diner feel – the waiters wear stone-washed denim and the patrons are dressed up like Bollywood stars. It has an extraordinary menu, including Popeye sizzlers (mushy cheese, spinach, noodles and tomato sauce; Rs 75), as well as more pedestrian pizzas (from Rs 40) and Indian dishes. Try one of the mocktails if you dare, like the apparently popular Fire & Ice, a fluorescent green potion made of mint, salt, green chillies and lemonade (Rs 35).

Gangaur Pizza Point *(☎ 621590; Sandar Patel Marg; open 9am-10pm daily)*, across the road from Mango Masala, serves the usual selection of fast food including pizzas (about Rs 55) and ice-cream sodas (around Rs 20). They will deliver free to your hotel.

Honeydew Restaurant *(☎ 622498; open 9am-11pm daily)*, next door to KEM Rest House, offers Indian, Chinese and continental veg and nonveg fare. There's also a variety of fast food such as fish and chips (Rs 50), pizzas (around Rs 50), chocolate milk shakes (Rs 25), and for the adventurous, brain pakoras (Rs 40). A favourite with travellers is the banana lassi (Rs 20). There are pool tables (Rs 40 per hour) and a choice of indoor or outdoor seating.

Bhola Hotel *(Agra Gate)*, at the top of a seedy staircase, has a good and reasonably priced vegetarian restaurant. There are delicious thalis for Rs 35, and a range of other dishes such as paneer kofta (curd cheese balls; Rs 40).

Madeena Hotel *(open 5am-11pm daily)* is handy if you're waiting for a train (the station is directly opposite). This very simple pale-green joint cooks up cheap fare, specialising in mutton korma (Rs 44), chicken mughlai (Rs 50) and rumali roti (Rs 52).

Sheesh Mahal *(☎ 425702; Mansingh Palace)* is the top restaurant in town. Pricey Indian, continental and Chinese dishes are on offer. There's also a pleasant bar. A malai kofta is Rs 120 and desserts hover around Rs 70.

Getting There & Away

Bus Call **Roadways** *(☎ 429398)* if you have inquiries about bus travel. There are buses from Jaipur to Ajmer every 30 minutes, some nonstop (Rs 53, 2½ hours). From Delhi, there are state transport buses which run daily in either direction (Rs 163, nine hours).

Buses leave from outside the Nasiyan Temple every 20 minutes for Pushkar (Rs 7, 45 minutes). There are also buses every hour from the bus stand (Rs 5). The trip

usually takes a bit longer during the Camel Fair, when roads can become congested.

State transport buses also go to:

destination	cost (Rs)	duration (hrs)
Abu Road	139	9
Ahmedabad	212	12
Alwar	111	6
Bharatpur	122	6
Bhopal	224	14
Bikaner	111	7
Bundi	71	4½
Chittorgarh	74	5
Indore	209	12
Jodhpur	82	5
Kota	87	6
Nagaur	63	5
Ranakpur	107	7½
Sawai Madhopur	74	6½
Sikar	97	6
Udaipur	115	7

In addition, buses leave for Agra (Rs 153, nine hours) and for Jaisalmer (Rs 190, 12 hours). Also, there are private buses to Ahmedabad (Rs 120), Udaipur (Rs 80), Jodhpur (Rs 80), Jaipur (Rs 60), Mt Abu (Rs 120), Bikaner (Rs 100) and Delhi (Rs 110). Most of the companies have offices on Kutchery Rd. If you book your ticket to one of these destinations through an agency in Pushkar, they should provide a free jeep-transfer to Ajmer to start your journey.

Train The telephone number for train inquiries is ☎ 131. Ajmer is on the Delhi-Jaipur-Marwar-Ahmedabad-Mumbai line and most trains stop at Ajmer. The 135km journey from Jaipur costs Rs 40 in 2nd class.

To Udaipur, there's a fast express train, which leaves at 1.50am daily (Rs 77/120 in 2nd-class seat/sleeper, 8½ hours) and a slower train at 7.50am (10 hours). The comfortable *Shatabdi Express* travels between Ajmer and Delhi (Rs 630/1250 in ordinary/executive-chair class, 6½ hours) via Jaipur (Rs 320/615). Refreshments and meals are included in the ticket price. The train leaves Delhi at 6.10am daily except Monday, departs Jaipur at 10.45pm and arrives in

Ajmer at 12.45pm. Going in the other direction, the train leaves Ajmer daily except Sunday at 3.50pm and arrives in Jaipur at 5.45pm and Delhi at 10.20pm.

Getting Around
There are plenty of autorickshaws, some cycle-rickshaws and quite a few tongas. To travel anywhere in town by autorickshaw should cost you around Rs 15. For longer trips, you can hire a car/jeep for Rs 3.5/4 per kilometre. A half/full day of sightseeing will cost Rs 600/1200.

AROUND AJMER
Kishangarh
Kishangarh is 27km northeast of Ajmer and was founded in the early 17th century by Kishan Singh, a Rathore prince. Since the 18th century, Kishangarh has had one of India's most famous schools of miniature painting. Among its renowned paintings is that of Krishna's consort, Radha, depicted as a beautiful woman with enchanting, almond-shaped eyes. Today local artists are trying to revive this magnificent school of painting by making copies of the originals on surfaces such as wood, stone and cloth; Kishangarh is also famous for painted wooden furniture. The original paintings were done on paper.

Kishangarh town is divided into the old city, which still has an old-world charm, and the new city, which is mainly commercial. Pollution is steadily increasing along with the growing number of dusty marble factories and textile mills.

Places to Stay About 25km out of town, **Roopangarh Fort** (*☎/fax 01463-42001 singles/doubles Rs 1190/1750, suites Rs 2500*) has been converted into an evocative hotel by the maharaja and maharani of Kishangarh. Roopangarh was the capital of this province for about 100 years and was never conquered despite being repeatedly attacked by neighbouring states. The fort was founded in 1653 by Maharaja Roop Singh, the fifth ruler of Kishangarh. He was inspired to make this site his capital after watching a mother sheep gallantly protect her lambs from a pack of hungry wolves. The road to the fort passes through an interesting village where you get a glimpse of everyday life as it was long ago. The hotel can arrange village tours, bird-watching and camel, horse or jeep safaris.

Getting There & Away There are frequently run daily buses between Ajmer and Kishangarh (Rs 12).

Tilonia
You can visit the inspiring **Barefoot College** (*☎ 1463-88207, fax 88206;* **W** *www.barefoot college.org*) in the small town of Tilonia (see

Barefoot College

Barefoot College is an NGO mixing radical change with a renewed respect for traditional knowledge systems. The college is pulling women out of purdah to teach them how to become solar-power engineers. But it has also sent 2000 puppeteers out into poor rural areas with shows on health, education and human rights. This is based on the long Rajasthani tradition of storytelling and education through puppet theatre, and is particularly effective in the semiliterate communities that Barefoot targets.

Officially known as the Social Work & Research Centre, Barefoot College was set up in 1972 and since then it has pioneered many creative ideas like this to promote self-reliance in poor communities. Other programmes include night schools that give working adults and children access to education, and a variety of schemes that promote the work of low-caste artisans on fair-trade principles.

The organisation is largely supported by the government and international donors, but 20% of its funds are generated through selling handicrafts and installing solar-power packs. You can support the college's efforts and check out the project by visiting the craft showroom at Tilonia.

the boxed text), about 25km east of Kishangarh, 7km off the Jaipur to Ajmer road. The impressive showroom is a great place to pick up high-quality, reasonably priced souvenirs, including everything from wall hangings to furniture and leather goods. There's also *bell totas* (colourful strings of stuffed birds; from Rs 25), ceramic painted bowls (from Rs 20) and wooden toys (from Rs 90).

Getting There & Away The easiest way to get to Tilonia is to hire a car, which will cost around Rs 400 to 500 return from Ajmer or Pushkar. From Ajmer you can take a Harmara bus (Rs 16) and ask to be dropped off at Tilonia. There are also buses from Kishangarh (Rs 6). The centre is about 1km from the bus stop.

Pachewar

This little village, about 90km east of Ajmer has a lake that attracts migratory birds in the winter.

Pachewar Garh (☎ *01437-28756, Jaipur ☎/fax 0141-601007; singles/doubles Rs 1000/ 1150)* is not as flash as many of Rajasthan's other fort-hotels, but is still comfortable enough. Rooms come with a private bathroom. The set breakfast/lunch/dinner is Rs 140/200/300. The hotel can also arrange jeep safaris.

PUSHKAR

☎ 014581 • postcode 305022 • pop 14,789
Pushkar is a very important pilgrimage centre and devout Hindus should visit it at least once in their lifetime. The town attracts a large number of *sadhus* (individuals on a spiritual search) who mainly congregate around the lake and temples. Unfortunately, after a poor monsoon the lake doesn't fill up. This is a pity, as it is a big factor in the town's appeal and is of great religious importance. Situated right on the edge of the desert, Pushkar is only 11km northwest of Ajmer but separated from it by Nag Pahar, the Snake Mountain.

Pushkar has become a major tourist hotbed. Many travellers who visit the place fall so deeply in love with it that they stay much longer than anticipated. The town has

Pushkar Passports

You can recognise travellers who've been to the ghats in Pushkar by the red ribbons (the 'Pushkar Passport') tied around their wrists. Getting one can be an expensive procedure if you allow yourself to be bullied into a more generous donation than you wanted to give. Priests, some genuine, some not, will approach you near the ghats and offer to do a *puja*. At some point during the prayers they'll ask you to tell Brahma how much you're going to give him, Rs 100 to 400 being the suggested figure (although some travellers have even been asked for US dollars!). Don't fall for this emotional blackmail – if you want to give just Rs 10, that's fine, although some 'priests' may tell you it doesn't even cover the cost of their 'materials'. It's best to say in advance how much you will give, Indians often give Rs 1 over a round figure (eg, Rs 11 or Rs 21) for good luck. Many visitors cop an earful of abuse if they do not shell out the cash demanded – keep your cool and don't let the pushy priest ruin your visit to the lake. Some travellers put on a red ribbon prior to visiting the lake to avoid being approached by a priest altogether.

A current scam involves 'priests' offering travellers a flower, or petals. Once you take this, you are asked to throw it into the holy lake – for a pretty price! It is best to firmly refuse any flowers that may be offered.

Obviously there are still some genuine, friendly priests in Pushkar, but unfortunately more and more travellers are reporting problems with the 'other half'. If you feel strongly about it, try lodging a complaint with the Tourist Information Centre.

a distinctly touristy ambience these days: its streets are lined with shops selling raver gear and the sounds of techno waft from the rooftop restaurants and places selling special lassis. Despite all this, the holy town still manages to retain its mystical charm – although many travellers who find the scene too high-profile have skipped it in favour of more mellow destinations.

EASTERN RAJASTHAN

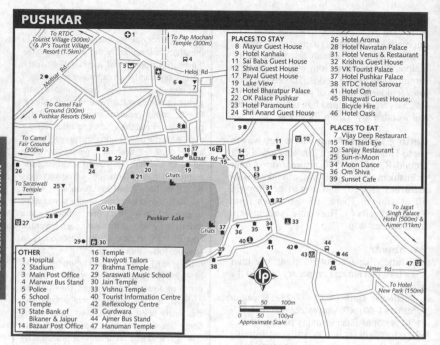

PUSHKAR

PLACES TO STAY
8 Mayur Guest House
9 Hotel Kanhaia
11 Sai Baba Guest House
12 Shiva Guest House
17 Payal Guest House
19 Lake View
21 Hotel Bharatpur Palace
22 OK Palace Pushkar
23 Hotel Paramount
24 Shri Anand Guest House
26 Hotel Aroma
28 Hotel Navratan Palace
31 Hotel Venus & Restaurant
32 Krishna Guest House
35 VK Tourist Palace
37 Hotel Pushkar Palace
38 RTDC Hotel Sarovar
41 Hotel Om
45 Bhagwati Guest House;
   Bicycle Hire
46 Hotel Oasis

PLACES TO EAT
7 Vijay Deep Restaurant
15 The Third Eye
20 Sanjay Restaurant
25 Sun-n-Moon
34 Moon Dance
36 Om Shiva
39 Sunset Cafe

OTHER
1 Hospital
2 Stadium
3 Main Post Office
4 Marwar Bus Stand
5 Police
6 School
10 Temple
13 State Bank of
   Bikaner & Jaipur
14 Bazaar Post Office
16 Temple
18 Navjyoti Tailors
27 Brahma Temple
29 Saraswati Music School
30 Jain Temple
33 Vishnu Temple
40 Tourist Information Centre
42 Reflexology Centre
43 Gurdwara
44 Ajmer Bus Stand
47 Hanuman Temple

Pushkar is world famous for its spectacular camel fair which takes place here in the Hindu lunar month of Kartika (see the boxed text 'Camel Fair' for exact dates). If you're anywhere within striking distance at the time, you'd be crazy to miss it.

During this period, the town is jam-packed with tribal people from all over Rajasthan, pilgrims from all over India and film-makers and tourists from all over the world. And of course there are plenty of camels and other livestock (it's best to arrive a few days before the official commencement date to see the most livestock).

Orientation

The desert town clings to the side of the small but beautiful Pushkar Lake with its many bathing ghats and temples. Pushkar town is a maze of narrow streets filled with interesting little shops, food stalls, hotels and temples. Fortunately there's virtually no motorised traffic in the main bazaar,

making it a pleasurable place to explore at leisure. The town is very tourist-friendly and most people speak some English, so you should have no problem finding your way around.

Information

The **Tourist Information Centre** (open 10am-5pm Mon-Fri & every 2nd Sat) is on the grounds of the Hotel Sarovar.

The **State Bank of Bikaner & Jaipur** (open 10am-2pm Mon-Fri & 10am-noon Sat) only changes travellers cheques (not currency). You may find the wait irritatingly long and the staff brusque. Currency (and travellers cheques) can be changed at moneychangers scattered along Sadar Bazaar Rd.

The main **post office** (open 9am-5pm Mon-Sat) is just south of the hospital. There's also a more convenient smaller post office (open 9am-5pm Mon-Sat) in the main bazaar.

On Sadar Bazaar Rd, there are plenty of places offering Internet access. The usual charge is around Rs 30 per hour – the places with ISDN connections are the fastest.

Temples

Pushkar boasts 400 temples, though few are as ancient as you'd expect at such an important pilgrimage site. Many were destroyed by Aurangzeb in the 17th century and subsequently rebuilt. Most famous is the **Brahma Temple**. It's marked by a red spire, and over the entrance gateway is the *hans*, or goose symbol, of Brahma. Inside, floor and walls are engraved with dedications to the dead.

The one-hour trek up to the hill top **Saraswati Temple** overlooking the lake is best made early in the morning; the view is magnificent.

Ghats

Numerous ghats run down to the lake and pilgrims are constantly bathing in the lake's holy waters. If you wish to join them, do it with respect – remove your shoes, don't smoke, refrain from kidding around and don't take photographs.

Horse & Camel Safaris

There are quite a few people in Pushkar who offer horse or camel safaris. It's best to ask your hotel, a travel agent, or other travellers to recommend somebody who organises good trips. For camels, the prices per hour/day are quoted at about Rs 70/300, or Rs 275 per day for two or more days. Horses per hour/day can be hired for around Rs 100/450.

Most organisers are happy to tailor-make a safari and have good suggestions about places of interest in and around Pushkar. If you want to get off the beaten track you can arrange a safari all the way to Jaisalmer, a journey of about four weeks. Camel safaris are a splendid way of taking in the sights and experiencing the rugged beauty of the desert. If it's your first time on a camel, take it easy and avoid galloping!

Massage & Yoga

For reiki, acupressure and yoga, try the **Reflexology Centre** (☎ 642818, ℮ *mathur_narenda@hotmail.com; open 10.30am-6.30pm*

EASTERN RAJASTHAN

Dreamer of the Universe

According to one Indian saying, GOD stands for Generation, Operation, Destruction; with the Hindu trinity of Brahma, Vishnu and Shiva respectively responsible for these three great tasks. Of the three, Brahma, the Creator, is the most mysterious. Unlike Vishnu and Shiva he is rarely worshipped, although reality itself is Brahma's dream. Each of his lifetimes spans 311,040,000,000,000 human years and corresponds to a great cycle of the universe, at the end of which it is destroyed by Shiva. Then Brahma is reborn to dream it all again.

Brahma is usually depicted with four bearded faces facing the four directions, and four hands, each holding one of the four books of the Vedas (Books of Knowledge). His vehicle is the swan and his consort is Saraswati, the Goddess of Education.

According to legend, the sacred lake of Pushkar sprang up at the spot where Brahma dropped a lotus flower from the sky. Pushkar takes its name from this incident – *pushp* means 'flower' and *kar* means 'hand'. Brahma wanted to perform a *yagna*, or holy sacrifice, at the lake on a full-moon night, a ceremony that required the presence of his consort. But Saraswati was late. Irritated, Brahma quickly married a convenient milkmaid named Gayatri and when Saraswati arrived she discovered Gayatri seated in her own honoured place beside Brahma. Saraswati was furious and vowed that Brahma would be forgotten by the people of the earth. It was a profound curse and the gods pleaded with her to reconsider. Finally she relented, decreeing that he could be worshipped, but only in Pushkar. Since then, the Brahma temple at Pushkar has remained one of the only temples in the world dedicated to Brahma and allegedly the only one in India. Meanwhile, Saraswati and Gayatri receive their *pujas* at separate temples, at opposite ends of the town.

daily), on the eastern side of town, where Dr NS Mathur offers treatments for Rs 100 per hour, or classes in treating others for the same price.

Music Schools

The **Saraswati Music School** (☎ 773124) is an excellent place to learn classical tabla (drums) and singing. Birju, with over 12 years of experience, charges Rs 100 for one hour or Rs 600 for three days of lessons. It's open from 10am to 10pm most days, but closes if the season is slow. If in doubt you can contact the school through Moon Dance restaurant (see Places to Eat later).

Tailors

Pushkar is an excellent place to get some clothes made up. One reliable place that has been recommended by a number of travellers is **Navjyoti Tailors** (☎ 72589, e yogeshnav jyoti@hotmail.com), opposite the Lake View (see Places to Stay – Budget). The relaxed Yogi can make just about anything you want in one to two days and is very reasonably priced.

Places to Stay

The bulk of Pushkar's budget hotels are nothing fancy (many budget places are spartan and have Indian-style toilets), but they're generally clean and freshly white-washed. You should ask to see a few rooms before deciding on one, as many have a cell-like atmosphere due to the small or nonexistent windows.

Although it is dominated by budget hotels, there are several upmarket accommodation

---

Camel Fair

The exact date on which the Pushkar Camel Fair is held depends on the lunar calendar but, in Hindu chronology, it falls on Kartik Purnima (the full moon of the Hindu month of Kartika) when devotees cleanse away their sins by bathing in the holy lake. Each year, more than 200,000 people flock to Pushkar for the camel fair, bringing with them some 50,000 camels and cattle for several days of pilgrimage, livestock trading, horse dealing and spirited festivities. There are camel races, street theatre and a variety of stalls selling handicrafts. The place becomes a flurry of activity with musicians, mystics, comedians, tourists, traders, animals and devotees all converging on the small town. It's truly a feast for the eyes, so don't forget to bring your camera. This fair is the only one of its kind on the planet and has featured in numerous magazines, travel shows and films.

Although Pushkar is transformed into a carnival, the camel fair is taken very seriously by livestock owners, who come from all over the country with the sole intent of trading. A good camel can fetch tens of thousands of rupees and is a vital source of income for many villagers.

It's strongly recommended that you get to the fair several days prior to the official commencement date, to see the camel and cattle trading at its peak. The real traders' fair is held in the first five days, or even before, while most of the events in the last five days are cultural activities organised by the tourist authorities.

Be warned that it can get noisy at night (and in the early morning when loud devotional music is often played), so if you're a light sleeper, bring along earplugs. Carry appropriate allergy medication if you are affected by dust and/or animal hair. Keep your valuables in a safe place – a moneybelt worn under the clothes is recommended.

Dates of the fair in forthcoming years are as follows:

2002	11 to 20 November
2003	31 October to 8 November
2004	18 to 26 November
2005	8 to 15 November
2006	29 October to 5 November

options in the town. But be warned that during the camel fair when demand is high, most hotels have ridiculously inflated prices. Unfortunately, there isn't much you can do about this, as it's usually a case of find what's available before it's all gone.

With thousands of tourists visiting each year, Pushkar has been exposed to the 'wicked ways of the West' and many hotels display prominent warning signs such as: 'In Pushkar, holding hands or kissing in public are not permitted'; 'Ladies and men should dress appropriately'; 'Drugs, alcohol and meat are not permitted'.

Places to Stay – Budget

Hotel Venus (☎ 772323; e venushotel@ yahoo.com; singles/doubles with private bathroom Rs 125/150), on the main drag, is a popular choice right in the middle of the action. It's set in a shady garden and there's a restaurant upstairs (see Places to Eat). The same owner runs the **Venus Holiday Resort** (☎ 773217, fax 772244; singles/doubles with private bathroom Rs 100/150, with air-con 400/500), north of the Hanuman Temple, which has a pool.

Krishna Guest House (☎ 772461; singles/ doubles with shared bathroom from Rs 75/ 120, with private bathroom from Rs 150/ 225), in the same area as Hotel Venus, is a good cheapie with decent, if bare, rooms. It's in a lovely old building and there's a nice garden area and a restaurant.

Payal Guest House (☎ 772163; singles/ doubles with private bathroom from Rs 75/ 100) is another favourite with travellers. It's in a multistorey block in the middle of the main bazaar, but maintains a laid-back atmosphere. The cool courtyard is shaded by a banana tree and meals are available – there's even a small bakery.

Lake View (☎ 773477, fax 772106; doubles with shared bathroom Rs 100-200, with private bathroom from Rs 200), across the street from Payal Guest House, is wonderfully located with superb views over the lake from the roof. Some of the rooms with a shared bathroom have a balcony overlooking the water.

Shri Anand Guest House (☎ 772562; e jotem2000@yahoo.com; singles/doubles

with shared bathroom Rs 30/50, doubles with private bathroom Rs 80) is a bargain, with basic rooms around a lovely garden.

Hotel Aroma (☎ 772729, fax 772244; singles/doubles Rs 75/100) is a welcoming place and one of the closest to the location of the camel fair.

Hotel Navratan Palace (☎ 772145, fax 772225; singles/doubles with private bathroom from Rs 150/200, with air-con Rs 500/600), close to the Brahma Temple, has a lovely enclosed garden and swimming pool. Nonguests can swim for Rs 50.

Hotel Bharatpur Palace (☎ 772320; singles/ doubles with shared bathroom from Rs 100/ 200, doubles with private bathroom Rs 500) occupies one of the best spots in Pushkar, literally on the upper levels of the western ghats. Room No 1 (Rs 500) wins the prize for the best place to wake up in the morning and is one of the most romantic choices in Pushkar. Although it doesn't have a private bathroom, it's surrounded on three sides by the lake (with doors that open out on each of these sides), it is possible to lie in bed with the doors open and have the lake and ghats laid out before you (with all of the attendant clamour and noise).

Hotel Kanhaia (☎ 772146; singles/doubles from Rs 60/80, best room Rs 250) is a fine place to stay, with small, clean, good-value rooms. Meals are available.

Mayur Guest House (☎ 772302; doubles with shared bathroom Rs 60, singles/doubles with private bathroom Rs 60/125) is a pleasant place with neat rooms around a leafy courtyard. Only breakfast is available.

Hotel Paramount (☎ 772428, fax 772244; doubles Rs 100-450) is in a peaceful location and has fine views over the town. The best rooms (Nos 106, 108, 109 and 111), with balconies and private bathrooms, are popular.

OK Palace Pushkar (☎ 772868, fax 772566; singles/doubles with shared bathroom Rs 40/ 80, doubles with private bathroom Rs 100), nearby, offers low prices and a friendly atmosphere.

Sai Baba Guest House (singles/doubles Rs 40/70) is another possibility if you're low on rupees. Rooms are simple and somewhat gloomy and have shared bathroom.

Shiva Guest House *(☎ 772120; singles/ doubles with private bathroom Rs 60/100)* has been recommended by a number of travellers. Simple rooms are set around a sandy courtyard, which seven pet tortoises call home.

VK Tourist Palace *(☎ 772174, fax 772662; singles/doubles with shared bathroom Rs 75/ 150, with private bathroom Rs 100/150, doubles with balcony Rs 200)* is a popular place with reasonable rooms and a good Tibetan rooftop restaurant (momos Rs 30).

Hotel Om *(☎ 772672; e hotelom@rediff mail.com; singles/doubles with shared bathroom Rs 100/150, with private bathroom Rs 200/400)* has lovely views over nearby fields, a relaxed owner and buffet lunch or dinner (Rs 40) available in the garden.

Bhagwati Guest House *(☎ 772423; singles/ doubles with shared bathroom Rs 40/50, doubles with private bathroom Rs 80-150)*, near the Ajmer bus stand, is a good option if you're going through a cash crunch. There are small but acceptable rooms or reasonable larger doubles. There's also a good restaurant with food like cheese onion pie (Rs 60), banana pancakes (Rs 25) and pizzas (Rs 45 to 70).

Hotel Oasis *(☎ 772100, fax 772557; singles/doubles Rs 130/150, with air-con Rs 400/500)* is across the road from Bhagwati and is a big place with large, bare rooms. There's a restaurant, Internet access (Rs 40 per hour) and a swimming pool, although the latter is made less appealing by the number of men who seem to lurk permanently around the entrance and reception area.

Places to Stay – Mid-Range & Top End

JP's Tourist Village Resort *(☎ 772067, fax 772026; e jpresorts@hotmail.com; treehouse singles/doubles Rs 120/150, doubles Rs 200-750)* is about 2km from the centre of town, but free transport to and from town is available. There are comfortable rooms furnished in a traditional style, set around a beautiful garden where the food served in the restaurant is grown. For those who want to relive their childhood, treehouse accommodation is available. In fact this is a very

child-friendly place, with a kiddie pool and play equipment.

RTDC Hotel Sarovar *(☎/fax 772040; dorm beds Rs 50, singles/doubles with shared bathroom Rs 150/250, with private bathroom Rs 350/450, with air-con Rs 800/900)* is set in its own spacious grounds at the far-eastern end of the lake. It's next to the Hotel Pushkar Palace, but approached from a different entrance. The rooms are ordinary, but it has more character than most RTDC places, due largely to its great location right on the lake. There's a swimming pool and a restaurant. Some travellers have complained about the lack of cleanliness and the quality of the service.

Hotel New Park *(☎ 772464, fax 772199; singles/doubles Rs 450/550, with air-con 650/ 750)*, a few kilometres from town, is a modern place surrounded by tranquil flower gardens and market gardens. It has clean rooms, great mountain views and its own swimming pool and restaurant.

Hotel Pushkar Palace *(☎ 772001, fax 772 226; e hppalace@datainfosys.net; singles/ doubles 1900/1995, suites 4000/5000)*, right on the lake, is an old favourite. Once belonging to the maharaja of Kishangarh, these days it's an upmarket hotel. It's got the best location in town but it's had some mixed reviews in recent years. There's a pleasant outdoor eating area overlooking the lake (see Places to Eat). Prices rise to US$200 during the fair, including all meals.

Jagat Singh Palace Hotel *(☎ 772953, fax 772952; e hppalace@datainfosys.net; singles/doubles Rs 1900/1995)*, a little out of the main town area, is terrific if you like your creature comforts. The sister hotel to the Hotel Pushkar Palace, this place is designed like a fort. It has plush rooms, a large garden area, a restaurant and a pool. Rates increase to US$200 during the fair.

Pushkar Resorts *(☎ 772017, fax 772946; e pushkar@pushkarresorts.com; singles/doubles Rs 1895/2195)* about 5km out of town, is also suitably luxurious. There are 40 modern cottages that are certainly clean and comfortable, although a little lacking in character. All have air-con and TV. The dining hall serves meat, since it's outside the town limits (guests only). There's also a swimming pool, billiard table and two telescopes for stargazing. Camel-cart picnics and camel/jeep safaris can be organised.

Tourist Village During the camel fair, the RTDC and many private operators set up a sea of tents near the *mela* (fair) ground. It can get cold at night, so bring something warm to wear. A torch (flashlight) may also be useful. Demand for tents is high so you're strongly urged to book well ahead.

RTDC Tourist Village (☎ 772074, fax 772 040; *dorm tents Rs 2000 per person, single/double tents with private bathroom Rs 5000/5500, double huts Rs 6600*) has dormitory tents and tents with private bathroom. There are also deluxe huts available, which are open year-round, and singles/doubles cost just Rs 200/300 (with air-con Rs 300/400) when the fair is not on. Prices during the fair include all meals. Full payment must be received one month in advance to be sure of accommodation.

Royal Tents (*singles/doubles with meals US$200/275*), owned by the maharaja of Jodhpur, seem to be the most luxurious tents available in Pushkar, but you'll pay for this privilege. Tents come with private bathroom (bucket hot water), and rates include all meals. Reservations should be made in advance at the Balsamand Palace in Jodhpur (☎ 0291-572322, fax 571240).

Royal Desert Camp (*doubles with meals US$75*), further away from the fairground, is another good option, the tents have private bathrooms (which even have showers). You'll need to pay well in advance through the Hotel Pushkar Palace in Pushkar (☎ 772001, fax 772226).

Places to Eat
Pushkar is one of those towns in which everyone has a favourite restaurant, and there's plenty to choose from. There are quite a few rooftop and garden restaurants, which are ideal for a leisurely meal. Being a holy place, alcohol, meat and even eggs are banned, but the cooks make up for this with imagination. You can even get an eggless omelette in some places!

Buffet meals are popular, with many places offering all-you-can-eat meals for Rs 35 to 45. It's safest to eat buffet meals at the busiest places where the food is more likely to be freshly cooked for each meal, rather than reheated. German bakeries are the latest rage around town.

There are a number of places where the view or location is better than the food. Surprisingly, one such place is the **Hotel Pushkar Palace** (*buffet lunch & dinner Rs 150*), – a great place for a drink at sunset (a rose shake is Rs 70), but eat elsewhere. Others include the **Venus Restaurant** (*open 8am-11pm daily*), which has a prime vantage point overlooking the main thoroughfare and its fascinating passing parade (a plain/special thali goes for Rs 35/40), and **Sanjay Restaurant** (*open 7am-10.30pm; curries Rs 20-40*) that has a great view over the lake.

Sunset Cafe (*open 8am-11pm daily*) has long been a popular hang-out with travellers: a good place to swap stories about Goa, Kathmandu and beyond. This simple café offers the usual have-a-go-at-anything menu, which includes dosas (Rs 15) and sizzlers (Rs 75 to 150). There's a German bakery; the lemon cake is pretty good (Rs 20 per slice). The location by the lakeshore is delightful, especially at sunset, but the service can be sluggish.

Om Shiva (*buffet lunch or dinner Rs 50; open 1pm-4pm & 5pm-10pm daily*) is another popular hang-out, serving up a tasty all-you-can-eat buffet for lunch and dinner.

Moon Dance (☎ 772606; *open 8am-11pm daily*) is an old favourite. This laid-back garden retreat serves a wide range of food, including good Indian, Mexican, Italian and even Thai dishes. A spinach and mushroom enchilada is Rs 55, a Kashmiri burger is Rs 50, and a cup of cinnamon tea is Rs 6. There's also a German bakery.

Sun-n-Moon (☎ 772883; *open 8am-11pm daily*), not far from the Brahma Temple, has tables around a bo tree, and there's a soothing calm about this place. It offers a variety of Western and Indian foods such as cheese kofta (Rs 45), veg pizza (Rs 60), and tantalising roasted banana with chocolate and honey (Rs 50).

The Third Eye *(open 10am-11pm)* is a funky place where you can play pool (per game/hour Rs 20/60) and listen to techno beats. Good Israeli food is served, but most falls under their menu category of 'munchies' rather than meals.

Vijay Deep Restaurant *(☎ 772477)* is a cosy local joint with a dirt floor near the Marwar bus stand. It has a simple menu (thalis from Rs 30) but is a good spot if you want to get away from the tourist scene.

Shopping

Pushkar's main bazaar is a tangle of narrow lanes lined with an assortment of interesting little shops – ideal for picking up gifts for friends back home. If it's sold in Rajasthan, you'll find it here – although you'll have to haggle over prices. The shopkeepers are used to tourists who accept the first price, so there's the usual nonsense about 'last price' quotes that aren't negotiable. Take your time and visit a few shops before you decide.

Particularly good buys include silver and beaded jewellery, embroidered fabrics, bed and cushion covers, wall-hangings, groovy shoulder bags, Rajasthani puppets and fusion music. A lot of what is stocked here actually comes from the Barmer district south of Jaisalmer and other tribal areas of Rajasthan.

In between are the inevitable clothing shops selling trendy Western designs based on clothes that travellers have brought in to have copied by tailors – see under Tailors earlier. There's also a lot of hippy stuff straight out of Goa circa 1960.

Pushkar is a great place to stock up on reading material, particularly if you're heading into more remote corners of Rajasthan. There's an excellent range of second-hand novels in various languages available, and the bookshops will buy them back for 50% of what you pay.

Getting There & Away

Frequent buses leave Ajmer for Pushkar (Rs 7; only Rs 5 when going *from* Pushkar *to* Ajmer because of the road toll). It's a spectacular climb up and over the hills and you never know quite what to expect around each turn.

There are a number of travel agencies in Pushkar offering tickets for private buses to various destinations – shop around for the best price. Private buses depart Pushkar for Jodhpur (Rs 90, five hours), Jaipur (Rs 60, 3½ hours), Delhi (Rs 169, 11 hours) and Udaipur (Rs 90, seven hours). Government buses to Jodhpur, Jaipur, and Delhi leave from the Marwar bus stand and are a shade cheaper, but less comfortable. Buses to Mt Abu, Jaisalmer and Agra leave from Ajmer, but if you book them through a Pushkar agent they should provide you with a free transfer to Ajmer. Some travel agencies will also book rail tickets for services leaving from Ajmer, for an additional booking fee (usually around Rs 30), which saves you the hassle of going down to the Ajmer station.

Getting Around

Fortunately, there are no autorickshaws in the town centre so it's a breeze to get around by foot. A bicycle is great to buzz around on and there are hire places near the Ajmer bus stand (Rs 5/25 per hour/day) and even a few places that rent scooters (from Rs 60/200). It's possible to get a wallah to carry your luggage on a hand-drawn cart to or from the bus stand for a small fee (Rs 10 is fine).

TONK

This town, 95km to the south of Jaipur, on the way to Ranthambhore National Park, was built in the mid-17th century. Tonk was originally ruled by a tribe of Afghani Pathans, and their prosperous Muslim descendants have left a legacy of fine mansions, a testament to the wealth they accumulated when they ruled as nawabs from this region. Tonk also served as an important administrative centre during the era of the Raj, and the British have left behind some well-preserved colonial buildings.

Attractions in Tonk include the early-19th-century **Sunehri Kothi**, with its beautiful coloured glass and inlay work; and the imposing **Jama Masjid**, an important place of worship. At the **Arabic & Persian Research Institute**, a rare collection of old Arabic and Persian manuscripts and books is housed.

Getting There & Away

There are many buses from Jaipur's main bus stand which pass through Tonk (Rs 30, 2½ hours) en route to Kota. There are also numerous buses between Tonk and Sawai Madhopur for Ranthambhore National Park (Rs 50, two hours).

RANTHAMBHORE NATIONAL PARK
☎ 07462

Accessed via the town of Sawai Madhopur, midway between Bharatpur and Kota, Ranthambhore National Park is one of the prime examples of Project Tiger's conservation efforts in Rajasthan. Sadly, it also demonstrates the programme's overall failure; for it was in this park that government officials were implicated in the poaching of tigers for the Chinese folk-medicine trade. In 2000 the visit of then US president Bill Clinton led to a rapid growth in the park's popularity, although sadly it also highlighted its problems. Bumbram, the tiger seen by President Clinton, could not be found when the park reopened after the monsoon in October 2000. This lead to fears that the now-famous tiger had been

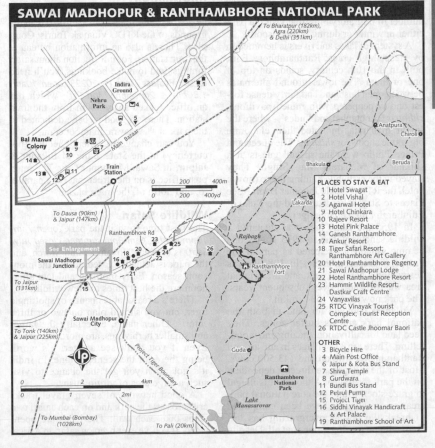

SAWAI MADHOPUR & RANTHAMBHORE NATIONAL PARK

To Bharatpur (182km),
Agra (220km)
& Delhi (351km)

Indira
Ground

Nehru
Park

Bal Mandir
Colony

Main Bazaar

Train
Station

0   200   400m
0   200   400yd

Anatpura

Chiroli

Bhakula

Beruda

Lakarda

To Dausa (90km)
& Jaipur (147km)

Ranthambhore Rd

See Enlargement

Sawai Madhopur
Junction

Rajbagh

Ranthambhore
Fort

To Jaipur
(131km)

Sawai Madhopur
City

To Tonk (140km)
& Jaipur (225km)

Guda

Ranthambhore
National
Park

Project Tiger Boundary

0   2   4km
0   1   2mi

To Mumbai (Bombay)
(1028km)

To Pali (20km)

Lake
Manasarovar

PLACES TO STAY & EAT
1 Hotel Swagat
2 Hotel Vishal
5 Agarwal Hotel
9 Hotel Chinkara
10 Rajeev Resort
13 Hotel Pink Palace
14 Ganesh Ranthambhore
17 Ankur Resort
18 Tiger Safari Resort;
   Ranthambhore Art Gallery
20 Hotel Ranthambhore Regency
21 Sawai Madhopur Lodge
22 Hotel Ranthambhore Resort
23 Hammir Wildlife Resort;
   Dastkar Craft Centre
24 Vanyavilas
25 RTDC Vinayak Tourist
   Complex; Tourist Reception
   Centre
26 RTDC Castle Jhoomar Baori

OTHER
3 Bicycle Hire
4 Main Post Office
6 Jaipur & Kota Bus Stand
7 Shiva Temple
8 Gurdwara
11 Bundi Bus Stand
12 Petrol Pump
15 Project Tiger
16 Siddhi Vinayak Handicraft
   & Art Palace
19 Ranthambhore School of Art

poached, although park authorities denied the reports.

According to a 2001 census, the park had a total of 33 to 35 tigers, including 11 cubs. Other animals inhabiting Ranthambhore include the endangered caracal, also a member of the cat family, the leopard and the jungle cat; several members of the dog family such as hyenas, foxes and jackals; the sloth bear and varieties of deer, including the chital (spotted deer) and the sambar, India's largest deer. There are also two species of antelope: the chinkara (Indian gazelle) and the nilgai (bluebull).

Ranthambhore National Park also boasts at least 260 species of birds, including a number of migratory birds that visit the park either in winter or during the monsoon.

A system of lakes and rivers is hemmed in by steep, high crags; Ranthambhore Fort, built in the 10th century, stands on top of one of them. The lower ground alternates between open bushland and fairly dense forest and is peppered with ruined pavilions, *chhatris* (cenotaphs) and 'hides' – where the Jaipur maharajas mounted their elaborate big-game shoots, or *shikhars*. The queen and Prince Philip were the special guests at a shikhar of Maharaja Man Singh. They stayed in the erstwhile hunting lodge (now a hotel, the RTDC Castle Jhoomar Baori – see Places to Stay & Eat later), and the Duke of Edinburgh killed a large tiger.

In 1955 the game park was declared a wildlife sanctuary, and in 1973 it was one of nine sanctuaries selected as part of the Project Tiger programme. In 1980 it was designated a national park, and the original area was expanded over subsequent years. The park now covers 1334 sq km.

Villagers compete for land in both the national park and its buffer zones. They need land for cultivation, grazing and woodfelling. There are 332 villages in and around Ranthambhore, with around 143,500 cows. Most of the villages are directly dependent on the park for fodder. Although it is illegal to graze stock within the core national park area, some villagers have been compelled to break the law as overgrazing has left them with no grazing grounds at all. Despite efforts of ecodevelopment and education within the local villages, the relationship between the villagers and park authorities remains strained.

Orientation

It's 10km from Sawai Madhopur to the first park gate, where you pay the entry fee, and a further 3km to the main gate and the Ranthambhore Fort. Accommodation is strung out along the road from the town to the park. Sawai Madhopur City is a residential area to the south of the park.

Information

The helpful **Tourist Reception Centre** (☎ 20808; open 10am-5pm Mon-Sat) is in the grounds of the RTDC Vinayak Tourist Complex. There's also an information bureau at the train station. For information about safari timings, and to make bookings, you'll need to see **Project Tiger** (☎ 20223; open 10am-1.30pm & 2pm-5pm Mon-Sat), which has an office tucked away 500m from the train station. There's a good website dedicated to the park at W www.ranthambor.com.

You can change travellers cheques (not currency) at the **State Bank of Bikaner & Jaipur**, in Sawai Madhopur City. The main post office is on the street that runs parallel to, and north of, the main bazaar.

Wildlife Safaris

The best time to visit the park (open 7am-10pm winter, 6am-9pm summer, closed July-Sept) is between November and March, and the park is actually closed during the monsoon season. Early morning and late afternoon are the best times to view wildlife.

There's a reasonable chance of spotting a tiger, but you should plan on two or three safaris. Other game, especially the larger and smaller herbivores, are more numerous. Even if you don't see a tiger, it's worth being there for the scenery alone: In India it's not often you get the chance to visit such a large area of virgin bush.

A good network of seven gravel tracks crisscrosses the park and on each safari two jeeps take each trail. The jeeps are open-sided. If you've ever been on safari in Africa, you might think this is unduly risky but the tigers appear unconcerned by garrulous tourists toting cameras only metres away from where they're lying. No one has been mauled or eaten – yet!

There are two ways to see the park – by jeep or by canter. Both must be booked at the Project Tiger office (☎ 20223).

Jeeps are almost impossible to obtain during most of the season because only 16 jeeps are allowed in the park at once – you usually need to book at least *two months* in advance. On top of this there are a number of separate charges for park entry by jeep. The admission fee for foreigner/citizen is Rs 200/25. A jeep costs Rs 700 and can be shared by up to five people. This includes all kilometre charges, so if you're staying further from the park entrance the trip isn't going to cost more. You'll also have to pay for vehicle entry (Rs 125 per jeep) and a (compulsory) guide (Rs 100). Many guides speak good English and there's currently one, **Yadvendra Singh** (☎ 34042, fax 21212), who is also semifluent in German.

Alternatively you can visit the park in a large, open-topped, 20-seater truck (called a canter). Canters are limited to only five of the trails. A seat for foreigner/citizen costs Rs 305/130 (including park admission and guide), and you can arrange to be picked up if your hotel is on the road between the town and the park. Up to 20 canters are allowed in the park, and you can usually get a seat on one.

Both jeep and canter tours go for three hours and run twice daily. The morning canter tour leaves half an hour before the park opens from the Project Tiger office. The afternoon tour leaves at 4pm in summer and 2.30pm in winter. If you're taking a morning safari in winter it's a good idea to bring something warm to wear, as it can get quite cold. According to several guides, red clothing should be avoided as it apparently irritates tigers! Take a hat and a bottle of water, but leave behind your torches and camera flashes. Mosquito repellent and sunscreen are also recommended, particularly in October and November. Some guides have binoculars that you may be able to use.

If you are taking photos, it's worthwhile bringing some 400 or 800 ASA film, as the undergrowth is dense and surprisingly dark in places. The prime time for photography is May to June, when there are fewer people around, and jeeps are better suited to photography than the canters. A still camera is free, but it's Rs 200 if you've got a video camera.

Ranthambhore Fort

The ancient Ranthambhore Fort *(admission free; open 6am-6pm daily)* in the heart of the national park, is believed to have been built by the Chauhan Rajputs in the 10th century AD, only a few years before the invasion of India by Mohammed Ghori. According to tradition, the fort was erected over the site at which two princes were engaged in a boar hunt. The boar eluded the princes and dived into a lake. Not to be thwarted, the princes prayed to Shiva to restore the boar. This Shiva deigned to do, on condition that the princes build a fort in his honour at the spot.

However, it is Ganesh who is most revered at the fort, and a temple in his honour can be found overlooking its southern ramparts. Traditionally when a marriage is to take place, invitations are forwarded to Ganesh before any other guests. The temple

Miniature paintings often portrayed the Rajasthani rulers, or the British, hunting tigers

SARAH JOLLY

at the fort receives hundreds of letters each week addressed to the elephant god, some of which include money to enable him to pay for his fare to the marriage celebration!

The fort is believed to be the site at which the first *jauhar* in Rajput history was performed. In the early 14th century, the ruler of the fort, Hammir Deva, was engaged in a protracted battle with the Muslim forces. Although Hammir repulsed the Muslim invaders, the women who were installed in the fort for their safety heard that he had succumbed on the battlefield. In usual Rajput style, preferring death to dishonour, they committed mass suicide. When confronted with the grisly news, the victorious Hammir beheaded himself before the image of Shiva in the temple at the fort.

From a distance, the fort is not an imposing edifice, being almost indiscernible on its hill top looking out over the lake of Padam Talab. However, it affords very fine views from the disintegrating walls of the Badal Mahal, on its northern side, and its seven enormous gateways are still intact. Inside the fort there are three Hindu temples, dedicated to Ganesh, Shiva and Ramlalaji. They date from the 12th and 13th centuries and are constructed with impressive blocks of red Karauli stone. Constructed of the same stone are a number of cenotaphs that can be seen in the precincts of the fort.

Places to Stay & Eat

The best places to stay are on Ranthambhore Rd, but 'shoestringers' will find much cheaper (and grimier and noisier) lodgings in uninspiring Sawai Madhopur. Many of the hotels offer hefty discounts during the low-season (up to 50%).

Ranthambhore Road All of the following places offer fixed-price meals, and some also offer an à la carte selection. Many of the places to stay along this strip close when the park is closed.

RTDC Castle Jhoomar Baori (*☎/fax 20 495; singles/doubles from Rs 600/700, suites Rs 1000/1900*), about 7km from the train station, is a former royal hunting lodge stunningly located on a hillside (you can see it

from the train). The multichamber rooms are loaded with character, although they're a bit shabby these days. There's a lounge, open-rooftop areas and a bar. Continental/Indian lunch or dinner is Rs 190/150.

Hotel Ranthambhore Resort (*☎ 21645, fax 21430; doubles with private bathroom Rs 200*), about 5km from the train station, is the cheapest place along Ranthambhore Rd with simple but clean, decent-sized rooms.

Ankur Resort (*☎ 20792, fax 20697; e ankur@ranthambor.com; singles/doubles Rs 650/750, cottages Rs 1000/1300*), 3km from the station, is a popular choice though a touch overpriced. Deluxe single/double cottages cost Rs 1200/1500 (the doubles have satellite TV).

Hotel Ranthambhore Regency (*☎ 21176, fax 21672; e ranthambhore@hotmail.com; doubles from Rs 800, cottages Rs 1500*), nearby Ankur Resort, has attractive rooms, or 'cottages' lining a long private courtyard. There are nightly puppet shows on the roof terrace.

Hammir Wildlife Resort (*☎ 20562, fax 21 842; singles/doubles Rs 600/700, air-con doubles Rs 900, cottages Rs 1100*), 5km from the train station, has rather neglected rooms.

RTDC Vinayak Tourist Complex (*☎ 21169, fax 20702; singles/doubles Rs 550/650, suites Rs 1300*), further along the road, has decent rooms with alcove windows. There's a nice lawn area and a campfire is lit in the winter. There's a dining hall where a fixed dinner is Rs 140.

Tiger Safari Resort (*☎ 21137, fax 22391; e arvinda@datainforsys.net; singles/doubles Rs 600/700, deluxe Rs 800/900*) is a relaxed, though rather pricey, choice, with pleasant doubles and very clean bathrooms. Go for a standard room – the deluxe rooms just have better paintings.

Sawai Madhopur Lodge (*☎ 20541, fax 20 718; tents with private bathroom per double Rs 4000, doubles Rs 5000, suites Rs 8000*) is 3km from the train station, the first on the strip and one of the most swanky places to stay. The lodge formerly belonged to the maharaja of Jaipur and is now managed by the Taj group. It is suitably luxurious, with a lending library, bar, restaurant, pool (open to nonguests for Rs 300), tennis court and beautiful garden. There are rooms or luxury tents (with private bathroom). Nonguests are welcome to dine at the restaurant with advance notice; the buffet lunch is Rs 280, and dinner is Rs 325.

Vanyavilas *(☎ 23999, fax 23988; e reser vations@vanyavilas.com; tents singles/doubles Rs 16,000/18,000)* is by far the flashest place to stay. The latest hotel to be opened by the Oberoi chain, this is a suitably sumptuous establishment, based on the design of the Raj Vilas in Jaipur. Accommodation includes all meals and is in luxury tents, complete with colonial-style baths. Each tent is in its own private compound on the 20-acre grounds, which are beautifully landscaped with lush gardens, artificial waterways and an orchard.

Sawai Madhopur As few travellers choose to stay in Sawai Madhopur, the accommodation options are limited and lacklustre – but a fraction of the price.

Hotel Chinkara *(☎ 20340; 13 Indira Colony, Civil Lines; singles/doubles Rs 150/ 200)* is a very good choice in Sawai Madhopur. It offers large quaint and quiet rooms with a private bathroom. Meals are available with advance notice.

Rajeev Resort *(☎ 21413, fax 33138; 16 Indira Colony, Civil Lines; singles with shared bathroom Rs 100, singles/doubles with private bathroom Rs 150/300)*, just a few doors away, has decent rooms and a pleasant atmosphere.

Hotel Vishal *(☎ 20504; singles/doubles from Rs 50/100)*, in the main bazaar, has a range of reasonable rooms if you're low on cash (hot water free by the bucket). Some rooms have balconies.

Hotel Swagat *(☎ 20601, fax 23687; singles/doubles with private bathroom Rs 60/ 80, better doubles Rs 150)*, further east, is a seedy place, not recommended for solo female travellers. The basic and rather grubby rooms come with private bathroom (hot water by the bucket).

Hotel Pink Palace *(☎ 20722, fax 21455; Tonk Rd, Bazaria; doubles with private bathroom Rs 150, with a private geyser from Rs 200)*

is on the western side of the overpass. Basic rooms have private bath with either buckets of hot water or geysers. Meals are also available here.

Ganesh Ranthambhore *(☎ 21124; 58 Bal Mandir Colony, Civil Lines; doubles Rs 500, with air-con Rs 700)* is a clean place with more air and light than most of the pokey options in Sawai Madhopur. All rooms have bathroom and TV (hot water is sometimes available through the geysers) and meals are available.

Retiring rooms *(doubles with private bathroom Rs 175)* can be found at the train station.

Agarwal Hotel *(☎ 20276)* is a small restaurant in the main bazaar which has a variety of cheap vegetarian eats. Thalis are Rs 40.

Shopping

The **Dastkar Craft Centre**, 3km beyond the park entrance on Ranthambhore Rd, is worth a visit. The handicrafts, all of which are produced by low-caste women in local villages, include bedspreads, clothes and other textile pieces.

The **Ranthambhore School of Art** *(☎ 34 813)* aims to promote conservation through art. The school's signature photo-realistic wildlife prints start at Rs 1200.

There are a couple of bookshops in the park including **Siddhi Vinayak Handicraft & Art Palace**, on the Ranthambhore road near the Sawai Madhopur Lodge. On the same road, near the Hotel Anurag Resort, is the **Ranthambhore Art Gallery** *(☎ 34813)*, which sells a similar range of books.

Getting There & Away

Bus There are buses every half hour to Jaipur (Rs 45, four hours) via Dausa (buses leave from the roundabout near the main post office) or Tonk (leaving from the Bundi Bus Stand, near the overpass), and there are four daily express buses (Rs 65, three hours) from either bus stand. Buses to Bundi (Rs 40, 3½ hours) leave from the Bundi bus stand, and go on to Kota (Rs 70, five hours). Travelling to Bharatpur by bus invariably involves a change in Dausa – the train is infinitely preferable.

EASTERN RAJASTHAN

Train There's a **computerised reservation office** (*open 8am-8pm Mon-Sat, 8am-1.45pm Sun*) at the train station.

For Delhi, the *2903 Golden Temple Mail* leaves Sawai Madhopur at 1.05pm daily, arriving in the capital at 7pm (Rs 84/131/378 general/sleeper/3A class). It goes via Bharatpur, arriving at 3.35pm (Rs 52/84/234). To Kota, there are seven trains daily, the most convenient of which is probably the *5063 Avadh Express*, which leaves Sawai Madhopur at 9.50am, arriving at 11.35am (Rs 34/84/183).

Getting Around

Bicycle hire is available at the shops just outside the main entrance to the train station. It's also available at the east end of the main bazaar. The cost per hour/day is usually around Rs 2/15.

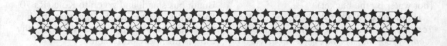

Southern Rajasthan

Bordering Gujarat and Madhya Pradesh, southern Rajasthan is one of the state's most fertile regions. It has a varied topography, with rolling hills, lush valleys and desolate plains. The region is also dotted with many lakes, including Jaisamand, one of the biggest artificial lakes in Asia. The south boasts some of Rajasthan's most important forts, including the huge hilltop fort of Chittorgarh. This sprawling fort occupies a paramount place in the annals of Rajput valour, for this was where tens of thousands of Rajput men, women and children perished in the name of honour. The imposing 15th-century fort of Kumbhalgarh is the second most significant in the Mewar (Udaipur) region after Chittorgarh.

Southern Rajasthan has one of India's best-known palace hotels, the breathtaking Lake Palace Hotel, in Udaipur. Superbly situated in the middle of a lake, this enchanting white palace once served as the royal summer residence.

Kota is one of the state's major industrial centres and has seen an increasing rate of industrialisation and pollution. This trend is not limited to Kota: over the past decade, many cities and towns in southern Rajasthan have suffered rising pollution levels, largely because of industrial growth and urban sprawl. Marble mining has burgeoned in the south and contributed to denuding the landscape of vegetation; it's not unusual to see white dust from the marble quarries blanketing the countryside. Although the government has taken measures to curtail industrial waste, a handful of historic monuments are believed to have already been adversely affected by pollution.

Southern Rajasthan has the state's only hill station, Mt Abu. Situated along a 1200m-high plateau, hordes of people from Rajasthan and Gujarat throng here during summer to escape the sweltering heat. Like many other hill stations in India, Mt Abu is very popular with honeymooners and young families. It is also home to the superb Dil-

- Bundi, a picturesque little town, with a ramshackle fort and medieval ambience

- Chittorgarh, Rajasthan's most historically significant fort, where tens of thousands of men, women and children died in the name of honour

- Udaipur, arguably India's most romantic city with its whitewashed temples and grand palaces in and around the lake

- The Jain temples at Mt Abu and Ranakpur, among the most exquisite in all of India

wara temples, which are an important Jain pilgrimage centre. These temples have some of the most amazing marble carvings in Rajasthan, if not India. Another impressive and important Jain temple at Ranakpur is renowned for its 1444 exquisite pillars, no two of which are alike.

This part of the state is rich in antiquities, with potentially many more undiscovered. Jhalawar, for instance, is an archaeologist's heaven, with historic relics being continually unearthed at a rare assortment of ancient sites, including extraordinary Buddhist caves and *stupas* (Buddhist religious monuments composed of a solid hemisphere topped by a spire) atop a hill.

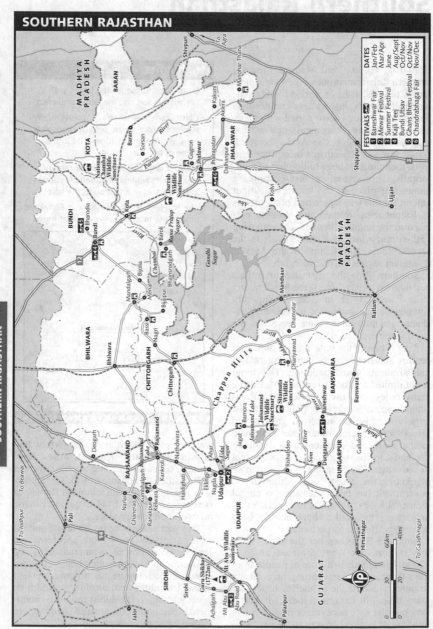

SOUTHERN RAJASTHAN

DATES	
Jan/Feb	
Mar/Apr	
June	
Aug/Sept	
Oct/Nov	
Nov/Dec	

FESTIVALS
1 Baneshwar Fair
2 Mewar Festival
3 Summer Festival
4 Kajli Teej
5 Bundi Utsav
6 Ghans Bheru Festival
6 Chandrabhaga Fair

Historically, Rajasthan has been a flourishing centre of art and culture, boasting many of India's finest schools of miniature painting. Former rulers were great patrons of the arts and employed local artists to develop unique styles. The famous Bundi school of painting had Mughal influences and specialised in hunting and palace scenes. The artists of Kota produced miniature paintings in the early 19th century that are acclaimed for their eloquent depictions of hunting and have featured at many international exhibitions. Mewar also developed its own style and was especially known for its highly detailed court scenes. Created from the early 18th century for the Mewar rulers, some of these paintings can be seen at the City Palace Museum in Udaipur. Also noteworthy are the vivid Nathdwara *pichwai* (cloth) paintings, which were produced in the 17th century after the revered black stone image of Krishna was brought here from Mathura. Other small towns, mostly those with royal connections, had their own schools of painting.

Many traditional tribal folk dances and songs have survived from southern Rajasthan's colourful past. For example the Bhil tribal people often perform their vibrant dances during special festivals such as Holi.

Southern Rajasthan has a handful of wildlife reserves there is abundant birdlife around the many lakes, particularly at Udaipur, Jaisamand and Dungarpur.

History

Southern Rajasthan's history is dominated by the kingdom of Mewar, which was wracked with both bloodshed and acts of astounding valour. The events at Chittorgarh, the former capital of Mewar, were undoubtedly the most catastrophic and poignant in all of Rajasthan, for it was here that countless Rajput men, women and children chose death over defeat. Chittorgarh was sacked three times from 1303 to 1568 and each defeat ended in immense carnage. While the men died in battle, the women committed *jauhar* (collective sacrifice) by throwing themselves into the flames of huge pyres to avoid the infamy of capture. After the third attack, Mewar's ruler, Maharana Udai Singh II, decided to leave Chittorgarh and establish his new capital in Udaipur.

Geographically, Udaipur was shielded by thick forests and the Aravalli Range, and was therefore far less vulnerable than the exposed Chittorgarh. But this did not stop invaders from trying to lay siege to the new capital of Mewar, and Udaipur also had its share of battles. These power struggles ended in the early 19th century when the British signed an alliance pledging to protect the Mewar rulers.

The rulers of the Mewar region, the illustrious Sisodia Rajput clan, are said to be descendants of the sun, and the symbol of the sun is a common motif in the palaces and forts of the region. Historically they have occupied the top of the Rajput hierarchy, making this an important region of Rajasthan. This dynasty is believed to be one of the oldest in the world, reigning in unbroken succession for over 1400 years. They staunchly defied foreign domination of any kind and were the only Hindu princes who refused to intermarry with the once-influential Mughal emperors. For them, honour, heritage and independence were of paramount importance, even if that meant deprivation and suffering.

Other princely states in southern Rajasthan, such as Kota and Bundi, were formed long after the region of Mewar. For example, the remote princely state of Jhalawar was only created in 1838.

BUNDI

☎ 0747 • postcode 323001 • pop 88,312

Visiting Bundi is like stepping back in time. It's a picturesque and captivating little town which has more or less retained a medieval atmosphere. Located only 39km northwest of Kota, it's more pleasant to stay here and visit Kota on a day trip.

Bundi is not a major tourist tramping ground, which is a big part of its appeal. The only place you may get a little hassled (by small children) is on the way up to the palace. In the evening, people throng to the colourful and bustling markets that meander through the town's lanes. Unlike many other

Festivals of Southern Rajasthan

Several colourful festivals are celebrated in southern Rajasthan. For statewide and nationwide festivals, see Public Holidays & Special Events in the Facts for the Visitor chapter.

January–February

Baneshwar Fair Celebrated by thousands of Bhil people at Baneshwar, in Dungarpur district, this festival honours Vishnu who is worshipped as Kalki. Festivities include acrobatic performances and cultural programmes, and a silver image of Kalki is paraded through the village on horseback.

February–March

Holi Udaipur is the place to be in Rajasthan during this happy celebration, which is celebrated across India in late February/early March. Holi marks the end of winter and the beginning of spring. It symbolises the victory of divine power over demonic strength. It is also known as the Festival of Colours, because of the exuberant throwing of coloured powder and water on the last day.

The Udaipur royal family hosts an elaborate function at the City Palace to celebrate Holi. There's an evening procession with decorated horses, a band, local nobility in traditional attire and, of course, the royal family. After performing an ancient religious ceremony, the royal family lights a huge sacred fire signifying the triumph of good over evil. Tribal people then commence a traditional dance. Afterwards, you get the chance to rub shoulders with nobility at a reception held in the Zenana Mahal at the City Palace. Tickets cost Rs 1500 per person and can be obtained at the **Shiv Niwas Palace Hotel** (☎ 0294-528008, fax 528006) in Udaipur.

March–April

Gangaur Essentially a festival for women, Gangaur is dedicated to the goddess Gauri (Parvati) and celebrated by women across Rajasthan. Wives pray for their spouses and unmarried women pray for good husbands. The Garasia tribes of the Mt Abu region add an interesting element to the festivities: they celebrate Gangaur for an entire month, and the image of Gauri is carried aloft from village to village. Young unmarried people are able to meet without social sanction and select marriage partners, with whom they elope. In Bundi, Kota and Jhalawar, unmarried girls collect poppies from the fields and make them into wreaths for the goddess.

places in Rajasthan, in Bundi you are unlikely to be hounded by persistent shopkeepers and it's a friendly place.

The Rajput legacy is well preserved in the shape of the massive Taragarh. The fort broods over the town, which is crowded into the narrow valley below. The old city has a number of blue-coloured houses, similar to those found in Jodhpur.

Bundi has a collection of interesting historic sites, but sadly many are in a crumbling state of disrepair.

History

The Hadoti Chauhans, who claim their descent from the sacred fires of Mt Abu,

conquered this area of Rajasthan in the 12th century, wresting it from the Mina and Bhil tribes. This occured after they were pushed south from their stronghold at Ajmer by Mohammed of Ghori. Bundi was chosen to be the capital of the new Hadoti kingdom, and Kota was the land grant of the ruler's eldest son.

In 1624, Kota was made into a separate state at the instigation of the Mughal emperor Jehangir. Although Bundi's importance dwindled with the rise of Kota, during Mughal times, it maintained its independence until it was finally incorpored into the state of Rajasthan after Independence in 1947.

Festivals of Southern Rajasthan

Mewar Festival In late March/early April, Udaipur hosts its own colourful version of the Gangaur Festival. People dressed in traditional costumes sing and dance in a lively procession which goes through the town to Gangaur Ghat at Lake Pichola. Idols of Gauri and Shiva, who represent the perfect couple, are carried in the procession. There are also free cultural programmes.

June
Summer Festival This festival takes place in Mt Abu, which registers the coolest temperatures in the state at this scorching time of the year, and so is not a bad place to be. The festival takes place over three days (1–3 June each year) and includes classical and traditional folk-music programmes.

August–September
Kajli Teej The onset of the monsoon is especially celebrated in Bundi, where it is observed on the third day of the month of Bhadra. A palanquin bearing the goddess Teej is carried through the streets. The celebrations merge with the festival of Janmashtami, Krishna's birthday.

October–November
Bundi Utsav This cultural festival showcases the colourful traditions of the region with a procession, classical raga performances, magic and fireworks.
Ghans Bheru Festival – held on the day after Diwali in the little village of Bharodia, about 10km northeast of Bundi, this festival honours the Hindu god Ghans Bheru. Almost unknown to most tourists, this colourful festival attracts thousands of villagers from the Bundi district, who converge on the village to celebrate a prosperous harvest. To find out the exact dates, contact the tourist office in Bundi.

November–December
Chandrabhaga Fair This large cattle fair takes place on the last day of the Hindu month of Kartika on the banks of the Chandrabhaga River near Jhalrapatan. Attracting villagers from Rajasthan and neighbouring states, it includes livestock trading and colourful stalls. The religious element involves pilgrims at this time bathing in a sacred part of the river known as Chandrawati.

Orientation
It's relatively easy to find your way to the palace on foot through the bazaar – once you pass through the city gates, there are only two main roads through town and the palace is visible from many points. The bus stand is at the Kota (southeast) end of town and the train station is about 2km south of town, across National Hwy 12.

Information
Tourist Offices There's a small **tourist office** (☎ 443697; Lanka Gate Rd; open 10am-1.30pm & 2pm-5pm Mon-Sat) near Raniji-ki-Baori. It sells a good map of Bundi for Rs 2. Mukesh Mehta, at the Haveli Braj Bhushanjee hotel (conveniently situated near the palace), is also a terrific source of information.

Money At the time of research, no banks in Bundi changed money or issued cash advances on credit cards. The small shopfront moneychanger just south of the palace will change US dollars for a few rupees less than the market rate, which could be useful if you're stuck.

Post The main post office is found near the cinema and there are smaller post offices opposite Charbhuja Temple in the old city and opposite Raniji-ki-Baori.

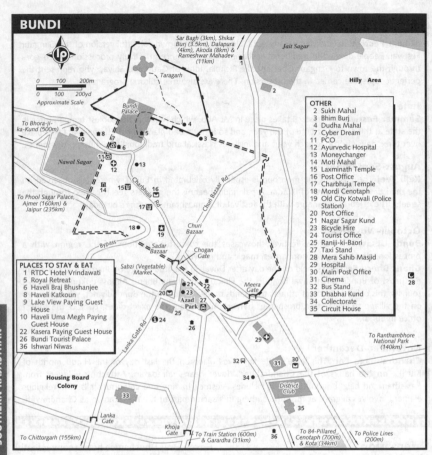

BUNDI

Sar Bagh (3km), Shikar Burj (3.5km), Dalapura (4km), Akoda (8km) & Rameshwar Mahadev (11km)

Jait Sagar

Hilly Area

Taragarh

Bundi Palace

To Bhora-ji-ka-Kund (500m)

Nawal Sagar

To Phool Sagar Palace, Ajmer (160km) & Jaipur (235km)

Charbhuja Rd

Churi Bazaar Rd

Churi Bazaar

Sadar Bazaar

Bypass

Chogan Gate

Sabzi (Vegetable) Market

Lanka Gate Rd

Azad Park

Meera Gate

To Ranthambhore National Park (140km)

Housing Board Colony

Lanka Gate

Khoja Gate

To Chittorgarh (155km)

To Train Station (600m) & Garardha (31km)

To 84-Pillared Cenotaph (700m) & Kota (34km)

To Police Lines (200m)

District Club

PLACES TO STAY & EAT
1 RTDC Hotel Vrindawati
5 Royal Retreat
6 Haveli Braj Bhushanjee
8 Haveli Katkoun
9 Lake View Paying Guest House
10 Haveli Uma Megh Paying Guest House
22 Kasera Paying Guest House
26 Bundi Tourist Palace
36 Ishwari Niwas

OTHER
2 Sukh Mahal
3 Bhim Burj
4 Dudha Mahal
7 Cyber Dream
11 PCO
12 Ayurvedic Hospital
13 Moneychanger
14 Moti Mahal
15 Laxminath Temple
16 Post Office
17 Charbhuja Temple
18 Mordi Cenotaph
19 Old City Kotwali (Police Station)
20 Post Office
21 Nagar Sagar Kund
23 Bicycle Hire
24 Tourist Office
25 Raniji-ki-Baori
27 Taxi Stand
28 Mera Sahib Masjid
29 Hospital
30 Main Post Office
31 Cinema
32 Bus Stand
33 Dhabhai Kund
34 Collectorate
35 Circuit House

0 100 200m
0 100 200yd
Approximate Scale

Email & Internet Access The Internet can be accessed at **Cyber Dream** (☎ 445280; open 5.30pm-9pm daily) or at the **public call office** (PCO; open 7am-10.30pm) across the road. Both charge Rs 60 per hour and are located near Haveli Braj Bhushanjee.

Medical Services If you're feeling a little off-colour, you may like to drop in at the **Ayurvedic Hospital** (☎ 443708; open 9am-1pm & 4pm-6pm Mon-Sat, 9am-1pm Sun), opposite the Haveli Braj Bhushanjee, which prescribes natural plant-based remedies. There are medicines for all sorts of ailments,

from upset tummies to arthritis, and many of them are free. The **government hospital** is in the south of town, near the bus stand.

Bundi Palace

The palace is reached from the north-western end of the bazaar, through a huge wooden gateway and up a steep cobbled ramp. Only one part of the outer perimeter of the palace, known as the **Chittra Shala** (admission free; open 8am-5pm daily), is officially open to the public. If you want to see the renowned **Bundi murals** (found in the Chattra Mahal and Badal Mahal within the palace complex), you could try contacting the secretary of the maharaja of Bundi at 'Mahal Palace', behind the Ayurvedic Hospital, or ask at your hotel. Flash photography is officially prohibited. The palace looks beautiful, from a distance and when it is illuminated at night.

Taragarh

The Taragarh *(Star Fort; admission free)* was built in 1354 and is a great place to ramble around at leisure. This rather ramshackle fort, with its overgrown vegetation and resident monkeys, is thankfully free of the souvenir shops and touts found at so many of Rajasthan's tourist attractions.

The views over the town and surrounding countryside from the top are magical, especially at sunset. Inside the ramparts are huge reservoirs carved out of solid rock, and the **Bhim Burj**, the largest of the battlements, on which there is mounted a famous cannon. It's just a shame that the national broadcaster, Doordarshan, decided to build an ugly concrete transmission tower right next to the fort.

Taragarh is reached by a steep road leading up the hillside to its enormous gateway. Take the path up behind the Chittra Shala, go east along the inside of the ramparts, then left up the steep stone ramp just before the **Dudha Mahal**, a small disused building 200m from the palace. It's also possible to take an autorickshaw to the top.

Baoris & Water Tanks

Bundi has around 60 beautiful *baoris* (step-wells), some right in the centre of town. The very impressive **Raniji-ki-Baori** is 46m deep and has some superb carving. One of the largest of its kind, it was built in 1699 by Rani Nathavatji. The **Nagar Sagar Kund**, nearby, is a pair of matching step-wells outside the Chogan Gate to the old city.

Visible from the fort is the square artificial lake of **Nawal Sagar**. In the centre is a temple to Varuna, the Aryan god of water. Also worth a look is the **Bhora-ji-ka-Kund**, which is 500m beyond Nawal Sagar, opposite one of Bundi's oldest Shiva temples, the Abhaynath Temple. This 16th-century tank attracts a variety of birdlife after a good monsoon, including kingfishers and hummingbirds. The **Dhabhai Kund**, south of the Raniji-ki-baori, is another imposing tank.

Other Attractions

Try to slot in time to visit the vibrant **sabzi (vegetable) market**, situated between the Raniji-ki-Baori and Nagar Sagar Kund. There are marvellous photo opportunities at this market, so don't forget your camera.

Bundi's other attractions are all out of town and are difficult to reach without a car,

The Step-Wells of Rajasthan

Building a step-well is lauded in the ancient Hindu scriptures as an act of great merit. Although the distinctions have become blurred, the term *kund* generally referred to a structural pond, while a *vapi* (also known as a *vav* or *wav*) indicated a water supply reached via a series of steps. Another generic term for step-wells is *baori*, which usually denotes a connection to a religious community.

In addition to their essential function as a water supply in arid areas, step-wells were frequently attached to temples and shrines, enabling devotees to bathe and purify themselves. Many formed part of a larger complex which included accommodation for weary travellers. The more elaborate *baoris* have intricate columns and pillars, steps built in artistic configurations, and rest rooms, corridors, galleries and platforms cut into the various levels. The spiritual and life-giving properties of step-wells, and their pivotal role in daily life, meant that many were adorned with carvings and statues of gods and goddesses, with Ganesh, Hanuman, Durga and Mahishasura the most commonly represented deities.

There are many impressive step-wells in Rajasthan, including the Raniji-ki-Baori in Bundi and the *baori* at Abhaneri (see the Jaipur chapter), although most towns and villages have at least one.

autorickshaw or bicycle. **Jait Sagar**, to the north, is a picturesque lake flanked by hills and strewn with pretty lotus flowers during the monsoon and winter months. The small **Sukh Mahal**, on the edge of Jait Sagar, is a cute pavilion where Rudyard Kipling once stayed. It's now the Irrigation Rest House. On the opposite side of the lake, the rather neglected **Sar Bagh** has a collection of royal cenotaphs, some with beautifully carved statues. **Shikar Burj**, nearby, is a small erstwhile royal hunting lodge and picnic spot. Many people hire a bike to visit these places (see Getting Around later for more details on bicycle hire).

If you're feeling energetic, you can ride on to visit six tiny **villages** in the pristine countryside – it's a good idea to take a picnic lunch. The first village you'll come to is Dalapura and the last is Akoda (around 8km from Bundi). About 3km beyond Akoda village is the Rameshwa Mahadev, a 16th-century Shiva temple.

To the west of Bundi is a modern palace known as the **Phool Sagar Palace**. There's a charming artificial tank in the gardens that's a good places for bird-watching, especially from November to February. The palace itself is currently closed.

South of town is the stunning **84-Pillared Cenotaph** (Chaurasi Khambon-ki-Chhatri), which is lit up at night. Set among well-maintained gardens, this architecturally impressive monument with its 84 pillars is certainly worth a look.

About 32km from Bundi at the village of Gararardha, there are ancient red-coloured **rock paintings**. Found on boulders flanking the river, these are believed to be over 15,000 years old. There's a curious depiction of a man riding a huge bird and some hunting scenes. There are also some stick figures of people holding hands – this is apparently how villagers crossed rivers long ago and is still practised today in some regions. To make the most of the trip out here, it's best to come with a local guide – contact Mukesh Mehta at the Haveli Braj Bhushanjee (see Places to Stay) for more information. A half-day return trip in a jeep costs around Rs 450. Carry water and wear strong shoes (so you can easily scramble across the rocks). This is likely to be of interest to prehistory fans only; the landscape itself is not worth the trip.

Places to Stay & Eat

You won't find any five-star hotels in Bundi. There are only budget and midrange accommodation options (which are also the best places to eat). There are some good budget places operating under Bundi's Paying Guest House Scheme, with prices ranging from Rs 100 to 450 per night – ask the tourist office for details.

The commission racket operates here in Bundi, so don't feel pressured into staying at the place of your taxi or autorickshaw driver's choice.

Haveli Katkoun (☎ 444311; e raghunandansingh@yahoo.com; doubles Rs 200-250), just outside the town's west gate, has comfortable, spotless rooms (with bucket hot water) off a pleasant garden. Good breakfasts and thalis (from Rs 80) are available, although the service is slow.

Lake View Paying Guest House (☎ 442326; e lakeviewbundi@yahoo.com; singles/doubles with shared bathroom from Rs 80/125, with private bathroom from Rs 150/200) is set in the modest 200-year-old Meghwahanji Haveli. Some rooms have lake views; room No 1 is particularly good. Home-cooked meals are available.

Haveli Uma Megh Paying Guest House (☎ 442191; doubles with shared bathroom from Rs 200, with private bathroom from Rs 250), almost next door, has a wide range of rooms; some of the cheaper ones also have a view. There's a nice garden restaurant by the water's edge.

Kasera Paying Guest House (☎ 444679, fax 443126; e kaserapayingguesthouse@usa.net; doubles with shared bathroom Rs 100-150, with private bathroom from Rs 250), near Chogan Gate in the main bazaar, is a great choice. Set in a delightful old haveli (mansion), it has a good rooftop restaurant with an extensive menu – excellent curries cost Rs 25 to 40 and desserts are around Rs 50.

Haveli Braj Bhushanjee (☎ 442322, fax 442142; w www.kiplingsbundi.com; doubles with private bathroom Rs 350-1400), just below the palace, is a funky, 150-year-old haveli run by the helpful Braj Bhushanjee family (descendants of the former prime ministers of Bundi). It's a cosy place with splendid views from the rooftop terrace, especially at night when the palace is illuminated. The cheaper rooms have bucket hot water; wholesome, but expensive, set veg meals are Rs 250. If you arrive after hours when the shop is closed, just ring the doorbell. Free pick-ups from the bus stand and train station are available (advance notice appreciated), as well as two-hour tours of Bundi by autorickshaw (Rs 250 for two people).

Ishwari Niwas (☎ 442411, fax 445014; e in_heritage@indiatimes.com; 1 Civil Lines; singles/doubles with private bathroom from Rs 200/250, suites Rs 500/600) is a family-run hotel that has royal associations. This graceful old colonial building has high ceilings and tidy, well-kept rooms around a pleasant courtyard. The rooms are excellent value, although the hotel's a long way from the old city, past the bus stand. Sightseeing excursions can be arranged.

Royal Retreat (☎ 444426, fax 443278; e royalretreat@123india.com; singles/doubles with private bathroom from Rs 250/550), ideally situated in the palace compound, is set around a quiet open-air courtyard. The vegetarian restaurant (open also to non-guests) is reasonably priced, with Indian dishes ranging from Rs 25 to 50. You can even get beer here (Rs 80 per bottle). There's an interesting collection of handicrafts for sale in its shop.

Bundi Tourist Palace (☎ 442650; singles/doubles with shared bathroom Rs 75/125), opposite Azad Park, is nothing fancy, but ideal if you're strapped for cash. There are six tiny rooms here; hot water is by the bucket.

RTDC Hotel Vrindawati (☎ 442473; singles/doubles with private bathroom Rs 100/200) is a tranquil place opposite Jait Sagar. It's a bit out of the way, but is good value, with basic rooms overlooking the lake. There's a small dining hall where curries cost around Rs 20.

Getting There & Away

Bus There are express buses heading for multiple destinations in Rajasthan including the following:

destination	fare (Rs)	duration (hrs)
Ajmer	71	4½
Bijolia	22	1¼
Bikaner	170	12
Chittorgarh	68	4
Jaipur	83	5
Jodhpur	150	9
Keshraipatan	16	1¼
Kota	15	1
Menal	30	2
Sawai Madhopur	44	4½
Udaipur	113	8

Some buses also go to places in neighbouring Madhya Pradesh state, such as Indore (Rs 147, nine hours) and Shivpuri (Rs 107, eight hours).

Train The train station is located about 2km south of the old city. There are rail connections between Bundi and Agra, Chittorgarh and Kota. From Kota, you can catch a connecting train to various destinations.

There's a slow overnight train to Agra, the *Agra Fort Passenger*. It leaves Chittorgarh daily at 3pm, stops in Bundi at 5.25pm and arrives in Kota at 7.30pm. It leaves Kota at 9pm arriving in Agra at 6am. The same train leaves Agra at 7.30pm and arrives in Bundi at 7.50am, then continues on to Chittorgarh, arriving at noon. From Bundi, it costs Rs 25 to Chittorgarh, Rs 9 to Kota and Rs 49/103 to Agra for a seat/sleeper.

Getting Around

Taxis can be hired from the stand near the Raniji-ki-Baori. Autorickshaw drivers will quote around Rs 15 to take you from the bus stand to Bundi Palace. For local sightseeing, expect to pay around Rs 50 per hour for an autorickshaw.

Bicycles are an ideal way to get around this area. They can be rented fairly cheaply near the bus stand. The charge is usually around Rs 2/10 per hour/day.

KOTA

☎ 0744 • postcode 324001 • pop 695,899

Kota is one of Rajasthan's less inspiring cities and today serves largely as an army headquarters. It is also Rajasthan's prime industrial centre (mainly producing chemicals), and is powered by the hydroelectric plants on the Chambal River – the only permanent river in Rajasthan – and a nearby nuclear plant that made headlines in 1992 when it was revealed that levels of radioactivity in the area were way above 'safe' levels. Kota also has one of Asia's largest fertiliser plants.

Growing industrialisation has led to increasing levels of pollution. Black smoke belches into the air from two huge chimneys across the river. Fortunately, there are a few leafy parks scattered throughout the town and an artificial lake with an enchanting palace on a little island in the middle.

Kota is well known for its saris, which are woven at the nearby village of Kaithoon.

Known as Kota *doria* saris, they are made of cotton or silk in an assortment of colours, many with delicate golden thread designs. The miniature paintings of Kota are also noteworthy, particularly the hunting scenes. These present a vivid and detailed portrayal of hunting expeditions in the once thickly wooded forests in and around Kota.

History

Building of the city began in 1264 following the Hadoti Chauhan defeat of Koteya, a Bhil chieftain who gave the city his name. Koteya was beheaded and on that very spot the foundation stone of the fort was laid. Kota didn't reach its present size until well into the 17th century, when Rao Madho Singh, a son of the ruler of Bundi, was made ruler of Kota by the Mughal emperor Jehangir. Kota remained a separate state until it was integrated into Rajasthan after Independence. Subsequent rulers have all added to the fort and palaces, and each also

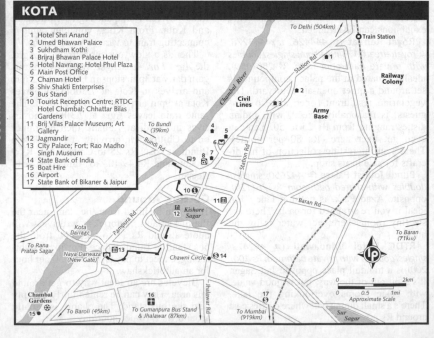

KOTA

1 Hotel Shri Anand
2 Umed Bhawan Palace
3 Sukhdham Kothi
4 Brijraj Bhawan Palace Hotel
5 Hotel Navrang; Hotel Phul Plaza
6 Main Post Office
7 Chaman Hotel
8 Shiv Shakti Enterprises
9 Bus Stand
10 Tourist Reception Centre; RTDC Hotel Chambal; Chhattar Bilas Gardens
11 Brij Vilas Palace Museum; Art Gallery
12 Jagmandir
13 City Palace; Fort; Rao Madho Singh Museum
14 State Bank of India
15 Boat Hire
16 Airport
17 State Bank of Bikaner & Jaipur

To Delhi (504km)
Train Station
Station Rd
Railway Colony
Chambal River
Civil Lines
Army Base
To Bundi (39km)
Bundi Rd
Station Rd
Baran Rd
To Baran (71km)
Pampura Rd
Kota Barrage
Kishore Sagar
To Rana Pratap Sagar
Naya Darwaza (New Gate)
Chawni Circle
Jhalawar Rd
Sur Sagar
Chambal Gardens
To Baroli (45km)
To Gumanpura Bus Stand & Jhalawar (87km)
To Mumbai (919km)

0   1   2km
0   0.5   1mi
Approximate Scale

SOUTHERN RAJASTHAN

contributed to making Kota a flourishing centre of art and culture.

Orientation

Kota is strung out along the east bank of the Chambal River. The train station is well to the north; the RTDC Hotel Chambal, a number of other hotels and the bus stand are in the middle; and Chambal Gardens, the fort and the Kota Barrage are to the south.

Information

The **Tourist Reception Centre** (☎ 327695; open 10am-5pm Mon-Sat) is in the grounds of the RTDC Hotel Chambal.

The **State Bank of Bikaner & Jaipur** (Industrial Estate), found opposite the Rajasthan Patrika newspaper office, changes travellers cheques and currency. The **State Bank of India** (Chawni Circle) only changes American Express travellers cheques, as well as major currencies.

The **main post office** (open 10.30am-1.30pm & 2pm-6pm Mon-Sat) is situated in the middle of town.

You can access the Internet at **Shiv Shakti Enterprises** (☎ 333205; Station Rd; open 9am-10pm daily) for Rs 20 per hour.

City Palace & Fort

Standing beside the Kota Barrage and overlooking the Chambal River, the City Palace and Fort is one of the largest such complexes in Rajasthan. The palace itself was the former residence of the Kota rulers and used to be the centre of power. The treasury, courts, arsenal, soldiers and various state offices were all located here. Some of its buildings are now occupied by schools. Entry is from the south side through the **Naya Darwaza** (New Gate).

Rao Madho Singh Museum (foreigner/citizen Rs 50/10, still camera/video Rs 50/75; open 10am-4.30pm Sat-Thur), in the City Palace, is impressive. It's on the right-hand side of the complex's huge central courtyard and is entered through a gateway topped by rampant elephants. Inside, there are displays of weapons, old costumes and some of the best-preserved murals in Raja-sthan. There's also a collection of animal trophies and

portraits of past rulers. The pieces are well displayed and it's an enjoyable place to take in the regional history. Guides are found near the ticket office.

After visiting the museum, wander around the rest of the complex just to appreciate how magnificent it must have been in its heyday. Unfortunately, a lot of it is falling into disrepair and the gardens are no more, but there are some excellent views over the old city, the river and the monstrous industrial complex across the river. Pollution is believed to be contributing to the deterioration of the fort. Some of the exterior murals are fading, which is a great pity. There's a small restaurant in the courtyard.

Jagmandir

Between the City Palace and the RTDC Hotel Chambal is the picturesque artificial tank of Kishore Sagar, constructed in 1346. Right in the middle of the tank, on a small island, is the beguiling little palace of Jagmandir. Built in 1740 by one of the maharanis of Kota, it's best seen early in the morning but is exquisite at any time of day. It's not currently open to the public.

Brij Vilas Palace Museum

This small government museum (admission Rs 3, Mon free; open 10am-4.30pm Sat-Thur), near the Kishore Sagar, is not as good as the museum at the City Palace. It has a collection of stone idols and other such fragments, mainly from the archaeological sites at Baroli and Jhalawar. There are also some weapons, paintings and old manuscripts. Photography is not allowed. Next door is a small modern **art gallery** (admission free; open 10am-5pm Mon-Sat) exhibiting works by local artists.

Gardens

There are several well-maintained, peaceful gardens in Kota which provide a splash of greenery to this rather drab industrial town. The **Chambal gardens** (admission Rs 2) are on the banks of the Chambal River, south of the fort. They're a popular place for picnics.

[Continued on page 226]

TRADITIONAL DRESS

Although it is not unusual to see Rajasthani women in saris, the traditional dress consists of a full, often brightly coloured, ankle-length skirt known as a *ghaghara* or *lehanga*, which is worn with a short blouse called a *choli* or *kanchali*. A looser blouse, a *kurti* or *angarkhi*, is worn over the *choli*. As well, an *odhni* (head scarf) of a bold, vibrant fabric, either plain or patterned and often with a fancy border in silver thread, is worn. Sometimes *odhnis* are also adorned with mirrorwork, beads and shells. If the woman is a widow, the *odhni* is not brightly coloured. The leather shoes worn by men and women are called *jootis* or *mojdis*. Women's *jootis* have no heel. Men's *jootis* curl up at the toes.

For special occasions such as weddings and festivals, women decorate their palms, feet and fingers with intricate henna designs known as *mehendi*. The *lehanga*, traditionally worn by a bride, is generally a Sanganeri or Jaipuri printed fabric, and the *odhni* is always red.

Everyday wear for men consists of a long shirt with either a short upright collar or no collar, which is known as a *kurta*. It is worn over a *dhoti*, which is simply a long piece of material wrapped around and drawn up between the legs. Today Rajasthani men have adopted the *jodhpuri*, a buttoned coat which is the official judicial dress of Rajasthan's courts. The turban is worn by men of most classes. It can be either plain or vividly coloured, and is tied in various ways according to the class of the wearer. Men also take pride in their moustaches. Rajputs are renowned for their long, bushy moustaches, which are supposed to suggest chivalry. As with turbans, the way the moustache is worn varies from region to region.

Bridegrooms traditionally carry a sword known as a *dalwar*.

Jewellery

Rajasthani women, most notably those in villages, bedeck themselves with heavy and ornate jewellery, generally of silver, the lavishness of which symbolises the relative affluence of their husbands. Even the poorest families ensure that their daughters are married appropriately adorned in silver ornaments, which form part of their dowries.

The ornament worn by women on their forehead is known as a *bor*, *tikka* or *rakhadi*. Ear ornaments have various names, including *jhela*, *bhujali*, or *bali*. Earrings are not just worn for decorative purposes, the manipulation of an earring is believed to restore equilibrium to internal organs. Nose pins and rings are known as *nathdis*, *laonghs* and *bhanvatiyas*, and are sometimes connected to earrings by silver chains.

Necklaces are sometimes known as *timania* and *galsadi*. They may be just a simple thread upon which a small token is hung, a beautiful and elaborate locket, or a heavy and chunky neckpiece of silver.

Inset: A Rajasthani woman in her customary jewellery (Photograph by Dallas Stribley)

DALLAS STRIBLEY

ANDERS BLOMQVIST

KAREN TRIST

Adornment is for both the everyday and special occasions: *chudas* (bangles), encasing the whole arm, are in plastic for the poor and ivory for the rich; nose rings can be connected to earrings by silver chains; and *mehendi* (henna patterning) is applied to palms, fingers and feet for festivals and weddings

ANTONY V GIBLIN

ANTONY V GIBLIN

JOHN BORTHWICK

Turbans come in many styles, colours and methods of tying, and are traditional for all Rajasthani men, from cameleers to distinguished Rajputs. Accessories are a matter of personal taste and style!

Bangles, which cover the entire arm, increasing in diameter from the wrist to just below the shoulder, are called *chudas*. Today, poorer women may wear *chudas* of plastic, while their richer sisters adorn their arms with ivory ones. A *chuda* may also consist of a single ornament, often of silver, which covers the entire upper arm.

Toe rings, known as *bichiyas*, are only worn by married women. The silver anklets worn by women are called *payal*. Silver ornaments worn on the back of the hand, and connected to four rings, one on each finger, are known as *hathphool*, from *phool*, meaning 'flower', and *hath*, for 'hand' – literally, 'hand flower'.

Rajasthani Turbans

The turbans of Rajasthan are perhaps the most colourful and impressive in the whole of India. Known as a *safa*, *paag* or *pagri*, the turban is a prominent and important part of a Rajput man's dress. It is said that turbans were first worn to protect the head from evil spirits. They were also worn in battle to protect the head against weapons such as swords and axes; a saffron-coloured turban signified chivalry, and was thus often worn by warriors. The exchange of turbans symbolises a bond of friendship and honour. There are a number of instances of wives burning themselves to death along with their husband's turban, the husband having fallen on a battlefield far from home. A male heir will don his deceased father's turban, a symbol of his assumption of duties as the head of the household. To knock off, kick or step over another man's turban is considered a big insult.

An average turban is about 9m long, but it can be much longer – a *pagri* is around 24.5m long! It is possible to identify which part of Rajasthan a man comes from and his caste according to the way his turban is tied, and there are around 1000 different turban-tying styles in Rajasthan. *Safa*-style turbans are favoured by Rajputs, while businessmen prefer the *pagri* style. Today, not only is it traditional to wear a turban, but it also serves as protection from the harsh desert sun.

The versatile turban has a wide variety of other practical uses. It can be used as a pillow or sheet, a rope to draw water from a well, a filter to remove sand from the water, or as protective headgear in case the wearer falls over or is hit on the head!

Today many young men, particularly in cities such as Jaipur and Jodhpur, reject the turban as a symbol of rural parochialism, although it is always worn by the groom at a marriage celebration.

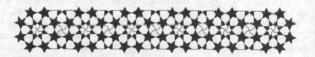

[Continued from page 223]

The centrepiece is a murky pond stocked with crocodiles, which you can walk over on a wobbly suspension bridge. Once common all along the river, by the middle of the 20th century crocodiles had been virtually exterminated by hunting. There are also some rare gharials (thin-snouted, fish-eating crocodiles). Beyond the crocodiles, on the riverfront, you can hire a **motor boat** (☎ 502832; open daily 10.30am-6pm) for Rs 400 per hour for up to six people.

Just beside the RTDC Hotel Chambal are the **Chhattar Bilas Gardens**, a curious collection of somewhat neglected, but still impressive, royal cenotaphs.

Places to Stay & Eat

As Kota is more a commercial centre than a tourist destination, it's hotels are generally rather bleak and expensive, although there are some pleasant top-end options. Most travellers prefer to base themselves in the more atmospheric town of Bundi. Mosquitoes can be a problem at some hotels in Kota, so come with a mossie net or repellent.

The best places to eat are in the hotels. For a cheaper feed, omelette stalls and other small eateries set up in the early evening on the footpath outside the main post office. If you do eat here, select food that has been freshly cooked, not reheated.

Hotel Shri Anand (☎ 441157, fax 441970; singles with shared bathroom Rs 80, singles/doubles with private bathroom Rs 125/175, deluxe Rs 175/250), 100m down the street opposite the train station, is good if you're catching an early train. The rooms (all with Indian-style toilet) are tiny, noisy and could be cleaner – ask them to change the sheets.

Chaman Hotel (☎ 320477; Station Rd; singles/doubles with private bathroom from Rs 100/120) is closer to the bus stand. It's one of the cheapest hotels in town, but be prepared for grubby sheets and rooms the size of cupboards. Single female travellers are advised to give this place a miss.

Hotel Phul Plaza (☎ 329350, fax 322614; singles/doubles with private bathroom & air-cooling Rs 275/350, with air-con Rs 500/600,

suites Rs 900/1100), next to Hotel Navrang, is a functional hotel for business travellers with ordinary rooms and overpriced suites.

Hotel Navrang (☎ 323294, fax 450044; singles/doubles with private bathroom & air-cooling Rs 400/500, with air-con Rs 600/1000), near the main post office, is one of Kota's best mid-range choices. Don't be deceived by the front of the hotel, which looks rather run-down. The rooms are arranged around an inner courtyard. Some have more character than others, so try to have a look at a few first. There's a reasonably priced veg restaurant serving Indian, continental and Chinese cuisine (dishes around Rs 40).

RTDC Hotel Chambal (☎ 326527; singles/doubles with private bathroom & air-cooling Rs 400/500, with air-con Rs 600/700) at Nayapura, near Kishore Sagar, has bland rooms. There's a small, grim restaurant; a veg thali is Rs 50 and chicken curry is Rs 57.

Brijraj Bhawan Palace Hotel (☎ 328701, fax 450057; e brijraja@datainfosys.net; Civil Lines; singles/doubles Rs 1380/1900, suites Rs 1950/2350) is an atmospheric palace that was once the British residency. Situated on an elevated site overlooking the Chambal River, this pleasant hotel has been named after the current maharao of Kota, Brijraj Singh, who converted part of this property into a hotel in 1964. Today the maharao and his family live in one portion of the palace. There are well-maintained gardens, a tennis court and an elegantly furnished lounge filled with pictures of former rulers and various dignitaries. There's an intimate dining room (for guests only) that, unlike most palaces, is homey rather than grand. Set breakfast/lunch/dinner is Rs 200/360/380.

Umed Bhawan Palace (☎ 325262, fax 451110; Station Rd; singles/doubles standard US$42/60, luxury US$42/70, suites US$82) is more grandiose than the Brijraj Bhawan Palace; while it might look OK, it lacks of attention to detail. Surrounded by sprawling gardens, this gracious palace has a restaurant, bar and billiard room. The single rate is the same for all the rooms, and some are excellent value for the price.

Situated near Umed Bhawan, **Sukhdham Kothi** (☎ 320081, fax 327781; singles/doubles

Rs 1050/1295; ℮ *sukhdham@datainfosys.net)* is over 100 years old and was once the home of the British Residents' surgeon. It's set in lovely gardens and is a friendly, family-run place. The set breakfast/lunch/dinner costs Rs 140/300/300. The hotel can arrange jeep safaris to places of interest around Kota and boat trips down the river.

Getting There & Away

Air There used to be flights to and from Kota, but these were discontinued a few years back. Flights may be rescheduled in the future, so ask a travel agent or at any airport.

Bus There are express-bus connections to major cities in Rajasthan and to Delhi.

destination	fare (Rs)	duration (hrs)
Ajmer	87	6
Alwar	160	9
Bikaner	190	12
Chittorgarh	98	6
Delhi	210	11
Jaipur	98	6
Jodhpur	163	10
Mt Abu	192	12
Udaipur	127	8

For Jaisalmer, you should change buses at Ajmer. Buses leave for Bundi (Rs 15, 45 minutes) and Jhalawar (Rs 35, two hours) every half-hour. To get to Madhya Pradesh, several buses a day go to such places as Gwalior, Ujjain, Bhopal and Indore.

Train Kota is on the main broad-gauge Mumbai to Delhi line via Sawai Madhopur, the gateway to the Ranthambhore National Park, so there are plenty of trains going to Sawai Madhopur (Rs 34/183 in 2nd/3-tier air-con, 109km, 1½ hrs), Jaipur (Rs 62/279, 4½ hours) and Delhi (Rs 104/468, 10 hours). There's a passenger train linking Kota with Chittorgarh via Bundi; the daily train departs at 7.05am, arriving in Bundi at 8am (Rs 10) and Chittorgarh at 11.20am (Rs 30).

Getting Around

Minibuses link the train station and bus stand (Rs 2). An autorickshaw should cost Rs 15 for this journey, although naturally you'll be asked for more. A cheaper alternative to travelling by autorickshaw is to take a cycle-rickshaw.

AROUND KOTA
Wildlife Sanctuaries

The 250-sq-km **Darrah Wildlife Sanctuary** *(foreigner/citizen Rs 100/20; open 10am-5pm daily)* is located about 50km from Kota. Here there are spotted deer, wild boars, bears, sambars, leopards, panthers and antelopes. The sanctuary is sometimes closed during the monsoon (usually from early July to mid-September). You need to get permission to visit from the local forest ranger, or contact the **District Forest Office** (☎ 0744-321263) in Kota. If that all fails, ask at the Kota **Tourist Reception Centre** (☎ 0744-327695).

Also accessible from Kota is the **National Chambal Wildlife Sanctuary**, which extends into neighbouring Madhya Pradesh. This 549-sq-km reserve is best known for its gharials which inhabit the Chambal River; blackbucks, chinkaras, wolves and the rarely seen caracals can also be found here.

About 45km east of Kota, flanking the main canal of the Chambal and Parvan Rivers, are the **Sorsan grasslands**. Covering 35 sq km, these grasslands are rich with insects during the monsoon and attract a good variety of resident and migratory birds, including the great Indian bustard – a reluctant flier which is more commonly seen stalking through the grasslands on its sturdy legs. Other birds of Sorsan include mynahs, orioles, quails, partridges, bulbuls, chats, drongos, shrikes, robins and weavers. Flocks of migrants, such as warblers, fly-catchers, larks, starlings and rosy pastors, winter at Sorsan between October and March. Indian rollers can be seen in early winter. The nearby canal and lakes attract waterfowl, such as bar-headed and greylag geese, common pochards, common teal and pintails.

You can hire a jeep to reach these parks from Kota for Rs 3.50 per kilometre with a minimum of 250km – ask about them at the Tourist Reception Centre for details.

Baroli

One of Rajasthan's oldest temple complexes is at Baroli, 45km southwest of Kota on the way to Rana Pratap Sagar. Set in a peaceful area, many of these 9th-century temples were vandalised by Muslim armies but much remains. The main temple is the **Ghateshvara Temple**, which features some impressive columns. Although it is one of the best preserved temples here, some of its figures have been damaged. Many of the sculptures from the temples are displayed in the Brij Vilas Palace Museum in Kota.

There are hourly buses from Kota to Baroli (Rs 20, 2 hrs). These leave from the Gumanpura bus stand, near the petrol pump.

Bhainsrodgarh

Not far from Baroli is the picturesque Bhainsrodgarh. This 14th-century fort was never besieged by an enemy force. Perched on a ridge overlooking the Chambal River, it is still occupied by descendants of a feudal family. Although you can't go inside, the views are superb. You must get permission to visit the fort – inquire at the **Tourist Reception Centre** (☎ 0744-327695) in Kota.

Get to Bhainsrodgarh by autorickshaw from Baroli (about Rs 100 return).

JHALAWAR

☎ 07432 • postcode 326001 • pop 48,049

Situated 87km south of Kota, at the centre of an opium-producing region, Jhalawar was the capital of a small princely state created in 1838 by Zalim Singh, the charismatic regent of Kota. Singh signed a treaty with the British on behalf of the young Kota prince, and in return he received the kingdom of Jhalawar to rule in his own right. This town is well and truly off the main tourist circuit, and only attracts a few travellers. During winter, many of the fields are carpeted with picturesque pink and white poppies.

Information

The **tourist office** (☎ 30081; open 10am-5pm Mon-Sat) is located at the RTDC Hotel Chandrawati (see Places to Stay) it is of limited help. The **main post office** (open 10am-1pm & 2pm-5pm Mon-Sat) is near the bus stand.

Carry enough rupees with you as, at the time of writing, there are no banks in Jhalawar that will change money.

Things to See & Do

In the centre of town is the **Jhalawar Fort** (admission free; open 10am-4.30pm Mon-Sat), built by Maharaja Madan Singh in 1838. Today it houses the government offices and is run-down. There's also the small **government museum** (admission Rs 3; open 10am-4.30pm Sat-Thur), which has a collection of 8th-century sculptures, gold coins, weapons and old paintings. The **Bhawan Natyashala**, inside the fort, is a theatre that was built in the 1920s and designed to allow horses and carriages into the lower floors.

Places to Stay & Eat

Attracting just a smattering of tourists, Jhalawar has very limited accommodation. The best places to eat are in the hotels.

Purvaj Hotel (☎ 31355; doubles with private bathroom Rs 200, doubles with geyser Rs 300), at Mangalpura near the clock tower, is the most homey place to stay. This simple 200-year-old haveli has basic but cheap rooms and more character than the other hotels in Jhalawar. Meals are available.

Hotel Dwarika (☎ 32626, fax 30588; Hospital Rd; singles/doubles Rs 200/250, deluxe Rs 250/300) has reasonably good rooms with private bathroom (bucket hot water) or deluxe rooms with constant hot water. There's a vegetarian restaurant.

The **RTDC Hotel Chandrawati** (Jhalrapatan Rd) was closed at the time of research, but was due to reopen in March 2002.

Getting There & Away

There are frequent buses going from Kota to Jhalawar (Rs 30, 2½ hrs).

Getting Around

If you plan to visit the historic sites out of town, it's best to hire a jeep because many of the roads are in a state of bumpy disrepair. Expect to pay Rs 3.50 per kilometre (minimum 250km). The tourist office can arrange jeep hire for you, otherwise, inquire at your hotel.

To travel anywhere in town by autorickshaw should cost Rs 15.

Bicycle is a good way of making your way around. Bicycles are available for hire from near the Purvaj Hotel for Rs 3 per hour.

AROUND JHALAWAR
Jhalrapatan

Seven kilometres south of Jhalawar on the Kota road is Jhalrapatan (City of Temple Bells). This walled town once had more than 100 temples, although far fewer remain. The best known is the huge 10th-century **Surya Temple**, which contains magnificent sculptures and one of the best-preserved idols of Surya (the sun god) in India. There's also the 12th-century **Shantinath Jain temple**, a colourful and well-maintained temple with intricately carved statues and two huge stone elephants, and **Sheetaleshvara Temple**, a fine example of Gupta architecture. About 3km outside Jhalrapatan, the 7th-century **Chandrabhaga Temple** is set in gardens on the banks of the Chandrabhaga River. There's also a small *baori* here.

There are regular daily buses from Jhalawar to Jhalrapatan (Rs 4, 15 mins). An autorickshaw from Jhalawar will cost around Rs 70 return.

Gagron Fort

While you're in this area, you should also look at the impressive Gagron Fort *(admission free; open sunrise-sunset daily)*, 10km from Jhalawar. Very few tourists even suspect its existence, and if you like to explore in peace and quiet this place is perfect. From the ramparts there are good views of the surrounding countryside. The 12th-century fort is situated at the confluence of two rivers. Though not as famous as the forts at Chittorgarh, Jodhpur and Jaisalmer, the huge fort occupies a prominent place in the annals of Rajput chivalry and has been fought over for centuries.

Near the fort walls there's a small village and the **shrine** of the Sufi saint Mittheshah.

Other Attractions

The Jhalawar region's other attractions are further out of town and difficult to reach without transport (a jeep is best as the roads are rough). About 54km (1½ hours) from Jhalawar at **Dalhanpur** are some temple ruins believed to be hundreds of years old. Located near the Chhapi River, this small collection of ruins includes some carved pillars with erotic figures. Take care not to damage the fragments of pillars and statues that have fallen over. About 11km from Dalhanpur, at **Kakuni**, are the ruins of an old township. There's also a small temple with a huge idol of Ganesh. Beyond Kakuni is the large **Fort of Manohar Thana**, once of great strategic importance. There are several small temples within its walls and a reafforestation program has filled the compound with vegetation and birdlife.

There are ancient **Buddhist caves and stupas** atop a desolate hill near the town of Kolvi, about 90km from Jhalawar. It's only a short climb to the top, where you'll find several enormous figures of Buddha. A narrow path winds past large stupas and numerous bat-filled meditation chambers. These remarkable caves are believed to date back to the 5th century and some contain weathered sculptures of Buddha – sadly, they are neglected and deteriorating.

BUNDI TO CHITTORGARH

Travelling by car, from Bundi to Chittorgarh, there are a few attractions worth visiting on the way. **Bijolia**, a large town 16km from Menal, was once a group of 100 temples. Most of these were destroyed by Mughal invaders and today only three are left standing.

Menal, 48km from Bundi, is a complex of crumbling Shiva temples built in the Gupta period. After a good monsoon, there's an impressive waterfall in this area that is also a big attraction.

To the west of Menal, **Mandalgarh** is the third fort of Mewar built by Rana Kumbha – the others are the great fort of Chittorgarh and the fort at Kumbhalgarh. There's a good view from the top.

Bassi

The town of Bassi, about 25km northeast of Chittorgarh and well off the tourist trail, is

SOUTHERN RAJASTHAN

Kavads

The artisans of Bassi are famous for their brightly painted wooden carvings, especially the amazing folding boxes known as *kavads*. These portable temples are made of a number of hinged doors that open outwards, each one covered in colourful pictures that illustrate the great Indian epics. They were the tools of professional bards, known as Kavadia Bhatts, who traditionally travelled from village to village chanting the tales of the Mahabharata, a skill that was handed down through the generations. As the stories unfolded, so did the boxes. At the climax of the tale, the last door opened to reveal the supreme deities – usually Rama, Lakshman and Sita, or Krishna. Somewhere near the bottom of the kavad there was always a slot where the audience could show their appreciation by depositing coins.

famous for its wood carvers. There's also the **Bassi Wildlife Sanctuary** to explore, with its panthers, antelope, wild boar and many birds – the hotels can arrange jeep safaris.

Seven kilometres from Bassi, on the Chittorgarh road, is **Nagri**, one of the oldest towns in Rajasthan. Hindu and Buddhist remains from the Mauryan to Gupta periods have been found here. Many old copper coins and sculptures discovered here are now at museums in Chittorgarh and Udaipur.

Places to Stay & Eat There are a couple of top-end accommodation options around Bassi, that are a far better bet than the dingy rooms on offer in Chittorgarh. **Bassi Fort Palace** (☎ 01472-25321, fax 40811; e bassifort palace@yahoo.com; singles/doubles Rs 1000/ 1250, deluxe tents Rs 1000) is situated in the town's 450-year-old fort, which was never defeated. There's a tree on the grounds that's said to grant wishes. It's a pleasant, peaceful spot with tastefully decorated rooms that are off a garden, or you can stay in a tented camp beside a lake in the wildlife sanctuary. The set breakfast/lunch/dinner here costs Rs 130/250/300.

Castle Bijaipur (singles/doubles Rs 1350/ 1435, Rs suites 1810/1890), 15km from Bassi, is a rustic 16th-century palace in the village of Bijaipur. It's an ideal place to kick back with a good book, do yoga, meditate, walk or do absolutely nothing! Rooms in this peaceful castle are traditionally decorated. There's a pleasant garden courtyard and an airy restaurant serving Rajasthani food – set lunch/dinner is Rs 230/345. The friendly owners can arrange jeep safaris to places of interest around Bijaipur, such as the nearby Bhil tribal village, or a visit to their cool jungle property, Thanderiberi. Bookings for the castle should be made through **Hotel Pratap Palace** (☎ 01472-40099, fax 41042) in Chittorgarh.

Getting There & Away Frequent buses travel daily from Chittorgarh to Bassi (Rs 10, 30 mins), passing through Nagri on the way. A jeep taxi to Bassi will cost around Rs 300. There are also buses from Chittor to Bijaipur (Rs 13, 1 hour).

CHITTORGARH
☎ 01472 • postcode 312001 • pop 96,028
The massive hilltop fort of Chittorgarh (Chittor) is one of the most historically significant in Rajasthan and epitomises the whole romantic, doomed ideal of Rajput chivalry. Three times in its long history, Chittor was sacked by a stronger enemy and, on each occasion, the end came in textbook Rajput fashion: *jauhar* was declared in the face of impossible odds. The men donned the saffron robes of martyrdom and rode out from the fort to certain death, while the women immolated themselves on a huge funeral pyre. Honour was always more important than death and Chittor still holds a special place in the hearts of many Rajputs.

The only real reason to come to Chittor is to see the fort – the town itself is quite crowded and really not of much interest. An increasing number of industries are based in and around Chittorgarh, some of which can be seen from the fort. Hopefully the pollution that usually comes with industrial growth will not affect the fort.

Despite the rugged fort's impressive location and colourful history, Chittor is well and truly off the main tourist circuit and sees surprisingly few visitors. If you're pressed for time, it's possible to squeeze in a visit to Chittor on a day trip from Udaipur. It's well worth the detour.

History

Chittor's first defeat occurred in 1303 when Ala-ud-din Khilji, the Pathan king of Delhi, besieged the fort in order to capture the beautiful Padmini (see the boxed text 'Death Before Dishonour').

In 1535 Bahadur Shah, the sultan of Gujarat, besieged the fort. Once again, the medieval dictates of chivalry determined the outcome and this time the carnage was immense. It is said that 13,000 Rajput women and 32,000 Rajput warriors died following the declaration of *jauhar*.

The final sack of Chittor came 33 years later, in 1568, when the Mughal emperor Akbar took the town. The fort was defended heroically against overwhelming odds. The women performed *jauhar*, the fort gates were flung open and 8000 orange-robed warriors rode out to their deaths. On this occasion, Maharana Udai Singh II fled Chittor for Udaipur, where he re-established his capital. In 1616, Jehangir returned Chittor to the Rajputs, however, there was no resettlement.

Orientation

The fort stands on a 280-hectare site on top of a 180m-high hill, which rises abruptly from the surrounding plain. Until 1568 the town of Chittor was also on the hilltop, within the fort walls, but today's modern town, known as Lower Town, sprawls to the west of the hill. A river separates it from the bus stand, railway line and the rest of the town.

Information

The **Tourist Reception Centre** (☎ 41089; open 10am-1.30pm & 2pm-5pm Mon-Sat) is near the train station.

Money can be changed at the **State Bank of Bikaner & Jaipur**, a short distance north

of the **main post office** (open 10am-1pm & 2pm-6pm Mon-Sat), which is located less than a kilometre south of the bus stand.

You can check your email at **Sanwariya Computers** (☎ 48552; open 8am-10.30pm daily), next to Hotel Mcera.

Fort

According to legend, Bhim, who was one of the Pandava heroes of the Mahabharata, is credited with the fort's original construction. All of Chittor's attractions are located within the fort (foreigner/citizen Rs 100/5; open sunrise-sunset). A zigzag ascent of over

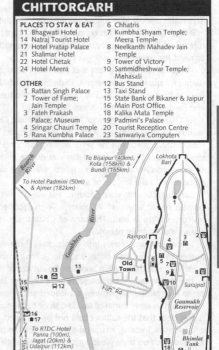

CHITTORGARH

PLACES TO STAY & EAT
11 Bhagwati Hotel
14 Natraj Tourist Hotel
17 Hotel Pratap Palace
21 Shalimar Hotel
22 Hotel Chetak
24 Hotel Meera

OTHER
1 Rattan Singh Palace
2 Tower of Fame; Jain Temple
3 Fateh Prakash Palace; Museum
4 Sringar Chauri Temple
5 Rana Kumbha Palace

6 Chhatris
7 Kumbha Shyam Temple; Meera Temple
8 Neelkanth Mahadev Jain Temple
9 Tower of Victory
10 Sammidheshwar Temple; Mahasati
12 Bus Stand
13 Taxi Stand
15 State Bank of Bikaner & Jaipur
16 Main Post Office
18 Kalika Mata Temple
19 Padmini's Palace
20 Tourist Reception Centre
23 Sanwariya Computers

SOUTHERN RAJASTHAN

1km leads through seven gateways to the main gate on the western side, the **Rampol** (*pol* means 'gate').

On the climb, you pass two **chhatris** (cenotaphs) between the second and third gates. They mark the spots where Jaimal and Kalla, heroes of the 1568 siege, fell during the struggle against Akbar. The main gate on the eastern side of the fort is the **Surajpol**. Within the actual fort itself, a circular road runs around the ruins and there's also a **deer park** situated at the southern end.

There are good views over the town, countryside and a huge cement factory from the western end of the fort; there's even a small village located here.

Today, the fort of Chittor is virtually a deserted ruin, but impressive reminders of its grandeur still stand. The main sites in the fort can all be seen in half a day (assuming you're not walking) but, if you like the atmosphere of ancient sites, then it is definitely worth spending longer as this is a very mellow place.

Death before Dishonour

History is kept alive by bards and folk songs in Rajasthan, and historical fact often merges with myth. This is the story that is told of the first sack of Chittor.

By the turn of the 14th century, much of North India had been conquered by the Mughals who ruled from Delhi. However the rana of Chittor, Rattan Singh, like many Rajput rulers, had managed to resist the invaders.

The jewel of the kingdom was Padmini, Rattan Singh's wife. Although she never left the *zenana* (women's quarters) uncovered, Padmini was admired far beyond the sturdy walls of the fortress, even as far away as Delhi. The rumours aroused the curiosity of the Sultan of Delhi, Ala-ud-din Khilji, and he decided to confirm them for himself.

In 1303 Ala-ud-din massed his armies around Chittorgarh and sent word to Rattan Singh that he wanted to meet Padmini. Knowing that his forces were no match for the sultan's armies, the rana reluctantly agreed, but he set a number of conditions. The sultan was required to enter the fort unarmed. Once inside, Ala-ud-din was not permitted to meet Padmini in person, but was only able to gaze upon her reflection in a mirror, while she sat well out of his reach inside a pavilion built (just to be sure) in the middle of a lotus pool.

But this glimpse was enough. Ala-ud-din was mesmerised by her beauty and resolved to possess her at any cost. As Rattan Singh escorted him to the gate, Ala-ud-din gave an order to his forces lying in wait. The rana of Chittor was taken hostage and the ransom demanded for his return was Padmini herself.

The court was thrown into panic, until Padmini came up with a plan. She sent word that she agreed to Ala-ud-din's terms and soon a long train of 150 beautiful curtained palanquins, befitting great ladies of the court in *purdah* (the custom of keeping women in seclusion), trundled slowly out of the fort. In fact, the palanquins were Chittor's Trojan Horse – as soon as they entered the sultan's camp four armed Rajput warriors leaped out of each palanquin and rescued their leader.

The sultan was infuriated and laid siege to the fort, patiently waiting as the Rajputs slowly starved. It was clear that the sultan could not be defeated, but the Rajputs couldn't consider the dishonour of surrender. Instead, a funeral pyre was lit in an underground tunnel. Padmini and all the ladies of the court put on their wedding saris and threw themselves into the fire as their husbands watched. The men then donned saffron robes, smeared the sacred ashes on their foreheads and rode out of the fort to face certain death.

Although it's clear that Ala-ud-din Khilji did lay siege to Chittor in 1303, and that the Rajput women committed *jauhar*, experts say that the beautiful Padmini may have been invented by a 16th-century bard.

A still camera is free, but there's a video charge of Rs 25 in the Tower of Victory. English-speaking guides are available inside the fort, usually at the Rana Kumbha Palace. The guides charge around Rs 230 for four people. Make sure you get a government-approved guide (they carry a guide licence).

Rana Kumbha Palace After entering the fort, turn right and will you arrive almost immediately to the ruins of this 15th-century palace. It contains both elephant and horse stables. Padmini's *jauhar* is said to have taken place in an underground tunnel between here and the Gaumukh Reservoir (see the boxed text 'Death before Dishonour'). Across the road is **Sringar Chauri Temple**, built in 1448.

Tower of Victory Erected between 1458 and 1468 by Rana Kumbha, the Tower of Victory *(Jaya Stambh; open 7am-sunset daily)* commemorates his victory over Mahmud Khilji of Malwa in 1440. It rises 37m in nine storeys and you can climb 157 narrow stairs to the top. Watch your head on the lintels! Hindu sculptures adorn the outside of the tower. The dome was damaged by lightning and repaired during the 19th century.

Close to the tower is **Mahasati**, a garden where the ranas were cremated during Chittorgarh's period as the Mewar capital. There are many *sati* stones, (which are stones that commemorate women who have committed *sati* by throwing themselves on their husbands' funeral pyres) here. The **Sammidheshwar Temple** stands in the same area, beside the Gaumukh Reservoir.

Gaumukh Reservoir Walk down beyond the temple and, at the very edge of the cliff, you'll see this deep tank where you can feed the fish. The reservoir takes its name from a spring that feeds the tank from a cow's mouth carved in the cliff-side. The opening here leads to the tunnel in which Padmini and her compatriots are said to have committed *jauhar*.

Padmini's Palace Continuing south, you come to Padmini's Palace, built beside the lotus pool with its pavilion in which Padmini sat reflected in Ala-ud-din's mirror.

The bronze gates in this pavilion were carried off by Akbar and can now be seen in the fort at Agra. Near Padmini's Palace is a small prison where captured invaders were kept and a sultan of Malwa and of Gujarat were once locked up.

Not far away are the former military training grounds for Rajput soldiers. Today the grounds are used as a helipad for visiting dignitaries. Continuing round the circular road, you pass the deer park, **Bhimlat Tank**, **Adhbudhnath Shiva Temple**, the **Surajpol** and the **Neelkanth Mahadev Jain temple** before reaching the Tower of Fame.

Tower of Fame Chittor's other famous tower, the Tower of Fame (Kirti Stambha), is older (probably built around the 12th century) and smaller (22m high) than the Tower of Victory. Built by a Jain merchant, it is dedicated to Adinath, the first Jain *tirthankar* (one of the 24 great Jain teachers), and is decorated with naked figures of the various *tirthankars*, thus indicating that it is a Digambara (SkyClad), monument. (Adherents of the Digambara Jain sect go naked.) A narrow stairway goes through seven storeys of the tower to the top. The tower stands beside a small Jain temple.

Rattan Singh Palace While Padmini's Palace was the summer abode of the Chittor royals, the winter palace takes the name of her husband, Rattan Singh. It overlooks a small lake and, although run-down, is an interesting place to explore.

Fateh Prakash Palace This palace is just beyond the Rana Kumbha Palace, and is much more modern (Maharana Fateh Singh died in 1930). It is closed except for a small **museum** *(admission Rs 3, free Mon; open 10am-4.30pm Sat-Thur)*.

Other Buildings Close to the Fateh Prakash Palace is the **Meera Temple**, built during the reign of Rana Kumbha in the ornate Indo-Aryan style and associated with the mystic-poetess Meerabai. The larger temple in this compound is the 15th-century **Kumbha Shyam Temple** (Temple of Varah).

Across from Padmini's Palace is **Kalika Mata Temple**, an 8th-century temple originally dedicated to Surya, but later converted to a temple to the goddess Kali. At the northern tip of the fort is another gate, the **Lokhota Bari**, while at the southern end is a small opening from which criminals and traitors were hurled into the abyss.

Places to Stay & Eat

Hotel standards in Chittor are generally disappointing; the cleanliness and service is usually below average and many of the cheaper places have miserable bathrooms (usually with an Indian-style toilet). Another option is the Paying Guest House Scheme, which operates in Chittor (ask about them at the Tourist Reception Centre; see Information earlier). If you would prefer to stay in top-end accommodation, you are better off staying in Bassi and visiting Chittor on a day trip.

Shalimar Hotel *(☎ 40842, fax 43942; singles/doubles with shared bathroom Rs 100/ 150, with private bathroom Rs 125/175)*, next to the train station, has small dull rooms with shared bathroom, or rooms with private bathroom. Hot water is available by the bucket (no charge).

Bhagwati Hotel *(☎ 46226; singles with shared bathroom Rs 80, singles/doubles with private bathroom Rs 100/150)*, just over the river, is better than the Natraj, but still not that great. The rooms are simple, but the main problem is the noise. Most rooms have hot water by the bucket. There's a basic restaurant here too (veg thali Rs 40).

Natraj Tourist Hotel *(☎ 41009; singles/ doubles with shared bathroom Rs 50/75, with private bathroom Rs 70/110, with geyser Rs 150/200)*, right by the bus stand, is very basic but undeniably cheap. Rooms are small, dark and dank; you'll probably have to get the staff to change the sheets. The cheaper rooms have hot water by the bucket. No meals are available.

Hotel Chetak *(☎ 41679; singles/doubles with private bathroom from Rs 200/300, deluxe Rs 350/450, with air-con Rs 600/700)*,

near the Shalimar, is not quite as good. Rooms are rather gloomy, but there's a restaurant.

Hotel Meera *(☎ 40934, fax 40466; singles/ doubles Rs 400/500)*, also situated near the train station, is a good option in this town low on hotel talent. It's a large, though rather impersonal, hotel with a restaurant (thalis Rs 40), snooker room and a bar.

RTDC Hotel Panna *(☎ 41238, fax 44024; dorm beds Rs 50, singles Rs 200-600, doubles Rs 300-700)* is closer to town (ie, further away from the fort). There are dorm beds and reasonable rooms with private bathroom; the cheaper options have hot water by the bucket. The hotel has a seedy little bar and a restaurant (the veg/nonveg thali is Rs 50/60).

Hotel Pratap Palace *(☎ 40099, fax 41042; e hpratap@hotmail.com; singles/doubles from Rs 250/300; deluxe Rs 690/740; super deluxe Rs 1325/1380)* is one of the most popular places to stay in Chittor. The deluxe and super-deluxe rooms are overpriced, but the ordinary rooms are reasonable value. There's a good restaurant near the pleasant garden; a half tandoori chicken costs Rs 70, *malai kofta* (meatballs in a creamy sauce) is Rs 35, a set breakfast is Rs 70. Village safaris can be arranged, and visits to its castle in Bijaipur (see Bundi to Chittorgarh earlier in this chapter).

Hotel Padmini *(☎ 41718, fax 47115; singles/doubles Rs 490/600, with air-con Rs 1000/1200, suites Rs 2500)* is a little out of town near the Bearch River, but is the most upmarket place in Chittor. It's owned by a marble magnate, and he's lined his hotel with his favourite stone. There's kids' play equipment on the grounds and a veg restaurant serving Indian and Chinese food; *paneer tikka* (spiced chunks of soft, unfermented cheese) is Rs 45. The hotel can also arrange horse safaris.

Retiring rooms *(doubles Rs 100, with air-con Rs 200)* can be found at the train station. A simple veg thali is available for Rs 20.

Getting There & Away

Bus Express buses travel to various destinations including Delhi (Rs 234, 16½ hours), Ajmer (Rs 74, five hours) and Jaipur

(Rs 125, eight hours). It's possible to take an early morning bus from Udaipur to Chittorgarh (Rs 45, 2½ hours), spend about three hours visiting the fort (by autorickshaw or tonga), and then take a late afternoon bus to Ajmer, but this is definitely pushing it.

Train The *Chetak Express* leaves Chittor at 10pm daily and travels to Ajmer (Rs 53/279 in 2nd/1st class, 4¼ hours), Jaipur (Rs 79/415, 7½ hours) and Delhi (Rs 131/688, 15 hours). There are also rail connections to Kota (4¼ hours) Ahmedabad (14 hours) and Udaipur (three hours).

Getting Around
It's about 6km from the train station to the fort (less from the bus stand) and 7km around the fort itself, not including the long southern loop out to the deer park. Autorickshaws charge around Rs 100 for a trip around the fort compound, and this includes waiting time at the various sites.

Bicycles can be rented near the train station (Rs 30 per day) to visit the fort but, as many Indian bikes lack gears, you may have to push the machine to the top. Still, they're great on the top and for the journey back down – but check the brakes first!

UDAIPUR
☎ 0294 • postcode 313001 • pop 389,317
Udaipur is the most romantic city in Rajasthan. This is quite a statement, given that the state is replete with grandiose palaces, fantastic hilltop forts and gripping legends of chivalry and heroism – but wait until you see it. In fact Colonel James Tod, in the *Annals & Antiquities of Rajasthan*, went even further, describing Udaipur as the 'most romantic spot on the continent of India'. Known as the Venice of the East, the Impressionist painters would have loved this place – Udaipur looks as though it has been lifted straight from the pages of a fairy-tale book.

The city is proud of its Rajput heritage. Udaipur's architecture rivals the famous creations of the Mughals, beautifully expressing the Rajput love of the whimsical. The best example of this cultural explosion

is, of course, the exquisite Lake Palace, on Jagniwas Island in the centre of Lake Pichola. It is complimented by Jagmandir, another island palace, the enormous City Palace on the shore, and the pretty Monsoon Palace (Sajjan Garh) high in the hills above.

Udaipur is also known as a centre for crafts and the performing arts, and its school of miniature painting is renowned. These paintings were produced for the maharanas of Udaipur from the early 18th to the mid-20th centuries and many examples can be seen at the City Palace Museum.

The old parts of the city are a jumble of tangled streets. Like most Indian cities, Udaipur's urban and industrial sprawl spreads beyond the city's original boundaries and pollution of various kinds can be discouraging. This will be your first impression of Udaipur if you arrive at the train or bus stations. Ignore it and head for the old city, where a different world awaits you.

This oasis in the desert has become a jewel of India's tourism industry and thousands of people flock here each year. There must be more rooftop restaurants here than any other place in Rajasthan. So sit back, relax and enjoy the views.

History
Udaipur was founded in 1568 by Maharana Udai Singh II following the final sacking of Chittorgarh by the Mughal emperor Akbar. According to legend, Udai Singh II found the site of his new capital some years before the last assault on Chittor, after coming across a holy man meditating on a hill near Lake Pichola. The old man advised the maharana to establish his capital on that very spot and that's how Udaipur came into existence. Surrounded by forests, lakes and the protective Aravalli Range, the new capital of Mewar was certainly in a much less vulnerable location than Chittor.

Maharana Udai Singh II died in 1572 and was succeeded by his son, Pratap, who bravely defended Udaipur from subsequent Mughal attacks, and gallantly fought at the battle of Haldighati in 1576. Unlike many other rulers in Rajasthan, the rulers of Mewar refused to be controlled by foreign

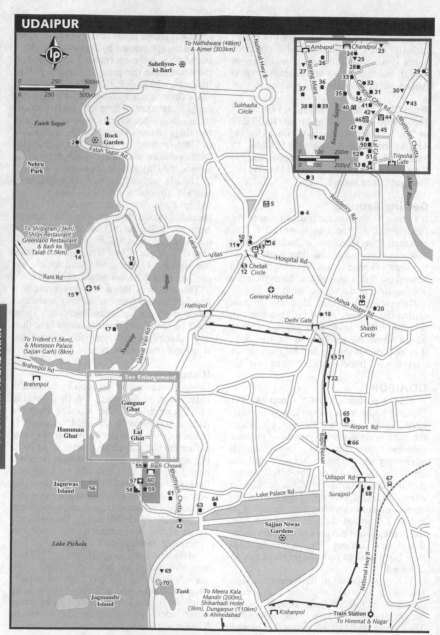

UDAIPUR

To Nathdwara (48km)
& Ajmer (303km)

Saheliyon-
ki-Bari

Sukhadia
Circle

Fateh Sagar

Rock
Garden

Fatah Sagar Rd

Nehru
Park

To Shilpgram (3km),
Shilpi Restaurant
Greenland Restaurant
& Badi ka
Talab (7.5km)

Rani Rd

Lakshmi
Vilas

Hospital Rd

Chetak
Circle

General Hospital

Hathipol

Delhi Gate

Ashok Nagar Rd

Shastri
Circle

To Trident (1.5km),
& Monsoon Palace
(Sajjan Garh) (8km)

Brahmpol Rd

Brahmpol

See Enlargement

Gangaur
Ghat

Lal Ghat

Hanuman
Ghat

Airport Rd

Bapu Bazaar

Badi Chowk

Bhattiyani Chotta

Jagniwas
Island

Lake Palace Rd

Udaipol Rd

Surajpol

Jagmandir
Island

Lake Pichola

Sajjan Niwas
Gardens

Tank

To Meera Kala
Mandir (200m),
Shikarbadi Hotel
(3km), Dungarpur (110km)
& Ahmedabad

Kishanpol

Train Station
To Himmat & Nagar

SOUTHERN RAJASTHAN

Ambapol   Chandpol

Barang Marg

Surajpol Ghat Rd

Swaroop Sagar

Lal Ghat

Bhattiyani Chotta

Ahar River

Tripolia
Gate

Residency Rd

PLACES TO STAY
3 Mewar Inn
13 Pahadi Palace
14 Hotel Ram Pratap Palace
17 Hotel Natural
20 RTDC Hotel Kajri
26 Dream Heaven Guest House
27 Queen Cafe & Guest House
28 Nukkad Guest House
31 Hotel Badi Haveli; Lehar Guest House; Heera
   Cycle Store
33 Hotel Minerwa
34 Hotel Gangaur Palace
35 Jheel Guest House
36 Hotel Sarovar
37 Panorama Guest House
38 Udai Kothi
39 Lake Shore Hotel
41 Jag Niwas Guest House
45 Pratap Bhawan Guest House
47 Lalghat Guest House; Evergreen Guest House;
   Restaurant Natural View
49 Lakeghat Palace; Hotel Caravanserai
50 Ratan Palace Guest House
51 Mughal Palace
52 Jagat Niwas Palace Hotel; Kankarwa Haveli
53 Lake Corner Soni Paying Guest House
54 Hotel Sai-Niwas
56 Lake Palace Hotel
59 Fateh Prakash Palace Hotel; Shiv Niwas Palace
   Hotel; Gallery Restaurant; Crystal Gallery
61 Hotel Raj Palace
63 Rang Niwas Palace Hotel
64 Hotel Mahendra Prakash
66 Apsara Hotel
68 Parn Kulti Hotel

PLACES TO EAT
10 Kwality Restaurant
11 Berry's Restaurant
15 El Parador
22 Park View
23 Savage Garden
25 Café Edelweiss
30 Maxim's Café
42 Coffee.com
43 Mayur Café
48 Ambrai Restaurant
62 Samor Bagh
69 Café Hill Park

OTHER
1 Moti Magri (Pratap Smarak)
2 Boats to Nehru Park; Paddle Boats
4 Jet Airways
5 Bhartiya Lok Kala Museum
6 Main Post Office
7 ATM
8 Cheetak Cinema
9 Rajasthali
12 ATM
16 Madan Mohan Malvai Ayurvedic College &
   Hospital
18 Indian Airlines
19 Poste Restante
21 Bank of Baroda
24 Ashtang Yoga Ashram
29 Clock Tower
32 Prem Musical Instruments
40 Bagore-ki-Haveli
44 Jagdish Temple
46 Mewar International
55 City Palace Museum; Government Museum
57 Sunset View Terrace
58 City Palace Jetty (Bansi Ghat)
60 City Palace; WWF; Vijaya Bank; Thomas Cook;
   Heritage Hotels Reservation Office
65 Tourist Reception Centre
67 Bus Stand
70 Sunset Point

To DHL
Worldwide
Express (500m)
& Ahar
Museum (2km)

To Airport
(25km) &
Chittorgarh
(112km)

To Pratap
Country Inn
(5km)

invaders, even though they were constantly attacked. After struggling against the Mughals, Udaipur was later attacked by the Marathas.

An end to bloody battles and instability came with British intervention in the early 19th century, when a treaty was signed which pledged to protect Udaipur from invaders. This umbrella of protection ended when India gained independence from the British. Along with all the other princely states, Udaipur surrendered its sovereignty and became part of a united India.

Orientation

The old city, bounded by the city-wall remains, is on the east side of Lake Pichola. The train station and bus stand are both just outside the city wall, to the southeast.

Information

Tourist Offices The **Tourist Reception Centre** (☎ 411535; open 10am-5pm Mon-Fri & every 2nd Sat) is located in the Fateh Memorial Building near Surajpol, less than 1km from the bus stand. Smaller tourist information counters operate at the train station and airport.

A more accessible source of information is *Out & About Udaipur*, an extremely informative magazine that's available in most bookshops (Rs 10), or ask at your hotel. There's a good website about Udaipur, with tourist and cultural information, at W www.udaipurplus.com.

Money You can change money at a number of places including the Vijaya Bank and Thomas Cook, both in the City Palace complex (near the museum). There's also the Bank of Baroda, the Bank of Rajasthan and the Punjab National Bank, all in Bapu Bazaar. At Chetak Circle, the State Bank of Bikaner & Jaipur changes money; there are also two 24-hour ATMs here where you can withdraw money against your credit card.

Post The main post office is north of the old city, at Chetak Circle; the poste restante facility is at the post office at Shastri Circle. In Badi Chowk, outside the City Palace

Tie The Knot With An Exotic Twist

Getting married? If you want to play prince and princess on your special day, you couldn't do much better than Udaipur, with its whimsical palaces. The city has become a favourite wedding venue for foreigners – many have travelled thousands of miles to tie the knot in this dreamy destination.

Situated in the middle of Lake Pichola, the gorgeous Lake Palace Hotel was once the exclusive summer residence of Udaipur's maharanas, but is today accessible to anyone (who can afford it!). There are a few sumptuous venues to choose from. If you like the thought of celebrating your marriage at one of the sets of *Octopussy*, then the Lily Pond may appeal to you. This is an inner open-air courtyard at the Lake Palace Hotel, complete with lily ponds and fountains. For those who like the idea of getting married on the move, there's the Gangaur Boat, an old royal barge belonging to the maharana of Udaipur.

All arrangements are made by the Lake Palace Hotel. Most types of wedding ceremonies are possible. If you intend getting married by a Christian priest, you must send a 'No Objection Certificate' (issued by a church in your country of residence) to Udaipur at least a month prior to your wedding date. If you opt for a Hindu ceremony, all arrangements can be made by the Lake Palace Hotel, including advice on where to get traditional Rajasthani wedding clothes. You will even get a certificate of marriage.

You're advised to make a reservation at least six months ahead. The most pleasant time to get married is during the cooler months between November and March. For prices and further information, contact the **Food & Beverage Manager, Lake Palace Hotel** (☎ 528800, fax 528700; e *lakepalace.udaipur@tajhotels.com; Post Box 5, Udaipur 313001, Rajasthan).*

In Udaipur, it's also possible to have weddings at the beautiful Shiv Niwas Palace Hotel (see Places to Stay), the grandiose Durbar Hall in the Fateh Prakash Palace Hotel in the City Palace complex (see the boxed text 'Durbar Hall') and the evocative Jagmandir Island. For these venues, you must contact the **Sales & Marketing Manager, HRH Group of Hotels, City Palace** (☎ 528008, fax 528012; e *resv@udaipur.hrhindia.com, Udaipur, 313001, Rajasthan).* If possible, have a look at all the venues before making a choice. Good luck!

Museum, there's a small **post office** *(open 10.30am-1pm & 1.30pm-4.30pm Mon-Sat).* An office of **DHL Worldwide Express** *(☎ 414388; 380 Ashok Nagar, Shree Niketan Bldg; open 9.30am-7pm Mon-Sat)* is near Ayer Bridge. It can arrange air freight around the world.

Email & Internet Access There are loads of places to surf the Internet, particularly in the Jagdish Temple area. Expect to pay around Rs 50 per hour. **Mewar International** *(☎ 419810)* has a good connection.

Travel Agencies Udaipur has scores of small travel agencies (concentrated in the tourist-laden old city), all promising the best deals in town. Shop around for the best price, as most will try to match or better the prices quoted to you by other agencies.

Bookshops There's a particularly good array of bookshops in the old city, as this is Udaipur's biggest tourist hang-out. Novels, guidebooks and books about Rajasthan are widely available, and some outlets have a small collection of music cassettes.

Medical Services The government-run **Madan Mohan Malvai Ayurvedic College & Hospital** *(☎ 431900; Ambamata Scheme; open 10am-5pm daily),* near Fateh Sagar, prescribes natural medicines and conducts free courses in Ayurveda. This hospital was opened in 1944 and specialises in joint pains, paralysis and neurological disorders.

For medical emergencies, head to the **general hospital** *(☎ 528811; Chetak Circle).*

Dangers & Annoyances If you have any trouble with hotels or rickshaw drivers (note their registration number), contact the **police** *(☎ 412693, ☎ 100 in the case of emergency)* or report it to the Tourist Reception Centre.

Lake Pichola

Beautiful Lake Pichola was enlarged by Maharana Udai Singh II after he founded the city. He built a masonry dam, known as the Badipol, and the lake is now 4km long and 3km wide. Nevertheless, it remains fairly shallow and can actually dry up – in severe droughts it's possible to walk to Jagniwas and Jagmandir. In recent years the monsoon has been poor and although there is still water in the lake, the 'petticoats' of the island palaces have been crudely exposed.

A handful of crocodiles are believed to inhabit the more remote parts of the lake, near uninhabited sections of the shore. Unfortunately the lake occasionally gets choked with that insidious weed, the water hyacinth. The City Palace extends for a long stretch along the east bank. South of the palace, a pleasant garden runs down to the shore. North of the palace, you can wander along the waterfront to some interesting bathing and *dhobi* (laundry) ghats – the slapping noise made by the *dhobi-wallahs* (washerpeople) echoes across the lake on all sides. Boat cruises on Lake Pichola leave from the City Palace – see City Palace Complex later for details.

Jagniwas Island The palace on Jagniwas Island, situated on Lake Pichola, was built by Maharana Jagat Singh II in 1743, and it covers the whole 1.5-hectare island. Once the royal summer palace, it was converted into a hotel in the 1960s by Maha-rana Bhagwat Singh. It is the ultimate in luxury hotels, with courtyards, fountains, restaurants and even a swimming pool. The gleaming white Lake Palace Hotel was largely responsible for putting Udaipur on the international tourist map. Its unparalleled location, majestic interior and exquisite architecture have placed it among the most exotic hotels in the world today. It's a magical place but casual visitors are discouraged. Nonguests can only come over

for lunch or dinner, and then only if the hotel is not full, which it often is (see Places to Eat for more details). Hotel launches cross to the island from the City Palace jetty. The Lake Palace and two other palaces in Udaipur, the Shiv Niwas Palace and the Monsoon

Mother

In Udaipur there is a woman who has been immortalised for her astounding loyalty to the royal family. Her name is Panna Dhai and her story is one of immense personal sacrifice and bravery, altruism and tragedy.

Prince Udai Singh II was just a baby when his father, Vikramaditya, the maharana of Mewar, was assassinated by a man called Banbir in 1535. Banbir wanted control of the kingdom and he was determined to eliminate anyone that stood in his way, including the young heir to the throne – Udai Singh. One night, Banbir managed to break into the prince's bedroom, planning to kill the baby boy.

However Udai Singh's devoted *dhai* (wet nurse), Panna, was one step ahead of him. At the time, Panna was also breastfeeding her own infant son, Chandan. She had already suspected Banbir's wicked intentions and had placed her Chandan in the prince's cradle. When Banbir demanded to know which child was the prince, Panna Dhai pointed to the prince's cradle where her own son slept. Banbir whipped out his sword and slaughtered the child.

Soon after the murder, Panna Dhai hid the prince in a basket and fled to the fort at Kumbhalgarh. She told the nobles and people of Mewar what had happened and the prince was promptly crowned, ensuring the unbroken lineage of the Mewar dynasty.

The current maharana of Udaipur has honoured the memory of Panna Dhai with a special award at the annual Maharana Mewar Foundation Awards ceremony. The Panna Dhai Award is given to an individual who 'ventures beyond the call of duty and sets an example in society of permanent value through sacrifice'.

Palace (Sajjan Garh), both appeared in the 1980s' James Bond film *Octopussy*.

Behind Jagniwas is a much smaller island known as **Arsi Vilas**. It was built by a former maharana of Udaipur to watch the sunset. There's a landing attached to this island, which has been used as a helipad in the past.

Jagmandir Island The other island palace, Jagmandir, was commenced by Maharana Karan Singh, but takes its name from Maha-rana Jagat Singh (r. 1628–52), who made a number of additions to it. It is said that the Mughal emperor, Shah Jahan, de-rived some of his ideas and inspiration for the Taj Mahal from this palace. He stayed here in 1623–24 while leading a revolt against his father, Jehangir. The island has some beautiful stone carvings, including a row of huge elephants that look as though they are guarding the island. An intricately carved *chhatri* made of grey-blue stone is also impressive. There's a small **museum** here detailing the history of the island, as well as frangipani trees, flowers and neat courtyards. Today the palace is primarily a venue for functions, but you can take a boat cruise to the island (see City Palace Complex). The view across the lake from the southern end, with the city and its glorious palace rising up behind the island palaces, is a scene of rare beauty.

City Palace Complex

The huge City Palace *(still camera/video Rs 75/300)*, which towers over the lake, is the largest palace complex in Rajasthan. Although it's a conglomeration of buildings added by various maharanas, the palace manages to retain a surprising uniformity of design. Building was started by Maharana Udai Singh II. The palace is surmounted by balconies, towers and cupolas and there are wonderful views over the lake and the city from the upper terraces.

Most people enter from the northern end through the **Baripol** of 1600 and the **Tripolia Gate** of 1725, with its eight carved marble arches. It was once a custom for maharanas to be weighed under the gate and their weight in gold or silver distributed to the populace. The main ticket office for the City Palace Museum is here.

Guides can be hired near the ticket office. An English-speaking guide costs Rs 70 (maximum five people), Rs 100 (maximum 10 people) or Rs 125 (maximum 15 people); the knowledgeable Kishan Das speaks French, English and Hindi and is currently learning Spanish. In the winter months (prime tourist season), the museum can get particularly crowded, so try to visit before 11am to avoid the rush.

In **Badi Chowk**, the large rectangular courtyard outside the museum, there are some shops selling rather pricey handicrafts and a money-exchange facility. There's also a small **Worldwide Fund for Nature shop** *(WWF; ☎ 524073; open 10am-5pm daily)*; the greeting cards (Rs 12) and playing cards (Rs 35) sold here are popular.

Inside the separate palace enclosure, entered from the south of Badi Chowk, are the Shiv Niwas and Fateh Prakash Palace Hotels, the Sunset View Terrace and Gallery Restaurants, the Crystal Gallery and the boat wharves for trips to Jagmandir and the Lake Palace. It costs Rs 25 for nonguests to enter this area, or you can buy a package ticket (adult/child Rs 435/175) that includes entry to the City Palace Museum and Crystal Gallery, a boat ride to Jagmandir and two free drinks. The ticket must be used within two days. There's another entrance to this enclosure on the southern side of the palace, more convenient if you're staying in the Lake Palace Road area.

City Palace Museum The main part of the palace is now preserved as the City Palace Museum *(adult/child under 12 years Rs 35/20, child under 5 free; open 9.30am-4.30pm daily)*, housing a large and varied collection of artefacts. Downstairs from the entrance is an armoury section, sporting a collection of old weapons including a lethal two-pronged sword. Usually after visiting the armoury, most people head straight for the City Palace Museum, which is through the Ganesh Deori, but you can also cross through the courtyard to get to the government museum (see later).

Durbar Hall

Many palaces in India have a durbar hall, or hall of audience. Historically, it was used by India's rulers for official occasions such as state banquets. It was also used to hold formal or informal meetings.

The restored Durbar Hall at the Fateh Prakash Palace Hotel, in the City Palace complex in Udaipur, is undoubtedly one of India's most impressive, with a lavish interior – just wait until you feast your eyes on the massive chandeliers. The walls display royal weapons and striking portraits of former maharanas of Mewar (a most distinguished looking lot). The illustrious Mewar rulers come from what is believed to be the oldest ruling dynasty in the world, spanning 76 generations.

The foundation stone was laid in 1909 by Lord Minto, the viceroy of India, during the reign of Maharana Fateh Singh. As a mark of honour to Lord Minto, it was originally named Minto Hall. The top floor of this high-ceilinged hall is surrounded by viewing galleries, where ladies of the palace could watch in veiled seclusion what was happening below. Nowadays, it's the Crystal Gallery museum; entry to the Durbar Hall is free with a ticket to the Crystal Gallery.

The hall still has the capacity to hold hundreds of people and can even be hired for conferences or social gatherings – for details, contact the Fateh Prakash Palace Hotel (☎ 528016, fax 528012).

The **Ganesh Deori** is the entrance to the museum and leads up to the **Rajya Angan**, or Royal Courtyard, the very spot where Udai Singh met the sage who told him to found his city here. The rooms of the museum are extravagantly decorated with mirrors, tiles and paintings. In the **Manak Mahal** (Ruby Palace) there is exquisite glass and mirror-work, while **Krishna Vilas** has a remarkable collection of miniatures (no photography is permitted here). The **Moti Mahal** has beautiful mirrorwork and the **Chini Mahal** is covered in ornamental tiles. The **Surya Chopar** has a huge, ornamental sun – the symbol of the Mewar dynasty, the origins of which are traced to the sun. The **Mor Chowk** (Peacock Square) has beautiful mosaics of peacocks, the favourite Rajasthani bird. In the **Bari Mahal** there is a fine central garden with good views over the old city.

More beautiful paintings can be seen in the **Zenana Mahal**, which opens onto **Laxmi Chowk**; there's a beautiful white pavilion in the centre of this square. Note the large tiger-catching cage near the Zenana Mahal entrance; a helpless goat or buffalo would be tied up inside the cage to lure the tiger in – gruesome.

Government Museum The government museum (admission Rs 5, free Mon; open 9.30am-5pm Sat-Thur) is outside the Ganesh Deori; photography is not allowed. The museum exhibits a collection of weapons, sculptures and paintings, plus a stuffed kangaroo that's coming apart at the legs, a freaky stuffed monkey holding a small lamp, and a Siamese-twin deer.

Crystal Gallery Situated at the Fateh Prakash Palace Hotel, the Crystal Gallery (admission Rs 200; open 10am-8pm daily in winter, 9am-8pm daily in summer), is breathtaking. This rare collection of Osler's crystal was ordered from England by Maharana Sajjan Singh in 1877, although the maharana never saw the crystal because of his untimely death. Items include crystal dressing tables, lamps, chairs, crockery, table fountains and even beds! There's an exquisite antique jewel-studded carpet, which has to be seen to be believed. Photography is strictly prohibited. The admission fee includes a soft drink, tea or coffee and entry to the grandiose Durbar Hall (see the boxed text). High tea is served daily at the restaurant in the Gallery – see Places to Eat.

Boat Cruises Boats leave regularly from 10am to 5pm daily from the City Palace jetty (known as Bansi Ghat), south of the Sunset View Terrace restaurant. There are 24-seater motorboats that cost Rs 100 per person for a 30-minute cruise and Rs 200 per person

SOUTHERN RAJASTHAN

for one hour; the latter includes a stop at Jagmandir Island. There are also eight-seater solar boats that cost Rs 1400 per hour; you can take these wherever you like.

Jagdish Temple
Located only 150m north of the entrance to the City Palace, this fine Indo-Aryan temple *(open 5am-2pm & 4pm-10pm daily)* was built by Maharana Jagat Singh in 1651 and enshrines a black stone image of Vishnu as Jagannath, Lord of the Universe. There is a brass image of the Garuda in a shrine in front of the temple and the steps up to the temple are flanked by elephants. You can donate money here, which is used to feed the hungry, between 11am and noon daily.

Bagore-ki-Haveli
The gracious old Bagore-ki-Haveli *(adult/child Rs 10/5; open 10am-7pm daily)*, right on the waterfront at Gangaur Ghat, was built by a former prime minister in the late 18th century. There are more than 100 rooms in the haveli, as well as courtyards, terraces and elegant balconies housing interesting exhibits including traditional Rajasthani costumes and modern art. There's also a nightly cultural performance here – see Entertainment, later, for details.

Fateh Sagar
North of Lake Pichola, this lake has become a popular hang-out as night falls for love-struck local youth. Overlooked by a number of hills, it was originally built in 1678 by Maharana Jai Singh, but was reconstructed by Maharana Fateh Singh after heavy rains destroyed the dam. A pleasant drive winds along the east bank and in the middle of the lake is **Nehru Park** *(open 8am-7pm in summer, 8am-6pm in winter)*, a popular garden island with a boat-shaped cafe. In dry years you can walk there, otherwise catch a boat near the bottom of Moti Magri for Rs 10 per person. Pedal boats (Rs 50/100 for half/one hour) are also available, but they don't operate when the water's low.

An autorickshaw from the old city to Fateh Sagar should only cost you around Rs 25 (one way).

Moti Magri
Atop the Moti Magri (Pearl Hill), overlooking Fateh Sagar, is a **statue** of the Rajput hero Maharana Pratap, who frequently defied the Mughals, riding his beloved horse Chetak. The path to the top traverses some pleasant **gardens** *(adult/child Rs 15/5; open 7.30am-7pm daily)*, including a Japanese rock garden. Car/rickshaw/motorcycle/bicycle entry is Rs 20/10/5/1.

Bhartiya Lok Kala Museum
The interesting collection exhibited by this small museum *(☎ 529296; foreigner/citizen Rs 25/25, camera/video Rs 10/50; open 9am-6pm daily)* and foundation for the preservation and promotion of local folk arts includes dresses, turbans, dolls, masks, musical instruments, paintings and – its high point – puppets. Regular 15-minute puppet shows are held daily (usually every half-hour) and are included in the admission charge. At noon and 6pm there are one-hour Rajasthani dance and puppet shows (foreigner/citizen Rs 30/50). An autorickshaw from the old city should cost Rs 20 (one way).

Saheliyon-ki-Bari
North of the city, Saheliyon-ki-Bari *(Garden of the Maids of Honour; admission Rs 5; open 8am-6.30pm daily)* is a small ornamental garden, built by Sangram Singh II in 1710 for the entertainment of the royal ladies. It's well maintained, with fountains (you may have to pay Rs 2 to see them turned on), kiosks, a delightful lotus pool and marble elephants. There's also a small **museum** *(open noon-5pm daily)* here, of which the main attraction are some stuffed cobras.

Shilpgram
A folk-culture village 3km west of Fateh Sagar, Shilpgram *(☎ 431304; adult/child Rs 10/5, still camera/video Rs 10/50; open 11am-7pm daily)* was inaugurated by Rajiv Gandhi in 1989. Although rather contrived, it's an interesting place with traditional houses from four states (Rajasthan, Gujarat, Goa and Maharashtra) and there are daily demonstrations by musicians, puppeteers, dancers and artisans from the various states.

There are also two small museums displaying musical instruments and household items – worth a look. Although it's much more animated during festival times (usually in early December, but check with the Tourist Reception Centre), the performance programme changes every few weeks. Camel rides (from Rs 10) are available.

Nearby there are a couple of restaurants – see Places to Eat. Some people walk out to Shilpgram; a return autorickshaw (including a one-hour wait) from the old city will cost you around Rs 80.

Ahar Museum
About 2km east of Udaipur are the remains of an ancient city. There's a **museum** (admission Rs 3, free Mon; open 10am-4.30pm Sat-Thur) here, where you'll find a limited, but very old collection of earthen pottery, sculptures and other archaeological finds. Some pieces date back to 1700 BC and there's a beautiful 10th-century metal figure of Buddha. Photography is not allowed.

Nearby is an impressive cluster of **cenotaphs** of the maharanas of Mewar, which have recently been restored. A total of around 19 former maharanas were cremated here. The most striking cenotaph is that of Maharana Amar Singh, who ruled from 1597 to 1620. Most tourists give these a miss, but they're worth a visit.

Monsoon Palace
On the distant mountain range, visible from the city, is the former maharana's Monsoon Palace (Sajjan Garh). It was built by Maharana Sajjan Singh in the late 19th century. This deserted and run-down palace is today owned by the government and in theory is closed to the public, but the caretaker has been charging Rs 10 to let tourists in for so long that the fee might as well be official. At the foot of the hill is the **Sajjan Garh Wildlife Sanctuary** (foreigner/citizen Rs 80/ 10, autorickshaw/car Rs 20/65; open 8am- 6pm daily).

This place is worth visiting just for the stunning views over Udaipur, especially at sunset. You can walk around the back of the palace for another fabulous view of the

surrounding hills. The palace is illuminated at night and is a popular conversation starter in Udaipur's rooftop restaurants.

The round trip takes about one hour by car. By autorickshaw/taxi it should cost around Rs 125/350 (including a 30-minute wait), but you'll probably be asked for more so bargain hard.

Other Attractions
The huge **fountain** in the centre of Sukhadia Circle, north of the city, is illuminated at night. **Sajjan Niwas Gardens** has a rose garden, the Gulab Bagh, pleasant lawns (beware of the unfriendly dogs here) and a zoo. Don't confuse **Nehru Park** opposite Bapu Bazaar with the island park of the same name in Fateh Sagar. The city park has some strange topiary work, a giant cement teapot and children's slides. **Sunset Point** (adult/child under 12 years Rs 5/2), not far from the Café Hill Park, is indeed delightful at sunset, with dazzling views over Lake Pichola, Jagmandir Island and the Monsoon Palace. There's a musical fountain, which plays a merry tune each evening.

Almost 5km beyond Shilpgram is **Badi Ka Talab** (Tiger Lake). This mammoth artificial lake, flanked by hills, is a pleasant picnic spot. The lake is at its most impressive after monsoon. Crocodiles lurk in parts of the lake, so swimmers beware! Near the lake there's a small Shiva and Hanuman temple. An autorickshaw to the lake should cost Rs 100/200 one way/return (with a one-hour wait).

Courses
At **Prem Musical Instruments**, (☎ 430599; 28 Ghadia Devara; open 9.30am-9pm), Bablu has been recommended by a number of travellers for his sitar, tabla and flute lessons (around Rs 100 an hour). He also sells and repairs those instruments and can arrange performances.

Mr Jaswant Tak offers yoga and meditation classes at the **Ashtang Yoga Ashram** (☎ 524872; 35 Ghadia Devara) for a donation; all proceeds go to an animal shelter. There are 1½-hour classes at 8am, 10am and 5pm daily – you need to book in advance.

Organised Tours

A five-hour tour starts at the RTDC Hotel Kajri at 8am each day. It costs Rs 73.50 (excluding admission fees to sites) and takes in all the main city sights. There's also an afternoon tour (2pm to 7pm) that goes out to Eklingji, Haldighati and Nathdwara (see North of Udaipur later); it costs Rs 105. Contact the **RTDC Hotel Kajri** (☎ 410501) for more details. See City Palace Complex earlier in this chapter for information about boat cruises.

Places to Stay

The most romantic place to stay is the Lal Ghat area, close to the shores of the lake and west of the Jagdish Temple, where there's a good range of places to suit most budgets. Quieter, and often with even better views, are the handful of excellent hotels and guesthouses just across the water in Hanuman Ghat.

Getting to the accommodation of your choice has been made easier by the police-supervised prepaid autorickshaw stands that are located outside the train and government bus stations (see Getting Around, later). Some unscrupulous operators will still try to take you to the hotel of their choice, but remember, they don't get reimbursed until you hand over the receipt at the end of your journey.

The commission system is in place with a vengeance, so if you get a rickshaw driver who insists that the hotel of your choice has burnt down or suddenly closed, or the owner has died in a freak accident, politely decline his kind offer. Unless your rickshaw is prepaid, ask for the Jagdish Temple when arriving as it's a good place to start looking for accommodation.

Places to Stay – Budget

Udaipur pioneered the Paying Guest House Scheme in Rajasthan, and there are now 41 families in it. Expect to pay Rs 100 to 200 per night. The Tourist Reception Centre (see Information earlier) has a list detailing all the places and the services offered.

In the low season the prices of budget hotels crumble – it's well worth bargaining.

Lal Ghat Area If you're booking a hotel near Lake Pichola, ask for a lake-facing room (they usually cost a bit more). Most places have fabulous views over the lake and the central location is ideal. If you are staying in this area, actively encourage your hotel to dispose of all rubbish in an environmentally friendly manner to prevent this magnificent place from being spoiled.

Lalghat Guest House (☎ 525301, fax 418508; e lalghat@hotmail.com; 33 Lal Ghat; dorm beds Rs 50, singles/doubles with shared bathroom Rs 75/100, with private bathroom from Rs 200/250, triples Rs 400), right by the lake, is a mellow place to hang out with other travellers. The rooftop areas (popular for sunbathing) have excellent views over the lake and there's a back terrace overlooking the ghats. All the rooms have fans and mosquito nets, and there's a small kitchen for self-caterers.

Hotel Gangaur Palace (☎ 422303; 3 Gangaur Ghat Rd; doubles with shared bathroom Rs 80, with private bathroom Rs 150-350) is a terrific choice in this area. It has large, clean rooms; the ones with a lake view are the most expensive. Hot water is a bit iffy. The rooftop restaurant has three tiers – one where *Octopussy* is screened, one showing a new movie and one playing classical Indian music. There's also a palmist from 2pm to 5pm daily, charging Rs 50 to 100.

Hotel Minerwa (☎ 523471; e minerwa 66@hotmail.com; singles/doubles with private bathroom from Rs 80/150), just down the street, has weary rooms but it's friendly and cheap.

Hotel Badi Haveli (☎/fax 412588; e hbha veli@datainfosys.net; 85 Gangaur Ghat Rd; singles/doubles with shared bathroom from Rs 150/200) is also good. The shared bathrooms are spotless (hot water is available morning and evening) and the ratio of toilets to rooms is high. There's a lovely sheltered and leafy courtyard surrounded by white-washed walls and the rooftop has spectacular views and a restaurant (mains are around Rs 60).

Lehar Guest House (☎ 417651; 86 Gangaur Ghat Rd; doubles with private bathroom Rs 80-200) is run by the friendly Manju. Th more expensive rooms are painted. There's a small rooftop restaurant, with good views, which serves Indian and continental food. You can also have your hands painted with *mehendi* (henna) here.

Lakeghat Palace (☎ *521636, fax 520023;* e *lakeghatanis@hotmail.com; singles Rs 300-500, doubles Rs 400-1000)* has OK rooms and an atrium filled with hanging plants. There are splendid views from the summit and a good restaurant (mains Rs 50).

Jag Niwas Guest House (☎ *416022, fax 412160; 21 Gangaur Ghat Rd; singles/ doubles with private bathroom from Rs 80/ 100)* is a friendly family-run place. The rooftop has a funky little nonveg restaurant offering cooking classes.

Evergreen Guest House (☎ *421585; 32 Lal Ghat; singles/doubles with shared bathroom Rs 50/70, with private bathroom Rs 100/ 150)* has seven simple, fairly clean rooms around a small courtyard with a manicured lawn. There's a popular restaurant here (see Places to Eat).

Lake Corner Soni Paying Guest House (☎ *525712; 27 Nav Ghat; doubles with shared bathroom Rs 80, with private bathroom Rs 100)* is nothing fancy (many rooms have Indian-style toilet), but the elderly couple who run it are lovely. There are fantastic views from the rooftop and veg food is available.

Jheel Guest House (☎ *421352; 56 Gangaur Ghat Rd; singles/doubles with shared bath-room from Rs 80/100, doubles with private bathroom Rs 200-600)* is right at the bottom of the hill by the ghat, and is housed in an old haveli. The newer annexe across the road has better (more expensive) rooms and a rooftop restaurant overlooking the lake.

Nukkad Guest House (*56 Ganesh Ghat; singles/doubles with shared bathroom Rs 50/ 60, with private bathroom Rs 70/80)*, run by a friendly family, has very basic but very cheap rooms. Meals are available.

Mughal Palace (☎ *417954;* e *mughal palace2001@hotmail.com; 46 Lal Ghat; singles/ doubles Rs 200/400)* is a modern hotel with traditional Rajasthani flourishes. It's a quiet place, close to the city palace, with a very pleasant rooftop restaurant (dishes Rs 35 to 40) sporting a great lake view.

Pratap Bhawan Guest House (☎/fax *560566;* e *pratapbhawan@yahoo.co.in; 12 Lal Ghat; singles/doubles 300/400)* offers comfortable, spotless rooms in a gracious family home. All the rooms are the same price, so ask for one upstairs from where you can glimpse the city palace.

Hanuman Ghat Area Directly across the water from Lal Ghat, Hanuman Ghat is a more peaceful place to stay.

Dream Heaven Guest House (☎ *431038;* e *deep_gb@yahoo.com; 22 Bhim Permash-ever Marg; doubles with private bathroom Rs 80-170)* is a fantastic choice. It has a lovely homey atmosphere and wins our vote for the best rooftop views in town – you can chill out here on a pile of cushions.

Lake Shore Hotel (☎ *431834; singles/ doubles with shared bathroom Rs 75/100, doubles with private bathroom from Rs 150/ 200)* is a laid-back place with fairly basic but good-value rooms and a terrace with fine views over Gangaur Ghat. The best rooms have window seats over the lake. There's a very good restaurant; baked pota-toes with garlic cheese are Rs 40.

Panorama Guest House (☎ *431027;* e *krishna2311@rediffmail.com; 47 Panch Devari Marg; singles/doubles Rs 60/100)* is a popular choice. Its pleasant, painted rooms have either a private bathroom or a view. It's in a quiet lane and there's a rooftop restaurant with an international menu.

Queen Cafe and Guest House (☎ *430875; 14 Bajrang Marg; doubles with shared bath-room Rs 100-150)* is another brilliant choice. There's a genuine family feel here, as well as cooking classes, henna painting and Hindi lessons. There are two simple rooms or you can sleep on the roof. There's also a great restaurant here – you can sit down-stairs on the pillow-strewn floor, or up on the roof.

Lake Palace Road Area This area is still central but further away from Lake Pichola than Lal Ghat.

Hotel Mahendra Prakash (☎ *419811; singles/doubles with private bathroom from Rs 250/300, doubles with air-con from Rs 500)*

SOUTHERN RAJASTHAN

has decent rooms, the ones in the new building have traditional-style decor. There's also a sparkling clean swimming pool, a restaurant and a rooftop with views of the City Palace.

Bus Stand Area This is a very noisy and polluted area, and you'd have to be desperate, totally lacking in imagination or have a (very) early departure to stay here.

Apsara Hotel *(☎ 420400; singles/doubles with private bathroom Rs 100/200),* north of the bus stand, is a huge and somewhat dreary place set back from the road. The rooms front onto an internal courtyard, making them relatively quiet. Hot water is by the bucket.

Parn Kulti Hotel *(☎ 586314, fax 521403; singles/doubles Rs 300/450)* has somewhat run-down but OK rooms with satellite TV.

Elsewhere If you don't mind staying away from the heart of the old city, there are some good budget options.

Hotel Natural *(☎ 527879; e hotelnat ural@hotmail.com; 55 Rang Sagar; doubles with private bathroom Rs 100/150)* is further away from Lake Pichola, but is good if you want to abscond from the tumult. Its basic doubles have bucket hot water and many of them have a shared balcony. There's good veg food cooked with tender loving care by Ritu, and a slice of cake, just like grandma used to bake, costs Rs 25 to 30. You can also order birthday cakes.

Pahadi Palace *(☎ 431699; 18 Ambargarh, Swaroop Sagar; doubles Rs 150-800),* not far away, has spotlessly clean rooms and is great value for money. There's also a good restaurant.

Mewar Inn *(☎ 522090; e mewarinn@hot mail.com; 42 Residency Rd; singles/doubles with shared bathroom Rs 39/49, with private bathroom from Rs 79/99)* is not in a thrilling location, but it's cheap and gets consistently good reports from travellers. Rooms are basic and a discount is given to YHA members. There's a rooftop veg restaurant and bicycles for hire (Rs 10 per day).

Pratap Country Inn *(☎ 583138, fax 583058; singles Rs 200-1100, doubles Rs 300-1200)*

is a serene and secluded country retreat at Titaradi village, about 5km outside Udaipur. Horse riding is available (learners' classes cost Rs 250 per day) and guests of more than one night get a free ride. It can be tough getting a rickshaw out here (Rs 50), but the hotel can pick you up from Udaipur with advance notice.

Places to Stay – Mid-Range
Lal Ghat Area It's wise to book ahead, as these places can fill up fast during the tourist season.

Jagat Niwas Palace Hotel *(☎ 422860, fax 418512; e mail@jagatniwaspalace.com; 25 Lal Ghat; doubles Rs 500-1850)* has long been a popular travellers hang-out. There are two wings to the hotel; one in a charming converted haveli right on the lakeshore and the other in a newer building with more mod cons. Ask for a room in the haveli – they're far more atmospheric and some overlook the lake. There's also a great restaurant here (see Places to Eat).

Kankarwa Haveli *(☎ 411457, fax 521403; e khaveli@yahoo.com; 26 Lal Ghat; doubles Rs 400-1200),* run by the helpful Janardan Singh, is a wonderful place to stay. Squeaky-clean doubles range in price; the more expensive rooms overlook Lake Pichola. Only veg breakfast is available, but you can pop next door to the Jagat Niwas Palace Hotel for a feed.

Hotel Sai-Niwas *(☎ 421586, fax 450009; e hotelsainiwas@yahoo.com; 75 Navghat Marg; doubles Rs 850-1250),* just down the hill towards the ghat from the City Palace entrance, is also heartily recommended. The seven double rooms are imaginatively decorated, even the toilet! There's a cute, if pricey, restaurant that serves Indian and continental food.

Ratan Palace Guest House *(☎/fax 561 153; 21 Lal Ghat; singles/doubles with private bathroom from Rs 200/250)* is a family-run place offering good rooms and lake views from the terrace. Meals are available.

Hotel Caravanserai *(☎ 411103, fax 521252; e hotelcaravanserai@hotmail.com; 14 Lal Ghat; doubles Rs 700-1200)* is modern place with clean, well-kept rooms. The food at the non-veg rooftop restaurant (curries Rs 35 to 90) is only average, but is compensated for by the lake views.

Hanuman Ghat A good choice in this area is **Udai Kothi** (☎ 432810, fax 430412, e udaikothi@yahoo.com; doubles Rs 850-1495), with stylish, beautifully appointed rooms in a building that looks like a wedding cake. The hotel also possesses one of the city's most spectacular rooftop terraces. It has 360° views, and you can swim in Udaipur's only rooftop swimming pool or dine well here. It's a tremendous place for a splurge.

Hotel Sarovar (☎ 432801, fax 431732; e sarovar@hotelsarovar.com; singles/doubles Rs 700/800, air-con Rs 1050/1200), on the same road, is a modern but impersonal motel-style place. There's a restaurant on the roof with good views and decent food.

Lake Palace Road Area Set in lovely gardens with a swimming pool is the **Rang Niwas Palace Hotel** (☎ 523890, fax 527884; e rangniwas75@hotmail.com; Lake Palace Rd; singles/doubles with shared bathroom Rs 300/350, with private bathroom from Rs 550/660, suites Rs 2500). It's a very relaxed hotel with evidence of attention to detail. There are two buildings – the old one is a former royal guesthouse.

Hotel Raj Palace (☎ 527092, fax 410395; 103 Bhattiyani Chotta; doubles with private bathroom Rs 450-1250) is not a bad choice, although it's looking a little weary these days. There's a lush courtyard restaurant which is a great place to chill out with a beer. The restaurant whips up delicious food, including chicken masala (Rs 75).

Elsewhere There are few other mid-range options.

Hotel Ram Pratap Palace (☎/fax 431700; e rpp_udr@vsnl.com; 5B Alkapuri; singles/ doubles Rs 985/1185, deluxe Rs 1585/1885) is an elegant modern haveli, in the Fateh Sagar area, although it's not fantastic value. Deluxe rooms face the lake. There's a good restaurant here and the rooftop terrace has romantic views.

RTDC Hotel Kajri (☎/fax 410503; Shastri Circle; singles/doubles with private bathroom from Rs 350/450) has overpriced rooms and a restaurant. The staff are helpful, and the RTDC tours of Udaipur start from here.

Places to Stay – Top End

Trident (☎ 432200, fax 432211; e reserva tions@tridentudp.com; singles/doubles from US$150/165) is rather out on a limb, beyond Chandpol, but is Udaipur's slickest hotel when it comes to service and attention to detail. Hidden in the hills, this modern property is part of the Oberoi Group and offers smart rooms. The multicuisine restaurant (nonguests welcome) is excellent and even has frothy cappuccinos. Other amenities include a swimming pool, bar, beauty parlour and health club. Don't miss the wild-boar feeding frenzy at 5.30pm daily – a truly awesome sight! The Oberoi Group is planning to open an upmarket boutique hotel in Udaipur (similar to the Raj Vilas in Jaipur) in August 2002.

Shikarbadi Hotel (☎ 584842, fax 584841; singles/doubles from Rs 1999/3300) is 4km out of town on the Ahmedabad road. Once a royal hunting lodge, it is set in wilderness and has a swimming pool and relaxing gardens. A stud farm on the premises offers short horse rides (Rs 250 for 45 minutes) and longer horse safaris (a half-day safari with breakfast is Rs 1500). Sip tea while you watch the wild boars gorge at 4pm each day (not far from the pool area). For room reservations book at the Heritage Hotels Reservation Office in the City Palace complex (☎ 528008).

Palace Hotels One of the world's most spectacular hotels must be the **Lake Palace Hotel** (☎ 528800, fax 528700; e lakepalace .udaipur@tajhotels.com; doubles US$230, with lake view US$300-325, suites US$400-750), which appears to be floating in the middle of Lake Pichola. It looks like something lifted straight out of a romantic novel and few people would pass up an opportunity to stay here, although the cheapest doubles don't have a lake view. This swanky white palace has a bar, two restaurants (see

Places to Eat), a little shopping arcade, open-air courtyards, lily ponds, an astrologer (Rs 625 per hour) and a small swimming pool shaded by mango trees. Needless to say, you will need to book well in advance.

Shiv Niwas Palace Hotel (☎ 528016, fax 528006; ℮ resv@hrhindia.com; doubles from US$125, doubles around the pool from US$300), part of the City Palace complex, is another atmospheric palace hotel. The cheapest rooms aren't really crash-hot value – it's much better to get a room around the pool (room No 16 has fine views over the lake). For a real splurge there are some lavish suites; the imperial suite (room No 19, US$600) doesn't have much of a lake view but is very romantic – it even has a small fountain near the dreamy four-poster bed. There's a good restaurant (see Places to Eat), bar, Ayurvedic massage centre and marble pool (open to nonguests for Rs 300 including a towel). A small bagpipe band (!) strikes up a merry tune each evening. You must book in advance.

Fateh Prakash Palace Hotel (☎ 528016, fax 528006; doubles US$125, suites US$250-300), also in the City Palace complex, was built in the early 1900s during the reign of Maharana Fateh Singh. The cheapest double rooms are not in the main palace wing, but all have a lake view. Far more ornate rooms furnished with traditional palace pieces are available (some with a lake view). The intimate Gallery Restaurant (see Places to Eat) has brilliant views across the lake.

Places to Eat

Udaipur has scores of sun-kissed rooftop cafés catering to budget travellers, as well as fine dining at the top-end hotels. Many restaurants also boast terrific lake views. At places offering multicuisine menus, the chefs generally do a better job of the Indian food. Some restaurants in Udaipur serve *bhang* lassis – see the boxed text 'Beware of Those Bhang Lassis' in the Facts for the Visitor chapter.

In the 1983, a James Bond movie was partly filmed in Udaipur, and no-one is allowed to forget it. As one of our readers,

Barbi Terpin of Slovenia, put it, 'I hope you like *Octopussy*, or else just don't go out for dinner at 7pm because you'll be forced to watch it day after day after day after day…' These days contemporary cult movies are also screened at Udaipur's restaurants.

Savage Garden (☎ 423316; open 8.30am-10pm; mains Rs 85-135), near Chandpol, gets rave reviews from travellers. It's a stylish place with well-designed lighting in a 250-year-old haveli painted peacock blue. The food is good; imaginative mains all come with rice and bread, and freshly ground coffee is served. It's tucked away in the backstreets but you can't miss the many signs erected by the enthusiastic management.

Ambrai (☎ 431085; mains around Rs 80) is also worth visiting for its superb location, across the water from Lal Ghat, with a great view of the City Palace. The beauty of this outdoor restaurant is that, unlike other places to eat, it sits right at water level. It's a great place to kick back with a cold beer or hot masala tea or an Indian, Chinese or continental meal.

El Parador (☎ 431443), out in the Fateh Sagar area (opposite the Ayurvedic hospital at Ranaji Chowk), is a cosy little place that looks like an Italian trattoria and even serves real Italian coffee (Rs 75 per heavenly pot). The restaurant is run by a family of women who send divine dishes from their kitchen, such as almondine chicken with cream sauce (Rs 98), vegetable moussaka (Rs 90) and nachos (Rs 80).

Mayur Café (☎ 412368; open 7.30am-10.30pm daily), by the Jagdish Temple, has long been popular, but more for the location than the atmosphere or the food. There are South Indian dishes and Western alternatives such as spaghetti with cheese (Rs 31).

Maxim's Café (open 7.30am-10pm daily), near the Mayur, is similar. Menu items include *paneer tikka* (Rs 30) and Rajasthani pizza (Rs 25).

Café Edelweiss (☎ 423316; 36 Gadiya Devra) is a German bakery; come straight here if you need a sugar hit from home. Its apple pie (Rs 50) is famous, and there are also sticky chocolate rum balls (Rs 10) and real coffee (Rs 20 a cup). The same owners run both **Coffee.com**, near the Jagdish Temple, and Savage Garden restaurant.

Samor Bagh *(☎ 427767; open 8am-10.30pm daily)*, near the Lake Palace Rd entrance to the City Palace, has slightly priccy Indian, Chinese and continental food. Its speciality is *paneer pasanda* (chunks of cheese in a nutty cream sauce, Rs 60). Other menu items include chicken steak sizzlers (Rs 150) and mushroom fried rice (Rs 55). You can sit in the large 'hut' or out in the garden; there are puppet shows between 11am and 6pm daily.

Restaurant Natural View *(open 8am-10.30pm)*, on the rooftop of the Evergreen Guest House, has fine lake views and is a deservedly popular travellers joint. It serves Indian, Chinese and continental fare; chicken *palak* (chicken with spinach) is Rs 50 and fish curry is Rs 60.

Café Hill Park *(☎ 529224; open noon-10pm)*, southwest of the Sajjan Niwas Gardens and on a hill that overlooks Lake Pichola, offers snacks to people who are visiting Sunset Point.

Park View *(☎ 528098; open 11am-11pm daily)*, one of Udaipur's oldest restaurants, is opposite the park in the main part of town and is often packed with middle-class Indian families. It's a dimly lit air-con restaurant, particularly known for its northern Indian cuisine. A half tandoori chicken is Rs 62 and fish curry is Rs 55.

Kwality Restaurant *(☎ 414927; Chetak Circle; open 10am-11pm)* is a bizarre retro salon with mood music, axe-shaped menus and a scary pink art installation on the wall. Beer is available (you may need it), as are 'chicken lollypops' (spicy chicken pieces served on the bone, Rs 90).

Berry's Restaurant *(Chetak Circle; open noon-4pm & 7pm-11pm daily; sizzlers Rs 85-135)* doesn't have much character but cooks up pretty good Indian food and is quite popular with the locals. The butter chicken is a hot seller (Rs 95/175 for a half/full bird).

Hotel Natural has a menu that offers a mishmash of veg Indian, Chinese, Mexican, Tibetan, Italian and Israeli food. An Israeli breakfast is Rs 50, an all-you-can-eat veg thali goes for Rs 40.

Shilpi Restaurant *(☎ 432495; Indian mains veg Rs 38-75, nonveg Rs 50-145)*, next to Shilpgram, serves snacks and good Indian, continental and Chinese food. It also has a swimming pool (admission Rs 100; open 11am to 5pm daily).

Greenland Restaurant *(☎ 432299; dishes Rs 25-55)* is not far from Shilpi Restaurant, but is less impressive. It serves veg Indian, continental and Chinese fare and offers a complimentary lemon squash.

Jagat Niwas Palace Hotel *(☎ 422860)* has an absolutely delightful restaurant which has superlative lake views – great for a minor splurge. Its Western dishes are a little pricey, but the Indian food is cheaper. It's wise to book ahead (especially for dinner), as this place can fill up in a flash.

Shiv Niwas Palace Hotel *(☎ 528016)*, inside the city palace enclosure (admission Rs 25), is highly recommended for a dose of pampering and is most captivating in the evening. There's seating indoors or in the pleasant open-air courtyard by the pool. The Indian food is best: try the *aloo chutneywale* (potatoes stuffed with Indian cottage cheese in a mango and mint chutney) for Rs 170. Indian classical music is performed each evening by the pool, creating a magical ambience. Nonguests are welcome, but it's always wise to book ahead, especially if you're going there for dinner. Before dinner, treat yourself to a drink at the plush poolside **Paanera Bar**.

Gallery Restaurant *(Fateh Prakash Palace Hotel; set lunch/dinner Rs 500/600)*, also in the palace enclosure (entry Rs 25), serves a set continental meal at lunch and dinner. Although the food here is nothing to write home about, this elegant little restaurant has beguiling views across Lake Pichola. For a really romantic evening, come here for a drink around sunset. For something more moneybelt-friendly, high tea is served daily between 3pm and 5pm. A cream tea costs Rs 150, while a pot of chocolate served with whipped cream is Rs 75.

Lake Palace Hotel *(buffet lunch/dinner Rs 500/750)* is, of course, the ultimate dining experience, although there's no guarantee you will get in since it's usually only possible to get a table when the hotel is not full. The buffet meal price includes the boat crossing and before your meal you can take a drink at the sophisticated bar. Special Rajasthani thalis are available with advance notice; they're mighty filling, so make sure you go on an empty stomach. Reservations are essential, and reasonably tidy dress is expected. For something different, ask about the tiny **floating pontoon** on Lake Pichola, which arranges lunch/dinner for US$50 (maximum four people). If you don't want a waiter hanging around, you can request a cordless phone to be left in case you need him for anything. Be sure to wear something warm if you are dining at night in winter.

Entertainment

Many hotels stage their own entertainment for guests – usually puppet shows or Rajasthani music/dance performances.

Meera Kala Mandir (☎ 583176; Sector 11, Hiran Magari; tickets Rs 60), near the Pars Theatre, has one-hour Rajasthani folk dance and music performances daily (except Sunday) at 7pm from August to April. It has a range of tribal folk dances. An autorickshaw to the auditorium from the City Palace area costs around Rs 25.

Bagore-ki-Haveli (Gangaur Ghat; adult/child Rs 35/20, camera/video Rs 10/50) stages nightly dance performances, also at 7pm, including traditional Mewari, Bhil and western Rajasthani dances. **Sunset View Terrace** (☎ 528016; open 7am-10.30pm daily; meals Rs 150-200), ideally situated on a terrace overlooking Lake Pichola, is the place to have a drink at sunset. Located near the Fateh Prakash Palace Hotel in the City Palace enclosure (admission Rs 25), this place is worth visiting for the views alone (don't forget your camera). Live Indian classical music is played from 7.30pm. A gin and tonic is Rs 90 while a glass of wine costs Rs 200. Light snacks are also available here.

There are a few cinemas in Udaipur if you feel like taking in the latest Bollywood hit, including the **Chetak Cinema** (Chetak Circle; admission Rs 38).

Shopping

Udaipur has oodles of small shops selling a jumble of items from funky Western clothing to exquisite antique jewellery. There are all sorts of local crafts, especially miniature paintings. The miniatures are painted on cloth, marble, wood, paper and even leaves. This is one of the best places to buy them. There are also many leather- and cloth-bound books of handmade paper for sale, in every design imaginable. Other things to buy in Udaipur include jewellery, carpets, block printed fabrics, marble items, wooden figures and papier mache. There's a good cluster of shops on Lake Palace Rd, near the Rang Niwas Palace Hotel, and also around the Jagdish Temple. Shops are usually open daily from 9.30am to 10pm.

Be warned that shops in Udaipur are used to dealing with tourists who have lots of money and little time to spend it, so be prepared to bargain hard (for some useful tips on how to bargain, see Tipping, Baksheesh & Bargaining under Money in the Facts for the Visitor chapter). The government fixed-price emporium **Rajasthali** (☎ 415346; Chetak Circle) is a good place to get an idea of prices before you hit the markets.

Getting There & Away

Air There are daily flights on **Indian Airlines** (☎ 410999; Delhi Gate; open 10am-1pm & 2pm-5pm daily) to Delhi (US$115), Jaipur (US$90), Jodhpur (US$75) and Mumbai (US$135). **Jet Airways** (☎ 561105; Blue Circle Business Centre) has daily flights to Delhi, Jaipur and Mumbai for the same prices.

You are strongly advised to make flight bookings well in advance during the busy tourist season.

Bus Frequent Rajasthan State Road Transport Corporation (RSRTC) buses run from Udaipur to other regional centres, as well as to Delhi and Ahmedabad. If you use these buses, take an express as the ordinary buses take forever, make innumerable detours to various towns off the main route and can be very uncomfortable. For long-distance travel, use deluxe or express buses but you'll need to book ahead. Destinations served by express bus include:

destination	fare (Rs)	duration (hrs)
Ahmedabad	100	6
Ajmer	115	7
Bundi	115	7
Chittorgarh	40	3
Delhi	263	14
Indore	162	10
Jaipur	163	9
Jodhpur	106	7
Kota	126	8
Mt Abu	75	6
Mumbai	232	16
Vadodara	115	7

There are quite a few private bus companies which operate services to Delhi (Rs 250, 14 hours), Jaipur (Rs 130, nine hours), Jodhpur (Rs 90, six hours), Mt Abu (Rs 90, five hours) and Mumbai (Rs 300, 16 hours).

Train Lines into Udaipur are currently metre gauge only, so there are very limited train services - you're better off getting a bus to most destinations. Work has begun to convert the line to broad gauge; it's scheduled to be completed in 2005.

The *Chetak Express* goes to Chittorgarh (Rs 35/184 in 2nd/1st class, 3½ hours), Ajmer (Rs 77/405, eight hours), Jaipur (Rs 99/520, 11½ hours) and on to Delhi (Rs 144/756, 19 hours).

Taxi If you hire a taxi, the drivers will show or quote you a list of 'official' rates to places such as Mt Abu and Jodhpur. Shop around for the most competitive rate. Taxis usually charge for a return trip even if you're only going one way. For useful tips on hiring a taxi and driver, see Car in the Getting Around chapter.

Getting Around
To/From the Airport The airport is 25km from the city. There's no airport bus; a taxi will cost around Rs 75.

Autorickshaw When hiring an autorickshaw you should agree on a fare before you

set off, as they are unmetered. The standard fare for tourists anywhere in the city appears to hover around Rs 20 to 25, and you'll be lucky to get it for less since too many tourists pay the first price asked. An autorickshaw charges around Rs 150/250 for a half/full day of local sightseeing.

There are prepaid autorickshaw booths run by the police at the bus and train stations. It's Rs 22/27 to Lal Ghat/Hanuman Ghat from the bus station and Rs 27/32 from the train station.

Bicycle & Motorcycle A cheap and environmentally friendly way to buzz around is by bike. You can hire them all over town for around Rs 25 per day. **Heera Cycle Store** (☎ 523525; open 7.30am-9pm daily) near Hotel Badi Haveli in the old city rents bicycles/mopeds/motorcycles from Rs 25/150/200 per day.

NORTH OF UDAIPUR
Eklingji & Nagda
The interesting village of Eklingji – only 22km and a short bus ride north of Udaipur – has a number of ancient temples. The **Shiva temple** (*admission free; open 4.15am-6.45am, 10.30am-1.30pm & 5.15pm-8.15pm daily*), with its 108 small shrines, was originally built in AD 734, although its present form dates from the rule of Maharana Raimal between 1473 and 1509. The walled complex has an elaborately pillared hall under a large pyramidal roof and features a four-faced Shiva image of black marble. Check the opening hours in case they have changed. Photography is not allowed. Avoid the temple on Monday (an auspicious day for devotees) as it can get very crowded. The maharana of Udaipur pays a private visit to the temple on Monday evening. Guides are available at the temple.

At Nagda, about 1km off the road and 1km before Eklingji, there are some 10th-century temples. The Jain temple of **Adbudji** is essentially ruined, but its architecture is interesting. About 500m away, the **Sas Bahu** has very fine and intricate carvings including some erotic figures. It is most convenient to reach these temples by hiring a bicycle in Eklingji itself. There are also some small temples that are submerged in the nearby lake.

Places to Stay & Eat At Lake Bagela in Nagda, **Heritage Resorts** (☎ 0294-440382, fax 441833; singles/doubles Rs 1850/3200), is set in lovely grounds on a hill overlooking the ruins. Prices include breakfast. Its restaurant (nonguests are welcome) has a buffet lunch or dinner for Rs 300. There's a small pool, and horse rides are available for Rs 30.

Getting There & Away Local buses run from Udaipur to Eklingji every hour from 5am to 10pm (Rs 7, 30 minutes).

Haldighati

This battlefield site, 40km north of Udaipur, is where Maharana Pratap defied the superior Mughal forces of Akbar in 1576. The site is marked by a small *chhatri* which commemorates the warrior's horse, Chetak. Although badly wounded and exhausted, this brave horse carried Maharana Pratap to safety before collapsing and dying. It is for this loyalty and courage that Chetak is honoured. There's not a lot to see, but the historical site attracts many Indian visitors. Haldighati can be reached by bus from Nathdwara (Rs 10, 30 minutes); the battle site is 2km from the town.

Nathdwara

The important 18th-century Krishna temple of **Sri Nathji** (admission free; open 5am-5.30am, 7.15am-7.45am, 9.15am-9.45am, 11.30am-noon, 3.30pm-4pm, 4.30pm-5pm & 6pm-6.30pm daily) stands at Nathdwara, 48km north of Udaipur. It's an important shrine for Vaishnavites. The black-stone Krishna image that is housed in the temple was brought here from Mathura in 1669 to protect it from the destructive impulses of Aurangzeb. According to legend, the getaway vehicle, a wagon, sank into the ground up to the axles as it was passing through Nathdwara. The priests realised that this was a sign from Krishna – the image did not want to travel any further! Accordingly, the Sri Nathji temple was built on the spot.

Attendants treat the image like a delicate child, getting it up in the morning, washing it, putting its clothes on, offering it specially prepared meals and putting it down to sleep, all at precise times throughout the day. It's a very popular pilgrimage site, and the temple opens and closes around the image's daily routine. It gets very crowded around 3.30pm to 4pm when Krishna gets up after a siesta. Do check that the listed temple timings have not changed. Photography is not permitted.

Nathdwara is also well known for its *pichwai* paintings, which were produced after the image of Krishna was brought to the town. These bright paintings, with their rather static images, were usually done on hand-spun fabric to be hung behind the idol. As with many other schools of painting, numerous inferior reproductions of the *pichwai* paintings are created specifically for the lucrative tourist trade.

Places to Stay & Eat Considering it's an RTDC establishment, **RTDC Hotel Gokul** (☎ 02953-30917; dorm beds Rs 50, singles/doubles Rs 400/500) is surprisingly good. It's set in quiet gardens around 4km from the temple. There's also a bar and a restaurant where vegetarian thalis cost Rs 60.

RTDC Hotel Yatrika Mangla (☎ 02953-31119; dorm beds Rs 50, singles/doubles Rs 300/400) is only around a kilometre from the temple, so is more convenient. There's a restaurant here.

Shreeji Resort (☎ 02953-31284, fax 30 400; singles/doubles from Rs 650/745) is a friendly place with reasonable rooms. The restaurant serves Indian vegetarian food.

Getting There & Away There are frequent daily buses going from Udaipur to Nathdwara (Rs 22, one hour). It costs Rs 10 to park a car at the temple.

Kankroli & Rajsamand Lake

At Kankroli, 66km from Udaipur, there is a **temple** devoted to Dwarkadhish (an incarnation of Vishnu), which is similar to the temple at Nathdwara; the opening hours are similarly erratic.

Nearby is the large Rajsamand Lake, created by a dam constructed in 1660 by Maharana Raj Singh (r. 1652–80). There are many ornamental arches and beautifully carved *chhatris* along the huge *bund* (embankment). It also has several interesting old inscriptions.

There are frequent RSRTC buses from Udaipur (Rs 25, 2½ hrs).

Kumbhalgarh

Kumbhalgarh *(foreigner/citizen Rs 100/5; open 9am-5pm daily)*, 64km north of Udaipur, is the most important fort in the Mewar region after Chittorgarh. It was here that the rulers of Mewar retreated in times of danger, and where a baby prince of Mewar was hidden from an assassin (see the boxed text 'Mewar's Most Honoured Mother' earlier). It's an isolated and fascinating place, built by Maharana Kumbha in the 15th century. Because of its inaccessibility – at 1100m on top of the Aravalli Range – it was taken only once in its history. Even then, it took the combined armies of the Mughal emperor Akbar, and of Amber and Marwar to breach its defences. The thick walls of this mighty fort stretch some 36km and are wide enough for eight horses to ride abreast. They enclose many temples, palaces, gardens and water storage facilities. The fort was renovated in the 19th century by Maharana Fateh Singh. It's worth taking a leisurely walk in the large compound, which has some interesting ruins and is very peaceful.

It's a steep climb up to the fort entrance, so don't forget to buy your ticket first, near the start of the road from the car park. It costs Rs 25 to park a car.

There's also the **Kumbhalgarh Wildlife Sanctuary** *(foreigner/citizen Rs 80/10, video Rs 200; open sunrise-sunset daily)* here, known for its wolves. The scarcity of waterholes between March and June makes this the best time to see animals, including chowsinghas (four-horned antelopes), leopards, panthers, sloth bears and various bird species. The best time for wildlife spotting is in the early morning or late afternoon. The Aodhi Hotel (see Places to Stay & Eat) can arrange horse and jeep hire for guests. You need to get permission to enter the reserve from the forest department in nearby Kelwara, or from the **Deputy Chief Wildlife Warden** *(☎ 0294-421361)* in Udaipur, but if you're staying at the Aodhi Hotel, it will be organised for you.

Places to Stay & Eat The best hotel in Kumbhalgarh is the **Aodhi Hotel** *(☎ 02954-42341, or book at Shiv Niwas Palace Hotel in Udaipur ☎ 0294-528016, fax 528006; singles/doubles Rs 1999/3300; suites Rs 5500)*. It's an ideal place to just read a book or play a leisurely game of cards. Built on the side of a hill, rooms are decorated in a wilderness theme and suites are available. Non-guests can dine in the restaurant; the set breakfast/lunch/dinner is Rs 225/300/375. Jeep safaris to the wildlife sanctuary can be arranged (Rs 2000 for three hours).

Kumbhalgarh Fort Hotel *(☎ 02954-42372, fax 0294-525106; singles/doubles from Rs 1195/2395)*, 5km from the fort, has comfortable rooms. The set breakfast/lunch/dinner is Rs 175/300/300 and there's a pool.

Hotel Ratnadeep *(☎ 02954-42217, fax 42340; dorm beds Rs 100, singles/doubles with private bathroom from Rs 400/500, with air-con Rs 800/1000)*, in nearby Kelwara, is a bit further away from the fort, but is a good option if you can't afford the above two hotels. The rooms are ordinary and most have Indian-style toilets. There's a small restaurant here. Near to this hotel is a Jain temple.

Thandiberi Forest Guest House *(doubles Rs 250)* is in the sanctuary. Bookings need to be made in advance through the **Deputy Chief Wildlife Warden** *(☎ 0294-421361)* in Udaipur.

Getting There & Away There are several daily buses from Udaipur (Rs 30, 3½ hours), but not all leave from the bus stand – some go from Chetak Circle. Some stop in Kelwara (Rs 30) and others stop at the Aodhi Hotel; the fort is a 2km walk from here.

If you want to hire a jeep, it's a good idea to come here as part of a small group and share the cost.

Ranakpur

☎ 02934

One of the biggest and most important Jain temples found in India, the extremely beautiful Ranakpur complex (admission free, still camera/video Rs 40/150; open to Jains 6.30am-7pm daily, to non-Jains 11.30am-5pm daily) is well worth seeing, and makes for a convenient stop between Jodhpur and Udaipur. It is tucked away in a remote and quiet valley of the Aravalli Range, 90km from Udaipur.

The main temple is **Chaumukha Temple**, or Four-Faced Temple, dedicated to Adinath, the first *tirthankar*. Built in 1439, this huge, superbly crafted and well-kept marble temple has 29 halls supported by 1444 pillars – no two are alike. Within the complex are two other Jain temples (dedicated to **Neminath** and **Parasnath**) and, a short distance away, a **Sun Temple**. **Amba Mata Temple** is 1km from the main complex.

Shoes and all leather articles must be left at the entrance.

Places to Stay & Eat The most upmarket place to stay is the **Maharani Bagh Orchard** (☎ 85105, fax 85151, or book at Umaid Bhawan Palace in Jodhpur ☎ 0291-510101, fax 510100; singles/doubles Rs 1700/2500), set in a lush mango orchard 4km from Ranakpur. It offers modern cottage-style accommodation and free bicycles for guests. Meals are available; the buffet lunch/dinner costs Rs 325/350 (nonguests welcome).

The Castle (☎ 952934; singles/doubles Rs 400/800) is set in large grounds and has comfortable rooms. There's a pleasant courtyard restaurant which serves Indian, continental and Chinese food; *dum aloo Kashmiri* (potatoes in an aromatic curd sauce) is Rs 60 and half a tandoori chicken is Rs 100. The hotel runs a daily tour to Kumbhalgarh (Rs 275).

Shivika Lake Hotel (☎ 85078; e shivi kalake@rediffmail.com; tents Rs 150, singles/doubles with private bathroom Rs 200/250) is a laid-back place with friendly staff and a nightly courtyard campfire. You can stay in a tent (with shared bathroom and bucket hot water) or in a room. Veg curries go for

Rs 35 to 45 and a bottle of beer usually costs about Rs 90.

RTDC Hotel Shilpi (☎ 85074; singles/doubles with private bathroom Rs 400/500, with air-con Rs 600/700) is the hotel closest to the temple. It's a quiet place with reasonable rooms. Vegetarian thalis are available in the dining room for Rs 60.

Roopam (☎ 85321; e roopaminn@hot mail.com; singles/doubles Rs 550/650; buffet Rs 150, mains Rs 35-90) has a few nice rooms. The restaurant offers a lunch buffet or à la carte dining. A bottle of beer is Rs 80.

The **dharamsala** (☎ 85019) is pilgrims' lodgings within the temple complex, offering very basic accommodation for just Rs 5 per bed. The rooms are simple (with shared bathroom and bucket hot water). At meal time veg thalis are served in the dining hall for Rs 15/20 for Jains/non-Jains.

Getting There & Around Frequent express buses from Udaipur (Rs 35, three hours) stop right outside the temple. Although it's just possible to travel through from Ranakpur to Jodhpur or Mt Abu on the same day, it's hardly worth it since you'll arrive well after dark. It's better to stay for the night and continue the next day. There are express buses to Mt Abu (Rs 75, five hours) and Jodhpur (Rs 72, five hours).

All the accommodation, except the Dharamsala and RTDC Hotel Shilpi, is too far from the bus stop to walk. Jeeps can sometimes be hired at the bus stop (ask at the shop), or call your hotel and see if you can be picked up.

Narlai

Narlai is an ideal base for exploring the various attractions around Udaipur. Opposite the Rawla Narlai hotel is a mammoth single granite rock with a small temple on top. There's also a good *baori* in Narlai, several old temples and lots of quiet walks.

Rawla Narlai (book at Ajit Bhawan in Jodhpur ☎ 0291-511410, fax 510674; singles/doubles Rs 1895/2295) is well kept with appealing rooms. Meals are available here and the set breakfast/lunch/dinner costs Rs 150/250/300).

There are buses from Udaipur (Rs 60, two hours) and Jodhpur (Rs 110, four hours).

Ghanerao

About 12km from Narlai is the little town of Ghanerao, which has a castle that has been converted into a hotel. **Mahavira Temple**, a 10th-century Jain temple, is also worth going to visit.

Ghanerao Royal Castle (☎ 02934-84035; singles/doubles Rs 1400/1800, suites Rs 2500) has a pavilion in a central courtyard of the castle where palace musicians used to perform. Near the castle are the cenotaphs of former rulers. A set meal in the dining room costs Rs 150/250/300 for breakfast/lunch/dinner.

Take an RSRTC bus from Udaipur to Sadri (Rs 70) or Desuri (Rs 70), then a jeep taxi (about Rs 75) from there to Ghanerao.

SOUTH OF UDAIPUR

Rishabdeo

At this village, about 65km south of Udaipur, there is a 15th-century **Jain temple to Rishabdeo** (admission free; open 6am-9.30pm daily). Rishabdeo is a reincarnation of Mahavir, the 24th and last of the Jain tirthankars, who founded Jainism around 500 BC and is also worshipped as a reincarnation of Vishnu. The temple, which is an important pilgrimage centre, features Rishabdeo's image, some beautiful carvings and two large black stone elephants at the temple's entrance. A short walk through a lane lined with small shops leads you there.

RTDC Hotel Gavri (☎ 02907-30145; singles/doubles with private bathroom from Rs 350/450, with air-con Rs 800/900), about 500m from the temple, has functional rooms and a vegetarian restaurant where veg thalis cost Rs 50.

There are buses to Rishabdeo from Udaipur (Rs 30, 1½ hours).

Bambora

About 45km southeast of Udaipur, this sleepy village has a 250-year-old fort that has been converted into an impressive hotel.

Karni Fort (☎ 0294-398283, or book at Hotel Karni Bhawan in Jodhpur ☎ 0291

512101, fax 512105; singles/doubles from Rs 2000/2750) has smart rooms but the best room (on the second floor, Rs 3700) has a blissfully soft round bed with panoramic views. There's a good restaurant, a secret tunnel, and an alluring swimming pool which has four water-spurting marble elephants and a central pavilion.

Jagat

At this small town, 56km southeast of Udaipur, is a small 10th-century **Durga temple**. There are some fine carvings, including a couple of erotic carvings which have inspired some people to call the town the Khajuraho of Rajasthan (total nonsense!).

Jaisamand Lake

Located in a stunning site 48km southeast of Udaipur, Jaisamand Lake is one of the largest artificial lakes in Asia. It was built by Maharana Jai Singh in the 17th century and created by damming the Gomti River; today it measures 14km long and 9km wide. There are beautiful marble *chhatris* around the embankment, each with an elephant in front. The summer palaces of the Udaipur maharanis are also here. The lake features a variety of birdlife and the nearby **Jaisamand Wildlife Sanctuary** (foreigner/citizen Rs 80/10; open 10am-5pm daily) is the home of panthers, leopards, deer, wild boars and crocodiles. The forests here used to be a favourite hunting ground for the former rulers of Mewar, and elaborate hunting expeditions would frequently take place here. It costs Rs 65 to take a car inside.

Boat rides (8am-7pm daily) on the lake start at Rs 20 per person for a short trip. A ride out to the Jaisamand Island Resort costs Rs 150.

Places to Stay The modern **Jaisamand Island Resort** (☎ 02906-34722, or book at Hotel Lakend in Udaipur ☎ 0294-431400, fax 431406; singles/doubles Rs 1800/2700, suites 3700) is in an isolated position, about 20 minutes by boat across the lake. The comfortable rooms here all have views over the water. Nonguests can visit the resort for a fee of Rs 150.

Forest Guest House *(rooms Rs 425)*, run by the wildlife sanctuary, has two huge rooms with double beds, although a lot more people could camp out on the floor. The views over the lake are fantastic but the bathrooms are a bit grotty, hot water is by the bucket. You must contact the deputy chief wildlife warden (☎ 0294-421361) in Udaipur for reservations.

Getting There & Away Hourly RSRTC buses travel from Udaipur to Jaisamand (Rs 15, 1 hour).

Sitamata Wildlife Sanctuary

Located 90km southeast of Udaipur, the Sitamata Wildlife Sanctuary covers 423 sq km of mainly deciduous forest, known for its ancient teak trees. Wildlife includes deer, sambars, leopards, caracals, flying squirrels and wild boars. Not many tourists make it out this way, which is part of the region's appeal. If you're in search of picturesque countryside, peace and plenty of fresh air, this place is ideal and there are two very different accommodation options available.

Places to Stay Simple accommodation is available at **Teekhi Magri Resort** *(☎ 0141-212235; cottages per double Rs 1100)*, a secluded jungle retreat 22km from the village of Dhamotar (160km from Udaipur). There are just three basic mudbrick cottages (lighting is by lantern). The jungle surrounding the cottages is home to a variety of wildlife, including leopards (look for paw prints in the morning). Meals are available and jeep safaris can be arranged. In winter be prepared for very cold nights. Bookings are essential.

Fort Dhariyawad *(☎ 02950-20050; singles/doubles Rs 1200/1300)* is also in the Sitamata sanctuary area, 120km from Udaipur. Although it does not have the same remote jungle appeal as the Teekhi Magri Resort, it is certainly recommended for those who prefer their creature comforts. The restaurant here serves tasty food; the set breakfast/lunch/dinner costs Rs 200/400/425. Jeep safaris can be arranged to places of interest in the area. The owners can also arrange

tented accommodation for the Baneshwar fair (see Baneshwar later).

There are RSRTC buses from Udaipur to Dhariyawad (Rs 50, 3½ hours).

Dungarpur

Situated about 110km south of Udaipur, Dungarpur, or City of Hills, was founded in the 13th century. You can visit the deserted old **Juna Mahal** *(admission Rs 100; open 9am-4.30pm daily)* after obtaining a ticket from the Udai Bilas Palace (see Places to Stay). Built in stages between the 13th and 18th centuries this crumbling, seven-storey palace is filled with old frescoes and paintings. The Aam Khas, or main living room, has impressive mirrorwork and glass inlays. The former royal hunting lodge, on a nearby hilltop, has sensational views over the town and its many temples.

Other points of interest in Dungarpur include the government-run **Rajmata Devendra Kunwer State Museum** *(admission Rs 3, free Mon; open 10am-5pm Sat-Thur)* near the hospital, which has pieces from the 6th century. They are well displayed but the captions are in Hindi. The beautiful **Deo Somnath Temple**, about 25km north of town, dates back to the 12th century. Note the amazing banyan tree opposite the temple, which must be hundreds of years old.

Places to Stay Maharaj Kumar Harshvardhan Singh of Dungarpur has partly converted an 18th-century palace constructed of *pareva* (Dungarpur's blue-grey stone) into a hotel, the **Udai Bilas Palace** *(☎ 02964-30808, fax 31008; singles/doubles Rs 2000/2650, suites Rs 3250-3800)*. There is a gruesome array of stuffed beasts in every conceivable corner of the hotel, including the long dining hall, where hollow eyes watch your every bite. The exquisite ceiling is made from Burmese teak. Another feature is the intricately carved Ek Thambia Mahal (One-Pillared Palace) in one of the courtyards. The property is ideally located near Gaibsagar lake, which is a good place for bird-watching. Many rooms are decorated in Art Deco style; suite No 9 has a mirror-floored dressing room. Bicycle hire and bird-watching excursions can also be organised for guests.

Hotel Pratibha Palace *(☎ 02964-30775; Shastri Colony; singles with private bathroom Rs 50-150, doubles with private bathroom Rs 100-250)* is the best budget hotel in town. Some rooms are quite small but it's otherwise OK considering the tariff. The toilets are Indian-style. Meals are available in the restaurant downstairs.

Getting There & Away Frequent RSRTC buses travel to Dungarpur from Udaipur (Rs 45/50 for express/deluxe, three hours).

Galiakot

About 50km southeast of Dungarpur is the important Muslim pilgrimage centre of Galiakot. This town is famous for the tomb of the saint Fakruddin, who spread the word of Mohammed in the 10th century. Each year, thousands of local and international Bohra Muslim pilgrims flock here to pay homage to the saint.

There are daily express buses from Udaipur (Rs 58, three hours).

Baneshwar

Baneshwar is at the confluence of three holy rivers: the Mahi, Som and Jakham. In January–February the week-long **Baneshwar Fair** is held at the Baneshwar Temple, about 80km from Dungarpur. It attracts thousands of Bhil tribal people.

Tents with attached bathroom (minimum booking of 10 tents, ie, a 20-person group; Rs 6000 a double for two days, including all meals) can be arranged through Fort Dhariyawad *(☎ 02950-20050)*. Bookings are essential at least two months in advance.

There are regular buses from Dungarpur to Baneshwar (Rs 10, one hour).

MT ABU

☎ 02974 ● postcode 307501 ● pop 22,045
Rajasthan's only hill station sprawls along a 1220m-high plateau in the south of the state, close to the Gujarat border. It's a popular hot-season retreat from the plains of both Rajasthan and Gujarat, but you won't find many Western travellers here – apart from those studying at the Brahma Kumaris World Spiritual University. The streets are filled with Indian tourists – starry-eyed honeymooners paddling boats around the lake and middle-class families wrapping their tongues around ice-cream cones.

Like most hill stations, it's best to avoid Mt Abu in summer, when hordes of people come to escape the heat. Tourism has greatly altered the natural environment here – vegetation has been cleared to make way for the many hotels that continue to crop up, and the temperatures are not as cool as they used to be. Nonetheless, Mt Abu has retained a certain green charm.

The Dilwara group of Jain temples, 5km from town, is a very important pilgrimage centre for Jains and the temples' superb marble carvings are among the best in Rajasthan, if not India. Also, like many hill stations, Mt Abu has its own lake, which is the hub of activity.

Myths and legends abound as to when or how Mt Abu came into existence. According to one, Mt Abu is as old as the Himalaya. It was named after Arbuda, a mighty serpent who saved Shiva's revered bull, Nandi, from plunging into an abyss. Another legend relates that in Mt Abu, the four Rajput fire clans, the Chauhans, Solankis, Pramaras and Pratiharas, were created from a fire pit by Brahmin priests.

Orientation

Mt Abu is a good place to simply wander around at leisure. It is on a hilly plateau about 22km long by 6km wide, 27km from the nearest train station at Abu Road. The main part of the town extends along the road in from Abu Road, down to Nakki Lake.

Information

Tourist Offices The **Tourist Reception Centre** *(☎ 35151; open 10am-1.30pm & 2pm-5pm daily)* is opposite the main bus stand.

Money The **State Bank of Bikaner & Jaipur**, situated in the same area as the main post office, changes travellers cheques and currency. The **Bank of Baroda**, near the southern part of the polo ground, changes

SOUTHERN RAJASTHAN

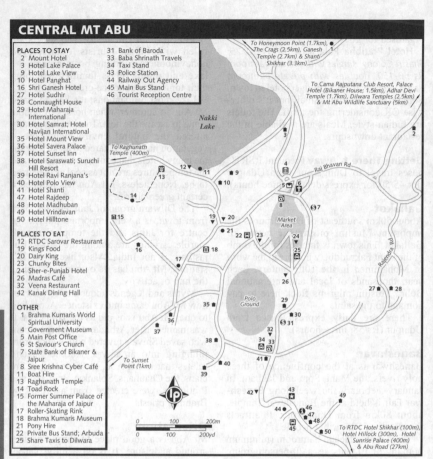

CENTRAL MT ABU

PLACES TO STAY
2 Mount Hotel
3 Hotel Lake Palace
9 Hotel Lake View
10 Hotel Panghat
16 Shri Ganesh Hotel
27 Hotel Sudhir
28 Connaught House
29 Hotel Maharaja International
30 Hotel Samrat; Hotel Navijan International
35 Hotel Mount View
36 Hotel Savera Palace
37 Hotel Sunset Inn
38 Hotel Saraswati; Suruchi Hill Resort
39 Hotel Ravi Ranjana's
40 Hotel Polo View
41 Hotel Shanti
47 Hotel Rajdeep
48 Hotel Madhuban
49 Hotel Vrindavan
50 Hotel Hilltone

PLACES TO EAT
12 RTDC Sarovar Restaurant
19 Kings Food
20 Dairy King
23 Chunky Bites
24 Sher-e-Punjab Hotel
26 Madras Café
32 Veena Restaurant
42 Kanak Dining Hall

OTHER
1 Brahma Kumaris World Spiritual University
4 Government Museum
5 Main Post Office
6 St Saviour's Church
7 State Bank of Bikaner & Jaipur
8 Sree Krishna Cyber Café
11 Boat Hire
13 Raghunath Temple
14 Toad Rock
15 Former Summer Palace of the Maharaja of Jaipur
17 Roller-Skating Rink
18 Brahma Kumaris Museum
21 Pony Hire
22 Private Bus Stand; Arbuda
25 Share Taxis to Dilwara
31 Bank of Baroda
33 Baba Shrinath Travels
34 Taxi Stand
43 Police Station
44 Railway Out Agency
45 Main Bus Stand
46 Tourist Reception Centre

travellers cheques and currency and offers advances on credit cards.

Post The **main post office** (Raj Bhavan Rd; open 9am-5pm Mon-Sat) is at the northern end of town.

Email & Internet Access There are a few places in town where you can check your email, including **Sree Krishna Cyber Café** (open 7am-9pm daily), near the post office, which charges Rs 60 per hour, and **Baba Shrinath Travels** (open 8.30am-10.30pm daily), offering the same rate.

Nakki Lake

Legend has it that this small lake, virtually in the centre of Mt Abu, was scooped out by a god using only his nails, or *nakh*. Some Hindus thus believe it to be a holy lake. The lake is surrounded by hills, parks and strange **rock formations**. The best known, **Toad Rock**, looks just like a toad about to hop into the lake. The 14th-century **Raghunath Temple** stands beside the lake. Several maharajas built lavish summer houses around Nakki Lake, and the maharaja of Jaipur's former **summer palace** is perched on a hill overlooking the water.

Nakki Lake is the heart of all activity in Mt Abu. It's a short and easy stroll around it and there are juice stalls, ice-cream parlours, balloon vendors, souvenir shops and small food stalls. You'll probably have to plough through the persistent photographers eager to take a happy snap of you by the water. The honeymooners are often approached by innovative sellers offering a range of aphrodisiacs that 'make big difference'.

One-hour horse rides cost Rs 50. From around 8am to 8pm daily, you can hire a pedal boat; it costs Rs 50/100 for a two-/four-person boat for 30 minutes. Six-person rowing boats cost Rs 180 for 30 minutes. On the edge of the lake there is a dilapidated, concrete, boat-shaped snack bar.

Viewpoints

Of the various viewpoints around town, **Sunset Point**, 1.5km from the tourist office, is the most popular. Hordes stroll out here every evening to catch the setting sun, the food stalls and all the usual entertainment. It's a 1km-walk from the road to the viewpoint, or you can hire a horse (Rs 20). Other popular spots include **Honeymoon Point**, which also offers a view of the sunset, and **The Crags**. Follow the white arrows along a rather overgrown path up to the summit of **Shanti Shikhar**, west of Adhar Devi Temple, where there are panoramic views.

Dilwara Temples

These remarkable Jain temples are Mt Abu's main attraction and among the finest examples of Jain architecture in India. The complex *(admission free; open to Jains sunrise -sunset daily, to non-Jains noon-6pm daily)* includes two temples with exquisite marble carvings – the art must surely have reached unsurpassed heights here.

The older of the temples is the **Vimal Vasahi**, built in 1031 by a Gujarati minister named Vimal. It is dedicated to the first *tirthankar*, Adinath. The central shrine contains an image of Adinath, while around the courtyard are 57 identical cells, each with a Buddha-like cross-legged image. Forty-eight elegantly carved pillars form the entrance to the courtyard. In front of the temple stands the **House of Elephants**, with figures of elephants marching in procession to the temple.

The later **Tejpal Temple** is dedicated to Neminath, the 22nd *tirthankar*, and was built in 1231 by the brothers Tejpal and Vastupal. Like Vimal, they were ministers in the government of the ruler of Gujarat. Although the Tejpal Temple is important as an extremely old and complete example of a Jain temple, its most notable feature is the intricacy and delicacy of the marble carving. It is so fine that, in places, the marble becomes almost transparent. In particular, the lotus flower that hangs from the centre of the dome is an incredible piece of work. It's difficult to believe that this huge lace-like filigree started as a solid block of marble. The temple employs several full-time stonecarvers to maintain and restore the work.

There are three other temples in the enclosure, but they all pale beside the Tejpal Temple and Vimal Vasahi.

Photography is not allowed, and bags are searched to prevent cameras being taken in. As at other Jain temples, all articles of leather (such as shoes and belts) have to be left at the entrance (where you pay Rs 1 per item when collecting them).

You can stroll out to Dilwara from the town in less than an hour, or take a share-taxi for Rs 4 per person (one way) from just opposite the Madras Café in the town centre.

Brahma Kumaris World Spiritual University & Museum

The Brahma Kumaris teach that all religions lead to God and so are equally valid, and the principles of each should be studied. The university's (W *www.bkwsu.com*) stated aim is the establishment of universal peace through spiritual knowledge and raja yoga meditation. The headquarters are in Mt Abu, and many followers come here each year to attend courses at the university.

For many people the teachings are immensely powerful, evidenced by the fact that there are over 6500 branches in 84 countries around the world. It even has consultative status on the Economic and Social Council of the UN. On the other hand, many travellers who visit the university come away feeling that this is a rather loony New Age sect. You can make up your own mind by paying a visit to the **Universal Peace Hall** (☎ 38261, fax 38952; open 8am-6pm daily) where free tours are available, including an introduction to the philosophy of the Brahma Kumaris. If you want to find out more, you can take an introductory course (seven lessons) for a minimum of three days, however a course of seven days is recommended. There's no fee or charge – the organisation is entirely supported by donations. To attend one of these residential courses, contact your local branch and arrange everything in advance.

The organisation also runs the **Peace Park** (admission free; open 8am-6pm daily), near Guru Shikhar, which is the highest point in Rajasthan, and a **museum** (admission free; open 8am-8pm daily) in the town, outlining the university's teachings through wonderfully kitsch light-up dioramas. Meditation sessions are also offered here.

Other Attractions

A small **government museum** (admission Rs 3, open 10am-4.30pm Sat-Thu), near the post office, features marble sculptures from the 12th century and other cultural displays. There's also a **roller-skating rink** (open 9am-10pm daily), which charges Rs 15/25 per 15/30 minutes, including skate hire. You can hire ponies nearby.

About 3km north of town, 365 steps lead to the ancient **Adhar Devi** temple, which is built in a natural cleft in the rock. You have to stoop to get through the low entrance to the temple. There are nice views over Mt Abu from up here.

Organised Tours

Rajasthan Roadways offers daily tours of all the main sites. Tours leave from the main bus stand (opposite the Tourist Reception Centre) and cost Rs 36; make your booking at the bus stand. This price does not include entry to the sites or camera charges. Tour times are 8.30am to 1pm and 1.30pm to 7pm (later in summer). The afternoon tour finishes at Sunset Point.

Places to Stay

There are plenty of hotels to choose from, with new ones springing up each year. Most are along or just off the main road through to Nakki Lake. The high season lasts from around mid-April to mid-November and most hotel owners raise prices to whatever the market will bear at those times. During the five days of Diwali (October–November), rooms are ridiculously expensive and virtually unobtainable without advance booking. Avoid the place at this time, when it is transformed from a quiet retreat to a congested and noisy hive of activity.

During the low season (with the exception of Christmas and New Year), discounts of up to 70% are available and mid-range accommodation can be an absolute bargain. Most places are definitely open to a bit of bargaining, and the rates get cheaper the longer you stay. Most of the budget hotels have an ungenerous 9am checkout time.

At all times of the year there are plenty of touts working the bus and taxi stands. In the low season you can safely ignore them; at peak times they can save you a lot of legwork as they'll know exactly where the last available room is. Hot water can be erratic at the budget places and the service is rather unenthusiastic at most places.

The Paying Guest House Scheme, which gives you the opportunity to live with a local family, operates in Mt Abu. It costs around Rs 100 to 500 per night – contact the Tourist Reception Centre (see Information earlier) for details.

Places to Stay – Budget

Shri Ganesh Hotel (☎ 35591; e lalit_gan esh@yahoo.com; dorm beds from Rs 50, singles from Rs 125, doubles high/low season Rs 300/100), up the hill towards the maharaja of Jaipur's old summer palace, is popular with travellers and deservedly so. It's in a quiet location, management is friendly and rooms are good value. The sitting area on the roof, complete with swing chair, is a great place to relax. There's a laundry service and Internet access, and Lalit Ganesh takes guests on excellent guided walks (Rs 20) into the surrounding hills every evening.

The restaurant serves good home-cooking at reasonable prices (veg thalis for Rs 40).

Hotel Lake View (*☎ 38659; doubles Rs 400-700)* overlooks picturesque Nakki Lake. The views are good, and the rooms are pretty good value. Hot water is by the bucket in the cheaper rooms, and available between 7am and 11am in the bathrooms of the more expensive ones. There's a pleasant terrace and veg meals are served.

Hotel Panghat (*☎ 38886; doubles with private bathroom Rs 150)*, close by Lake View, is also good if you want to be where the action is – Nakki Lake. Its average rooms have a lake view and TV. Hot water is available from 7am to 9am.

Hotel Shanti (*☎ 38031, singles/doubles with private bathroom from Rs 100/150)* is a huge pale-blue concoction with simple, clean rooms (some with Indian toilets) accessed by a maze of terraces and staircases.

Hotel Vrindavan (*☎ 35147; doubles with private bathroom Rs 300-700, triples Rs 500)*, near the bus stand, is set back from the main road, making it relatively quiet. The rooms are clean, light and spacious and there are pleasant gardens and terraces. Hot water is available from 6.30am to 10am. There's a vegetarian restaurant here that serves thalis for Rs 50.

Hotel Rajdeep (*☎ 35525; doubles with private bathroom in low season from Rs 150-500)* is right opposite the bus stand, so can get a bit noisy. The cheaper rooms have hot water by the bucket. A small Punjabi and South Indian restaurant at the front of this hotel doubles as reception.

Hotel Sudhir (*☎ 35311, fax 38259; doubles with private bathroom Rs 350-550)* offers basic doubles with constant hot water. There are good views from the terrace and veg meals are available.

RTDC Hotel Shikhar (*☎ 38944, fax 37069; singles/doubles with private bathroom from Rs 210/270)*, set back from the main road and up a steepish path, is a huge hollow place. Although fairly popular, it's certainly not the best value in town and the service leaves a little to be desired.

Hotel Polo View (*☎ 35487, fax 38900; doubles with private bathroom Rs 80-150)* is

excellent value, offering rooms that have 24-hour hot water.

Hotel Mount View (*☎ 37121; doubles with private bathroom Rs 250)* is an older building; the clean, no-frills rooms have hot water from 7am to 10am.

Hotel Saraswati (*☎ 38887, fax 37377; doubles with private bathroom Rs 100-400)*, near Hotel New Mount View, is pretty good value. Reasonable doubles have hot water from 7am to noon, and there's a vegetarian restaurant that serves Gujarati thalis (famous for their sweet curry dishes) for Rs 45.

Places to Stay – Mid-Range

Mount Hotel (*☎ 35150; doubles Rs 400-600)*, run by the affable Jehangir Bharucha (fondly known as 'Jimmy'), is a homey place in a tranquil location along the road to the Dilwara temples. It once belonged to a British army officer and has changed little since those days. The handful of rooms are a bit worn and weary, but you'll have no hassles whatsoever. Vegetarian lunch or dinner is Rs 90, available with advance notice, and Jimmy can organise horse safaris (Rs 140 per hour). His dog, Spots, is a friendly creature.

Hotel Lake Palace (*☎ 37154, fax 38817; e savshanti@hotmail.com; singles/doubles/ triples in high season Rs 800/900/1100)* makes the most of its excellent location – just across from Nakki Lake – with rather high prices. You should be able to get at least 50% off the high-season prices in the low season, if you bargain hard. Indian food is available (veg curries Rs 25 to 55).

Hotel Sunset Inn (*☎ 35194, fax 35515; e thomasg1956@yahoo.com; doubles in high season Rs 1250-1700)*, on the western edge of Mt Abu, is a modern hotel that's well run but rather overpriced. The restaurant serves Punjabi and Gujarati food. Low-season discounts of 40% are available.

Hotel Savera Palace (*☎ 35354, fax 38900; e savshanti@hotmail.com; singles/doubles Rs 900/1000)*, near Hotel Sunset Inn, has decent rooms with 24-hour hot water. There's a restaurant and swimming pool.

Suruchi Hill Resort (*☎ 35577; doubles in high season Rs 690)* is near Hotel Saraswati at the bottom end of the polo ground. It has a pool and a restaurant serving Indian and Chinese food.

Hotel Ravi Ranjana's *(☎ 38277, fax 38 900; doubles in low season Rs 500-900)*, at the end of this road, is rather scruffy for the price. There's a restaurant which serves Indian, Chinese and continental cuisine.

Hotel Madhuban *(☎ 38822, fax 38900, e hotmadhuban@yahoo.com; doubles in low season Rs 600-750)* has doubles with hot water from 7am to 2pm, or there are super-deluxe rooms with geysers. There are only snacks available here.

Hotel Samrat *(☎ 35173; singles/doubles low season from Rs 290/350)* and **Hotel Navijan International** *(☎ 35153; singles/doubles Rs 150/250)*, both on the main road, are basically the same hotel, although they appear to be separate. Both have rooms with hot water from 6am to 11am. The Navijan is cheaper, but not quite as good.

Hotel Maharaja International *(☎ 35161, fax 38627; singles/doubles in low season Rs 590/700)* is a little more upmarket than the Samrat and Navijan, which are directly opposite, but it is not remarkable. Punjabi and Gujarati food is cooked here.

Places to Stay – Top End

Palace Hotel *(Bikaner House; ☎ 35121, fax 38674; singles/doubles Rs 1700/2200, suites Rs 2200/2850)* is a worthwhile treat and a very pleasant place to chill out. The hotel was once the summer residence of the maharaja of Bikaner and is now run by the maharaja's amiable son-in-law. The hotel is in a picturesque location near the Dilwara temples and has shady gardens, a private lake, two tennis courts, and pony rides by arrangement. There are 35 tastefully decorated rooms; the ones in the old wing have the most character. Delicious meals are also available in the dining room (see Places to Eat).

Cama Rajputana Club Resort *(☎ 38205, fax 38412; doubles Rs 2100, with air-con Rs 2600, suites Rs 3600)*, nearby, was once a private club but is now a large hotel. Set in its own gardens, it's a classy place with nice views over the hills. It also has a good

restaurant serving Chinese, continental and Punjabi food. Ayurvedic massage is available (Rs 600 per hour).

Connaught House *(☎ 38560, fax 38900, or book at Umaid Bhawan Palace in Jodhpur ☎ 0291-510101, fax 510100; singles/doubles in old wing Rs 1600/2100, in new wing Rs 1400/1900)* belongs to the maharaja of Jodhpur and has a relaxing atmosphere. It's more like an English cottage than a hotel and is set in shady gardens. The rooms in the old building have more charm than those in the new wing. Meals are available but should be ordered in advance; the set lunch or dinner is Rs 225.

Hotel Sunrise Palace *(☎ 35573, fax 38775, e sunrisepalace@gnahd.global.net.in; doubles Rs 780-1410, suites from Rs 1740)*, found at the southern end of Mt Abu, is yet another former summer residence of a Rajput maharaja (this time the maharaja of Bharatpur). Although it lacks the panache of Connaught House and the Palace Hotel, it's a very tranquil hotel with fabulous views. The rooms are well furnished and the restaurant has excellent views.

Hotel Hilltone *(☎ 38391, fax 38395; e hilltone@sancharnet.in; doubles Rs 1600-2400, cottages Rs 3200)* is centrally located, but doesn't quite make the grade of its famous namesake. Within the hotel complex there's a swimming pool, a sauna, a good restaurant and a cocktail bar (Long Island iced tea Rs 120, screwdriver Rs 80).

Hotel Hillock *(☎ 38463, fax 38467; rooms in high season Rs 2190-3390)* is a large, swanky place that's spotlessly clean and quite well decorated. There's a restaurant serving Indian, Chinese and continental food, a bar, a coffee shop, a swimming pool and pleasant gardens. A 30% discount is offered in the low season.

Places to Eat
Kanak Dining Hall *(☎ 38305)*, near the main bus stand, is a popular place to eat. The all-you-can-eat Gujarati thalis (Rs 45) served here are perhaps the best in Mt Abu; there's seating indoors and outdoors.

Veena Restaurant *(☎ 38022; open 7am-11.30pm daily)* is further uphill, next to the junction at the bottom end of the polo ground. Its refillable Gujarati thalis (Rs 45) are also excellent.

Sher-e-Punjab Hotel *(open 8am-12.30am daily)*, in the market area, has reasonably priced Punjabi and Chinese food. It takes delight in its brain preparations (brain masala is Rs 40). There are also some more conventional creations such as chicken curry (Rs 40).

Madras Café *(open 8am-11pm daily)*, also in this area, offers an assortment of Indian and Western veg and nonveg fare. There are even Jain pizzas (no garlic, onion or cheese) for Rs 35. *Masala dosas* (lentil-flour crepes stuffed with potatoes cooked with onions and curry leaves) are Rs 25 and a glass of lassi is Rs 15.

Arbuda *(☎ 35358; open 7.30am-10.30pm daily; dishes around Rs 50)*, near the entrance to the private bus stand, is a pleasant pure veg restaurant on an open-air terrace.

Chunky Bites, across the road is a good place to grab a snack. It has loud music and regional delicacies such as *bhelpuri* (a popular Mumbai snack) for Rs 20 and Delhi *chaat* (snacks such as samosas and fried potato patties seasoned with spices and served with chutney) for Rs 25.

Kings Food, found on the road leading down to the lake, has the usual have-a-go-at-anything menu and is good for a light bite. Across the road, **Dairy King** sells ice cream.

RTDC Sarovar Restaurant *(dishes under Rs 40)* is right on the water's edge. The food is nothing special but it's a pleasant place from which to view the lake; the effect is diminished somewhat by the Hindi rock music blaring from loudspeakers. There are pool tables inside (Rs 50 per hour).

Palace Hotel *(☎ 38684; Bikaner House; open 7.30am-11pm daily; set lunch or dinner veg/nonveg Rs 350/375)* is the best place for a special meal and has a set lunch or dinner. It's best to make advance reservations.

Shopping

Around Nakki Lake there are lots of colourful little shops and stalls flogging all sorts of kitsch curios. In the evening, the town really comes to life and this is an enjoyable time to do some leisurely browsing and people watching.

Getting There & Away

As you enter Mt Abu, there's a toll gate where bus and car passengers are charged Rs 10, plus Rs 10 for a car. If you're travelling by bus, this is an irksome hold-up, as you have to wait until the collector painstakingly gathers the toll from each and every passenger (keep small change handy).

Bus Regular buses make the 27km climb from Abu Road up to Mt Abu (Rs 15, one hour) – you never know quite what to expect as the bus spirals up the mountain. Some RSRTC buses go all the way to Mt Abu, while others terminate at Abu Road, so make sure you get the one you want.

The bus schedule from Mt Abu is extensive, and for many destinations you will find a direct bus faster and more convenient than going down to Abu Road and waiting for a train.

destination	express (Rs)	deluxe (Rs)	duration (hrs)
Ahmedabad	87	120	6
Ajmer	154	140	8
Baroda	–	160	8
Jaipur	202	150	11
Jodhpur	120	120	7
Mumbai	–	350	18
Surat	–	180	10
Udaipur	75	100	5

Bus tickets can be bought from travel agencies, such as **Gujarat Travels** *(☎ 37123; open 6am-midnight daily)*, near the bus stand, which can also arrange local sightseeing (a half/full day costs Rs 40/80 per person).

Train Abu Road, the railhead for Mt Abu, is located on the broad-gauge line between Delhi and Mumbai via Ahmedabad.

In Mt Abu there's a **Railway Out Agency** *(☎ 38383; open 9am-1pm & 2pm-4pm Mon-Sat, 9am-noon Sun)* near the main bus stand (which is opposite the police station) which has quotas on most of the express trains out of Abu Road.

From Abu Road, direct trains run to various destinations including Ajmer, Jodhpur, Jaipur and Ahmedabad. For Bhuj and the rest of the Kathiawar peninsula in Gujarat, change trains at Palanpur, 53km south of Abu Road.

Taxi A taxi, which you can share with up to five people, costs about Rs 200 from Abu Road. To hire a jeep for local sightseeing costs around Rs 350/700 for a half/full day (bargain hard and you just may bring it down). Many hotels can arrange jeep hire, or they can be rented in the town centre.

Getting Around
Buses from the bus stand go to the various sites in Mt Abu, but it takes a little planning to get out and back without too much hanging around. For Dilwara it's easier to take a share-taxi. These buses leave, when full, from opposite the Madras Café, in the centre of town; the fare is Rs 4 per person.

There are no autorickshaws in Mt Abu, but it's relatively easy to get around on foot. Porters with trolleys can be hired for a small charge to transport your luggage – weary travellers can even be transported there on the trolley!

AROUND MT ABU
Achalgarh
Eleven kilometres north of Mt Abu, the Shiva temple of **Achaleshwar Mahandeva**, in Achalgarh, boasts a number of interesting features, including what's said to be a toe of Shiva, as well as a brass Nandi (Shiva's vehicle, a bull) and, where the Shiva lingam would normally be, there's a deep hole that is said to extend all the way down to the underworld.

Just outside the temple, beside the car park, three stone buffaloes stand around a tank, while the figure of a king shoots at them with his bow and arrows. A legend states that the tank was once filled with ghee, but demons, in the form of the buffaloes, came down and polluted the ghee that is until the king shot them. A path leads up the hillside to a group of colourful **Jain temples**, which all have fine views out over the plains.

Guru Shikhar
At the end of the plateau, 15km from Mt Abu, is Guru Shikhar, the highest point in Rajasthan at 1722m. A road goes almost all the way to the summit. At the top is the **Atri Rishi Temple**, complete with a priest and good views all around.

Mt Abu Wildlife Sanctuary
The 290-sq-km Mt Abu Wildlife Sanctuary *(Trevor Tank; foreigner/citizen Rs 80/10; open sunrise-sunset daily)*, 8km northeast of Mt Abu, is home to animals such as panthers, bears, sambars, foxes, wild boars, crocodiles and birds.

A sign at the sanctuary gives the following advice to visitors: 'Use your eyes to observe the plants, birds and animals, use your ears to hear birds and animals call, use your legs to walk – the more you walk the more you see and hear'.

Gaumukh Temple
Down on the Abu Road side of Mt Abu, a small stream flows from the mouth of a marble cow, giving the shrine its name. There is also a marble figure of the bull Nandi, Shiva's vehicle. The tank here, Agni Kund, is said to be the site of the sacrificial fire, made by the sage Vasishta, from which four of the great Rajput clans were born. An image of Vasishta is flanked by figures of Rama and Krishna.

To reach the temple you must take a path with 750 steps down into the valley (and then climb those 750 steps back out again!).

ABU ROAD
This station, 27km down the hill from Mt Abu on the plains, is the rail junction for Mt Abu. The train station and bus stand are conveniently located right next to each other on the edge of town.

Although there are RSRTC buses from Abu Road to other cities such as Jodhpur, Jaipur, Udaipur and Ahmedabad, there is little point in catching them from here as these services are all available from Mt Abu itself. Alternatively, private bus companies also operate their services from Mt Abu to several destinations.

There's a sprinkling of cheap hotels along Abu Road and most are located only a short walk from the train station. These places are satisfactory and OK for a night's stay, but the accommodation available in

Mt Abu is the better choice in terms of comfort and price.

Retiring rooms *(doubles Rs 120)* at the Abu Road train station are convenient if catching an early train (veg thali is Rs 40).

Northern Rajasthan (Shekhawati)

The semidesert Shekhawati region lies in the triangular area between Delhi, Jaipur and Bikaner. Around the 14th century, a number of Muslim clans moved into the area, and the towns that developed became important trading posts on caravan routes from the ports of Gujarat. The name of the region and its inhabitants can be traced to a 15th-century Rajput Kachhwaha chieftain by the name of Rao Shekha.

Although the towns have long since lost their importance, they have not lost the amazing painted havelis (mansions), with internal courtyards, built by the merchants of the region. Most of the buildings date from the 18th century to the early 20th century, and such is their splendour that the area has been dubbed by some as the 'open-air gallery of Rajasthan'. Shekhawati sees fewer tourists than many other parts of Rajasthan, so facilities at most places can be limited. But for many people this is its greatest appeal. Tracking down painted havelis is something like a treasure hunt, taking you through the ever-changing backstreets of traditional Indian towns. Some people go in search of a particular haveli, while others just wander at random through these small, dusty towns. There's no chance of getting lost, and there are surprises around every corner. The houses mentioned here are just a small sample of the many beautiful painted homes that you may stumble across. There are also the obligatory (for Rajasthan) forts, a couple of minor castles, distinctive wells, *baoris* (step-wells), *chhatris* (cenotaphs) and a handful of mosques to discover.

The major towns of interest in the region are Nawalgarh, Fatehpur, Mandawa, Ramgarh and Jhunjhunu, although at least a few havelis survive in nearly every town.

History

As the Mughal empire fell into decline after the death of Aurangzeb in 1707, the

PAKISTAN

DELHI

Mandawa p287 Jhunjhunu p278
Fatehpur p285

Nawalgarh p272

Northern Rajasthan (Shekhawati) p267

RAJASTHAN

descendants of Rao Shekha, who had already installed themselves in the area to the east of the Aravalli Range, encroached on the regions to the north and west. Covering an area of approximately 30,000 sq km, the Shekhawati region encompasses the administrative districts of Churu, Jhunjhunu and Sikar.

The chieftains of the region retained a nominal loyalty to the Rajput states of Jaipur and Amber, which in turn honoured them with the hereditary titles of *tazimi sardars*. It was probably exposure to the courts of

Jaipur and Amber that encouraged the chieftains, known as *thakurs*, or barons, to commission the first of the thousands of murals to decorate their havelis.

By 1732, two of these chieftains, Sardul Singh and Shiv Singh, had overthrown the nawabs of Fatehpur and Jhunjhunu and carved their territories up between them. Their descendants, particularly the sons of Sardul Singh, installed themselves in surrounding villages, where they commanded the allegiance and respect of the villagers. Their coffers were filled by heavy taxes imposed on the poor farmers of the area and

duties levied on the caravans carrying goods from the ports of Gujarat overland to northern India and the countries bordering India to the north, northwest and northeast. The merchants travelled via Shekhawati because the Rajput royal states on either side imposed even greater levies on traders. The arid region of Shekhawati thus saw a great deal of trading activity, encouraging merchants to establish themselves here.

The rise of the British Raj following the eclipse of the Mughal empire could have sounded the death knell for Shekhawati. The British ports at Bombay (present-day

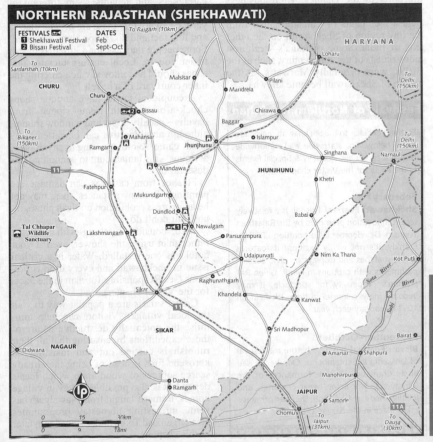

NORTHERN RAJASTHAN (SHEKHAWATI)

FESTIVALS 🎪 DATES
1 Shekhawati Festival Feb
2 Bissau Festival Sept-Oct

Mumbai) and Calcutta (present-day Kolkata) were able to handle a higher volume of trade than those at Gujarat. Pressure by the British East India Company compelled Jaipur state to drastically reduce its levies, and it became no longer necessary for traders to travel via Shekhawati. However, the Shekhawat merchants had received a good grounding in the practices and principles of trade, and were reluctant to relinquish what was obviously a lucrative source of income.

Towards the end of the 19th century, men emigrated en masse from their desert homes to the thriving trading centres emerging on the ports of the Ganges. Their business acumen was unparalleled, and some of the richest merchants of Calcutta hailed from the tiny region of Shekhawati on the other side of India. Some of India's wealthiest industrialists of the 20th century, such as the Birlas, were originally Marwaris (as the people of Shekhawati became known).

Festivals of Northern Rajasthan

Festivals peculiar to the Shekhawati region are given below. For statewide and nationwide festivals, see Public Holidays & Special Events in the Facts for the Visitor chapter.

February
Shekhawati Festival This fair is a relatively recent innovation promoted by the Rajasthan Tourism Development Corporation (RTDC). Frankly, it's not wildly exciting: it features sports matches and displays on civic accomplishments with captions in Hindi. Given Rajasthan's propensity for spectacle, it may become more colourful in time. It's held on 10–11 February each year.

September–October
Bissau Festival Ten days before the festival of Dussehra in September or October, Bissau hosts dramatic mime performances of the Ramayana. The actors wear costumes and locally made masks, and the performance takes place in the bazaar at twilight.

Responsible Tourism

The tourist boom has still not really caught up with Shekhawati. There is a basic infrastructure to accommodate the increasing number of foreign visitors, but tourism here is still in its infancy. While tourism can play a positive role in promoting interest in Shekhawati's great legacy of beautifully painted buildings and so generating the political will to preserve them, this is an ecologically and culturally sensitive region.

Few havelis are open as museums or for display, and consequently many are either totally or partially locked up. While the caretakers and tenants seem tolerant of strangers wandering into their front courtyard, be aware that these are private places, and that tact and discretion should be used. Some people may ask for a little baksheesh to let you in. Local custom dictates that shoes should be removed when entering the inner courtyard of a haveli.

A couple of towns have antique shops chock-a-block with items ripped from havelis – usually doors and window frames, although anything that can be carted away is fair game. Avoid investing in any of these antiques – it's tantamount to condoning this desecration.

Flashes from cameras can damage the paintings. In many instances, there may not be an express prohibition on flash photography, but don't do it!

Also, consider washing with a bucket rather than using the shower, even if your hotel has one installed. Water is a critical issue in Shekhawati and every drop is precious (see Responsible Tourism in the Facts for the Visitor chapter).

Camel safaris are a popular way to visit the local villages. Visitors can help minimise the potentially destructive nature of these expeditions by ensuring that all their rubbish is carried out and insisting on kerosene fires instead of using the already scarce sources of wood upon which locals depend. It is also possible to stay in village homes: Ramesh Jangid from Nawalgarh has some interesting homestay programmes (see Organised Tours under Nawalgarh later in this chapter).

Ramesh is also a terrific source of information on the havelis. He is the president of Les Amis du Shekhawati (Friends of Shekhawati) – for more information about the society and its endeavours to protect the paintings of Shekhawati, see Volunteer Work in the Facts for the Visitor chapter. Ramesh has initiated some visionary conservation measures at Apani Dhani in Nawalgarh.

Another good source of information on the painted havelis of Shekhawati is Laxmi Kant Jangid at the Hotel Shiv Shekhawati in Jhunjhunu.

Guidebooks

For a full rundown on the history, people, towns and buildings of the area, it's well worth investing in a copy of *The Guide to the Painted Towns of Shekhawati* by Ilay Cooper. This publication gives details of the buildings of interest in each town, precise locations of interesting paintings and fine sketch maps of the larger tours of the area.

Getting There & Away

Access to the region is easiest from Jaipur or Bikaner. The towns of Sikar (gateway to the region, but with no notable havelis) and Fatehpur are on the main Jaipur to Bikaner road and are served by many buses. Churu is on the main Delhi to Bikaner train line, while Sikar, Nawalgarh and Jhunjhunu have several daily passenger train links with Jaipur and Delhi. For more details, see the relevant Getting There & Away sections.

Getting Around

The Shekhawati region is crisscrossed by narrow bitumen roads and all towns are served by government or private buses and jam-packed shared jeeps. Old 1950s round-snouted Tata Mercedes buses ply the routes, with turbaned villagers riding 'upper class' (on the roof!). Many of the roads are in poor condition, so be prepared for a bumpy journey at times.

If you have a group of four or five, it is worth hiring a taxi for the day to take you around the area. It's easy to arrange in the towns that have accommodation, although finding a driver who speaks English is more of a challenge. The official rate for a taxi is Rs 4 per kilometre with a minimum of 300km per day. Some of the larger towns have autorickshaws and tongas.

A number of operators are now offering camel safaris in the Shekhawati region. See Organised Tours in the Nawalgarh and Dundlod sections for details.

The best way to explore the towns themselves is on foot. Bring a hat and water to stave off the heat, and, if you have one, a compass is handy to find your way around.

NAWALGARH

☎ 0159 • postcode 333042 • pop 56,482

Nawalgarh was founded in 1737 by Nawal Singh, one of the five sons of the Rajput ruler Sardul Singh. The arrival of merchants from Jaipur increased the town's prosperity, and some of India's most successful merchants, such as the wealthy Goenka family, (which built many havelis), hailed from Nawalgarh. The town is built in a depression where a number of rivers terminate. The accumulated silt carried by these rivers was used to make the bricks (some of the best-preserved in Shekhawati) for local havelis.

Orientation & Information

Nawalgarh's havelis are spread throughout the town, but you can reach most of them on foot. The train station is at the western end of town and accommodation is concentrated in the north and west.

The best source of information on Nawalgarh and its painted havelis is Ramesh Jangid at Apani Dhani (see Places to Stay). He is actively involved in the preservation of Shekhawati's havelis, and has initiated educational programmes to raise local awareness about the rich cultural legacy they represent. Ramesh can speak Hindi, English, French and German.

Bala Qila

The main building in this town is the fort, founded in 1737. Today it is largely disfigured by modern accretions. It houses a fruit and vegetable market and two banks. One room in the southeastern quarter of the fort retains mirrorwork and beautiful paintings

NORTHERN RAJASTHAN

The Havelis of Shekhawati

Shekhawati's magnificent havelis are the result of the burgeoning wealth and pride of the Marwari merchants as they built their new lives in India's developing commercial centres. They lived frugally in their adopted homes, sending the bulk of their vast fortunes back to their families in Shekhawati to be used to construct grand havelis commensurate with their new station in life. Merchants competed with one another to build ever more grand edifices – homes, temples, step-wells – and these were richly decorated, both inside and out, with thousands of painted murals.

Many of the artists, masons and craftsmen, known as *chajeras*, were commissioned from beyond Shekhawati – particularly from Jaipur, where they had been employed decorating the palaces of the new capital – and others flooded into the region to offer their skills. There was a cross-pollination of ideas and techniques, with local artists learning skills from the new arrivals and adopting their designs.

These days most of the havelis are not inhabited by their owners, who find that the small towns in rural Rajasthan have little appeal. Many are occupied just by a single *chowkidar* (caretaker), while others may be home to a local family. They are pale reflections of the time when they accommodated the large households of the Marwari merchant families. A few havelis have been restored, some now house schools, and some lie derelict, crumbling slowly into elegant ruin.

Architecture

Shekhawati's havelis are usually architecturally unremarkable on the outside; rather the focus is on one or more internal courtyards, which are designed to provide security and privacy for the women, and offer some relief from the fierce heat that grips the area in summer. The plain exteriors also made the houses easy to defend.

The main entrance is a large wooden gate, which is usually locked. In this gate is a smaller doorway that gives access to the outer courtyard. Often an enormous ramp leads to the entrance, up which a prospective groom could ascend in appropriate grandeur on horseback or, in some cases, on elephantback. Above the entrance you can usually see one or more small shield-shaped devices called *torans*. These are generally wrought of wood and silver, and often feature a parrot – the bird of love. In a mock show of conquest, the groom was required to pierce the *toran* with his sword before claiming his bride. Each *toran* over a doorway represents the marriage of a woman from the household.

To one side of the outer courtyard is the *baithak*, or salon, in which the merchant could receive guests. In order to impress visitors, this room was generally the most elaborately crafted and often featured marble or mock-marble walls. Here the merchant and his guests reclined against bolsters as they discussed their business.

Between the outer and inner courtyards is a type of vestibule, traversed by a blank wall in which is a small window. Through this window the women of the household, who were kept in strict

on its ceiling, which depict street scenes of both Jaipur and Nawalgarh from the mid-19th century. To find it, climb a small greenish staircase in the southeast corner of the fort to the second floor. The room is hidden behind a sweet shop, where you will be asked for Rs 10 to let you through.

Havelis

To the west of Bala Qila is a group of six havelis known as the **Aath Havelis**. The in-congruous name – *aath* means 'eight' – refers to the fact that originally eight havelis were planned. The paintings are not technically as proficient as some others in this town, but they illustrate the transition in painting styles over the decades. As you approach the group through the gate from the road, the first haveli to the left is a case in point: there are older paintings on the front of the side external wall, while newer paintings, with synthetic colours, are at the rear.

The Havelis of Shekhawati

purdah (isolation), could peep at prospective guests. Entry into the inner courtyard was restricted to women, members of the family and, very occasionally, privileged male guests. Access was gained on either side of the partitioning wall. This courtyard was the main domestic arena – the walls are often smoke-stained by countless kitchen fires. Rooms off this courtyard served as bedrooms or store rooms, and staircases led to upper levels, mostly comprised of bedrooms. The largest of the mansions had as many as four courtyards and were up to six storeys high.

Paintings

The early Mughal influence manifested in floral arabesques and geometric designs (according to the dictates of their religion, the Mughals never created a representation of an animal or human). This gave way to influences from the Rajput royal courts. Later the walls were embellished with paintings of the new British technological marvels to which the Shekhawat merchants were exposed in centres such as Calcutta. Many of the pictures of motor cars and steam trains that adorn the buildings of Shekhawati were painted by artisans who had probably never even seen a motorised vehicle!

Originally the colours used in the murals were all ochre based, but in the 1860s artificial pigments were introduced from Germany. The predominant colours are blue and maroon, but other colours such as yellow, green and indigo are also featured.

The major themes used by artists, who were known as chiteras, were scenes from Hindu mythology, history, folk tales, eroticism (many of these works have been defaced or destroyed), and – among the most interesting – foreigners and their modern inventions such as trains, planes, telephones, gramophones and bicycles. Animals and landscapes were also popular. The colourful paintings were a response to the arid landscape, and served to both educate and entertain. Religious themes mostly featured the legends of Krishna and Rama, and were used as moral teachings in which good prevailed over evil.

The paintings also served as social documents depicting the concerns of the day. The advent of photography and exposure to European art had a dramatic influence on the execution of art in Shekhawati. Previously, subjects were depicted two-dimensionally, with little emphasis on anatomical accuracy or shading for perspective, and more emphasis on the imagination. With the influence of photography, artists sought a more faithful rendering of their subjects.

The paintings of Shekhawati are thus an extraordinary synthesis of Eastern and Western influences. A haveli in Fatehpur perfectly illustrates this cultural collision: in one painting, Krishna is depicted playing a gramophone for his consort Radha. Some of the paintings of the early 20th century exhibit an extraordinary technical expertise; others are florid, grotesque and executed in lurid colours. But all are interesting.

The front section depicts a steam locomotive, while the back section features some monumental pictures of elephants, horses and camels.

Opposite this group of havelis is the **Murarka Haveli**, which has some very fine paintings including, above the entrance, miniatures depicting the Krishna legends. The haveli is no longer inhabited, but is hired out for marriage celebrations. Unfortunately, unless a marriage is taking place,

the richly painted inner courtyard is usually locked.

About 10 minutes' walk to the north is the **Hem Raj Kulwal Haveli**, which was built in 1931. Above the entrance are portraits of members of the Kulwal family, as well as portraits of Gandhi and Nehru. Very colourful architraves surround the windows, and an ornate silver door leads to the inner courtyard. This features paintings depicting mostly religious themes. The *chowkidar*

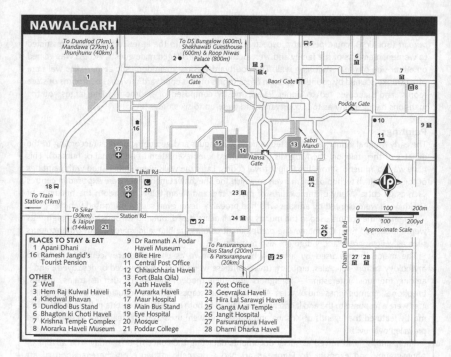

NAWALGARH

PLACES TO STAY & EAT
1 Apani Dhani
16 Ramesh Jangid's
   Tourist Pension

OTHER
2 Well
3 Hem Raj Kulwal Haveli
4 Khedwal Bhavan
5 Dundlod Bus Stand
6 Bhagton ki Choti Haveli
7 Krishna Temple Complex
8 Morarka Haveli Museum

9 Dr Ramnath A Podar
  Haveli Museum
10 Bike Hire
11 Central Post Office
12 Chhauchharia Haveli
13 Fort (Bala Qila)
14 Aath Havelis
15 Murarka Haveli
17 Maur Hospital
18 Main Bus Stand
19 Eye Hospital
20 Mosque
21 Poddar College

22 Post Office
23 Geevrajka Haveli
24 Hira Lal Sarawgi Haveli
25 Ganga Mai Temple
26 Jangit Hospital
27 Parsurampura Haveli
28 Dharni Dharka Haveli

will ask Rs 10 to let you in. Opposite is a guesthouse with distinctly European architecture, in which guests of the Kulwal family were accommodated.

Nearby is the **Khedwal Bhavan**, which features beautiful mirrorwork above the entrance to the inner courtyard, and fine blue tilework. A locomotive is depicted above the archway, and a frieze along the north wall shows the Teej festival (note the women on swings). On the west wall is a large locomotive crossing a bridge and underneath are portraits of English people. On the outside north wall is the story of Dhola Maru in two frames. (See the boxed text 'The Legend of Dhola Maru', later, for details of the story.) In the first frame, soldiers chase the fleeing camel-borne lovers. Maru fires arrows at the assailants while Dhola urges the camel on. Above can be seen a smaller painting of an English woman with an infant. The lane between the Hem Raj Kulwal Haveli and the Khedwal Bhavan

leads to three more beautifully painted havelis that are worth checking out.

To the northeast of the Baori Gate is **Bhagton ki Choti Haveli**. On the external west wall is a locomotive and a steamship. On the wall above elephant-bodied *gopis* (milkmaids) dance. Adjacent, women perform a dance during the Holi festival.

Above the doorway to the inner courtyard is a very detailed picture of the marriage of Rukmani. Krishna cheated the groom Sisupal of his prospective wife by touching the *toran* first, thus claiming her for himself. The walls of the salon resemble marble – the wall was first painted black then decorative incisions were made. The inner chamber upstairs contains the family quarters, also elaborately painted. A room on the west side has a picture of a European man with a cane and pipe and a small dog on his shoulder. Adjacent, a melancholy English woman plays an accordion. A donation of Rs 10 to 20 is requested.

About 200m east is the **Morarka Haveli Museum** (admission Rs 15), which has only recently been opened and has very well-presented original paintings, preserved for decades behind doorways blocked with cement. On the western external wall, under the eaves, is a picture of Jesus Christ. The inner walls depict scenes from the Ramayana. Despite the sign declaring that this is a tourist information centre, you won't find much help here. Across the road are a Krishna temple complex and a well.

On Dharni Dharka Rd is the **Parsurampura Haveli**, which dates from the early 20th century and belongs to a merchant from Parsurampura. The paintings are very grand, and almost *too* perfect – the European influence is evident. Themes include both the religious and the secular.

In the street behind this haveli is the **Dharni Dharka Haveli**, which dates from 1930. There is an ornate painted carving above the arches and there are portraits of Gandhi, Nehru in an automobile, and Krishna and Radha on a swing.

A short distance to the south of the fort are a number of interesting buildings, including the **Chhauchharia Haveli**, behind Jangit Hospital, with paintings dating from the last decade of the 19th century. Some of the more interesting pictures include those of a hot-air balloon being inflated by several Europeans blowing vigorously through pipes, and a man who on first glance appears to be, well, exposing himself. A closer examination reveals that he is holding out his finger! The very elaborate floral motifs over the enormous doorway have been restored with oil paints.

To the southwest of the fort is the **Hira Lal Sarawgi Haveli**, which is famous for its different representations of cars. Other pictures on its external walls include an English couple sitting stiffly on a bench and a tractor with a tip-tray – a new invention – and a woman trying to distract a *sadhu* (ascetic or holy person) with an erotic dance.

A short distance to the north is the **Geevrajka Haveli**, which has very fine paintings on the ceiling of the entrance, depicting various Hindu deities.

The **Dr Ramnath A Podar Haveli Museum** (admission Rs 40), which dates from 1920, is now a secondary school. The paintings of this haveli have been well restored, and new additions added – they represent some of the few actively preserved paintings in Nawalgarh. On the ground floor there are several displays, including one room with examples of different schools of Rajasthani painting and one with dolls in the wedding dress of different castes. These are neatly presented but there are some questions about the accuracy of the subject matter in some of the displays. Lessons are held on the floor above.

Ganga Mai Temple

Several hundred metres to the south of the Nansa Gate is Ganga Mai Temple, which, as its name suggests, is dedicated to the goddess Ganga. There is some fine mirrorwork around the inner sanctum. The courtyard is surrounded by four aisles, each formed by five archways with floral motifs above the arches. There are some good, small paintings above the *mandapa* (courtyard before the inner sanctum). The temple was built by the wealthy Chhauchharia merchants in 1868 and devotees come here regularly in the morning and evening.

Organised Tours

Ramesh Jangid and his son Rajesh are keen to promote rural tourism, eg, staying with families in small villages in the Shekhawati region. Numbers are kept to a minimum (a maximum of two couples only per host family) and an English-speaking interpreter is provided. They also organise three-day treks in the Aravalli Range, camel safaris around Rajasthan (see Organised Tours in the Getting Around Chapter), and informative guided tours around the painted havelis of Shekhawati, including trips by bicycle.

Treks start at Rs 1750 per person per day for up to two people, Rs 1500 per person for three people, and Rs 1250 for four people. Treks include food, accommodation, transfers and a guide.

Prices for jeep tours to the villages of Shekhawati from Nawalgarh are as follows:

a three-hour trip taking in Dundlod and Parsurampura is Rs 1000 for up to four people; a five-hour trip taking in Mandawa, Dundlod and Fatehpur is Rs 1250 for up to four people; a seven- to eight-hour trip visiting Bissau, Churu, Ramgarh and Mahansar is Rs 1500. Guided tours of Nawalgarh cost Rs 200, plus Rs 100 for a car, and take two to three hours. See Places to Stay for Ramesh Jangid's contact details.

Roop Niwas Palace provides English-speaking guides for walking tours of the painted walls of Nawalgarh for two-hour/full-day tours for about Rs 100/400. Horse rides cost Rs 350 for one hour, or Rs 1350/2700 for a half/full day. Camel rides are Rs 300/600/12002 for one hour/half day/full day.

Places to Stay & Eat

Near the Maur Hospital, **Ramesh Jangid's Tourist Pension** (☎ 7424060, fax 7422129; e touristpension@yahoo.com; singles/doubles upstairs from Rs 180/200, downstairs Rs 280/300) is well known, so if you get lost, just ask one of the locals to point you in the right direction. This family-run guesthouse has a warm atmosphere and is within easy walking distance of some of Nawalgarh's best havelis. It's great value for money and you'll have no hassles whatsoever. Upstairs rooms have hot water by the bucket (no charge). Internet access and pure veg meals are available (veg thalis cost Rs 70).

Apani Dhani (☎ 7422239, fax 7424061; w www.apanidhani.com; singles/doubles with private bathroom Rs 600/725) is also owned by Ramesh. Near the TV tower, on the west side of the main Jaipur road, Apani Dhani is a delightful ecofarm and Ramesh has implemented his various experiments in alternative energy, such as solar water heaters, compost toilets, biogas and solar cookers. Accommodation is in comfortable cottages, all decorated in traditional style with thatched roofs and mud plaster. These are arranged around a peaceful courtyard hung with bougainvillea. The farm has buffaloes, cows and goats; their manure is used on the vegetable garden and to produce biogas for cooking. Fresh organic vegies from the garden make up the bulk of the pure veg meals; a set breakfast/lunch/dinner costs Rs 100/150/200.

DS Bungalow (☎ 7422703; singles/doubles with private bathroom Rs 250/400) is a quiet, comfortable place, a little out of town, with a pleasant rooftop restaurant (veg thalis Rs 125). The rooms upstairs are better than the ones below.

Shekhawati Guesthouse (☎/fax 7424658; e gss2@stayam.net.in; singles/doubles with private bathroom Rs 300/400), next door to DS Bungalow, is a clean, family-run place with a lovely garden restaurant in a thatched bungalow. Free pick-up from the bus or train station can be arranged.

Roop Niwas Palace (☎ 7422008, fax 7423388; singles/doubles from Rs 1200/1400) is on the northern edge of town, about 1km from the fort. It has comfortable rooms, although the decor is somewhat eclectic. This was the rural retreat of the thakur of Nawalgarh, Nawal Singh (1880–1926). Amenities include a swimming pool and restaurant (the set lunch or dinner is Rs 250). See Organised Tours, earlier, for more information about camel and horse excursions.

Getting There & Away

Bus There are buses every 15 minutes between Nawalgarh and Jaipur (Rs 58, 3½ hours), and several services each day to Delhi (Rs 115, seven hours) and Jodhpur (Rs 136, nine hours).

Buses for destinations in Shekhawati leave every few minutes and shared jeeps leave according to demand (Rs 12 to Sikar, Rs 15 to Jhunjhunu). Private buses run to Fatehpur (Rs 20) and Mandawa (Rs 12).

There are two daily private services that go to Ahmedabad (Rs 250, 15 hours), Ajmer (Rs 80, six hours) and Chittorgarh (Rs 137, 10 hours), and three buses daily to Udaipur (Rs 250, 12 hours).

Train There are rail connections to several destinations in Shekhawati. The 9734 *Shekhawati Express* leaves Nawalgarh at 9.54pm, arriving at Delhi's Sarai Rohilla station at 5.30am (Rs 69/134 in 2nd-class seat/sleeper). To Jaipur, the 9733 *Shekhawati*

The Legend of Dhola Maru

One of the most popular paintings to be seen on the walls of Shekhawati havelis depicts the legend of Dhola Maru, the Shekhawat equivalent of Romeo and Juliet.

The princess Maru hailed from Pugal, near Bikaner, and Dhola was a young prince from Gwalior. When Maru was two years old there was a bad drought in her homeland, so her father, the maharaja, shifted to Gwalior where his friend, Dhola's father, ruled. He stayed for three years, returning to Pugal when he learned that the drought had broken. Before he left, as a token of friendship between the two rulers, a marriage alliance was contracted between their children. However, after 20 years the promise had been forgotten and Maru was contracted to marry a man by the name of Umra.

Wedding plans would have proceeded but a bard, who had travelled from Pugal to Gwalior, sang at the royal court of the childhood marriage of Dhola and Maru. In this way Dhola came to hear of the beautiful Maru, with whom he immediately fell in love after simply hearing her virtues described, and resolved to meet her. Of course, when Maru laid eyes on her champion she fell in love with him, and they decided to flee together.

Her betrothed, Umra, heard of their flight and set chase with his brother, Sumra. They pursued the camel-borne lovers on horseback, and it was the brave princess Maru who fired at them with arrows, although they proved of little use against the brothers, who had guns. They were able to temporarily elude the brothers and took shelter in a forest. However, Dhola was bitten by a snake and succumbed on the spot. Maru, thus thwarted by death, proceeded to weep for her lost lover, and her lamentations were heard by Shiva and Gauri (Parvati) who were walking nearby. Parvati beseeched Shiva to restore the dead Dhola to life and the couple was reunited.

Express leaves Nawalgarh at 6.30am, reaching Jaipur at 10am (Rs 42 in 2nd-class seat). The inquiries number is ☎ 7422025.

Getting Around

Bicycles can be hired near Poddar Gate (Rs 5/25 per hour/day). If you're staying at Ramesh Jangid's Tourist Pension, bicycle hire can also be organised there. The cost is approximately Rs 25 per day.

A shared autorickshaw from the train or bus station to the main market is Rs 4; you can wave them down anywhere along this route. To hire an autorickshaw or a horse-drawn tonga from either the bus or train station to the fort costs about Rs 30.

PARSURAMPURA

This tiny village, 20km southeast of Nawalgarh, has some of the best-preserved and oldest paintings in the Shekhawati region. The **Shamji Sharaf Haveli**, just south of the bus stand, dates from the end of the 18th century. Pictures include a grandmother having her hair dressed, a woman spinning and an English woman in shiny patent-leather shoes carrying a parasol. A frieze shows a celebration, probably of a marriage, and on one side is a frame showing a priest presiding over the ceremony. The opposite wall depicts Europeans in a car. Above the lintel are some very well-preserved portraits, and below, portrayals of Ganesh, Vishnu, Krishna and Radha. Saraswati is riding a peacock in the right-hand corner.

The paintings on the interior of the dome of the **Chhatri of Thakur Sardul Singh**, 50m to the south, date from the mid-18th century. The very fine and detailed work here is reminiscent of miniature painting. The antiquity of the paintings is evident in the muted, russet colours used. Pictures include those of the *thakur* and his five sons, graphic battle scenes from the Ramayana, and the love story of Dhola Maru, a common theme employed by the painters of Shekhawati. To visit the cenotaph you must obtain the key from the caretaker, Sri Banwari Lal (nicknamed Maharaj), who sits in the little booth under the peepul tree outside the gate of the Shamji Sharaf Haveli. Maharaj is a Brahmin priest, and it's almost entirely through his efforts that the *chhatri* is so well maintained. He is responsible for the pretty flower beds of roses and jasmine that surround the *chhatri*, and there's a toilet here. A small donation would be welcome – it will be put to good use.

Also found in Parsurampura is the small **Gopinathji Mandir**, on the left just before you leave the village on the road to Nawalgarh. The temple was built by Sardul Singh in 1742 and it is believed that the same artist responsible for the paintings on the Chhatri of Thakur Sardul Singh executed the fine paintings here. According to local lore, the artist had half completed the work when the son of Sardul Singh chopped his hands off because he wanted the artist's work to be exclusive to his father's *chhatri*. Not to be deterred, the valiant artist completed the work with his feet!

Getting There & Away

There are numerous buses throughout the day to Parsurampura from Nawalgarh, which depart from the Parsurampura bus stand. The trip can take up to one hour (because of the many stops en route) and costs Rs 8. You'll probably have to fight for a seat (or roof space!). The road is dusty and corrugated, and crosses a dry riverbed just before the village.

DUNDLOD
☎ 01594

Dundlod is a tiny village lying about 7km north of Nawalgarh. Its small fort was built in 1750 by Keshri Singh, the fifth and youngest son of Sardul Singh. Major additions were made in the early 19th century by his descendant Sheo Singh, who resettled in the region despite attempts on his life by Shyam Singh of Bissau (Shyam Singh murdered his father and brother in an endeavour to claim the region for himself). Members of the wealthy Goenka merchant family also settled here, and their prosperity is evident in their richly painted havelis.

Things to See

The **Dundlod Fort** dates from 1750 and features a blend of the Rajput and Mughal

styles of art and architecture. The Diwan-i-Khas (Hall of Private Audiences) has stained-glass windows, fine Louis XIV antiques and an impressive collection of rare books. Above the Diwan-i-Khas is the *duchatta*, or women's gallery, from where the women in *purdah* could view all of the proceedings below. The *zenana*, or women's quarters, features walls of duck-egg blue, and opens out onto the reading room of the *thakurani* (noblewoman). This room has a hand-carved wooden writing table, which bears oriental motifs in the form of dragons.

The beautiful **Chhatri of Ram Dutt Goenka** and the adjacent well were both built by Ram Chandra Goenka in 1888. They lie about five minutes' walk to the southeast of the fort. The caretaker is usually around in the morning, otherwise you'll need to borrow the key from the caretaker at the Ram Chandra Goenka Haveli. The interior of the dome has floral motifs extending in banners down from its centre. The dome is encircled by a frieze depicting Krishna dancing with the *gopis*, interspersed with peacocks and musicians. The dominant colours are blue, red, yellow, turquoise and brown. Paintings around the inner base of the dome illustrate a battle scene from the Mahabharata, a marriage celebration and Vishnu reclining on a snake.

The **Bhagirath Mal Goenka Haveli** is often locked, but you can see fine mirror-work above the windows on the upper walls of the courtyard. Finely preserved paintings under the eaves mostly comprise portraits in round frames. The haveli opposite it is interesting, as the work has not been completed, and it is possible to see how the artist sketched the drawings before adding colour. Pictures include those of an elephant, camel and rider, and a horse.

In a small square to the right just before the fort entrance is **Satyanarayan Temple**, which was built by a member of the Goenka family in 1911. On the west wall of the temple is a long frieze showing Europeans on bicycles and in cars, and a long train, above which telegraph lines extend. The portraits under the eaves show the nobles engaged in leisure pursuits, such as smelling flowers and reading. One fine moustachioed and turquoise-turbaned fellow has a bird in his hand, and another painting shows a woman admiring herself in a mirror.

A short distance to the south of the temple is a **Goenka Haveli** built by Arjun Dass Goenka in 1875, although it's usually locked. Above the window arches, mirrors are arranged in florets. Better-preserved paintings can be seen on the east wall of the nearby **Jagathia Haveli**. There is a good train station scene – in one carriage, a man appears to be in a passionate embrace with his wife, but closer inspection reveals his angry expression and that he is in fact beating her. A man hurries along on a bicycle parallel to the train, pursued by a dog.

Just to the south of here, the **Ram Chandra Goenka Haveli** is painted a soft yellow colour, featuring florets and birds in the outer courtyard.

Organised Tours

Dundlod Fort (see Places to Stay) can organise horse safaris around the Shekhawati region. It's also possible to hire a camel and an English-speaking guide to visit the havelis of Dundlod (Rs 150 per hour). Jeep safaris (minimum of four people) can also be organised at a cost of Rs 1500/2000 for a half/full day.

Places to Stay & Eat

Dundlod Fort (☎/fax 52180, in Jaipur ☎/fax 0141-213224; singles/doubles Rs 1500/1800, suites Rs 2800), at the fort, is still owned by the family of Dundlod's founder. It has air-cooled standard rooms. Each room is different; thogh it's not luxurious but it is certainly cosy and comfortable. Breakfast is Rs 150 and lunch/dinner is Rs 300/325.

Getting There & Away

It's possible to walk all the way from Nawalgarh to Dundlod, although it's a hot walk along a busy, dusty road. For just a few rupees, you can catch one of the many local buses that ply the route between these two towns every 15 minutes. Catch one at the Dundlod bus stand.

MUKUNDGARH

There are some interesting painted havelis to be seen in this town, about 5km north of Dundlod.

Mukundgarh Fort (☎ 01594-7252397, in Delhi ☎ 6372565, fax 011-6814954; singles/doubles from Rs 1000/2000, Maharaja suite Rs 6000) has 46 rooms and the Maharaja suite, which can accommodate up to eight people. The set lunch/dinner in the restaurant costs Rs 200/250. There's a pool here and camel safaris can be arranged for the adventurous. A two-hour trip in a camel cart is Rs 300 per person.

JHUNJHUNU

☎ 0159 • postcode 333001 • pop 100,476
Jhunjhunu lies 245km from Delhi and 180km from Jaipur, and is one of the largest towns of Shekhawati. It is currently the district headquarters of the region.

The town was founded by the Kaimkhani nawabs in the middle of the 15th century, and remained under their control until it was taken by the Rajput ruler Sardul Singh in 1730. It was in Jhunjhunu that the British based their Shekhawati brigade, a troop raised locally in the 1830s to try to halt the activities of *dacoits* (bandits). The dacoits were largely local petty rulers who had decided it was easier to become wealthy by pinching other people's money than by earning their own.

Information

The **Tourist Reception Centre** (☎ 7232909; open 10am-5pm Mon-Fri & every 2nd Sat) is a little out of the town centre at the Churu bypass, Mandawa Circle. It can arrange taxi hire and jeep and camel safaris.

Currently, the only government-approved guide in town is the knowledgeable Laxmi Kant Jangid (owner of the Hotel Shiv Shekhawati – see Places to Stay & Eat). He provides free guided tours around Jhunjhunu, or charges Rs 1000 for a car tour of surrounding towns.

You can check your email at **Cyber World** (Station Rd; open 9am-9pm daily), a small cramped place near Nehru Bazaar, for Rs 30 per hour.

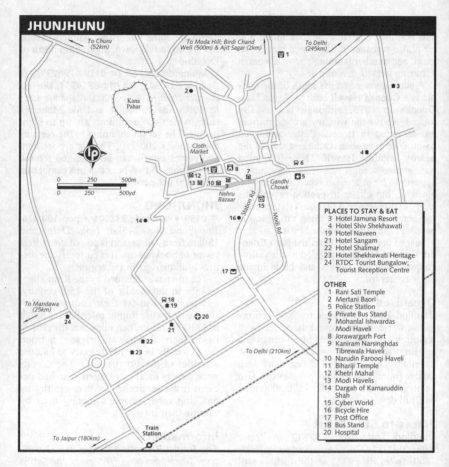

JHUNJHUNU

To Churu (52km)

To Moda Hill; Birdi Chand Well (500m) & Ajit Sagar (2km)

To Delhi (245km)

Kana Pahar

Cloth Market

Nehru Bazaar

Gandhi Chowk

To Mandawa (25km)

To Delhi (210km)

To Jaipur (180km)

Train Station

0   250   500m
0   250   500yd

PLACES TO STAY & EAT
3   Hotel Jamuna Resort
4   Hotel Shiv Shekhawati
19 Hotel Naveen
21 Hotel Sangam
22 Hotel Shalimar
23 Hotel Shekhawati Heritage
24 RTDC Tourist Bungalow;
     Tourist Reception Centre

OTHER
1   Rani Sati Temple
2   Mertani Baori
5   Police Station
6   Private Bus Stand
7   Mohanlal Ishwardas
     Modi Haveli
8   Jorawargarh Fort
9   Kaniram Narsinghdas
     Tibrewala Haveli
10 Narudin Farooqi Haveli
11 Bihariji Temple
12 Khetri Mahal
13 Modi Havelis
14 Dargah of Kamaruddin
     Shah
15 Cyber World
16 Bicycle Hire
17 Post Office
18 Bus Stand
20 Hospital

At the time of writing, no banks in Jhunjhunu changed money, but this may change.

Rani Sati Temple

In the northeast corner of town is the enormous Rani Sati Temple (admission free, photography permitted; open 4am-10pm daily), commemorating an act of sati (self-immolation) by a merchant's wife in 1595. It apparently receives the second-highest number of donations of any temple in India and is particularly revered by the wealthy merchant class. Rani Sati Temple has long been embroiled in a national debate about

sati, especially since the 19-year-old widow Roop Kanwar committed sati in nearby Sikar district in 1987 (see the boxed text 'Glorifying the Burning Widow' in the Facts about Rajasthan chapter). It's fronted by two courtyards, around which 300 rooms offer shelter to pilgrims. The main hall is of marble with elaborate silver repoussé work before the inner sanctum.

There is a tile-and-mirror mosaic on the ceiling of the mandapa depicting Rani Sati, while Shiva, Ganesh and Durga watch over her. A relief frieze on the north wall shows her story. Her husband is killed by the nawab's army; after battling the soldiers (one of whom has been decapitated), Rani Sati the funeral pyre; she is consumed by flames while Durga sends her power to withstand the pain. In the next panel Rani commands a chariot driver to place her ashes on a horse, and to build a temple over the spot where the horse halts. The final panel shows the ostentatious temple built in her honour. Rani Sati is the patron goddess of the merchant class, which is believed to hold 60% of the wealth in India and control all the major newspapers.

Khetri Mahal

A series of small laneways leads to the **Khetri Mahal**, considered by some people to be one of the finest buildings in Shekhawati. This graceful palace dates from around 1770 and is believed to have been built by Bhopal Singh, who founded Khetri. Unfortunately it is now overrun with goats and has a desolate, forlorn atmosphere, but the architecture is superb. There are no doors or windows in the palace. Instead, the rooms are connected by an intricate series of arches and columns that lend an elegant symmetry to the building. The lime plaster has not been painted, and has a rosy cast.

In the private chamber of the *thakur* are two small alcoves that retain fragments of paintings in natural earth pigments. The various levels of the palace are connected by a series of ramps along which the *thakur* and *thakurani* could be pulled – the *thakur* could reach the rooftop, where he could gaze down over his subjects, without even having to take a single step! There are good views over the town from the rooftop.

Havelis

Near the Khetri Mahal are two havelis that are opposite each other, and known as the **Modi Havelis**. The haveli on the eastern side has a painting of a woman in a blue sari sitting before a gramophone; a frieze depicts a train, alongside which soldiers race on horses. The spaces between the brackets above show the Krishna legends. Part of the haveli facade on the eastern side of the road has been painted over. Still remaining,

however, are a few portrayals of rabbits that are quite lifelike; rabbits were introduced by the British. The enormous ramp enabled the bridegroom to ride into the haveli on elephant back to claim his bride.

The haveli on the western side has pictures with an almost comic appeal – the facial expressions are remarkable. Note the different styles and colours of turbans on the inside of the archway between the outer and inner courtyard here. Some of the subjects have enormous bushy moustaches, others wear perky little pencil moustaches.

A short distance away is the **Kaniram Narsinghdas Tibrewala Haveli** *(admission Rs 10)*, fronted by a vegetable market. On the west wall of the first courtyard there is a frieze depicting two trains approaching each other. That on the left is a passenger train and the one on the right is a goods train whose carriages contain livestock. The artist had probably never seen a real train and used his imagination. On the north wall, a man ties his turban while another man holds a looking glass in front of him. Close by, a man and woman pass a child between them.

A short distance to the west is the **Narudin Farooqi Haveli**, close to the Noor Mosque. In usual Muslim style, only floral motifs are depicted – there are no animal or human representations – and blue is the dominant colour. Unfortunately, the arches leading to the salons off the first courtyard have been sealed off with concrete.

On the north side of Nehru Bazaar is the **Mohanlal Ishwardas Modi Haveli** *(admission Rs 10)*, which dates from 1896. There is the inevitable train on the front facade. Above the entrance to the outer courtyard are scenes from the legend of Krishna. In the centre is Krishna stealing the clothes of the *gopis*, who stand waist-deep in water. Krishna is hiding up a tree with the *gopis'* saris around him. On a smaller, adjacent arch can be seen British imperial figures, including monarchs and judges in robes. On the opposite side are Indian rulers, including maharajas and nawabs.

Around the archway, between the inner and outer courtyards, there are some portrait miniatures behind glass. There's also some fine mirror-and-glass tile work. In the second half of the antechamber, Krishna dances with the *gopis* while angels fly overhead. This is very fine work. In the inner courtyard, the hierarchy of the universe is shown, with deities in the upper frieze, humans in the middle band, and animal and floral motifs below.

Other Attractions
On the northwest side of town is the **Birdi Chand Well**, surmounted by four imposing minarets (two minarets generally symbolise the presence of a step-well). Because water is such a precious commodity in the desert, wells were treated almost like temples, and in fact it is not unusual to see a temple at a well – there is a small temple at this well that is sacred to Hanuman. Wells were often decorated in rich paintings, with one or two pavilions erected nearby at which women could gather and exchange news – the local village served as an important social centre. As at this well, you will often find a neem tree nearby, the twigs from which are used to clean the teeth.

Unfortunately, the paintings that are on the minarets at this well have faded. Nearby, on its west side, is an old inn at which caravans would once have halted.

A few kilometres further north is the picturesque artificial **Ajit Sagar**, built by Jitmal Khaitan in 1902.

The **Mertani Baori**, to the northwest of the fort, is named after the woman who commissioned it: Mertani, the widow of Sardul Singh. It was built in 1783 and recently restored. The step-well is about 30m deep, and its sulphuric waters are said to cure skin diseases. On either side of the well, steps lead to a series of cool resting rooms for visitors.

To the south of Kana Pahar is the **Dargah of Kamaruddin Shah**, a complex consisting of a *madrasa* (Islamic college), a mosque and a *mehfilkhana*, at which religious songs are sung. Fragments of paintings depicting floral motifs remain around the courtyard, particularly on the eastern and northern sides (although many have been whitewashed). Blue – a favourite colour of the Muslims – is the predominant colour used.

A short distance northwest of Jorawargarh Fort is the fine **Bihariji Temple**, which dates from approximately 1776 and is dedicated to Krishna. On the inside of the dome, Krishna and the *gopis* are rendered in natural pigments. The circular form of domes makes the dance of Krishna and the *gopis*, called the *rasalila*, a popular theme here.

Painting Classes
For tuition in traditional Shekhawati painting, contact Laxmi Kant Jangid at the Hotel Shiv Shekhawati (see Places to Stay & Eat). Laxmi can organise lessons with a local artist in traditional Shekhawati painting, and offers accommodation by donation at the Hotel Shiv Shekhawati for anybody who stays at least 16 days (two months is ideal).

Organised Tours
Camel and jeep safaris can be arranged at the Hotel Shiv Shekhawati. For a half/full day camel safari the charge per person is Rs 300/400. Jeep safaris are Rs 1000 per day (maximum of six people). A packed lunch (Rs 40) or snacks (Rs 35) to take along can also be arranged.

Places to Stay & Eat
Hotel Shiv Shekhawati (☎ 7232651, fax 7234070; ᴡ www.shivshekhawati.com; singles/ doubles with air-cooling Rs 600/800, with air-con Rs 1000/1200) is 2km from the bus stand in a quiet area on the eastern edge of town and a red-hot favourite with travellers. The rooms are well kept and Internet access is available (Rs 60 per hour). The affable owner, Laxmi Kant Jangid, is a wealth of knowledge on the villages of Shekhawati (see Information earlier). Discounts of up to 50% are available in the low season.

Hotel Jamuna Resort (☎ 7232871, fax 7234070; singles/doubles Rs 1000/1200, painted room Rs 1500), about 1km away from Shekhawati, is also run by Laxmi Kant Jangid and is set in a pleasant garden. The traditionally decorated air-con cottages feature mirrorwork while the vibrant 'painted room' is a little more expensive. There's a small swimming pool (open to nonguests for free); pool-side oil massages are also available. The charming mirrored dining hall welcomes nonguests; you can sit indoors or out on the lawn. The set veg/nonveg meal is Rs 150/200. You can dine à la carte also; most dishes are below Rs 45; a dish called 'mixed vegetables' is Rs 30 and *raita* (yogurt side dish) is Rs 25.

RTDC Tourist Bungalow *(☎ 7238266; dorm beds Rs 50; singles/doubles Rs 200/300, with geyser Rs 400/500)*, just next door to the tourist reception centre, has nondescript rooms and is a long way from town. There's a restaurant serving up veg/nonveg thalis for Rs 55/65.

Hotel Naveen *(☎ 7232527; singles/doubles with shared bathroom Rs 70/125, with private bathroom Rs 80/150, with air-con Rs 450/500)* is next to the bus stand and has fairly dreary rooms.

Hotel Shekhawati Heritage *(☎ 7237134, fax 7233077; singles/doubles with private bathroom Rs 200/300, with air-con Rs 700/800)* has reasonable rooms with colour TV. Vegetarian meals are available.

Hotel Shalimar *(☎ 7237809, fax 7235225; singles/doubles with private bathroom Rs 200/500, with air-con Rs 700/800)* has some rooms with air-con. There's a grim veg dining hall (open to nonguests) with most main dishes for below Rs 50; a special thali is Rs 50, a *dosa* (lentil-flour pancake) is Rs 20 and a veg sandwich is Rs 15.

Hotel Sangam *(☎ 7232544; singles with shared bathroom Rs 100, singles/doubles with private bathroom Rs 150/300, with air-con Rs 600)*, behind the bus stand, has basic rooms, most with bucket hot water. Only room-service meals are served. This is a large, somewhat impersonal hotel; budget rooms are at the front and could be noisy.

Getting There & Away
Bus There are regular buses between Jhunjhunu and Jaipur (Rs 75, five hours). There are buses every hour to Churu (Rs 22, 1½ hours) and Bissau (Rs 15, 1½ hours). There are numerous buses to Mandawa from 6.30am (Rs 8, one hour) and Nawalgarh (Rs 15, one hour).

Buses leave for Delhi every 30 minutes from 5am (Rs 100, six hours). There are also buses to Jodhpur (Rs 149, 10 hours), Ajmer (Rs 122, seven hours) and Bikaner (Rs 96, five hours). The Roadways inquiries number is ☎ 7232664.

Train There are several daily passenger trains going between Jaipur and Jhunjhunu (Rs 114/820 in 2nd/1st class, 5¼ hours). The *Shekhawati Express* runs between Jhunjhunu and Delhi (Rs 125/964 in 2nd/1st class). It leaves Jhunjhunu at 11pm and arrives at Delhi Sarai Rohilla station at 5.30am. For inquiries call ☎ 7232251.

Getting Around
Autorickshaw For local sightseeing, you'll pay about Rs 30 per hour for an autorickshaw. A rickshaw from the train or bus station to the Hotel Shiv Shekhawati costs about Rs 20.

Bicycle Bicycles can be rented on Station Rd (near Nehru Bazaar) for around Rs 4/20 per hour/day.

BAGGAR
This small village is located about 15km from Jhunjhunu.

Piramal Haveli *(☎ 01572-21220; singles/doubles Rs 1500/2000)* has just eight rooms so advance bookings are essential. Pure veg meals are available at this atmospheric old haveli.

BISSAU
☎ 01595 ● pop 21,133
The small town of Bissau lies about 32km to the northwest of Jhunjhunu. It was founded in 1746 by the last of Sardul Singh's sons, Keshri Singh. The town prospered under Keshri, but fell into brigandry during the rule of his grandson Shyam Singh. According to local lore, the merchants of Bissau, who had been encouraged to set up in the town by Keshri, promptly packed up and left when Shyam extracted vast sums of money from them. The *thakur* then resorted to brigandry, embarking on raids with *dacoits* to neighbouring regions. The British called on the Shekhawati brigade to restore order in the anarchic town, although by the

time the expedition was mounted, Shyam Singh had expired and his heir, Hammir Singh, had driven out the brigands and encouraged the merchants to return to the town. The British were impressed by the town's prosperity and left without a single shot being fired.

Things to See
On the facade of the **Chhatri of Hammir Singh**, which is near the private bus stand and dates from 1875, you can see British folk in various fancy carriages, including one in the shape of a lion and another in the form of a hybrid lion-elephant. The *chhatri* is now a primary school, with lessons held under the dome and even in the sandy courtyard. Some of the rooms are used to store fodder. On the external back wall is a portrayal of Dhola Maru, and unusually, the bard who features in the love story is also depicted. On the south wall, a man on a horse dispatches a lion with a sword. The paintings on the four corner pavilions are badly deteriorated.

If you walk north from the bus stand and take the first street to the right, on the left-hand side at the next intersection is the **Haveli of Girdarilal Sigtia**. The paintings on the external walls have been destroyed, but the rooms retain some vibrant paintings in bright oranges, blues, reds and greens. A room in the northeast corner of the haveli shows Shiva (who is unusually depicted with a moustache) with the Ganges flowing from his hair. There is also a woman nursing a tiny child. Note the orange handprints on the outer courtyard wall, signifying the birth of a male child. The handprints are a peculiarly Shekhawat custom.

On the opposite side of this lane is the **Motiram Jasraj Sigtia Haveli**, which is now a junior school. On the north wall, Krishna has stolen the *gopis'* clothes. The maidens have been modestly covered by the artist in the coils of snakes, although one reptile can be seen emerging from between a *gopi's* legs! Over the top of some of the old paintings the children have taped diagrams of their science experiments, full of beakers and bunsen burners.

Getting There & Away
There are daily buses from Bissau to Jhunjhunu every 30 minutes (Rs 15, 1½ hours) and to Mahansar (Rs 5, 20 minutes), Mandawa (Rs 12, 1½ hours) and Churu (Rs 6, 30 minutes).

Getting Around
Bicycles can be hired for Rs 20 per day (bargain hard) from the shops near the Chhatri of Hammir Singh. They are an excellent way to tour this region, and are particularly good for the 6km trip to Mahansar.

MAHANSAR
A turn-off to the left as you leave Bissau on the Churu road leads 6km to the sleepy little village of Mahansar. This is a dusty place, where donkeys outnumber motorised vehicles. There is not an overabundance of painted havelis here, although the wealthy Poddar clan have left a legacy of very fine paintings in those that can be seen. Mahansar is peaceful and pristine, and a good place to break a journey.

Mahansar was founded by Nawal Singh in 1768, and the town prospered for several decades until one of the Poddars lost his livelihood when two shiploads of opium sunk without trace.

Things to See
The **Raghunath Mandir**, in the town centre, dates from the mid-19th century. It has fine floral arabesques beneath the arches around the courtyard and a very fine facade.

A short distance to the northeast of the Raghunath Temple is the **Sone ki Dukan Haveli** *(admission Rs 100)*, which has a steep admission fee. It is famous for the gold leaf incorporated into its paintings, which is unusual for Shekhawati. You can see the gold leaf particularly around the alcoves in the first chamber. The scenes from the Ramayana in the southern section of the ceiling in the first chamber are particularly fine and detailed. The lower walls are richly adorned with floral and bird motifs, creating an almost utopian fantasy with butterflies, trees laden with fruit, and flowers. Painted in gold script on panels on the west wall of this chamber are the names of the gods. Carved wooden beams divide the ceiling into three sections: on the north side, the life of Krishna is portrayed. A golden river connects the holy cities of Vrindavan, where Krishna spent his childhood, and Mathura, where he lived as a king.

About 10 minutes' walk from the bus stand, past the fort on the right-hand side of Ramgarh Rd, is the **Sahaj Ram Poddar Chhatri**. Unfortunately, some of the archways have been bricked in, but there are still some well-preserved paintings on the lower walls, and this is a well-proportioned and attractive building.

Places to Stay & Eat
Narayan Niwas Castle (*☎ 0159-7564322; basic singles/doubles with private bathroom Rs 450/600, standard rooms with private bathroom Rs 700/900)*, in the old fort, about 100m north of the bus stand, is the only place to stay in this remote village. It is an authentic Rajasthani castle (without the commercial trappings of many of today's royal hotels – thank goodness!). This creaky castle is run by the down-to-earth *thakur* of Mahansar and his wife, an elderly couple who have interesting stories to tell about days long gone. Hot water is by the bucket. Breakfast is Rs 100, and lunch/dinner costs Rs 200/225. Some of the rooms have fine antique furniture and one room is completely covered in paintings. Ask to see several rooms before checking in, as some are better than others (room No 5 is very atmospheric). There are some smaller, cheaper rooms in a separate portion of the castle. Camel safaris into the local sand dunes can be arranged for Rs 150/450 per hour/day.

Getting There & Away
There are regular bus services between Mahansar and Ramgarh (Rs 4), Churu (Rs 8), Fatehpur (Rs 13) and Bissau (Rs 3). Change at Bissau for buses to Jhunjhunu.

RAMGARH
Sixteen kilometres south of Churu and 20km north of Fatehpur is Ramgarh, which was founded by a disaffected group from

the wealthy Poddar family in 1791. The Poddars defected from nearby Churu after the *thakur* of that town imposed an extortionate wool levy on the merchants. The town prospered until the late 19th century, but is today a fairly quiet place. It retains a rich legacy of painted buildings.

The town is easy to explore on foot. The bus stand is at the western edge of town. In the northern section, about 600m from the bus stand, there is a concentration of havelis, as well as the main Shani Temple and the Ganga Temple. There is currently nowhere to stay in Ramgarh.

Things to See
The imposing **Ram Gopal Poddar Chhatri**, to the south of the bus stand, was built in 1872. The main dome of the *chhatri* is encompassed by a series of smaller domes. On the west side of the outer rim of the main dome, one of the projecting braces bears a picture of a naked woman stepping into her *lehanga* (skirt), while another woman shields her from the eyes of a man by holding the hem of her own skirt before her. The drum of the main dome is very brightly painted and has well-preserved paintings in blues and reds depicting the battle from the Ramayana. The building on the north side of the *chhatri* was where family members paying homage to their dead ancestor could rest. Unfortunately, the *chhatri* is in a sorry state – the northeast corner of the building is badly water damaged. To enter the compound, you will need to find the caretaker, who will ask about Rs 50 to let you in.

Just a short distance to the north of the town wall, on the east side of the road, is the fine **Ganga Temple**. It was built by one of the Poddar clan in 1845, and is an imposing building with large elephant murals on its facade. The right side of the facade is deteriorating – the foundations are crumbling. The temple is open only for morning and evening *puja* (prayers). Other paintings depict religious themes, including some depicting Krishna.

About 20m further north, on the left-hand side, is a **Ganesh Temple**. It has a densely painted forecourt and a series of interesting paintings between the brackets under the eaves, most of which feature birds and religious themes.

From here, a road heads east to the beautiful, tiny **Shani Mandir** (Saturn Temple). This temple was built in 1840, and features some crude paintings on its facade. However, this exterior belies the temple's richly ornate interior, which is completely covered in fantastic mirrorwork. There are some fine murals in the chamber before the inner sanctum, incorporating gold paint, and the overall effect is dazzling. Some scenes from the Mahabharata, and depictions of Krishna and Radha are featured. To the south (left) of the inner sanctum there is a painting on the ceiling featuring the marriage of Shiva and Guari (Parvati). Unfortunately, the ceiling in the chamber on the right-hand side of the inner sanctum is badly damaged, apparently by damp.

If you go back to the main Churu Gate, and continue past the gate for about 50m then turn left, you'll come to a group of **Poddar havelis**. Popular motifs include soldiers, trains, and an unusual design, peculiar to Ramgarh, of three fish arranged in a circle with their faces touching each other. One haveli has a painting of women carrying water in pitchers on their heads, and there is an interesting portrayal of the Dhola Maru legend on the west wall of another: while Maru fires at the advancing assailants, Dhola nonchalantly smokes a hookah!

Getting There & Away
There are buses to Nawalgarh (Rs 25, 2½ hours), Bissau (Rs 7, 45 minutes) and Fatehpur (Rs 8, 45 minutes). Ramgarh is on the narrow-gauge line that runs between Sikar and Churu; daily services connect these towns.

FATEHPUR
☎ 01571 • postcode 332310 • pop 78,471
Fatehpur was established in 1451 as a capital for Muslim nawabs, but it was taken by the Shekhawat Rajputs in the 18th century. The relative wealth of the community of merchants here, who counted among their numbers the rich Poddar, Choudhari and

Ganeriwala families, is evident in the many vibrantly painted havelis and fine *chhatris*. Unfortunately, the best of these are generally locked. The town does, however, serve as a good base for visiting the nearby villages of Mandawa and Lakshmangarh.

Mahesh Yogi (☎ 2014) is a government-approved guide based in Fatehpur. He charges about Rs 50 per hour, or Rs 380 for a full day (up to four people). You can reach him through RTDC Hotel Haveli.

Things to See
On the right of the Mandawa road, about 50m east of the main intersection with the Churu–Sikar road, is the badly deteriorating **Choudharia Haveli** – extreme caution is needed, as the entire edifice looks as if it will soon be a heap of rubble. Poor drainage has caused water damage and is responsible for the haveli's sorry state. On the eastern wall is an interesting erotic painting. A woman is embracing a man with one hand and holding a glass in the other, while she is being ravished, as a servant stands by.

On the western side of Mandawa road, about 50m west of the Churu to Sikar road, and on the left-hand side past the lac bangle vendors, is the **Geori Shankar Haveli**. There are very good mirror mosaics on the ceiling of the antechamber. You'll probably be asked for a donation to enter this haveli.

Nearby on the same road is the **Mahavir Prasad Goenka Haveli**, built in 1885, which is considered by some to have the very best paintings of Shekhawati, as it combines a perfect synthesis of colour and design. Unfortunately, it is usually locked.

At the first intersection to the north past the intersection of the Mandawa road and the Churu to Sikar road, turn right and you'll soon come to **Haveli Nadine**, formerly known as the Nand Lal Devra Haveli, on your right. This house was purchased by French artist Nadine Le Prince in 2000 and she is restoring the haveli, although visitors are no longer welcome inside. The facade retains some paintings, predominantly in tones of red and blue. There is a finely carved lintel with Ganesh sculpted over the centre (Ganesh, the protector of households, is often depicted here). Fifty metres south of this haveli is the small **Chauhan Well**, which dates from the early 18th century. There is some uninspiring painting around the windows and a couple of the pavilions, and the minarets retain fragments of geometric and floral designs.

Return to the Haveli Nadine, and from there, retrace your steps back to the main Churu–Sikar road. Cross this and continue along the same road, then turn right up the first lane. On the right-hand side of the lane is the **Jagannath Singhania Haveli**. It is often locked, but has some interesting paintings on its facade, including those of Krishna and Radha, who are framed by four elephants, and above this, some British men with guns.

In the northwest of the town (take the turn to the left off the Churu to Sikar road opposite the large Jagannath Singhania Chhatri) are **two large havelis** which were built by the Barthia family. The paintings are not exceptional, but are excellently preserved and maintained. These havelis are reminiscent of Victorian-era theatres.

The **Jagannath Singhania Chhatri**, on the east side of the Churu to Sikar road (enter through a gateway behind the *chhatri*), has very pretty and well-tended gardens. This is an imposing building, although not very comprehensively painted. Paintings, some of which appear to be unfinished, include hunting scenes. There is a small Shiva shrine in the *chhatri* at which villagers still pay homage. Opposite is the small Singhania well, which is still in use.

Near the private bus stand is a large **baorl** which was built by Sheikh Mohammed of Nagaur in 1614. There's a path to the *baori* from a lane opposite the private bus stand. Unfortunately, the *baori* is in a shocking state of disrepair. In fact, it's downright dangerous, and you shouldn't approach too close to the edges. It was obviously a feat of some magnitude to dig to this depth, and around the sides there is a series of arched galleries, most of which have collapsed. The *baori* is now used as a rubbish dump. On the south side of it a haveli has half fallen into the well, and its courtyard paintings are

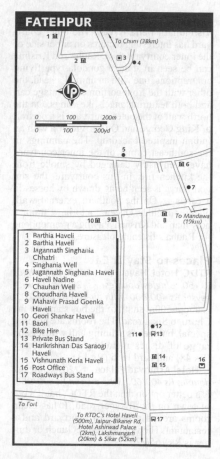

FATEHPUR

To Churu (38km)

0   100   200m
0   100   200yd

To Mandawa (19km)

To Fort

To RTDC's Hotel Haveli (500m), Jaipur-Bikaner Rd, Hotel Ashirwad Palace (2km), Lakshmangarh (20km) & Sikar (52km)

1 Barthia Haveli
2 Barthia Haveli
3 Jagannath Singhania Chhatri
4 Singhania Well
5 Jagannath Singhania Haveli
6 Haveli Nadine
7 Chauhan Well
8 Choudharia Haveli
9 Mahavir Prasad Goenka Haveli
10 Geori Shankar Haveli
11 Baori
12 Bike Hire
13 Private Bus Stand
14 Harikrishnan Das Saraogi Haveli
15 Vishnunath Keria Haveli
16 Post Office
17 Roadways Bus Stand

exposed. Two ornate columns hang poised precariously over the abyss. The minarets of the *baori* still stand as a testament to its obvious former grandeur.

Diagonally opposite the *baori*, situated on the south side of the private bus stand, the **Harikrishnan Das Saraogi Haveli** features a colourful facade with iron lacework on the upper verandas and shops at street level. There's a vibrantly coloured outer courtyard. In one picture, a woman appears to be smoking a hookah. The inner courtyard has an interesting juxtaposition: a camel-drawn cart next to a motorcar.

NORTHERN RAJASTHAN

Adjacent to this haveli (to the south) is the **Vishnunath Keria Haveli**. The outer courtyard has interesting pictures on either side of the inner courtyard door. Radha and Krishna can be seen in strange gondola-type flying contraptions, one with an animal's head, the other with the front portion of a vintage car, and both featuring angel-like wings. On the north wall of the outer courtyard is a portrait of King George and Queen Victoria with an Indian-inspired backdrop. The paintings in the southeast corner of the inner courtyard have been badly damaged by smoke from the kitchen fire. In this courtyard, the sun god Surya is seen being drawn by horses in a carriage. On the southern external wall, pictures include Queen Victoria, a train, a holy man and Krishna playing a gramophone for Radha's listening pleasure.

Places to Stay & Eat

RTDC Hotel Haveli *(☎ 20293; dorm beds Rs 50, singles/doubles Rs 200/300, with geyser Rs 400/500, with air-con Rs 600/700)* is about 500m south of the bus stand on the Churu to Sikar road. The rooms are nothing special, but there's a dining hall with a good range of dishes including chicken curry (Rs 48) and curd lassi (Rs 13).

Hotel Ashirwad Palace *(☎ 22635; singles/doubles Rs 400/600, with air-con Rs 800/950)* is a better option than the RTDC, but it's out of town on the Bikaner road. It has clean rooms around a peaceful courtyard and a restaurant. The veg/nonveg set lunch or dinner is Rs 165/220.

Getting There & Away

At the private bus stand, on the Churu to Sikar road, buses leave for Jhunjhunu (Rs 18, one hour), Mandawa (Rs 10, 20 minutes), Churu (Rs 15, one hour), Ramgarh (Rs 10, 45 minutes) and Sikar (Rs 22, one hour).

From the Roadways bus stand, which is further south down this road, buses leave for Jaipur (Rs 66, 3½ hours), Delhi (Rs 125, seven hours) and Bikaner (Rs 73, 3½ hours).

Getting Around

Bicycles can be hired (Rs 5/25 per hour/day) near the private bus stand.

MANDAWA

☎ 01592 • postcode 333704 • pop 20,717

The compact and busy little market town of Mandawa, 19km northeast of Fatehpur, was settled in the 18th century and fortified by the dominant merchant families. It has some fine painted havelis and is becoming increasingly popular with travellers, which accounts for the alarming number of antique shops cropping up along the main drag.

Information

The State Bank of Bikaner & Jaipur, in Binsidhar Newatia Haveli, changes travellers cheques and currency.

Things to See

The **Binsidhar Newatia Haveli**, on the northern side of the Fatehpur to Jhunjhunu road, is now the premises of the State Bank of Bikaner & Jaipur. The interior paintings have been whitewashed, but there are still some interesting paintings on the external eastern wall (accessible through the bank). These include a European woman in a car driven by a chauffeur; a man on a bicycle; the Wright brothers evoking much excitement in their aeroplane as women in saris, among others, point with astonishment; a boy using a telephone; and a birdman flying by in a winged device. The paintings date from the 1920s.

Continue west and turn right at the bus stand and left again. About 50m along are several havelis belonging to the Goenka family. To the right of the entrance to the **Hanuman Prasad Goenka Haveli** is an unusual composite picture that shows either Indra on an elephant, or Shiva on his bull, depending on which way you look at it. Across the road is the **Goenka Double Haveli**, which has two entrance gates and monumental pictures, including elephants and horses, on the facade. The paintings on the haveli to the left are badly deteriorated.

Adjacent is the **Murmuria Haveli**. From the sandy courtyard in front of this haveli, you can get a good view of the southern external wall of the adjacent double haveli: it features a long frieze depicting a train with a crow flying above the engine and much activity at the railway crossing. The Murmuria Haveli also reflects a strong European influence in its paintings. Nehru is depicted on horseback holding the Indian flag. Above the arches on the south side of the courtyard are two paintings of gondolas on the canals of Venice.

From here a road leads south, and 50m along you can take a short detour to the right to see the impressive **Harlalka well**, marked by four pillars and its old pulley and camel ramp. Back on the road heading south, you come to a T-junction and turn left. On the next corner is the **Jhunjhunwala Haveli** *(admission Rs 10)*, with an impressive gold leaf–painted room to the right of the main courtyard.

About 50m east is the **Mohan Lal Saraf Haveli**. On the south wall, a maharaja is depicted grooming his bushy moustache. There is fine mirror-and-mosaic work around the door to the inner courtyard, and Surya, the sun god, can be seen over the lintel.

Further south on the same street is the **Lakshminarayan Ladia Haveli**. On the west wall is a faded picture of a man enjoying a hookah, and a good procession frieze. Between the wall brackets, *gopis* emerge from the tentacles of a sea monster upon whose head Krishna dances. Other pictures include that of Rama slaying Ravana.

Unfortunately, many of the erotic images on the **Gulab Rai Ladia Haveli**, a short distance to the east, have been systematically defaced by prudish souls. In the last pair of brackets on the first half of the southern wall a woman can be seen giving birth, attended by maidservants. There is an erotic image in the fifth niche from the end on this wall, but don't draw too much attention to it, or it might suffer the same fate as the other erotic art on this building. There is also something untoward happening in a train carriage on this wall.

About 150m past this haveli to the south is the **Chokhani Double Haveli**. The pictures

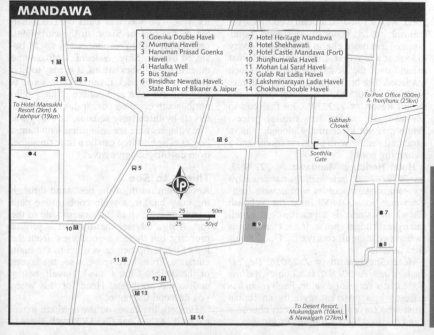

MANDAWA

1	Goenka Double Haveli
2	Murmuria Haveli
3	Hanuman Prasad Goenka Haveli
4	Harlalka Well
5	Bus Stand
6	Binsidhar Newatia Haveli; State Bank of Bikaner & Jaipur
7	Hotel Heritage Mandawa
8	Hotel Shekhawati
9	Hotel Castle Mandawa (Fort)
10	Jhunjhunwala Haveli
11	Mohan Lal Saraf Haveli
12	Gulab Rai Ladia Haveli
13	Lakshminarayan Ladia Haveli
14	Chokhani Double Haveli

To Hotel Mansukhi Resort (2km) & Fatehpur (19km)

To Post Office (500m) & Jhunjhunu (25km)

Subhash Chowk

Sonthlia Gate

0   25   50m
0   25   50yd

To Desert Resort, Mukundgarh (10km), & Nawalgarh (27km)

NORTHERN RAJASTHAN

are not that special, but the building is rather grand. The paintings inside include floral arabesques and peacocks above the archways, as well as the Krishna legends.

Organised Tours

You can organise camel and horse rides at the **Hotel Castle Mandawa** (see Places to Stay & Eat). A one-hour camel ride is Rs 450 and a half-/full-day trip is Rs 750/1000. Another option is the Hotel Heritage Mandawa (see Places to Stay & Eat), which organises camel rides for Rs 400/800 per half/full day. A three-day safari costs Rs 2500, including all meals, tents, bedding and camels. It can also arrange jeep hire for Rs 800 per day (maximum of six people), plus Rs 250 per day for a guide.

Places to Stay & Eat

Hotel Castle Mandawa (✆ 7223124, fax 7223171; ℮ information@castlemandaw.com; singles Rs 1850-1975, doubles Rs 2400-3500, suites Rs 3995) is one of the most upmarket places to stay in Shekhawati. This large hotel, with a somewhat contrived medieval atmosphere, has tastefully designed rooms – some have more charm than others, so try to look at a few first. Like many hotels that expand over the years, the personal touch has faded. The buffet breakfast/lunch/dinner is Rs 275/450/500. The hotel also runs **Desert Resort** (✆ 7223245), on the road to Mukundgarh, which has similar prices. While it is not as centrally placed, it is in a tranquil setting with pleasant rooms and a swimming pool.

Hotel Heritage Mandawa (✆ 7223743, fax 7223742; ℮ hotelheritagemandawa@yahoo.com; singles/doubles with private bathroom from Rs 300/400), near the Subhash Chowk bus stand, is a gracious old haveli and a great budget choice. It has clean rooms around two tranquil courtyards. Good meals are available.

Hotel Shekhawati (✆ 7223036; singles/doubles from Rs 50/100) is a homey, yellow place that's very good value. Each room has a fresco in a different style by an Italian artist who stayed here – you can choose a room inspired by the Rajputs or Picasso.

Hotel Mansukhi Resort (✆ 7223181, fax 7223884; singles/doubles Rs 100/150) is about 2km from Mandawa, with a handful of romantic round huts or odd rooms on three levels. Free pick-up from the town is offered – contact its office on the road to the fort. You can hire a bicycle/motorcycle for Rs 25/100 per day. Camel safaris can also be organised.

Getting There & Away

There are buses to Nawalgarh (Rs 12, 45 minutes), Fatehpur (Rs 9, one hour), Bissau (Rs 15, 1½ hours) and Ramgarh (Rs 13, 1½ hours). There are also direct buses to Jaipur (Rs 50, four hours) and Bikaner (Rs 40, 3½ hours). A taxi between Mandawa and Fatehpur costs Rs 200 (one way), or you can take a crammed jeep taxi for Rs 10.

LAKSHMANGARH

✆ 01573 • pop 47,288

The most imposing building in this town, only 20km south of Fatehpur, is its small fortress, which looms over the township to its west. The fort was built by Lakshman Singh, the raja of Sikar, in the early 19th century after the prosperous town was besieged by Kan Singh Saledhi. Unlike some other towns of Shekhawati, it is easy to find your way around Lakshmangarh, as it is well laid out on a grid pattern, with a main north–south oriented bazaar dissected at intervals by three busy squares, or *chaupars*. The villagers here are unfamiliar with tourist hordes. The children can be a little tiresome, even downright aggressive!

Things to See

About 50m north of the bus stand through the busy bazaar, a wide cobblestone path wends its way up to the eastern side of the **fort**. A sign advises that the fort is private property, but there's a good view from the top of the ramp before you get to the main entrance. From here you can see the layout of the double Char Chowk Haveli, below and to the northeast. Head for this when you descend the ramp.

Beneath the eaves on the northern external wall of the **Char Chowk Haveli**, there is a picture of a bird standing on an elephant with another elephant in its beak. The large paintings on the facade of the northern face have mostly faded, and the paintings in the outer downstairs courtyard are covered by blue wash. The paintings in the inner courtyard are well preserved. The walls and ceiling of a small upstairs room on the east side of the northern haveli are completely covered with paintings. It has some explicit erotic images, but is very badly illuminated, so although they're well preserved you'll need a flashlight to see them properly.

In the same building, a room in the northwest corner retains floral swirls and motifs on the ceiling with scenes from the Krishna legends interspersed with inlaid mirrors. The black-and-white rectangular designs on the lower walls create a marbled effect. No-one lives in the haveli, but the caretaker may open it for you (for a small fee). The front facade is in very poor condition at the lower levels, with the plaster crumbling and the bricks exposed. The southern haveli is still inhabited by about 30 people.

About 50m east of this haveli is the large **Radhi Murlimanohar Temple**, which dates from 1845. It retains a few paintings beneath the eaves and some sculptures of deities around the external walls.

If you take the road west from the temple, on the corner of the second laneway on the right is the **Chetram Sanganeeria Haveli**. The lower paintings on the west wall are badly damaged: the plaster has peeled away and concrete rendering has been applied. Paintings on this wall include a woman in a swing suspended from a tree, a woman spinning, a man dancing on a pole balancing knives, people enjoying a ride on a Ferris wheel, a man ploughing fields with oxen, and men sawing timber.

A little to the south of the temple is the busy bazaar, flanked by a series of shops whose overhanging balconies have three scalloped open arches between two blank arches with lattice friezes. The shops were constructed during the mid-19th century by a branch of the Poddar family known as Ganeriwala, who actually hailed from the village of Ganeri.

On the northeast corner of the clock tower square, which is about 100m south of the temple via the busy bazaar, is the **Rathi Family Haveli**. On the west wall, a European woman in a smart red frock sews on a treadle machine. The European influence is very much in evidence here, with painted roses and a Grecian column effect. On the south side of this haveli are ostentatious flourishes and the British crown flanked by unicorns. On the east side are some blue-eyed British soldiers.

There is a busy set of *chai* (tea) stalls on the west side of the haveli, and this is a good place to sit down and admire these extraordinarily over-the-top paintings.

Getting There & Away
There are many buses between Lakshmangarh and both Sikar (Rs 10) and Fatehpur (Rs 8), as well as Nawalgarh (Rs 8).

Getting Around
A bicycle shop just to the south of Radhi Murlimanohar Temple hires bikes for a nominal price.

CHURU
☎ 01562 • postcode 331001 • pop 97,627
Churu is not technically part of Shekhawati, falling within the administrative district of Bikaner. However, it is usually included in discussions of the painted walls of Shekhawati, as it was also a centre of trade and commerce, and the many rich merchant families who hailed from here left a legacy of fine painted havelis. About 95km to the southwest of Churu is the small Tal Chhapar Wildlife Sanctuary (see Around Churu), home to a substantial population of blackbucks and other mammals and birds.

Arvind Sharma (☎ 51024), based in Churu, is a government-approved guide.

Things to See
You'll need help to find the **Malji ka Kamra**, which is to the north of the bus stand, down a lane on the west side of the main bazaar. It's well worth the effort to find this place: it's an extraordinary edifice covered in pale-blue stucco and perched on green pillars

like some baroque travesty of a wedding cake. This once-grand building is now covered in pigeon pooh and is home to rubbish-grazing cows. Statues on the facade include a bored-looking woman dressed in a sari (and with a handbag and wings), turbaned men, and angels. It was built in 1925, but its days of glory are long gone.

A short distance to the northwest (within easy walking distance) is the **Surana Double Haveli**. This five-storey edifice with its hundreds of windows achieves something of a Georgian effect. On the lower levels of the west wall are fragments of paintings, including processions and peacocks. The haveli is beyond an archway at the end of a narrow laneway.

A further 100m to the northwest is the **Surajmal Banthia Haveli**, which was built in the 1920s. It is best known for its infamous picture of Christ with a cigar, on the external north wall, rather incongruously juxtaposed beside a British lady. Across the lane to the north is a haveli with what may well be the most bizarre paintings on any of the havelis of Shekhawati – beneath the eaves on the eastern side is a series of inverted paintings of naked men fondling rabbits!

Places to Stay & Eat
Not many travellers choose to stay in Churu, but if you do find yourself here for a night there is one reasonably decent hotel, although English can be a problem.

Hotel Deluxe (☎ 51114; doubles with private bathroom Rs 160) is directly opposite the private bus stand. It has small, grimy rooms and hot water by the bucket. There's a restaurant downstairs that cooks up veg fare at modest prices.

Getting There & Away
The Roadways bus stand is 500m west of the private one. Regular services to destinations in Shekhawati from the private bus stand include Fatehpur (Rs 15, one hour), Jhunjhunu (Rs 20, 1½ hours) and Sikar (Rs 35, two hours). From the Roadways stand there are services to Delhi (Rs 119, six hours) and Jaipur (Rs 81, five hours).

The train station is located 100m north of the private bus stand. To Bikaner, the train takes approximately four hours (Rs 54/318 in 2nd/1st class). There are trains to Delhi (Rs 73/393, 6½ hours) and to Jaipur (Rs 56/329, six hours).

AROUND CHURU
Tal Chhapar Wildlife Sanctuary
This small grassland sanctuary, which lies about 95km southwest of Churu and 210km northwest of Jaipur, covers 70 sq km and has healthy populations of blackbucks, as well as chinkaras (Indian gazelles) and smaller mammals, such as desert foxes. The sanctuary lies on the migration route of a number of bird species, most notably harriers, which descend here during September. Other birds include various types of eagle (tawny, imperial, short-toed), which migrate here in winter, and the demoiselle crane, which also descends in large numbers during the winter months (early September to late March). Throughout the year there are populations of crested larks, ring and brown doves and skylarks.

It is best to visit the sanctuary between September and March. There is a **forest resthouse** at Chhapar. For more information, contact the Deputy Conservator of Forests (Wildlife) in Jodhpur.

Western Rajasthan

Encompassing a vast area, which includes the districts of Jodhpur, Jaisalmer, Bikaner and Barmer, this desolate and arid land was believed to have been created by the falling of an arrow fired by Rama, hero of the Ramayana. The arrow was destined for the sea god who inhabited the straits between India and Lanka (Sri Lanka). However, when the sea god apologised to Rama for opposing his desire to cross the straits, Rama fired the arrow to the northwest, and thus rendered this region a desolate wasteland.

Western Rajasthan includes the vast Thar Desert, which extends through the adjacent states of Punjab, Haryana and Gujarat and into Pakistan, and is the world's most populous arid zone. It was the scene of bloody conflicts over the ages, as feudal kings fought both with each other and against external invaders such as the Muslims.

Western Rajasthan has two of the most stunning palace-fort complexes in India at Jodhpur and Jaisalmer. Nothing rivals Meherangarh at Jodhpur for sheer awe-inspiring majesty, while the Jaisalmer fort is romance incarnate, an extraordinary edifice in yellow sandstone which rises from the desert landscape. It is a tribute to the valour of the Bhatti Rajputs, who ruled here for centuries. Enormous rocks can still be seen perched precariously across the top of the battlements; they were intended for the heads of advancing enemies, and those who escaped these missiles would then have to dodge the cauldrons of boiling oil poured from the ramparts.

Bikaner's fort, Junagarh, is only slightly less impressive, and you can lose yourself for hours in the colourful bazaars of its old walled city, which also encompasses two exquisite Jain temples.

Ancient Osiyan, northwest of Jodhpur, also has ancient temples, and from late August/early September until the end of March, at nearby Khichan, you can see hundreds of graceful demoiselle cranes, which descend morning and evening on the fields

Highlights

- The mighty Meherangarh, one of Rajasthan's most impressive forts
- Exquisite havelis, beautifully crafted outdoor works of art
- Jaisalmer's glorious fort, rising from the stark desert landscape
- Camel safaris, a unique way to see the dunes and lonely plains of Rajasthan's desert
- The bizarre Karni Mata Temple, a sanctuary for myriad holy rats in Deshnok

surrounding this village to feed on grain distributed by villagers.

History

The district of Jodhpur was, until comparatively recent times, known as the ancient kingdom of Marwar, the largest kingdom in Rajputana and the third largest of the Indian kingdoms, after Kashmir and Hyderabad.

Little historical evidence remains of the period prior to the 3rd century BC. In 231 BC, Chandragupta Maurya's empire came to power, extending its dominion across northern India from its capital at present-day Patna, in Bihar. The indigenous inhabitants were subjugated by the Aryans during

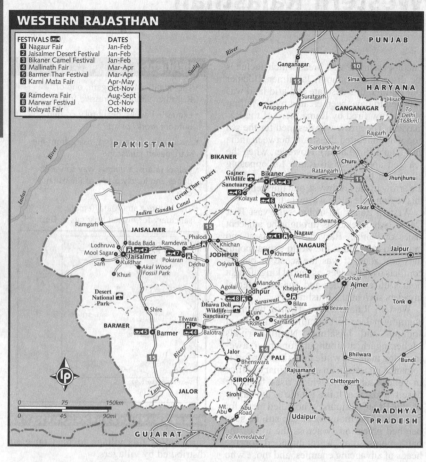

WESTERN RAJASTHAN

FESTIVALS	DATES
1 Nagaur Fair	Jan-Feb
2 Jaisalmer Desert Festival	Jan-Feb
3 Bikaner Camel Festival	Jan-Feb
4 Mallinath Fair	Mar-Apr
5 Barmer Thar Festival	Mar-Apr
6 Karni Mata Fair	Apr-May, Oct-Nov
7 Ramdevra Fair	Aug-Sept
8 Marwar Festival	Oct-Nov
9 Kolayat Fair	Oct-Nov

their invasion of northern India between 1500 and 200 BC. In subsequent centuries, the region fell to the Kushanas, the Hunas and the Guhilas. However, it was ultimately the Rajput Rathores, who hailed from Kannauj in present-day Uttar Pradesh, and consolidated themselves in this region, ousting the local tribal leaders. From them, historians can more accurately trace the emergence of the state of Marwar. The Rathores originally settled at Pali, which is southeast of present-day Jodhpur, however in 1381 they shifted their capital to Mandore. In 1459 Rao Jodha, the Rathore leader, shifted the capital about 9km to the south and founded the city of Jodhpur.

Meanwhile, the Muslims were entrenched at Nagaur, after Mohammad Bahlim, the governor of Sind, erected a fort here in 1122 upon subduing the local Hindu chief, Ajayaraja. The rule of Nagaur fell variously to Ajayaraja (again), the sultanate of Delhi, the Rathores, an independent local dynasty led by Shams Khan Dandani, the Lodi sultans of Delhi and the Mughals under Akbar. In 1572, Akbar granted it to the chief of Bikaner, Raisimha. In the early 18th century, Nagaur was acquired by the maharaja of Jodhpur.

The desert city of Bikaner was founded by one of the sons of Rao Jodha, founder of Jodhpur, following a schism in the ruling Rathore family.

JODHPUR
☎ 0291 • postcode 342001 • pop 846,408
Jodhpur stands at the edge of the Thar Desert and is the largest city in Rajasthan after Jaipur. This bustling desert city is dominated by a massive fort, topping a sheer rocky ridge which rises right in the middle of the town.

The old city of Jodhpur is surrounded by a 10km-long wall, which was built about a century after the city was founded. From the fort, you can clearly see where the old city ends and the new one begins. It's fascinating to wander around the jumble of winding streets in the old city, out of which eight gates lead. Part of the film *Rudyard Kipling's Jungle Book*, starring Sam Neill and John Cleese, was shot in Jodhpur and yes, it was from here that those baggy-tight horse-riding trousers, jodhpurs, took their name.

As one of the closest major Indian cities to the border with Pakistan, Jodhpur has a large defence contingent. When tensions on the border are high you might have a strong impulse to dive for cover when you hear booming jet fighter planes above, but they're probably just doing routine training exercises.

History
Founded in 1459 by Rao Jodha, a chief of the Rajput clan, the Rathores, Jodhpur was the capital of the Rathore kingdom once known as Marwar, the Land of Death. The Rathores were driven from their homeland of Kannauj by Afghans serving Mohammed of Ghori, and fled west to the region around Pali, a short distance to the south of Jodhpur. An expedient marriage alliance between the Rathore Siahaji and the sister of a local prince enabled the Rathores to consolidate themselves in this region. In fact, they prospered to such a degree that they managed to oust the Pratiharas of Mandore, 9km to the north of present-day Jodhpur.

By 1459, it became evident that a more secure headquarters was required. The high rocky ridge 9km to the south of Mandore was an obvious choice for the new city of Jodhpur, with the natural fortifications afforded by its steep flanks greatly enhanced by a fortress of staggering proportions (see Mcherangarh later).

Orientation
The Tourist Reception Centre, train stations and bus stand are all outside the old city. High Court Rd runs from the Raika Bagh train station, past Umaid Gardens, the RTDC Hotel Ghoomar and Tourist Reception Centre, and beside the city wall towards the main station and the main post office. Trains from the east stop at the Raika Bagh station before heading on to the main station, which is handy if you're staying at a hotel on the eastern side of town.

Information
Tourist Offices The **Tourist Reception Centre** (*☎ 1364, 545083; High Court Rd; open 8am-8pm Mon-Sat*) is adjacent to RTDC Hotel Ghoomar. It sells a good map of Jodhpur (Rs 2) and supplies various tourist brochures. A smaller tourist office at the airport is being planned.

At the main train station is an **International Tourists Bureau** (*☎ 439052; open 5am-11.30pm Mon-Sat*), which provides help for foreign passengers – a handy place to hang around while waiting for a train. There are comfortable armchairs and a shower and toilet here. Unattended luggage must be deposited in the train station cloakroom (Rs 10 per piece for 24 hours).

Money The **State Bank of India** (*High Court Rd*) changes travellers cheques and currency. **LKP Forex** (*☎ 512532*), opposite Circuit House, changes a wider range of currencies. You can get cash advances on your credit card at the **Bank of Baroda** (*open 10am-3pm Mon-Fri & 10am-12.30pm Sat*) at Sojati Gate. There's also an ATM at Ratanada Circle where you can withdraw cash against your MasterCard.

Post The **main post office** (*Station Rd; open 10am-5pm Mon-Fri, 10am-1pm Sat*) is less

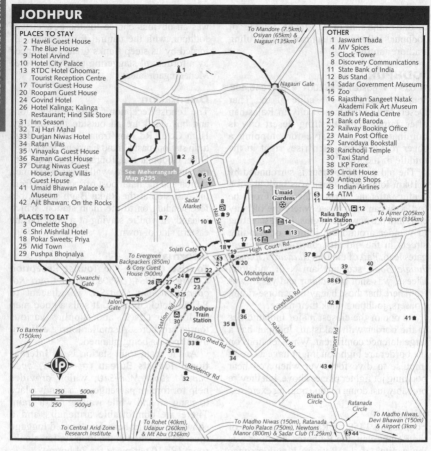

JODHPUR

PLACES TO STAY
2 Haveli Guest House
7 The Blue House
9 Hotel Arvind
10 Hotel City Palace
13 RTDC Hotel Ghoomar;
   Tourist Reception Centre
17 Tourist Guest House
20 Roopam Guest House
24 Govind Hotel
26 Hotel Kalinga; Kalinga
   Restaurant; Hind Silk Store
31 Inn Season
32 Taj Hari Mahal
33 Durjan Niwas Hotel
34 Ratan Vilas
35 Vinayaka Guest House
36 Raman Guest House
37 Durag Niwas Guest
   House; Durag Villas
   Guest House
41 Umaid Bhawan Palace &
   Museum
42 Ajit Bhawan; On the Rocks

PLACES TO EAT
3 Omelette Shop
6 Shri Mishrilal Hotel
18 Pokar Sweets; Priya
25 Mid Town
29 Pushpa Bhojnalya

OTHER
1 Jaswant Thada
4 MV Spices
5 Clock Tower
8 Discovery Communications
11 State Bank of India
12 Bus Stand
14 Sadar Government Museum
15 Zoo
16 Rajasthan Sangeet Natak
   Akademi Folk Art Museum
19 Rathi's Media Centre
21 Bank of Baroda
22 Railway Booking Office
23 Main Post Office
27 Sarvodaya Bookstall
28 Ranchodji Temple
30 Taxi Stand
38 LKP Forex
39 Circuit House
40 Antique Shops
43 Indian Airlines
44 ATM

To Mandore (7.5km),
Osiyan (65km) &
Nagaur (135km)

Nagauri Gate

*See Meherangarh
Map p295*

Sadar
Market

Umaid
Gardens

Raika Bagh
Train Station

To Ajmer (205km)
& Jaipur (336km)

Sojati Gate

High Court Rd

To Evergreen
Backpackers (850m)
& Cosy Guest
House (900m)

Mohanpura
Overbridge

Siwanchi
Gate

Jalori
Gate

Gavshala Rd

Ratanada Rd

Airport Rd

To Barmer
(150km)

Jodhpur
Train
Station

Station Rd

Old Loco Shed Rd

Residency Rd

To Central Arid Zone
Research Institute

To Rohet (40km),
Udaipur (260km)
& Mt Abu (326km)

To Madho Niwas (150m), Ratanada
Polo Palace (750m), Newtons
Manor (800m) & Sadar Club (1.25km)

Bhatia
Circle

Ratanada
Circle

To Madho Niwas,
Devi Bhawan (150m)
& Airport (3km)

0   250   500m
0   250   500yd

---

than half a kilometre north of the main train station.

Email & Internet Access There are loads of places where you can access the Internet around town; the going rate at the time of writing was Rs 40 per hour. **Discovery Communications** (☎ 548339; 122 Nai Sarak) has a generator in case of blackouts.

Bookshops Off Station Rd, opposite Ranchodji Temple, is the **Sarvodaya Bookstall** (☎ 622734; 70 Station Rd; open 8.30am-10.30pm daily). It has English-language

newspapers, magazines, a good range of books on India and a few Western novels. It also stocks some good maps of Rajasthan. On the Mohanpura Overbridge is **Rathi's Media Centre** (☎ 513580; open 8.30am-8.30pm daily), which stocks a reasonable range of books in English, including novels and recent releases.

Meherangarh

Still operated by the maharaja of Jodhpur, Meherangarh (Majestic Fort; foreigner/citizen Rs 50/15, camera/video Rs 50/100; open 9am-1pm & 2pm-5pm daily) is majestic indeed.

Sprawled across a 125m-high hill, this is perhaps the most formidable fort in all of Rajasthan. It has been added to over the centuries by reigning Jodhpur maharajas, but the original fort was built in 1459 by Rao Jodha, after whom the city takes its name. A winding road leads up to the entrance from the city, 5km below. The second gate is still scarred by cannonball hits, showing that this was a fort that earned its keep. To the left, just beyond the ticket office, is the **Chhatri of Kiratsingh Sodha**. This cenotaph was built over the site where a soldier fell defending Jodhpur against Jaipurians in 1806.

The gates, of which there are seven, include the **Jayapol** (*pol* means 'gate') built by Maharaja Man Singh in 1806 following his victory over the armies of Jaipur and Bikaner. This is the main entrance to the fort. The **Fatehpol** (Victory Gate), at the southwest side of the fort, was erected by Maharaja Ajit Singh to commemorate his defeat of the Mughals.

The **Lohapol** (Iron Gate) has beside it 15 handprints, the *sati* (self-immolation) marks of Maharaja Man Singh's widows, who threw themselves upon his funeral pyre in 1843. These marks still attract devotional attention and are usually covered in red powder (and paper-thin silver during special festivals).

Inside the fort is a series of courtyards and palaces. The **palace apartments** have evocative names such as Moti Mahal, or Pearl Palace, Sukh Mahal, or Pleasure Palace and Phool Mahal, or Flower Palace. These days the apartments house one of Rajasthan's most fascinating collections of artefacts, in the **museum**. The exhibits may have been rearranged (and may not be in the sequence described here). Entry to the museum is via the Surajpol. To the right, just beyond the entrance, there is a collection of elephant carriages. Some of the *howdahs* (seats for carrying people on elephants' backs) feature the most exquisite repoussé (raised relief) silverwork, with designs such as rampant lions. In the next room are the maharajas' palanquins, including covered palanquins for the women in *purdah* (seclusion). In the

armoury, which has exhibits dating from the 17th to the 19th centuries, is an assortment of deadly weapons, each of which is a remarkable work of art.

Upstairs is the **Phool Mahal**, in which traditional dances were performed. It was also used as a durbar hall by former maharajas. The fine paintings adorning the walls of this palace were executed by a single artist, and took over 10 years to complete. In fact, the artist died before the work was finished, evident in the bare patch to the left of the hallway. The gold ceiling is embellished with over 80kg of gold plate, and around it the various maharajas of Jodhpur are depicted. The stained glass in this room further accentuates the room's opulence. To the north is a palace that was a place of prayer. It is covered with glass tiles and extraordinary modern Christmas ball-like decorations suspended from the ceiling.

In the **Ajit Vilas** there's an excellent display of miniatures from the Marwari school

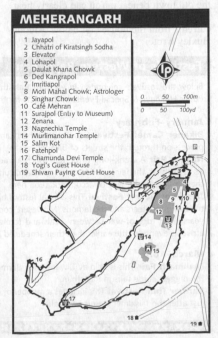

MEHERANGARH

1 Jayapol
2 Chhatri of Kiratsingh Sodha
3 Elevator
4 Lohapol
5 Daulat Khana Chowk
6 Ded Kangrapol
7 Imritiapol
8 Moti Mahal Chowk; Astrologer
9 Singhar Chowk
10 Café Mehran
11 Surajpol (Entry to Museum)
12 Zenana
13 Nagnechia Temple
14 Murlimanohar Temple
15 Salim Kot
16 Fatehpol
17 Chamunda Devi Temple
18 Yogi's Guest House
19 Shivam Paying Guest House

of art, including a particularly fine painting of the wedding procession of Shiva. Nearby, **Umaid Bhavan**, which usually houses the collection, was under restoration at the time of writing, and due to reopen in 2003.

The next room is the private chamber of Maharaja Thakhat Singh (r. 1843–73), who had no less than 30 maharanis and numerous concubines. There's a beautiful ceiling adorned with lac painting, and the walls are painted. Nearby, in the *zenana* (women's apartments), the **Zhanki Mahal** has cradles of infant princes, including that of the current maharaja. In the **Moti Mahal** are five alcoves along the west wall. The other tiny alcoves around the wall were for oil lamps. The ceiling is embellished with glass tiles and gold paint. An astrologer can be consulted here (see Astrology later). The *zenana* is adorned with fine latticework screens, featuring over 150 different designs.

At the southern end of the fort, cannons on the ramparts overlook the sheer drop to the old town beneath. You can clearly hear voices and city sounds carried up by the air currents from the houses far below. Aldous Huxley wrote:

From the bastions of the Jodhpur Fort one hears as the Gods must hear from Olympus – the Gods to whom each separate word uttered in the innumerable peopled world below, comes up distinct and individual to be recorded in the books of omniscience.

The views from these ramparts are nothing less than magical. You can see the many houses painted blue, traditionally to distinguish them as those of Brahmins. **Chamunda Devi Temple**, dedicated to Durga in her wrathful aspect, stands at this end of the fort.

There's an elevator near the ticket office, which costs Rs 10 one way (but it's free for mobility-impaired visitors). If possible, walk rather than take the lift, as you see more. For a guided tour of the fort, expect to pay Rs 100 (maximum of four people).

The tours operated by the Rajasthan Tourism Development Corporation (RTDC; see Organised Tours, later) will only give you an hour at the fort, so if you want to stay here longer (there's plenty to see), get here under your own steam. There is a classy restaurant, **Café Mehran**, at the fort, just near the Surajpol, where you can get a veg thali for Rs 65.

Festivals of Western Rajasthan

Below are festivals celebrated in western Rajasthan. For statewide and nationwide festivals, see Public Holidays & Special Events in the Facts for the Visitor chapter.

January–February
Bikaner Camel Festival Gaily caparisoned camels are proudly displayed by their owners in a procession through the streets of Bikaner.

Nagaur Fair A week-long cattle fair which attracts thousands of rural people from far and wide. As at Pushkar, the fair includes camel races and cultural entertainment programmes. Unlike Pushkar, there is little in the way of accommodation here.

Jaisalmer Desert Festival This annual festival has camel races and dances, folk music, traditional ballads, puppeteers and the famous 'Mr Desert' competition. It's become a lot more touristy over the years, with tugs-of-war between locals and foreigners and turban-tying competitions. It's best to arrive at events a little earlier than their scheduled time, to get a seat and avoid the chaotic crowds.

March–April
Mallinath Fair This is held at Tilwara, near Barmer, over a fortnight in March–April and is one of the biggest cattle fairs in Rajasthan.

Barmer Thar Festival This includes a number of cultural shows, dancing and puppetry and is held just after the Jaisalmer Desert Festival.

Jaswant Thada

This white marble memorial to Maharaja Jaswant Singh II *(foreigner/citizen Rs 10/5; open 9am-1pm & 2pm-5pm daily)* is situated about 400m northeast of the fort, just off the fort road. The cenotaph, built in 1899, was followed by the royal crematorium and another three cenotaphs, which stand nearby. There is marble *jali* (lattice) work over the windows and carved wooden doors. Some parts of the white marble are translucent. There are some good views to take in from the terrace in front of the cenotaph, which is fronted by a little garden of flowering shrubs. Swimming in the Devakund, just a short distance to the west of the cenotaph, is prohibited.

Clock Tower & Markets

The clock tower is a popular landmark in the bustling old city and a wonderful place to simply ramble around. The vibrant Sadar Market is close to the tower, and narrow alleys lead from here to the bazaars selling textiles, silver, handicrafts, aromatic spices (see Shopping later), vegetables and colourful Indian sweets.

Rajasthan Sangeet Natak Akademi Folk Art Museum

This academy, established in 1938, has the gigantic task of preserving the traditional folk art, dance, drama and music of Rajasthan. You might need to rustle someone up to open the little museum *(☎ 544090; W www.sangeetraj.com; Town Hall, High Court Rd; admission Rs 5; open 10am-5pm daily)* for you, but it's well worth it. There are beautiful puppets, an amazing array of rare traditional instruments and other exhibits on the performing arts. Unfortunately, there's not much information in English. The academy also organises performances of music, dance and theatre every fortnight or so (call for details). It costs around Rs 10 for a ticket.

Umaid Gardens & Sadar Government Museum

The pleasant Umaid Gardens *(admission free)* contain the Sadar Government Museum *(admission Rs 3; open 10am-4.30pm Sat-Thur)*, the zoo *(admission Rs 4)* and the library. There is the usual collection of sculptures, weapons and moth-eaten stuffed

---

Festivals of Western Rajasthan

April–May
Karni Mata Fair Devotees throng to the Karni Mata Temple in Deshnok, near Bikaner, where rats are worshipped as the reincarnations of local people. The fair is celebrated twice yearly, in April–May and October–November.

August–September
Ramdevra Fair Ramdev Temple in the village of Ramdevra, near Pokaran, is the focus of this fair, which takes place each year in either August or September, and is celebrated by both Hindus and Muslims. Devotees place small embroidered horses in the temple in honour of the holy man's trusty steed, who carried him to villages where he administered to the poor. Female performers, who have 13 small cymbals attached to their costumes, dance the *terahtal* (a traditional dance), while balancing pitchers of water on their heads.

October–November
Marwar Festival In Jodhpur, the rich cultural legacy of Marwar (Jodhpur) is celebrated, with turban tying, a moustache competition and traditional dance and drama from the region. It is held over two days, one of which coincides with the full moon.

Kolayat Fair Near Bikaner, this fair takes place around the same time as the Pushkar Camel Fair. Devotees take a dip in the holy lake on the full moon.

animals, including a number of almost featherless desert birds in two glass cases. The military section includes wooden biplane models.

Umaid Bhawan Palace & Museum

Constructed of marble and pink sandstone, this immense palace is also known as the Chhittar Palace because it uses local Chhittar sandstone. Begun in 1929, it was designed by the president of the British Royal Institute of Architects for Maharaja Umaid Singh, and took 15 years to complete.

Probably the most surprising thing about this grandiose palace is that it was built so close to Independence, after which the maharajas and their grand extravagances were a thing of the past. It has been suggested that the palace was built as some sort of royal job-creation programme.

Umaid Singh died in 1947, four years after the palace was completed; the current maharaja, Maharaja Gaj Singh II (known as Bapji), still lives in part of the building. The rest has been turned into a hotel. The palace (not including the museum) is only open to nonguests if you pay a visitor fee of Rs 330, which is then deducted from any food or drink you might purchase (see Places to Eat for dining options in the palace).

The museum *(foreigner/citizen Rs 50/15; open 9am-5.30pm daily)* is open to everyone and well worth a visit. It has beautifully crafted weapons; an array of stuffed leopards; an enormous banner presented by Queen Victoria to Maharaja Jaswant Singh Bahadur in 1877; human-sized Chinese urns and other fine china; and a fantastic clock collection, including specimens shaped like windmills and lighthouses.

Astrology

Astrologer Mr Sharma *(☎ 548790, ext 39, mobile ☎ 9829022591; e slsharma@satyam.net .in; Meherangarh; open 9am-1pm & 2.30pm-5pm daily)* offers palm reading (Rs 150/300 for main lines/details) from his office in the Moti Mahal section of the fort. Mr Sharma has been studying astrology for over 30 years and can also offer a private consultation,

for which you will need an advance booking. Don't wear nail polish if you intend getting a reading, as the nails are used to ascertain your state of health.

Golf

At **Sadar Club** *(open 1pm-11pm daily)*, in Ratanada, there's a recently revamped golf course. These brown grounds offer some challenging shots for golfers. Expect to pay Rs 300 for 18 holes, including equipment. A caddie costs Rs 10 and you bring your own balls. This club, popular with the British during the Raj, is about 100 years old. You can still see the damage inflicted on part of the building, which was bombed during the first war between India and Pakistan!

Organised Tours

The **Tourist Reception Centre** *(☎ 545083)* operates daily tours of Jodhpur from 9am to 1pm and 2pm to 6pm. These take in all the main sites including the Umaid Bhawan Palace, Meherangarh, Jaswant Thada, and the Mandore Gardens north of Jodhpur. They start from the Tourist Reception Centre (see Information) and cost Rs 85 per person (not including entry fees). Bookings are essential.

Jodhpur is known for its interesting village safaris, which visit villages of the Bishnoi, a people whose belief in the sanctity of the environment and the need to protect trees and animals dates from the 15th century. See Bishnoi Villages under Around Jodhpur, later, for more information.

Most safaris include a visit to a couple of villages, where you have the chance to meet the local people as they go about their daily lives, have a traditional lunch at one of the villages and stop at a few crafts outlets. Visitors are sometimes invited to share *amal* (an opium preparation), which is traditionally offered to guests. The cheaper tours cost around Rs 400 per person (including jeep, guide and lunch) and can be organised through most hotels and travel agencies. Competition is fierce and readers have cautioned to choose carefully, as some are overpriced and poorly organised. A budget option is the Tourist Reception Centre jeep tours; a five-hour tour costs Rs 1100 for up to seven people, plus Rs 50 per person for lunch. Bookings are essential.

Trips out to Osiyan by camel are also popular and can be arranged through **Cosy Guest House** (☎ 612066) and the **Govind Hotel** (☎ 622758).

Places to Stay

A number of families are registered with the Paying Guest House Scheme in Jodhpur. Costs per night range from Rs 200 to 1000. Inquire at the Tourist Reception Centre (see Information earlier).

Places to Stay – Budget

Yogi's Guest House (☎ 643436, fax 619808; e yogiguesthouse@hotmail.com; doubles with shared bathroom Rs 100, singles/doubles with private bathroom from Rs 100/150), right at the base of the fort walls, is a good choice with a chilled-out atmosphere. Set in the 500-year-old Rajpurohitji-ki-Haveli, this place has been recommended by many travellers. The rooms are simple but clean and comfortable. There's a restaurant on the roof, where you can enjoy good views while you eat. It's well signposted off the lanes leading to the fort.

Cosy Guest House (☎ 612066; Novechokiya Rd, Brahm Puri, Chuna-ki-Choki; singles/doubles with shared bathroom Rs 50/100, singles/doubles with private bathroom Rs 150/250), formerly known as Joshi's Blue House, is an unpretentious little place deep in the old city. This family-run, blue-coloured house has bucket loads of character and is said to be 500 years old (don't expect modern gadgets). Go to the rooftop for a splendid view at sunset. Camel safaris can be arranged here.

Evergreen Backpackers (☎ 628290; singles/doubles with shared bathroom Rs 40/80, doubles with private bathroom Rs 100), nearby, has fairly basic but undeniably cheap rooms, and a fabulous view from its rooftop, which has a lawn area. Internet access is available here (Rs 1 per minute) and a new dorm is planned, in which beds will only cost around Rs 20 per person.

Madho Niwas (Bhenswara House; ☎ 51 2486, fax 512086; e madhoniwas@satyam.net

.in; New Airport Rd, Ratanada; singles/doubles with private bathroom Rs 150/200, with air-con Rs 650/700) is run by Dalvir Singh and is a homey place to stay, with a quiet lawn area. It's a few kilometres from the centre of town, but it's good value, with comfortable rooms, a pool and a restaurant. The Marwari-style barbecue chicken (Rs 300), with a squeeze of lemon, is delicious and the set lunch or dinner is Rs 125. Good village safaris are available (Rs 500 with lunch) and the hotel can also arrange a sojourn at Ravla Bhenswara (see Around Jodhpur later in this chapter).

Shivam Paying Guest House (☎ 610688; e shivamgh@hotmail.com; doubles with private bathroom Rs 200, with air-con Rs 400), not far from the clock tower, is one place to go if you want a traditional family atmosphere. It's a relaxed place where you'll have no hassles at all.

The Blue House (☎ 621396, fax 619133; e bluehouse36@hotmail.com; singles/doubles with shared bathroom from Rs 150/200, doubles with private bathroom Rs 200-600), in the heart of the old city, is also good. The rooms are atmospheric (the cheapest ones are in thatched huts on the roof) and Internet access and home-cooked meals are also available.

Govind Hotel (☎ 622758; e govindhotel2000@yahoo.com; dorm beds Rs 60, singles/doubles with private bathroom Rs 130/250, with air-con Rs 600/650), opposite the main post office, is just five minutes' walk from the train station – ideal if you've got an early morning train departure. Run by the helpful Jagdish Sadarangani, this is a very traveller-friendly place. The rooms at the back are the quietest although some have no external window. The rooftop veg restaurant has wonderful views of the palace and fort – veg pizza costs Rs 55. Camel safaris (Rs 600) and budget village tours (from Rs 250 per person for five people) can be organised.

Haveli Guest House (☎ 614615; e havelighj@sify.com, Makrana Mohalla; doubles with private bathroom Rs 200-800) gets very mixed reviews. The hotel offers fat commissions to rickshaw drivers who will try every trick in the book to get you to stay here – a marketing ploy that has made Haveli the subject of irritated conversation wherever two travellers meet in Jodhpur. However, Lonely Planet has also received many letters of praise about this guesthouse, which readers find friendly, clean and a good place to meet other backpackers. It's a large hotel with a rooftop veg restaurant sporting good views of the fort, Jaswant Thada and the 'Blue City'. The food is home-cooked and menu items include *paneer pasanda* (chunks of cheese in a nutty cream sauce, Rs 60) and *dum aloo* (Rs 45).

Durag Niwas Guest House (☎ 510 692; e maharaja_m2k_4u@hotmai.com; 1 Old Public Park; doubles with private bathroom from Rs 150-200) is another family-run place, and offers decent double rooms. The restaurant serves thalis for Rs 80 to 100. Camel and village safaris are available.

Durag Villas Guest House (☎ 512298; e harshita_2000@rediffmail.com; doubles with private bathroom Rs 150-300), next door, is very good value for money. Veg and nonveg meals are available and it can organise village safaris (a half-day jeep safari with lunch is Rs 350 per person).

Roopam Guest House (☎ 513374; e roopamguesthouse@rediffmail.com; 7 Jagannath Bldg, Mohanpura Overbridge; singles/doubles with shared bathroom Rs 150/250, with private bathroom from Rs 350/400) is opposite a small pink sandstone Shiva temple. Run by retired Major TS Rathore, it has a handful of rooms, including two with small balconies, and one with air-con. Meals are available with notice.

Hotel Arvind (☎ 619538, fax 547423; 135 Nai Sarak; singles/doubles with shared bathroom Rs 100/150, with private bathroom Rs 160/200, with balcony Rs 200/250) has rather dim rooms, although some have private balconies. Most rooms are furnished with an Indian-style toilet.

Tourist Guest House (☎ 541235; e udai bedi@hotmail.com; doubles with private bathroom from Rs 200) is a great choice outside the old city on High Court Rd. It has a welcoming family atmosphere with rooms to match.

Raman Guest House (☎ 513980; singles/doubles with shared bathroom Rs 125/150, with private bathroom Rs 150/200, with air-con Rs 550/600), opposite Kesar Bagh on Shiv Rd, is also run by a friendly family and is an increasingly popular place to stay in the area. Village safaris can be arranged and there's a restaurant; a continental breakfast costs Rs 90.

Vinayaka Guest House (☎ 514420, Shiv Rd; singles/doubles with private bathroom Rs 300/400, with air-con Rs 600/700), nearby, is a friendly, family-run place with simple rooms and a shady garden. A home-cooked veg/non-veg lunch or dinner is Rs 95/115.

RTDC Hotel Ghoomar (☎ 548010, fax 545010; High Court Rd; dorm beds Rs 50, singles/doubles from Rs 350/450) houses a reasonable nonveg restaurant and a bar (a bottle of beer is Rs 65).

Retiring rooms (dorm beds Rs 75, doubles Rs 150, with air-con Rs 350) are available at the main train station.

Places to Stay – Mid-Range

Devi Bhawan (☎ 511067, fax 512215; e devibhawan@satyamonline.com; 1 Ratanada Circle; singles/doubles Rs 700/750, suites Rs 800/875, bungalow Rs 800) is a splendid place to stay and you'll have no hassles here whatsoever. Run by a charming couple, this green oasis has fresh rooms and a cottage. There's a good restaurant and the garden there would have to be one of the loveliest in Jodhpur.

Ratan Vilas (☎ 613011, fax 614418; e ratanvilas_jod@rediffmail.com; Loco Shed Rd, Ratanada; singles/doubles from Rs 700/750, suite Rs 1500) is another very well-kept family villa set in a pleasant garden. Rooms are comfortable and meals are available in the homey dining room. The set lunch or dinner is Rs 200 (available with advance notice). If you're interested in getting authentic jodhpur trousers made, ask the owner's son, Brijraj. Some of the tailors are quite elderly, so allow at least a week for your jodhpurs to be stitched.

Durjan Niwas Hotel (☎ 649546, fax 616 991; e daspan@email.com; singles/doubles Rs 1200/1500), off Old Loco Shed Rd, has elegant, quiet rooms, and will usually negotiate the price if things are quiet.

Newtons Manor (☎ 430686, fax 610603; ℮ info@newtonsmanor.com; 86 Jawahar Colony, Ratanada; doubles with private bathroom from Rs 895, with bathtub Rs 1195), opposite Green Gate No 8, is also a good choice, although the location is far from ideal. The hotel is crammed with kitsch knick-knacks and there are just five doubles, one of which is a bigger room with a bathtub. The rooms are clean, the outdoor area is nice and there's even a fish tank. Scrumptious home-cooked meals are available; the set lunch/dinner is Rs 180 (veg), or Rs 230 (nonveg).

Hotel Kalinga (☎ 627338, fax 627314, ℮ kalingahotel@satyam.net.in; singles/doubles Rs 490/700, with breakfast Rs 540/800) is convenient as it is close to the main train station. The rooms are dull but comfortable and spacious. Check out is 24 hours.

Hotel City Palace (☎ 431933, fax 639033; ℮ hotel@satyam.net.in; 32 Nai Sarak; singles/doubles with air-con Rs 990/1190), near Sojati Gate, is a reasonable choice in this area, though some rooms are a bit dark and dismal. You can eat at **Gossip**, the veg restaurant, or have a drink in the underground **Classic Bar**, which has a nautical theme and sometimes has live music. If you're a woman, you'll be the only one in here.

Inn Season (☎/fax 616400; ℮ innseason@hotmail.com; rooms from Rs 1200, suites Rs 1800), opposite the PWD office, is another fine choice, with well-kept rooms and a lovely suite. There's a pool and the restaurant serves Indian and continental food; the set lunch/dinner is Rs 200 (veg), or Rs 250 (nonveg). Check out the funky old German record player with an equally funky collection of classic records, including Louis Armstrong and Ella Fitzgerald.

Places to Stay – Top End
Ajit Bhawan (☎ 511410, fax 510674; ℮ ab hawan@del3.vsnl.net.in; Circuit House Rd; cottage singles/doubles from Rs 1995/2400, suites Rs 3500) has long been a favourite with travellers. It has a series of modern stone cottages and suites arranged around a relaxing garden. There's an over-the-top swimming pool (nonguests pay Rs 250), meals are available and village safaris can be arranged. Other services include babysitting (Rs 100 an hour), Internet access and a wonderful collection of vintage cars which can be rented for a small fortune – the 1939 Chevrolet convertible costs Rs 2400/4000 for a half/full day.

Taj Hari Mahal (☎ 439700, fax 614451; ℮ harimahal.jodhpur@tajhotels.com; 5 Residency Rd; singles/doubles with garden view US$135/150, with pool view US$150/170, suites US$250) is a newly constructed place with all the mod-cons. The facilities in all the rooms are the same, with tasteful decor, bathtubs, TVs, air-con and safes; but the cheaper rooms look out on the garden and the pricier ones have a pool view. There are three restaurants here, including a Chinese restaurant specialising in Sichuan cuisine and a classy bar. Prices drop by up to two-thirds in the off season.

Ratanada Polo Palace (☎ 431910, fax 433118; ℮ serena@ndf.vsnl.net.in; Residency Rd; singles/doubles Rs 700/1000) is in its own spacious grounds, but is a bit low on character. It has a pool and restaurant. The set breakfast/lunch/dinner is Rs 100/200/200.

Umaid Bhawan Palace (☎ 510101, fax 510100; ℮ ubp@ndf.vsnl.net.in; singles/doubles US$165/185, suites US$325-750), east of the city centre, is the place to stay in Jodhpur if you have a passion for pure luxury. This very elegant, and very snooty, palace has an indoor swimming pool, a tennis court, a billiards room, lush lawns and several restaurants (see Places to Eat). A wing of the palace is still occupied by the current maharaja of Jodhpur and his family. The cheaper rooms are suitably comfortable, but hardly what you would call palatial.

Places to Eat
While you're in Jodhpur, try a glass of makhania lassi, a filling saffron-flavoured variety of that most refreshing of drinks.

Shri Mishrilal Hotel, at the clock tower, is nothing fancy in terms of decor, but whips up the best lassis in town. A delicious glass of creamy special makhania lassi is Rs 12. One glass can do you for lunch!

Pokar Sweets (☎ 547087; open 6am-midnight daily), on the corner of Nai Sarak and High Court Rd, has a huge selection of sweet treats. You can pick out a box of five or six for around Rs 20.

Priya (☎ 547879, 181 Nai Sarak), nearby, is a hotel with a popular restaurant open to the chaos of Nai Sarak. It's usually crowded with locals and you can get an excellent, quick thali for Rs 40.

Omelette Shop (omelette Rs 12), just through the gate behind the clock tower on the northern side of the square, claims to go through 1000 eggs a day. It's a small stall and it's usually packed with locals. The standard serving is a two-egg omelette with chilli, coriander and four pieces of bread.

Kalinga Restaurant (☎ 624066; open 7am-10.30pm daily), at the hotel of the same name near the train station, is a pleasant place to eat (and kill time while waiting for a train). The service is quick and you can get Indian, Chinese and continental dishes. The 'Hunters Paradise' section on the menu includes chicken *hakim* for Rs 130.

Mid Town (☎ 637001; mains Rs 40-65; open 7am-11pm daily), near Kalinga, is a bit pricey but not bad. There are Rajasthani specials such as *chakki-ka-sagh* (wheat sponge cooked in rich gravy – a speciality of Jodhpur) and roti for Rs 55, or *bajara-ki-roti pachkuta* (*bajara* wheat roti with local dry vegetables), also for Rs 55. A Gujarati or Rajasthani thali is Rs 80.

On the Rocks (☎ 302701; Ajit Bhawan Hotel; open 12.30pm-3pm & 7pm-11pm daily) is very popular, if a little on the pricey side, serving tasty Indian cuisine in a candle-lit courtyard – half a tandoori chicken is Rs 140 and a veg *biryani* (fragrant steamed rice with vegetables) is Rs 55. The service can be a tad sluggish, particularly when it's busy, and reservations are recommended. In the same compound, there's an attractive little **bar** (women should be prepared for stares by the predominantly male clientele). There's also an excellent **bakery** with fresh muffins, bread, biscuits and cakes (birthday cakes can be made with advance notice).

Umaid Bhawan Palace has four restaurants (the nonguest visiting fee of Rs 330 is deducted from any food or drink purchased), including the very grand **Marwar Hall** (although the buffet here is pretty average). Overlooking the back lawn and with a view of the fort is **The Pillars**, a pleasant informal Indian and continental eatery. There's also the more formal **Risala**, specialising in continental cuisine, and **Kebab Konner**, a casual open-air restaurant which is especially popular with the locals, serving moderately priced barbecue Indian food (dinner only). If you're just feeling thirsty, you can have a drop of amber fluid at the **Trophy Bar**.

Pushpa Bhojnalya (☎ 641205; open 8am-11pm daily), a tiny place close to Jalori Gate and about 10 minutes' walk from the train station, serves authentic Rajasthani cuisine such as *churma* (Rs 10).

The **refreshment room** (open 6am-10.30pm daily), found on the first floor of the main train station, is surprisingly good. It's a cool, quiet haven, and the food is cheap. The veg/nonveg thali is Rs 20/25. There are also lighter options such as cheese sandwiches and sweet lassis.

Shopping

Jodhpur specialises in antiques, with the greatest concentration of antique shops along the roads connecting the Ajit Bhawan with the Umaid Bhawan Palace. These shops are well known to Western antique dealers who come here with wallets stuffed with plastic cards. As a result, you'll be hard pressed to find any bargains. The trade in antique architectural fixtures is contributing towards the desecration of India's cultural heritage – don't support this trade with your shopping dollars. Most of these warehouse-sized showrooms also deal in antique reproductions, catering for a growing number of overseas export houses. They're fascinating places to wander around.

Certain restrictions apply to the export of Indian items over 100 years old – see Antiques under Shopping in the Facts for the Visitor chapter.

For excellent Indian spices, go to **MV Spices** (☎/fax 615846; ⓦ www.mvspices .com), shop 209B at the *sabzi* (vegetable) market, near the clock tower. There are a few imitators in this area, so look out for the MV sign. Its enthusiastic owner, Mohanlal Verhomal, sells a tantalising array, including a 'winter tonic' that apparently enhances sexual appetite (Rs 175). He even has before and after shots from satisfied customers to prove it. Buy spices to make mulled wine, various teas and curries, and a packet of 'spice for cold (bad sneeze)' for Rs 175. Mohanlal has a deep passion for spices, and will happily answer your questions.

Getting There & Away
Air The domestic carrier, **Indian Airlines** (☎ 510757; 2 West Patel Nagar, Circuit House Rd, Ratanada; open 10am-1.15pm & 2pm-4.30pm daily), has an office near the Ajit Bhawan hotel. It has daily flights to Jaipur (US$90), Delhi (US$115), Udaipur (US$75) and Mumbai (US$160).

Jet Airways (☎ 625094) flies daily to Mumbai (US$165) and Delhi (US$115).

The telephone number of the Jodhpur airport is ☎ 512617.

Bus The Rajasthan State Road Transport Corporation (RSRTC) buses leave from the Roadways bus stand (☎ 544686, 544989).

There are a number of private bus companies opposite the train station. Quoted rates for deluxe buses with 2 x 2 (two seat by two seat) pushback seats are:

destination	fare (Rs)	duration (hrs)
Agra	180	13
Ahmedabad	140	10
Ajmer	80	4½
Delhi	180	13
Jaipur	100	7
Jaisalmer	80	5
Udaipur	110	7

The main highway between Jodhpur and Jaisalmer is via Agolai, Dechu and Pokaran, but it's more interesting to go on the less frequently travelled route via Osiyan and Phalodi (for Khichan), which meets the main route at Pokaran.

Train The booking office (☎ 636407; Station Rd; open 8am-8pm Mon-Sat & 8am-1.45pm

Sun), is between the train station and Sojati Gate. Demand for tickets is heavy, so come here soon after you arrive. There's a tourist quota for trains to Delhi and Jaisalmer – go to counter No 788. At the main train station there is an International Tourist Bureau (see Information, earlier).

Make sure you find out what the current train times are, as they have a tendency to change. The 2466 Jodhpur–Jaipur *Intercity* leaves at 5.45am (Rs 106/312 in 2nd/1st class, 4¾ hours). There are trains to Bikaner at 10.15am and 8.35pm daily (Rs 70/525, 5 hours). There's a train to Delhi at 7.30pm daily (Rs 142/370, 11 hours), as well as services to Agra, Varanasi and Mumbai.

There are two trains from Jodhpur to Jaisalmer – one leaves at 8am and arrives in Jaisalmer at 4.30pm, and the other leaves at 11.30pm and arrives in Jaisalmer at 5.45am. A ticket costs Rs 142/370 in 2nd/1st class.

Taxi There is a taxi stand to the right as you exit the main train station. A one-way taxi trip to Jaisalmer will cost around Rs 1800, Rs 1700 to Udaipur and Rs 2100 to Jaipur.

Getting Around
To/From the Airport The airport is only 5km from the city centre. It costs Rs 50 in an autorickshaw and Rs 100 in a taxi.

Taxi To hire a taxi for sightseeing in Jodhpur, expect to be quoted around Rs 500/750 per half/full day. To Mandore, a taxi costs about Rs 200 including a one-hour wait. To Osiyan it is Rs 700 return, including a three-hour stay there. You might bring these prices down with determined bargaining.

Autorickshaw Most journeys in the town area by autorickshaw should cost no more than Rs 25 to 30. A day's sightseeing costs around Rs 500.

Bicycle It is possible to hire a bike from several places near the Kalinga Restaurant, including **Hind Silk Store** (open 8am-9pm daily), which charges Rs 3/15 per hour/day, or Rs 20 for 24 hours.

AROUND JODHPUR
Maha Mandir & Balsamand Lake
About 4km northeast of the city is the Maha Mandir (Great Temple). It's built around a 100-pillared Shiva temple but is nothing to write home about. The picturesque Balsamand Lake is 5km further north.

Balsamand Palace (✆ 572321, fax 571240; or book through the Delhi office ✆ 011-656 1869, fax 6868994; e welcom@ndf.vsnl .net.in; singles/doubles Rs 1990/2900, suites Rs3900), near the lake, offers comfort in a lush and serene setting not too far away from Jodhpur. Rooms are in the former stables, all with a private terrace area. There are two restaurants which serve Indian and continental cuisine; the buffet lunch/dinner is Rs 300/350.

Mandore
Mandore, 9km to the north of Jodhpur, was the capital of Marwar before the foundation of Jodhpur. It was founded in the 6th century, and passed to the Rathore Rajputs in 1381 after a marriage alliance between a princess of the original founders, the Pratiharas, and the Rathore raja, Rao Chandor.

Today the only attraction here is the extensive **Mandore Gardens** with their high rock terraces. The gardens also contain the *chhatris* of the Rathore rulers. One of the most imposing is the **Chhatri of Maharaja Dhiraj Ajit Singh** (1793), an enormous edifice with carved elephants, *amalaka* (disk-shaped flourishes with fluted edges), a pillared forechamber and fine sculpture. You can climb to the third storey up a peculiar set of staircases. Opposite is the 17th-century **Chhatri of Maharaja Dhiraj Jaswant Singh**, an enormous octagonal pavilion with a vast dome and huge pillars. It achieves a remarkable symmetry, with a gallery supported by pillars and sculptures of Krishna and the *gopis* (milkmaids).

At the rear of the complex, to the right, is the small **government museum** (admission Rs 5; open 10am-4pm Sat-Thur). To the left is the **Hall of Heroes**, with 15 figures carved out of a rock wall. The brightly painted figures represent Hindu deities or local Rajput heroes on horseback. The **Shrine of 33 Crore Gods** is painted with figures of deities and spirits (1 *crore* = 10 million).

It costs Rs 10 to park a car outside the Mandore Gardens.

Places to Stay Set in a shady garden, **Mandore Guest House** (✆ 0291-545210, fax 571620; singles/doubles with private bathroom from Rs 300/500) is a delightful place. The rooms are good value and you can even opt to dine with the owner and his family at their house next door.

Getting There & Away There are many buses throughout the day between Jodhpur and Mandore (Rs 5), which is on the main road between Jodhpur and Nagaur. Catch one on High Court Rd. Mandore is also included on the RTDC city tours (see Organised Tours, earlier).

Bishnoi Villages
A number of Bishnoi and other traditional villages are strung along and off the Pali road, to the southeast of Jodhpur. Various operators, including the RTDC in Jodhpur, conduct jeep safaris to the villages – see Organised Tours under Jodhpur for details. A tour is essential to visit this region: some of these villages are tiny, along tracks which can be barely made out in the sand, and which you will be hard pressed to find on any maps.

Tours offer a glimpse into timeless Indian village life – many villagers live in handmade thatched huts following the traditions of their ancestors. Tours usually include a meal cooked over the fire in one of the villages. Unfortunately, the increase in tourism is starting to cause tension in some of the villages. Remember that you are visiting a private community and make sure you ask before taking photographs.

Many visitors are surprised by the density, and fearlessness, of the wildlife around the Bishnoi villages. The relationship between the villagers and the animals has been carefully nurtured for hundreds of years. The 1730 sacrifice of 363 villagers to protect the khejri trees (see the boxed text) is commemorated in September at **Khejadali** village, where there is a memorial to the victims fronted by a small grove of khejri trees.

At **Guda Bishnoi**, locals are traditionally engaged in animal husbandry; there is a small artificial lake here where migratory birds and mammals such as blackbucks and chinkaras can be seen, particularly at dusk, when they feed at the lake. The lake is full only after a good monsoon (July and August). There are plans to shift Jodhpur airport here within the next decade.

The village of **Salawas** is traditionally a centre for weaving *dhurries* (carpets). Today a cooperative of 48 weavers runs the efficient **Roopraj Dhurry Udyog** (☎ 0291-896658; e *rooprajdurry@sify.com*) from Salawas, with all profits going to the artisan. A beautiful 1.3m x 2m *dhurrie* can take about one month to complete, depending on the intricacy of the design and the number

of colours used, and costs from Rs 2500 to 3000. The coordinator, Roopraj, will happily answer your questions about this craft.

These days, chemical rather than natural dyes are used. *Dhurries* are usually of cotton, but sometimes camel or goat hair, or silk, is used. After the weaving is completed, the *dhurries* are sometimes stonewashed to give an antique effect. The *dhurrie* weavers can arrange post by sea or air (shipping costs around Rs 1050 for one piece).

Also in Salawas, several families, mostly of the Muslim community, are engaged in block printing. The hand-woven, block-printed cloth is known as *fetia*. A single bed sheet costs around Rs 300, and a double sheet is about Rs 450, depending on the design.

At the villages of **Zhalamand**, **Salawas** and **Kakani**, potters can be seen at work using hand-turned wheels.

Village Activists

The Bishnoi are perhaps the most dedicated conservationists in the world. They hold all animal life sacred, in particular the endangered blackbuck, or Indian antelope. The Bishnoi sometimes bury dead blackbuck and mark their graves with stones, and the women are said to suckle blackbuck fawns that have been orphaned. They also have a long history of protecting the sacred khejri tree – sometimes with their lives.

The sect was founded in the 15th century, when a severe drought was crippling the desert regions near Jodhpur. A villager named Jambeshwar had a vision that the drought had been caused by humans meddling with the natural order. He laid down 29 tenets for conserving nature, including not killing animals, not felling trees and not using wood for funeral pyres. Jambeshwar became known as Guru Jambhoji, and his followers became known as the Bishnoi (meaning 29) after the principles they followed.

The most famous Bishnoi act of self-sacrifice occurred in 1730 when the maharaja of Jodhpur sent woodcutters into their villages to cut khejri trees for his lime kilns. A woman named Amritdevi clung to one of the trees and refused to be removed, so the axeman cut her head off. Before she died she uttered this famous Bishnoi couplet: 'A chopped head is cheaper than a felled tree'. One by one, other Bishnoi villagers followed Amritdevi's lead, and each in turn was killed by the axemen until 363 people lay dead. The maharaja, hearing of the carnage, declared a conservation zone around the Bishnoi villages, prohibiting tree felling or poaching in the area.

Today the site at Khejadali is a quiet grove of khejri trees and a temple commemorates the sacrifice. The Bishnoi continue to live by their strict code and to defend native wildlife. In 1996, a Bishnoi villager named Nihal Chand Bishnoi was shot and killed by poachers near Bikaner as he tried to save the lives of some chinkaras (Indian gazelles). In October 1998 Bollywood superstar Salman Khan was arrested for killing two blackbucks near a Bishnoi village. The authorities were allegedly alerted to the crime by the villagers who chased Khan from the scene and presented the dead blackbucks as evidence. Today around 90% of the blackbucks in India live under Bishnoi protection.

Sardar Samand Lake

The route to this wildlife centre, 66km southeast of Jodhpur, passes through a number of colourful little villages. Blackbucks, chinkaras and birdlife are found in this area.

Sardar Samand Palace *(☎ 02960-45003, or book at the Umaid Bhawan Palace in Jodhpur ☎ 0291-510101, fax 510100; singles/ doubles Rs 1990/2800)*, formerly the maharaja of Jodhpur's summer palace, is now a hotel. There's a restaurant and a stylish lakeside swimming pool to enjoy. This place is a world away from the clamour of Jodhpur. Village safaris are available.

Rohet

In this village, 40km south of Jodhpur, the former local ruler has converted his 350-year-old manor into a heritage hotel. **Rohet Garh** *(☎ 02936-68231; singles/doubles Rs 1275/1850, with air-con Rs 1850/2000)* has a fantastic swimming pool and a relaxing garden to sit back with a good book; you can buy a cook book (Rs 150) of local Rajasthani recipes. All rooms have a special character of their own. Village safaris and horse rides can be arranged. The place seems to attract travel writers: Bruce Chatwin wrote *The Songlines* here and William Dalrymple began *City of Djinns* in the same room (No 15).

From Jodhpur, there are local daily buses to Rohet (Rs 13) or you can get a taxi for around Rs 650.

Bhenswara

Bhenswara, which translates as 'the place where buffaloes were kept', is located about 130km south of Jodhpur.

Ravla Bhenswara *(☎ 02978-22080, fax 22187 or book through the Jodhpur office ☎ 0291-512486, fax 512086; singles/doubles from Rs 995/1195)* is an unpretentious rural manor, perfect if you want some respite from travelling. This place is run by a lovely young couple, Shiv Pratap Singh and Uma Kumari, who give this hotel a homey appeal. The rooms are quaint and each has a personality of its own. The set veg/nonveg lunch or dinner is Rs 225/275. There's also a swimming pool there and jeep village safaris can

be organised for Rs 500 per person (minimum of two people). A village bullock cart ride is Rs 225 per person (minimum of two people). The hotel owners can arrange a visit to the nearby **Jalor Fort**. The climb up to the fort takes about 45 minutes (carry water as the ascent can be a hot one).

The closest bus route goes to Jalor (Rs 70 from Jodhpur); from there you should catch a taxi.

Dhawa Doli Wildlife Sanctuary

This sanctuary is about 40km southwest of Jodhpur, on the road to Barmer, and has populations of blackbucks, partridges, desert foxes and nilgais. There is no accommodation here, but it is possible to take a half-day tour from Jodhpur for Rs 700. Check at the **Tourist Reception Centre** *(☎ 0291-545083)* in Jodhpur. Animals and birds which can be seen here include blackbucks, partridges, desert foxes and nilgais.

Khejarla

Fort Khejarla *(☎ 02930-58311; singles/doubles Rs 950/1150)*, 85km east of Jodhpur en route to Ajmer, is a 400-year-old fort. It's not as swish as most of the other fort-hotels in Rajasthan, but it has a certain rustic charm. The set breakfast/lunch/dinner here costs Rs 175/350/450.

Village safaris can be arranged, as well as a visit to an old step-well (ask Dalip Singh about the ghost).

Khimsar

Khimsar Fort *(☎ 01585-62345, fax 62228; e khimfort@satyam.net.in; singles/doubles US$42/82)*, about 95km northeast of Jodhpur, dates back to 1523, and has been converted into an upmarket hotel. Rooms are well appointed and there's a sauna, yoga centre, pool (with a nearby hammock to laze away the day), a good restaurant (buffet breakfast/lunch is US$ 8/11, dinner is US$12) and pleasant gardens. It is possible to arrange a jeep safari or a horse/camel ride, for US$10 per person. Ayurvedic massage costs US$14 for one hour.

A local bus from Jodhpur costs Rs 40. A taxi is about Rs 800.

NAGAUR
☎ 01582 • postcode 341001 • pop 88,313
Nagaur, 135km northeast of Jodhpur, has the historic **Ahhichatragarh** *(foreigner/citizen Rs 10/30, camera/video Rs 25/50; open 10am-5pm daily)*, an ancient fort that is currently being restored. The fort is protected by massive double walls which encompass a richly painted **palace**. Within the walls of the old city are several **mosques**, including one commissioned by Akbar for a disciple of the Sufi saint Khwaja Muin-ud-din Chishti, who roamed India in the 13th century. An English-speaking guide costs Rs 100 and car parking is Rs 15.

Nagaur also hosts a fair, which is a smaller version of Pushkar Camel Fair – see the boxed text 'Festivals of Western Rajasthan', earlier in this chapter. During this time a tourist information office is set up at the festival grounds.

Places to Stay & Eat
Hotel Bhaskar *(☎ 40100; singles/doubles Rs 100/250, doubles with air-con Rs 600)*, near the train station, has ordinary rooms with private bathroom.

Hotel Mahaveer International *(☎ 43158; singles/doubles from Rs 250/350, with air-con Rs 350/450)* is at Vijai Vallabh Chowk, about 1km from the fort. This hotel has fairly uninspiring but comfortable rooms aimed at the business traveller. There's also a restaurant and bar.

Royal tents *(singles/doubles with all meals US$95/125)* are available during the fair. These luxurious tents must be booked in advance through the Umaid Bhawan Palace in Jodhpur *(☎ 0291-510101, fax 510100; e udp@ndf.vsnl.net.in)*.

During the festival, the RTDC opens a hotel. For details contact the General Manager, **Central Reservations** *(☎ 0141-202586, fax 204065; RTDC Hotel Swagatam Campus, near train station, Jaipur, 302006)*.

Getting There & Away
Nagaur is connected by express buses to Jodhpur (Rs 57, 2 hrs) and Bikaner (Rs 55, 2½ hrs). A taxi from Jodhpur costs about Rs 825 (one way).

JODHPUR TO JAISALMER
The most direct route by road to Jaisalmer is the southern route via Agolai, Dechu and Pokaran. There are, however, some interesting places to visit on the lesser-travelled northern route, which goes via Osiyan and Phalodi and meets up with the main route at Pokaran. The exquisite temples at Osiyan, the feeding grounds of the demoiselle cranes at Khichan and the important pilgrimage site of Ramdevra all lie on or just off this southern route, which numerous buses ply every day.

Osiyan
If you can't make it to Jaisalmer and are desperate to get a taste of the desert, this is a good alternative. The ancient Thar Desert town of Osiyan, 65km north of Jodhpur, was a great trading centre between the 8th and 12th centuries, when it was dominated by the Jains and known as Upkeshpur. The wealth of Osiyan's medieval inhabitants enabled them to build lavish and beautifully sculpted temples. The village of Osiyan is inhabited mostly by Brahmins, as evidenced by the predominance of blue-painted houses there.

Temples The temples of Osiyan rival the Hoysala temples of Karnataka and the Sun Temple of Konark in Orissa. About 200m north of the bus stand is **Sachiya Mata Temple** *(admission free)* – Sachiya Mata is the ninth and last incarnation of the goddess Durga. A long flight of steps takes you to the forechamber. Before the *mandapu* (chamber before the inner sanctum), and beyond the impressive *torana* (gateway), are sandstone statues of various incarnations of Durga which were excavated by archaeologists and installed here. The main temple is flanked by nine smaller temples, each dedicated to an incarnation of the goddess. Abutting the sides of the main temple is a series of ancient temples contemporary with Sachiya Mata Temple.

Five minutes' walk from Sachiya Mata Temple is **Mahavira Temple** *(admission Rs 5, camera/video Rs 30/100; open 5am-9pm daily)*, which was dedicated to the last of the

WESTERN RAJASTHAN

Jain *tirthankars* (teachers). This is a more spacious temple than Sachiya Mata Temple, and it features an open-air pavilion-style *mandapa* supported by carved pillars. As at the Sachiya Mata Temple, the drum of the dome features sculptures of *apsaras* (celestial maidens). There is also a beautiful *torana* before the temple, with very intricate sculptural work.

The image of Mahavira is quite difficult to make out in the dimly lit inner sanctum. According to legend it is over 2500 years old, and is made of sand and milk and coated in gold. In the right-hand corner there is an ancient frieze, which retains fragments of colour.

Among the other temples in Osiyan are those dedicated to Surya, Shiva and Harihara, but they are in poor condition and are being restored. There is also a badly deteriorating *baori* (step-well).

Places to Stay & Eat Few travellers stay overnight in Osiyan, which accounts for the lack of accommodation. A Brahmin priest, the energetic Bhanu Prakash Sharma, has a small **guesthouse** (☎ 02922-74260; *rooms around Rs 100*), just near the Mahavira Temple. This place has just two very simple rooms with *charpoys* (Indian string beds) and bucket hot water. A veg lunch or dinner is Rs 80 to 100. The owner can arrange jeep excursions and camel rides, and is also a guide to the temples. You can usually find him sitting at the gateway to the temple, or ask any of the village children who will happily track him down for you.

The Camel Camp (☎ 02922-74333; e *camelcamposian@yahoo.com; single/double tents with shared bathroom Rs 300/600, deluxe tents US$180/200*) in Osiyan offers a range of tented accommodation in a very magical location: atop a secluded sand dune overlooking the town. Deluxe tents come with private bathroom (and shower!), all meals and a camel safari. The cool and casual owner, Reggie, is here most of the time and is planning to build a pool on a dune! Contact The Safari Club (☎/fax 0291-437023; High Court Colony, Jodhpur). Let Reggie know when you will be arriving in Osiyan,

and he can arrange for a jeep to pick you up from the train station or bus stand.

Getting There & Away Although few people travel to Osiyan, buses to Jodhpur depart every 30 minutes or so, (Rs 26, 1½ hrs); and to Phalodi (Rs 31, 2 hrs).

There's also a daily train from Jodhpur (Rs 15/135 in 2nd/1st class, 1½ hrs). A taxi from Jodhpur costs about Rs 400 (return).

Phalodi

Phalodi is a fairly nondescript large town lying about midway between Jodhpur and Jaisalmer. The main attraction here is the tiny village of **Khichan**, about 10km east of Phalodi, a feeding ground during the winter months for the beautiful demoiselle crane (see the boxed text 'The Demoiselle Cranes of Khichan'). Khichan also has some beautiful red sandstone havelis (mansions), some around 100 years old, an attractive Jain temple and a crumbling fort. A series of sand dunes affords a stunning desert panorama. Your hotel can organise a guide to take you to Khichan.

Places to Stay & Eat Directly opposite the Roadways bus stand is **Hotel Sunrise** (☎/fax 02925-22257; *singles/doubles with shared bathroom Rs 100/150, with private bathroom Rs 200/250*). It has basic but acceptable rooms with bucket hot water. There's also a restaurant here.

Lal Niwas Days Inn (☎ 02925-23813, fax 22017; e *saranghaveli@hotmail.com; singles/doubles Rs 1300/1500, suites Rs 1700*) is a beautiful old red haveli in the old part of town, with balconies, courtyards and a tangle of passages. All the rooms are different, tastefully decorated in the traditional style. The family suite is fantastic, especially if you have kids, with a number of rooms divided by carved arches. There's also a restaurant (curries Rs 45 to 70), a bar and a swimming pool.

Getting There & Away Phalodi is 135km from Jodhpur, 165km from Jaisalmer and 150km from Bikaner. There are many buses (from the Roadways bus stand) to Jodhpur

The Demoiselle Cranes of Khichan

During the season, over 7000 demoiselle cranes (*Anthropoides virgo*), known locally as kurjas, make a dramatic descent every morning and evening to the fields around Khichan to feed on the grain which has been spread there by villagers.

The demoiselle cranes winter in Khichan, from the last week of August or the first week of September until the last week of March. They stand about 76cm high, have a long neck and short beak and are a brown-grey colour with a black chest and throat. In traditional Marwari songs, women beseech the cranes to bring back messages from their loved ones when they return from distant lands. The flock consumes a phenomenal 600kg of grain each day, distributed at the Birds Feeding Home, all of which is funded by (very welcome) donations.

The practice of feeding the cranes dates back some 150 years, and the number of cranes is increasing by about 10% to 15% each year. The grain is spread at night, ready for the birds to feed at sunrise (about 7am), and again around 5pm, in time for the birds' return in the afternoon. The sight of these wonderful birds in such large numbers descending on the feeding ground is truly awe-inspiring, and shouldn't be missed if you're in the area. Please keep a distance from the birds and refrain from making a noise, so as not to scare them.

The demoiselle cranes winter in India, Pakistan and Africa. To migrate they must cross the Himalaya from their breeding range, which extends over a wide belt traversing eastern Europe, Central Asia and eastern China.

For more information about the demoiselle cranes and the feeding programme at Khichan, contact the **International Crane Foundation** (☎ 608-3569462, fax 3569465; **W** www .savingcranes.org; PO Box 447, E-11376 Shady Lane Rd, Baraboo, WI 53913-0447, USA).

(Rs 47/56 for a local/express bus, 3½ hours) and Bikaner (Rs 59/69, 3½ hours) and express buses to Jaisalmer (Rs 59, 3½ hours).

Phalodi is on the broad-gauge line and has rail connections with Jodhpur (Rs 26/43 for the day/night train, 3 hours) and Jaisalmer (Rs 28/50 for the day/night train, 3 hours).

Getting Around There are daily buses between Phalodi and Khichan (Rs 2, 15 minutes). An autorickshaw will cost Rs 50 (return) to Khichan.

Ramdevra

This tiny, desolate and windswept desert village lies 10km north of Pokaran and, while it's probably not the most salubrious place to stay at, it has a very important temple dedicated to a deified local hero Ramdev from the Middle Ages. Ramdev was born in Tanwar village to a Rajput family and was opposed to all forms of untouchability, believing that all human beings are equal.

Ramdev Mandir The temple itself, with its brightly coloured facade, is not architecturally of great interest, but the devotional activities of the hundreds of pilgrims who pay homage at this shrine certainly are. The streets outside the temple are lined with tea shops and souvenir-wallahs. Pilgrims leave tiny models of horses at the temple; there are sometimes hundreds of embroidered horses, like the ones for sale all over Rajasthan. They commemorate Ramdev's trusty horse, who went with him from village to village as he helped ailing villagers.

You'll probably be assailed by people with receipt books demanding donations, both as you enter the temple complex and within the temple itself, even by men who 'guard' your shoes!

Places to Stay & Eat Near the temple and the bus stand, **Hotel Sohan Palace** (☎ 02996-37025; singles/doubles with private bathroom Rs 150/200) has simple rooms with hot water by the bucket. No meals are available here.

Getting There & Away Most buses between Phalodi and Pokaran pass through Ramdevra – Phalodi to Ramdevra costs Rs 18. Jeep taxis leave when full along the main street for Pokaran (Rs 5, 20 minutes).

Pokaran

At the junction of the Jaisalmer, Jodhpur and Bikaner roads, 110km from Jaisalmer, is this desert town, site of another fort, although not of the formidable dimensions of the Jodhpur and Jaisalmer forts. The bus stand is on the Jodhpur road at the southern edge of town. The fort is 1.5km to the northeast of the bus stand. There is nowhere to change money in Pokaran, so take enough rupees.

It was in the Pokaran area, in May 1998, that India detonated five nuclear devices, heightening tension between India and neighbouring Pakistan – rivals since Partition in 1947. The crux of the contention between the two countries has long been the disputed territory of Kashmir, which is claimed by both India and Pakistan. While world leaders vehemently condemned the Indian nuclear tests, hundreds of thousands of Hindu loyalists celebrated Prime Minister Atal Behari Vajpayee's controversial decision. Pakistan swiftly responded to India by detonating its own nuclear devices, igniting global concern about a nuclear arms race in south Asia. In late September 2001, the US lifted the sanctions against India that were imposed after the nuclear tests. Analysts saw this as a reward for India's support in the 'war against terror' after the 11 September attacks on the United States.

Pokaran Fort & Museum Though it's an evocative place, Pokaran Fort (admission Rs 30, camera & video Rs 20; open 7am-6pm daily) has a rather ramshackle and abandoned atmosphere. The museum is nothing special, with an assortment of weaponry, some brocaded clothes, old wooden printing blocks and various games of former rulers of Pokaran, including dice and dominoes. There's also a small shrine to Durga.

There is no entry charge to the fort if you have a meal at the Fort Pokaran hotel.

Places to Stay & Eat A stop at Pokaran breaks the long journey between Jodhpur and Jaisalmer, but accommodation is lacklustre so most travellers stop here for lunch rather than overnight.

RTDC Motel Godawan (☎ 02994-22275; doubles with private bathroom half/full day Rs 100/200, cottages Rs 250/500), 3km west of the bus stand, conveniently rents out cottages and rooms for half or full days. An Indian lunch or dinner is Rs 60/100 for veg/nonveg. The continental veg/nonveg lunch or dinner is Rs 165/200. This place is a lot better than most other RTDC hotels.

Fort Pokaran (☎ 02994-22274, fax 22388; singles/doubles Rs 950/1150, doubles with air-con Rs 1500, suite Rs 2000), within the fort itself, offers overpriced accommodation that's not nearly as grand as that offered in some of Rajasthan's other amazing fort-palace complexes. It does have a certain faded appeal, and may be more luxurious once the restoration is complete. Breakfast is Rs 150, the veg/nonveg lunch or dinner is Rs 250/300. Jeep safaris can be arranged.

Getting There & Away There are regular RSRTC buses to Jaisalmer (Rs 30, 2 hours). There are buses to Bikaner (Rs 80, 5 hours) and to Jodhpur (Rs 58, 3 hours).

There are daily rail services to Jaisalmer (Rs 103/359 in 2nd/1st class, 5 hours) and Jodhpur (Rs 104/213, 4 hours).

JAISALMER

☎ 02992 • postcode 345001 • pop 58,286

Jaisalmer is a place that should exist only in the imagination. Nothing else in India is remotely similar to this enchanting city, which has been dubbed the 'Golden City' because of the honey colour imparted to its stone ramparts by the setting sun. The vision of Jaisalmer's massive fort thrusting heavenwards out of the barren desertscape is un-forgettable, and the magic doesn't diminish as you approach its walls and bastions, and lose yourself in its labyrinthine streets and bazaars. The fort, which resembles a

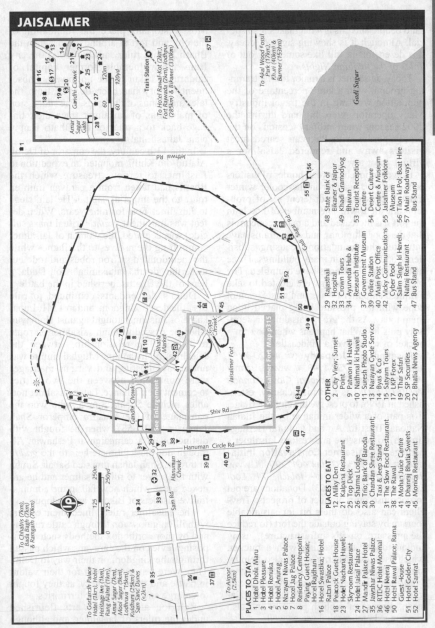

JAISALMER

PLACES TO STAY
1 Hotel Dhola Maru
3 Hotel Pleasure
4 Hotel Renuka
5 Hotel Anurag
6 Narayan Niwas Palace
7 Hotel Jag Palace
8 Residency Centrepoint
   Paying Guest House;
   Ho el Rajdhani
16 Hotel Swastika; Hotel
   Ratan Palace
18 Peacock Guest House
23 Hotel Nachana Haveli;
   Skyroom Restaurant
24 Hotel Jaisal Palace
27 Ma idir Palace Hotel
35 Jawahar Niwas Palace
36 RTDC Hotel Moomal
46 Hotel Meera
50 Hotel Rawal Palace; Rama
   Guest-iouse
51 Hotel Golden City
52 Hotel Samrat

PLACES TO EAT
12 Milky Den
21 Kalpana Restaurant
25 Top Deck
26 Sharma Lodge
28 Trio; Bank of Baroda
30 Chandan Shree Restaurant;
   Taxi & Jeep Stand
31 The Slow Food Restaurant
38 The Rawal
41 Moha i Juice Centre
43 Dhanraj Bhatia Sweets
45 Monica Restaurant

OTHER
2 City View; Sunset
   Point
9 Patwon ki Haveli
10 Nathmal ki Haveli
11 Suresh Photo Studio
13 Narayan Cycle Service
14 Byas & Co
15 Satyam Tours
17 LKP Forex
19 Thar Safari
20 SP Securities
22 Bhatia News Agency
29 Rajasthali
32 Hospital
33 Crown Tours
34 Ayurveda Hub &
   Research Institute
37 Government Museum
39 Police Station
40 Main Post Office
42 Vicky Communications
44 Salim Singh ki Haveli;
   Cyber Pool
47 Bus Stand
48 State Bank of
   Bikaner & Jaipur
49 Khadi Gramodyog
   Bhavan
53 Tourist Reception
   Centre
54 Desert Culture
   Centre & Museum
55 Jaisalmer Folklore
   Museum
56 Tilon ki Pol; Boat Hire
57 Main Roadways
   Bus Stand

To Gorbandh Palace
Hotel (1km); Hotel
Heritage Inn (1km);
Rang Mahal (1km);
Amar Sagar (7km);
Mool Sagar (9km);
Lodhruva (15km);
Kuldhara (25km) &
Sam San¢ Dures
(~2km)

To Chhatris (7km);
Bada Bagh (7km)
& Ramgarh (70km)

To Airport
(2.5km)

To Gadi Sagar Rd

To Akal Wood Fossil
Park (17km);
Khuri (40km) &
Barmer (153km)

Train Station

To Hotel Rawal-kot (2km);
Fort Rajwada (3km); Jodhpur
(285km) & Bikaner (330km)

Gadi Sagar

Jaisalmer Fort

See Jaisalmer Fort Map p315

Gopa
Chowk

Bhatia
Market

Shiv Rd

Hanuman Circle Rd

Hanuman
Chowk

Sam Rd

Gandhi Chowk

See Enlargement

Jethwal Rd

Amar
Sagar
Gate

Gandhi Chowk

gigantic sandcastle, is home to several thousand people and this is what makes it so special. Although it is showing signs of decay, this desert fort is still like something out of *Tales of the Arabian Nights*.

Today, Jaisalmer is a major tourist tramping ground, with a large percentage of the population working in the travel industry. Many operators were hit hard during the 2002 season, when military tensions on the nearby border with Pakistan scared most visitors away and rendered Jaisalmer a virtual ghost town.

However, in a busy year, hordes of visitors converge on Jaisalmer in the cooler winter months, presenting a different set of problems for the town. The number of hotels in the fort has increased and a major concern is that the poor plumbing and open drains have saturated the foundations, causing subsidence and collapse in many buildings. Three of the fort's 99 bastions have crumbled. The old open drains, which were created to take a limited amount of water and waste, cannot cope with the pressure being placed upon them today. As the group Jaisalmer in Jeopardy puts it: 'What happens when you tip a bucket of water over a sandcastle?'

Jaisalmer in Jeopardy (☎ 44-20-7352 4336, fax 44-20-7737 4948; W www.jaisalmer -in-jeopardy.org; 3 Brickbarn Close, London SW10 0TP, UK) is a British charity, established in 1996, to preserve the city's heritage. It is part of a wider initiative by the Indian National Trust for Art and Cultural Heritage (Intach) to conserve and restore Jaisalmer's heritage, the **Jaisalmer Conservation Initiative** (☎ 011-4645482, fax 4611290; W www .intach.org/jaisal.htm; c/- Intach, 71, Lodi Estate, New Delhi 110003). Donations are put to good use on a number of projects. Travellers can also do their bit for sustainable tourism by staying outside the fort (to reduce the pressure on it's infrastructure), using Indian toilets and bathing with a bucket, which uses less water. You can also help by simply showing an interest in conserving Jaisal-mer's heritage and encouraging locals to take pride in it. As in other parts of Rajasthan, dispose of rubbish properly and also encourage hoteliers to do so as well.

History

Most historians place the foundation of the city and fort at around 1156, when the Bhatti Rajput ruler Jaisala moved the city from the vulnerable former capital of Lodhruva, 15km to the northwest. Subsequent history has been derived from the tales and songs of the bards. The succession of maharajas of Jaisalmer trace their lineage back to a ruler of the Bhatti Rajput clan, Jaitasimha.

In the 13th century, the emperor of Delhi, Ala-ud-din Khilji, mounted an expedition to Jaisalmer to retrieve treasure which the Bhattis had taken from a caravan train en route to the imperial capital. He laid siege to Jaisalmer Fort for nine years. When defeat was imminent, *jauhar* (ritual mass suicide) was declared, the women of Jaisalmer committing themselves to the flames while the men donned saffron robes and rode out to certain death. Jaitasimha's son Duda, a hero of the Bhattis, perished in the battle.

Duda's descendants continued to rule over the desert kingdom, and in 1541, Lunakarna of Jaisalmer fought against Humayun when he passed through Jaisalmer en route to Ajmer. The relationship between the Jaisalmer rulers and the Mughal empire was not always hostile, and various marriages were contracted between the two parties to cement their alliance. Later Jaisalmer notables include Sabala Simha, who won the patronage of the Muslim emperor Shah Jahan (r. 1627–58), when he fought with distinction in a campaign at Peshawar. Although not the legitimate heir to the *gaddi*, or throne, Shah Jahan invested Sabala Simha with the power to rule Jaisalmer and he annexed areas which now fall in the administrative districts of Bikaner and Jodhpur.

The Jaisalmer rulers lined their coffers with illicit gains won through cattle rustling and by more orthodox methods such as imposing levies on the caravans which passed through the kingdom on their way to Delhi. They were renowned both for their valour in battle and their treachery, as they fought to enlarge and secure their territories.

Religion and the fine arts flourished under the rulers of Jaisalmer, and although professing Hinduism, they were tolerant of Jainism, encouraging the construction of the beautiful temples which now grace the old city within the fort walls. Sculptural depictions of both Hindu and Jain deities and holy men stand side by side on the walls of these fine edifices. The visionary rulers commissioned scholars to copy precious sacred manuscripts and books of ancient learning which may otherwise have been lost during Muslim raids.

Jaisalmer's strategic position on the camel train routes between India and Central Asia brought it great wealth. The merchants and townspeople built magnificent houses and mansions, all carved from wood and golden-yellow sandstone. These havelis can be found elsewhere in Rajasthan (notably in Shekhawati), but nowhere are they quite as exquisite as in Jaisalmer. Even the humblest of shops and houses display something of the Rajput love of the decorative arts in its most whimsical form. It's likely to remain that way too, since the city planners are keen to ensure that all new buildings blend in with the old.

The rise of shipping trade and the port of Mumbai saw the decline of Jaisalmer. At Independence, Partition and the cutting of trade routes through to Pakistan seemingly sealed the city's fate, and water shortages could have pronounced the death sentence. However, the 1965 and 1971 wars between India and Pakistan revealed Jaisalmer's strategic importance, and the Indira Gandhi Canal to the north is restoring life to the desert.

Today, tourism rivals the military base as the pillar of the city's economy. The presence of the Border Security Force sometimes impinges on the tourist trade in the old city, with thousands of soldiers stationed in the Jaisalmer area and the occasional sound of war planes in the distance disturbing the tranquillity of this desert gem.

Orientation

This old city was once completely surrounded by an extensive wall, much of which has sadly been torn down in recent years for building material. Some of it remains,

however, including the city gates and, inside them, the massive fort which rises above the city and is the essence of Jaisalmer. The fort itself, which is entered via the First Fort Gate, is a warren of narrow, paved streets complete with Jain temples and the old palace of the former ruler.

The main market, Bhatia Market, is right below the hill, while the banks, the new palace and several other shops and offices are near the Amar Sagar Gate to the west.

Information

Tourist Offices The **Tourist Reception Centre** (☎ 52406; Gadi Sagar Rd; open 10am-5pm Mon-Sat), about 2km southeast of the First Fort Gate, supplies various brochures, including a map of Jaisalmer (Rs 2). It opens 8am to 8pm in the high season. There's also a smaller tourist information counter at the train station in the high season.

Money Next to Trio restaurant, the **Bank of Baroda** (Gandhi Chowk; open 10am-2pm Mon-Fri) changes Amex travellers cheques and issues cash advances on Visa and MasterCard. The **State Bank of Bikaner & Jaipur**, opposite the Hotel Neeraj, can change travellers cheques and major currencies. The more professional and reliable private moneychangers include **LKP Forex** (☎ 53679; open 9.30am-6.30pm daily) and **SP Securities** (☎ 50025; open 9.30am-8pm daily); both have offices on Gandhi Chowk.

Post The **main post office** (Hanuman Circle Rd; open 10am-6pm Mon-Sat) is just west of the fort. Inside the fort is a **small post office** (open 10am-3pm Mon-Sat), which only sells stamps.

At the time of writing, STD and international calls out of Jaisalmer were restricted due to the military tensions in the region. Previously, there were ample phone booths (both inside and outside the fort), from which you could call home.

Email & Internet Access From no Internet places just a few years ago, Jaisalmer now has dozens of places where you can surf the Net, both inside and outside the fort.

Connections vary from instant to painfully slow – morning and late evening are your best chance of seeing your inbox within the hour. **Vicky Communications Cyber Pool** (*☎ 52022; open 8am-11pm*) has a reasonably fast connection and charges Rs 20 per hour.

Photography In Bhatia Market (opposite the Bhatia News Agency) is **Byas & Co** (*☎ 51884; open 8.30am-9pm daily*), where you can buy fresh slide and print film and batteries for still and movie cameras. A pack of Fuji print film (36 shots) costs Rs 90, Rs 225 for slide film. To develop print film the charge is Rs 15 for developing, plus Rs 3 per print. It takes two hours. Video 8 cassettes (Rs 325) and mini digital video cassettes (Rs 450) are also available, as well as lithium batteries.

Suresh Photo Studio (*☎ 51382; open 9am-8.30pm daily*), 50m to the east, is similar, but also sells an excellent range of large black-and-white prints of Jaisalmer from the early 20th century.

Bookshops Daily newspapers as well as postcards can be bought at the well-stocked **Bhatia News Agency** (*☎ 52671; open 9am-9pm daily*), in Bhatia Market. There is an excellent selection of new books (especially novels) here, as well as some second-hand books (in English, French, German, Spanish and several other languages), which can be either bought or swapped.

Jaisalmer Fort

Built in 1156 by the Bhatti Rajput ruler Jaisala, and reinforced by later rulers, the fort crowns the 80m-high Trikuta Hill. Over the centuries it was the focus of a number of battles between the Bhattis, the Mughals of Delhi and the Rathores of Jodhpur. This is one of the planet's only living forts, with about a quarter of the old city's population residing in it. The fort has 99 bastions around its circumference and is protected by three walls. The lower wall is of solid stone blocks which reinforce the loose rubble of which Trikuta Hill is composed. The second wall snakes around the fort, and between this and the third, or inner, wall,

the warrior Rajputs hurled boiling oil and water, and massive round missiles on their unwitting enemies below.

Above the fort flies the Jaisalmer standard, which features a *chhatri* against a red and yellow background. The fort looks especially magical when it is lit up at night.

It's fascinating to wander around this living fort. It's packed with houses, temples, handicraft shops and beauty parlours, and honeycombed with narrow, winding lanes, all of them paved in stone. It's also quiet – vehicles are not allowed up here and even building materials have to be carried up by camel cart. The fort walls provide superb views over the old city and surrounding desert. Strolling around the outer fort ramparts is a popular activity at sunset.

The fort is entered from First Fort Gate through a forbidding series of massive gates via an enormous stone-paved ramp, which leads to a large courtyard. The former maharaja's seven-storey palace, Rajmahal, fronts onto this. The square was formerly used to review troops, hear petitions and present extravagant entertainment for important visitors.

Rajmahal Part of this palace is open to the public (*admission Rs 10, camera/video Rs 20/50; open 8am-1pm & 2pm-5pm daily*), although it's not comparable to the museum housed within the palaces at Meherangarh in Jodhpur. At the time of writing the palace was under restoration, with extra rooms in the *zenana* due to open in 2003. The entrance is to the right just after you pass through the last gate into the fort proper.

On the eastern wall is a sculpted pavilion-style balcony. Here drummers raised the alarm when the fort was under siege. The doorways connecting the rooms of the palace are quite low – not a reflection on the stature of the Rajputs, but to force those walking through to adopt a humble, stooped position, in case the room they were entering contained the maharaja.

In the **Diwan-i-Khas** (Hall of Private Audience), on the east side of the palace, there's a display of stamps from the former Rajput states. The room affords fine views out over

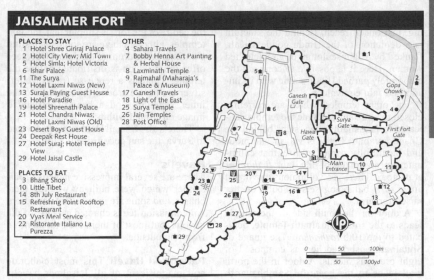

JAISALMER FORT

PLACES TO STAY
1 Hotel Shree Giriraj Palace
2 Hotel City View; Mid Town
5 Hotel Simla; Hotel Victoria
6 Ishar Palace
11 The Surya
12 Hotel Laxmi Niwas (New)
13 Suraja Paying Guest House
16 Hotel Paradise
19 Hotel Shreenath Palace
21 Hotel Chandra Niwas;
   Hotel Laxmi Niwas (Old)
23 Desert Boys Guest House
24 Deepak Rest House
27 Hotel Suraj; Hotel Temple
   View
29 Hotel Jaisal Castle

PLACES TO EAT
3 Bhang Shop
10 Little Tibet
14 8th July Restaurant
15 Refreshing Point Rooftop
   Restaurant
20 Vyas Meal Service
22 Ristorante Italiano La
   Purezza

OTHER
4 Sahara Travels
7 Bobby Henna Art Painting
   & Herbal House
8 Laxminath Temple
9 Rajmahal (Maharaja's
   Palace & Museum)
17 Ganesh Travels
25 Surya Temple
26 Jain Temples
28 Post Office

the entrance ramp to the fort and the town spread beneath it. From here you can clearly see the numerous round rocks piled on top of the battlements, ready to be rolled onto advancing enemies. There's a small **Diwan-i-Am** (Hall of Public Audience) with lower walls lined with porcelain tiles.

The adjacent room is lined with blue and white tiles. Upstairs, in a room close to the maharaja's private chamber on the east side of the palace, is a room which has some exquisite stone-panel friezes, which on first glance appear to be carved from wood. The views from the top of the palace are superb.

Jain Temples Within the fort walls, there are seven beautifully carved Jain temples *(foreigner/citizen Rs 10/free, camera/video Rs 50/100; open 7am-noon daily)* built between the 12th and 15th centuries. Only the Chandraprabhu and Rikhabdev Temples are currently open to non-Jains, although the priests are considering opening all of them between 11am and 1pm daily – ask the care-takers for an update. The cluster of temples is connected by a series of corridors and walkways. Shoes and all leather items must be removed before entering the temple.

The first temple you come to is the one dedicated to **Chandraprabhu**, the eighth *tirthankar* (Jain teacher), whose symbol is the moon. It was built in 1509 and features fine sculpture in sandstone in the *mandapa*. Around the inside of the drum are 12 statues of Ganesh, and around the hall which encompasses the inner sanctum are numerous statues of *tirthankars*. The *mandapa* is supported by elaborately sculpted pillars which form a series of *toranas*. No mortar was used in the construction of this temple; blocks of masonry are held together by iron staples. Around the upper gallery are 108 marble images of Parasnath, the 22nd *tirthankar*. In the inner sanctum are four images of Chandraprabhu. Note that the statues are unclothed. This is typical of Jain statues; in contrast those of Hindu deities are always elaborately garbed.

To the right of the Chandraprabhu Temple is **Rikhabdev Temple**. There are some fine sculptures around the walls protected by glass cabinets, and the pillars are beautifully sculpted with *apsaras* and gods. This temple has a lovely, tranquil atmosphere. On the south side of the inner sanctum, a carving depicts a mother holding a child who is reaching up for the fruit she is holding, just out of reach. Behind the sanctum is a depiction of the Hindu goddess Kali, flanked by a Jain sculpture of an unclothed woman. Here it is possible to compare the elaborately garbed Hindu statue with its unadorned Jain equivalent.

The other temples, which are currently closed to non-Jains, include the temple dedicated to **Parasnath**, a few steps behind the Chandraprabhu. Entry is via an enormous and beautifully carved *torana* that culminates in an image of the Jain *tirthankar* at its apex. There is a voluptuous carving of an *apsara* balancing sets of balls on her raised forearm.

A door on the south side of the temple leads to the small **Shitalnath Temple**, dedicated to the 10th *tirthankar*. The image of Shitalnath enshrined here is composed of eight precious metals. A door in the north wall leads to the beautiful **Sambhavanth Temple**. In the courtyard before this temple, Jain priests grind sandalwood in mortars for devotional use inside. Steps in the courtyard of this temple lead to the **Gyan Bhandar**, a library founded in 1500 by Acharya Maharaj Jin Bhadra Suri. This small underground vault houses priceless ancient illustrated manuscripts, some dating from the 11th century. Other exhibits include astrological charts and the Jain version of the Shroud of Turin: the Shroud of Gindhasuri, a Jain hermit and holy man who died in Ajmer. When his body was placed on the funeral pyre, the shroud was miraculously unsinged. In a small locked cabinet are images of Parasnath made of ivory and various precious stones including emerald and crystal. There are plans to shift the library outside the temple so it can be visited.

Steps lead from the courtyard before Sambhavanth Temple to **Shantinath Temple**, which was built in 1536. The enclosed gallery around this temple is flanked by hundreds of images of saints, some of marble and some of Jaisalmer sandstone. Steps lead below this temple to **Kunthunath Temple**, which was also built in 1536.

Guides are available outside the temples for around Rs 50.

Laxminath Temple This Hindu temple, in the centre of the fort, is simpler than the Jain temples, although there are some interesting paintings in the drum of the dome. Devotees offer grain which is distributed before the temple. There is a repoussé (raised relief) silver architrave around the entrance to the inner sanctum, and a heavily garlanded image enshrined within.

There's also a small Hindu temple devoted to Surya, the sun god, inside the fort.

Havelis

There are several impressive havelis in Jaisalmer which were built by wealthy merchants, and some are in excellent condition. An admission fee is charged at some of the havelis, but most of them are best admired from the outside.

Patwon-ki-Haveli This most elaborate and magnificent of all Jaisalmer havelis stands in a narrow lane. It's divided into five apartments: two are owned by the Archaeological Survey of India; one is a private home; and two contain craft shops. The havelis were built between 1800 and 1860 by five Jain brothers who made their fortunes trading jewellery and fine brocades. They have remnants of paintings in vibrant reds and gold, as well as fine mirrorwork.

The first haveli is a private museum and shop *(admission Rs 10, camera/video Rs 10/ 20)*, featuring displays of old furnishings and household items. The second and fifth havelis *(admission Rs 2 for both)* are government run. They are empty but you can wander around and soak in the atmosphere. Only the ground floor is open on the second haveli. The third haveli is an antique shop and the fourth, a private residence, is not open to the public.

Salim Singh-ki-Haveli This private haveli *(admission Rs 15; open 8am-6pm daily)* was built about 400 years ago and part of it is still occupied. Salim Singh was the prime minister when Jaisalmer was the capital of a princely state, and his mansion has a beautifully arched roof with superb carved brackets in the form of peacocks. There are stone elephants before the haveli; these were traditionally erected before the homes of prime ministers. The mansion is constructed with no mortar or cement – the stones are connected with tongue-and-groove joints. The admission fee includes a free guided tour, although language can be a bit of a problem.

Nathmal-ki-Haveli This late-19th-century haveli (admission free; open 8.30am-8pm daily) was also used as a prime minister's house and has a superb exterior. The left and right wings of the building were carved by brothers and are very similar, but not identical. Yellow sandstone elephants guard the building, and even the front door is a work of art.

Gadi Sagar
This tank, south of the city walls, once held the town's water supply, and, befitting its importance in providing precious water to the inhabitants of this arid city, it is surrounded by small temples and shrines. A wide variety of waterfowl flock here in winter. The tank was built in 1367 by Maharaja Gadsi Singh, taking advantage of a natural declivity that already retained some water.

The beautiful yellow sandstone gateway arching across the road down to the tank is the **Tilon-ki-Pol**, and is said to have been built by a famous prostitute, Tilon. When she offered to pay to have this gateway constructed, the maharaja refused permission on the grounds that he would have to pass under it to go down to the tank, and he felt that this would be beneath his dignity. While he was away, she built the gate anyway, adding a Krishna temple on top so that the king could not tear it down.

Boats can be hired from 8am to 9pm daily at the Tilon-ki-Pol; a rowboat is Rs 10 per person, a two-seater pedal boat is Rs 50 per half-hour and a four-seater is Rs 100.

Museums
There are two very good museums, which are not far from each other and house very similar displays (a visit to one is enough). They were founded by NK Sharma, a local

historian and folklorist. Next to the Tourist Reception Centre is the **Desert Culture Centre & Museum** (☎ 53723; foreigner/citizen Rs 10/5; open 8am-8.30pm daily) which has textiles, old coins, fossils, traditional Rajasthani musical instruments and a karal (opium-mixing box), among other things. Its aim is to preserve cultural heritage and conduct research on local history. A daily puppet show is performed here at 6.30pm, costing Rs 30/20 for foreigners/citizens.

The admission fee to this museum also includes entry to the **Jaisalmer Folklore Museum** (☎ 52188; open 8am-7pm daily), located on the road leading down to the lake. Here there's a model made of horse dung and clay model of the legendary Moomal Palace and exhibits of Rajasthani household items. Informative booklets about Jaisalmer in English, French, German and Italian are available here. The hill near here is a tremendous place to soak up the sunset.

Next to the RTDC Hotel Moomal is the small **Government Museum** (adult/student Rs 3/1, free Monday; open 10am-4.30pm Sat-Thur), which has a limited though interesting collection of fossils, some of which date back to the Jurassic era (160 to 180 million years ago!), and other artefacts. Other exhibits include examples of ancient script, coins, religious sculptures (some from the 11th century), puppets and textiles. There is even a stuffed great Indian bustard, the state bird of Rajasthan, which thrives in the Thar Desert but is declining in numbers elsewhere. Photography is not allowed.

Ayurvedic Centres
After a long camel trek you can soothe your jangled body with some Ayurvedic massage and herbal healing. Most people come to the **Ayurveda Hub & Research Institute** (☎ 54692; e drprathmeshvyas@yahoo.co.in; 62 CV Singh Colony, off Sam Rd; open 9am-6.30pm daily) for a massage (Rs 400 for 45 minutes) or a steam bath (Rs 150 for 20 minutes), but the centre offers a wide range of other treatments to cure everything from asthma to arthritis. A full day of purification and relaxation therapy costs Rs 1800. The

Arrival in Jaisalmer

You realise that Jaisalmer is a tourist hotbed long before you arrive. Hotel and camel safari touts may even approach you in Bikaner or Jodhpur. If you're travelling by bus you'll find the number of passengers suddenly increases about an hour before arrival; the touts know that they have a captive audience.

In the past few years, the local authorities have introduced policies designed to keep the touts at bay. Most carriages on the overnight train carry at least a couple of soldiers to try to ensure you get a good night's sleep and they also patrol the train station platforms in Jodhpur with varying degrees of vigilance. Perhaps the most surreal experience is stumbling out of the train in the predawn light to find a small army of hotel owners kept behind a barricade about 20m from the station exit, holding up their signs and champing at the bit. Once you cross that line, you're on your own.

Don't believe anyone who offers to take you 'anywhere you like' for just a few rupees, and take with a grain of salt claims that the hotel you want to stay in is 'full', 'closed', 'no good any more' or has suffered some other inglorious fate. If the hotel of your choice has a representative waiting for you, by all means accept the free ride. Alternatively, take a rickshaw and hope you get an honest driver (they do exist) – pay no more than Rs 30.

institute also offers courses in Ayurveda, which last from seven days to six months. A seven-day course costs Rs 4500, including free treatments. Longer courses are free, but you must volunteer at the centre.

There are loads of other places offering Ayurvedic massage and henna painting, including **Bobby Henna Art Painting & Herbal House** (*☎ 54468*), in the fort. This place is run by women, so female travellers will feel comfortable here.

Organised Tours

Few travellers visit Jaisalmer without taking a camel safari into the desert. For details,

see the boxed text 'Camel Safaris Around Jaisalmer', later.

The Tourist Reception Centre offers a morning and evening city sightseeing tour (Rs 75 per person), and sunset tour to the Sam sand dunes (Rs 125 per person), leaving at 3.30pm daily in summer, 3pm in winter. On request, the tours to Sam may stop at Kanoi, 5km before the dunes, from where it's possible to get a camel to the dunes in time for sunset (about Rs 100).

Places to Stay

Tourist authorities are encouraging tourists to choose a hotel outside the fort to relieve some of the pressure on the delicate infrastructure. A plan to add a levy to the hotels in the fort has even been mooted in an attempt to slow the water deterioration. Motorised traffic is not permitted within the fort at most times, which means you'll have to lug your backpack up the steep ramp and cart it around with you while you check out the options. Many hotels in Jaisalmer have an ungenerous 9am check-out time.

Unfortunately, quite a few of the cheap hotels are really into the high-pressure selling of camel safaris. Some places can get quite ugly if you book a safari through someone else. Not only will they refuse to hold your baggage, they'll actually evict you from the hotel! Before you check in, make it clear that you will only stay if you don't have to do a safari – if they do hassle you, simply move on.

If there's a festival on, prices skyrocket and accommodation of any kind can be hard to get. Many places do offer low-season discounts between April and August – but you'd be crazy to come here during this time, as Jaisalmer becomes hellishly hot.

Places to Stay – Budget

There are plenty of budget hotels to choose from. Most of the rock-bottom places are pretty similar in standard. Many have bucket hot water and Indian-style toilets. The Paying Guest House Scheme has just seven participating families in Jaisalmer. Expect to pay Rs 150 to 300 – contact the Tourist Reception Centre for details.

Town Area There's a good choice of budget hotels along the two streets that run parallel to each other north of the Trio Restaurant, which is about five minutes' walk east of the city bus stand.

Hotel Swastika (☎ 52483; singles/doubles with shared bathroom Rs 90/120, singles/doubles with private bathroom Rs 150/200), opposite the Peacock Guest House, gets good reports. It has a friendly atmosphere, clean rooms and it even throws in a free cup of *chai* (tea) in the morning. It costs a steep Rs 10 pr piece per day to store luggage if you take a camel safari, unless you book through the hotel, when it's free.

Hotel Anurag (☎ 50276; singles/doubles with private bathroom from Rs 50/70) has good views from its rooftop restaurant. It also offers a free cup of *chai*.

Hotel Renuka (☎ 52757; e hotelrenuka@rediffmail.com; singles/doubles with shared bathroom Rs 60/80, with private bathroom from Rs 80/120), near Hotel Anurag, is a family-run place. The best room has a balcony and all the rooms have Indian-style toilets. There's a roof terrace here with great fort views, and a reasonably priced rooftop restaurant. The same family runs **Hotel Ratan Palace** (☎ 53615; dorm beds Rs 30, singles/doubles with shared bathroom from Rs 60/80, with private bathroom from Rs 100/150), closer to Gandhi Chowk on the same street, with larger, newer rooms.

Peacock Guest House (☎ 50039; singles/doubles with private bathroom from Rs 40/80) does get mixed reports from travellers, although it is certainly cheap and has a relaxed atmosphere.

Hotel Pleasure (☎ 52323; e didiballani@yahoo.com; singles/doubles with shared bathroom Rs 60/70, with private bathroom from Rs 120/150), in the same area, has small, basic rooms. You can use the washing machine for free (supply your own powder).

There are quite a few good budget options in the southern section of the walled city, just off Gadi Sagar Rd.

Hotel Golden City (☎/fax 51664; bed on roof Rs 15, singles/doubles with private bathroom from Rs 40/55) is a laid-back place offering rooms with grubby sheets. You can also sleep on the roof. There's a pleasant, reasonably priced rooftop restaurant here with a tandoori oven; a half tandoori chicken costs Rs 90.

Hotel Samrat (☎ 51498; dorm beds Rs 15, singles/doubles with shared bathroom from Rs 30/40, with private bathroom from Rs 40/50), in the same area as Golden City, is a real bargain, with very clean rooms and a rooftop restaurant.

Hotel Rawal Palace (☎ 51966; singles/doubles with private bathroom from Rs 150/200) is a little lacking in atmosphere, but not a bad choice. The rooms are tidy and spacious and come with a balcony and TV.

Rama Guest House (☎ 53609; singles/doubles from Rs 30/50), just next door, has basic but cheap rooms; hot water is by the bucket here.

Hotel City View (☎ 52804; singles/doubles from Rs 50/70, with balcony Rs 100/125) doesn't offer safaris, which means you won't be hassled to take one. The rooms are tidy and have Indian-style toilets and hot water with advanced notice.

Hotel Shree Giriraj Palace (☎ 52268, fax 55158; singles/doubles with shared bathroom Rs 20/30, with private bathroom from Rs 50/65) is a little bit further west (towards Bhatia Market). This is a cheap and cheerful place with good-value rooms and a restaurant upstairs that sports fort views.

Residency Centrepoint Paying Guest House (☎/fax 52883; singles/doubles with private bathroom from Rs 150/200), near Patwon-ki-Haveli, has five clean and spacious doubles. Room No 101 has a lovely antique balcony and nice internal fittings. This friendly, family-run place serves good home-cooked meals on the rooftop with superb views of the fort.

Hotel Rajdhani (☎ 52746, fax 51474; dorm beds Rs 50; singles/doubles with shared bathroom Rs 80/100, with private bathroom Rs 150/200, rooms with air-cooling Rs 300), nearby, has small, spartan but clean rooms. There are larger rooms with balcony and air-cooling. Climb right to the top of the hotel for the veg restaurant and a fabulous fort view. The same owner runs the **Hotel Jag Palace** (☎ 50438; singles/doubles with shared bathroom Rs 60/80, with private bath-room from Rs 125/150), across the road. It has decent rooms and vegetarian meals are served on the roof terrace.

Retiring rooms (doubles with private bathroom Rs 150) at the train station are not bad at all. Try to get one of the thatched huts which are set back from the station. No meals are available.

Fort In the north corner of the fort, **Hotel Simla** (☎ 53061 ⓔ sunnypawar@yahoo.com; bed on roof Rs 30, singles/doubles from Rs 80/100) is a wonderful place – you'll have no hassles here whatsoever. There are some rooms with private and some with shared bathroom, and it's possible to sleep on the roof, which includes a blanket, mattress and great view. There's also a restaurant on the roof. The owners also run the **Hotel Victoria** (singles/doubles from Rs 100/200), next door, which has more modern rooms, all with private bathroom.

Deepak Rest House (☎ 52665, fax 52070; ⓔ vyasdinesh@yahoo.com; dorm beds Rs 20, singles/doubles with shared bathroom Rs 40/50, with private bathroom from Rs 80/100), in the western part of the fort, is quite a popular place, although the service does get mixed reports. The bathrooms in some rooms are not the cleanest. The hotel is actually part of the fort wall, so the views from some rooms are stunning, as are those from the rooftop. Some rooms are in old circular bastions and there's a tatty dorm. The rooftop veg restaurant has pillows on the ground to sit on and a good range of dishes; veg biryani is Rs 40, special muesli is Rs 35.

Hotel Chandra Niwas (☎ 54477; doubles with shared bathroom from Rs 70, with pri-vate bathroom up to Rs 200) is a splendid place to stay with just a handful of well-maintained double rooms. You'll be very well looked after here by the friendly owners. Veg meals are available.

Ishar Palace (☎ 53062; bed on roof Rs 15, doubles with shared bathroom Rs 50, doubles with private bathroom from Rs 100) is near Laxminath Temple. It's a bit rundown but it has loads of character. Rooms are spartan

but quite clean, or you might like to sleep on the roof. This was the home of a 19th-century prime minister, Ishar Singh, as evi-denced by the statues of elephants before the building. Meals can be arranged with advance notice and you can take cooking classes here for Rs 500 per person (includ-ing the dinner you cook).

Hotel Laxmi Niwas (old) (☎ 52758, fax 52269; singles/doubles with shared bathroom Rs 30/60) has very small rooms. The shared shower is a bit primitive, and the toilet is tiny. The same owner runs **Hotel Laxmi Niwas (new)** (☎ 52758; doubles with shared bathroom from Rs 250, with private bathroom Rs 300), in the southeast corner of the fort. It has only six ordinary rooms, but they are all well kept.

Hotel Paradise (☎ 52674, fax 52259; bed on roof Rs 40, singles/doubles with shared bathroom from Rs 80/150, doubles with pri-vate bathroom Rs 300-850) is a very popular place with travellers, but gets very poor reviews from some people. You'll see it on the far side of the main square from the palace as you come through the last gate into the fort. It's a kind of haveli, with 23 rooms arranged around a leafy courtyard, and has excellent views from the roof. It's also possible to sleep on the roof; a blanket and mattress are provided. Only breakfast is available and prices rise steeply in the high season.

Hotel Temple View (☎ 52832; singles/doubles/triples with shared bathroom Rs 80/100/150, singles/doubles with private bath-room from Rs 150/250) has small but decent rooms and a friendly owner, Sunny. You can use the kitchen on the roof and examine the carvings on the roof of the Jain temples, next door.

The Surya (☎ 50647; doubles with shared bathroom Rs 100-250) is tucked away in the southeast corner of the fort and is a lovely, quiet, family place. There's a cute little restaurant with loads of charm.

Suraja Paying Guest House (☎ 50617, fax 52259; doubles from Rs 100/150), in the far southeast of the fort, has rooms in the fort wall with balconies and a veg and nonveg restaurant on the roof.

Places to Stay – Mid-Range

Town Area Just inside the town walls, **Mandir Palace Hotel** (☎ 52788, fax 51677; Gandhi Chowk; singles/doubles Rs 1200/2000, suites Rs 3000/4250) was once a royal palace, and part of it is still home to the erstwhile royal family. The intricate stone latticcwork is exquisite and all rooms ooze an old-world charm with antique furniture and fittings – check out a few to see which suits your taste as some have more character than others. There's a pricey restaurant here and a swimming pool is planned.

Hotel Nachana Haveli (☎ 52110, fax 52 778; e nachana_haveli@yahoo.com; Gandhi Chowk; singles/doubles Rs 750/900, with air-con Rs 1350/1500) is a 200-year-old haveli that has been converted into a charming hotel, with rooms set around a courtyard. The hotel is guarded by a protective Great Dane called Ruby, but her bark is worse than her bite. Meals are available with advance notice.

Hotel Jaisal Palace (☎ 52717, fax 50 257; e hoteljaisalpalace@yahoo.com; singles/doubles/triples Rs 500/600/900), near Hotel Nachana Haveli, is clean and wellrun. Go up to the chair-swing on the roof terrace to soak up the view. Meals are available.

RTDC Hotel Moomal (☎ 52392, fax 52545; dorm beds Rs 50, singles/doubles Rs 450/500, with air-con Rs 900/1000, huts Rs 600/750) is west of the walled city and the exterior is more impressive than the interior. There are ordinary (and rather musty) rooms in the main complex and air-cooled thatched huts in the grounds. There's also a bar (a bottle of beer is Rs 50) and a restaurant serving veg and nonveg fare.

Hotel Neeraj (☎ 52442, fax 52545; Shiv Rd; singles/doubles Rs 650/900, with air-con Rs 800/1050) is outside the town walls, southwest of the fort, fronting a busy road. Rooms are unremarkable, but it's right beside the bus stand. The set breakfast/lunch/dinner is Rs 85/150/175.

Fort The beautifully decorated **Desert Boys Guest House** (☎ 53091; e desert_p@yahoo.com; singles/doubles with private bathroom from Rs 100/150) is great value. All rooms have a private sitting room. There's a pleasant restaurant where you can lounge around on pillows and listen to the nightly folk music performances.

Hotel Shreenath Palace (☎ 52907; e shree nath52907@hotmail.com; singles/doubles with shared bathroom Rs 350/400), close to the Jain temples, is a family-run establishment in a beautiful 450-year-old haveli. The rooms are rich in atmosphere, with little alcoves and balconies, and some with magnificent sunset views over the temple. Omjee, the owner, claims descent from one of Jaisalmer's past prime ministers. Rooms have free bucket hot water (No 4 is particularly nice with an inlaid ceiling).

Hotel Suraj (☎ 51623, fax 53614; e hotel surajjaisalmer@hotmail.com; singles with private bathroom Rs 300-550, doubles with private bathroom Rs 350-650), near Hotel Shreenath, is another atmospheric old haveli which features fine sculpture on the facade and good views from the roof. The sparsely furnished rooms are all different, and are a bit rough around the edges, but the architecture is fantastic and all bathrooms have a hot shower. The restaurant serves basic veg fare; the set lunch/dinner is Rs 50/75.

Hotel Jaisal Castle (☎ 52362, fax 52101; e nnpjsm@sancharnet.in; singles/doubles from Rs 700/850), in the southwest corner of the fort, is another restored haveli. The rooms are a tad musty but its biggest attraction is its position, high on the ramparts overlooking the desert. Both veg and nonveg meals are available. This is also one of the only places in the fort where you can purchase a beer (Rs 90).

Places to Stay – Top End

Most of the top-end hotels are inconveniently located a long way from town.

Fort Rajwada (☎ 53233, fax 53733; e sales@rajwadafort.com; singles/doubles Rs 1800/3000; suites up to Rs 7500), 3.5km from the old city, is a new place built on the principles of vaastu, an ancient Indian art of design similar to feng shui – all the materials in the hotel are natural except the plastic shower caps. Carved sandstone balconies, taken from royal havelis in Jaisalmer, have been installed in the foyer. The rooms are stylish and there's a pool, a billiards room, a coffee shop and a pure white bar.

Hotel Rawal-Kot (☎ 51874, fax 50444; e kotjsm@sancharnet.in; singles/doubles US$45/70), next to Fort Rajwada, is another good choice. It's a tasteful sandstone hotel with rooms around a well-tended garden.

Jawahar Niwas Palace (☎ 52208, fax 52611; e jawaharniwaspalace@yahoo.com; Bada Bagh Rd; singles/doubles Rs 2000/ 2750, doubles with a view Rs 3500), about 1km west of the fort, is a stunning sandstone palace standing rather forlornly in its sandy grounds. The elegant rooms are spacious (upstairs has the best fort views). A set breakfast/lunch/dinner is Rs 225/400/450.

Narayan Niwas Palace (☎ 52408, fax 52101; e nnpjsm@sancharnet.in; singles/ doubles from Rs 1500/2500), north of the fort, is the most centrally located of the top-end hotels. It counts among its former guests Britain's Princess Anne. However, these days the rooms get mixed reports from travellers. There's a rather gloomy indoor swimming pool. Every evening there is a cultural programme including traditional Rajasthani dancing, which nonguests are welcome to attend (Rs 400, including a buffet dinner). The rooftop has a superb view of the fort and the old city. Hot water is available 6am to 10am and 6pm to 10pm.

Hotel Dhola Maru (☎ 52863, fax 52 761; e hoteldholamaru@hotmail.com; Jethwai Rd; singles/doubles Rs 1800/2000, suites Rs 2500), to the northeast of the walled city, is a few kilometres from the fort entrance. It's a popular choice, although the location is not great and it doesn't have the polish of the other top-end hotels. The design on some of the passage floor tiles can make you downright dizzy – so don't look down when you walk! There's an extraordinary little bar, which has incorporated tree roots and saddle-shaped bar stools into its decor, and a restaurant.

The rest of the top-end hotels are strung along Sam Rd, about 2.5km west of the fort.

Gorbandh Palace Hotel (☎ 53801, fax 53811; e jaisalmer@hrhindia.com; singles/ doubles Rs 1999/3300) is a modern upmarket hotel with traditional design elements. Constructed of local sandstone, the friezes around the hotel were sculpted by local artisans. The rooms are fairly nondescript, but have good facilities, and there's a coffee shop, bar, restaurant and pool (open to nonguests for Rs 200).

Hotel Heritage Inn (☎ 501901, fax 51638; e hhijsl_jp1@snacharnet.in; singles/doubles Rs 1700/2900, family suite Rs 3900), next door to Gorbandh Palace Hotel, has comfortable cottage-style rooms around a courtyard and a pool, but not much character.

Rang Mahal (☎ 50907, fax 51305; e info@ hotelrangmahal.com; singles/doubles from Rs 1850/2250, deluxe doubles Rs 3150, suites Rs 4500), nearby, is a dramatic building with impressive rooms. The deluxe rooms and suites are divine and there's a pool with a poolside bar.

Places to Eat

With so many tourists visiting Jaisalmer, you may find service at some restaurants rather lackadaisical. Nonetheless, there are plenty of places where you can kick back.

Town Area Probably the best restaurant in town is **Natraj Restaurant** (☎ 52667; open 8am-11pm). The decor is nothing fancy, but the food is consistently excellent, the service is good and the prices are very reasonable. Chicken Mughlai is Rs 65, vegetable au gratin is Rs 50, palak paneer (unfermented cheese in a spinach gravy) is Rs 45, and a beer will set you back Rs 80. For sweet tooths, apple pie (Rs 40) and fried ice cream (Rs 40) feature on the dessert list. The open-air top floor has a nice view of the upper part of the Salim Singh-ki-Haveli next door, and away to the south of town.

Mid Town (☎ 50242; Gopa Chowk; open 7am-11pm daily; mains under Rs 50), outside the fort, is a cosy place that cooks up vegetarian food. A Rajasthani special thali is Rs 50. The food here is OK, but nothing to rave about.

Monica Restaurant (☎ 51586; open 8am-11pm daily) is a short distance away and gets lots of good reports from travellers. There's live music nightly and an extensive menu with Indian (including Rajasthani), continental and Chinese food. To taste authentic local specialities, try the Rajasthani thali (Rs 70), *kadhan* chicken (Rs 60) and the potato peas curry (Rs 35).

Trio (☎ 52733; open 7am-10.30pm daily), near the Amar Sagar Gate, is worth a try. This long-running Indian and continental restaurant is pricier than its neighbours, but the food is excellent, and musicians play in the evening. You can sit in a charming tent or on couches under the stars. The *saagwala* mutton (mutton with creamed spinach) for Rs 105 is delicious. There's even mashed potato (Rs 45) – ideal for tender tummies.

Skyroom Restaurant (☎ 52765; open 7am-10.30pm daily), above the Hotel Nachana Haveli, is a little rundown but it has pretty good fort views. A mutton or chicken sizzler is Rs 80, half a tandoori chicken is Rs 90 and a banana pancake is Rs 30.

Kalpana Restaurant (☎ 52469; open 8am-10pm daily), in the same area, is quite frankly nothing special when it comes to the food, but it's a good place to just watch the world go by while sipping on a banana lassi (Rs 15) or snacking on a toasted chicken sandwich (Rs 30).

Top Deck (☎ 51444; open 8am-11pm daily), also in the area, has reasonably priced veg and nonveg Indian, Chinese and continental cuisine, such as ginger chicken (Rs 70), egg curry (Rs 30) and sizzlers (Rs 60 to 80). Its fruit lassi (Rs 20) is refreshing.

Sharma Lodge (☎ 50480; open 5.30am-10.30pm daily) is a very simple restaurant with a filling Indian thali for Rs 25.

Milky Den (☎ 52125; open 9am-9pm in winter, 9am-11.30pm in summer) is a spotless ice-cream shop that serves 'softy cones' (Rs 20), thick shakes (Rs 25 to 55) and sundaes (Rs 40).

Mohan Juice Centre (Bhatia Market; open 8am-9.30pm daily) sells an amazing assortment of interesting lassi flavours, although some, such as the mocha lassi (Rs 13), don't really work. A glass of fresh orange juice is Rs 6 to 15, and you can get home-made peanut butter here (Rs 10 for 100g).

Dhanraj Bhatia Sweets (Sadar Bazaar, Bhatia Market; open 6am-9pm daily) has been churning out traditional sweet treats for the past 10 generations. It is renowned in Jaisalmer and beyond, for its local speciality sweets such as *ghotua ladoos* (sweetmeat balls made with gram flour) and *panchadhuri ladoos* (made with wheat flour), which cost Rs 5 each. This simple little shop is worth visiting just to watch the sweet makers ply their trade. There's no English sign, but you can recognise it by the small wooden platform out the front and the many locals stopping in to buy sweets.

Chandan Shree Restaurant (☎ 53965; open 8am-11pm daily; thali Rs 30), next to the taxi stand, is an authentic thali joint that's very popular with locals.

The Rawal, beside Hanuman Chowk, whips up interesting Indian dishes such as a tandoori thali (Rs 125) which contains tandoori chicken, chicken tikka, vegetable kebab, *paneer tikka* (spiced *paneer*, or unfermented cheese), butter naan and pappadam. There's also an array of continental and Chinese fare and the lassis (Rs 25) are positively divine. There are fine fort views from this rooftop restaurant.

The Slow Food Restaurant (☎ 51637; open 8am-10.45pm daily) is a good restaurant on Hanuman Chowk serving up Rajasthani favourites such as *dahi sangri* (desert bean curry, Rs 45). Don't let the name deter you – the service is actually quite prompt and you can sit under the tented canopy or outside, where there's a fire in winter.

Fort Just east of the main square, **Little Tibet** (☎ 54243; open 9am-11pm daily) has a cosy dining area, friendly service and large servings. The menu is extensive with hearty soups (a serve of pumpkin and garlic soup costs Rs 30), a large plate of veg *momos* (Tibetan dumplings) for Rs 40 and good enchiladas for around Rs 50. It's often full so get there early or be prepared to wait.

Ristorante Italiano La Purezza (☎ 50566; open 9am-11pm), near the Desert Boys Guest House, serves excellent authentic pasta dishes for Rs 70 to 100 – if you've been travelling in Rajasthan for a while, you'll appreciate what a treat this is. The bruschetta is also good (Rs 15 to 30) and it does tiramisu (Rs 45), as well as espresso coffee and cappucino! It's a brilliant place to watch the sunset. The service is also good.

8th July Restaurant *(☎ 52814; open 7am-10pm daily)*, above the main square in the fort, is certainly centrally located, however the food and service are variable. The menu largely caters to Western tastes and is purely vegetarian. Vegemite-deprived Aussies can get the black wonder-spread here (Rs 35 for three slices of toast). Other menu items include veg cheese pizza (Rs 45), *palak paneer* (Rs 45) and apple pie (Rs 45). Average filtered coffee is Rs 25/50 for a cup/pot.

Refreshing Point Rooftop Restaurant *(☎ 54519; open 7.30am-11pm daily)*, nearby, is a good place to watch the passing human and bovine traffic in the main square. The menu offers Indian, continental, Italian, Mexican, Tibetan, Chinese and even Greek cuisine. Moussaka is Rs 50 and enchiladas with rice and salad are Rs 55. It also serves hearty breakfasts. On the premises is a small German bakery that's only open during the high season.

Vyas Meal Service *(☎ 51264; open 10am-10pm daily; thalis Rs 50-200)*, near the Jain temples, is a brilliant place to eat homemade food. This small, family-run veg restaurant offers traditional cuisine from Jaisalmer. It does wholesome thalis and also brews a jolly good *masala* (spice) tea. You can buy a packet of this tea for Rs 60 (makes 40 cups).

Bhang Shop *(open 9am-10pm daily)*, outside the First Fort Gate, not far from Sahara Travels, is a government-authorised *bhang* (derivative of marijuana) shop! A medium/strong *bhang* lassi or tea is Rs 35/40, fruit juice with *bhang* is Rs 40/45. *Bhang* cookies, cakes and candy can be baked with advance notice and the shop specialises in packing supplies for camel safaris. *Bhang* does not agree with everyone – see the boxed text 'Beware of Those *Bhang* Lassis!' under Drinks in the Facts for the Visitor chapter.

Shopping

Jaisalmer is famous for its embroidery, Rajasthani mirrorwork, rugs, blankets, antiques

and old stonework. Watch out for silver items as the metal may sometimes be adulterated with bronze.

Tie-dye and other fabrics are made at the **Khadi Gramodyog Bhavan (Seemagram)** *(Dhibba Para)*, not far from the fort. There's a **Rajasthali** *(☎ 52461; open 9.30am-8.30pm Mon-Sat)* handicraft emporium just outside Amar Sagar Gate, which sells all sorts of products, from embroidered cushion covers to wooden ornaments. It's a government-run fixed-price emporium, and you can get a good idea of prices here. In the high season there's a smaller branch on Gandhi Chowk.

On the laneway leading up to the Jain temples within the fort, is an enthralling little shop, **Light of the East**, which sells crystals and rare mineral specimens, including zeolite, which can fetch up to Rs 5000 depending on the quality. Ask the owner to show you the amazing apophyllite piece which is carefully hidden away in a box. Don't set your heart on it – unfortunately, it's not for sale.

Getting There & Away

Air The airport is only open during the high season, from 1 October to 31 March, although at the time of writing it was closed year-round due to the tensions with Pakistan. **Crown Tours** *(☎ 51912; Sam Rd; open 9.30am-5.30pm daily)*, opposite the Collectorate, is the agent for Indian Airlines. There are three weekly flights between Jaisalmer and Jodhpur (US$80), Jaipur (US$135), Udaipur (US$110), Mumbai (US$205) and Delhi (US$165).

Bus Located near the train station, the main **Roadways bus stand** *(☎ 51541)* is some distance from the centre of town. Fortunately, all buses start from a bus depot just behind the Hotel Neeraj, which is more conveniently located.

There are frequent buses going to Jodhpur (Rs 92/109 for express/deluxe, 5 hours). There is one daily deluxe bus which runs direct to Jaipur (Rs 239, 12 hours) and several daily direct express buses which run to Bikaner (Rs 113, 6 hours). Express buses for Barmer leave every hour (Rs 62, 3 hours).

You can book luxury buses through most of the travel agencies. Quoted rates at the time of research were:

destination	fare (Rs)	duration (hrs)
Ajmer	150	12
Bikaner	100	6
Delhi	250	20
Jaipur	170	11
Jodhpur	80	5
Mt Abu	190	12
Udaipur	170	10

The trip to Udaipur sometimes requires a change of bus at Jodhpur. Others may also require a change en route, so check when making your booking.

Train The reservation office at the train station is open 8am to 8pm Monday to Saturday, 8am to 2pm on Sunday.

The passenger train *1JPJ* leaves Jaisalmer daily at 7.15am, arriving in Jodhpur at 2.15pm (Rs 44 in 2nd-class seat). The *Jodhpur Express* leaves Jaisalmer at 11pm and arrives in Jodhpur at 4.30am (Rs 74/142/379 in 2nd-class seat/2nd-class sleeper/three-tier air-con). From Jodhpur you can get train connections to other destinations (see Getting There & Away under Jodhpur, earlier).

Jeep It's possible to hire jeeps from the stand outside the Amar Sagar Gate. To Khuri or the Sam sand dunes expect to pay Rs 400 return with a one-hour wait. For Lodhruva, you'll pay Rs 200 return with a one-hour stop. A full day of sightseeing of the sights around Jaisalmer will cost around Rs 1000. To cut the cost, find other people to share with (maximum of six people per jeep).

Getting Around
Autorickshaw Jaisalmer's rickshaw drivers can be rapacious, so bargain hard. An autorickshaw to Gadi Sagar costs about Rs 15 one way from the fort entrance. From the fort to the airport it costs around Rs 50 (a taxi will cost Rs 100).

Bicycle A good way to get around is by bicycle. There are a number of hire places,

including **Narayan Cycle Service** (*Gandhi Chowk; open 8am-9pm*), which charges Rs 4/25 per hour/day. With 30 minutes' notice motorcycle hire can also be organised for Rs 100/400 per hour/day.

AROUND JAISALMER
There are fascinating places to see around Jaisalmer, although the landscape soon fades into a barren sand-dune desert stretching across the lonely border into Pakistan.

Due to the alleged arms smuggling across that border, most of Rajasthan west of National Hwy No 15 is a restricted area. Special permission is required from the **district magistrate** (☎ 02992-52201) in Jaisalmer to go there, and is usually only issued in exceptional circumstances. Places exempted are Amar Sagar, Bada Bagh, Lodhruva, Kuldhara, Akal, Sam, Ramkund, Khuri and Mool Sagar.

Bada Bagh
About 7km north of Jaisalmer, Bada Bagh is a fertile oasis with a huge old dam. It was built by Maharaja Jai Singh II and completed after his death by his son.

Above the gardens (currently closed to visitors) are picturesque royal *chhatris* (*admission Rs 10*) with beautifully carved ceilings and equestrian statues of former rulers. Bada Bagh is now surrounded by windmills used to generate electricity.

Amar Sagar
This once pleasant formal garden, 7km northwest of Jaisalmer, has now fallen into ruin. The lake here dries up several months into the dry season. According to locals, the step-wells here were built by prostitutes.

Nearby is a finely carved Jain temple (*foreigner/citizen Rs 10/free, camera/video Rs 50/100*; open 8am-7.30pm daily) that is well worth a look. Restoration commenced in the 1970s with craftspeople brought from Agra in Uttar Pradesh.

Lodhruva
Further out beyond Amar Sagar, 15km northwest of Jaisalmer, are the deserted ruins of Lodhruva, which was the ancient

Camel Safaris Around Jaisalmer

Exploring the desert around Jaisalmer by camel safari is undoubtedly the most evocative way to sample desert life. If you follow a few simple precautions before setting out, you might just find it a highlight of your time in India. October to February is the best time.

Before Setting Out

Competition between safari organisers is cut-throat and standards vary considerably. None of the hotels have their own camels – these are all independently owned – so most of the hoteliers and travel agencies are just go-betweens.

Hotel owners typically pay the camel drivers around Rs 150 per camel per day to hire them, so if you're offered a safari at Rs 200 or even Rs 250 per day, this leaves only a small margin for food and the agent's profit. It's obvious that you can't possibly expect three reasonable meals a day on these margins, but this is frequently what is promised. A lot of travellers feel ripped off when the food isn't what was offered. Beware of operators who claim to offer (and charge for) three-day safaris when in actual fact you return after breakfast on the third day – hardly value for money.

Another precaution suggested by the tourist office is to ask your booking agent for the camel or jeep driver's identity card and note down the registration number (written in red). If they can't produce one, you may want to look elsewhere.

The realistic minimum price for a basic safari is about Rs 400 per person per day. For this you can expect a breakfast of porridge, tea and toast, and a lunch and dinner of rice, daal and chappatis – pretty unexciting stuff. Blankets are also supplied. You must sometimes bring your own mineral water. Of course you can pay more for greater levels of comfort – tents, stretcher beds, better food, beer etc.

However much you decide to spend, make sure you know exactly what is being provided and make sure it's there before you leave Jaisalmer. Ensure you know where you're going to be taken. Attempting to get a refund for services not provided is a waste of time. Take care of possessions, particularly on the return journey. A recent scam involves the drivers suggesting that you walk to some nearby ruins while they stay with the camels and keep an eye on your bags. The police station in Jaisalmer receives numerous reports of items missing from luggage but seems unwilling to help. Nonetheless, any complaints you do have should be reported, either to the **superintendent of police** (☎ 52233) or to the **Tourist Reception Centre** (☎ 52406).

If you're on your own it's worth getting a group of at least four people together before looking for a safari. Organisers will make up groups, but four days is a long time to spend with people you might not get on with. Usually each person is assigned their own camel, but check this as some agencies might try to save money by hiring fewer camels, meaning you'll find yourself sharing your camel with a camel driver or cook, which is not nearly as much fun.

What to Take

Take something comfortable to sit on – many travellers fail to do this and come back with very sore legs or backsides or both! Women should consider wearing a sports bra, as the trotting momentum of the camels can cause some discomfort after even just a few hours. A wide-brimmed hat (or Rajput-style turban), long trousers, toilet paper, sunscreen cream and a personal water bottle (with a strap so you can secure it easily) are also recommended. It can get very cold at night, so if you have a sleeping bag take it along even if you're told that lots of blankets will be supplied.

Safari Agents

There are several independent camel-safari agents (not linked to any hotels). **Sahara Travels** (☎ 52609; c sahara_travels@yahoo.com), by the First Fort Gate, is run by Mr Bissa, alias Mr Desert

Camel Safaris Around Jaisalmer

or India's Marlboro Man – the rugged model in the Jaisalmer cigarette ads. He's been getting good reports from travellers for years and charges Rs 450 per day for two to four days. **Ganesh Travels** (☎ 50138; e *ganeshtravel45@hotmail.com*), inside the fort, is wholly owned by former and current camel drivers, although it gets mixed reviews from travellers. Standard tours cost Rs 400 a day for two to four days (you get your own camel).

Remember that no place is perfect and recommendations here ought not be a substitute for doing your own research to see what suits your particular needs and budget. The Tourist Reception Centre can recommend an operator, based on your requirements. In the past, Lonely Planet has recommended **Satyam Tours** (☎ 50773; e *ummedsatyam@yahoo.co.in*) and **Thar Safari** (☎/fax 54296, fax 52722; e *tharsafari@hotmail.com*), both on Gandhi Chowk. These still get overwhelmingly positive reports, although not everyone has found that their safari lived up to expectations. **KK Travels** and **Adventure Travel Agency**, near the fort gate, have also been recommended. Of the hotels, Hotel Renuka runs good safaris and Hotel Paradise offers 'happy camels', a claim we were unable to verify.

Whoever you book your safari through, make sure that you insist that all rubbish is carried back to Jaisalmer, and not left at the Sam sand dunes or in remote villages where the wind will carry it across the desert.

Out on the Trail

The desert is surprisingly well populated and sprinkled with ruins. You often come across tiny fields of millet, girls picking berries or boys herding flocks of sheep or goats. The flocks are usually fitted with tinkling neck bells and, in the desert silence, it's music to the ears. Unfortunately the same cannot be said for the noises emitted by the notoriously flatulent camels!

Camping out at night, huddling around a tiny fire beneath the stars and listening to the camel drivers' yarns can be quite romantic. The camel drivers will expect a tip or gift at the end of the trip. Don't neglect to give one.

The reins are fastened to the camel's nose peg, so the animals are easily steered. At resting points, the camels are completely unsaddled and hobbled. They limp away to browse on nearby shrubs while the camel drivers brew sweet *chai* or prepare food. The whole crew rests in the shade of thorn trees by a tank or well.

Most safaris last three to four days, and if you want to get to the most interesting places, this is a bare minimum unless a significant jeep component is included. The usual circuit takes in such places as Amar Sagar, Lodhruva, Mool Sagar, Bada Bagh and Sam, as well as various abandoned villages along the way. It's not possible to ride by camel to the Sam sand dunes in one day; in 1½ days you could get a jeep to Sam, stay there overnight, and take a camel from there to either Kuldahra (then a jeep back to Jaisalmer) or Kanoi (and catch a jeep from there to Jaisalmer). If you're really pressed for time, you could opt for a half-day camel safari (which involves jeep transfers).

In 2½ days you could travel by camel to Lodhruva, spend the second night at the Sam sand dunes, and return the following day to Jaisalmer by jeep. If you have more time, obviously you can travel at a more leisurely pace through these regions and forgo the jeep component.

With the amount of tourist traffic in the desert around Jaisalmer these days (until recently), some adventurous travellers opt to head off the beaten track altogether. It's possible to travel overland by camel to destinations such as Pokaran (one week), Barmer (one week), Bikaner (three weeks) and Pushkar (four weeks). Camels can travel around 15km to 20km per day and you must pay for the number of days it takes to reach your chosen destination, and then half as many again to enable to camels to get back to Jaisalmer.

capital before the move to Jaisalmer. It was probably founded by the Lodra Rajputs, and passed to the ruler of Devagarh, Bhatti Devaraja, in the 10th century. In 1025, Mahmud of Ghazni laid siege to the town, and it was sacked various times over subsequent decades, prompting Jaisala to shift the capital to a new location, resulting in the foundation of Jaisalmer in 1156.

The **Jain temples** *(foreigner/citizen Rs 10/ free, camera/video Rs 50/100; open 6.30am-7.30pm daily)*, rebuilt in the late 1970s, are the only reminders of the city's former magnificence. The main temple enshrines an image of Parasnath, the 23rd *tirthankar*, and is finely wrought in silver and surrounded by fine sculptures.

The ornate rosette in the centre of the drum of the dome over the *mandapa* was carved from a single piece of stone, and before the temple is a beautiful *torana*. The small sculptures around the lower course of the inner sanctum are badly damaged, and still bear the scars of Muslim raids. Behind the inner sanctum is a 200-year-old carved Jaisalmer stone slab which bears carvings of the *tirthankars'* feet in miniature.

The temple has its own resident cobra, which is said to be 1.5m long and over 400 years old. It lives in a hole on the north side of the main temple. It's supposed to be very auspicious to see the cobra, but probably as close as you'll get to one is viewing the photograph of it, which is separately housed inside the temple. The small temple to the right is dedicated to Adinath, the first *tirthankar*.

There is nowhere to stay in Lodhruva – the *dharamsala* (pilgrims' lodging) beside the temple is for Jains only. Three daily buses go from Jaisalmer to Lodhruva (Rs 5).

Mool Sagar

Situated 9km west of Jaisalmer, this is another pleasant, but rather neglected, small garden and tank *(admission Rs 5; open 8am-7pm daily)*. It belongs to the royal family of Jaisalmer and was originally built as a cool summer retreat. In the lemon grove there's a small Shiva temple carved from two pieces of sandstone.

Kuldhara

This small village *(admission Rs 10; open 8am-6pm daily)* is located 25km west of Jaisalmer. Around 400 years ago, all the inhabitants of the 84 villages in the area left after a dispute with the prime minister. However, according to legend, they couldn't carry all their gold and silver, so they buried it. Several years ago some Westerners arrived at Kuldhara on motorcycles armed with gold detectors and found hundreds of gold and silver coins. However, local villagers became suspicious and called the police, and the treasure hunters were apprehended and divested of their booty! Kuldhara is included on some of the extended camel treks. It costs Rs 50 to bring in a car or a jeep, or you can cover the 500m from the gate on foot. Restoration work is being done here.

Desert National Park & Sanctuary

This national park lies 42km to the southwest of Jaisalmer, and was established in 1980 in order to preserve the fragile desert ecosystem and thus protect the range of drought-resistant species that inhabit it, including the critically endangered Indian bustard *(Choriotis niergceps)*, known locally as godawan. It encompasses an area of 3162 sq km, an arid zone of sand dunes, thorn forest, scrub and sandy wastelands between Jaisalmer and Barmer, including the areas around Sam and Khuri.

The park should be avoided during the summer months, when temperatures soar to over 50°C. You need to bring a good supply of drinking water at any time. For more information contact the Desert National Park's **deputy director** (☎ 02992-52489) in Jaisalmer.

Sam Sand Dunes

Sam village *(admission Rs 3)* is on the edge of the Desert National Park. One of the most popular excursions is to the sand dunes on the edge of the park, 42km from Jaisalmer along a very good sealed road (maintained by the Indian army). The vehicle admission fee is Rs 5, and the camel admission fee is Rs 70.

This is Jaisalmer's nearest real Sahara-like desert. It's best to be here at sunrise or sunset, and many camel safaris spend a night at the dunes. Just before sunset jeep loads of day-trippers arrive from Jaisalmer to be chased across the sands by tenacious camel owners offering short rides and young boys selling soft drinks. Yes, this place has become a massive tourist attraction, so don't set your heart on a solitary desert sunset experience. The hordes of people here at sunset lend the place something of a carnival atmosphere. If you want a less touristy sand dunes experience, Khuri is a much more peaceful and pristine alternative (see following).

Despite the tourist hype, it is still quite a magical place, and it's possible to frame pictures of solitary camels against lonely dunes. The desert dung beetles are fascinating to watch. These industrious little creatures can roll lumps of dung twice their size. It's a heartbreaking sight to see a beetle lose control of a piece of dung it has rolled halfway up a sand dune.

One tragic consequence of the increasing number of visitors to the dunes is the debris and rubbish lying at their base. Visitors are now charged a fee to visit the dunes, money which could be put to good use to clean them up, but is more likely lining the pocket of some local official. If you feel strongly about the rubbish here, a letter to the **Chief Tourism Officer** (RTDC Tourism, Swagatam Campus, near train station, Jaipur 302006, Rajasthan) might have some effect. For further information, contact the Desert National Park's **deputy director** (☎ 02992-52489) in Jaisalmer.

Places to Stay & Eat There are a few places to stay at while visiting the dunes. However most travellers prefer to visit the dunes on a day trip from Jaisalmer or as part of a camel safari.

RTDC Hotel Sam Dhani (dorm beds Rs 50, doubles with private bathroom Rs 300) has eight good rooms and dorm beds. There is currently no power, but lanterns are provided. Veg meals are available. It's a good idea to book ahead, through RTDC Hotel

Moomal (☎ 02992-52392) in Jaisalmer, as the manager is not always around.

Dune Safari Camp (☎ 02992-54463, Delhi office ☎ 011-686 6167, fax 652 97562; e dunesafari@vsnl.net; doubles Rs 2500) has comfortable tents with bathrooms; currently hot water is supplied by the bucket but showers are planned. Prices include breakfast and dinner and camel safaris can be arranged; it costs Rs 1000 for a full-day safari, including lunch. Nonguests can dine here; the set veg/nonveg lunch or dinner is Rs 500/800.

There are a few other restaurants and tea shops at the dunes.

Getting There & Away There are three daily buses to Sam from Jaisalmer (Rs 15, 45 minutes).

Khuri

Khuri is a small village 40km southwest of Jaisalmer, with its own desert sand dunes about 2km from the town. It has far less tourist hype (at least for now) than the Sam sand dunes, and is becoming increasingly popular for camel/jeep safaris. It's a peaceful place with houses of mud and straw decorated like the patterns on Persian carpets. There are, thankfully, no craftshop-lined streets or banana pancake restaurants. The attraction out here is the desert solitude and the brilliant star-studded sky at night.

Places to Stay & Eat Places to stay in Khuri are pretty basic, and have charpoys and bucket hot water. All provide meals and most can arrange camel safaris. Accommodation is limited and you won't find any bargains; basically you're paying for the peace and quiet rather than the facilities, which are minimal.

Khuri Guest House (☎ 03104-74044; doubles with shared bathroom Rs 100, hut doubles with private/shared bathroom Rs 150/100) is on the left of the main road as you enter the village. It's run by a friendly fellow and has conventional rooms or huts. Camel safaris are Rs 300 per person per day. Meals and sunset camel trips to the dunes are available.

WESTERN RAJASTHAN

Mama's Guest House (*☎ 03014-74023; huts in high season Rs 150/200, rooms around Rs 150*) is actually several clusters of thatched huts. The cheapest huts are set in a semicircle around a campfire, or you can pay a little more and take a hut that's better thatched (so will be cooler) in a cluster with a greater number of shared bathrooms. It's also possible to stay in a very basic conventional room with shared bathroom (but not nearly so romantic!). Camel safaris in the region start at Rs 350 per day. Good food is available and there's a relaxing common dining area.

Gangaur Guest House (*☎ 03014-74056, fax 52453; e hameersingh@yahoo.com; huts Rs 500*) has cosy huts. Rates include all meals and a sunset trip to the sand dunes.

Getting There & Away Several buses go daily to Khuri (Rs 20, 1 hour).

Akal Wood Fossil Park

One kilometre off the road to Barmer, 17km from Jaisalmer, are the fossilised remains of a 180-million-year-old forest (*foreigner/citizen Rs 20/5, plus Rs 10 per vehicle; open 8am-1pm & 2pm-5pm daily*). To the untrained eye it's not very interesting, but there are beautiful desert vistas. One of the foresters will show you around.

BARMER

☎ 02982 • postcode 344001 • pop 83,517

Barmer is famous for its woodcarving, carpets, embroidery, block printing and other crafts – handicrafts produced here are found in shops throughout Rajasthan. The centre for embroidery is Sadar Bazaar; crafts are for sale on Station Rd at more reasonable prices than elsewhere. Otherwise this desert town, 153km south of Jaisalmer, isn't very interesting, and few travellers make the trek out here. There's no fortress and perhaps the best part is the journey here through peaceful, small villages, their mud-walled houses decorated with geometric designs.

Places to Stay & Eat

RTDC Hotel Khartal (*☎ 22956; singles/doubles with private bathroom Rs 300/400*),

out of the town centre, is nothing flash but it has adequate rooms. Meals are available.

Hotel Krishna (*☎ 20785, fax 24326; Station Rd; singles/doubles with shared bathroom Rs 100/175, singles/doubles with private bathroom from Rs 150/300, doubles with air-con Rs 550*) has small, clean rooms. Hot water is by the bucket.

Kailash Sarover Hotel (*☎ 20730, fax 20141; Station Rd; singles/doubles with shared bathroom from Rs 200/250, with private bathroom Rs 225/375, with air-con Rs 500/700*), further away from the station and on the opposite side of Station Rd, offers rather overpriced rooms. Veg food is also available here. This place is not quite as impressive as Hotel Krishna.

Raj Restaurant (*Station Rd; open 7am-midnight daily*), between the train station and Hotel Krishna, has vegetarian dishes at reasonable prices.

Getting There & Away

There are several daily express buses to Jodhpur (Rs 84, 4 hours) from in front of the train station. To Jaisalmer, there are frequent daily express buses (Rs 62, 2½ hours). They leave from the main bus stand, which is about 1km north of the train station. The bus stops for a break at the small highway town of Shive, where there's a renowned *pakora* (vegetable fritter) maker.

There is a local train which goes to Luni (Rs 28), from where you can catch a connecting train to nearby Jodhpur. Barmer should soon be converted to broad gauge, enabling greater rail connections.

AROUND BARMER

About 35km from Barmer, the **Kiradu Temples** feature some very fine sculpture. These five temples conform to a style of architecture known as Solanki, and the most impressive is **Someshvara Temple**, which has a multi-turreted spire and beautiful sculpture. However, it's located in the sensitive border region near Pakistan, so you'll first need to contact the **district magistrate** (*☎ 02992-20003*) who will obtain the necessary permission for you to visit, from the superintendent of police.

BIKANER
☎ 0151 • postcode 334001 • pop 529,007

Bikaner holds a secondary rank amongst the principalities of Rajputana. It is an offset of Marwar, its princes being scions of the house of Jodha, who established themselves by conquest on the northern frontier of the parent state; and its position in the heart of the desert, has contributed to the maintenance of their independence.

Colonel James Tod, *Annals & Antiquities of Rajasthan*

This desert town in the north was founded in 1488 by Rao Bika, a descendant of Jodha, the founder of Jodhpur. Like many in Rajasthan, the old city is surrounded by a high crenellated wall and, like Jaisalmer, it was once an important staging post on the great caravan trade routes. The Ganga Canal, built between 1925 and 1927, irrigates a large area of previously arid land around Bikaner.

As the tourist hype in Jaisalmer heightens, Bikaner is becoming increasingly appealing to travellers. It's easy to see why – Bikaner has a brilliant fort and offers camel safaris (see Organised Tours later), and 30km to the south is the extraordinary Karni Mata Temple in Deshnok, where thousands of holy rats are worshipped. The town is also known for its traditional fire dances, performed by members of a religious sect called the Jas Naths, which can be seen at festival time (see the boxed text 'Festivals of Western Rajasthan' earlier in this chapter).

Orientation
The old city is encircled by a 7km-long city wall with five entrance gates, constructed in the 18th century. The fort and palace, built of the same reddish-pink sandstone as Jaipur's famous buildings, are outside the city walls.

Information
Tourist Offices The **Tourist Reception Centre** (☎ *544125; open 10am-5pm Mon-Fri & every 2nd Sat*), is near Pooran Singh Circle,

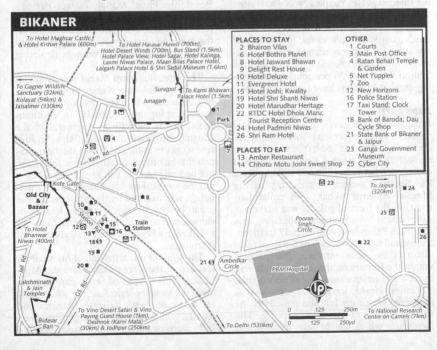

BIKANER

To Hotel Meghsar Castle & Hotel Kishan Palace (600m)
To Hotel Harasar Haveli (700m),
Hotel Desert Winds (700m), Bus Stand (1.5km),
Hotel Palace View, Hotel Sagar, Hotel Kalinga,
Laxmi Niwas Palace, Maan Bilas Palace Hotel,
Lalgarh Palace Hotel & Shri Sadul Museum (1.6km)

To Gagner Wildlife Sanctuary (32km), Kolayat (54km) & Jaisalmer (330km)

Surajpol   To Karni Bhawan Palace Hotel (1.5km)
Junagarh
Park

Kem Rd.

Kote Gate

Old City & Bazaar

To Hotel Bhanwar Niwas (400m)

Lakshminath & Jain Temples

Station Rd.
Train Station

Jail Rd.

GS Rd.

Bidasar Bari

To Vino Desert Safari & Vino Paying Guest House (1km), Deshnok (Karni Mata) (30km) & Jodhpur (250km)

To Delhi (530km)

Pooran Singh Circle

Ambedkar Circle

PBM Hospital

To Jaipur (320km)

To National Research Centre on Camels (7km)

0   125   250m
0   125   250yd

PLACES TO STAY
2 Bhairon Vilas
6 Hotel Bothra Planet
8 Hotel Jaswant Bhawan
9 Delight Rest House
10 Hotel Deluxe
12 Evergreen Hotel
15 Hotel Joshi; Kwality
19 Hotel Shri Shanti Niwas
20 Hotel Marudhar Heritage
22 RTDC Hotel Dhola Maru;
   Tourist Reception Centre
24 Hotel Padmini Niwas
26 Shri Ram Hotel

PLACES TO EAT
13 Amber Restaurant
14 Chhotu Motu Joshi Sweet Shop

OTHER
1 Courts
3 Main Post Office
4 Ratan Behari Temple
   & Garden
5 Net Yuppies
7 Zoo
12 New Horizons
16 Police Station
17 Taxi Stand; Clock
   Tower
18 Bank of Baroda; Dau
   Cycle Shop
21 State Bank of Bikaner
   & Jaipur
23 Ganga Government
   Museum
25 Cyber City

in the RTDC Hotel Dhola Maru compound, about 1km from the city centre. It has various brochures (including a good map of Bikaner for Rs 2) and a toilet that can be used by tourists.

Money You can change US dollars and pound sterling (cash and travellers cheques) at the **State Bank of Bikaner & Jaipur** *(open noon-4 pm Mon-Fri)* and at its branch near Junagarh *(open 10am-2pm Mon-Fri)*. The **Bank of Baroda** *(open 10am-3pm Mon-Fri, 10am-12.30pm Sat)*, opposite the train station on the first floor, changes travellers cheques only. At the time of writing, no banks in Bikaner issued cash advances on credit cards.

Post The **main post office** *(open 10am-1pm & 2pm-3pm Mon-Fri, 10am-1pm Sat)* is near Junagarh.

Email & Internet Access You can access the Internet at **Net Yuppies** *(☎ 204801; open 9.30am-11pm)*, off Kem Rd, for Rs 20 per hour; at **Cyber City** *(☎ 529078; A49 Sadul Ganj; open 9am-10pm daily)*, in the east of town, for Rs 50 per hour; and at **New Horizons** *(Biscuit Gali; open 9am-10pm daily)*, off Station Rd, for Rs 30 per hour. An increasing number of hotels have Internet access.

Junagarh

Junagarh would have to be one of Rajasthan's most impressive fort complexes *(foreigner/citizen Rs 50/10, camera/video Rs 30/100; open 10am-4.30pm daily)*. It was constructed between 1588 and 1593 by Raja Rai Singh, a general in the army of the Mughal emperor Akbar, with embellishments in the form of palaces and luxurious suites added by subsequent maharajas. This fort has a 986m-long wall with 37 bastions, a moat and two entrances. The **Surajpol** (Sun Gate) is the main entrance. The palaces within the fort are on the southern side and make a picturesque ensemble of courtyards, balconies, kiosks, towers and windows. A major feature of the fort and palaces is the superb quality of the stone carving. The handprints which can be seen close to the

Daulatpol commemorate the wives of Rajput soldiers lost in battles, who committed *sati* on their husbands' funeral pyres.

Despite the fact that Junagarh doesn't command a hilltop position, as do some of Rajasthan's other grand forts, it is no less imposing and – a credit to its planners and architects – has never been conquered.

You may be besieged by 'guides' offering their services before you arrive at the ticket counter. Unless you want an individual tour, this is unnecessary, as the ticket price includes a tour with a group and official guide. Tours leave every 15 to 20 minutes and take one hour.

The gold-painted ceiling of the beautiful **Diwan-i-Khas** (Hall of Private Audience) was executed in 1631, and the silver *gaddi* (throne) of the maharajas can still be seen here. There is a fine courtyard paved with Italian tiles. Through the fine lattice screens around the courtyard, the women of the *zenana* could watch the activities below. Beside the **Phool Mahal** (Flower Palace), which was built during the reign of Maharaja Gaj Singh, is a marble statue of Surya, the sun god, and around the upper edges of the walls there are paintings depicting Hindu gods.

The beautiful **Anup Mahal** was commissioned by Maharaja Karan Singh (1631–69). According to local lore, the maharaja was camping at Golkonda, in southern India, in his capacity as a general in the Mughal army, when an artist showed him fine works in gold. The artist told the maharaja that he originally hailed from Jaisalmer, but had migrated to southern India when a famine swept over his homeland. The maharaja was inspired by the proficiency and great beauty of the work he had been shown, and so he invited the artist to return to Bikaner where the artist was given royal patronage.

The work of this artist and of his students features in the Karan Mahal and the Anup Mahal. Three types of work can be seen here: the *sonakin* style features white plaster decorated with delicate patterns and painted with gold leaf; the *jangali sunthari* style features plaster with a green backing that depicts floral motifs; and the *manovat* style features a pillar of clay which is embossed on plaster, the entire work painted with gold leaf.

In the **Badal Mahal** (Cloud Palace), the walls are painted with blue cloud motifs and there is a statue here of Vishnu and Laxmi. The large pillars beside the Karan Mahal were installed with the aid of elephants nearly 400 years ago.

The **Gaj Mandir** was the private chambers of Maharaja Gaj Singh. The maharani's chamber is decorated with mirror tiles and gold painting, and on the ceiling there is wooden lac painting. The maharaja's chamber has a beautiful painted wood ceiling featuring florets and geometric motifs, and carved ivory doors.

In the **Hawa Mahal** (Summer Palace), there is an ingenious device said to have alerted the maharaja to potential enemies: a mirror positioned over the bed enabled Maharaja Dunga Singh to see the reflections of people walking across the courtyard below – or at least this is the purpose of the mirror according to the official fort guides! The ceiling features floral arabesques and scenes of Krishna dancing. The blue tiles inside were imported from both Europe and China.

There's an interesting museum exhibition (included in the ticket price) housed in several of the newer rooms of the palace. In the armoury are enormous bore guns which were used for shooting from the backs of camels, as well as the usual collection of sinister-looking pistols and swords.

In the Diwan-i-Khas of Ganga Singh there are three massive, intricately carved arches and a throne of sandalwood. Here also can be seen a 56kg suit of armour, including chain mail, and sculptures of Krishna dancing and stealing the clothes of the *gopis*. Beautiful if deadly weapons, each an exquisite work of art – swords with ivory and crystal handles, some in the shape of lions – can also be seen here. In a separate chamber are the royal vestments of Maharaja Ganga Singh, as well as items from his office including a paper weight and his briefcase. There's also an old biplane which was presented to Ganga Singh by the British government during WWI. This is one of only two models of this kind of plane in the world.

Prachina Cultural Centre & Museum

There's a museum (☎ 525609; foreigner/ citizen Rs 25/10, camera/video Rs 10/75; open 9am-6pm daily) across the main courtyard from Surajpol. It focuses on the Western influence on the Bikaner royals prior to Independence, including crockery from England and France and menu cards from 1936. There's also an excellent display of Rajasthani textiles and clothing, handicrafts, and items from everyday life.

There's a small shop and café at the museum and a reference library containing a small collection of books on Rajasthan, which is open to the public.

Jain Temples

Two Jain temples can be found just inside the walled city. **Bhandasar Jain Temple** (admission free; open 6am-7pm daily) is dedicated to the fifth *tirthankar*, Sumtinath, and the building was commissioned in 1468 by a wealthy Jain merchant, Bhandasa Oswal. It was completed after his death, in 1514.

The interior of the temple is stunning, with, unusually for a Jain temple, a series of vibrant paintings. The pillars bear floral arabesques and stories that depict the lives of the 24 Jain *tirthankars*. It is said that 40,000kg of ghee was used instead of water in the mortar, which locals insist seeps through the floor on hot days.

On the first floor of the three-storey temple are beautiful miniatures of the sentries of the gods. There are fine views out over the city from the third floor, with the desert stretching behind it to the west.

The second Jain temple here is **Sandesh-war Temple** (admission free, camera/video Rs 20/30; open 6am-noon & 6pm-7pm daily). It is smaller than Bhandasar Temple, and has good carving around the door architraves and columns, and ornately carved painted pillars. Inside the drum of the *sikhara* (spire) are almost ethereal paintings, and the sanctum itself has a marble image of Sandeshwar flanked by smaller marble statues of other Jain *tirthankars*.

Lakshminath Temple

Behind Bhandasar Temple, to the right, is the Hindu Lakshminath Temple. It was built during the reign of Rao Lunkaran between 1505 and 1526. Lakshminath was the patron god of the rulers of Bikaner, and during major religious festivals a royal procession led by the maharaja paid homage at the temple. The elaborate edifice was maintained with tributes received from five villages and several shops, which were granted to the temple by Maharaja Ganga Singh (1887–1943). Photography at this temple is not permitted.

Lalgarh Palace

This red sandstone palace, 3km north of the city centre, was built by Maharaja Ganga Singh in memory of his father, Maharaja Lal Singh. Although it's an imposing building with overhanging balconies and delicate latticework, it's not the most beautiful of Rajasthani royal residences.

The **Shri Sadul Museum** *(foreigner/citizen Rs 20/10; open 10am-5pm Mon-Sat)* covers the entire first floor of the palace. The museum was established in 1976 and there's a reasonable collection of artefacts and personal possessions of the Bikaner maharajas reflecting the privileged lifestyles of these rulers, including (empty!) wine and sherry bottles and a brass vessel known as a *tokna* used to collect revenue which was transported by camel to the Bikaner state treasury. There's even a funky old film projector made in New York in 1921. Other more pedestrian exhibits include Maharaja Karni Singh's golf tees, roller skates and typewriters. There is also a somewhat disturbing pictorial display of tiger carnage, including a shot of the five tigers shot in three minutes by Maharaja Ganga Singh in 1937.

In front of the palace is a carriage from the maharaja's royal train.

Ganga Government Museum

This interesting museum *(admission Rs 3, free Mon; open 10am-4.30pm Sat-Thur)* is on the Jaipur road. Exhibits include terracotta ware from the Gupta period, a range of Rajasthani traditional musical instruments, miniature wooden models of the Gajner and Lalgarh palaces and a miniature of the Royal Bikaner train with the roof folded back to reveal its comfortable amenities. There is a separate exhibition hall with antique carpets and royal vestments.

Other interesting exhibits include decrees issued by the Mughals to the maharajas of Bikaner, including one advising Rai Singh to proceed to Delhi 'without any delay and with utmost expedition and speed, travelling over as great a distance as possible during the day time as well as by night' as 'Emperor Akbar is dying'. It was issued by Crown Prince (who would shortly become Emperor) Jehangir.

There are also some fine oil paintings, including one entitled *Maharaja Padam Singh avenging…the death of his brother, Maharaja Mohan Singhji by killing the Emperor's brother-in-law…He drew his sword, rushed upon his enemy…and severed him in two with a blow which also left a mark upon the pillar*!

The sculptures include a beautiful and voluptuous image of Devi, and a marble Jain sculpture of Saraswati which dates from the 11th century.

Only still cameras (no videos) are permitted (no charge).

Organised Tours & Camel Safaris

The **Tourist Reception Centre** (see Information earlier) can arrange English-speaking guides (Rs 250 per day, with a maximum of four people).

If you wanted to take a camel safari in Jaisalmer but didn't because it was too much of a scene, Bikaner is an excellent alternative. One good operator is **Vino Desert Safari** (☎ 270445, fax 525150, W *www.vino desertsafari.com*), opposite Gopeshwar Temple. It's run by the helpful Vinod Bhojak. There are at least eight different camel treks available (they include trips to Khichan, home of the demoiselle cranes, and the rat temple at Deshnok), ranging from two to seven days' duration. Costs are from Rs 400 per person per day (minimum of six people and only for shorter treks) up to Rs 800. Vinod, who speaks English, French and German, has rooms available at Vino Paying Guest House (see Places to Stay – Budget) and can also pick you up from town for free. Other operators include **Thar Desert Safari** (☎ 521661, fax 522041, e thardesertsafari@ rediffmail.com), with safaris for Rs 400 per day (minimum two days) and **Rajasthan Safaris & Treks** (☎ 527072; w www.real bikaner.com/tourism/rajsafari; 138, Gandhi Nagar, near Narendra Bhawan), which offers more upmarket safaris.

Places to Stay
The Tourist Reception Centre at the RTDC Hotel Dhola Maru (☎ 544125) has a list of families registered with Bikaner's Paying Guest House Scheme. It costs from around Rs 150 to 400 per night.

Places to Stay – Budget
There are numerous budget options, many near the train station. Station Rd is an amazingly busy thoroughfare, so the noise level in any room fronting it can be diabolical so make sure you choose carefully. Many places in the rock-bottom bracket have Indian-style toilets.

Hotel Meghsar Castle (☎ 527315, fax 52 2041; e meghsarcastle@yahoo.com; 9 Gajner Rd; singles with private bathroom Rs 250-500, doubles with private bathroom Rs 300-600) is popular with travellers and has clean, spacious rooms. Meals are available in the pleasant courtyard; you can get a chicken curry for Rs 90.

Hotel Kishan Palace (☎ 527762, fax 522041; 8B Gajner Rd; singles/doubles from Rs 250/300, doubles with air-con Rs 650), next door, has spacious, comfortable rooms. On Sunday morning Mr Chander Prakash Singh does pressure-point liver healings from the hotel. Meals are available and there's free pick-up from the bus station.

Hotel Marudhar Heritage (☎ 522524, fax 523673; e hmheritage@rediffmail.com; singles Rs 250-900, doubles Rs 350-999) is a great with rooms to suit most budgets. It's a friendly place with nice views from the roof

and Internet access (Rs 60 per hour). Hot water is available only from 6am to 1pm.

Shri Ram Hotel (☎ 522651, fax 209181; e shriramhotel@yahoo.com; singles/doubles from Rs 150/200) is another excellent place. Located in a quiet area east of town, all rooms are spotless and most have satellite TV. There's a real family atmosphere.

Vino Paying Guest House (☎ 270445; e vino_desertsafari@yahoo.com; singles/doubles from Rs 80/125), south of town, is another homey place. If you enjoy the cooking, the operators run cooking classes (free for guests) and can also adorn you with henna painting.

Hotel Harasar Haveli (☎ 209891, fax 509160; e harasar_haveli@yahoo.com, singles/ doubles from Rs 150/200), near the Karni Singh Stadium, is excellent value, with clean, uncluttered rooms. It's almost worth staying in this lovely haveli for the rooftop area with its swing chairs and attractive restaurant. Camel safaris are available.

Hotel Desert Winds (☎ 542202; singles/ doubles with private bathroom Rs 150/ 200, with air-con Rs 400/550) is next door to Hotel Harasar Haveli. Meals are available and the owner, a retired deputy director of tourism with the RTDC, can give you plenty of information about the town.

Evergreen Hotel (☎ 542061; e evergreen hotel@yahoo.co.in; singles/doubles with shared bathroom Rs 80/125, singles/doubles/ triples with private bathroom Rs 125/175/ 200) is not a bad choice. Rooms are small and clean and have a TV. All rooms have hot water by the bucket (Rs 5). There's a restaurant downstairs, which serves veg Indian, Chinese and continental food. A veg biryani is Rs 35, cheese pizza is Rs 40, and an almond milk shake is Rs 20.

Hotel Deluxe (☎ 528127; singles/doubles from Rs 90/140), nearby, is not as good – travellers have complained about the lack of cleanliness. The cheaper rooms have hot water by the bucket for Rs 5. Veg meals are available.

Delight Rest House (☎ 542313, fax 209338; singles/doubles with shared bath-room Rs 65/90, with private bathroom Rs 75/ 100) is in the laneway behind the Hotel

Deluxe. It's a dingy flophouse that's cleaned occasionally – it's the place to go if you're short on rupees. Hot water is available in buckets for Rs 5.

Hotel Shri Shanti Niwas (☎ 521925; e shrishanti@vsnl.com; singles with private bathroom Rs 80-450, doubles with private bathroom Rs 165-600), on the road directly opposite the train station, has clean rooms aimed at the business traveller. No meals are served here.

RTDC Hotel Dhola Maru (☎ 529621, fax 522109; singles/doubles Rs 200/300, with air-cooling Rs 400/500, with air-con Rs 600/700) is near Pooran Singh Circle, about 1km from the centre of the city. There are bland rooms and a restaurant; a veg/nonveg thali is Rs 60/80.

Retiring rooms (dorm beds 12/24 hours Rs 30/35, rooms with private bathroom Rs 35/50) at the train station are reasonable, and you can get one for half a day.

Places to Stay – Mid-Range

Bhairon Vilas (☎/fax 544751, fax 529227; e hbhairon@rediffmail.com; singles/doubles with private bathroom from Rs 300/500; doubles with air-con Rs 800), near Junagarh, opposite the main post office, is the most funky place to stay in Bikaner and is managed by the equally funky Harshvardhan Singh. The rooms have loads of character and imaginative decor. Some of the cheaper ones are quite small, but still good. Meals are available (dishes around Rs 40) in the distinctive dining room, which is filled with old photos and paraphernalia. Camel safaris can also be arranged.

Hotel Palace View (☎ 543625, fax 522741; Lalgarh Palace Campus; singles/doubles from Rs 200/300, with air-con Rs 400/600) is the closest hotel to the palace. There are, as you would expect, views of the palace, and this is a peaceful and well-run place. Breakfast is Rs 100 and veg/nonveg lunch or dinner is Rs 150/175.

Hotel Sagar (☎ 520677, fax 201877; e hsagar@nda.vsnl.net.in; singles/doubles Rs 300/500, with air-con Rs 700/900) is a large salmon-pink building – the first place to the left of the driveway as you approach the palace. There are air-cooled rooms, or for the same price you can have a thatched hut. Air-con rooms are also available. A set lunch/dinner in the restaurant costs Rs 125/150.

Hotel Kalinga (☎ 209751; singles/doubles with private bathroom Rs 200/300, with air-con Rs 400/500), opposite the Hotel Sagar, is OK but not exceptional. Rooms are spartan but reasonable.

Hotel Padmini Niwas (☎ 522794, 148 Sadul Ganj; singles/doubles from Rs 400/450, with air-con Rs 550/750) has clean rooms and is a good place to stay. There's a restaurant and nice lawn area.

Hotel Joshi (☎ 527700, fax 521213; e hoteljoshi@rediffmail.com; Station Rd; singles/doubles with air-cooling Rs 350/450, with air-con Rs 600/700, best doubles Rs 745) is close to the train station. It's more salubrious than the budget flophouses further north. There's a veg restaurant, or a couple of good thali places across the road which all charge Rs 30.

Hotel Jaswant Bhawan (☎ 948848, fax 521834; e jashwant@sancharnet.net; Alakh Sagar Rd; singles/doubles from Rs 500/600, with air-con Rs 600/745) is a pleasant place to stay – handy for the train station without the noise of Station Rd. The rooms are attractive and you can use the excellent kitchen for self-catering.

Hotel Bothra Planet (☎ 544502, fax 54 4501; e bothraplanet@hotmail.com; singles/doubles Rs 650/800, with air-con Rs 900/1100), nearby, is modern and comfortable if a tad sterile. There's a restaurant here, some rooms have a bathtub, and major credit cards are accepted. It's on top of a shopping complex and you enter from round the back.

Places to Stay – Top End

Hotel Bhanwar Niwas (Rampuri Haveli; ☎ 201043, fax 200880; e bhanwarniwas@rediffmail.com; Rampuria St; singles/doubles Rs 1600/2000) is a very interesting place. It's in the old city near the kotwali (police station). Turn left at the Kote Gate, and take the first right at Lady Elgin School. The hotel is close to a community of kite makers, who can be seen practising their craft. It's a beautiful pink sandstone building, with rooms set around a courtyard. There are 26 atmospheric air-con rooms and each one is different. The set breakfast/ lunch/dinner is Rs 165/325/350. The haveli was completed in 1927 for Seth Bhanwarlal Rampura, heir to a textile and real-estate fortune. In the foyer is a stunning 1927 blue Buick with a silver horn in the shape of a dragon, and an immaculate 1942 Indian Ambassador.

Lalgarh Palace Hotel *(☎ 540201, fax 52 2253; e gm.bikaner@itchotels.co.in; singles/ doubles US$42/82)*, 3km north of the city centre, is set in its own pleasant grounds, and has well-appointed rooms. Ask for a VIP room, as they're all the same price. There's a resident masseur (Rs 150 for 30 minutes) and a consultation with the astrologer, including casting your horoscope, is Rs 600. Residents have exclusive use of the indoor swimming pool, billiard room and croquet facilities. The hotel can organise a three-hour camel safari for Rs 500 per person (minimum of four people).

Laxmi Niwas Palace *(☎ 202777, fax 52 5219; singles/doubles from Rs 2500/4500)*, beside the Lalgarh Palace Hotel, is in a beautifully restored part of the palace, with comfortable painted rooms. There's an evocative dining hall and a courtyard overlooked by the old *zenana*. Also on the grounds is the smaller **Maan Bilas Palace Hotel** *(☎ 524711, fax 547940; singles/doubles Rs 1250/1750)*, to the right of the main gate. It's a relaxed little place with just nine rooms and can be booked through the Karni Bhawan Palace Hotel.

Karni Bhawan Palace Hotel *(☎ 524701, fax 522408; e mgrgaj@gagner.hrhindia.com; Gandhi Colony; singles/doubles Rs 1999/3000, suites Rs 1999/5500)* is about 800m east of the Lalgarh Palace Hotel and was briefly the residence of Maharaja Karni Singh. Although it's a rather ugly building, it's homey and well run. Rooms are Art Deco style and suites are huge. There's a good restaurant; the buffet lunch or dinner is Rs 375. A visit to stunning Gajner Palace Hotel can be arranged (see Around Bikaner later).

Places to Eat

Bikaner is noted for the *bhujiya*, which is a special kind of *namkeen* (spicy snack) sold in the shops along Station Rd, among other places.

Amber Restaurant *(☎ 201122; open 7am-10pm daily; dishes under Rs 60)* is opposite Hotel Joshi and is popular for its vegetarian food. There are some continental creations such as baked macaroni (Rs 55). South Indian snacks are also available and there is a variety of Indian sweets including delicious *gulab jamuns* (deep-fried balls of dough soaked in a rose-flavoured syrup) for Rs 18.

Hotel Bhanwar Niwas *(see Places to Stay; set breakfast/lunch/dinner Rs 165/325/350)* welcomes nonguests to its vegetarian dining hall (advance notice is essential). You can have a drink before dinner in the courtyard.

Lalgarh Palace Hotel *(see Places to Stay)* is open to nonguests. Curries range from Rs 65 to 200, or you may just prefer to sip on a beer (Rs 150 a bottle) in the bar, with stuffed beasts peering down at you. Snacks, such as vegetable *pakoras* (Rs 75), are available.

Chhotu Motu Joshi Sweet Shop *(Station Rd; open 6am-6.30pm daily)* is the town's most loved Indian sweet shop. It is a very busy place, selling a range of sweets including the milk-based *rasmalai* (Rs 12) and *kesar cham cham* (Rs 10 for three); the latter is a sausage-shaped sticky confection of milk, sugar and saffron which, when bitten, oozes a sweet sugar syrup. Fresh samosas are available out the front in the mornings and *bhujiya* is available for Rs 5 per plate.

Shopping

The Urmul Trust is planning to relocate its shop, **Abhivyakti**, to the trust's campus in Lunkaransar, near the bus stand, although at the time of writing it was temporarily located at the National Research Centre on Camels (see Around Bikaner). The trust, founded in 1986, aims to provide primary health care and education to the people of the remote villages of Rajasthan, raise awareness of poor women's rights and promote the handicrafts of rural artisans, thus cutting out middlemen and commissions. Items sold here are of high quality and are made by people from surrounding villages. Proceeds go directly to health and education projects in these villages. You can pick up some *pattus* (lovely handloom shawls) from Rs 300, cushion covers (Rs 100 to 200) and traditional folding chairs known as *pidas* from Rs 200. It also sells *jootis* (traditional Rajasthani shoes), hand-printed cotton garments, puppets, cotton birds and more.

Go to Usta St in the old city to see artisans making *usta* (camel leather) products.

Getting There & Away

Bus The bus stand is north of the city centre, almost opposite the road leading to the Lalgarh Palace Hotel (if your bus is coming from the south and you want to be dropped off in the town centre, ask the driver).

There are frequent express buses to the following destinations:

destination	fare (Rs)	duration (hrs)
Agra	160	10
Ahmedabad	250	12
Ajmer	90	6
Barmer	140	10
Delhi	170	10
Jaipur	80	6
Jaisalmer	113	6
Jhunjhunu	60	4
Jodhpur	80	6
Kota	170	10
Udaipur	170	10

For Roadways inquiries ring ☎ 523800.

Train Bikaner has train connections to several destinations, including Jaipur, Churu, Jodhpur and Delhi – the Tourist Reception Centre has a useful chart with details of timings and costs. The train inquiry number is ☎ 131.

Getting Around

Autorickshaw An autorickshaw from the train station to the fort costs about Rs 10, but you'll probably be asked for more.

Bicycle You can hire bicycles at the Dau Cycle Shop, opposite the police station on Station Rd (Rs 3/20 per hour/day).

AROUND BIKANER
Devi Kund

Eight kilometres east of Bikaner, this is the site of the royal *chhatris* of many of the Bika dynasty rulers. The white marble *chhatri* of Maharaja Surat Singh is among the most imposing.

National Research Centre on Camels

This government-managed station, 8km from Bikaner, is probably unique in Asia. There are about 230 camels at the National Research Centre on Camels *(☎/fax 0151-230183; admission free, camera Rs 10; open 3pm-5pm daily)* and three different breeds are reared here. The British army had a camel corps drawn from Bikaner during WWI. There's not a great deal to see here, unless you have a camel fetish, but you can take a camel ride (Rs 30 per person), visit the baby camels and look around the small museum. The Urmul trust shop Abhivyakti was also located here at the time of writing.

For the round trip including a half-hour wait at the camel farm, it's around Rs 60 for an autorickshaw, or Rs 100 for a taxi.

Gajner Wildlife Sanctuary

The lake and forested hills of this reserve *(admission per jeep Rs 1000)*, 32km from Bikaner on the Jaisalmer road, are inhabited by wildfowl, hares, wild boar, desert foxes and a number of deer and antelopes including blackbucks and bluebulls. Imperial sand grouse migrate here in winter. There are no authorised guides at the sanctuary and, apart from the Gajner Palace Hotel, no accommodation or infrastructure for visitors. The reserve is only accessible by Gajner Palace Hotel vehicles (which can be hired by non-guests). Jeeps can take a maximum of six people.

Places to Stay & Eat Ideally situated on the banks of a lake, **Gajner Palace Hotel** *(☎ 01534-55065, fax 55060, book through Karni Bhawan Palace Hotel in Bikaner ☎ 0151-524701, fax 522408; e mgrgaj@gagner.hrh india.com; singles/doubles Rs 1999/3300, suites Rs 5500)* is the erstwhile royal winter

Get to Know Your Camel

The camels reared at Bikaner's National Research Centre on Camels are of three breeds. The long-haired camels with hair in their ears are local camels from the Bikaner district; they are renowned for their strength. The light-coloured camels are from the Jaisalmer district, and are renowned for their speed – up to 22km/h! The dark-coloured camels are from Gujarat, and the females are renowned for the quantity of milk they produce – an average of 4L to 6L at each milking. The milk tastes a little salty and is reputedly good for the liver. If you have a cup of *chai* in a small desert village, you're quite possibly drinking camel milk. The stout of heart might even like to try fresh, warm camel milk at the farm. The camels on the farm are crossbred so, in theory, they should be the strongest, fastest and best milk-producing camels you'll find anywhere! Breeding season is from around December to March, and at this time the male camels froth disconcertingly at the mouth.

This is also a stud farm; locals bring their female camels here to be serviced free of charge. Female camels give birth every 1½ years depending on their age and health, following a long (13-month) gestation period. A male camel can inseminate up to five cows per day.

Adult camels consume about 16kg of fodder in summer, and drink around 30L of water per day; in winter, they drink about 20L per day. In winter a healthy camel can work up to one month without food or water, and in summer, up to one week.

palace. It's an impressive building made of red sandstone and is set in serene, lush surroundings – ideal for some serious rest and relaxation. Some of the rugs in the main palace were woven by prisoners of the Bikaner jail. There's an indoor restaurant, or you can eat outdoors as you watch the birds bobbing on the calm lake; the buffet lunch/dinner is Rs 375/425. If you are not staying at the hotel, you will have to pay Rs 100 per person to visit, which includes a soft drink, tea or coffee. No admission fee is levied if you are taking a safari or having a meal at the palace (advance bookings are recommended).

Getting There & Away There are frequent daily buses (Rs 20) to Gajner village, located about 1km away from the hotel. A return taxi from Bikaner should cost around Rs 450 return, including the two hours' waiting time.

Kolayat

This small temple town set around a lake, 22km south of Gajner, is often referred to as a mini-Pushkar. It lacks the vibrant character of Pushkar, but is far less touristy. There's a *mela* (fair) held here around the same time as the Pushkar Camel Fair in October–November (minus the camels and cattle, but with plenty of *sadhus*, or holy persons). The main temple at Kolayat is **Kapil Muni Temple** *(closed between 3pm-5pm)*.

There are frequent daily buses from Bikaner to Kolayat Rs (20, 1½ hours).

Deshnok

Deshnok is a village 30km south of Bikaner along the Jodhpur road. A visit to Deshnok's fascinating temple of Karni Mata, an incarnation of Durga, is not for the squeamish. Here the holy rodents are considered to be incarnations of storytellers, and run riot over the temple complex.

Karni Mata lived in the 14th century and performed many miracles during her lifetime. When her youngest son, Lakhan, drowned, Karni Mata ordered Yama, the god of death, to bring him back to life. Yama replied that he was unable to do this, but that Karni Mata, as an incarnation of Durga, could restore Lakhan's life. This she did, and decreed that members of her family would no longer die, but would be reincarnated as *kabas* (rats), and these *kabas* would return as members of her family. There are around 600 families in Deshnok who claim both descent from Karni Mata and that they will be reincarnated as *kabas*.

Karni Mata Temple The temple (W www
.karnimata.com; admission free, camera/video
Rs 20/50; open 4am-10pm daily) is an important place of pilgrimage, with pilgrims
being disgorged every few minutes from
buses. Once at the village, they buy *prasaad*
in the form of sugar balls to feed to the rats.
The pilgrims are anointed with a *tikka* made
with ash from a holy fire in the inner sanctum, while the objects of their devotion run
over their toes (sorry, no shoes permitted!).
Before the temple is a beautiful marble
facade with solid silver doors donated by
Maharaja Ganga Singh. Across the doorway
to the inner sanctum are repoussé (raised
relief) silver doors – one panel shows the
goddess with her holy charges at her feet. An
image of the goddess is enshrined in the
inner sanctum. There are special holes
around the side of the temple courtyard to
facilitate the rats' movements, and a wire
grille has been placed over the courtyard to
prevent birds of prey and other predators
consuming the holy rodents.

It is considered highly auspicious to have
a *kaba* run across your feet – you'll probably find you'll be inadvertently graced in
this manner whether you want it or not!
White *kabas* are quite rare, although there
are one or two at the temple, and sighting
one augurs well for your spiritual progress.
Frankly, the holy charges here are a rather

moth-eaten assortment, who engage in decidedly unholy behaviour as they fight each
other to get the best position around the
enormous bowls of milk that are constantly
replenished by the temple priests.

There are two special festivals at this
temple around April–May and October–
November – ask at the **Tourist Reception
Centre** (☎ 0151-544125) in Bikaner for the
exact dates.

Shri Karni Centenary Auditorium Across
the square from the temple, the pictorial
display in this auditorium (admission Rs 2;
open 7am-7pm daily) is worth a look. It tells
the story of Karni Mata's life with descriptions in English and Hindi.

Places to Stay The best place to stay in
Deshnok is **Shri Karni Yatri Niwas** (doubles
Rs 150), but you are much better off staying
in Bikaner and visiting Deshnok on a day
trip. Rooms are dusty and poorly maintained. The service provided is minimal and
no meals are available.

Getting There & Away Buses from the bus
stand in Bikaner depart daily every hour for
Deshnok (Rs 10, 30 minutes). A slow rickshaw from the train station can be arranged
for Rs 100 return, but Rs 150 is more common. A taxi (Rs 250) is better and safer.

Agra

☎ 0562 • postcode 282001 • pop 1.3 million

In the 16th and 17th centuries, Agra was the capital of India under the Mughals, and its superb monuments date from this era. They include a magnificent fort and the building that many people come to India solely to see – the Taj Mahal.

Badal Singh is credited with building a fort on the site of the present Agra Fort in 1475. Sikander Lodi made his capital on the opposite bank of the Yamuna in 1501. Agra became the Mughal capital after Babur defeated the last Lodi sultan in 1526 at Panipat. It reached its glorious peak between the mid-16th and mid-17th centuries under the reigns of Akbar, Jehangir and Shah Jahan, when the fort, the Taj Mahal and Agra's major tombs were built. In 1638 Shah Jahan built a new city in Delhi, and Aurangzeb moved the capital there 10 years later.

In 1761 Agra fell to the Jats, who looted its monuments, including the Taj Mahal. It was taken by the Marathas in 1770, before the British wrested control in 1803. There was heavy fighting around the fort during the Uprising of 1857, and after the British regained control, they shifted the administration of the northwestern provinces to Allahabad. The city has since developed as an industrial centre.

Agra is worth more than a flying visit, particularly if you intend to see the nearby deserted city of Fatehpur Sikri.

Orientation

Agra is on the western bank of the Yamuna River, 204km south of Delhi. The old part of the city and main marketplace (Kinari Bazaar) are northwest of the fort. The spacious British-built cantonment is south, and the main road running through it is called The Mall. The commercial centre of the cantonment is Sadar Bazaar.

The labourers and artisans who toiled on the Taj set up home immediately south of the mausoleum. This area, full of congested alleyways, is known as Taj Ganj and today

Highlights

- The Taj Mahal, truly one of the wonders of the world
- Agra Fort, a huge and intriguing complex
- Itimad-ud-Daulah, the tomb of Mirza Ghiyas Beg, with its impressive Mughal architecture
- Fatehpur Sikri, a romantic deserted city

★★★★★★★★★★★★★★★★★★★★★★★★★★★★★★★★

it contains most of Agra's budget hotels. The 'tourist class' hotels are predominantly in the area south of here.

Information

The **Government of India tourist office** (☎ 226378; 191 The Mall; e goitoagra@sancharnet.in; open 9am-5.30pm Mon-Fri, 9am-4.30pm Sat) produces an informative brochure on Fatehpur Sikri. The **tourist information counter** (open 7.55am-8.20pm) is found at Agra Cantonment train station.

The State Bank of India branch south of Taj Ganj and the Andhra Bank in Sadar Bazaar (next to the Hotel Pawan) are the best banks for changing money.

You'll find the **main post office** (The Mall; open 10am-6pm Mon-Sat) with its lax poste restante facility opposite the Government of India tourist office. **Cyberlink** (3/14

AGRA

PLACES TO STAY
8 Lauries Hotel
10 Tourist Rest House
12 Agra Ashok Hotel
15 Hotel Pawan; Andhra Bank
18 Clarks Shiraz Hotel; Indian Airlines
22 Hotel Atithi
23 Taj View; Mayur Tourist Complex

PLACES TO EAT
14 Zorba the Buddha
17 Lakshmi Vilas
20 Only Restaurant

OTHER
1 Itimad-ud-Daulah
2 SN Hospital
3 Jama Masjid
4 Power House Bus Stand
5 Foreigners Registration Office
6 Idgah Bus Stand
7 Buses to Jaipur
9 District Hospital
11 Main Post Office
13 Government of India Tourist Office
16 Police Station
19 Archaeological Survey of India
21 State Bank of India

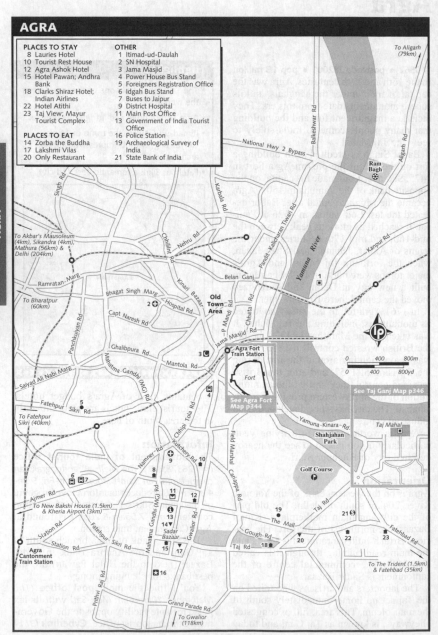

Thana Chowk; open 8am-10pm daily), in Taj Ganj, has an ISDN Internet link and charges Rs 60 per hour.

If you're looking for reading material, the small bookshop in the Taj View hotel carries stock in English and French.

Some private clinics have been mixed up in medical insurance fraud (see the boxed text 'Agra-Phobia'), so stick with the government hospitals: the **District Hospital** (☎ 363043; *Mahatma Gandhi (MG) Rd)* and **SN Hospital** (☎ 361313; *Hospital Rd)*.

Taj Mahal

Described as the most extravagant monument ever built for love, this poignant Mughal mausoleum has become the tourist emblem of India. The Taj Mahal *(foreigner/ citizen Rs 750/20, children under 15 free; open 6am-7.30pm Sat-Thur)* was constructed by Emperor Shah Jahan in memory of his second wife, Mumtaz Mahal, whose death in childbirth in 1631 left the emperor so heartbroken that his hair is said to have turned grey overnight.

Gone are the days of a cheap, or even free, visit; not only does the Archaeological Survey of India take Rs 500, but the local government also dips into your pocket for Rs 250. Some argue that this ensures the world's most famous building is kept in good condition, but for backpackers it can represent several days' budget.

Construction of the Taj began in 1631 and was not completed until 1653. In total, 20,000 people from India and Central Asia worked on the building (some later had their hands or thumbs amputated, so as to ensure that the perfection of the Taj could never be repeated). The main architect is believed to have been Isa Khan, who was from Shiraz in Iran. Experts were also brought from Europe – Austin of Bordeaux and Veroneo of Venice were both involved in the Taj's decoration.

The Taj is definitely worth more than a single visit, as its character changes with the light during the day. Dawn, when the Taj is virtually deserted, is a magical time.

There are three entrances to the Taj (east, south and west); the main entrance is on the

western side. The grand red sandstone **gateway** on the south side of the interior forecourt is inscribed with verses from the Quran in Arabic. It would make a stunning entrance to the Taj, but unfortunately these days you only exit through here. The entrance is now through a small door to the right of the gate, where everyone has to undergo a security check. Food, tobacco, matches and other specified items (including, thankfully, the red-staining betel-nut chewing preparation *paan*), cannot be taken inside. There's a cloakroom nearby for depositing your belongings for safekeeping.

Paths leading from the gate are divided by a long **watercourse** in which the Taj is reflected. The ornamental gardens the paths lead you through are set out along classical Mughal *charbagh* lines – a square quartered by watercourses. To the west is a small **museum** *(Rs 5; open 10am-5pm Sat-Thur)*. It houses original architectural drawings of the Taj, information on the semiprecious stones used in its construction, and some nifty celadon plates, said to split into pieces or change colour if the food served on them contains poison.

The Taj Mahal itself stands on a raised marble platform on the northern edge of the ornamental gardens. Tall, purely decorative white **minarets** grace each corner of the platform. Twin red sandstone buildings frame it; the one on the western side is a **mosque**, while the identical one on the eastern side is for symmetry. It cannot be used as a mosque, as it faces the wrong direction.

The central Taj structure has four small domes surrounding the bulbous central dome. The **tombs of Mumtaz Mahal and Shah Jahan** are in a basement. Above them in the main chamber are false tombs, which were commonly included in mausoleums of this type. Ironically, the perfect symmetry of the Taj is disrupted only by the tomb of the man who built it. When Shah Jahan died in 1666, Aurangzeb placed his casket next to that of Mumtaz Mahal. His presence, which was never intended, unbalances the mausoleum's interior.

Light is admitted into the central chamber by finely cut marble screens. The echo in this high-domed chamber is superb, and there is always someone there to demonstrate it. The lamp hanging from the centre of the dome was an unrefusable 'gift' from the British viceroy Lord Curzon.

Although the Taj is amazingly graceful from almost any angle, it's the close-up detail that is really astounding. Semiprecious stones are inlaid into the marble in beautiful patterns using a process known as *pietra dura*. As many as 43 different types of gems were used for Mumtaz's tomb alone.

Agra Fort

Construction of the massive red sandstone Agra Fort *(foreigner/citizen Rs 300/20, child under 15 free, video Rs 25; open sunrise-sunset)* on the bank of the Yamuna River was begun by Emperor Akbar in 1565, and additions were made up until the rule of his grandson Shah Jahan.

The auricular fort's colossal double walls rise over 20m in height and measure 2.5km in circumference. They are encircled by a fetid moat and contain a maze of buildings which form a small city within a city. Unfortunately, not all buildings are open to visitors, including the white marble Moti Masjid (Pearl Mosque), regarded by some as the most beautiful mosque in India. The Amar Singh Gate to the south is the sole entry point. Knowledgeable guides are available just inside the gate. Expect to pay from Rs 150 to 200.

Diwan-i-Am Built by Shah Jahan, the Hall of Public Audiences, or Diwan-i-Am, and replaced an earlier wooden structure. His predecessors played a part in the hall's construction, but the throne room, with its inlaid marble work, indisputably bears Shah Jahan's influence. This is where the emperor met officials and listened to petitioners. Beside the Diwan-i-Am is the small **Nagina Masjid** (Gem Mosque). A door leads from here into the **Ladies' Bazaar**, where female merchants came to sell goods to the ladies of the Mughal court. No males were allowed to enter the bazaar, except for Akbar, though

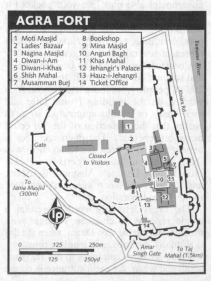

AGRA FORT

1 Moti Masjid
2 Ladies' Bazaar
3 Nagina Masjid
4 Diwan-i-Am
5 Diwan-i-Khas
6 Shish Mahal
7 Musamman Burj
8 Bookshop
9 Mina Masjid
10 Anguri Bagh
11 Khas Mahal
12 Jehangir's Palace
13 Hauz-i-Jehangri
14 Ticket Office

Yamuna River

Kinara Rd

Gate

Closed to Visitors

To Jama Masjid (300m)

0   125   250m
0   125   250yd

Amar Singh Gate

To Taj Mahal (1.5km)

according to one apocryphal story he still enjoyed visiting in female disguise.

Diwan-i-Khas The Hall of Private Audiences, or Diwan-i-Khas, was also built by Shah Jahan, between 1636 and 1637. It is where the emperor received important dignitaries and foreign ambassadors. The famous Peacock Throne was kept here before being moved to Delhi by Aurangzeb. It was later carted off to Iran by Nadir Shah.

Musamman Burj The exquisite Musamman Burj (Octagonal Tower) stands close to the Diwan-i-Khas. This is where Shah Jahan died after seven years' imprisonment in the fort. The tower looks out over the Yamuna and is traditionally considered to offer one of the most poignant views of the Taj, but Agra's pollution is now so thick that it's difficult to see the Taj from here. The small **Mina Masjid** was Shah Jahan's private mosque during his imprisonment.

Jehangir's Palace Akbar is believed to have built this palace, the largest private residence in the fort, for his son. This was one of the first signs of the fort's changing emphasis from military purposes to luxurious living quarters. The palace also displays an interesting blend of Hindu and Central Asian architectural styles – a contrast to the unique Mughal style used by Shah Jahan.

Jama Masjid

Across the train tracks from the Delhi Gate of Agra Fort is the Jama Masjid, built by Shah Jahan in 1648. Over the main gate, an inscription indicates that it was built in the name of Jahanara, Shah Jahan's favourite daughter, who was eventually imprisoned with Shah Jahan by Aurangzeb.

Itimad-ud-Daulah

On the opposite bank of the Yamuna, north of the fort, is the exquisite Itimad-ud-Daulah (foreigner/citizen Rs 110/10, video Rs 25; open sunrise-sunset), the tomb of Mirza Ghiyas Beg. This Persian gentleman was Jehangir's wazir, or chief minister, and his beautiful daughter Nur Jahan (Light of the World) later married the emperor. Nur Jahan constructed the tomb from 1622 to 1628 in a style similar to the tomb she built for Jehangir near Lahore in present-day Pakistan.

Interestingly, many of its design elements foreshadow the Taj, construction of which began only a few years later. The Itimad-ud-Daulah was the first Mughal structure that was totally built from marble, and the first to make extensive use of *pietra dura*, the marble inlay work that is so characteristic of the Taj. Though small and squat compared with its more famous cousin (it's known as the 'baby Taj'), its human scale is attractive. Extremely fine marble latticework passages admit light to the interior, and the beautifully patterned surface of the tomb is superb.

Akbar's Mausoleum

The sandstone and marble tomb of Akbar (foreigner/citizen Rs 110/15, video Rs 25; open sunrise-sunset), who was the greatest of the Mughal emperors, lies in the centre of a peaceful garden grazed by deer at Sikandra, 4km northwest of Agra. Akbar started its construction himself, blending Islamic, Hindu, Buddhist, Jain and Christian motifs and styles, much like the syncretic religious philosophy he developed called Deen Ilahi.

When Akbar died, the mausoleum was completed by his son Jehangir, who made significant modifications to the original plans. This accounts for its somewhat cluttered architectural lines.

Local buses heading to Sikandra run along Mahatma Gandhi (MG) Rd from the Agra Fort bus stand. They cost Rs 4. Autorickshaws should charge around Rs 85 for the return trip with an hour's waiting time at the tomb.

Other Attractions

The alleyways of **Kinari Bazaar** (Old Marketplace) start near the Jama Masjid. There are several distinct areas, the names of which are relics of the Mughal period and don't always bear relation to the goods that are sold there today.

The **Loha Mandi** (Iron Market) and **Sabji Mandi** (Vegetable Market) still operate, and

AGRA

the **Nai ki Mandi** (Barber's Market) is now famous for textiles.

Organised Tours

Guided tours depart from Agra Cantonment train station, where passengers arriving from Delhi on the *Taj Express* are collected at 9.47am. The tours include a visit to the Taj Mahal, Agra Fort and a rather hasty one to Fatehpur Sikri. They finish at 6pm so day-trippers can catch the *Taj Express* back to Delhi at 6.25pm. Tickets are available from the tourist information counter at the train station and cost Rs 1500/250 for foreigners/citizens; this includes all admission fees and a guide.

An afternoon tour to Fatehpur Sikri leaves Agra Cantonment at 10.15am and returns at 1.30pm. Tickets cost Rs 450/175 for foreigners/Indians; this includes admission fees and a guide.

Places to Stay – Budget

The two main areas for cheap accommodation are the Taj Ganj area and the Sadar Bazaar area. However, the government is currently struggling to stop hotels in Taj Ganj from 'encroaching' on the monument and ruining the skyline around it, so you may want to think twice about encouraging their skyward growth.

Agra's Paying Guest Scheme enables you to stay with local families for between Rs 200 and 500. Contact the tourist information counter at the train station for details.

Hotel Kamal (☎ *330126; Taj Ganj;* e *hotel kamal@hotmail.com; singles with private bathroom Rs 120-300, doubles with private bathroom Rs 170-350)* has helpful staff and OK rooms. The more expensive ones have 24-hour hot showers. There's a prime view of the Taj from the sitting area on the roof and this place gets positive reviews from travellers. Checkout is an unfriendly 10am.

Hotel Sidhartha (☎ *331238; Western Gate; singles Rs 100-150, doubles Rs 150-250)* is a clean, spacious place built motel-style around a garden courtyard; the rooms have decent-sized windows. The cheaper rooms have bucket hot water and the more expensive ones have hot water on tap.

Tourist Rest House (☎ *363961, fax 366910;* e *trh@sancharnet.in; Kachahari Rd; singles Rs 120-450, doubles Rs 150-550)* is a well-known, guest-friendly place. The rooms over Rs 200 have 24-hour hot water and air-conditioning and the best room comes with a TV and fridge. It's managed by two benign brothers who make train and air reservations, provide good local information and also run tours to Rajasthan. Internet access is available. Decent vegetarian food is served in the candle-lit courtyard or in the rooftop restaurant. Don't confuse this place with the nearby (and inferior) Kapoor Tourist Rest House on Fatehpur Sikri Rd or the Tourist Guest House near Agra Fort bus stand.

Hotel Pawan (☎ *225506, fax 225604;* e *paw anhotel@sancharnet.in; air-cooled singles/doubles from Rs 250-350, air-con singles/doubles from Rs 500/600),* also known as Hotel Jaiwal, is found on the main drag of Sadar Bazaar close to shops and restaurants.

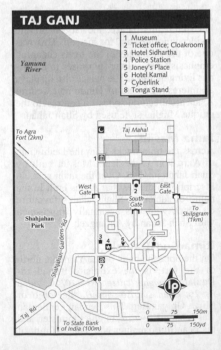

TAJ GANJ

1 Museum
2 Ticket office; Cloakroom
3 Hotel Sidhartha
4 Police Station
5 Joney's Place
6 Hotel Kamal
7 Cyberlink
8 Tonga Stand

Yamuna River

To Agra Fort (2km)

Taj Mahal

West Gate

East Gate

South Gate

To Shilpgram (1km)

Shahjahan Park

Shahjahan Gardens Rd

Taj Rd

To State Bank of India (100m)

0   75   150m
0   75   150yd

The rooms are fine and children under 12 stay here for free.

Places to Stay – Mid-Range

Mayur Tourist Complex (☎ 332302, fax 332 907; Fatehbad Rd; air-cooled singles/doubles Rs 900/1050, air-con singles/doubles Rs 1200/1500) has pleasant cottage-style rooms set around a lawn with a swimming pool, but beware of the mosquitoes. The hotel also has a pretty good restaurant and a bar.

Hotel Atithi (☎ 230040, fax 330878; e hotelatithi@hotmail.com; Fatehbad Rd; singles/doubles with air-con from Rs 1200/1450) has good-sized, well-equipped rooms plus a swimming pool. There's no restaurant but there are plenty of eateries nearby.

Lauries Hotel (☎ 364536, fax 268045; e laurieshotel@hotmail.com; Mahatma Gandhi (MG) Rd; camping Rs 50, singles/doubles Rs 725/900) is where Queen Elizabeth II's party stayed on a visit to India in 1961 when presumably there was little better. Any regal pretensions have long since faded into old-age decline, though the hotel retains its spacious arcaded corridors and extensive grounds. Its swimming pool is open during the hotter months.

New Bakshi House (☎ 302176, fax 301448; e bakshivilla@hotmail.com; 5 Laxman Nagar; rooms Rs 1100-1300) is between the train station and the airport. It's effectively a private home and you can use the family's lounge. Some of the comfortable doubles in this clean place have air-con.

Places to Stay – Top End

All the top-end hotels are air-conditioned and have pools.

Agra Ashok Hotel (☎ 361223, fax 361620; e itdcagra@sancharnet.in; 6B The Mall; singles/doubles Rs 1995/2995) is a pleasant place to stay and well-managed, despite being part of the Indian Tourism Development Corporation chain.

The Trident (☎ 331818, fax 331812; e reservations@tridentag.com; Tajnagri Scheme, Fatehbad Rd; singles/doubles US$95/100) is a low-rise, Mughal-style hotel with a garden and restaurant. Rooms are excellent value in summer, but from October to April prices

soar. It caters for nonsmokers and has two rooms for people with disabilities.

Clarks Shiraz Hotel (☎ 226121, fax 226 128, e clarkraz@sancharnet.in; 54 Taj Rd; singles/doubles US$44/48) is a long-standing Agra landmark. Rooms have the expected comforts, including a fridge, and are good value. The inquisitive can consult the resident astrologer every morning.

Taj View (☎ 232400, fax 232420; w www.tajhotels.com; Fatehbad Rd; singles/doubles US$90/95, with view US$105/115 Oct-Apr, US$42/70 May-Sept) is a five-star member of the Taj Group of hotels. Rooms have either a view of the Taj Mahal or the hotel's extensive gardens and pool. Regardless of the view the charge is the same. In the hot season, room prices are typically discounted by half. The hotel has the usual upmarket shopping arcade, a fitness centre and an astrologer.

Amarvilas (☎ 231515, fax 231516, e rooms div@amarvilas.com; Taj East Gate Rd; singles US$322, doubles US$345-368) is the top-notch place in Agra and is really only for those with bulging wallets or no sense of budgeting. What a place it is, with a huge swimming pool set into an immense baori-like construction with flights of shallow steps, landings and small pavilions. It could be some lavish film set. The rooms have all you could imagine and there are two excellent **restaurants** where a three-course meal will set you back Rs 2000. If you're desperate for a bit of hedonism you could get away with a single course for Rs 600 with a view of the Taj and a sneak around the hotel.

Places to Eat

Don't forget to try peitha, the local speciality made of ultrasweet candied pumpkin, and dalmoth, a tangy-flavoured snack made from pulses. If you want to sample Agra's fine tradition of Mughlai food you'll need to dip into the luxury hotels – and deep into your wallet.

Joney's Place (meals Rs 20-50) is one of the longest-running establishments in the Taj Ganj area. This tiny place serves great Western breakfasts and good Indian and Israeli food; its banana lassis are famous.

Joney's Place should not be confused with Joinus just down the road.

Zorba the Buddha (☎ 225055; E-13 Shopping Arcade, Sadar Bazaar; open noon-3pm & 6pm-9pm July-Apr; dishes around Rs 70-80) is a spotlessly clean, nonsmoking, Osho-run vegetarian restaurant. You can polish off an excellent main dish with a coffee flavoured with cinnamon and cashews. It's very popular with travellers, so it can be hard to get a table here in the evening.

Lakshmi Vilas (50-A Taj Rd; meals from Rs 30-40) is a cheap South Indian veg restaurant that's popular with the locals. It's recommended for its 23 varieties of *dosa* (lentil pancakes), which start at Rs 25. Shakes, lassis, ice creams and real filter coffee are also served here, making it a good place for dessert.

Only Restaurant (☎ 226834; 45 Taj Rd; dishes Rs 75-105), at the Taj Ganj end of The Mall, is highly rated by locals and visitors. Mughlai, continental and Chinese cuisine are on offer. A budget-smasher is the *dum-e-raan*, a whole leg of mutton simmered in a thick creamy curry with spices, herbs and dry fruits (Rs 775). There's live Indian music in the evening.

Shopping
Agra is well known for its leather goods, jewellery, *dhurrie* (rug) weaving and marble items inlaid with coloured stones, similar to the *pietra-dura* work on the Taj. Both Sadar Bazaar and the area south of Taj Ganj are full of emporiums, but prices are more expensive than in the bazaars in the old part of the city. The best jewellery shops are around Pratapur, also in the old part, though precious stones are cheaper in Jaipur.

About 1km along the road running from the eastern gate of the Taj is Shilpgram, a crafts village and open-air emporium. Prices are on the high side, but the quality and range are good.

Don't let rickshaw-wallahs persuade you to visit shops on the way to your destination. If you don't, you'll pay inflated prices to cover their commission.

Getting There & Away
Air The office for **Indian Airlines** (☎ 360948; open 10am-1.15pm & 2pm-5pm Mon-Sat) is at Clarks Shiraz Hotel.

Fares from Agra are: Delhi US$65, Khajuraho US$90 and Varanasi US$115.

Bus Most buses leave from the **Idgah bus stand** (☎ 366588). Deluxe buses to Delhi leave every 15 minutes and cost Rs 90; the trip takes about five hours.

There are deluxe buses to Jaipur every half-hour for Rs 98; there are also air-con buses for Rs 112. The journey takes about six hours. They leave from a small booth right outside the Hotel Sheetal on Ajmer Rd, very close to the Idgah bus stand; you should book a day in advance.

Train Agra Cantonment is the city's main train station. The *Taj Express*, leaving New Delhi at 7.15am daily, conveniently connects

Major Trains from Agra Cantonment

destination	train No & name	departure time (daily)	fare (Rs)	duration (hrs)	distance (km)
Delhi	2001 *Shatabdi Express*	8.18pm	760/390★	2½	194
Delhi (Nizamuddin)	2179 *Taj Express*	6.35pm	54/284✦	3¼	194
Jaipur	4853/4863 *Marudhar Express*	7.15am	77/120/347✳	6¾	308
Jodhpur	4853/4863 *Marudhar Express*	7.15am	132/205/594✳	13½	621

★ air-con chair/executive chair   ✦ 2nd-/1st-class seat
✳ general/2nd-class sleeper/3-tier air-con

with the guided tour of the Taj, Agra Fort and Fatehpur Sikri (see Organised Tours earlier). Agra Fort train station has services to Jaipur, Fatehpur Sikri and Bharatpur.

Take great care at New Delhi station; pickpockets, muggers and others are very aware that this is a popular tourist route and they work overtime at parting unwary visitors from their goods.

Getting Around
The Taj is surrounded by a no-go zone for the internal combustion engine. The nearest you can get to the western entrance is the roundabout by Shahjahan Park. From there it's about a 10-minute walk or a Rs 15 cycle-rickshaw ride.

To/From the Airport Agra's Kheria airport is 7km from the centre of town. Taxis charge around Rs 75; in an autorickshaw it's Rs 40.

Taxi & Autorickshaw Prepaid transport is available from Agra Cantonment train station to Taj Ganj (Rs 40/150 by autorickshaw/taxi) and to the Taj Mahal and Agra Fort with waiting time (Rs 250/350). A prepaid rickshaw for local sightseeing costs Rs 250 for a full day and Rs 135 for four hours. Taxis cost Rs 500 for a full day (8am to 4pm) within a 40km radius, or Rs 650 to include Fatehpur Sikri.

Cycle-Rickshaw Agra is very spread out and not conducive to walking, since hordes of cycle-rickshaw-wallahs pursue would-be pedestrians with unbelievable persistence. Don't take any nonsense from rickshaw-wallahs who offer to take you from A to B via a few marble or jewellery shops.

A trip from Taj Ganj to Sadar Bazaar costs less than Rs 15 and to Agra Cantonment less than Rs 20, which is about the most you should pay to get anywhere in Agra.

Bicycle The simple solution to Agra's transport problem is to hire a bicycle. The city is sufficiently traffic-free to make cycling an easy proposition, and avoiding rickshaw-wallahs will increase your enjoyment of the

city three-fold. **Usmani Cycle Store**, near the Taj Ganj tonga and rickshaw stand, hires bicycles for Rs 15 for half a day and Rs 35 for a full day.

Around Agra

FATEHPUR SIKRI
Between 1571 and 1585, during the reign of Emperor Akbar, the capital of the Mughal empire was situated here, 40km west of Agra. Then, as suddenly and dramatically as this new city had been built, it was abandoned, mainly due to difficulties with the water supply. Today it's a perfectly preserved example of a Mughal city at the height of the empire's splendour.

Legend has it that Akbar was without a male heir and made a pilgrimage to this spot to see the saint Shaikh Salim Chishti. The saint foretold the birth of Akbar's son, the future emperor Jehangir, and in gratitude Akbar named his son Salim. Furthermore, Akbar transferred his capital to Sikri and built a new and splendid city.

Orientation & Information
The deserted city lies along the top of a ridge, 40km west of Agra. The village, with its bus stand and train station, is at the bottom of the ridge's southern face.

The old city consists of two parts, a central paid enclosure that has been extensively restored, and the many ruins outside, mostly to the north.

Old City
There are two ticket offices for the historic enclosure (foreigner/citizen Rs 260/20, video Rs 25; open sunrise-sunset) one in the car park by the Jama Masjid in the southwest and the other in the northeast by the Diwan-i-Am.

The function and even the names of many buildings remain contentious, so you may find it useful to hire a guide. Licensed guides (around Rs 150 for 90 minutes for up to six people) are available from the area around the ticket office and at the entrance to the Jama Masjid; unlicensed guides will charge around Rs 10 to 20.

The first building inside the southwest gate is the **Palace of Jodh Bai**. On the outer north wall is a projecting pavilion, the **Hawa Mahal** (Palace of the Winds), made entirely of stone latticework. Built either by or for Raja Birbal, Akbar's favourite courtier, the small **Birbal Bhavan** palace is extremely elegant in its design and execution.

Not far from the Palace of Jodh Bai, is **Mariam's House** (Palace of the Christian Wife) used by Akbar's Goan Christian wife, Mariam; at one time this place was gilded throughout – earning it the name 'Golden House'.

The exterior of the **Diwan-i-Khas** is reasonably plain, but its interior design is unique. A stone column in the centre of the building supports a flat-topped 'throne' some 6m high, with narrow stone bridges radiating to the corners of the room.

Just inside the gates at the northeast end of the deserted city is the **Diwan-i-Am**. This consists of a large open courtyard surrounded by cloisters. Beside the Diwan-i-Am is the **Pachisi Courtyard**, set out like a gigantic gameboard. It is said that Akbar played the game *pachisi* here, using slave girls as the pieces.

Jama Masjid & Tomb of Shaikh Salim Chishti

The Jama Masjid *(Dargah Mosque; admission free)*, said to be a copy of the mosque at Mecca, is a beautiful building containing elements of Persian and Hindu design.

In the northern part of the courtyard is the superb white marble *dargah* or tomb of Shaikh Salim Chishti, built in 1570. The carved-marble lattice screens are probably the finest examples of such work you'll see anywhere in the country.

Places to Stay & Eat

Goverdhan Tourist Complex (☎ 882643; *dorm beds Rs 100, singles/doubles with private bathroom & bucket hot water from Rs 100/*150, triples Rs 600) has a pleasant atmosphere with a range of clean but basic rooms. Food is served on the garden terrace.

Gulistan Tourist Complex (☎ 882490; *singles/doubles from Rs 400/450, with aircon from Rs 700/850*) is a sympathetically designed, upmarket Uttar Pradesh Tourism operation. It's a nice place to stay, but not great value; prices drop by Rs 100 between March and September. It has a courtyard garden, a nonveg restaurant and a bar.

Shere Punjab *(meals from Rs 40)*, opposite the petrol station on the bypass road, is an excellent road-side *dhaba* (basic restaurant or snack bar) that does a good *masala dosa* (lentil-flour crepe stuffed with potatoes cooked with onions and curry leaves).

There are plenty of snack and soft-drink vendors to be found around all the entrances to the enclosures. Fatehpur Sikri's speciality is *khataie*, the biscuits you'll see piled high in the bazaar.

Getting There & Away

The tour buses stop for only an hour or so at Fatehpur Sikri. If you want to spend longer (which is recommended), it's worth taking the bus from Agra's Idgah bus stand (Rs 16, 1 hour). Buses depart every 30 minutes between 7am and 7pm. There are also four trains a day to Fatehpur Sikri from Agra Fort (Rs 8, one hour).

DHOLPUR

Situated almost midway between Agra (in Uttar Pradesh) and Gwalior (in Madhya Pradesh), on an eastward thrusting spur of Rajasthan, is Dholpur. It was near here that Aurangzeb's sons fought a pitched battle to determine who would succeed him as the emperor of the rapidly declining Mughal empire. The Shergarh fort in Dholpur is very old and is now in ruins.

There are regular train and bus connections from Agra to Dholpur, as well as from Dausa and Gwalior.

Delhi

☎ 011 • postcode 110001 • pop 9.8 million

Most visitors to Rajasthan fly into Delhi, a major international gateway. Delhi is the capital of India, northern India's industrial hub and the country's third-largest city.

Few travellers have much that is good to say about India's fastest-growing city; the intense air pollution and persistent touts often make it an unsettling experience for newcomers. It does, however, have a long and fascinating history and there's a tangible energy and confidence that only comes with a history as rich and varied as Delhi's.

Admission prices for foreigners to Delhi's monuments went up dramatically a few years back, creating storms of protest from both visitors and tour operators. Now prices have been readjusted downwards. There are basically two prices for foreigners, US$2/Rs 100 or US$5/Rs 250, depending on the monument (mosques are free). There are also fees for using cameras and there are no longer free days once a week. Indian citizens pay a lower admission fee and children under 15 enter free.

There have been at least eight cities around modern Delhi, beginning with Indraprastha, which featured in the epic Mahabharata over 3000 years ago.

Old Delhi was the capital of Muslim India between the 17th and 19th centuries. New Delhi was built as the imperial capital of India by the British. They announced their intention to shift the capital from Calcutta (present-day Kolkata) in 1911, and New Delhi was finally inaugurated in 1931. Following Independence in 1947, Delhi became the capital of the new republic of India.

For a much more in-depth guide to the city, get a copy of Lonely Planet's *Delhi*.

Orientation

Delhi is a relatively easy city to find your way around although it is very spread out. The section of most interest to visitors is on the west bank of the Yamuna River and is

Highlights

- The Red Fort, Delhi's massive Mughal-era monument
- The Qutb Minar, a magnificent tower built to proclaim the arrival of Islam in India
- The Jama Masjid, the largest mosque in India
- Connaught Place, the thriving heart of New Delhi
- Humayun's tomb, a fine example of early Mughal architecture

divided basically into two parts – the tightly packed streets of Old Delhi and the more spacious, planned areas of New Delhi.

Old Delhi is the 17th-century walled city of Shahjahanabad, with city gates, narrow alleys, constant traffic jams, terrible air pollution, the enormous Red Fort and Jama Masjid, temples, mosques, bazaars and the famous street known as Chandni Chowk. Here you will find the Delhi train station and, a little further north, the Interstate Bus Terminal (ISBT) near Kashmiri Gate.

Near New Delhi train station there is the crowded market area of Paharganj. This has become the budget travellers' hang-out – it has many good budget hotels, cafés and restaurants.

DELHI

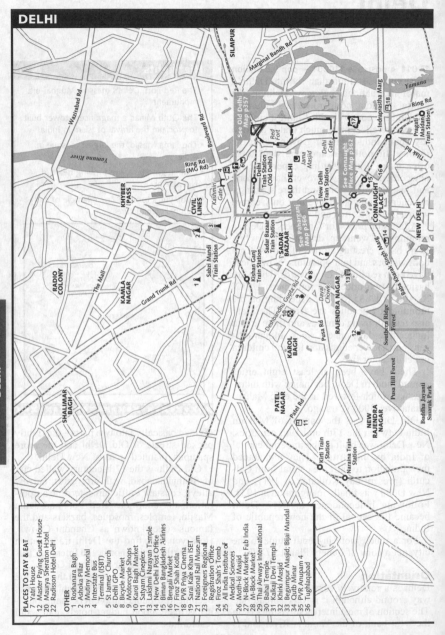

SILMPUR

Marginal Bandh Rd

Yamuna

Indraprastha Marg

Ring Rd

See Old Delhi
Map p357

Red
Fort

Pragati
Maidan
Train Station

18

17

Tilak Rd

Wazirabad Rd

Boulevard Rd

Yamuna River

KHYBER
PASS

Ring Rd
(MG Rd)

4

Kashmiri
Gate

Delhi
Train Station
(Old Delhi)

5
6

Delhi
Gate

Jama
Masjid

OLD DELHI

New Delhi
Train Station

See Connaught
Place Map p362

16

15
C

14

CONNAUGHT
PLACE

NEW DELHI

CIVIL
LINES

2
3

3

Sabzi Mandi
Train Station

Sadar Bazaar
Train Station

SADAR
BAZAAR

See Paharganj
Map p366

7

Kishan Ganj
Train Station

Baba Kharak Singh Marg

RADIO
COLONY

The Mall

KAMLA
NAGAR

Grand Trunk Rd

1

1

Deshbandhu Gupta Rd

Dayal
Chowk

8

13

RAJENDRA NAGAR

Southern Ridge
Forest

SHALIMAR
BAGH

10

KAROL
BAGH

Pusa Rd

12

Pusa Hill Forest

Buddha Jayanti
Smarak Park

PATEL
NAGAR

Patel Rd

11

NEW
RAJENDRA
NAGAR

11

Kirti Train
Station

Naraina Train
Station

DELHI

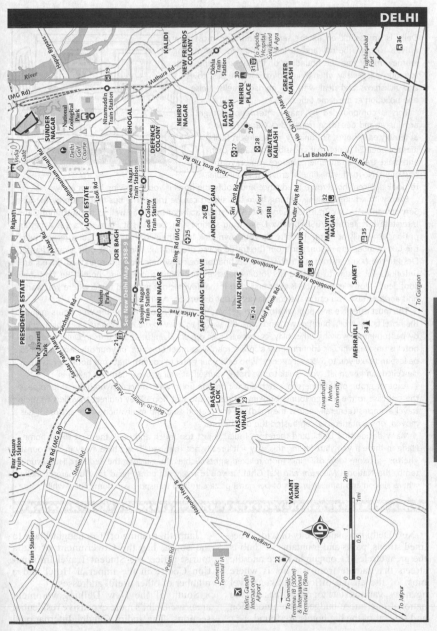

DELHI

To Apollo Hospital, Sultankund (& Agra)

KALIDI

NEW FRIENDS COLONY

Hapal Bypass

River

(MG Rd)

SUNDER NAGAR

India Gate

Delhi Golf Course

PRESIDENT'S ESTATE

Rajpath

Subramanium Bharti Rd

Lodi Rd

LODI ESTATE

JOR BAGH

Nehru Park

Panchsheel Rd

Akbar Rd

Mahavir Javanti Park

Sardar Patel Marg

Ring Rd (MG Rd)

Brar Square Train Station

Station Rd

National Hwy 8

Benj-to-Juret- Marg

VASANT VIHAR

VASANT KUNJ

Jawarharlal Nehru University

Palam Rd

To Domestic, Terminal-IB (300m) & International Terminal 1a (5km)

Domestic Terminal IA

Indira Gandhi International Airport

Gurgaon Rd

To Jaipur

Mathura Rd

BHOGAL

Nizamuddin Train Station

National Zoological Park

DEFENCE COLONY

Sewa Nagar Train Station

Lodi Colony Train Station

Ring Rd (MG Rd)

Sarojini Nagar Train Station

SAROJINI NAGAR

SAFDARJANG ENCLAVE

Africa Ave

HAUZ KHAS

Olof Palme Rd

BASANT LOK

NEHRU NAGAR

Josip Broz Tito Rd

ANDREW'S GANJ

Aurobindo Marg

Siri Fort Rd

SIRI

Siri Fort

Aurobindo Marg

BEGUMPUR

EAST OF KAILASH

Okhla Train Station

NEHRU PLACE

GREATER KAILASH II

Ho Chi Minh Marg

GREATER KAILASH I

Lal Bahadur — Shastri Rd

Outer Ring Rd

MALVIYA NAGAR

SAKET

MEHRAULI

To Gurgaon

Tughlaqabad Fort

See New Delhi Map p358-9

19

20

21

22

23

24

25

26

27

28

29

30

31

32

33

34

35

36

2km
1mi
0   0.5   1

DELHI

Dodgy Delhi

Delhi is an assault on all the senses, daunting most new arrivals to both the city and to India. Frazzled from a long journey, many find the hounding of the beggars and touts too much, especially when trying to manoeuvre past cows and rickshaws and deal with the myriad smells, noise and pollution at the same time.

This is compounded by many international flights arriving at and departing from Indira Gandhi airport at terribly early hours. Fortunately, most airport facilities are open 24 hours, so it's possible to change cash and make travel arrangements before you brave the onslaught. No matter the time of arrival, it's advisable to book a decent hotel room in advance and notify the hotel if you're arriving late or early.

MICK WELDON

Even with a hotel booking, getting from the airport can be tricky. The bus that is run by the Ex-Servicemen's Air Link Transport Service (EATS) stops at large hotels as well as the Kashmiri Gate Interstate Bus Terminal (ISBT), New Delhi train station and Connaught Place. A taxi is a better option, especially at night; if you're on your own look for others to share with. Get a receipt with the taxi number and destination from the traffic police prepaid taxi booth – the others overcharge. Despite the taxi registration number and destination being written down, airport taxi drivers are notorious for scams to get tourists into expensive and commission-paying hotels. Be firm and confident – don't let on if this is your first visit; if the driver is not prepared to go where you want, find another taxi. You can make complaints about drivers on ☎ 6101197.

The most effective and popular stories to get you to another hotel during the wee hours include the hotel being 'full', 'burnt down' and 'closed', as well as a few more extravagant tales, backed up by pantomimes involving other players – sometimes drivers claim there are riots in Delhi and your hotel is unsafe, which is confirmed by a 'policeman' you meet en route, or your driver will claim to be lost and take you to a 'travel agency' who calls your hotel to confirm that your booking has been cancelled, and even lets you speak to the hotel yourself. It's all a ruse – don't be taken in.

Another group of scammers to watch out for are the uniformed 'officials' who hang around near the staircase to the foreign tourist-booking office on the first floor. They redirect travellers to their travel agencies (generally across the road) on the pretext that the reservation office is closed, has moved, or spontaneously combusted the day before.

Many decide that Delhi (and therefore India) is just too much and book the next flight home. Hang in there if you start feeling this way – it's really not that bad. Don't hide away in the tourist ghettos – explore some of Delhi's more relaxed sights such as the gardens, the Red Fort, Humayun's tomb, the National Museum and Raj Ghat. If you're really suffering, head for Connaught Place where air-con and familiar brands of beer and pizza can help transport you home for a while.

New Delhi is a planned city of wide, tree-lined streets, parks and fountains. Its hub is the great circle of Connaught Place and the streets that radiate from it. This is where most of the airline offices, banks, travel agencies, various state tourist offices and the national one, more budget accommodation and several of the big hotels are found.

Janpath, running off Connaught Place to the south, has the Government of India tourist office, the Student Travel Information Centre in the Imperial Hotel and a number of other useful addresses.

South of the New Delhi government areas are Delhi's more expensive residential sections. The Indira Gandhi International

Airport is to the southwest of the city, and about halfway between the airport and Connaught Place is Chanakyapuri, the diplomatic enclave.

Information

Tourist Offices The **Government of India tourist office** (☎ 3320005, fax 3320109, W www.india-tourism.com; 88 Janpath; open 9am-6pm Mon-Fri, 9am-2pm Sat & most public holidays), off Connaught Place, has a good free map of the city.

In the arrivals hall of the international terminal at Indira Ghandi airport there is a **tourist counter** (open 24 hrs).

Delhi Tourism and Transportation Development Corporation (DTTDC; ☎ 3314229; W www.delhitourism.nic.in; N-Block, Middle Circle; open 7am-9pm Mon-Fri) also has counters at New Delhi and Old Delhi train stations, as well as at the interstate bus station at Kashmiri Gate and the international and domestic terminals at the airport.

There are several listings and general information guides – Delhi Cityinfo (free), Delhi City Guide (Rs 20) and Delhi Diary (Rs 10) are the best and come out fortnightly.

Most of the state governments have information centres in Delhi. The **Rajasthan tourist information centre** (☎ 3383837; Bikaner House, Pandara Rd) is near India Gate.

Money Central Bank has a 24-hour branch at the Ashok Hotel in Chanakyapuri, New Delhi, although it doesn't accept all currencies. There are also 24-hour branches of the State Bank of India and Thomas Cook in the arrival and departure areas of the international terminal at Indira Ghandi airport. There are half a dozen ATMs where you can get cash advances on your credit card at Connaught Place. In Paharganj there's an ICICI ATM next to the Hotel Kelson in Rajguru Rd.

There are several moneychangers located around Connaught Place. **American Express** (☎ 3325221, fax 3715352; A-Block, Inner Circle; open 9.30am-5.45pm Mon-Sat) is usually crowded, but the service is fast. You don't have to have AmEx cheques to change money here.

Post There are small post offices in Paharganj and A-Block, Connaught Place, but the main post offices are the **New Delhi GPO** (Baba Kharak Singh Marg; open 10am-8pm Mon-Sat, 10am-5pm Sun), on the traffic circle 1km southwest of Connaught Place, and the **Delhi GPO** (Lothian Rd), between the Red Fort and Kashmiri Gate.

Poste restante mail is held at the New Delhi post office. Mail is held here for about six weeks. Poste restante mail addressed simply to 'GPO Delhi' will end up at the inconveniently situated old Delhi GPO, so ask your correspondents to specify 'New Delhi post office, 110001'.

Email & Internet Access Internet and email cafés are multiplying rapidly and improving in their quality of connection. Email/Internet facilities at luxury hotels are too expensive to consider. There's an Internet office at the **British Council** (17 Kasturba Gandhi Marg), southeast of Connaught Place, while at Connaught Place there's **DSIDC Cyber Cafe** (N-Block Middle Circle; open 9am-8pm Mon-Sat), which charges Rs 20/30 for 30 minutes/one hour.

In Paharganj there's the **Internet Centre**, near the Hotel Vishal and a centre in the Hotel Ajay charging Rs 30 an hour.

Visa Extensions Lodge applications at the **Foreigners Regional Registration Office** (FRRO) in Delhi – see Visas & Documents in the Facts for the Visitor chapter.

Travel Agencies In New Delhi the **Student Travel Information Centre** (☎ 3368161, fax 3369694; W www.isicweb.net) has an office in Hotel Janpath that many travellers use to renew or obtain student cards, although their tickets are not usually as cheap as elsewhere. **Ashok Travels & Tours** (☎ 3325035; L-Block, Connaught Place) is the travel agency arm of the Indian Tourism Development Corporation (ITDC). It can book tickets as well as arranges tours.

Southwest of Connaught Place, **VINstring Holidays** (☎ 3368717, fax 3368901; W www .vinstring.com; YWCA International Guest House, 10 Sansad Marg) and **Y Tours & Travel**

(☎ 3711662; YMCA Tourist Hotel, Ashoka Rd) have been recommended by readers.

In Paharganj, **Hotel Namaskar** (☎ 3621234; e namaskarhotel@yahoo.com; 917 Chandiwalan), just off Main Bazaar, and the travel agency at the **Hotel Ajanta** (☎ 7520925; Arakashan Rd) are also recommended.

For upmarket travel arrangements, try **Cox & Kings** (☎ 3736031; w www.coxandkings.com; H-Block, Connaught Place) and **Sita World Travels** (☎ 3311133; F-Block, Connaught Place).

Photography If you're wanting to get film processed in Delhi, the **Delhi Photo Company** (☎ 3320577; 78 Janpath), off Connaught Place, processes both print and slide film competently.

Bookshops Around Connaught Place, some good bookshops include **Bookworm** (☎ 3322260; e bookworm@vsnl.com; B-29 Radial Rd No 4), **New Book Depot** (☎ 3320020; e rakeshchandra@mantraonline.com; B-18 Inner Circle), **English Book Store** (☎ 332 9126; L-17, Connaught Circus) and **People Tree** (☎ 3734877; 8 Regal Bldg, Sansad Marg), which sells books about the environment and ecofriendly products.

Medical Services Reliable places include **East West Medical Centre** (☎ 6293701/2; B-28 Greater Kailash, New Delhi), near the Delhi Golf Course; **Dr Ram Manohar Lohia Hospital** (☎ 3365525; Baba Kharak Singh Marg); and **All India Institute of Medical Sciences** (☎ 6561123; Ansari Nagar, Andrew's Ganj). Embassies have lists of doctors and dentists. There's a 24-hour **pharmacy** (☎ 3318163; opposite M-Block, Connaught Circus) at Super Bazaar.

Old Delhi

The old walled city of Shahjahanabad stands to the west of the Red Fort and was, at one time, surrounded by a sturdy defensive wall, only fragments of which are now in existence.

The **Kashmiri Gate**, at the northern end of the walled city, was the scene of desperate fighting when the British retook Delhi

during the 1857 Uprising. West of here, near Sabzi Mandi, is the British-erected **Mutiny Memorial** to the soldiers who lost their lives during the 1857 Uprising. Near the monument is an **Ashoka pillar**.

Red Fort The red sandstone walls of the Red Fort (Lal Qila; foreigner/citizen/child under 15 Rs 100/5/free; video Rs 25) extend for 2km. Emperor Shah Jahan began the construction of the fort in 1638 and it was completed in 1648. He never completely moved here from Agra, as he was deposed and imprisoned by his son Aurangzeb, the first and last great Mughal emperor to rule from here. You can wander around on your own: hire an audio guide inside for Rs 20.

You enter the fort through the **Lahore Gate**, so named because it faces Lahore, now in Pakistan, and find yourself in a vaulted arcade, the **Chatta Chowk** (Covered Bazaar), which once sold the quality items required by the royal household – silks, jewellery and gold. This leads to the **Naubat Khana** (Drum House), where musicians used to play for the emperor. The first floor now houses a small **military museum**.

The elegant **Diwan-i-Am** (Hall of Public Audiences) was where the emperor heard complaints or disputes. The **Diwan-i-Khas** (Hall of Private Audiences), built of white marble, was the luxurious chamber where the emperor held private meetings. The centrepiece of the hall was the magnificent Peacock Throne, which the Persian emperor Nadir Shah carted off to Iran in 1739. In 1760 the Marathas removed the silver ceiling, so today the hall is a pale shadow of its former glorious self.

The modest building with a graceful roof at the northeastern edge of the fort is the **Shahi Burj**, Shah Jahan's private working area and a favourite place for emperors to hold conclaves. From here the **Nahr-i-Bhisht** (Stream of Paradise) water channel used to flow through the Royal Baths, the Diwan-i-Khas, the Khas Mahal and the Rang Mahal.

The **Khas Mahal** was the emperor's private palace, divided into rooms for worship, sleeping and living. Spanning the Nahr-i-Bhisht

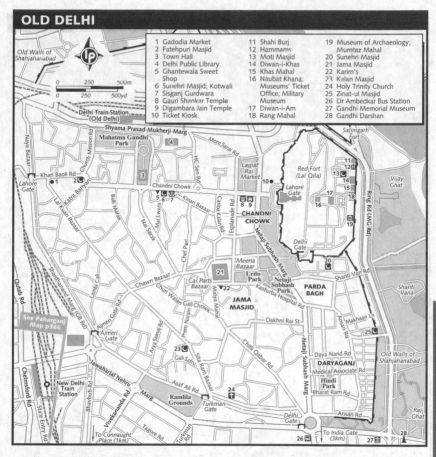

OLD DELHI

1 Gadodia Market	11 Shahi Burj	19 Museum of Archaeology;
2 Fatehpuri Masjid	12 Hammams	Mumtaz Mahal
3 Town Hall	13 Moti Masjid	20 Sunehri Masjid
4 Delhi Public Library	14 Diwan-i-Khas	21 Jama Masjid
5 Ghantewala Sweet	15 Khas Mahal	22 Karim's
Shop	16 Naubat Khana;	23 Kalan Masjid
6 Sunehri Masjid; Kotwali	Museums' Ticket	24 Holy Trinity Church
7 Sisganj Gurdwara	Office; Military	25 Zinat-ul Masjid
8 Gauri Shankar Temple	Museum	26 Dr Ambedkar Bus Station
9 Digambara Jain Temple	17 Diwan-i-Am	27 Gandhi Memorial Museum
10 Ticket Kiosk	18 Rang Mahal	28 Gandhi Darshan

DELHI

is a fine inlaid marble *jali* (carved lattice screen) depicting the sun, moon and stars, as well as the scales of justice.

The **Rang Mahal** (Palace of Colour) took its name from the painted interior (now sadly gone) and was the residence of the emperor's chief wife.

The most southern of the pavilions along the eastern wall is the **Mumtaz Mahal**, formerly the residence Jahanara Begum, Shah Jahan's favourite daughter and boss of the royal harem. Today this building houses the small and tatty, but interesting, **Museum of Archaeology** *(admission free; open 9am-5pm*

Sat-Thur) which displays weapons, carpets, textiles and scenes of courtly life.

Chandni Chowk The main street of Old Delhi is the colourful shopping bazaar known as Chandni Chowk. Next to the *kotwali* (police station) is the **Sunehri Masjid**. In 1739, Nadir Shah, who carried off the Peacock Throne when he sacked Delhi, stood on this roof to watch his soldiers massacre Delhi's residents. The west end of Chandni Chowk is marked by the **Fatehpuri Masjid**, which was erected in 1650 by one of Shah Jahan's wives. **Khari Baoli**, the road

NEW DELHI

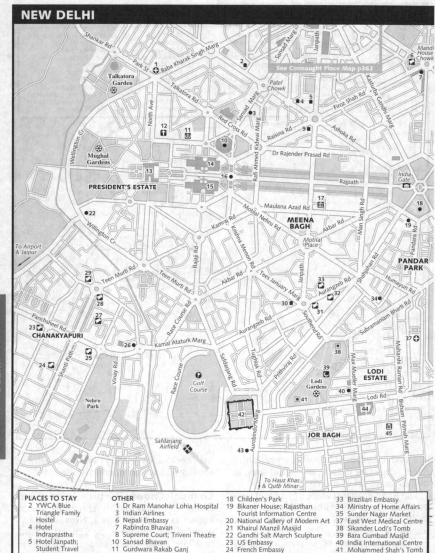

See Connaught Place Map p362

PLACES TO STAY
2 YWCA Blue
   Triangle Family
   Hostel
4 Hotel
   Indraprastha
5 Hotel Janpath;
   Student Travel
   Information Centre;
   SriLankan Airlines;
   Virgin Atlantiz; STIC;
   Kazakhstan Airlines
9 Hotel Le Meridien;
   CJ's Nightclub
30 Claridges Hotel
36 The Oberoi

OTHER
1 Dr Ram Manohar Lohia Hospital
3 Indian Airlines
6 Nepali Embassy
7 Rabindra Bhavan
8 Supreme Court; Triveni Theatre
10 Sansad Bhavan
11 Gurdwara Rakab Ganj
12 Cathedral Church of the
   Redemption
13 Rashtrapati Bhavan
14 Secretariat (North Block)
15 Secretariat (South Block)
16 Vijay Chowk
17 National Museum;
   Archaeological Survey of India

18 Children's Park
19 Bikaner House; Rajasthan
   Tourist Information Centre
20 National Gallery of Modern Art
21 Khairul Manzil Masjid
22 Gandhi Salt March Sculpture
23 US Embassy
24 French Embassy
25 Australian Embassy
26 Ashok Hotel; Iran Air;
   Central Bank
27 UK Embassy
28 Norwegian Embassy
29 Sri Lankan High Commission
31 Danish Embassy
32 Israeli Embassy

33 Brazilian Embassy
34 Ministry of Home Affairs
35 Sunder Nagar Market
37 East West Medical Centre
38 Sikander Lodi's Tomb
39 Bara Gumbad Masjid
40 India International Centre
41 Mohammed Shah's Tomb
42 Safdarjang's Tomb
43 Indian Airlines
   (24 Hours)
44 Indian Habitat Centre;
   Habitat World
45 Tibet House
46 Nizam-ud-din's Shrine
47 Humayun's Tomb

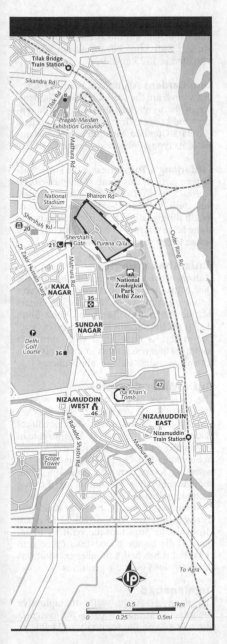

running from the Fatehpuri Masjid to the western edge of the old city, is where you'll find Delhi's hectic wholesale spice market.

Jama Masjid The great Jama Masjid *(Friday Mosque; admission free, still camera or video Rs 100; open 7am-12.15pm & 1.45pm-half hr before sunset, open 9.30am winter)* of Old Delhi is both the largest mosque in India and the final architectural extravagance of Shah Jahan, who also built the Taj Mahal and Delhi's Red Fort. Begun in 1644, it was not completed until 1658. You can enter by either the north or south gate.

Firoz Shah Kotla Built by Firoz Shah Tughlaq in 1354, the ruins of Firozabad, the fifth city of Delhi, are at Firoz Shah Kotla, just off Bahadur Shah Zafar Marg between Old and New Delhi. In the fortress-palace is a 13m-high sandstone Ashoka pillar inscribed with Ashoka's edicts.

Raj Ghat Northeast of Firoz Shah Kotla, on the banks of the Yamuna, a simple square platform of black marble marks the spot where Mahatma Gandhi was cremated following his assassination in 1948. A commemorative ceremony takes place each Friday, the day on which he was killed.

Gandhi Darshan & Gandhi Memorial Museum Across the road from Raj Ghat, the **Gandhi Darshan** *(☎ 3319001; admission free; open 10am-5pm Mon-Fri & every 2nd Sat)* is a huge but poorly patronised display of paintings and photos about the Mahatma's life and deeds.

On the opposite corner is the **Gandhi National Museum** *(☎ 3310168; admission free; open 10am-5.30pm daily)*, with yet more Gandhi memorabilia, including the bamboo staff Gandhi carried on the Salt March in Gujarat, the bullet that killed him and even two of his lower teeth, which were extracted in 1936.

New Delhi

Only a short stroll down Sansad Marg from **Connaught Place** is the **Jantar Mantar** *(Sansad Marg; foreigner/citizen Rs 100/5;*

DELHI

open sunrise-sunset), a strange collection of salmon-coloured structures that comprise one of Maharaja Jai Singh II's observatories, built in 1725. It is dominated by a huge sundial known as the Prince of Dials.

The immensely broad **Rajpath** (Kingsway), is a feature of architect Lutyens' New Delhi. The Republic Day parade is held here every 26 January, attracting millions.

The 42m-high **India Gate** is at the eastern end of Rajpath. The official residence of the president of India, **Rashtrapati Bhavan**, stands at the western end. Completed in 1929, it is an interesting blend of Mughal and Western architecture. Prior to Independence this was the viceroy's residence. He had 418 gardeners, 50 of whom were boys employed to chase away birds!

Sansad Bhavan, the Indian parliament building, stands almost hidden at the end of Sansad Marg, just north of Rajpath. After the 13 December 2001 terrorist attack on the parliament it may be very difficult to visit.

Purana Qila Just southeast of India Gate and north of Humayun's tomb is the old fort, Purana Qila (foreigner/citizen Rs 100/5, video Rs 25; open sunrise-sunset). This is the supposed site of Indraprastha, the original city of Delhi. The Afghan ruler Sher Shah completed the fort during his reign from 1538 to 1545.

There's a small **archaeological museum** just inside the main gate, and good views of New Delhi from atop the gate. There's also a **sound-and-light show** (☎ 4629365; Rs 25; English show 8.30pm Feb-Apr, 9pm May-Aug, 8.30pm Sept-Oct, 7.30pm Nov-Jan) here that's better than you might expect. It goes for an hour, with the Hindi show starting one-and-a-half hours earlier than the English show.

Humayun's Tomb Built in the mid-16th century by Haji Begum, the Persian-born wife of the Mughal emperor Humayun, this is a wonderful early example of Mughal architecture (foreigner/citizen Rs 250/5, video Rs 25; open sunrise-sunset daily). Haji Begum is buried in the tomb of red-and-white sandstone and black-and-yellow marble.

Nizam-ud-din's Shrine Across the road from Humayun's tomb is the shrine of the Muslim Sufi saint Nizam-ud-din Chishti, who died in 1325 aged 92.

Lodi Gardens About 3km west of Humayun's tomb are the well-kept Lodi Gardens, site of the tombs of the Sayyid (15th century) and Lodi (15th to 16th century) rulers. The **Bara Gumbad Mosque** is a fine example of its type of plaster decoration.

Safdarjang's Tomb Beside the small Safdarjang airport, this tomb (foreigner/citizen Rs 100/5, video Rs 25; open sunrise-sunset) was built in 1753–54 by the nawab of Avadh for his father, Safdarjang, and is one of the last examples of Mughal architecture before the great empire collapsed.

Hauz Khas Village

Midway between Safdarjang's tomb and the Qutb Minar, this area was once the reservoir for the second city of Delhi – Siri. Sights include the domed **Tomb of Firoz Shah** (1398) and the remains of an ancient college. The village is now filled with upmarket boutiques and restaurants in a slightly fake but still pleasant 'village' atmosphere.

Qutb Minar Complex

The buildings in this complex (foreigner/citizen Rs 250/10, video Rs 25; open sunrise-sunset daily), 15km south of Connaught Place, date from the onset of Muslim rule in India and are fine examples of early Afghan architecture. The **Qutb Minar** is a soaring tower of victory that was started in 1193, immediately after the defeat of the last Hindu kingdom in Delhi.

At the foot of the Qutb Minar stands the **Quwwat-ul-Islam Masjid** (Might of Islam Mosque), the first mosque built in India. Qutb-ud-din began its construction on it in 1193, but it has had a number of additions and extensions over the centuries.

Tughlaqabad

The massively strong walls of impressive Tughlaqabad (Mehrauli Badarpur Rd; foreigner/citizen Rs 100/5), the third city of Delhi, lie

8km east of the Qutb Minar. The walled city and fort with its 13 gateways was built by Ghiyas-ud-din Tughlaq and its construction involved a legendary quarrel with the saint Nizam-ud-din. When the Tughlaq ruler took the workers Nizam-ud-din wanted for work on his tank, the saint cursed the king with the warning that his city would be inhabited only by Gujars (shepherds). Today that is indeed the situation.

Museums & Galleries

The **National Museum** (☎ 3019272; Janpath; foreigner/citizen Rs 150/10, camera 300/20; open 10am-5pm Tues-Sun) is just south of Rajpath. It has exhibits dating back to the Mauryan period (2nd to 3rd century BC); from South India's Vijayanagar period (14th to 16th centuries); miniature and mural paintings; and costumes of India's Adivasis (tribal peoples). There are free guided tours conducted at 10.30am, 11.30am, noon, 2pm and 3.30pm.

The **National Gallery of Modern Art** (☎ 3382835; foreigner/citizen Rs 150/10; open 10am-5pm Tues-Sat) is near India Gate. It has excellent works by Indian and colonial artists.

The **National Rail Museum** (☎ 6881816; Chanakyapuri; adult/child Rs 5/3, camera Rs 10; open 9.30am-1pm & 1.30pm-7.30pm Tues-Sun Apr-Sept, 9.30am-1pm & 1.30pm-5.30pm Tue-Sun Oct-Mar) will be of great interest to anyone even remotely interested in railways. In the park are a large number of retired locomotives spanning the years of India's railway system.

Tibet House (☎ 4611515; Lodi Rd; admission Rs 10; open 9.30am-5.30pm Mon-Fri), just over 1km southeast of Lodi Garden, has a fascinating collection of ceremonial items brought out of Tibet when the Dalai Lama fled from the Chinese occupation forces.

Organised Tours

The ITDC, under the name **Ashok Travels & Tours** (☎ 3325035; L-Block, Connaught Place), near Nirula's Hotel, has half-day (Rs 130 to 150) and full-day (Rs 240) tours. You can also book at the **Government of India tourist office** (☎ 3320005; 88 Janpath)

or at major hotels. The **Delhi Tourism & Transportation Development Corporation** (DTTDC; ☎ 3314229; N-Block, Middle Circle) also has half-/full-day tours for Rs 95/180.

Places to Stay

If Delhi is your first stop in India, it's very wise to make an advance accommodation booking. Good hotels fill up fast, leaving you prey to hotel touts who earn their commissions by luring you into the rip-off joints.

Places to Stay – Budget

Many travellers head for Paharganj near New Delhi train station – midway between Old Delhi and New Delhi. The alternative area is around Janpath at the southern side of Connaught Place in New Delhi, but there's less choice there.

Homestays The **Government of India tourist office** (see Information earlier) and the **Student Travel Information Centre** at the Hotel Janpath (see Travel Agencies earlier), have lists of families who offer homestays, which usually cost between Rs 500 and 1500 per night.

Connaught Place & Janpath Area The ever popular **Ringo Guest House** (☎ 3310605; Connaught Lane; dorm beds Rs 90, singles/doubles with shared bathroom Rs 125/250, doubles with private bathroom Rs 350-400) has had its fair share of detractors as well as fans, but it's safe and the staff are friendly. The rooms are very small but it's clean enough.

Sunny Guest House (☎ 3312909; Connaught Lane; dorm beds Rs 90, singles/doubles with shared bathroom from Rs 125/250, doubles with private bathroom Rs 280-400) is not far away from Ringo Guest House, but the place has less of a communal feel.

Paharganj Area The good-value **Kailash Guest House** (☎ 3674993; 4469 Main Bazaar; singles/doubles with shared bathroom Rs 110/200, doubles with private bathroom & hot water Rs 250) is a modern, clean and quite friendly place, although many of the rooms face inwards and tend to be a bit stuffy.

DELHI

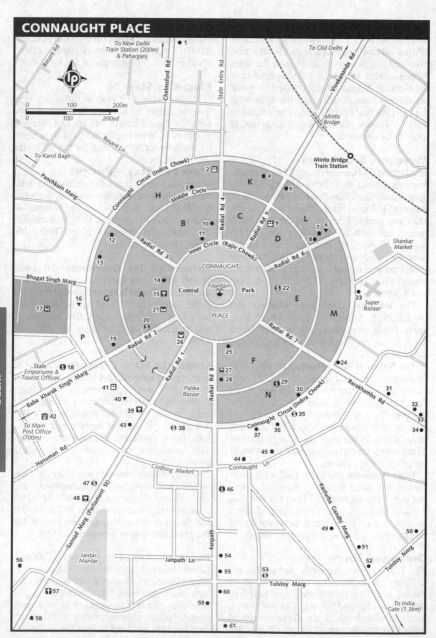

CONNAUGHT PLACE

CONNAUGHT PLACE

PLACES TO STAY
4   York Hotel
7   Nirula's Hotel
12 Hotel Marina
44 Ringo Guest House; Don't
    Pass Me By Cafe
45 Sunny Guest House
56 YMCA Tourist Hotel; Y Tours
    & Travels
58 YWCA International Guest
    House; VINstring Holidays

PLACES TO EAT
6   Nirula's Complex; Pot Pourri;
    Chinese Room; Pegasus
16 Vega
40 Gaylord

OTHER
1   Railway Booking Office
2   Plaza Cinema
3   Cox & Kings
5   English Book Store
8   Ashok Travels & Tours
9   Odeon Cinema
10 Bookworm
11 New Book Depot
13 Gulf Air

14 American Express
15 El Rodeo
17 Local Bus Station
18 Delhi Tourism Corporation
19 Royal Jordanian; SriLankan
    Airlines
20 American Express Bank ATM
21 Post Office
22 24-Hour Standard Chartered
    Grindlays Bank ATM
23 24-Hour Pharmacy
24 British Airways; Qantas
    Airways
25 Sita World Travels
26 Prepaid Autorickshaw Kiosk
27 EATS Airport Bus
28 Indian Airlines
29 Delhi Tourism and Transporta-
    tion Development Corporation
    (DTTDC); DSIDC Cyber Cafe
30 Jet Airways
31 Malaysia Airlines; Singapore
    Airlines
32 Emirates; Wheels
33 Kuwait Airways
34 Saudi Arabian Airlines
35 Hong Kong & Shanghai Bank
    ATM

36 Air France
37 Delhi Transport Corporation
38 Jeevan Bharati Building (24-
    Hour Citibank ATM; Air India)
39 DV8
41 Regal Cinema
42 Hanuman Mandir
43 People Tree
46 Government of India Tourist
    Office; Delhi Photo Company
47 Standard Chartered Grindlays
    Bank ATM
48 Someplace Else
49 British Council
50 KLM; El Al Israel Airlines
51 Kuwait Airways
52 United Airlines; Scandinavian
    Airlines
53 Deutsche Bank ATM; Aeroflot
54 Lufthansa Airlines; Air Canada
55 Royal Nepal Airlines
    Corporation (RNAC)
57 Free Church
59 Imperial Hotel
60 Central Cottage Industries
    Emporium
61 Chandralok Building (Druk Air;
    Japan Airlines)

DELHI

Major's Den (☎ 3629599; e majorsden@
hotmail.com; 2314 Lakshmi Narain St; singles
with private bathroom Rs 150-350, doubles
with private bathroom Rs 250-450), in an
alleyway leading off Rajguru Rd, is clean,
well run and a good place to stay. All bathrooms are advertised as having 'modern
gadgets' and two rooms have air-con.

Lord's Hotel (☎ 3558703; e jassal@ndf
.vsnl.net.in; 51 Main Bazaar; singles/doubles
Rs 395/495) is a bright new hotel built with
copious amounts of white marble. Rooms
here are good value.

Hotel Soma (☎ 3621002, fax 3552634; 33
Arakashan Rd; singles/doubles Rs 400/450,
rooms with air-con Rs 700), about 500m
north of Main Bazaar, has clean and modern rooms of a decent size.

Krishna Hotel (☎ 3610252, fax 3632033;
45 Arakashan Rd; singles/doubles Rs 300/
350, air-con rooms with private bathroom
Rs 800) has smallish but quite acceptable
rooms. The bathrooms are serviced with
24-hour hot water.

Airport For those who have a confirmed
departure within 24 hours of arrival, consider staying at the airport **retiring rooms**
(dorm beds Rs 80), conveniently located at
both the domestic (Terminal I; ☎ 3295126;
dorm beds Rs 250) and the international (Terminal II; ☎ 5452011; dorm beds Rs 90, twin
share Rs 450) terminals.

Places to Stay – Mid-Range
There's a luxury tax of 10% on rooms over
Rs 500, and some places also levy a service
charge of 5% to 10%.

The Ys The Ys are popular so book ahead.
YMCA Tourist Hotel (☎ 3361915, fax
3746032; e ymca@ndf.vsnl.net.in; Jai Singh
Rd; singles/doubles with shared bathroom
Rs 450/800, with air-con & private bathroom
Rs 900/1500; open 24 hrs) is near the Jantar
Mantar (south of Connaught Place) and
gets very mixed reports from travellers.
Breakfast is included in the rates and there's
also a pool.

YWCA International Guest House (☎ 336 1561, fax 3341763; ⓦ www.ywcaindia.org; 10 Sansad Marg; singles/doubles with private bathroom Rs 800/1100) is near Connaught Place and has a good restaurant and travel agency. Rates include breakfast.

YWCA Blue Triangle Family Hostel (☎ 3360133, fax 3360202; Ashoka Rd; singles/doubles Rs 575/1035, with air-con Rs 805/1150) is just west off Sansad Marg. It's clean, well run and has a restaurant, but the rooms are basic and starting to decay. Rates include breakfast.

Connaught Place & Janpath Area The clean, comfortable **York Hotel** (☎ 3323769, fax 3352419; K-Block, Connaught Circus; singles/doubles Rs 1800/2950) has helpful management. The rooms at the back are quieter. For Rs 500 you can be collected from the airport.

Hotel Marina (☎ 3324658, fax 3328609; ⓔ marina@nde.vsnl.net.in; G-59 Block, Connaught Circus; singles/doubles Rs 2600/3200) is quite smart. The rooms, mostly with windows, are of a good standard and comfortable. They come with phones, TV and 24-hour room service.

Nirula's Hotel (☎ 3322419, fax 3353957; ⓔ delhihotel@nirulas.com; L-Block, Radial Rd 6; singles/doubles from Rs 1995/3700) is right beside the Nirula restaurants and snack bars. It is a small, comfortable and clean three-star hotel, which has been decorated with a certain flair. Advance bookings are advisable.

Other Areas There are two excellent private guesthouses to the west of Connaught Place.

Master Paying Guest House (☎ 5741089; ⓔ urvashi@del2.vsnl.net.in; R-500 New Rajendra Nagar; singles Rs 400-700, doubles Rs 500-800) is a homey and friendly place. The beautifully furnished rooms are large and airy and the service is excellent; in winter you get hot-water bottles in your bed.

Yatri House (☎ 3625563; ⓔ yatri@nde.vsnl.net.in; 3/4 Panchkuian Rd; singles/doubles Rs 1125/1400) is a calm and secure guest house with spotlessly clean rooms.

Hotel Indraprastha (☎ 3344511, fax 336 8153; ⓔ indraprastha@vsnl.net; cnr Ashoka Rd & Janpath; nonair-con singles/doubles from Rs 650/800, air-con singles/doubles from Rs 1100/1200) is just a 10-minute walk from Connaught Place. Rooms in this high-rise, government-run hotel are a reasonable size and some have been renovated, but none have a phone, TV or room service. There's a self-service café, restaurant and air-conditioned bar. Ashok Travels & Tours (the ITDC tourist outfit) has a desk at this hotel. The Indraprastha gets very mixed reviews from travellers depending on the room, but don't expect any ambience.

Hotel Janpath (☎ 3320070, fax 3327083; ⓔ janpath@ndf.vsnl.net.in; Janpath; 4-star; singles/doubles from US$60/75) is a large rambling 1950s ITDC hotel that looks as if it's been declining since its opening day. Now really only deserving two stars, its redeeming feature is its central position.

Places to Stay – Top End

Many of the best restaurants and most exclusive boutiques are at the top-end hotels.

Claridges Hotel (☎ 3010211, fax 3010625; ⓔ claridges.hotel@genu.vsnl.net.in; 12 Aurangzeb Rd, New Delhi; singles/doubles from US$175/200) is a very comfortable, older establishment that boasts four good restaurants, a swimming pool and a health club. This place is probably the best-value five-star hotel in town.

Radisson Hotel Delhi (☎ 6137373; National Hwy 8; rooms from US$225) is a flashy new place just 3km from the international terminal and it has a complimentary transfer service between hotel and airport.

Maurya Sheraton Hotel (☎ 6112233, fax 6153333; ⓦ www.welcomgroup.com; Sardar Patel Marg; singles/doubles from US$195/220) is west of Chanakyapuri, on the road to the airport, and has a high level of comfort as well as several excellent restaurants, a solar-heated swimming pool, and a disco.

Hotel Le Meridien (☎ 3710101, fax 3714545; ⓦ www.lemeridien-newdelhi.com; Janpath, New Delhi; singles/doubles from US$275/300) is another very modern place to stay and it features a stunning atrium.

The Oberoi (☎ 4363030, fax 4360484; W www.oberoihotels.com; Dr Zakir Hussain Marg, New Delhi; singles/doubles from US$357/387), on the edge of the Delhi Golf Course, is southeast of India Gate. Services include a business centre, travel desk and secretarial services – all 24-hour.

Places to Eat

Delhi has an excellent array of places to eat – from cheap *dhabas* (road-side restaurant) with dishes for less than Rs 15 to swanky restaurants where a meal for two can top Rs 3500.

Connaught Place & Janpath Area A wide variety of snacks, both Indian and Western, is available at **Nirula's** (☎ 3322419; L-Block, Connaught Circus). Above it are a sit-down restaurant called **Pot Pourri** (open 7.30am-midnight; smorgasbord Rs 90, breakfast Rs 60-120) and the **Chinese Room** (open 12.30pm-11pm), with meals for two in the Rs 400 region. Downstairs there's the congenial British-style pub **Pegasus**.

Don't Pass Me By (Connaught Lane; dishes Rs 20-45), in the same lane as the Ringo and Sunny guesthouses, is both popular and cheap. It caters to international tastes and is great for breakfast. There are other cheap eateries along the lane.

Vega (☎ 3344328; P-Block; meals Rs 200, breakfast Rs 65-125), at the Hotel Alka, specialises in veg food cooked Delhi style (in pure ghee but without onion and garlic).

fabcafe (N-1; open 11am-11pm Mon-Sat, 11.30am-4.30pm Sun; mains Rs 135-195) has a very cosmopolitan menu and offers such treats as Creole chicken and wild mushrooms in thyme sauce. The salad bar allows you to construct your own salad.

Gaylord (☎ 3360717; 18 Regal Bldg Connaught Circus; mains around Rs 230) is one of the priciest, plushest restaurants in the area, with big mirrors, chandeliers and excellent Indian food. The high quality of the ingredients makes this a worthwhile splurge.

Paharganj Area Main Bazaar in Paharganj has a handful of cheap restaurants that cater to foreign travellers.

German Bakery, in the foyer of the Hotel Ajay, is a 24-hour place that makes sandwiches, snacks and a wide range of sugar-laden cakes, for about Rs 35 per piece.

Malhotra Restaurant (1833 Laxmi Narain St; dishes Rs 40-130; open daily) is a well-established restaurant that regularly gets good reports. The cuisine is Indian, Chinese and continental.

Vatika (1836 Laxmi Narain St; dishes Rs 35-120; open daily), close to Malhotra, is a new restaurant with a Japanese co-owner. There are authentic Japanese dishes and you can even get a Japanese breakfast for Rs 50. Apart from this there's a plentiful Thai, Indian and Chinese selection.

Old Delhi For really cheap eating, there are food stalls that set up in the evening on the southern side of the Jama Masjid. They really only serve fried fish, fried chicken or mutton kebabs, which are accompanied by *rumali roti* ('handkerchief' bread). It's fairly chaotic but you can eat really well here for Rs 30.

Ghantewala Sweet Shop (Chandni Chowk), near the Sisganj Gurdwara, has been running for 200 years and is reputed to have the best Indian sweets in Delhi.

Karim's (☎ 3269880; Matya Mahal; mains Rs 50-70; open 6am-midnight) is without doubt the first choice in Old Delhi. It has been serving excellent Mughal food to Delhi-wallahs for 80-odd years and has a well-deserved reputation.

Entertainment

First City magazine lists what's going on in town. Major theatre, dance and live-music venues include **Habitat World** (☎ 4682222; W www.habitatworld.com; Lodi Rd, New Delhi), at the India Habitat Centre; the nearby **India International Centre** (☎ 4619431; 40 Max Mueller Marg, New Delhi); **Kamani Auditorium** (☎ 3388084; Copernicus Marg); and the **Triveni Chamber Theatre** (☎ 3718833; 205 Tansen Marg), at Triveni Kala Sangam, close to Rabindra Bhavan.

There are a number of cinemas around Connaught Place, showing Hindi mass-appeal movies; seats range from Rs 25 to 50.

DELHI

DELHI

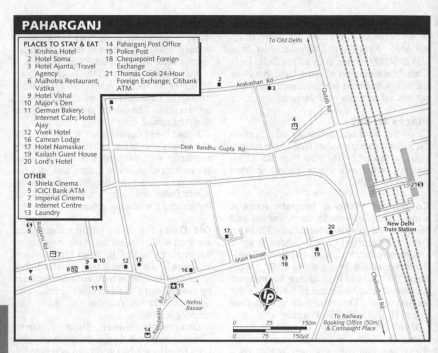

PAHARGANJ

PLACES TO STAY & EAT
1 Krishna Hotel
2 Hotel Soma
3 Hotel Ajanta; Travel Agency
6 Malhotra Restaurant; Vatika
9 Hotel Vishal
10 Major's Den
11 German Bakery; Internet Cafe; Hotel Ajay
12 Vivek Hotel
16 Camran Lodge
17 Hotel Namaskar
19 Kailash Guest House
20 Lord's Hotel

14 Paharganj Post Office
15 Police Post
18 Chequepoint Foreign Exchange
21 Thomas Cook 24-Hour Foreign Exchange; Citibank ATM

OTHER
4 Shiela Cinema
5 ICICI Bank ATM
7 Imperial Cinema
8 Internet Centre
13 Laundry

To Old Delhi
Arakashan Rd
Qutab Rd
Desh Bandhu Gupta Rd
Raiguru Rd
Main Bazaar
Ramdwara Rd
Nehru Bazaar
Chelmsford Rd
New Delhi Train Station
To Railway Booking Office (50m) & Connaught Place

0   75   150m
0   75   150yd

Habitat World has a cinema showing Indian documentaries and arthouse films.

DV8 (*Deviate;* ☎ *3361444; 13 Regal Bldg, Connaught Circus*) is a new bar-restaurant that has the ambience but not the stuffiness of a modern gentleman's club. Contemporary and classic pop is played but not at a level to inhibit conversation.

El Rodeo (*A-12 Inner Circle, Connaught Place*) is a bar-restaurant and it has a cover charge of Rs 200 after 7.30pm if you only want to drink and not eat. Draught beer is around Rs 80.

CJ's Nightclub (*Hotel Le Meridien; Janpath, New Delhi; Rs 500 a couple*) is a popular disco that usually pumps out Western, Indian, techno or pop, depending on what the crowd demands.

The gay and lesbian scene meets every Tuesday at **Someplace Else** (*Park Hotel, Sansad Marg*), near Connaught Place, and the **Mirage Disco** (*Crowne Plaza, New Friends Colony*) on Thursday.

Shopping

Good buys include silk products, precious stones, leather and woodwork. At **Central Cottage Industries Emporium** (☎ *3326790; Janpath*) you'll find items from across India. Along Baba Kharak Singh Marg, two streets from Janpath, are a number of state emporiums. Each sells handicrafts from its state.

In Old Delhi, Chandni Chowk is the famous shopping street. Here you'll find carpets and jewellery of all descriptions. Perfumes are made in the narrow Cariba Kalan.

Main Bazaar in Paharganj has an interesting variety of perfumes, oils, soaps and incense at two places (both signposted), one near Hotel Vivek and another near Camran Lodge. Monday is the official weekly holiday for the shops in Main Bazaar, but you'll find many shops are actually open seven days a week.

Fab India (☎ *6212183; 14 N-Block Market, Greater Kailash I*) is a famous clothing, fabric and furnishings store. (In Dehli young

Indian parliamentarians are sometimes referred to as the 'Fab India gang'.)

Getting There & Away

Delhi is a major international gateway to India; for details on arriving from overseas see the Getting There & Away chapter at the beginning of this book.

Delhi is also a major centre for domestic travel, and you'll find extensive bus, rail and air connections there.

Air The domestic terminal (Terminal I) is 7km from the centre, and the newer international terminal (Terminal II) is a further 4km out. There is a free Indian Airlines bus between the two terminals, or you can use the EATS service (see Getting Around later).

If you're arriving at the airport from overseas, after passing through customs you'll find yourself in an arrivals hall containing various booths. Here you'll find the State Bank of India and Thomas Cook foreign-exchange counters, open 24 hours; a **train booking counter** *(open 8am-8pm Mon-Sat, 8am-2pm Sun)*; at least two 24-hour prepaid taxi counters (you want the one signed 'Prepaid Taxi Local'); two tourist information counters; and a booth where you can hire mobile phones. After this area you'll reach the arrivals public waiting hall, where there's an ICICI bank ATM. Then it's out into open mayhem.

Several airlines require you to have the baggage you're checking in X-rayed and sealed, so do this at the machines just inside the departure hall before you queue to check in. Nearly all tickets have the departure tax included in the price; if not you must pay at the State Bank of India counter in the departures hall, also before checking in.

Indian Airlines The **Malhotra Building office** *(☎ 3310517, 3310141; W www.indian-airlines.nic.in; F-Block, Connaught Place; open 10am-5pm Mon-Sat)* is probably the most convenient, though it's mostly busy.

At **Safdarjang airport** *(☎ 4620566, 141; Aurobindo Marg; open 7am-11pm)* there's a late-opening office and this can be a quick place to make bookings.

Note that if you have an onward connection to another city in India, it may be with Air India, the country's international carrier, rather than the domestic carrier, Indian Airlines. If this is the case, you must check in at the international terminal (Terminal II) rather than the domestic terminal.

Jet Airways The only other domestic airline that services Rajasthan is **Jet Airways** *(☎ 6853700, airport ☎ 5665404, W www.jetairways.com; N-40 Connaught Circus; open 9am-6pm daily)*. Domestic airlines servicing other areas have offices at the airport's domestic terminal.

International Airlines International airlines in Delhi include the following:

Aeroflot (☎ 3312843) Tolstoy House, Tolstoy Marg
Air Canada (☎ 3720014) 56 Janpath
Air France (☎ 3312853) 7 Atma Ram Mansion, Connaught Circus
Air India (☎ 3736446) Jeevan Bharati Bldg, Connaught Circus
Biman Bangladesh Airlines (☎ 3354401) World Trade Centre, Babar Rd, Connaught Place
British Airways (☎ 3316611) Dr Gopal Das Bhavan, Barakhamba Rd
Delta Airlines (☎ 6388979) First India Place, Sushant Lok-l, Mehrauli Gurgaon Rd, Gurgaon
Druk Air (☎ 3310990) Chandralok Bldg, 36 Janpath
El Al Israel Airlines (☎ 3357965) Prakash Deep Bldg, 7 Tolstoy Marg
Emirates (☎ 3328080) Kanchenjunga Bldg, 18 Barakhamba Rd
Gulf Air (☎ 3324293) G-12, Connaught Circus
Japan Airlines (☎ 3327108) Chandralok Bldg, 36 Janpath
KLM (☎ 3357747) Prakash Deep Bldg, 7 Tolstoy Marg
Kuwait Airways (☎ 3354373) Ansal Bhavan, 309 Kasturba Gandhi Marg
Lufthansa Airlines (☎ 3323310) 56 Janpath
Malaysia Airlines (☎ 3313448) Ashoka Estate Bldg, Barakhamba Rd
Royal Jordanian Airlines (☎ 3320635) G-56 Connaught Place
Royal Nepal Airlines Corporation (RNAC, ☎ 3320817) 44 Janpath
Scandinavian Airlines (SAS; ☎ 3352299) Ambadeep Bldg, Kasturba Gandhi Marg

DELHI

Flights to Rajasthan from Delhi

flight	service	departs	arrives	cost (US$)
Indian Airlines				
Delhi–Jaipur	CD7471	5.45am daily	6.25am	65
Delhi–Jaipur	IC896	6.50pm daily	7.30pm	65
Delhi–Jodhpur	CD7471	5.45am daily	7am	115
Delhi–Udaipur	CD7471	5.45am daily	8.50am	115
Jet Airways				
Delhi–Jaipur	9W3401	5.55am daily	6.55am	65
Delhi–Jaipur	9W721	4.50pm daily	5.30pm	65
Delhi–Jodhpur	9W3315	7.05am daily	8.25am	115
Delhi–Udaipur	9W3401	5.55am daily	8.40am	115
Delhi–Udaipur	9W3311	10.55am daily	12.35pm	115

Singapore Airlines (☎ 3329036) Ashoka Estate Bldg, Barakhamba Rd
SriLankan Airlines (☎ 3711334) G-55 Connaught Circus
Swiss (☎ 6388911) First India Place, Block A, Sushant Lok-l, Mehrauli Gurgaon Rd, Gurgaon
Thai International Airways (☎ 6239988) Park Royal Intercontinental Hotel, America Plaza, Nehru Place
United Airlines (☎ 3352986) Ambadeep Bldg, Kasturba Gandhi Marg

Bus The main bus station is the Interstate Bus Terminal at Kashmiri Gate, north of the Old Delhi train station. It has 24-hour left-luggage facilities, a post office, pharmacy and restaurant. Outside there is a 24-hour prepaid taxi counter. City buses leave here for locations all over Delhi.

There are a number of state government bus companies that operate from here, including **Rajasthan Roadways** (☎ 3868709), at counter No 36. Bookings can also be made at Bikaner House just south of Rajpath. There are express buses to many other destinations in Rajasthan, including Alwar (Rs 64, four hours), Bikaner (Rs 170, 10 hours), Kota (Rs 210, 11 hours), Udaipur (Rs 263, 14 hours) and Jhunjhunu (Rs 100, six hours). Private buses run to Ajmer (Rs 110, nine hours), Jodhpur (Rs 180, 13 hours) and Jaisalmer (Rs 250, 20 hours) – book these through a travel agency.

Deluxe buses for Jaipur leave from **Bikaner House** (☎ 3383469; Pandara Rd), between 6.30am and midnight. The trip takes 5½ hours and costs Rs 216, or Rs 348 for the less-frequent air-con services.

From the **Sarai Kale Khan ISBT**, close to Nizamuddin train station, there are frequent departures for Agra (from Rs 75 to Rs 100 depending on class, five hours).

Train The best place to make bookings is the special **foreign tourist booking office** (open 7.30am-5pm Mon-Sat, 8am-2pm Sun) upstairs in New Delhi train station. Ignore the touts lurking around the station who may try to lead you astray. This is the place to go if you want a tourist-quota allocation. Tickets must be paid with rupees backed up by a bank exchange certificate, or in US dollars or pounds sterling, with any change given in rupees.

Other foreigners reservation offices include the one at the airport (open 24 hours) and another located at the **Delhi Tourism and Transportation Development Corporation** (N-Block, Connaught Place; open 7.30am-5pm Mon-Sat).

The **Railway Booking Office** (Chelmsford Rd; open 7.45am-9pm Mon-Sat & 7.45am-1.50pm Sun) is between New Delhi train station and Connaught Place. Take a number as you enter the building, and wait at the allotted window. It's best to arrive first thing in the morning, or when it reopens after lunch.

Remember that there are two main train stations – Delhi train station in Old Delhi, and New Delhi train station at Paharganj. If you're departing from the Old Delhi station allow up to an hour to wind your way through the traffic snarls. Between the Old Delhi and New Delhi stations you can take the No 6 bus.

There's also the Nizamuddin train station south of the New Delhi area. It's worth getting off here if you are staying south of Connaught Place.

Some trains to Jaipur, Jodhpur and Udaipur operate out of Sarai Rohilla station rather than Old Delhi – it's about 3.5km northwest of Connaught Place on Guru Govind Singh Marg. The exception is the *Shatabdi Express* to Jaipur, which operates from New Delhi station. Check out the Indian Railways website (W www.indian rail.gov.ind).

Car & Motorcycle Given Delhi's mind-boggling traffic (there are about six road deaths per day on average), you're better off getting someone to drive you. You'll also save money. If you must rent a car, try **Wheels Rent-a-Car** (☎ 3722150; *Kanchenjunga Bldg, 18 Barakhamba Rd*) or **Hertz** (☎ 6786681, fax 6786615; W www.hertz.com; *RZ-A/43 Mahipalpur Extension*) on National Hwy 8 just before the turn-off to the international airport.

The range of motorcycles available for hire when you get to Rajasthan is rather limited, so you may wish to make your motorcycle arrangements in Delhi.

If you are in the market for a new Enfield motorcycle, Karol Bagh is the place to look. Try **Inder Motors** (☎ 5728579, fax 5755812; e lalli@ndf.vsnl.net.in; *1744 Hari Singh Nalwa St, Karol Bagh*), off Abdul Aziz Rd or, for second-hand bikes and parts, **Madaan Motors** (☎ 5735801, fax 5755812; e madaan motors@yahoo.com; *1767 Naiwala Gali, Har Kishan Das Rd*). Typically a 350cc Enfield will cost Rs 300 a day to hire, and a 500cc will cost Rs 500.

See the Getting Around chapter for advice on travelling by motorcycle.

Getting Around
Delhi is large and congested, and the buses get hopelessly crowded. The alternative is a

DELHI

Major Trains to Rajasthan & Agra from Delhi

destination	train No & name	departure time & station	distance (km)	duration (hrs)	fare (Rs 2nd/1st)
Agra	2180 *Taj Express*	7.15am HN	199	2½	54/284
	2002 *Shatabdi Express*∗	6am ND		2	390/760
Ajmer	2015 *Shatabdi Express*∗	6.10am ND	442	6½	630/1250
	9615 *Chetak Express*	2.10pm SR		12	194/580
Alwar	2015 *Shatabdi Express*∗	6.10am ND	157	2½	350/670
Bikaner	9733 *Shekhawati Express*	11pm SR		12	203/610
Chittorgarh	9615 *Chetak Express*	2.10pm SR	612	16½	131/688
Jaipur	2413 *Delhi–Jaipur Express*	5.15am OD	304	5¼	77/405
	2015 *Shatabdi Express*∗	6.10am ND		4½	495/985
Jodhpur	2461 *Mandor Express*	9pm ND		11	142/370
Udaipur	9615 *Chetak Express*	2.10pm SR	727	19	144/756

Abbreviations for train stations:
ND – New Delhi, OD – Old Delhi, HN – Hazrat Nizamuddin, SR – Sarai Rohilla
∗ *Shatabdi Express* fares are for air-con chair/air con executive classes – fares include meals and drinks

taxi, an autorickshaw, or, for the truly brave, a bicycle.

To/From the Airport The Ex-Servicemen's Air Link Transport Service *(EATS; ☎ 3316530)* has a regular bus service that goes between between the airport (both terminals) and Connaught Place (Rs 50 plus Rs 10 per large piece of luggage). It will drop you off at major hotels en route and at the entrance to New Delhi train station for Paharganj. In Connaught Place the service leaves from near the Indian Airlines office, between 4am and 11.30pm.

When leaving the international terminal, the counter for the EATS bus is just to the right as you exit the building. This is probably the best, although not the quickest, way into the city if you arrive late at night.

On the left, as you leave the customs area, is the 'Prepaid Taxi Local' booth (make sure you don't get taken in by a fake one), where you'll get the lowest prices (Rs 170 to Paharganj). You'll be given a voucher to present at the booth just outside the airport building.

At the domestic terminal, the taxi booking desk is just inside the terminal and it usually charges Rs 170 to Paharganj, plus Rs 5 per bag.

Bus Avoid buses during the rush hours. Whenever possible try to board (and leave) at a starting or finishing point, such as the Regal and Plaza cinemas in Connaught Place. There are some seats reserved for women on the left-hand side of the bus. The White Line and Green Line buses are slightly more expensive and thus usually a little less crowded. Private buses and minibuses also run on these routes.

Taxi & Autorickshaw All taxis and autorickshaws are metered, but the meters are invariably out of date or 'not working', or the drivers simply refuse to use them.

At the end of a metered journey you will have to pay according to a perversely complicated scale of revised charges. There are fare charts printed in the *Delhi City Guide* (Rs 15, available from newsagents). If you have one, pay what you think is the right price and leave it at that. There are prepaid autorickshaw booths at all the train and bus stations, at Palika Bazaar in Connaught Place, near the Government of India tourist office on Janpath, Nehru Place and Basant Lok, as well as another 15 throughout the city itself.

A trip from Connaught Place to the Red Fort by autorickshaw/taxi should cost you around Rs 30/80. From Connaught Place to Paharganj is Rs 20/30 and to Humayun's tomb it's Rs 40/150. From 11pm to 5am there is a 20% surcharge for autorickshaws.

To hire a taxi for eight hours should cost around Rs 500, though the driver will expect a tip of around Rs 100.

Cycle-Rickshaw Although they are banned from Connaught Place and New Delhi, these are ideal for travelling around Old Delhi (they're as fast as any other traffic and more manoeuvrable in this area). Bargain hard and expect to pay about Rs 15 for a trip between Paharganj and Old Delhi.

Language

Hindi, spoken by over 90% of the population, is the most widely spoken language in Rajasthan, and the most useful language with which to communicate across the state.

Rajasthani is the collective name for the various dialects spoken in Rajasthan. There are five main regional dialects: Marwari, Mewari, Dhundhari, Mewati and Hadoti. Marwari is the most commonly spoken.

English is widely spoken by people working in the hospitality industry, such as hotels and restaurants, and at important tourist attractions such as forts and palaces. English-speaking guides are available in towns and cities such as Jaipur, Udaipur, Jodhpur, Bikaner and Jaisalmer. In some places, it's also possible to hire Spanish, German and French-speaking guides.

In the rural areas, little if any English is spoken, and attempts at a few Hindi phrases will greatly enhance your enjoyment of travelling through the more remote regions.

One word which you will probably hear frequently during your travels in Rajasthan is *padharo*, meaning 'Please come/You're welcome'. The small hole-in-the-wall eateries known elsewhere in India as *dhabas* are often referred to as *bhojnalyas* in Rajasthan. Beware of *acha*, that all-purpose word for 'OK'. It can also mean 'OK, I understand what you mean, but it isn't OK'.

Hindi is written in Devanagari script from left to right. All nouns in Hindi have a gender, either masculine or feminine. Different forms of verbs or adjectives are used depending on the gender of the noun. Where necessary, these forms are indicated by (m) or (f).

For a more in-depth guide to the Hindi language, get a copy of Lonely Planet's *Hindi & Urdu phrasebook*.

Pronunciation

Most of the sounds in Hindi correspond to the Roman letters used to represent them in the transliteration.

Vowels & Diphthongs

It's important to pay attention to the pronunciation of vowels and especially to their length. A line over a vowel (eg, $\bar{a}$, $\bar{i}$, $\bar{u}$) indicates a longer vowel sound. The symbol ~ over a vowel (eg, $\tilde{a}$, $\tilde{i}$, $\bar{\tilde{i}}$, $\tilde{u}$, $\bar{\tilde{u}}$) indicates that it should be spoken through the nose.

a	as the 'u' in 'sun'
ā	as in 'father'
e	as in 'bet'
i	as in 'sit'
ī	as the 'ee' in 'feet'
o	as in 'both'
u	as in 'put'
ū	as the 'oo' in 'fool'
ai	as the 'a' in 'bad'
au	as the 'aw' in 'saw'

Note that **ai** is pronounced as a diphthong when followed by **ya**, and **au** is pronounced as a diphthong when followed by **va**.

ai	as the 'i' in 'high'
au	as the 'ou' in 'ouch'

Consonants

Most consonants in the transliterations are pronounced as in English, with the following exceptions:

c	as the 'ch' in 'cheese'
ḍ	pronounced with the tongue curled back towards the roof of the mouth
g	always as in 'gun', never as in 'age'
q	as the 'k' in 'king', but pronounced further back
r	slightly trilled
ṛ	an 'r' with the tongue placed near the roof of the mouth and flapped quickly down, touching the roof as it moves
ṭ	pronounced with the tongue further back than in English. Curl the tongue back towards the roof of the mouth.
y	as in 'yak'

gh like the 'g' in 'go' but pronounced further back in the throat

kh similar to the 'ch' in Scottish loch

Aspirated consonants are pronounced with a breath of air, represented by an **h** after the consonant (except for **sh**, pronounced as in 'ship', and **kh** and **gh**).

Essentials

Hello.	*namaste/namskār*
Goodbye.	*namaste/namskār*
Yes.	*jī hã̄*
No.	*jī nahī̃*

Please – usually conveyed through the polite form of the imperative, or through other expressions. This book uses polite expressions and the polite forms of words.

Thank you.	*shukriyā/dhanyavād*
You're welcome.	*koī bāt nahī̃*
Excuse me/Sorry.	*kshamā kījiye*
How are you?	*āp kaise/ī haĩ?* (m/f)
Fine, and you?	*bas āp sunāiye*
What's your name?	*āp kā shubh nām kyā hai?*
My name is ...	*merā nām ... hai*

Language Difficulties

Do you speak English?	*kyā āp ko angrezī ātī hai?*
Does anyone here speak English?	*kyā kisī ko angrezī ātī hai?*
I understand.	*maĩ samjhā/ī* (m/f)
I don't understand.	*maĩ nahī̃ samjhā/ samjhī* (m/f)
Could you speak more slowly?	*dhīre dhīre boliye*
Please write it down.	*zarā likh dījiye*

Getting Around

How do we get to ...?	*... kaise jāte haĩ?*

When is the ... bus?	*... bas kab jāegī?*
first	*pehlī*
next	*aglī*
last	*ākhirī*

Signs

प्रवेश/अन्दर	**Entrance**
निकार/बाहर	**Exit**
खुला	**Open**
बन्द	**Closed**
अन्दर आना [निषिि/मना] है	**No Entry**
धूम्रपान करना [निषिि/मना] है	**No Smoking**
निषिि	**Prohibited**
गर्म	**Hot**
ठंडा	**Cold**
शोचालय	**Toilets**

What time does the ... leave/arrive?	*... kitne baje jāyegā/ pahũcegā?* (m)
	... kitne baje jāyegī/ pahũcegī? (f)
plane	*havāī jahāz* (m)
boat	*nāv* (f)
bus	*bas* (f)
train	*relgāṛī* (f)

I'd like a ... ticket.	*mujhe ek ... ṭikaṭ*
one-way	*ek-tarafā*
return	*do-tarafā*
1st-class	*pratham shrēni*
2nd-class	*dvitīy shrēni*

Accommodation

Where is the (best/ cheapest) hotel?	*sab se (acchā/sastā) hoṭal kahã̄ hai?*
Could you write the address, please?	*zarā us kā patā likh dījiye*
Do you have any rooms available?	*kyā koī kamrā khālī hai?*

How much for ...?	*... kā kirāyā kitnā hai?*
one night	*ek din*
one week	*ek hafte*

I'd like a ...	*mujhe ... cāhiye*
single room	*singal kamrā*
double room	*ḍabal kamrā*
room with a bathroom	*ghusalkhānevālā kamrā*

I'd like to share a dorm.	*maī ḍorm mē ṭheharnā cāhtā/ī hū* (m/f)
May I see it?	*kyā maī kamrā saktā/ī hū?* (m/f)
Is there any other room?	*koī aur kamrā hai?*
Where's the bathroom?	*ghusalkhānā kahā hai?*

Around Town

Where's a/the ...?	*... kahā hai?*
bank	*baink*
consulate	*kaūnsal*
embassy	*dūtāvās*
Hindu temple	*mandir*
mosque	*masjid*
post office	*ḍākkhānā*
public phone	*sārvajanik fon*
public toilet	*shaucālay*
Sikh temple	*gurudvārā*
town square	*cauk*

Is it far from/near here?	*kyā nvoh yahā se dūr/ nazdīk hai?*
Can I change money here?	*kyā yahā ḍālar badal jaa saktā/ī hū?* (m/f)
How much is ...?	*... ka dam kyā hai?*
This is expensive.	*yeh bahut mahēgā hai*

market	*bāzār*
shop	*dukān*

Health

I'm sick.	*maī bīmār hū*

Where's a/the ...?	*... kahā hai?*
chemist	*davākhānā*
dentist	*ḍenṭisṭ*
doctor	*ḍākṭar*
hospital	*aspatāl*

antiseptic	*ainṭīsepṭik*
asprin	*(esprin) sirdard kī davā*
condoms	*nirodhak*
contraceptives	*garbnirodhak*
diarrhoea	*dast*
medicine	*davā*
nausea	*ghin*
syringe	*sūī*
tampons	*ṭaimpon*

Emergencies

Help!	*mada kījiye!*
Stop!	*ruko!*
Thief!	*cor!*
Call a doctor!	*ḍākṭar ko bulāo!*
Call an ambulance!	*embulains le ānā!*
Call the police!	*pulis ko bulāo!*
I'm lost.	*maī rāstā bhūl gayā/ gayī hū* (f/m)

Where is the ...?	*... kahā hai?*
police station	*thānā*
toilet	*ghusalkhānā*

I wish to contact my embassy/ consulate.	*maī apne dūtāvās ke logõ se bāt karnā cāhtā/cāhtī hū* (f/m)

Time & Date

When?	*kab?*
What time is it?	*kitne baje haī?/ ṭāim kyā hai?*
It's (ten) o'clock	*(das) baje haī*
today	*āj*
tomorrow/yesterday	*kal*
(meaning is made clear by context)	
now	*ab*

morning	*saverā*
evening	*shām*
night	*rāt*
day	*din*
week	*hafte*
month	*mahīnā*
year	*sāl/baras*

Monday	*somvār*
Tuesday	*mangalvār*
Wednesday	*budhvār*
Thursday	*guruvār/brihaspativār*
Friday	*shukravār*
Saturday	*shanivār*
Sunday	*itvār/ravivār*

Numbers

Whereas in English we count in tens, hundreds, thousands, millions and billions, the Indian numbering system goes tens, hundreds, thousands, hundred thousands, ten millions. A hundred thousand is a *lākh*, and 10 million is a *karoṛ*.

LANGUAGE

These two words are almost always used in place of their English equivalent. Thus you will see 10 lakh rather than one million and one karor rather than 10 million. Furthermore, the numerals are generally written that way too – thus three hundred thousand appears as 3,00,000 not 300,000, and ten million, five hundred thousand would appear numerically as 1,05,00,000 (one karor, five lakh) not 10,500,000. If you say something costs five karor or is worth 10 lakh, it always means 'of rupees'. Many of Rajasthan's younger generation fondly refer to rupees as 'bucks'.

1	*ek*
2	*do*
3	*tīn*
4	*cār*
5	*pā̃c*
6	*chai*
7	*sāt*
8	*āṭh*
9	*nau*
10	*das*
11	*gyārah*
12	*bara*
13	*terah*
14	*caudah*
15	*pandrah*
16	*solah*
17	*satrah*
18	*aṭṭhārah*
19	*unnīs*
20	*bīs*
21	*ikkīs*
22	*bāīs*
30	*tīs*
40	*cālīs*
50	*pacās*
60	*sāṭh*
70	*sattar*
80	*assī*
90	*nabbe/navve*
100	*sau*
200	*do so*
1000	*hazār*

100,000		*ek lākh*
(written 1,00,000)		
10 million		*ek karor*
(written 1,00,00,000)		

FOOD

breakfast	*nāshtā*
lunch	*din kā khānā*
dinner	*rāt kā khānā*
Can we see the menu?	*menyū kārḍ dījiye*
I'm a vegetarian.	*maī shākāhārī hū̃*
Please bring the bill.	*bil lāiye*
Do you have ...?	*kyā āp ke pās ... hai?*
I am hungry.	*mujhe bhūkh lagī hai*
I am thirsty.	*mujhe pyās lagī hai*
I (don't) like hot and spicy food.	*mujhe tīkhā khānā acchā (nahī̃) lagtā hai*

fork	*kā̃ṭā*
knife	*churī*
glass	*glās*
plate	*pleṭ*

food	*khānā*
bread	*roṭī*
fried bread	*parā̃ṭhā*
tandoori rounds	*nān or tandūrī roṭī*
sliced bread	*ḍabal (double) roṭī*
butter	*makkhan*
cheese	*panār*
chillies	*mārc*
without chillies	*mirc ke binā*
rice	*cāval*
fried rice	*pulāv*
salt	*namak*
spices	*masāle*
sugar	*cīnī*
yogurt	*dahī*

Meat & Poultry

beef	*gāy kā māns*
chicken	*murgh*
fish	*machlī*
goat	*bakrī kā māns*
meat	*māns/gosht*
mutton	*beṛ kā māns*
pork	*suar kā māns*

Vegetables

cabbage	*band gobhī*
eggplant	*baīgan*
lentils	*dāl*
peas	*maṭar*

potato	*ālū*		mango	*ām*
pumpkin	*kaddū*		orange	*nārangi*
spinach	*pālak*			
vegetable	*sabzī/sāg*			

Fruit

apple	*seb*
apricot	*khubānī*
banana	*kelā*
fruit	*phal*
grapes	*angūr*

DRINKS

coffee	*kāfī*
milk	*dūdh*
soft drink	*sauft drink*
(cup of) tea	*cāy*
tea with milk	*dūdhvālī cāy*
tea with sugar	*cīnī ke sāth*
(boiled) water	*(ūblā) pānī*

Glossary

agarbathi – incense

Agnikula – 'Fire Born', the name of the mythological race of four *Rajput* clans who were manifested from a sacred fire on Mt Abu; one of the three principal races from which Rajputs claim descent

ahimsa – nonviolence and reverence for all life

andhi – dust storm in the Thar Desert

angrezi – foreigner

apsara – celestial maiden

Aryan – Sanskrit word for noble; refers to those who migrated from Persia and settled in northern India

ashram – spiritual community or retreat

autorickshaw – noisy three-wheel device with a motorbike engine and seats for two passengers behind the driver

Ayurveda – Indian herbal medicine

azan – Muslim call to prayer

bagh – garden

baithak – salon in a *haveli* where merchants met their clients

baksheesh – tip, bribe or donation

bandh – general strike

bandhani – popular form of tie-dye

Banjaras – nomad tribe, believed to be the ancestors of Europe's gypsies

banyan – Indian fig tree

baori – well; particularly a step-well with landings and galleries

baraat – marriage party

bazaar – market area (or market town)

betel – nut of the betel tree; chewed as a stimulant and digestive, and added to *paan*

bhang – dried leaves and flowering shoots of the marijuana plant

bhavan – house; also spelt 'bhawan'

Bhils – a tribal people from southern Rajasthan

bhojanalya – basic restaurant or snack bar; known elsewhere in India as a *dhaba*

Bhopa – Bhil priest; also traditional storytellers of Rajasthan

bhuut – ghost

bichiya – toe ring

bidi – small, hand-rolled cigarette; really just a rolled-up leaf; also known as beedi

bindi – forehead mark; also known as *tika*

Bishnoi – a nomadic tribe, known for their reverence for the environment

bor – forehead ornament; also known as a *rakhadi*

bo tree – *Ficus religiosa*, under which the Buddha attained enlightenment

Brahma – source of all existence and worshipped as the Creator in the Hindu triad; Brahma is depicted with four heads (a fifth was burnt by Shiva's central eye when he spoke disrespectfully), and his vehicle is a swan or goose

Brahmin – member of the priest caste, the highest Hindu caste

Buddha – Awakened One; originator of Buddhism, who lived in the 5th century BC; regarded by Hindus as the ninth reincarnation of Vishnu

bund – embankment or dyke

bunti – wooden block used for the block-printing of fabric

cantonment – administrative and military area of a Raj-era town

caste – a Hindu person's hereditary station in life

chai – tea

chajera – mason employed by Marwari businessmen of Shekhawati to build *havelis*

chakki – handmill used to grind grain

chappals – sandals

chappati – unleavened Indian bread; also known as *roti*

charbagh – formal Persian garden, divided into quarters (literally 'four gardens')

charpoy – Indian rope bed

chaupar – town square formed by the intersection of major roads

chhapa – wooden block, also known as a *bunti*, used to block-print fabric

chhatri – cenotaph (literally 'umbrella')

chitera – painter of *havelis* in Shekhawati

choli – cropped blouse worn by Indian women

chowk – a town square, intersection or marketplace

chowkidar – caretaker

chudas – bangles of Rajasthani women

chureil – evil spirit; also known as a *dakin*

crore – 10 million

cycle-rickshaw – three-wheeler bicycle with two passengers behind the rider

dacoit – bandit

Dalit – preferred term for India's Untouchable caste

dalwar – sword

dargah – shrine or place of burial of a Muslim saint

darwaza – gateway or door

Devi – *Shiva's* wife

dhaba – hole-in-the-wall restaurant or snack bar; boxed lunches delivered to office workers

dahal – lentil soup

dhobi ghat – where clothes are washed

dhobi-wallah – person who washes clothes for a living

dhoti – length of fabric worn by men which is drawn up between the legs

dhurrie – rug, usually cotton

Digambara – literally 'SkyClad'; a Jain sect whose monks may show their disdain for worldly goods by going naked

diwan-i-am – public audience hall in a palace

diwan-i-khas – private audience hall

dogla – building adjacent to a village dwelling in which livestock and grain are kept; also known as a *chhan*

dosa – paper-thin pancakes made from lentil flour (curried vegetables wrapped inside a dosa make it a *masala dosa*)

dowry – money and goods paid by a bride's parents to their son-in-law's family; it's illegal but no arranged marriage can be made without it

dupatta – scarf worn by Punjabi women

durbar – royal court, or *maharajas* meeting hall; also used to describe a government

Durga – the Inaccessible; a form of *Shiva's* wife, *Parvati*, a beautiful but fierce woman riding a tiger; major goddess of the Shakti cult

gaddi – throne of a Hindu prince

Ganesh – god of good fortune; elephant-headed son of *Shiva* and *Parvati*, and probably the most popular god in the Hindu pantheon

ganja – dried flowering tips of marijuana plant; which are highly potent

gaon – village

garh – fort

Garuda – man-bird vehicle of *Vishnu*

geyser – hot-water heater

ghaghara – traditional ankle-length skirt of Rajasthani women

ghat – steps or landing on a river; range of hills, or road up hills

ghazal – Urdu songs derived from poetry; sad love themes

ghee – clarified butter

ghoomer – dance performed by women during festivals and weddings

godown – warehouse

goondas – ruffians or toughs

gopis – milkmaids; *Krishna* was very fond of them

gram panchayat – government at the village level

gufa – cave

Gujjars – people traditionally engaged in animal husbandry

gur – sweetmeat made from unrefined sugar

gurdwara – Sikh temple

guru – teacher or holy person

halwa – cereal or lentils fried and cooked in a sugar syrup

Hanuman – Hindu monkey god

hathi – elephant

hathphool – ornament worn on the back of the hand by Rajasthani women

haveli – traditional mansion with interior courtyards

hijra – eunuch

hookah – water pipe

howdah – seat for carrying people on an elephant's back

IMFL – Indian-made foreign liquor; beer or spirits produced in India

Induvansa – Race of the Moon (Lunar Race); one of the three principal races from which *Rajputs* claim descent

jagirdari – feudal system of serfdom which is imposed on the peasants of Rajasthan

Jagirdars – feudal lords of Rajasthan

Jajman – patron of folk entertainers

jali – carved-marble lattice screen; also used to refer to the holes or spaces produced through carving timber

Jats – traditionally, people engaged in agriculture; these days, Jats play a strong role in administration and politics

jauhar – ritual mass suicide by immolation, used by *Rajput* women after military defeat to avoid dishonour

jhonpa – village hut with mud walls and thatched roof

jogi – priest

jootis – traditional leather shoes of Rajasthan; men's jootis often have curled-up toes; also known as *mojdis*

Julaha – weaver caste

kaarkhana – embroidery workshop; established during the Mughal era

kabas – the holy rats believed to be the incarnations of local families at Karni Mata Temple at Deshnok

Kalbelias – a nomadic tribal group associated with snake charming

Kali – the Black; a terrible form of *Devi*

karma – the Hindu-Buddhist principle of retributive justice for past deeds

kashida – embroidery on *jootis*

kathputli – puppeteer; also known as a *putli-wallah*

khadi – homespun cloth; Mahatma Gandhi encouraged people to spin khadi rather than buy English cloth

kheis – shawl; also known as a *pattu*

kot – fort

kotwali – police station

Krishna – *Vishnu's* eighth incarnation, often coloured blue; a popular Hindu deity, he revealed the Bhagavad Gita to Arjuna

Kshatriya – the caste of soldiers and governors; second in the caste hierarchy; *Rajputs* claim lineage to the Kshatriyas

kuldevi – clan goddess; every family pays homage to a clan goddess

kulfi – pistachio-flavoured iced sweet, which is similar to ice cream

kund – lake or *tank*

kundan – type of jewellery featuring enamelwork *(meenakari)* on one side and precious stones on the other

kurta – long cotton shirt with either short collar or no collar

lakh – 100,000

Lakshmi – *Vishnu's* consort; Hindu goddess of wealth

lassi – yogurt and iced-water drink

lingam – phallic symbol; symbol of *Shiva*

loharia – form of *bandhani* tie-dye, which gives a ripple effect

lungi – like a sarong

madrasa – Islamic college

Mahabharata – Vedic epic poem of the Bharata dynasty, which describes the battle between the Pandavas and the Kauravas

mahal – house or palace

maharaja – princely ruler or king

maharaj kumar – son of a *maharaja*; prince

maharani – wife of a princely ruler or a ruler in her own right

Mahavir – the 24th and last *tirthankar* (Jain teacher, or prophet)

mahout – elephant rider or master

mandana – folk paintings in red chalk on village dwellings

mandapa – forechamber of the inner sanctum of a temple

mandir – temple

mantra – sacred word or syllable used by Buddhists and Hindus to aid concentration; metric psalms of praise found in the *Vedas*

Maratha – warlike central Indians who controlled much of India at times and fought against the *Mughals* and *Rajputs*

marg – major road

Marwar – kingdom of the Rathore dynasty, which ruled first from Mandore, and later from Jodhpur

masjid – mosque

mataji – female priest; also a respectful form of address to a mother or older woman

meenakari – type of enamelwork used on ornaments and jewellery

mehendi – intricate henna designs applied by women to their hands and feet

mela – a fair

Mewar – kingdom of the Sisodia dynasty; ruled Udaipur and Chittorgarh
Moghul – another spelling for *Mughal*
moksha – release from birth and death cycle
monsoon – rainy season; June to October
moosal – pestle
mosar – death feast
Mughal – Muslim dynasty of Indian emperors from Babur to Aurangzeb (16th–18th centuries)

namaz – Muslim prayers
Nandi – bull vehicle of *Shiva*
nathdi – nose ornament; also known as a *laongh* and a *bhanvatiya*
nautch girls – dancing girls; a nautch is a dance
nawab – Muslim ruling prince or powerful landowner
nilgai – antelope
niwas – house, building
NRI – Nonresident Indian

odhni – headscarf
okhli – mortar; bowl for grinding grain with a pestle, or *moosal*
Om – sacred invocation that represents the essence of the divine principle

paag – turban; also called *pagri* and *safa*
paan – chewable preparation made from *betel* leaves, nuts and lime
Pabuji – deified folk hero; particularly revered by the nomadic *Bhopas*
pagri – see *paag*
pahar – hill
panchayat sammiti – local government representing several villages
panghat poojan – ceremony performed at a village well following the birth of a child
Parvati – another form of *Devi*
pattu – shawl; also known as a *kheis*
payal – anklet worn by Rajasthani women
PCO – public call office
phad – the painted scroll used in *Bhopa* performances to illustrate legends concerned with the life of *Pabuji*
pichwai – religious paintings on homespun cloth, generally of events from the life of *Krishna*, which are hung behind the image of Sri Nathji at Nathdwara

pida – low, folding chair featuring decorative woodcarving, traditionally made in Shekhawati and Bikaner
pitar – soul of a dead man
pitari – soul of a woman who has died before her husband
pol – gate
poori – flat pieces of dough that puff up when deep fried
prasaad – sacred food offered to the gods
puja – literally 'respect'; offering or prayer
purdah – seclusion; wives of *Rajputs* were kept in purdah and seen by no man other than their husbands
putli-wallah – puppeteer; also known as a *kathputli*

Rabaris – nomadic tribe from Jodhpur area
raga – any conventional pattern of melody and rhythm that forms the basis for free composition
raj – rule or sovereignty
raja – king
Rajput – 'Sons of Princes'; Hindu warrior caste, rulers of western India
Rama – seventh incarnation of *Vishnu*; whose life story is the central theme of the Ramayana
Ramdev – deified folk hero, who, along with his horse, is worshipped in a temple at Ramdevra, near Pokaran
rani – wife of a king
ras gullas – balls of sweet cream cheese flavoured with rose water
rawal – nobleman
reet – bride price; opposite of dowry
road – railway town, which serves as a communication point to a larger town off the line, eg, Mt Abu and Abu Road
RSTC – Rajasthan State Transport Corporation
RTDC – Rajasthan Tourism Development Corporation

sabzi – vegetables
sadar – main
sadhu – ascetic, holy person; one who is trying to achieve enlightenment; usually addressed as 'swamiji' or 'babaji'
sagar – lake, reservoir
sahib – title applied to any gentleman

sal – gallery in a palace

sambar – deer

Sanganeri print – block-printed fabric of Sanganer village, near Jaipur

sapera – a snake charmer; traditionally associated with the Kalbelias tribe

sarangi – stringed folk instrument

sati – suicide by immolation; banned more than a century ago, sati is still occasionally performed

Scheduled Tribes – government classification for tribal groups of Rajasthan; the tribes are grouped with the lowest casteless class, the *Dalits*

sheesh mahal – mirror palace

shikhar – hunting expedition

Shiva – the Destroyer; also the Creator, in which form he is worshipped as a *lingam* (phallic symbol)

Sikh – member of the monotheistic religion of Sikhism, which separated from Hinduism in the 16th century and has a military tradition

sikhara – Hindu temple spire or temple

silavat – stonecarvers

singh – literally 'lion'; a surname adopted by *Rajputs* and *Sikhs*

sitar – Indian stringed instrument

sonf – aniseed seeds; come complimentary with the restaurant bill, after a meal, for digestive purposes

Sufi – Muslim mystic

Surya – the sun; a major deity in the *Vedas*

Suryavansa – Race of the Sun (Solar Race); one of the three principal races from which *Rajputs* claim descent

tabla – pair of drums

tank – reservoir

Tejaji – deified folk hero believed to cure snakebite

tempo – noisy three-wheel form of public transport; bigger than an autorickshaw

thakur – nobleman

thali – all-you-can-eat meal; literally the plate on which the meal is served

tika – a mark devout Hindus put on their foreheads with tika powder

tirthankar – one of the group of 24 great Jain teachers

tokna – large vessel in which the *maharajas*' treasurers collected taxes

tonga – two-wheeled passenger vehicle drawn by horse or pony

toran – shield-shaped device above a lintel which a bridegroom pierces with his sword before claiming his bride

torana – an elaborately sculpted gateway before temples

Vaisya – the caste comprising tradespeople and farmers; the third caste in the hierarchy

Varuna – supreme Vedic god; Aryan god of water

Vedas – the Hindu sacred books; a collection of hymns composed during the 2nd millennium BC and divided into four books: Rig-Veda, Yajur-Veda, Sama-Veda and Atharva-Veda

Vishnu – the third in the Hindu trinity of gods with Brahma and Shiva; the Preserver and Restorer, who has nine *avatars* (incarnations)

wallah – literally 'man', thus taxi-wallah, Delhi-wallah

yagna – self-mortification; holy offering

zenana – women's quarters

zila parishad – government at the district level

LONELY PLANET

You already know that Lonely Planet produces more than this one guidebook, but you might not be aware of the other products we have on this region. Here is a selection of titles that you may want to check out as well:

India
ISBN 1 86450 246 0
US$24.99 • UK£14.99

Hindu & Urdu phrasebook
ISBN 0 86442 425 6
US$6.95 • UK£4.50

Read This First: Asia & India
ISBN 1 86450 049 2
US$14.95 • UK£8.99

South India
ISBN 1 86450 161 8
US$19.99 • UK£12.99

Healthy Travel Asia & India
ISBN 1 86450 051 4
US$5.95 • UK£3.99

India and Bangladesh Road Atlas
ISBN 1 74059 019 8
US$15.99 • UK£9.99

Goa
ISBN 0 86442 681 X
US$16.99 • UK£10.99

World Food India
ISBN 1 86450 328 9
US$13.99 • UK£8.99

Sacred India (paperback)
ISBN 1 74059 366 9
US$19.99 • UK£12.99

In Rajasthan
ISBN 0 86442 457 4
US$10.95 • UK£6.99

Available wherever books are sold

LONELY PLANET

ON THE ROAD

Travel Guides explore cities, regions and countries, and supply information on transport, restaurants and accommodation, covering all budgets. They come with reliable, easy-to-use maps, practical advice, cultural and historical facts and a rundown on attractions both on and off the beaten track. There are over 200 titles in this classic series, covering nearly every country in the world.

 Lonely Planet Upgrades extend the shelf life of existing travel guides by detailing any changes that may affect travel in a region since a book has been published. Upgrades can be downloaded for free from **www.lonelyplanet.com/upgrades**

For travellers with more time than money, **Shoestring** guides offer dependable, first-hand information with hundreds of detailed maps, plus insider tips for stretching money as far as possible. Covering entire continents in most cases, the six-volume shoestring guides are known around the world as 'backpackers bibles'.

For the discerning short-term visitor, **Condensed** guides highlight the best a destination has to offer in a full-colour, pocket-sized format designed for quick access. They include everything from top sights and walking tours to opinionated reviews of where to eat, stay, shop and have fun.

CitySync lets travellers use their Palm™ or Visor™ hand-held computers to guide them through a city with handy tips on transport, history, cultural life, major sights, and shopping and entertainment options. It can also quickly search and sort hundreds of reviews of hotels, restaurants and attractions, and pinpoint their location on scrollable street maps. CitySync can be downloaded from **www.citysync.com**

MAPS & ATLASES

Lonely Planet's **City Maps** feature downtown and metropolitan maps, as well as transit routes and walking tours. The maps come complete with an index of streets, a listing of sights and a plastic coat for extra durability.

Road Atlases are an essential navigation tool for serious travellers. Cross-referenced with the guidebooks, they also feature distance and climate charts and a complete site index.

LONELY PLANET

ESSENTIALS

Read This First books help new travellers to hit the road with confidence. These invaluable predeparture guides give step-by-step advice on preparing for a trip, budgeting, arranging a visa, planning an itinerary and staying safe while still getting off the beaten track.

Healthy Travel pocket guides offer a regional rundown on disease hot spots and practical advice on predeparture health measures, staying well on the road and what to do in emergencies. The guides come with a user-friendly design and helpful diagrams and tables.

Lonely Planet's **Phrasebooks** cover the essential words and phrases travellers need when they're strangers in a strange land. They come in a pocket-sized format with colour tabs for quick reference, extensive vocabulary lists, easy-to-follow pronunciation keys and two-way dictionaries.

Miffed by blurry photos of the Taj Mahal? Tired of the classic 'top of the head cut off' shot? **Travel Photography: A Guide to Taking Better Pictures** will help you turn ordinary holiday snaps into striking images and give you the know-how to capture every scene, from frenetic festivals to peaceful beach sunrises.

Lonely Planet's **Travel Journal** is a lightweight but sturdy travel diary for jotting down all those on-the-road observations and significant travel moments. It comes with a handy time-zone wheel, a world map and useful travel information.

Lonely Planet's eKno is an all-in-one communication service developed especially for travellers. It offers low-cost international calls and free email and voicemail so that you can keep in touch while on the road. Check it out on **www.ekno.lonelyplanet.com**

FOOD & RESTAURANT GUIDES

Lonely Planet's **Out to Eat** guides recommend the brightest and best places to eat and drink in top international cities. These gourmet companions are arranged by neighbourhood, packed with dependable maps, garnished with scene-setting photos and served with quirky features.

For people who live to eat, drink and travel, **World Food** guides explore the culinary culture of each country. Entertaining and adventurous, each guide is packed with detail on staples and specialities, regional cuisine and local markets, as well as sumptuous recipes, comprehensive culinary dictionaries and lavish photos good enough to eat.

LONELY PLANET

OUTDOOR GUIDES

For those who believe the best way to see the world is on foot, Lonely Planet's **Walking Guides** detail everything from family strolls to difficult treks, with 'when to go and how to do it' advice supplemented by reliable maps and essential travel information.

Cycling Guides map a destination's best bike tours, long and short, in day-by-day detail. They contain all the information a cyclist needs, including advice on bike maintenance, places to eat and stay, innovative maps with detailed cues to the rides, and elevation charts.

The **Watching Wildlife** series is perfect for travellers who want authoritative information but don't want to tote a heavy field guide. Packed with advice on where, when and how to view a region's wildlife, each title features photos of over 300 species and contains engaging comments on the local flora and fauna.

With underwater colour photos throughout, **Pisces Books** explore the world's best diving and snorkelling areas. Each book contains listings of diving services and dive resorts, detailed information on depth, visibility and difficulty of dives, and a roundup of the marine life you're likely to see through your mask.

LONELY PLANET

OFF THE ROAD

Journeys, the travel literature series written by renowned travel authors, capture the spirit of a place or illuminate a culture with a journalist's attention to detail and a novelist's flair for words. These are tales to soak up while you're actually on the road or dip into as an at-home armchair indulgence.

The range of lavishly illustrated **Pictorial** books is just the ticket for both travellers and dreamers. Off-beat tales and vivid photographs bring the adventure of travel to your doorstep long before the journey begins and long after it is over.

Lonely Planet **Videos** encourage the same independent, tough-minded approach as the guidebooks. Currently airing throughout the world, this award-winning series features innovative footage and an original soundtrack.

Yes, we know, work is tough, so do a little bit of deskside dreaming with the spiral-bound Lonely Planet **Diary** or a Lonely Planet **Wall Calendar**, filled with great photos from around the world.

TRAVELLERS NETWORK

Lonely Planet Online. Lonely Planet's award-winning Web site has insider information on hundreds of destinations, from Amsterdam to Zimbabwe, complete with interactive maps and relevant links. The site also offers the latest travel news, recent reports from travellers on the road, guidebook upgrades, a travel links site, an online book-buying option and a lively travellers bulletin board. It can be viewed at **www.lonelyplanet.com** or AOL keyword: lp.

Planet Talk is a quarterly print newsletter, full of gossip, advice, anecdotes and author articles. It provides an antidote to the being-at-home blues and lets you plan and dream for the next trip. Contact the nearest Lonely Planet office for your free copy.

Comet, the free Lonely Planet newsletter, comes via email once a month. It's loaded with travel news, advice, dispatches from authors, travel competitions and letters from readers. To subscribe, click on the Comet subscription link on the front page of the Web site.

Lonely Planet Guides by Region

Lonely Planet is known worldwide for publishing practical, reliable and no-nonsense travel information in our guides and on our Web site. The Lonely Planet list covers just about every accessible part of the world. Currently there are 16 series: Travel guides, Shoestring guides, Condensed guides, Phrasebooks, Read This First, Healthy Travel, Walking guides, Cycling guides, Watching Wildlife guides, Pisces Diving & Snorkeling guides, City Maps, Road Atlases, Out to Eat, World Food, Journeys travel literature and Pictorials.

AFRICA Africa on a shoestring • Botswana • Cairo • Cairo City Map • Cape Town • Cape Town City Map • East Africa • Egypt • Egyptian Arabic phrasebook • Ethiopia, Eritrea & Djibouti • Ethiopian Amharic phrasebook • The Gambia & Senegal • Healthy Travel Africa • Kenya • Malawi • Morocco • Moroccan Arabic phrasebook • Mozambique • Namibia • Read This First: Africa • South Africa, Lesotho & Swaziland • Southern Africa • Southern Africa Road Atlas • Swahili phrasebook • Tanzania, Zanzibar & Pemba • Trekking in East Africa • Tunisia • Watching Wildlife East Africa • Watching Wildlife Southern Africa • West Africa • World Food Morocco • Zambia • Zimbabwe, Botswana & Namibia
Travel Literature: Mali Blues: Traveling to an African Beat • The Rainbird: A Central African Journey • Songs to an African Sunset: A Zimbabwean Story

AUSTRALIA & THE PACIFIC Aboriginal Australia & the Torres Strait Islands •Auckland • Australia • Australian phrasebook • Australia Road Atlas • Cycling Australia • Cycling New Zealand • Fiji • Fijian phrasebook • Healthy Travel Australia, NZ & the Pacific • Islands of Australia's Great Barrier Reef • Melbourne • Melbourne City Map • Micronesia • New Caledonia • New South Wales • New Zealand • Northern Territory • Outback Australia • Out to Eat – Melbourne • Out to Eat – Sydney • Papua New Guinea • Pidgin phrasebook • Queensland • Rarotonga & the Cook Islands • Samoa • Solomon Islands • South Australia • South Pacific • South Pacific phrasebook • Sydney • Sydney City Map • Sydney Condensed • Tahiti & French Polynesia • Tasmania • Tonga • Tramping in New Zealand • Vanuatu • Victoria • Walking in Australia • Watching Wildlife Australia • Western Australia
Travel Literature: Islands in the Clouds: Travels in the Highlands of New Guinea • Kiwi Tracks: A New Zealand Journey • Sean & David's Long Drive

CENTRAL AMERICA & THE CARIBBEAN Bahamas, Turks & Caicos • Baja California • Belize, Guatemala & Yucatán • Bermuda • Central America on a shoestring • Costa Rica • Costa Rica Spanish phrasebook • Cuba • Cycling Cuba • Dominican Republic & Haiti • Eastern Caribbean • Guatemala • Havana • Healthy Travel Central & South America • Jamaica • Mexico • Mexico City • Panama • Puerto Rico • Read This First: Central & South America • Virgin Islands • World Food Caribbean • World Food Mexico • Yucatán
Travel Literature: Green Dreams: Travels in Central America

EUROPE Amsterdam • Amsterdam City Map • Amsterdam Condensed • Andalucía • Athens • Austria • Baltic States phrasebook • Barcelona • Barcelona City Map • Belgium & Luxembourg • Berlin • Berlin City Map • Britain • British phrasebook • Brussels, Bruges & Antwerp • Brussels City Map • Budapest • Budapest City Map • Canary Islands • Catalunya & the Costa Brava • Central Europe • Central Europe phrasebook • Copenhagen • Corfu & the Ionians • Corsica • Crete • Crete Condensed • Croatia • Cycling Britain • Cycling France • Cyprus • Czech & Slovak Republics • Czech phrasebook • Denmark • Dublin • Dublin City Map • Dublin Condensed • Eastern Europe • Eastern Europe phrasebook • Edinburgh • Edinburgh City Map • England • Estonia, Latvia & Lithuania • Europe on a shoestring • Europe phrasebook • Finland • Florence • Florence City Map • France • Frankfurt City Map • Frankfurt Condensed • French phrasebook • Georgia, Armenia & Azerbaijan • Germany • German phrasebook • Greece • Greek Islands • Greek phrasebook • Hungary • Iceland, Greenland & the Faroe Islands • Ireland • Italian phrasebook • Italy • Kraków • Lisbon • The Loire • London • London City Map • London Condensed • Madrid • Madrid City Map • Malta • Mediterranean Europe • Milan, Turin & Genoa • Moscow • Munich • Netherlands • Normandy • Norway • Out to Eat – London • Out to Eat – Paris • Paris • Paris City Map • Paris Condensed • Poland • Polish phrasebook • Portugal • Portuguese phrasebook • Prague • Prague City Map • Provence & the Côte d'Azur • Read This First: Europe • Rhodes & the Dodecanese • Romania & Moldova • Rome • Rome City Map • Rome Condensed • Russia, Ukraine & Belarus • Russian phrasebook • Scandinavian & Baltic Europe • Scandinavian phrasebook • Scotland • Sicily • Slovenia • South-West France • Spain • Spanish phrasebook • Stockholm • St Petersburg • St Petersburg City Map • Sweden • Switzerland • Tuscany • Ukrainian phrasebook • Venice • Vienna • Wales • Walking in Britain • Walking in France • Walking in Ireland • Walking in Italy • Walking in Scotland • Walking in Spain • Walking in Switzerland • Western Europe • World Food France • World Food Greece • World Food Ireland • World Food Italy • World Food Spain **Travel Literature:** After Yugoslavia • Love and War in the Apennines • The Olive Grove: Travels in Greece • On the Shores of the Mediterranean • Round Ireland in Low Gear • A Small Place in Italy

Lonely Planet Mail Order

Lonely Planet products are distributed worldwide. They are also available by mail order from Lonely Planet, so if you have difficulty finding a title please write to us. North and South American residents should write to 150 Linden St, Oakland, CA 94607, USA; European and African residents should write to 10a Spring Place, London NW5 3BH, UK; and residents of other countries to Locked Bag 1, Footscray, Victoria 3011, Australia.

INDIAN SUBCONTINENT & THE INDIAN OCEAN Bangladesh • Bengali phrasebook • Bhutan • Delhi • Goa • Healthy Travel Asia & India • Hindi & Urdu phrasebook • India • India & Bangladesh City Map • Indian Himalaya • Karakoram Highway • Kathmandu City Map • Kerala • Madagascar • Maldives • Mauritius, Réunion & Seychelles • Mumbai (Bombay) • Nepal • Nepali phrasebook • North India • Pakistan • Rajasthan • Read This First: Asia & India • South India • Sri Lanka • Sri Lanka phrasebook • Tibet • Tibetan phrasebook • Trekking in the Indian Himalaya • Trekking in the Karakoram & Hindukush • Trekking in the Nepal Himalaya • World Food India **Travel Literature**: The Age of Kali: Indian Travels and Encounters • Hello Goodnight: A Life of Goa • In Rajasthan • Maverick in Madagascar • A Season in Heaven: True Tales from the Road to Kathmandu • Shopping for Buddhas • A Short Walk in the Hindu Kush • Slowly Down the Ganges

MIDDLE EAST & CENTRAL ASIA Bahrain, Kuwait & Qatar • Central Asia • Central Asia phrasebook • Dubai • Farsi (Persian) phrasebook • Hebrew phrasebook • Iran • Israel & the Palestinian Territories • Istanbul • Istanbul City Map • Istanbul to Cairo • Istanbul to Kathmandu • Jerusalem • Jerusalem City Map • Jordan • Lebanon • Middle East • Oman & the United Arab Emirates • Syria • Turkey • Turkish phrasebook • World Food Turkey • Yemen **Travel Literature**: Black on Black: Iran Revisited • Breaking Ranks: Turbulent Travels in the Promised Land • The Gates of Damascus • Kingdom of the Film Stars: Journey into Jordan

NORTH AMERICA Alaska • Boston • Boston City Map • Boston Condensed • British Columbia • California & Nevada • California Condensed • Canada • Chicago • Chicago City Map • Chicago Condensed • Florida • Georgia & the Carolinas • Great Lakes • Hawaii • Hiking in Alaska • Hiking in the USA • Honolulu & Oahu City Map • Las Vegas • Los Angeles • Los Angeles City Map • Louisiana & the Deep South • Miami • Miami City Map • Montreal • New England • New Orleans • New Orleans City Map • New York City • New York City City Map • New York City Condensed • New York, New Jersey & Pennsylvania • Oahu • Out to Eat – San Francisco • Pacific Northwest • Rocky Mountains • San Diego & Tijuana • San Francisco • San Francisco City Map • Seattle • Seattle City Map • Southwest • Texas • Toronto • USA • USA phrasebook • Vancouver • Vancouver City Map • Virginia & the Capital Region • Washington, DC • Washington, DC City Map • World Food New Orleans **Travel Literature**: Caught Inside: A Surfer's Year on the California Coast • Drive Thru America

NORTH-EAST ASIA Beijing • Beijing City Map • Cantonese phrasebook • China • Hiking in Japan • Hong Kong & Macau • Hong Kong City Map • Hong Kong Condensed • Japan • Japanese phrasebook • Korea • Korean phrasebook • Kyoto • Mandarin phrasebook • Mongolia • Mongolian phrasebook • Seoul • Shanghai • South-West China • Taiwan • Tokyo • Tokyo Condensed • World Food Hong Kong • World Food Japan **Travel Literature**: In Xanadu: A Quest • Lost Japan

SOUTH AMERICA Argentina, Uruguay & Paraguay • Bolivia • Brazil • Brazilian phrasebook • Buenos Aires • Buenos Aires City Map • Chile & Easter Island • Colombia • Ecuador & the Galapagos Islands • Healthy Travel Central & South America • Latin American Spanish phrasebook • Peru • Quechua phrasebook • Read This First: Central & South America • Rio de Janeiro • Rio de Janeiro City Map • Santiago de Chile • South America on a shoestring • Trekking in the Patagonian Andes • Venezuela **Travel Literature**: Full Circle: A South American Journey

SOUTH-EAST ASIA Bali & Lombok • Bangkok • Bangkok City Map • Burmese phrasebook • Cambodia • Cycling Vietnam, Laos & Cambodia • East Timor phrasebook • Hanoi • Healthy Travel Asia & India • Hill Tribes phrasebook • Ho Chi Minh City (Saigon) • Indonesia • Indonesian phrasebook • Indonesia's Eastern Islands • Java • Lao phrasebook • Laos • Malay phrasebook • Malaysia, Singapore & Brunei • Myanmar (Burma) • Philippines • Pilipino (Tagalog) phrasebook • Read This First: Asia & India • Singapore • Singapore City Map • South-East Asia on a shoestring • South-East Asia phrasebook • Thailand • Thailand's Islands & Beaches • Thailand, Vietnam, Laos & Cambodia Road Atlas • Thai phrasebook • Vietnam • Vietnamese phrasebook • World Food Thailand • World Food Vietnam

ALSO AVAILABLE: Antarctica • The Arctic • The Blue Man: Tales of Travel, Love and Coffee • Brief Encounters: Stories of Love, Sex & Travel • Buddhist Stupas in Asia: The Shape of Perfection • Chasing Rickshaws • The Last Grain Race • Lonely Planet ... On the Edge: Adventurous Escapades from Around the World • Lonely Planet Unpacked • Lonely Planet Unpacked Again • Not the Only Planet: Science Fiction Travel Stories • Ports of Call: A Journey by Sea • Sacred India • Travel Photography: A Guide to Taking Better Pictures • Travel with Children • Tuvalu: Portrait of an Island Nation

Index

Text

Boxed Text

MAP LEGEND

CITY ROUTES

Freeway .... Freeway	Unsealed Road
Highway .... Primary Road	One-Way Street
Road .... Secondary Road	Pedestrian Street
Street .... Street	Stepped Street
Lane .... Lane	Tunnel
.... Roadblocks	Footbridge

HYDROGRAPHY

.... River, Creek	Dry Lake, Salt Lake
.... Canal	Spring, Rapids
.... Lake, Tank	Waterfalls

REGIONAL ROUTES

Tollway, Freeway	
Primary Road	
Secondary Road	
Minor Road	

BOUNDARIES

International	
State	
Disputed	
Fortified Wall	

TRANSPORT ROUTES & STATIONS

Train	Cable Car, Chairlift
Metro	Ferry
Tramway	Path in Park
Bus Route	Walking Trail
Monorail	Walking Tour

AREA FEATURES

Building	National Park
Park, Garden	Market
	Beach
	Campus
	Cemetery
	Urban

MAP SYMBOLS

○ **CAPITAL** National Capital	Cathedral, Church	Jain Temple	Shopping Centre
◉ **CAPITAL** State Capital	Cave	Lighthouse	Sikh Temple
○ **City** City, Large Town	Cinema	Lookout	Ski Field
○ Town Town	Embassy, Consulate	Monument	Stately Home, Haveli
○ Village Village	Festival	Mosque	Stupa
■ Place to Stay	Fort	Mountain, Hill	Swimming Pool
▼ Place to Eat	Fountain	Mountain Range	Taxi
● Point of Interest	Gate	Museum, Gallery	Transport (General)
Airfield, Airport	Ghat	Parking Area	Telephone
⊖ Bank	Golf Course	Pass	Temple
Bird Sanctuary	Hammam	Petrol/Gas Station	Theatre
Border Crossing	Hindu Temple	Police Station	Toilet
Buddhist Temple	Hospital	Post Office	Tomb
Bus Terminal, Stop	Internet Cafe	Pub, Bar	Tourist Information
Camping Ground	Islamic Shrine	Ruins	Zoo

Note: not all symbols displayed above appear in this book

LONELY PLANET OFFICES

Australia
Locked Bag 1, Footscray, Victoria 3011
☎ 03 8379 8000 fax 03 8379 8111
email: talk2us@lonelyplanet.com.au

USA
150 Linden St, Oakland, CA 94607
☎ 510 893 8555 TOLL FREE: 800 275 8555
fax 510 893 8572
email: info@lonelyplanet.com

UK
10a Spring Place, London NW5 3BH
☎ 020 7428 4800 fax 020 7428 4828
email: go@lonelyplanet.co.uk

France
1 rue du Dahomey, 75011 Paris
☎ 01 55 25 33 00 fax 01 55 25 33 01
email: bip@lonelyplanet.fr
www.lonelyplanet.fr

World Wide Web: www.lonelyplanet.com *or* AOL keyword: lp
Lonely Planet Images: www.lonelyplanetimages.com